Beginnings of Interior Environment

7TH EDITION

Beginnings of Interior Environment

PHYLLIS SLOAN ALLEN

MIRIAM F. STIMPSON

Prentice Hall
Upper Saddle River, NJ 07458

Dedicated to all beginning interior designers, professional and nonprofessional, on whom the quality of America's future interior environment depends.

Phyllis Sloan Allen
Miriam F. Stimpson

Library of Congress Cataloging-in-Publication Data
Allen, Phyllis Sloan.
    Beginnings of interior environment / Phyllis Sloan Allen,
    Miriam F. Stimpson.—7th ed.
        p.   cm.
    Includes bibliographical references and index.
    ISBN 0-02-301821-6
    1. Interior decoration—Handbooks, manuals, etc.
    I. Stimpson, Miriam F.   II. Title   III. Title: Interior
    Environment.
NK2115.A59   1994   93-27012
728—dc20   CIP

Cover photo: © 1992 Tibor Fischl/Photobank, Inc.

Editor: Kevin M. Davis
Developmental Editor: Molly Kyle
Production Editor: Mary Harlan
Art Coordinator: Lorraine Woost
Text Designer: Anne Flanagan
Cover Designer: Thomas Mack
Production Buyer: Patricia A. Tonneman
Illustrations: Rolin Graphics, Inc.

This book was set in Garamond by Carlisle Communications, Ltd., and was printed and bound by Von Hoffmann Press, Inc. The cover was printed by Von Hoffmann Press, Inc.

© 1994 by Prentice-Hall, Inc.
A Simon & Schuster Company
Upper Saddle River, New Jersey 07458

Earlier editions copyright © 1968, 1969, 1972, 1977 by Burgess Publishing Company; 1985, 1990 by Macmillan Publishing Company

Printed in the United States of America
10 9 8 7

ISBN 0-02-301821-6

Prentice-Hall International (UK) Limited, *London*
Prentice-Hall of Australia Pty. Limited, *Sydney*
Prentice-Hall Canada Inc., *Toronto*
Prentice-Hall Hispanoamericana, S.A., *Mexico*
Prentice-Hall of India Private Limited, *New Delhi*
Prentice-Hall of Japan, Inc., *Tokyo*
Simon & Schuster Asia Pte. Ltd., *Singapore*
Editora Prentice-Hall do Brasil, Ltda., *Rio de Janeiro*

PREFACE

Interior design has a profound and direct influence on our everyday lives—privately, at home, and in public, when we shop, dine, conduct business, enjoy recreation, and go to work. Our surroundings can lift our spirits, give us comfort, and enhance our lives. Because of its pervasive influence, interior design is a subject that should hold some interest for everyone. *Beginnings of Interior Environment,* Seventh Edition, approaches the subject of interior design practically and comprehensively. Our aim is to help the student learn easily and to become interested in and excited about each topic.

The design process can be exhilarating, rewarding, and fun. Students who pursue design as a profession will find that to attain excellence, they will have to make intelligent and appropriate decisions. Perhaps the most important responsibility of the designer is to be sensitive to individual needs and to human comfort and well-being.

GOALS OF THE TEXT

In the field of interior design, technology, materials, and design expression are constantly changing. Today's designer is increasingly concerned with the need to address social and global issues. We have made a special effort in this new edition to include the most current information on such topics as greening the environment, recycling, healthy environments, energy conservation, preservation of endangered materials, government codes and regulations, design for special-needs users, and computer aided design (CAD).

Beginnings of Interior Environment, Seventh Edition, establishes a solid framework for students' future careers. We illustrate ways to enrich interior spaces while taking into account the challenges that confront professional designers today: space limitations of apartments and condominiums; growing demands for convenience and efficiency; and the responsibility for planning the wise use of natural resources. The book is also intended to act as a catalyst for further study into the different topics of interior design that are introduced here.

NEW MATERIAL

The seventh edition has been significantly revised and expanded to include new chapters on lighting and accessories and to incorporate practical information on nonresidential design, with emphasis on the need for the highest quality design in public settings. Students will learn that the creation of residential and nonresidential (commercial and institutional) space involves similar design processes.

Half the photos and line drawings are new to this edition, enhancing the text throughout with hundreds of full-color and black-and-white photos that support and heighten the design concepts presented in the narrative.

ORGANIZATION OF THE TEXT

The text is organized into six parts. Part One, Design Theory and Application, includes the first three chapters: Chapter 1, The Principles and Elements of Design, focuses on developing the ability to discriminate between fine and poor design. The fundamental principles and design elements emphasized in this chapter are applied throughout the text. Chapter 2, Color, concerns the single most stimulating element of design. Chapter 3, Lighting, is new to this edition. Chapter 4 comprises Part Two, Space Planning, in which we cover the basic goals of design and space planning: functional needs, physical and psychological comfort, economic considerations, aesthetics, and individuality. Information on programming and the design process emphasizes seeking the best solution to problems in the use of space.

Part Three, Interior Materials and Components, begins with a chapter on Textiles (Chapter 5), which concentrates on fibers, construction, coloring, finishing, and types and uses of fabrics. There is also discussion of textiles for period and contemporary rooms, along with information about specifications, safety codes, government labeling, and environmental concerns. Chapter 6, Floors, Walls, and Ceilings, includes a history of rugs and carpets and machine and handmade rugs and how they are integrated into a design. Chapter 7, Windows, Doors, Stairways, and Fireplaces, introduces types of windows and methods of treatment and design and materials for the other important interior details.

Part Four concerns Furniture and Furnishings. Chapter 8, Furniture Selection, explains the necessity for attention to the human factor. Important topics include furniture categories, materials, quality, and finish. In Chapter 9, Furniture Styles, illustrations provide an overall visual concept of principal furniture periods. Furniture Arrangement and Wall Composition are explained in Chapter 10, and Chapter 11, Accessories, focuses on both functional and decorative accessories and how to integrate them into a room's design.

Part Five, Interior and Exterior Styles, includes Chapter 12, Historic Heritage of Architecture and Design and Chapter 13, Modern Architecture and Design, giving a brief but important overview of the timelessness of fine design and architecture.

Finally, in Part Six, we discuss The Profession of Interior Design: professional classifications, qualifications, responsibilities, preparations, procedures, opportunities, and future challenges for those who choose a career in interior design.

Treatment of topics is flexible, so that the instructor can introduce them at whatever level or point he or she chooses. Relevant projects listed at the ends of Chapters 1, 2, 3, 4, 5, 7, 9, and 10 will help test students on the chapter topics. The worksheets are included in the text's accompanying Student Packet. A coordinated Instructor's Manual suggests supplementary materials for class demonstrations and projects and contains a complete test bank.

ACKNOWLEDGMENTS

Special appreciation is extended to the architects, designers, manufacturers, museums, and galleries who contributed photographs of architecture, interior design, and products for this text. These photographs have provided most effective support to the written material. I am particularly grateful to Sally Sharp Adams for her precise and engaging illustrations throughout the text.

The following reviewers contributed immensely to the seventh edition of *Beginnings of Interior Environment* with their ideas, comments, and professional advice:

- Jerry Beitel, Fullerton College
- Stephanie A. Clemons, Colorado State University
- Marcia Gonzales, Scottsdale Community College
- Susan S. Reedy, Michigan State University
- Janice M. Rogers, Interior Design Institute, Inc.
- JoAnn M. Thomas, Portland Community College
- Lisa Waxman, Florida State University
- Bonadine Woods, Bowling Green State University

Kevin Davis, Mary Harlan, and the staff at Macmillan have handled the monumental task of coordinating and completing this text with sincere commitment and professionalism. For all their efforts the authors are truly appreciative.

Finally, to my family and my colleagues and students at Brigham Young University I express my love, gratitude, and appreciation for their wholehearted support and encouragement.

—M.F.S.

CONTENTS

CHAPTER 2

PART TWO
Space Planning

PART THREE
Interior Materials and Components

CHAPTER 5

CHAPTER 6

PART FOUR
Furniture and Furnishings

CHAPTER 11

PART FIVE
Interior and Exterior Styles

CHAPTER 12

PART SIX
The Profession of Interior Design

CHAPTER 14

Contents ▬▬▬▬▬▬▬▬▬▬▬▬▬▬▬▬▬▬▬▬▬▬▬▬▬ *xvii*

CHAPTER 1

Elements and Principles of Design

FIGURE 1.1 A dramatic and visually pleasing environment such as this does not happen by accident. Knowledge of the elements and principles of design and the ability to apply them are essential for solving design problems. (Photograph by Mark Boisclair.)

Good Taste and Style

Guidelines for Developing Style

The Human Factor

Definition of Design

Goals of Design

Two Basic Design Directions

Structural Design

Applied Ornamentation or Decorative Design

Elements of Design

Texture

Pattern

Line

Form and Shape

Space

Color

Light

Principles of Design

Proportion

Scale

Balance

Rhythm

Emphasis

Harmony

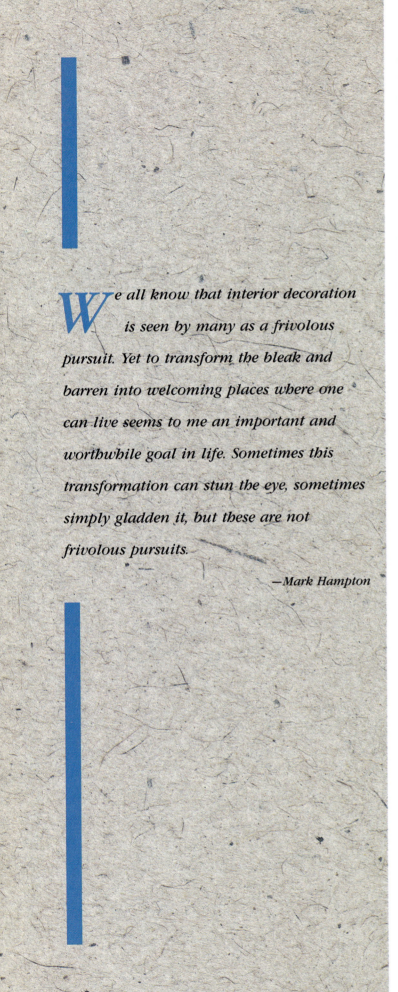

We all know that interior decoration is seen by many as a frivolous pursuit. Yet to transform the bleak and barren into welcoming places where one can live seems to me an important and worthwhile goal in life. Sometimes this transformation can stun the eye, sometimes simply gladden it, but these are not frivolous pursuits.

—*Mark Hampton*

GOOD TASTE AND STYLE

People are not born with that elusive element called "good taste"; it is a capability for making *aesthetic judgments* that develops over years of learning and experience. Anyone can express personal preference, but the acquisition of good aesthetic judgment requires a *knowledge of the elements and principles of design.* This knowledge can serve as a basis for *visual appreciation* and *intelligent selection.* Although acquiring this knowledge informally or through exposure is possible, more formal training is usually required. Once knowledge of the basic principles is established, new media and modern technology can be applied in original and creative ways to produce appropriate solutions to design problems. The use of innovative forms and proportions can be exciting, but to attempt innovative applications without first understanding the basic principles of design would be folly.

Various styles come and go, but personal style remains. Personal style can be identified, developed, and enriched through the years. Determining the most appropriate style for a particular individual and his or her environment requires careful consideration of many criteria including lifestyle and experiences, physiological and psychological needs, and preferences for colors, textures, patterns, and other elements. Discovering personal style can be a fulfilling endeavor. When a designer is attempting to create a sense of style in a residential or nonresidential setting, these values and considerations also apply.

Guidelines for Developing Style

Good design has no absolute formula. However, the successful employment of **aesthetic** principles—scale and proportion, rhythm, balance, harmony, and emphasis—enhances the designer's skill and provides a sound background for decision making (Figure 1.1). Integrity and simplicity are important ingredients in good design, along with consideration for the design's function and its relationship to the environment and to people. Whatever the design, its basic intention should be to enrich people's lives and enhance the human experience. Good design is a long-term investment; although at times expensive, it is worth the cost. Mediocre design will always be mediocre, and good design will always be good, no matter what the change in fashion. The best design should be demanded and expected in all areas.

For the student anticipating a career in interior design, certain guidelines can help in acquiring the capability to choose design of lasting beauty and enjoyment.

- *Acquiring knowledge* of the principles and elements of design is fundamental. Deliberate application of these principles will make them part of your consciousness.
- *Carefully and constantly observing objects in nature*—light and shadow, shape and texture, pattern and color—can develop personal awareness (Figure 1.2).

Gradation

Asymmetrical balance

Bisymmetrical balance

FIGURE 1.2 Design in nature.

These elements can be viewed not only in and of themselves but also with respect to how they interrelate. Looking for balance, rhythm, emphasis, scale, and proportion in nature can help you develop a sense of the harmony these principles produce.

- *Studying and researching historical, modern, and contemporary architecture and furnishing styles* will provide the design student with a knowledgeable background for current application.
- *Critically examining the excellent design periodicals* available is beneficial.
- *Asking questions of experienced professionals* in furniture stores and design studios is invaluable.
- *Acquiring knowledge of accessories* is important, particularly with regard to items appropriate for each style of furniture, as well as their use for enhancing rooms.
- *Realizing that fashion is not a good criterion of design.* Like fashion in clothes, fashion in home furnishings may often become outdated. Individual taste can be influenced by national trends, events, and celebrities. Trendsetters like famous designers, political figures, actors, rock stars, and others have sometimes inspired novel ideas in many mediums and in residential and nonresidential design in varying degrees.

Knowledge of what constitutes good design enables designers to guide their clients toward making purchases wisely, no matter how small. Whether the purchase is a crystal goblet, a chair, or a house, good taste is not determined by cost alone. Ultimately, taste is a sense of what is appropriate to a particular lifestyle, and the success of interior design depends on the choice of ingredients and the way they are blended together.

THE HUMAN FACTOR

Although numerous approaches to design theory and application exist, no design plan can be successful without consideration of the human factor. Taking into account the personal needs of the end users—including physical, emotional, and spiritual needs—is of utmost importance from the beginning of the design process to the completion of the project. Whether the project is for residential or nonresidential use, human needs for comfort, security, privacy, and aesthetic satisfaction should always be considered. The goals of a good design process (outlined in Chapter 4) always incorporate these basic human needs.

Definition of Design

Webster's Dictionary defines design as "the arrangement of details which make up a work of art." According to the *Encyclopaedia Britannica*, design is "the arrangement of lines or forms which make up the plan of a work of art with special regard to the proportions, structure, movement, and beauty of line of the whole." Generally the creator of a well-planned and well-executed design— whether for a silver spoon, a rug, or a complete house— has carefully considered the principles and elements of design to achieve a successful solution.

Goals of Design

Before approaching the actual design process, designers must define and consider certain values and attitudes in relation to the end users and their environment. These values or goals should be evaluated throughout the design process. As mentioned above, the goals of design take into consideration the human factor. Successful designers consider all aspects of the needs and preferences of their clients before commencing the project. The basic goals of design include: (1) creating designs that *function* for a particular purpose or use, keeping in mind the psychological as well as physiological needs of the occupants or users, (2) considering the *economic factors* involved with the project, or in other words working within the projected budget, (3) creating an environment that is

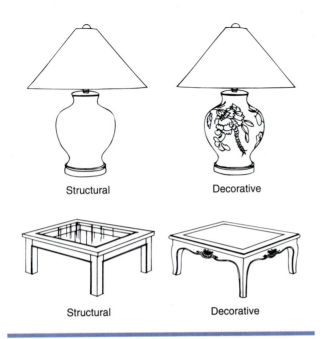

Structural   Decorative

Structural   Decorative

FIGURE 1.3 Structural design and applied ornamentation or decorative design.

aesthetically pleasing or beautiful, and (4) incorporating the intrinsic values of *character and individuality.* These goals are what the designer hopes to achieve by completing the design process. (The steps involved in the design process are covered in Chapter 4.)

TWO BASIC DESIGN DIRECTIONS

Becoming familiar with the two basic types of design, *structural* and *decorative,* is a helpful introduction to the principles and elements of design (Figure 1.3).

Structural Design

Structural design relates to the size and shape of an object; the design is an integral part of the structure itself. For example, the ancient pyramids of Egypt are structural designs because they expose the stone blocks from which they were made. Contemporary architecture, both inside and out, frankly reveals the materials that make up the basic structure, such as wood or metal beams, brick, stone, and concrete (Figure 1.4). The design of modern furniture is seen in the form itself, such as the metal frame of the Barcelona chair and the molded plastic of a pedestal table.

The attributes essential to successful structural design are *simplicity, good proportion,* and *appropriateness of materials used.*

Simplicity

Whether the structure itself is to stand as the finished product or is only the supporting element for design, it should be kept simple. For example, a room with too many or poorly placed openings, arches, and niches will seldom be pleasing until some elimination or simplification has been accomplished.

Good Proportion

Any object that is structurally well proportioned is intrinsically pleasing, whether it remains plain or is appropriately decorated. For example, when a room is well proportioned, it is a pleasure to plan the interior; one that is badly proportioned is difficult to correct. An upholstered chair with armrests that overpower the rest of the design must often be completely rebuilt to be attractive.

Appropriateness of Materials

Different materials lend themselves to various objects and construction methods. Glass may be blown and intricately decorated by skilled craftspeople, and molded plastic chairs may be turned out on an assembly line. Interchanging the procedures and materials for produc-

FIGURE 1.4 In this living room designed by Laurence Lake, both the architectural background and the furnishings demonstrate clean structural design. Pillows and other accessories soften the geometric effect and add a decorative quality. (Photograph by Pam Singleton.)

FIGURE 1.5 Applied pattern, or ornamentation, is found on virtually every surface in this elegant bedroom, from the patterned rug and the brocade spread to the delicate carving on the chairs, paneled walls, and fireplace. (Courtesy of F. J. Hakiman, Inc., N.Y. Design by Ron Grimaldi for Rose Cumming, Inc. Photograph by Phillip Ennis.)

ing an object may not be feasible or may not achieve the desired result. Material selected for a design should be chosen for the intended purpose without sacrificing the aesthetic goal.

Applied Ornamentation or Decorative Design

Decorative design relates to the ornamentation of the basic structure, which may be achieved through the selection and placement of color, line, and texture. For example, the exterior surfaces of East Indian temples are completely covered with embellishment. Victorian-style houses often display fanciful decoration added to the structure. Furniture may be handsomely carved to add charm and dignity. Fabrics, wallpapers, rugs, accessories, and other furnishings can be attractively enhanced by decorative design (Figure 1.5).

Four classifications apply to applied ornamentation or decorative design: **naturalistic**, **conventionalized** or **stylized**, **abstract**, and **geometric** (Figure 1.6).

1. *Naturalistic,* realistic, or photographic design reproduces a motif from nature in its natural form. For

example, flowers look exactly like flowers as they are seen in the garden.

2. *Conventionalized* or *stylized* design creates a motif taken from nature but adapted to suit the shape or purpose of the object to be decorated. For example, flowers are recognizable but are modified or slightly changed. This type of design is often used for interior furnishings.

3. *Abstract* design departs from nature. The elements, which may or may not be recognizable, are transformed into nonrepresentational design.

4. *Geometric* design is made up of geometric motifs such as stripes, plaids, chevron patterns, and zigzags.

The attributes essential to successful decorative design are suitability, appropriateness, and placement.

Suitability

An item's purpose should be immediately recognizable. A lamp should be designed to look like an object for giving light and not like a **Dresden** doll holding an umbrella. A salad bowl should look like an article to contain something.

Naturalistic

Conventional

Abstract

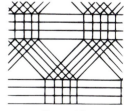

Geometric

FIGURE 1.6 Types of applied ornamentation.

FIGURE 1.7 A bed that is primarily structural is constructed of simple pine and metal components devoid of ornamentation. A small design on the headboard adds a contrasting decorative detail. (Courtesy of *The Naturalist.*)

FIGURE 1.8 With traditional carvings from the Tudor period in England, this bed is an example of applied ornamentation. (Courtesy of Stuart Interiors.)

Appropriateness

Any decoration added to the basic structure should accent its shape and beauty. For example, vertical fluting on a supporting column makes it seem higher, but crossbars appear to cut its height and reduce its dignity. Classic figures on a Wedgwood vase emphasize its rounded contour, but harsh lines destroy its beauty.

Placement

The embellishment of any item should be placed with purpose in mind. **Bas-relief** on the seat of a chair is uncomfortable to the occupant, but such carving on a wall plaque can be attractive and is more suitable.

The amount of surface decoration should be placed with great care, while keeping the basic structure in mind.

Figures 1.7 and 1.8 show contrasting examples of structural and decorative design.

ELEMENTS OF DESIGN

The basic components that make up a total design are known as the **elements of design**: *texture, pattern, line, form* and *shape, space, color,* and *lighting.* These elements aid the designer when creating a visual environment and are often referred to as *tools.* Organization and arrangement of these elements or tools relate closely to the principles of design.

Texture

Texture refers to the surface quality of objects—the quality that not only can be seen and touched but also can be sensed in memory. For example, the roughness of sandstone, the softness of a deep-pile rug, the smoothness of glass, and the shininess of growing leaves all produce for us a particular sensation because of our previous associations with these textures. Basically, textures fall into the following categories: *soft, smooth, shiny, dull,* and *rough.* Throughout history, smooth, highly polished surfaces, lustrous metals, and fabrics of satin, silk, and fine linen have been symbolic of wealth and high status, whereas rough, hand-hewn textures and homespun fabrics have characterized the homes of those in lower economic classes. Today this is no longer the case. Many wealthy individuals prefer the handcrafted look, which may well cost as much as the most refined look. Additionally, smooth and shiny surfaces have been reserved for formal interiors, while dull and rough textures have been associated with informal treatments. Regardless of style, a knowledgeable use of texture is a sure way to bring character to a room (Figure 1.9). Textures in the interior environment often combine several characteristics. For example, a wool carpet can have a soft and dull texture. Properties of and considerations regarding texture are discussed here.

Visual Interest, Beauty, and Character

Texture adds much visual interest in the environment. Cave dwellers enjoyed the feel of animal skins under their feet. The early Greeks delighted in the smoothness and beauty of mosaic floors. The people of Iran have always taken pride in the fine texture of their hand-knotted rugs, and the Japanese enjoy the freshness of grass mats called *tatami*. Modern interiors depend on the physical impression of texture to create variety and interest. The texture of a surface reflects a particular character and unique beauty that provides a physical or psychological impression.

Light Reflection

Each texture has a surface quality that affects light reflection. Smooth, shiny surfaces like glass, mirrors, satin, porcelain, and highly polished wood reflect more light than rough and dull textures like brick, concrete, stone, and coarse wood.

Maintenance

Surfaces in the home require upkeep. The choice of a particular texture determines the amount of maintenance.

Acoustics

Textures can absorb or reflect sound. Smooth and hard surfaces tend to magnify sound; soft and rough textures have a tendency to absorb sound. Walking through an unfurnished room with a hard floor produces a high level of sound. When the same room is furnished with rugs, fabrics, draperies, and furniture, the sound is greatly muffled. Designers can control the **acoustics** of a particular space with wise textural combinations.

A Combination of Textures

Formal textures like satin and polished marble and informal textures like burlap and brick are generally not mixed in the same environment unless a specific effect is desired. The dominant texture of a room is often established by the architectural background. For example, a room paneled in fine-grained and polished wood or papered in a traditional formal wall covering generally requires furniture woods and fabrics with a smoother and shinier texture than that required of a room paneled with natural coarse-grained wood or constructed of masonry. Contemporary use of texture may break these traditional rules, providing an element of surprise. A combination of textures, whether employed for an avant-garde or conservative environment, enhances the total visual experience. For example, a room may contain the textures of glass, wood, stone, plants, and fabrics, thus providing variety, interest, and character.

FIGURE 1.9 Smooth, shiny, dull, soft, and rough textures of the wicker, travertine, fabrics, ceramics, glass, wood, flowers, and rug combine to provide interest and variety. (Courtesy of Hasbrook Interiors, Phoenix).

FIGURE 1.10 Soaring verticals and intersecting diagonals silhouetted against the sky carry the eyes, and spirit, upward in the Thorncrown Wayfarer's chapel in Arkansas, designed by E. Fay Jones. (Courtesy of E. Fay Jones, FAIA, Maurice J. Jennings, AIA, and David W. McKee, AIA.)

Pattern

Pattern is a decorative design, figure, or motif created through the use of line, form, space, light, and color. Pattern can be effectively employed to create interest (see Figures 1.1 and 1.5). Too much pattern can make a room too "busy" and uncomfortable, and a room devoid of pattern may be stark and uninviting. The total arrangement of the components of a room creates an overall pattern, but more obvious patterns are seen in fabric and wallpaper. The use of pattern and pattern combinations are more thoroughly covered in Chapter 5.

Line

Line is the *direction* of an art creation and is particularly dominant in contemporary art and interiors. The feeling of a composition—a room—is established by the lines that give it motion or repose. Skillful use of line is therefore of utmost importance (Figure 1.10).

Line can seemingly alter the proportion of an object or of an entire room. For example, in Figure 1.11, two identical rectangles are divided, one vertically and the other horizontally. As the eye travels upward along the vertical line, the area seems higher. Along the horizontally divided area the eye is directed across, making the rectangle appear wider. Each kind of line has a particular psychological effect on a room. To achieve the desired result, the interior designer should keep in mind the distinct effects of each line.

- *Vertical lines* tend to provide a feeling of height, strength, and dignity. These lines are particularly evident on the exterior of a building where columns are used and in the interior where upright architectural members are conspicuous, in tall pieces of furniture, and in the long straight lines of vertical louvers or folds of drapery.
- *Horizontal lines* create a feeling of repose, solidity, and strength. These lines are often seen in cornices, dadoes, bookshelves, and long, low pieces of straight-lined furniture. Falling Water, a famous Frank Lloyd Wright house, is an excellent example of horizontal architecture (see Figure 13.1 in Chapter 13).
- *Diagonal lines* give a room a feeling of action and movement. They are evident in slanting ceilings, staircases, Gothic arches, and sloping furniture. Too many diagonals may give a room a feeling of unrest.
- *Curved lines* have a graceful and delicate effect on a room. They are found in arches and other curved architectural treatment, drapery **swags**, rounded and curved furniture, and rounded accessories. The Taj Mahal is a supreme example of graceful architecture primarily employing curved lines. Curved lines fall into four general categories: (1) Large convex (upward) curves tend to provide an uplifting feeling. (2) Large concave (downward) curves often give a feeling of solidity or even sadness. (Artists have used this line to evoke a feeling of mourning or unhappiness.) Downward curves may also be very dramatic, especially when used in modern design. (3) Horizontal curves can imply restfulness. (4) Small curves often express lightness and merriment.

Too much line movement in a room may evoke a feeling of instability. A careful balance of line is essential to the feeling of comfort and harmony in a room. Vertical, horizontal, diagonal, and curved lines, with their various psychological and physical properties, can be used throughout the home and work environment to provide interest, comfort, and unity. For example, a designer can use line to create a mood or feeling, to give direction to a room, to create an optical illusion, to achieve a feeling of balance and rhythm, to support a room's focal point by directing the eye toward that feature, and to give variety and unity to a room through the skillful blending of the various line types.

FIGURE 1.11 Line.

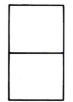

When two identical rectangles are divided differently—one horizontally and one vertically—the proportion seems to change.

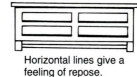

Horizontal lines give a feeling of repose.

Diagonal lines are lines of movement.

Vertical lines add height and dignity.

Vertical lines emphasize and enhance the basic structure.

Zigzag lines detract from the basic structure.

The curved line was used by Eero Saarinen to create the classic pedestal chair.

Form and Shape

The contour of an object is represented by its shape, which is made up of lines. When a two-dimensional shape takes on a third dimension, it becomes form or mass. In the planning of interiors, mass is perceived as objects of furniture that require space and may be moved to various locations. The arrangement of form within a room—furniture arrangement—is discussed in Chapter 10.

Basic forms or shapes fall into three categories:

1. *Rectangles and squares* are the most dominant shapes used in architecture and interior design. They provide a sense of unity and stability, are easy to work with, and may be arranged to conserve space. Too many rectangular and square forms may produce monotony, however. Introducing circular and angular forms into the space alters this effect.
2. *Triangular shapes* have three sides. The diamond shape results when triangles are arranged base to base. A variety of other shapes using the diagonal line may be created. These forms are often seen in sloping ceilings of contemporary homes and motifs applied to fabrics and wallpapers. Triangular, diamond, and other diagonal shapes may be used for flooring materials, furniture, and accessories, providing a dynamic effect.
3. *Curved forms* include the sphere, circle, cone, and cylinder. Curved forms are found everywhere in nature. Even our own bodies are curved. This form is constant, unifying, and pleasing. When used in the home environment, curved forms may be dramatic, like a sweeping staircase or domed ceiling, or used for accessories like a piece of pottery, a plate, a lamp, a

round table, or a sculpture. Curved forms may also give relief and variety to a room with a predominance of angular and rectilinear forms.

Very few homes employ only one shape or form. The environment is most often enhanced by skillfully combining the three basic forms for architecture and furnishings (Figure 1.12). However, too much variety of form

FIGURE 1.12 This fireplace in a contemporary Santa Fe style house is given prominence through form, color, texture, and space. (Photograph by Peter Paige.)

and shape may produce a room with a feeling of confusion. The transition from one object to another as the eye moves about the room should be easy and pleasurable. The emphasis created when a curved form is placed against a rectangular panel, however—for example, a pair of ornately carved Belter chairs against a plain paneled wall in a modern room—may provide unexpected and agreeable relief to a room's otherwise severe lines. The sophisticated combination of forms is currently evident in both modern and traditional styles.

Space

Space is perhaps the most important element of domestic architecture. *Funk & Wagnalls' Dictionary* defines *space* as "an interval or area between or within points or objects." Space may be characterized as the opposite of form or mass. Well-planned and well-organized space makes

FIGURE 1.13 Architecturally dynamic forms enclose a soaring living space in this private residence designed by architect Eduard Dreier. (Courtesy of Gayl Baddeley/Associates.)

for a smooth-working home (Figure 1.13). When walls are erected for a living area, space has been defined—a particular space that can be articulated to create a functional and livable environment for the occupants. Today, most homes lack adequate space, and the challenge of making the most of available space is a designer's prime concern. By utilizing all the elements of design—line, form, color, light, pattern, and texture—rooms can be furnished and arranged to increase the sense of space. Following are some suggestions for achieving this goal:

- Arrange space so the eye can easily travel through a room to outside areas like a garden, terrace, or view.
- Choose unobtrusive patterns and textures.
- Use few pieces of furniture, ones that are lightly scaled and placed close to walls.
- Select colors that are light in value, muted, and cool and that blend with each other to visually increase space.
- Use artificial lighting around the **perimeter** of the room both on the ceiling and with uplighters on the floor. This treatment enhances a small space, giving the illusion of depth.
- Provide wall-to-wall floor treatment and ceiling-to-floor window treatment. Consider simple window treatment like shutters, shades, or blinds rather than heavy draperies.
- Create the illusion of more space through the use of mirrors.
- Explore the possibilities of open planning, a projecting window, or a skylight.
- Select furnishings with a "see-through" look, like pieces with clear glass, plastic, or caning components. Avoid furniture with bases that are flush with the floor. Instead, select furniture that is supported by legs or pedestals or is wall-hung.
- Keep rooms free of clutter, with an occasional empty corner.
- Use a few well-chosen accessories.

The designer faced with the problem of space that is too expansive and lacks definition may simply reverse the preceding guidelines. Again, the elements of design are the tools to achieve the desired outcome. Furnishings can be grouped to divide the space. The challenge of working with a vast space is to create a visual composition that provides a sense of comfort and security suited to human scale.

The arrangement of space within the interior framework of the home and working environments is discussed in Chapters 4 and 10, which deal with design principles, floor plans, and furniture arrangement.

Color

Color, considered the most important element of design, is covered in detail in Chapter 2.

FIGURE 1.14 A floor plan, drafted by the designer, indicates the size and proportion of the rooms and how the furnishings are to be arranged within the spaces. Placement of built-in cabinets, seating, tables, beds, and storage units is determined by the basic rules of good proportion. (Courtesy of Jennifer Budd, designer.)

Light

The element of light, both natural and artificial, and its importance in the environment are presented in Chapter 3.

PRINCIPLES OF DESIGN

Through the centuries certain principles of design have evolved through careful observation of both nature and art. When these **principles of design**—proportion, scale, balance, rhythm, emphasis, and harmony—are thoughtfully considered and sensitively applied, they contribute to achieving the goals of design. The elements of design discussed in the first part of the chapter are the "tools" employed by the designer to accomplish the desired outcome.

Although there are no absolute rules when creating a design project, most interiors are enhanced by adhering to these basic guidelines. Understanding and using these principles, a designer can achieve excellence, whether the design involves a painting, a room, or an entire house. Although some successful contemporary designs violate these time-tested principles, understanding them is central to the interior designer's creativity and is essential for a beginning designer.

Proportion

Proportion encompasses both the relationship of one part of an object to the other parts or to the whole, and the relationship of one object to another—both aspects involving shape or form (Figure 1.14). Proportion has been a major concern of creative minds through the ages. Although no absolute formula for good proportion works in all design projects, over 2,000 years ago the Greeks discovered some secrets of good proportion and set down rules that students of design have accepted and incorporated into their compositions for centuries.

The Greeks found that the square was the least satisfactory proportion for an enclosure and that the rectangle was better. Their standard for good proportion was a rectangle or oblong with its sides in a ratio of 2:3 (Figure 1.15). This shape is called the **golden rectangle**. The **golden section** involves the division of a line or form in such a way that the ratio of the smaller portion to the larger is the same as that of the larger portion to the whole. The progression 2, 3, 5, 8, 13, 21, 34, and so on, in which each number is the sum of the two preceding numbers, provides a close approximation to this relationship. For example, 2:3 is roughly the same ratio as 3:5, 5:8 is roughly the same ratio as 8:13, and so forth. Another pleasing space relationship is 4:7. By multiplying any of these combinations of figures, the interior designer can plan larger areas with similar relationships.

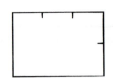

The golden rectangle. The Greek standard for good proportion is a rectangle with its sides in a ratio of 2:3.

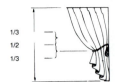

The golden mean. The division of a line somewhere between one half and one third is the most pleasing.

The Parthenon at Athens—based on a mathematical ratio of 1:1.6—fits almost precisely into a golden rectangle. Because of the frequency with which it occurs in the arts, the golden rectangle has mystified experts for centuries.

The golden section. 3:5 is roughly the same ratio as 5:8

4:7 is a pleasing proportion.

FIGURE 1.15 Greek proportions.

Perhaps the most important application of these proportions in house planning and furnishing lies in the relationship of sizes or areas. These proportions can be applied when planning the dimensions of a room or when selecting a piece of furniture for a particular area. For example, if the length of the living room measures 25 ft, a desirable width would be 15 ft. This measurement is determined by using the following process. Since the length of the living room (25 ft) is divisible by 5, the 3:5 ratio may be used. If

$$\frac{W \text{ (width)}}{L \text{ (length)}} = \frac{3}{5}$$

and L equals 25, then W would equal 15.

In another example, a piece of furniture 4 ft long would be a good size to place against a 7-ft wall space. These dimensions have the desirable ratio of 4:7.

Another Greek discovery was that the division of a line somewhere between one-half and one-third its length is the most desirable. This division is still retained as a **golden mean** and can be applied when planning any wall composition, such as determining the height for a

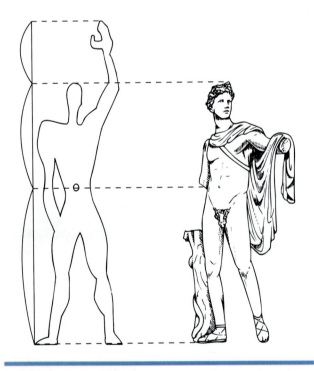

FIGURE 1.17 Le Corbusier planned his architectural projects to be consistent with the proportions of his human Modular (left). The same ideal proportions can be applied to the famous marble statue of the Apollo Belvedere (right) of ancient Greece or Rome (4th or 1st Century B.C.).

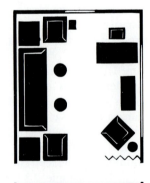

Poor   Better

FIGURE 1.16 Furniture should be in the right scale for a room.

mantel, tying back drapery, or hanging pictures, mirrors, or wall sconces.

The Greeks also discovered that odd numbers are preferable to even ones. A group of 3 objects to 3 is more pleasing than 2:2 or 4:4, and 2:3 is better than 2:4. These ratios might be applied, for example, when selecting pillows for the sofa or arranging pictures on a wall.

Scale

Scale refers to the overall size of an object or its parts compared with other objects or their parts, regardless of shape. A house is large, but it may be large or small in scale. A table is a smaller item, but it may be large or small in scale. It is only large or small when compared to another object.

The correct use of scale and proportion is important to the success of a house and its furnishings (Figure 1.16). Yet, because scale is a relative quality, mathematical correctness is not the solution, because weight and measurement do not always produce a feeling of rightness. For example, two love seats may have identical overall dimensions, yet may not look compatible if one has heavier arms and shorter legs than the other.

Interior design deals with size relationships geared to human scale, which determines the design of homes and furnishings (Figures 1.17 and 1.18). Considering that human beings usually weigh between 100 and 200 pounds and are between 5 and 6 ft in height, an interior environment can be planned and scaled accordingly. Successfully scaled rooms and furnishings make adults and children feel comfortable—the rooms are not too large or too small, but well suited to the occupants (Figure 1.19).

Good scale and proportion begin with the choice of the house on the lot and must be taken into account until

FIGURE 1.18 The beautiful lines and proportions of the highly acclaimed Barcelona chair, designed by Mies van der Rohe in 1929 for the Barcelona Exhibiton, have made the modern piece a timeless classic. (Courtesy of Knoll international.)

the last accessory is put in place. A tiny house on a spacious lot looks lost, and a large house looks cramped and uncomfortable on a small plot of ground. The size of trees and shrubs, carefully selected, can complement the overall plan.

The material used in construction should be in scale with the house itself. For example, a Cape Cod cottage would not look right made of large cinder block. The heavy material is not compatible with the refined scale of this particular home style.

Architectural features on the exterior of the house should be carefully designed and located. Because the door is the focal point of the facade, perfect scale is important. Windows should be carefully positioned and suitably scaled and proportioned.

FIGURE 1.19 In a large living space, the furnishings and architecture relate well in scale and proportion, creating an aesthetic composition that is enjoyable and comfortable for the occupants. (Courtesy of Milo Baughman, designer.)

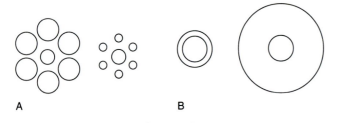

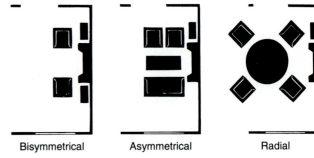

Bisymmetrical   Asymmetrical   Radial

FIGURE 1.20 Perception: The center circles in each of the diagrams are identical. The apparent change in size is due to the difference in size of the surrounding circles.

FIGURE 1.21 Three types of balance.

An object is perceived in relation to the area around it (Figure 1.20). Objects that are too large crowd a small room and make it appear smaller; furniture that is too small seems even smaller in an oversized room. When surrounded by small-scaled furniture, a large piece of furniture appears larger than when surrounded by large-scaled pieces. A small table with spindly legs placed at the end of a heavy sofa or chair looks out of place, and a large-scaled table placed near a dainty chair is not enhanced. The proper combination of large and small com-

FIGURE 1.22 Italian designer Vico Magistretti's famous Sindbad chairs are bisymmetrically arranged at the sides of a symmetrically designed fireplace. The windows and window treatments are also symmetrically arranged. This eclectic room combines both traditional and modern styles. (Photograph by Norman McGrath.)

Chapter 1

FIGURE 1.23 Sofas, accessories, and other furnishings are placed to achieve a sense of balance and harmony throughout this living area. The geometry of the asymmetric fireplace wall and the irregular curves of the stone and wood divider add interest and complexity. (Courtesy of Steve Chase and Associates. Photograph by Arthur Coleman.)

ponents in a room can often enhance all of the components in a room through the effective use of contrast.

Accessories such as mirrors, pictures, and lamps need to be scaled for the items with which they are to be used. A lamp generally must not overpower a table, nor should it be so small that it looks ridiculous. Both the lamp shade and base must be suitably scaled.

Not only form but also color, texture, and pattern are important in the consideration of scale and proportion. Whatever attracts the eye seems larger. Coarse textures, large patterns, and bold colors cause the object on which they are used to appear larger than an object with smooth textures, small patterns, and soft, light colors.

Through the skillful use of these and other principles, the apparent size and proportion of rooms and objects may be altered. The decor of a room succeeds largely through knowledgeable use of the principles of design.

Balance

Balance is that quality in a room that gives a sense of equilibrium and repose. It is a sense of weight as the eye perceives it. Generally, human beings have a need for balance in many aspects of their lives, and in the interior environment balance is necessary to achieve a comfortable atmosphere. The three types of balance are **bisymmetrical**, **asymmetrical**, and **radial** (Figure 1.21).

Bisymmetrical, or Formal, Balance

In **bisymmetrical balance** identical objects are arranged equally on each side of an imaginary line (Figure 1.22). This type of balance has the following characteristics:

- Often employed in traditionally styled environments
- Predominantly formal and dignified in feeling
- Contrasts with nature, since much in nature is asymmetrical
- Conveys a restful and peaceful sensation, since this type of balance is easily perceived and appreciated.

Asymmetrical Balance

Asymmetrical balance, sometimes called approximate symmetry, is more subtle than bisymmetrical balance, and it is often referred to as **occult** or optical. It requires more thought and imagination, but once achieved, remains interesting for a longer time (Figure 1.23). In this type of balance objects of different sizes, shapes, and colors may be used in an infinite number of ways. Two small objects may balance one large item, a small, shiny object may balance a larger dull one, a spot of bright color may balance a large area of neutral color, and a large object moved closer to a central point may balance a smaller one pushed farther away. No measurement indicates at what point these different items must be placed. The point at which balance is achieved must be sensed. General aspects of asymmetrical balance include the following:

- Tends to shift the focus from the center and achieve balance by visual tension created between dissimilar objects.
- Predominant in modern interiors
- Tends to be informal
- Generally more active than symmetrical balance
- Is more compatible with nature
- Provides a more spacious appearance.

FIGURE 1.24 Radial balance is seen in this Country French room that seems to radiate outward from a central core. Chairs are arranged around a circular table with a central centerpiece and chandelier. (Courtesy of Century Furniture Co.)

Radial Balance

In *radial balance* all elements of the design radiate from a central point like the spokes of a wheel radiating out from the hub. This balance is most often seen in a room where chairs surround a round table, in flower arrangements, and in chandeliers (Figure 1.24). Radial balance is often a visually pleasing alternative and combines effectively with the other two types of balance.

Other Considerations Involving Balance

The architectural background including doors, windows, paneling, and fireplaces, along with all accompanying furnishings, can be effectively arranged to provide a feeling of equilibrium. Some considerations include the following:

- Opposite walls and interior spaces and objects should have a comfortable feeling of balance through the distribution of high and low, and large and small objects.
- Most rooms need both bisymmetrical and asymmetrical balance.
- When furnishings are positioned above eye level, they appear heavier than items positioned below.
- Bright colors, heavy textures, unusual shapes, bold patterns, and strong lighting readily attract attention and can be manipulated to achieve balance within a space.
- Large furnishings in a space can be complemented by placing them next to small items, and vice versa, creating a refreshing contrast.

Rhythm

Rhythm is an intangible component of a composition. To most people rhythm suggests a flowing quality, but in interiors it is something that assists the eye in moving easily about a room from one area to another. This principle can be achieved through repetition, opposition, transition, gradation or progression, radiation, contrast, and alternation (Figure 1.25). By effectively creating rhythm, a designer can produce continuity and interest (Figure 1.26).

Repetition is rhythm established by repeating color, pattern, texture, line, light, or form. For example, a color in the upholstery fabric of a sofa can be repeated on a chair, the drapery, and a pillow, thus introducing rhythm. Too much repetition—or in some cases too little repetition—can produce confusion, monotony, or lack of stability. Repetition is a common means of achieving rhythm in a room because it is a relatively easy approach.

Opposition, a type of repetition, is found in a composition wherever lines come together at right angles (as in the corners of a square window frame). Other examples might include where a straight fireplace lintel meets

Gradation

Repetition

Transition

Opposition

Radiation

FIGURE 1.25 Types of rhythm.

an upright support or wherever a horizontal line of furniture meets a vertical architectural member.

- **Transition**, still another type of repetition, is rhythm found in a curved line that carries the eye easily over an architectural element, such as an arched window, or around items of furnishings, like drapery swags or a circular chair.
- **Gradation or progression** is rhythm produced by the succession of the size of an object from large to small or of a color from dark to light. Examples include the progression of one step up to another step; the gradation of a small salt container to a medium-sized sugar container up to a large flour container; and a rug that might have a dark border, a medium inner border, and a light interior area.
- **Radiation** is a method of rhythm in which lines extend outward from a central axis. This pattern is usually found in the accessories of a room, such as in lighting fixtures or a bouquet of flowers, but it also may be seen when furnishings or architecture radiate outward from a central core.
- **Contrast** is achieved when opposites are placed in close proximity, arousing the visual senses; for example, placing white against black or a rough texture against a smooth one, or putting a square glass piece on top of a cylindrical coffee-table base. Contrast can also be achieved by putting an ornately carved antique against a simple structural wall — currently a popular treatment in the contemporary home.
- **Alternation** is a type of rhythm in which two forms or lines alternate to create movement; for example, a striped pattern or a motif employing a repeating square, circle, square, and so on.

Emphasis

Emphasis in a room refers to its *dominant* and *subordinate* components or to the focal point and supportive furnishings of this center of interest. In every well-

FIGURE 1.26 The six types of rhythm are dramatically combined in this library foyer of a private home. (1) Gradation or progression is seen in the arrangement of the books, cabinets, and steps. (2) Repetition occurs with the use of the rectangle, colors, and lines of the ceiling. (3) Contrast is evident with the use of traditional furniture in a modern setting as well as contrasting light and dark colors. (4) Radiation is seen in the ceiling design. (5) Opposition is found where the right angles of the wall-hung bookshelves meet. (6) Transition, although limited, can be seen in the curves of the furniture, pottery, and finials on the cabinets. (Courtesy of Charles Moore Associates. Photograph by Gabriel Benzur, Inc.)

planned room, it is effective to have one feature repeatedly draw the eye (Figure 1.27). This emphasis or focal point can bring a feeling of order and unity into a room,

FIGURE 1.27 In this large room, the focal point of the architecture is the fireplace wall. The stunning painting by J. D. Challenger commands attention as a result of its location and the elements of design used to draw the eye to this feature from any area in the room. (Photograph by Mark Boisclair. Interior designer: Carol Conway. Architect: Kevin Bain.)

with all other groupings subordinated to it. When there is a lack of emphasis in a room, boredom and an uninteresting space can result. Too much emphasis (i.e., more than one or several centers of interest) can produce chaos and unrest. Analyzing a room and determining what components to emphasize and subordinate can be a challenging task. A general approach includes viewing the room on four basic levels of emphasis and then determining what components will be featured.

1. *Emphatic.* These features may include a dramatic view, fireplace, or architectural feature. For example, if a fireplace is prominently placed and designed, it naturally becomes a focal point; in addition, a burning fire radiates warmth, movement, color, and hospitality—a natural site for a main seating arrangement. Many rooms may not have an emphatic feature.
2. *Dominant.* In many instances this is the level where most designers begin. In the absence of dramatic features in a room, a dominant focal point may exist or be created. A fireplace in this case may not be an architecturally dramatic feature, but it certainly can be played up and designed to dominate a room. Other dominant features might include a wall of books, a composition of paintings, a beautiful piece of furniture, or a garden view (Figure 1.28).
3. *Subdominant.* This category includes the level of furnishings that support the focal point and might include large pieces of furniture or the window, ceiling, and floor treatment. Of course, if the designer treats the window or floor coverings and furniture so that they dominate a room, these items would move up to the dominant category.

4. *Subordinate.* This level most often includes accessories like lamps, plants, art objects, and small furnishings. Accessories chosen with discrimination can be artistically arranged and can give importance and individuality to a room.

This method of analyzing a room and breaking it down into various levels of importance can aid the designer; however, great flexibility is possible. Furnishings and architectural features can be rearranged within this framework depending on the desired outcome—in other words, the designer can determine what components will be emphasized and subordinated.

As emphasis in a room is planned and even manipulated through the use of the elements of design, it is essential that all parts relate to and support each other. Whatever the choice for a focal point, it can be important but not overpowering. Although some elements dominate, it is necessary to let the eye move easily about the room without one aspect completely controlling the environment. The room is enhanced when the elements are linked to other furnishings within a space.

- *Color* is probably the most important element by which a grouping may be brought into immediate focus. Color can be used artfully in achieving the desired amount of emphasis.
- *Form* usually involves arranging furniture within the space—placing furnishings so they focus on the point of emphasis. Unusual or strong form used for furnishings or architectural background can be dominant or even dramatic.

- *Texture,* whether rough, smooth, shiny, or dull, can help draw the eye to a particular item. The designer can use this tool to create dominance or to allow a component in the room to blend into the background.
- *Lighting* can be used creatively to tie the group together, dramatize, attract attention, or create a focal point.
- *Pattern,* especially a distinctive design with strong color or value contrast, can attract the eye to a desired focal point. For example, a dramatic patterned fabric canopy or valance over a headboard in a bedroom draws emphasis to that area. Using an attractive pattern on a sofa, patterned wallpaper, or patterned draperies are other effective ways of creating dominant features within a space.

Harmony

Harmony is an essential ingredient in any well-designed room. A unifying theme—a *common denominator*—should run through all the component parts and blend them together. Two goals are combined to create harmony: *unity* and *variety*. Exteriors and interiors are attractive when there is a pleasant relationship that provides unity, yet the aspect of variety is essential to provide interest. *Harmony* results when all other principles of design come into play, aided by the basic elements of design (Figure 1.29). Following are some of the most common and important considerations when seeking a harmonious living environment:

- In every room, the *interior architecture* is a determining factor. Just as the exterior and interior architecture should be consistent, the furnishings of a room must also be in harmony with the background. For example, molded plastic chairs do not belong against formal eighteenth-century paneling, nor is a classic Louis XVI chair desirable against a heavy block wall. A surprising juxtaposition of seemingly unrelated objects may occasionally add relief, but this practice requires sophisticated judgment.
- *Furniture* in the room should seem to belong there. Whether the room is large or small, furniture should be scaled accordingly. Whether the architectural background is strong—perhaps with exposed beams and masonry construction—or more formal and refined, the furniture should reflect the same feeling.
- *Colors* appropriate to the style and scale of furnishings should be considered; however, today's interiors often show great flexibility in color usage. A sensitive approach to color harmonies in relationship to furnishings, background, and style is important in achieving a unified result.

FIGURE 1.29   All the elements and principles of design are effectively used in this exquisite private residence in Georgia, designed by C. Smith Grubbs. The eclectic room combines eighteenth-century English and French styles in a fresh contemporary interpretation. (Photograph by David Schilling/Atlanta.)

- The *textures* of surfaces (i.e., smooth, rough, shiny, or dull) help determine the success of a room's harmony. Textures should be compatible with the design and style of all furnishings. For instance, a heavy homespun fabric is generally not suitable on a highly formal Queen Anne chair, nor is delicate silk damask usually at home on rough-hewn ranch oak.
- A *window treatment* can contribute to the room's total harmony, and planning a hard or soft line treatment suitable for the theme and style is essential. For example, ruffled cottage curtains are out of place in an Oriental-style house, and elegant silk damask swags are inappropriate for a rustic cottage.
- Carefully selected *floor coverings* help unify the scheme. Hard floor surfaces like wood, tile, and stone are extremely versatile and enhance most living areas. Area rugs, such as Persian Orientals, are at home in any decor, and wall-to-wall carpeting can tie an entire room together.
- Consistency or harmony is best achieved by carrying out a basic *theme* or *style*. The basic style need not be followed slavishly, but a general feeling of unity should be maintained throughout. Basic themes usually fall into the categories of *formal modern, informal modern, formal traditional,* or *informal traditional.* This allows the designer to combine good design from many periods with one theme dominating. Within this overall theme, an occasional surprise to give variety and interest can provide charm and individuality.
- *Accessories* can enhance a room or completely destroy the desired effect. If an accessory is not beautiful, useful, or meaningful to the person using it, it does not belong. The final touches added to a room reveal individual personality more readily than any other items of furnishing and cannot be overlooked in creating rooms of beauty and interest. Items that are essentially good, however, can lose their charm when not well used. For example, a gracefully scrolled wrought-iron wall sconce can add much to a room of Spanish or Mediterranean styling but would look heavy and out of place in a pastel room with delicate furnishings (see Chapter 9).

ASSIGNMENT

The following assignment is aimed at promoting awareness of the many principles and elements involved in the complete design of a room.

Select a *clear, colored* picture of a living room. The view should be complete, not just a corner of the room. Mount the picture on white paper, allowing a margin sufficiently wide for answering question 1. Write the answers to the remaining questions below the picture.

1. Point out the following by drawing a line from the correct object or objects in the picture to the explanation in the margin:

   An example of structural design

   An example of decorative design

   The use of the golden mean (explain briefly)

   A vertical line

   A horizontal line

   A curved line

   A diagonal line

   An example of bisymmetrical balance (explain briefly)

   An example of asymmetrical balance (explain briefly)

   Rhythm by repetition

   Rhythm by gradation

   Rhythm by opposition

   Rhythm by transition

   Rhythm by radiation

   Rhythm by contrast

2. Is there a predominance of one line, or are lines pleasingly distributed?
3. Are the elements of the room more strong or more delicate, or is neither effect predominant?
4. What kinds of designs are used in the fabrics in the room (e.g., naturalistic, conventional, abstract, geometric)? If the fabrics have no design, point out two specific textures used.
5. What is the focal point of the room? Point out four ways through which elements were used to bring this area into focus (see the section on emphasis).
6. Does the room have a feeling of unity and harmony? Examine the room carefully: backgrounds, furniture, fabrics, and accessories. Point out six specific elements of the room that contribute to the overall feeling of unity (see the section on harmony).
7. Does the lighting appear to be adequate? Are lighting fixtures and lamps artfully and conveniently located?

Make comments specifically related to the picture submitted. Selection and presentation will be considered in evaluating this project.

CHAPTER 2

Color

FIGURE 2.1 A color scheme of gray, gray-blue, and silver, popular during the Art Deco period, has been used in the Palm Court at the historic Omni Netherland Plaza Hotel in Cincinnati. (Courtesy of White House Publishing Co., Cincinnati.)

Color in History

The Psychology and Physiology of Color

Color Groups

Warm Colors
Cool Colors
Neutral and Neutralized Colors

Psychological and Physiological Effects of Individual Colors

Color and Pigment

Color Systems

The Brewster System
The Ostwald System
The Munsell System
Other Color Systems

Color's Three Dimensions

Hue
Value
Intensity or Chroma
Computer Applications

Creating Livable Color Harmonies

Monochromatic
Neutral (Achromatic) and Neutralized or Monotone
Analogous
Complementary

Additional Ways of Creating Color Harmony

The Shibui Color Harmony
Natural Earth Colors

Other Considerations in Color Application

The Effect of Adjacent Colors on Each Other
The Effect of Natural and Artificial Light on Color
The Effect of Texture on Color
The Effect of Distance and Area on Color
The Effect of Color on Temperature
Some Uses of Color for the Interior
Reflecting the Mood of the Room
Reflecting Personality
Color in Wood

Color Considerations for Nonresidential Settings

Color Forecasts for the 1990s

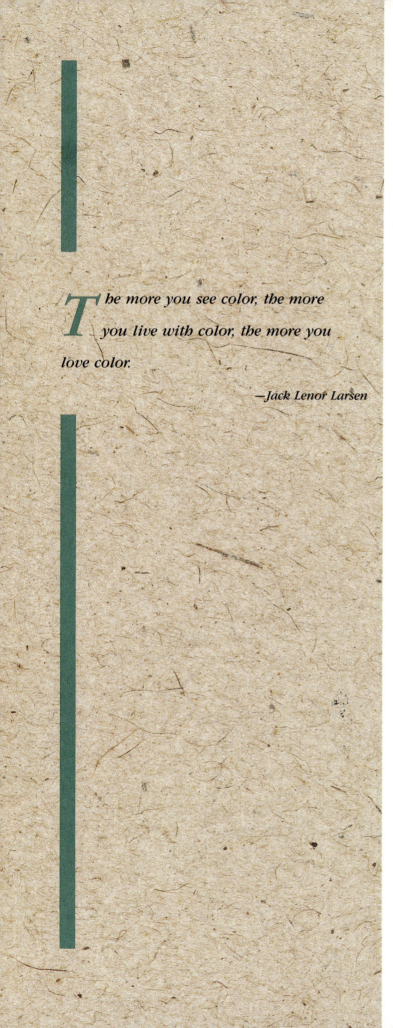

*T*he more you see color, the more you live with color, the more you love color.

—*Jack Lenor Larsen*

*T*he great nineteenth-century writer and critic John Ruskin said, "Color is the most sacred element in all visual things." Designers agree that color provides a visual sensation that is considered the most vital and expressive of the seven elements of design, as demonstrated in Figure 2.1. Therefore, it is essential that designers have a thorough knowledge of color associations, color theory, the properties and character of various colors, historic colors, color systems, and other considerations of color for use in planning both residential and nonresidential design.

Color, like music, is an international language. Throughout the world, birds, animals, trees, flowers, jewels, signals, and many other objects are identified by their coloring. The red-breasted robin, the green pine tree, and the blue sapphire look much the same wherever they are found. A red signal is recognized everywhere as a warning of danger, a green signal as an assurance of safety.

Color has always had symbolic importance. In early China, yellow had religious significance. In early Greece and Rome, red was believed to have protective powers. Purple was the imperial color of the ancients and was restricted for the use of nobility—hence the term *royal purple.* When the remains of Charlemagne (742–814) were disinterred in the middle of the twelfth century, the coffin was found to contain robes of sumptuous purple velvet. To the present time, purple is identified with royalty.

Among English-speaking people, many colors signify certain character traits, and expressions using color names have specific meanings commonly used and understood. When someone has the blues, the interpretation is that the person is unhappy or depressed. When a person has a green thumb, the meaning is an unusual ability to make plants grow. Other common color expressions and descriptive associations include caught red-handed, red-letter day, red tape, red alert, green with envy, green men from Mars, yellow coward, yellow journalism, blue blood, blue ribbon, blue chip, blue moon, born to the purple, white lies, white elephant, black magic, blackball, black market, and blackmail.

COLOR IN HISTORY

Color can reveal much about the civilizations of people in both primitive tribes and highly developed cultures, but perhaps the greatest value of color is its power to create beauty. Since the dawn of history, humans have toiled to bring beauty into their environment through the use of color. Following are some of the cultures that have had a significant influence on color use through the centuries.

Ancient Egypt (ca. 4000–660 B.C.). The ancient Egyptians adorned the walls of tombs and temples with brilliant hues of blue, tangerine, green, and *carmine.* Other colors they used were dull reds, various browns, rust, yellow, white, and black. Colors were derived from natural sources like red soil, soot, and lime.

Ancient Greece and Rome (ca. 6th Century B.C.–450 A.D.). The great temples and dwellings of Greece and Rome were decorated with colored marble and mosaic floors, brightly painted walls and ceilings, and richly colored tapestries and silks. Much of our information comes from surviving pottery and mosaic floors that show colors of cream, brown, white, black, purple, mauve, pink, deep green, and red. Particularly associated with ancient Italy are gold, blue, and a dull red called Pompeian red (named after the ancient city of Pompeii), which was often complemented with blue-green or used side by side with black and gold.

Medieval Europe (ca. 500–1500). The great cathedrals of medieval Europe, with their gloriously colored stained-glass windows, brought beauty into people's drab lives and remain today as supreme creative achievements of Western culture. Dominant colors were brilliant blues, reds, purples, yellows, golds, and greens.

Renaissance (ca. 1400–1600). During the Italian Renaissance the vibrant reds, greens, golds, and blues used by master artists were carried into the sumptuous villas of the reigning families in Italy and later into the great palaces of France, Germany, and England. Other colors include deep browns, greens, blues, golds, and reds with cream and some pale blue.

Louis XV and Rococo (1730–1774). With the **rococo** extravagance of Louis XV in France, where feminine tastes had great influence, colors became less vibrant. Courtiers such as Madame du Pompadour and Madame du Barry favored the use of lighter colors.

Neoclassic France (1760–1789). During the latter part of the eighteenth century, when Marie Antoinette reigned at the court of Louis XVI, colors became even more delicate and softly pastel. Throughout the late seventeenth and eighteenth centuries, when France dominated the arts of the Western world, French colors were in vogue wherever beauty and luxury were cherished.

Early Colonial America (1607–1700). This period is marked by the use of colors popular in Renaissance England, but somewhat lighter in value. Typical colors used were cupboard red (dark reddish brown), various greens ranging from deep green to pale yellow green, dark grayish blue, and natural colors such as cream, brown, and white.

Eighteenth-Century Georgian (1714–1790). This elegant period in England is well known for its great cabinetmakers—Chippendale, Hepplewhite, Sheraton, and the Adam brothers. The first half of the century witnessed the Chinese influence in the use of rich reds and golds, particularly found in the work of Thomas Chippendale. Also popular were dull medium tones of Williamsburg green and Williamsburg blue.

Neoclassic England and America (ca. 1790–1820). Toward the latter part of the century, the excavation of Pompeii in Italy inspired the Adam brothers in England

FIGURE 2.2 Understanding historic use of color helps the designer create settings that evoke the look and feel of a particular period. (Courtesy of Schumacher.)

and Thomas Jefferson and others in America to introduce the neoclassic style. Colors became more delicate, with Adam green (sharp, light green), peach, pink, soft yellow, and Wedgewood blue as favorites. Often these colors were combined with ivory or cream. In America the style was known as **Federal** (see Figure 2.2).

Empire and Greek Revival (ca. 1804–1860). The grand use of classical architecture and furnishings, particularly inspired by ancient Greece and Egypt, was popular during the first half of the nineteenth century. The Emperor Napoleon in France promoted the colors black, white, Empire green (deep emerald green), gold, and intense, vibrant colors like purple, red, yellow, and blue, which in turn influenced both European and American interiors.

China. Colors used in China for centuries have had a tremendous impact on the Western world that continues today. They include peacock blue, white, gold, chrysanthemum yellow, cherry blossom pink, celadon green (medium to light green), jade green, red-orange, red, and black.

Japan. The complex color theory called *shibui* employs colors derived from nature (see p. 46). American architect Frank Lloyd Wright was one of the first designers to introduce this color concept to the Western world.

Spain and Mexico (1600 to present). Vivid colors—blue, red, gold, pink, and orange—coupled with white and black have long been expressive of the Spanish and Mexican cultures, and these colors contribute to this style in traditional and contemporary Spanish American homes.

Southwest (ca. 1500 to present). Colors used for centuries by Native Americans in New Mexico and Arizona on blankets, rugs, and pottery continue to be popular, such as deep red, turquoise, gray, purple, black, and cream.

Victorian period (1837 to the turn of the century). The Victorian era was a period of eclecticism, known for its abundance of furnishings and accessories in the home. Colors were predominantly dull or vivid reds, bottle greens, tobacco browns, and deep purple mauves, which prompted the use of the term *the Mauve Decades* to refer to this era. Accent colors were brighter.

Arts and Crafts period. From about 1860 until the turn of the century, the **Arts and Crafts Movement** was popular in England and America. The movement, founded by William Morris, advocated a return to hand-crafted articles for home use inspired by medieval times. Popular colors were inspired by nature and made only with natural dyes. Colors were blue-greens, deep orange, rich greens, reds, blues, and golds.

Art Nouveau. During the opening decades of the twentieth century, the revolutionary ideas of the **Art Nouveau** style introduced plant forms and other influences from nature interpreted in exaggerated flowing forms. Soft afternoon colors of apricot, greens, and golds were made popular by French graphic designer Alphonse Mucha and others. Stained glass in rich colors was used by Louis Comfort Tiffany, and Charles Rennie Mackintosh in Scotland introduced the "modern" use of white, rose, pink, purple, and black for furnishings and interiors. Other avant-garde designers in Europe and America involved with Art Nouveau also combined unusual color schemes considered innovative for the time.

Sante Fe style (1920s to present). This style was made popular by East Coast residents "weekending" in Santa Fe, who brought furnishings from the East Coast and mixed them with local Native American, Mexican, and desert themes. The result was a sophisticated use of color including desert colors of sand, soft purples, blues, blue-greens, greens, corals, cream, and white.

Bauhaus, International Style (1919 to present). The famous experimental German design school, the **Bauhaus**, which flourished from 1919 to 1933, Swiss/French modern designer Le Corbusier, and others in Europe and America advocated clean, simple, white color schemes. This movement introduced modernism on a grand scale. In 1917 the modern Dutch group De Stijl introduced the use of white interiors accented by red, blue, yellow, gray, and black furnishings.

Art Deco (ca. 1909 to outbreak of World War II). A decorative style of the "Roaring Twenties" and thirties in America and Europe, **Art Deco** employed inspiration from many sources including the cinema, new modernism, ancient Egypt, and new technology. Colors included white, black, gray, silver, red, purple, chocolate brown,

turquoise, gray-blue, gray-green, peach, and pink. The style remains popular today, interpreted in contemporary terms.

Post–World War II (1940s–1960s). Light colors were generally preferred through the fifties; particularly popular were beige or off-white walls. Turquoise, orange, brown, rose, and blue were also popular for furnishings. American interest also turned to Mexico, and a shift to brighter colors with more contrast occurred, paving the way for a vivid palette of color that found favor with lovers of Spanish colonial. Scandinavian modern design and colors were introduced in America during this time, and blue and green and other "new" color combinations were used. Other modern movements with new color possibilities arose during the 1950s and 1960s. Particularly in the 1960s, a renewed interest in English furnishings of the sixteenth and seventeenth centuries brought with it rich, blended color schemes employing blue, green, gold, and red. French country and court style furnishings and colors continued to be popular in America during the postwar period.

The 1970s. The decade of the seventies witnessed a wide range of color fashions. One direction had to do with the patriotism generated by the American bicentennial, producing a renewed interest in the ever-popular combination of red, white, and blue. These colors were used not only for color schemes in many rooms of the house but also for many areas of industry and the arts. Color was used dramatically. For example, three extremes were fashionable: one employed shiny black walls with strong colors throughout the room, another used a silvery look for all furnishings and backgrounds, and still another was the all-over white look.

The 1980s. With the advent of new architectural and design styles such as **Post-Modernism**, **Memphis**, and **High Tech**, color trends increasingly incorporated many choices for both residential and nonresidential design. For example, the Memphis influence incorporated strong, vivid primary and secondary colors. Post-Modernism popularized muted purples, blues, pinks, greens, and peach. A great freedom in the use of color in the home and work environment was evident. Although they stay in vogue for only a short time, color fads and trends continue to influence designers and consumers. One trend that remained strong throughout the 1980s was the use of gray, pastel hues, and muted colors made popular by the Post-Modern style and neutral schemes. (See Color Forecasts for the 1990s at the end of the chapter.)

THE PSYCHOLOGY AND PHYSIOLOGY OF COLOR

Research has shown that the human body responds to color both psychologically and physiologically. Some major studies have shown that: (1) Color affects an individual's moods or feelings in regard to space. Therefore, the color of a particular space can be chosen to suit the activities of that area. Light and cool colors seem to expand space; dark and warm colors seem to enclose space. (2) Color affects the eye's perception of weight and size. Dark and bright colors seem heavier than light and cool colors. (3) Color affects a person's perception of temperature. Studies have indicated that the body's temperature actually fluctuates in response to various colors. For example, red, orange and yellow can raise one's temperature 5 to 7 degrees; cool colors have the opposite reaction. (4) Color can cause feelings of boredom and calmness, or stimulation and liveliness. Colors may cause the nervous system to become agitated, and the body reacts in negative ways to this stimulus. (5) Colors can even affect the body's reaction to sounds, taste, odors, and time perception.

It is understandable, then, that knowledge of the psychological and physiological effects of each color and its relationship to people are of immense value to the designer when planning both residential and nonresidential spaces. For example, experiments have shown that workers function more efficiently in surroundings of pleasant colors than they do in drab environments. Young people in detention homes have been found to respond more positively when dull-colored walls have been repainted with a bright color. The color pink has been found to have a soothing and calming effect.

Responding to the generally accepted notion that red will excite one to action and blue will calm one's nerves, some athletic directors have painted their players' dressing rooms in bright reds and oranges and visitors' dressing rooms in pale blues. The directors claim that it works.

Emotional reactions associated with color are spontaneous. The reaction is often due to the perception of a color rather than to the color itself, and the reaction produced may be positive or negative.

One such situation occurred in a meat market in Chicago, which, when painted a bright and cheerful yellow, lost business. A color consultant quickly informed the owner that the yellow walls caused a blue afterimage. It gave meat a purplish cast, making it appear old and spoiled. The walls were repainted bluish green, creating a red afterimage that enhanced the appearance of meat, and sales zoomed (John Dreyfuss, *Los Angeles Times*, 1977).

Some other popular color studies have indicated that:

- Drivers of brightly painted sports cars have higher insurance premiums and receive more traffic tickets than drivers of cars painted in more conservative colors.
- Most people prefer to eat from a white dinner plate rather than a colored one.
- Most flags of the world use one or more of only seven traditional colors: red, white, blue, green, yellow, orange, and black.

- Bulls, which are color-blind, react to the movement of the matador's cape rather than the color red—the crowd reacts to the excitement of red.
- Doctors tend to paint the walls of their offices soft calming colors, as opposed to the traditional stark white walls, which used to have a frightening and cold effect on patients.
- Fast-food restaurants tend to use bright warm colors for interior surfaces in order to stimulate the appetite and hurry patrons through their meals.
- After factory workers complained how heavy their black boxes were to carry, a color expert painted the boxes light blue. The workers congratulated management on making the boxes lighter.

Despite these popular studies, however, the knowledge on which popular assumptions about color are based is often superficial. Serious research on the subject is inconclusive and often contradictory. Authorities in the field generally agree that color and emotion are closely related and that people react differently to color. They do not, however, agree on the emotional effects of color, nor do they know whether emotional reactions to colors are inherent or learned.

That individuals have definite color preferences is common knowledge. We all have favorite colors that we find attractive and comfortable. Because of this, it makes sense to fashion our personal environment with these colors.

COLOR GROUPS

The simplest psychological division of color results in two major groups: *warm* and *cool,* with *neutral* in between.

Warm Colors

The warm colors of the spectrum include red, red-orange, orange, yellow-orange, yellow, and yellow-green. These colors have certain identifiable psychological and physiological attributes, especially when of a strong intensity. (See Figure 2.3.) Generally, these warm colors are considered engaging, active, positive, cheery, cozy, advancing, stimulating, and somewhat informal, tending to blend objects together (soften outlines) and to close in space. If used in strong intensity in large areas, warm colors may cause psychological irritation.

Cool Colors

The cool colors are blue, blue-green, green, violet, and blue-violet. Particularly in tints, cool colors are generally felt to be relaxing, restful, soothing, receding, and somewhat formal, tending to make individual objects stand out (reinforce outlines) and to expand space. Rooms done in

FIGURE 2.3 A warm color harmony of orange, yellow, and gold conveys a cheerful, optimistic, and lively atmosphere. The mirrored wall behind the sofa visually expands the space of this inviting living area. (Courtesy of Lynn McGhie & Associates.)

all cool colors may be perceived as too cool and unfriendly and may lack unity. (See Figure 2.4.)

Neutral and Neutralized Colors

Neutral Colors

Technically, neutral colors are gray, white, and black because they are without identifiable hue. These neutral colors are often called "achromatic," which in Greek means "without color."

Neutralized Colors

Colors falling midway between the warm and cool color groups are called **neutralized colors**. A warm neutralized color is a tint, tone, or shade of a warm hue; a cool neutralized color is a tint, tone, or shade of a cool hue. Warm neutralized colors are generally easier to work with than cool neutralized colors. Large background areas of warm neutralized tones tend to produce the most livable and lasting color schemes. (See Figure 2.5.)

Neutralized colors are generally important to every color scheme. They tend to be restful, tranquil, livable, unobtrusive, and supportive. However, if not used effectively, neutral and neutralized colors can produce feelings of boredom and weariness.

Many designers regard neutralized colors as neutrals too since the distinction between neutral and neutralized colors is confusing. In addition, colors like beige, brown, taupe, cream, ivory, off-black, and off-white (white with any small amount of hue added) are often regarded by designers as neutral colors because they possess very little chroma.

FIGURE 2.4 Cool colors of green and blue are combined in a bold Post-Modern design for a commercial space. The psychological effect is one of serenity, formality, and spaciousness. (Courtesy of Nishiyama Corporation of America.)

FIGURE 2.5 Neutral white and a number of neutralized colors create serene and harmonious living spaces in this Manhattan apartment. The lack of dramatic color allows attention to center on the wonderful variety of textures and surfaces. (Courtesy of Ron Wilson, designer, Beverly Hills.)

PSYCHOLOGICAL AND PHYSIOLOGICAL EFFECTS OF INDIVIDUAL COLORS

In addition to the division of colors into warm and cool, each color contains peculiar properties that produce certain psychological effects.

Hue: **Red** (warm group—primary color). *Psychological and physiological associations:* Courage, passion, love, excitement, danger, martyrdom, anger, fire, strength. *Application:* Red is conspicuous wherever it appears, and since it is lively and stimulating, it should be used with care. Red mixes well and most rooms are enhanced by a touch of one of its tones. A variety of popular colors are derived from red when it is lightened or darkened or brightened or dulled. For example, when red is darkened and muted it becomes maroon, and when it is lightened becomes pink. Pink is delicate and flattering. Pink is often enhanced by a stronger contrasting color and blends especially well with grays, browns, greens, blues, and purples.

Hue: **Yellow** (warm group—primary color). *Psychological and physiological associations:* Cowardice, deceit, sunlight, optimism, warmth, enlightenment, communication. *Application:* High-noon yellows are the most revealing and demanding and merit careful attention. Gray-yellows of early dawn are foils for more fragile colors—pinks, blues, pale greens. Warm afternoon yellow is a foil for rich, warm woods. Burnished yellows of brass give a cast of copper gilt and bring life to a room. Gold, inspired by the precious metal, provides an elegant and luxurious touch, especially for accents or accessories. All yellows are reflective, take on tones of other colors, and add flattering highlights.

Hue: **Orange** (warm group—secondary color). *Psychological and physiological associations:* Cheerfulness, stimulation, sunset, excitement. *Application:* Orange has similar stimulating properties as red, but is not as demanding. When lightened and muted, orange becomes a peach tone. Orange mixes well with cool colors.

Hue: **Blue** (cool group—primary color). *Psychological and physiological associations:* Honesty, truth, loyalty, masculinity, formality, repose, tranquility, sobriety, sky, depth of sea. *Application:* Blue is cool and soothing, recalling sky, water, and ice. It is difficult to mix and varies greatly under different lighting. More than any other color, blue is affected by the different materials it colors. Lacquer and glass, for example, have a reflective quality that intensifies blue. In deep-pile carpet, blue has great depth. Nubby fabrics soften blue. Shiny materials make blue look frosted. Light blue can give a ceiling a cool and celestial appearance. Blue can be somber, cold, and even depressing if not used effectively.

Hue: **Green** (cool group—secondary color). *Psychological and physiological associations:* Nature, serenity, hope, envy, safety, peace, passivity, security. *Application:* Fresh and friendly, green is nature's color and is a good mixer, especially yellow-green and spruce or forest green. White brings out green's best qualities. When grayed, warmed, or cooled, green makes an excellent background. When lightened, it is retiring and restful. Deep dark green is a favorite color for floor coverings.

Hue: **Violet** (cool group—secondary color). *Psychological and physiological associations:* Royalty, nobility, snobbery, power, drama, opulence, mystery, worship, dignity. *Application:* Naturally a dark value, violet is a blend of blue and red. When pink is added, it becomes warm, and a touch of blue makes it cool. It combines well with both pink and blue. A light value of violet produces lavender, a popular pastel employed in today's interiors. Other popular violet hues are plum, eggplant, and lilac. Often violet is used in small amounts as accents. It can be dramatic or even disturbing when used on large surfaces.

Hue: **White** (neutral color) and **off-white** (neutralized color). *Psychological and physiological associations:* Purity, cleanliness, sterility, sophistication, and freshness. *Application:* White and off-white have the psychological quality of making all colors in a room look cleaner and livelier. Warm off-white is considered unequaled as a mellow background color and works wonders in blending furniture of different woods and styles. Changes of light from day to night are kind to off-white and give it quiet vitality. White and off-white are at home in either traditional or modern styles. They can also give a mood of sterility and emptiness.

Hue: **Black** (neutral color—achromatic) and **off-black** (black-brown, neutralized color). *Psychological and physiological associations:* Mourning, sorrow, depression, sophistication, mystery, magic, night. *Application:* Black and off-black (a rich black-brown) in furniture finishes, small areas of fabric, or accessories add an important accent that makes other colors crisp and clear. When used for larger areas, black can be extremely dramatic but can also be oppressive and claustrophobic.

Hue: **Gray** (neutral color—achromatic). *Psychological and physiological associations:* Penance, gloom, storm, fog, depression, wisdom, intelligence, business, high-tech, sophistication. *Application:* Gray is used when a neutral appearance is desired. It may be tiring or monotonous without colorful accents for other furnishings. Gray is a good mixer with other colors, especially pinks, purples, and blues. Dark gray on large areas may be depressing. Light gray provides a nice background color.

Hue: **Brown** (neutralized color). *Psychological and physiological associations:* Earth, wood, warmth, comfort, security, support, stability. *Application:* The homeyness of brown tones makes them universal favorites, especially for furnishings made of wood. Ranging from pale cream beige to deeper chocolate brown, these tones, tints, and shades can be used together in a room to give infinite variety. Light browns, beige for example, make excellent supportive backgrounds.

COLOR AND PIGMENT

Over 300 years ago Sir Isaac Newton began a series of experiments that provided the foundation for our modern knowledge of color. Ever since, scientists have been developing new color theories and systems. Many different scientific approaches to color exist. The *physicist* works with colors in *light,* the *chemist* is mainly concerned with the production of *pigments,* and the *psychologist* has theories based on *visual perception* and the effects of color on the emotions. The artist—and particularly the student of interior design—benefits from an understanding of all three approaches, especially regarding color in pigments.

The most practical approach to the understanding of color derives from personal experience. Individuals are constantly surrounded by color. The colors in objects are referred to as *pigment colors* and the colors from the sun and from lamps are called *light colors.*

The process of combining the primary colors of light (red, green, and blue) is said to be an **additive** one (i.e., the sensations produced by different wavelengths of light, or **spectral** colors, are added together). When pigments are mixed, however, the resulting sensations differ from those of the spectral colors. In this case, the method is a *subtractive* one, since subtraction or absorption of the wavelengths of light occurs.

In reality, *a ray of light* is the source of all color, for without light, color does not exist. Color is light broken down into **electromagnetic** vibrations of varying wavelengths, which cause the viewer to see different colors. This phenomenon can be demonstrated by passing a beam of light through a glass prism. (See Figure 2.6.) The beam divides into the colors of the spectrum, proving that white light contains these colors. The longest wavelength is perceived as red and the shortest as violet. Everyone has had the experience of seeing these rainbow colors in a variety of places. A bright beam of light striking a soap bubble or the **bevel** edge of a mirror reflects the spectrum hues.

For the designer, however, pigment colors are of greater concern than spectral colors. Pigments are substances of various kinds that can be ground into fine powder and used for coloring dyes and paints. Certain pigments are combined to get certain colors, such as red and yellow to obtain orange, or blue and yellow to obtain green. Before people learned how to produce pigments

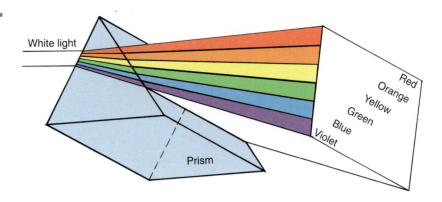

FIGURE 2.6 A ray of white light passed through a prism separates into distinct bands of color. The longest wavelength in the visible spectrum is red, followed by orange, yellow, green, blue, and violet, the shortest visible wavelength.

by chemical means, they were derived from *animal, mineral,* and *vegetable* sources. The Mayans in Central America extracted purple from shellfish. The highly prized Tyrian purple, which was used to color the robes of early Roman emperors, was obtained by the Phoenicians from shellfish found in the Mediterranean Sea. Another important dye of the Middle East was a red dye extracted from kermes, the dried bodies of scale insects.

The East Indians, who are usually credited with having first developed a thriving dyeing trade, were skilled in securing dyes from many plants, such as madder for red and indigo for blue. The ancient Chinese and Arabs were also familiar with natural sources of various pigments. Until the mid-nineteenth century, nature was the only source of dyes, many of which did not hold up well. Modern technology has improved the sharpness of color, the range of hues available, and the fastness and durability of dyes.

As a designer you will find a basic understanding of the derivation and development of color pigments both essential and rewarding. Many excellent books on the subject are available for in-depth study. (See the Bibliography.)

COLOR SYSTEMS

A number of color theories, or systems, have been developed and are in use today. Some incorporate psychological as well as physical factors. A variety of color wheels have been produced, each based on a different group of basic colors. The most common are: (1) the Ostwald color system, based on four principal hues: yellow, red, blue, and green, plus black and white; (2) the Munsell system, which begins with five hues: yellow, red, blue, green, and purple; and (3) the Brewster system, based on the three primaries: yellow, red, and blue.

The Brewster System

Developed by David Brewster, the **Brewster system** is the simplest and best known of the color systems. (It is often

referred to as the Prang color wheel or the *standard color wheel.*) (See Figure 2.7.) The Brewster system is a pigment theory employing the familiar color wheel based on *three primary colors: yellow, red,* and *blue.* **Primary** means the colors cannot be mixed from other pigments, nor can they be broken down into component colors. Theoretically, with five tubes of paint—the three primaries plus black and white—one could produce the entire range of colors, although the degree of precision needed makes this almost impossible. By using the three primaries, however, the twelve colors of the complete wheel can be derived.

Equal amounts of any two of the primary colors result in a **secondary** color. The Brewster wheel has three such colors: green, which is produced by mixing yellow and blue; violet, by mixing blue and red; and orange, by mixing red and yellow. The secondary color lies midway between the primary colors from which it is formed.

In similar fashion **tertiary**, or *intermediary,* hues are composed by mixing equal amounts of a primary color and a secondary color. These hues are also situated midway between the two hues that produced them and are identified by hyphenated names such as blue-green, red-orange, and red-violet. The last one, red-violet, is a combination of the two extreme hues of the spectrum. These twelve hues make up the full color wheel and include all the spectrum colors plus red-violet. The Brewster Color Wheel is a simple and useful tool for the designer.

The Ostwald System

The **Ostwald system** was named after its creator, the German scientist Friedrich Wilhelm Ostwald (1853–1932). The Ostwald Color Wheel, which uses yellow, orange, red, purple, blue, turquoise, sea green, and leaf green, is based on hue plus the white content and the black content of the hue. Theoretically, 24 hues can be derived from mixing these hues plus pure white and black. There are 28 variations of these 24 hues with a resulting total of 672 hues and 8 neutrals. The cool group of hues is on one half of the circle and the warm group of hues is arranged on the other half of the circle. Ostwald arranged the hues in a conical configuration with a value and

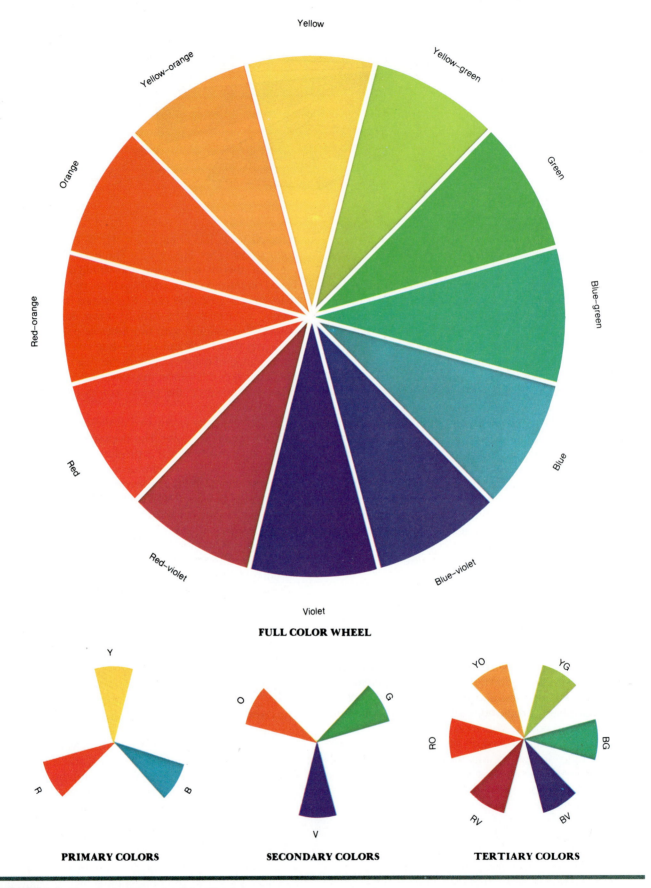

Yellow

Yellow–green

Yellow–orange

Green

Orange

Blue–green

Red–orange

Blue

Red

Blue–violet

Red–violet

Violet

FULL COLOR WHEEL

Y

R   B

PRIMARY COLORS

O   G

V

SECONDARY COLORS

YO   YG

RO   BG

RV   BV

TERTIARY COLORS

FIGURE 2.7 The standard Brewster Color Wheel.

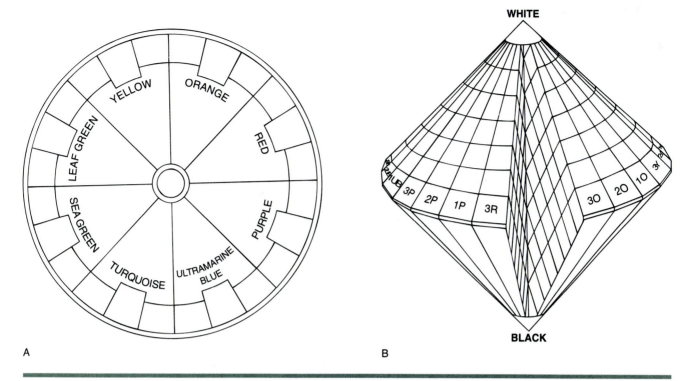

A

B

WHITE

BLACK

FIGURE 2.8 The Ostwald color system. *A,* the Ostwald color wheel is based on 24 hues that are either a pure hue or mixed with a pure hue plus white and black. The principal hues are yellow, orange, red, purple, ultramarine blue, turquoise, sea green, and leaf green. The other 16 hues are intermediate hues of these colors. *B,* the hues and their ranges of value and chroma are arranged to form a three-dimensional double cone.

chroma scale similar to Munsell's system, discussed next. (See Figure 2.8.)

The Munsell System

The **Munsell system** of color notation is essentially a scientific concept of describing and analyzing color in terms of three attributes: hue, value, and chroma. The designation of each color is written as H v/c. (See Figure 2.9.)

- **Hue,** or the color name, is indicated by the capital letter *H,* followed by a fraction in which the numerator represents the value and the denominator indicates the chroma. In the figure, hue is indicated by the circular band.
- **Value,** or the lightness and darkness of a color, is indicated by the central axis, which shows nine visible steps, from darkest value at the bottom to lightest value at the top, with 5/ for middle gray. Pure black would be designated as 0/ and pure white as 10/.
- The **chroma** notation is shown by the horizontal band extending outward from the value axis. It indicates the degree of departure of a given hue from a neutral gray of the same value. Since hues vary in their saturation strength, the number of chroma steps also varies. For example, yellow has the smallest number, and red has

the greatest number. Since yellow is nearest to white, it is placed nearest the top of the color tree at step 8; thus, normal yellow is Y 8/chroma. Other hues are placed at their natural values' levels, such as 5 red is natural at R 4/. Thus, the value of 5R and step 4 on the value scale are equal, designated as R 4/c. Purple is the darkest hue and is normal at step 3 on the value scale: P 3/c. The complete notation for a sample of vermillion might be 5R 4/14, meaning that 5R = pure red, 4/ = natural value, and /14 = strongest chroma.

In the Munsell system, *chroma,* the Greek word for "color," is used instead of intensity. This complex color system can be simplified to the following basics:

1. The chromatic colors are based on *five principal hues: red, yellow, green, blue,* and *purple.* The five intermediate colors that lie between these hues are yellow-red, green-yellow, blue-green, purple-blue, and red-purple, these being combinations of the five principal hues.
2. Each of these 10 hues is subdivided into four parts, indicated by the numerals 2.5, 5, 7.5, and 10. These hue names are symbolized by capitalized initials, such as R for red or YR for yellow-red.
3. When finer subdivisions are required, these 10 hues may again be combined, such as R-YR, which may be combined into still finer divisions.

FIGURE 2.9 Munsell Color System, including hue, value, and chroma relationships. *A,* The circular band represents the hues in their proper sequences. The upright, center axis is the scale of value. The paths pointing outward from the center show the steps of chroma increasing in strength, as indicated by the numerals. *B,* Hue notations of the five principal and the five intermediate hue families are encircled. A breakdown into 100 hues is indicated by the outer circle of markings, and the breakdown of each hue family into four parts (2.5., 5, 7.5, and 10) indicates the 40 constant-hue charts appearing in the *Munsell Book of Color. C,* Hue, value, and chroma are shown in relation to one another. The circular band represents the hues in their proper sequences. The upright center axis is the scale of value. The paths pointing outward from the center show the steps of chroma, increasing in strength as indicated by the numerals. (Courtesy of Munsell Color Company, Inc.)

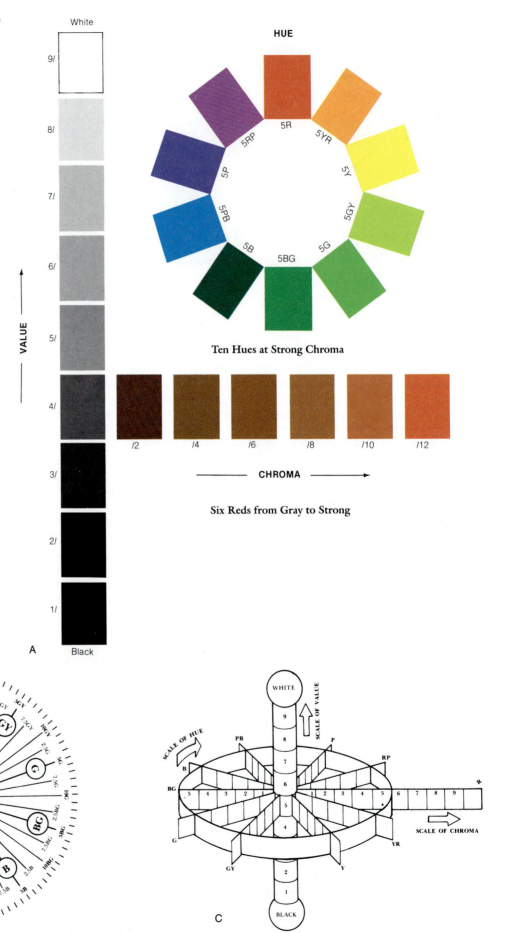

White

9/

8/

7/

6/

5/

4/

3/

2/

1/

VALUE

A

Black

HUE

5R

5RP

5YR

5P

5Y

5PB

5GY

5B

5G

5BG

Ten Hues at Strong Chroma

/2   /4   /6   /8   /10   /12

CHROMA

Six Reds from Gray to Strong

B

N

C

WHITE

SCALE OF VALUE

SCALE OF HUE

SCALE OF CHROMA

BLACK

4. The segment lying between each of the 10 color hues is divided into 10 color steps. In each case, the basic and intermediate color is in the center and is marked by the number 5, which indicates it is the strongest degree of pure color of that particular hue. Each of the 10 different hues, such as red, is designated by a number using the decimal system to indicate its degree of redness or intensity. For example, 2.5R has more red than 10RP, but both have much less red than 5R. Because this designation is done with the 10 color segments, the Munsell Color Wheel has a total of 100 different colors.

5. By using the correct letters and numbers, one can describe any given hue and locate it on the color tree. Through this practical method colors can be identified and standardized for professional purposes. This notation is useful to the interior designer, because it makes it possible to communicate color information in a precise manner.

Other Color Systems

Those working with color generally use the type of color system that best suits the needs of a particular project. In addition to the Brewster, Ostwald, and Munsell systems, other color systems are available to the designer. To present all these systems goes beyond the scope of this introductory text, but two of the best known include the *Gerritsen Color System,* based on color perception and six primary colors, and the *Kuppers Color System,* based on six primary colors: blue, green, yellow, red, cyan (a blue-green), and magenta.

Paint Manufacturer Color Systems
Many major paint manufacturers, such as Ameritone and DeVoe, have made available convenient color systems, color keys, and color codes that coordinate colors in particular ways with their products. The colors usually are coded according to cool, warm, and neutral harmonies.

Johannes Itten's Color Theories
Itten (1889–1967) originated his ideas on color while a teacher at the Bauhaus in Germany during the 1920s. One of his theories is the popular "Four Seasons—Personal Color Analysis" based on color palettes associated with the four seasons of the year.

Josef Albers
Josef Albers (1888–1976) was a pioneer of modern design and a teacher and color theorist at the Bauhaus in Germany and later at Yale University. He is particularly known for his theories on color perception. Albers's series of paintings entitled "Homage to the Square" demonstrate how one color reacts when placed next to another color. He found that color changes greatly as a result of its environment. His book *Interaction with Color* (1963) is still a popular reference.

Color Consultant Manufacturers
Currently a number of corporations offer designers and other clients color matching based on the latest computerized matching technology. These systems contain thousands of color samples for project specifications.

No one color system is universally accepted. Most industrial nations have their own systems of color classification and, regrettably, these systems are not interchangeable. Most designers select a system they feel comfortable with and that has a variety of colors available. It is also important that the system be organized and capable of accommodating specific design tasks.

COLOR'S THREE DIMENSIONS

The three dimensions of color have already been referred to in the Munsell notation. These major characteristics, basic to all colors, can be accurately measured and are essential in visualizing and describing any color. These qualities are hue, value, and intensity (or chroma).

Hue

Hue, or the *color name,* is the singular characteristic that sets each color apart from all the others. A color may be lightened or darkened, made more intense or less intense. If blue is the hue used, the result will be light blue, dark blue, bright blue, or gray-blue, but each will be of a blue hue. In all, about 150 variations of full chroma of hue exist, of which only 24 basic hues of full chroma have enough variation to be of practical use.

When neighboring hues on the color wheel are mixed, they produce new hues that are harmonious and closely related. When hues opposite from each other on the color wheel are mixed, the result is a neutral hue.

In beginning a color scheme for any room, generally one dominant hue is the starting point against which all other colors are gauged. The choice of color is personal, but in each case the room's size, proportion, function, style, mood, and the exposure and amount of light should be considered. Since color frequently produces the first and most lasting impression on those entering a room, selecting and combining hues is probably the greatest challenge to the interior designer.

Value

Value is the degree of *luminosity,* or *lightness or darkness* of a hue in relation to black and white. Nine such gradations are easily visible to the eye (see Figure 2.10).

The value of any hue can be raised by adding white and lowered by adding black. When black or another

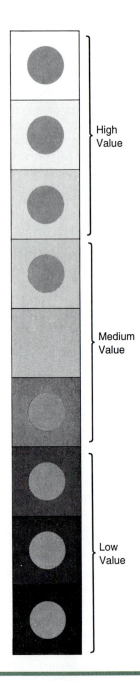

FIGURE 2.10 In the nine gradations of value from white to black, the small circles are identical in shade, demonstrating that the eye perceives color not in itself but in relation to its environment.

TABLE 2.1 To get a clear tint of a color

Basic Hue	Resultant Color	Correction	Tint
white + red	= light blue-pink	+ yellow	= red tint
white + yellow	= light violet-yellow	+ orange	= yellow tint
white + blue	= light violet-blue	+ yellow	= blue tint
white + green	= light blue-green	+ yellow	= green tint
white + orange	= light red-orange	+ yellow	= orange tint
white + violet	= light blue-violet	+ orange	= violet tint

Note: To get a clear tint of a color, use yellow to correct the color. For yellow or purple, however, use orange to correct the color.

tains a lot of red, and blue has some violet. You must correct for these imperfections to get a perfect tint of the desired hue. Table 2.1 points out the procedure for mixing tints by correcting imperfect pigments.

In addition to shades and tints, a third classification is **tone**. A tone is formed by adding both black and white to the hue or a pigment of the color directly opposite from it on the standard color wheel. These grayed hues are extremely useful in working out color schemes in which muted colors are necessary to tone down the brighter hues. Any tint may become a tone with the addition of a touch of black or of some of the hue's complement. (See Figure 2.11.)

Value may be applied in many ways when designing and furnishing a house. As an object is raised in value, its apparent size increases. A fabric colored in low value makes a chair seem smaller than one in light or high value. Since light colors recede and dark colors advance, one may, with skill, alter the apparent size and proportion of individual items or of an entire room (see Figure 2.12).

darkening agent is added to a hue, the value is lowered and the result is a **shade** of that particular hue. When white is added to a hue, the value is raised, and the result is a **tint**. Many value steps may be created in any hue between normal value and black and white.

Tints, either clear or neutralized, are most frequently used for large background areas such as walls and ceilings. When mixing tints, remember that certain pigments are not perfect, that is, they contain other hues. For example, white contains blue and a little violet, orange con-

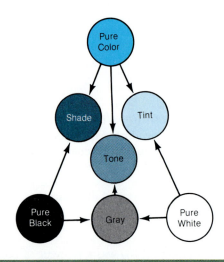

FIGURE 2.11 Although black and white pigments are not considered true colors, their addition to colored pigments produces tints, shades, and tones. Adding black to a pigment color produces a shade; adding white produces a tint. When gray (a mixture of black and white pigments) is added to a color, a tone is produced. (Courtesy of General Electric Company.)

A chair in light value blends into a similar background.

A chair in dark value placed against a light background produces a contrast.

A chair in light value placed against a dark background creates a more pronounced contrast.

FIGURE 2.12 Value effects—three treatments.

In small rooms, light values expand walls and ceilings. In long narrow rooms, colors in darker value pull in end walls and make the room appear shorter.

The use of sharp value contrast emphasizes an object. For example, the fine lines of a dark piece of furniture are accentuated if placed against a light background. The dark seems darker and the light background seems lighter. A piece of furniture seems unobtrusive if it is the same value as the background.

Black and white have a strong visible effect on other colors when brought into juxtaposition. Black tends to make adjacent colors look richer. White reflects light into adjacent colors. Rooms that seem lifeless may often be given sparkle and interest by the addition of black, white, or both.

The manner in which tonal value is distributed throughout a room is important. Each room usually contains three tonal values: light, medium, and dark, with varying amounts of each, as seen in Figure 2.13. The amounts of light and dark should not be equal. In most cases, having large areas of light set off by small areas of dark is wise. However, a client may prefer a room that is predominantly dark in value, as seen in Figure 2.14, to achieve a more cloistered, cozy feeling. When colors for backgrounds and furnishings are selected, careful consideration of value distribution contributes to the success of the environment.

Intensity or Chroma

Intensity, or chroma, is the *degree of saturation of pure color.* It describes the brightness or dullness and strength or weakness of the pure color that a hue contains. As any color may be raised and lowered in value by the addition of white or black, so the intensity may be strengthened by the addition of pure chroma or lessened by the addition of that color's complement, which is the color directly across from it on the standard color wheel. The more of

the color's complement that is added, the less pure color the original hue contains. Two colors may have similar hue (both blue) and the same value (neither darker nor

FIGURE 2.13 Black, the darkest value, is used as an accent throughout this sunroom. The strong contrast of black and white provides an effective background for green foliage. Touches of bright color, provided by flowers, will vary with the season. (Courtesy of Century Furniture Co.)

FIGURE 2.14 Predominantly dark and medium values have been used in this masculine retreat, establishing a cozy effect. Light values such as the pictures and coffee table accessories function as accents. The entire room is dramatized with pools of artificial light. (Courtesy of F. J. Hakimian, Inc. Design by Renny B. Saltzman, Inc. Photograph by Phillip Ennis.)

lighter), yet may be markedly different because of the different color strength or intensity.

A color is visually made more intense by adding more of the dominant hue to it. A color may also be made to appear more intense by placing it against its complementary color, whether of the same intensity or neutralized. For example, a painting with predominantly orange hues seems more orange if hung against a blue wall.

When two complementary colors are mixed in equal amounts, they tend to neutralize each other. Therefore, to decrease the intensity of a color, some of that color's complement, black, black and white, or another neutralizing agent should be added. A color *appears* more neutral or less intense if placed against an object that is of the same hue more saturated in chroma. For example, a muted green vase placed against a bright green background appears even more muted.

When planning color schemes for rooms, keep in mind that strong chroma is conspicuous and size-increasing. Furniture seems larger and fills up a room more if intense colors are used. (See Figure 2.15.) Walls in strong chroma, as with dark value, seem to advance and make the room appear smaller. Since rooms are backgrounds for people, color is generally most pleasing when not too demanding. The psychological effect of large areas of intense color can be irritating, so it may be wise to select colors in softly neutralized tones for large background areas in rooms where the occupants spend considerable time. Intense colors can work well when reserved for small areas and accents. A safe guide in planning a color scheme is the **law of chromatic distribution**: "The large areas should be covered in the most neutralized colors of the scheme. As the areas reduce in size, the chromatic intensity may be proportionally increased" (Whiton, *Interior Design and Decoration,* 1963).

Color is a great mood setter. Strong chroma tends to create a feeling of informality; soft neutralized tones are generally reserved for a more formal atmosphere. In today's interiors, however, when design rules are often considered and then broken, the opposite treatment may prevail.

The skillful application of color value and intensity can play a vital role in creating exciting and livable interiors. Even when all the hues in a room are correct, it may still be boring. Adding a contrasting value or intensity to the color harmony can provide interest and variety. For example, a medium blue room can come alive with the addition of pillows dark in value and artwork with bright hues.

Computer Applications

The computer is capable of performing many design-related tasks. Designers now have access to computer networks that connect with screens and with large computer processing systems, making a vast amount of information available instantly for design application (see Chapter 14). For example, colorant formulation systems can reproduce and record approximately 16 million colors; can accurately combine and reproduce these colors, showing such criteria as light reflection and textural effects; and can even deal with metamerism—the tendency of samples that match under one light to appear mismatched under a different light source. Printouts can communicate how the specified colors will appear in a particular setting—a valuable tool for the designer.

CREATING LIVABLE COLOR HARMONIES

Planning and organizing color schemes for the home can be a challenging and satisfying task. Endless color possibilities are available to the designer and consumer, derived from traditional organized methods or sparked by original ideas. Individual color preferences are naturally a consideration. Harmonizing colors from the standard

FIGURE 2.15 Bright chroma in red, blue, yellow, green, and purple are creatively combined for this bookcase, mirror, and table. Because of the strong chroma, these pieces attract the eye first, seem to advance, make the furniture seem larger in comparison to neutral surfaces, and make a lasting visual impression. (Courtesy of *The Naturalist.*)

FIGURE 2.16 A vivid monochromatic color scheme of a rich red wallcovering is seen in this stimulating dining room. The floral outline and border of gold and white provide variety and interest, which are often needed to make a one-color scheme successful. (Courtesy of The Jack Denst Designs, Inc.)

color wheel is a popular approach and may aid in color selections. In general, color schemes derived from the color wheel fall into two categories: *related* and *contrasting.* Within these categories the variations are endless. Related colors produce harmonious schemes that may be cool, warm, or a combination. Contrasting schemes have great variety and tend to be more exciting, particularly if strong chroma is used. In any scheme, black, white, or neutrals may be added without changing the scheme.

The basic color schemes are monochromatic, neutral and neutralized (monotone), analogous, and complementary. Although professional interior designers seldom select a specific scheme initially, the final scheme often falls into one of these categories.

Monochromatic

Monochromatic color schemes are developed from a *single hue,* but with a range of values and different degrees of intensity (see Figure 2.16). Unity is probably the most notable element in this type of scheme, and if light values predominate, space will be expanded. A danger in the one-color scheme may be monotony; however, if one looks to nature, where monotony is never present, the guidelines are clearly apparent. When examining the petals of a rose, one may see shadings from soft, delicate pink to deep red. The variety of tones, tints, and chroma of the green leaf can be combined in a room using the subtle neutralized tones for large wall areas, slightly deeper tones for the carpet, medium tones for large furniture, and vivid chroma for accents.

Monochromatic schemes are often further enhanced by the use of textures such as fabrics, woods, stones,

metals, and glass. Pattern can also add variety and character to the one-color scheme. Black and white can be used without changing the character of the plan and, in fact, may sharpen the scheme and add interest.

Neutral (Achromatic) and Neutralized or Monotone

A *neutral color scheme* is created by utilizing black, white, or variations of gray. It contains no identifiable hue, only values. The term **achromatic** is also used to describe the neutral black, white, or gray color scheme. (See Figures 2.17 and 2.18.)

Neutralized or monotone color schemes are created from colors with low chroma. In other words, they contain some chroma as opposed to the neutral or achromatic, no-chroma scheme. Neutralized colors fall halfway between warm and cool colors and can be employed as tints, tones, or shades. They can also be categorized as a type of monochromatic scheme. The most typical neutralized or monotone colors include off-white (white with a small amount of any hue), off-black (a rich brown-black), beige, cream, tan, and brown. These popular schemes are easy to live with and relatively simple to create. Accents of stronger chroma may be used for smaller furnishings and accessories without changing the neutral scheme and can add visual interest.

Analogous

Analogous, *adjacent,* or *related* color schemes are produced from any segment of colors that are in juxtaposition but contain no more than half the colors on the

FIGURE 2.17 A neutral white (achromatic) scheme dominates the background surfaces in this kitchen. Bright red is used as an accent, which emphasizes the forms and makes the room less formal. Compare this treatment with Figure 2.18. (Courtesy of Allmilmo Corporation.)

FIGURE 2.18 A neutralized off-white (white with a small amount of chroma) monochromatic scheme has been employed for this kitchen. Sleek formality pervades the room. (Courtesy of Allmilmo Corporation.)

standard color wheel, as seen in Figure 2.19. This color scheme is interesting, widely used, and easy to achieve, with successful results. The colors may be warm, cool, or a combination. Harmony is easily established with analogous colors because they usually have one color in common. Yellow, for example, is the common factor in orange and green, and by using the intermediate colors of yellow-orange and yellow-green, an interior designer can achieve a close relationship with a great variety of values and intensities. Generally, one dominant color should be present.

Complementary

Complementary, or *contrasting*, color schemes are probably the most widely used of all the color schemes because they have more variety. These may be developed in a number of ways, but each scheme uses colors of contrasting hues. Values and intensities may vary depending on the use and amount of area to be covered. All contrasting hues placed side by side enhance each other, and if they are in the same intensity, each makes the other seem more intense. When added together, however, con-

FIGURE 2.19 An analogous color scheme achieves harmony by employing hues close together on the color wheel. In this room orange, red, and gold, neighbors on the color wheel, have been used for the principal furnishings and background. A small amount of blue provides contrast. (Courtesy of Bill E. Coleman and J. H. Armer Company.)

trasting hues subtract from each other, as in color neutralization. When equal amounts of two complementary colors are used, they produce a neutral. Complementary schemes always have some warm and cool colors, since they are opposite on the color wheel. These schemes can work well for either traditional or modern interiors. In strong chroma they are lively and vigorous; in grayed tones they may be subtle and restful (refer to Figure 5.1). One dominant hue usually sets the mood.

Six types of complementary schemes are direct complement, split complement, triad, double complement, alternate complement, and tetrad, illustrated in Figure 2.20.

Direct Complement

The *direct complement,* the simplest of the contrasting color schemes, is formed by using any two colors that lie directly opposite each other on the color wheel. One of the hues should dominate. Used in equal amounts and in strong intensity, complementary colors clash, thus creating an unpleasant element in a room. The secondary

FIGURE 2.20 Basic color schemes derived from the color wheel.

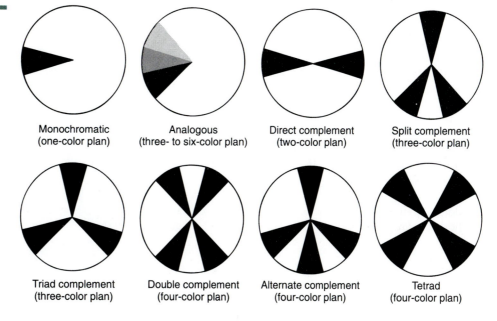

Monochromatic
(one-color plan)

Analogous
(three- to six-color plan)

Direct complement
(two-color plan)

Split complement
(three-color plan)

Triad complement
(three-color plan)

Double complement
(four-color plan)

Alternate complement
(four-color plan)

Tetrad
(four-color plan)

color, therefore, works best when neutralized or used in small areas.

Split Complement

The *split complement* is a three-color scheme composed of any hue plus the two hues next to its complement. For example, if yellow is selected as the dominant color, red-violet and blue-violet are the complementary colors. These colors contrast less than the direct complement, which is violet. Red has been added to one and blue to the other, giving a softness to the scheme and at the same time adding variety.

Triad Complement

The *triad complement* is another three-color contrasting scheme. The triad is made up of any three colors that are equidistant on the color wheel. These colors may be sharp in contrast, using strong chroma such as the three primaries—red, yellow, and blue, or red-orange, yellow-green, and blue-violet—or they may be neutralized, raised, or lowered in value to produce a tranquil scheme or any variant.

Double Complement

The *double complement* is a four-color scheme in which two pairs of complementary colors are used. This scheme doubles the possible combination of colors, offering a wide variety of decorative effects.

Alternate Complement

The *alternate complement* is another four-color scheme combining the triad and the direct complement. Many different interiors can be created by using this scheme.

Tetrad

The *tetrad* scheme combines any four hues that are equally spaced on the color wheel. An example would be the combination of orange, yellow-green, blue, and red-violet. Although usually more difficult to work with, this grouping of unexpected colors can add excitement and variety to the decor.

ADDITIONAL WAYS OF CREATING COLOR HARMONY

In addition to the basic color schemes and systems, other methods can inspire a room's color combinations.

- An attractive *fabric* might be a starting point for a color scheme. Following the law of chromatic distribution, for example, one of the lightest and most neutral colors can be selected for the room's background and other colors from the fabric can be used for various objects in the room. The most intense colors might be reserved for accents.
- A color scheme can be established drawing colors from a favored *wallpaper*.
- An *area rug, art rug, custom rug,* or *wall-to-wall carpeting*—patterned or plain—can be the inspiration for a room's color scheme.
- A prized *painting, print,* or *art object* can determine a color scheme.
- *Nature* can provide an unlimited number of color schemes. One popular color theory is called *shibui* (or *shibusa*).

The Shibui Color Harmony

Shibui (or *shibusa*) expresses in one word the *Japanese approach* to beauty as well as the intrinsic nature of Japanese culture. No single word in the English language precisely describes shibui, an elusive Japanese adjective (*shibumi* is the noun). The word *shibui*, however, sug-

FIGURE 2.21 In this assemblage of fabrics and carpets, textures and colors are drawn from nature to create the essence of shibui. (Courtesy of Rosecare Carpet Company.)

FIGURE 2.22 The shibui concept of color scheming is translated into an American interior by Jack Lenor Larsen with an emphasis on texture and simple colors. Flowers provide touches of brightness. The effect is subtle and unpretentious. (Photograph by Norman McGrath.)

gests an appreciation of *serenity* and a protest against ostentation. Belief in the power of the *understated and unobtrusive* dominates the sophisticated philosophy of the Japanese.

The color scheme essential in producing a shibui effect is one in which colors are brought together to enhance each other in a harmonious whole that will be deeply satisfying to live with for a long time, as demonstrated in Figure 2.21. Schemes must have depth and complexity, or they will soon become tiresome. A shibui color scheme has such qualities. The following ideas are incorporated in achieving a shibui effect.

- Understanding the shibui concept of color scheming requires *looking to nature, on which the color scheme is based.* Shibui uses colors found in nature, combining them in the same ratios. Colors found in the largest areas are quiet and undemanding (neutralized). Bright, vibrant colors are found in a small proportion.
- *Nature has thousands of colors, but none of them match or are uniform.*
- In nature the darker, more *solid colors occur underfoot.* As one looks upward, colors become lighter and more delicate.

- Most of the natural landscape shows a *matte finish with little high shininess or glitter,* such as the sun sparkling on a ripple in a stream.
- *Pattern and texture in nature are everywhere*—in every stone, leaf, and tree trunk—but they have to be discovered through close examination. This subtlety accounts for the absence of uniformity and the dimension of nature's colors.
- *Pattern in nature is not uniform.* No two patterns are identical, yet unity prevails throughout. Nature's colors, textures, and patterns appear simple and natural, but on close scrutiny prove highly complex.

Translating the shibui concept into today's decorating means following principles found in nature and applying them to the interior. American architect Frank Lloyd Wright greatly admired the shibui design philosophy and incorporated its concepts into many of his works. In recent years interest in Japanese design has been gaining momentum. New expressions of old Asian themes and soft, earthy colors mix pleasantly with today's contemporary furnishings, producing depths of beauty and an atmosphere of serenity essential to contemporary homes. (See Figure 2.22.)

Natural Earth Colors

Natural earth colors are inorganic pigments found in minerals, principally iron oxides, from the soil. They are washed and ground, then mixed with other substances to create paints or dyes. Earth colors usually include ocher (yellow), sienna, red oxide (red), umber (brown), and terra verde (green).

Earth colors have been used for millennia. For example, these pigments were used by the ancient Egyptians to paint the walls of their tombs, and by the artists of the Middle Ages and Renaissance in their paintings.

Earth colors are still used today for many purposes, especially to help protect from corrosion. Earth colors are the most permanent colors available, are usually non-toxic, and are not affected by atmospheric conditions.

OTHER CONSIDERATIONS IN COLOR APPLICATION

The Effect of Adjacent Colors on Each Other

Perhaps the most significant thing to remember about color is that a color is not important in itself. What is important is what happens when different colors are brought together. The eye perceives color in relation to its environment, as diagrammed in Figure 2.23.

Physiologists have shown that people are not color blind to one color only but to two or four, and the eye is sensitive to colors not singly but in pairs. The familiar **afterimage** effect demonstrates this perception. If a person looks at any one color for about 30 seconds, then looks at a white page, the complement of that color appears. (See Figure 2.24.) Also, when the eye sees a colored object, it induces that color's complement in the environment. For example, when a green chair is placed against a light neutralized background, the eye sees a tinge of red in that background.

When two primary colors are placed side by side, they appear tinted with the omitted primary; for example, when placed near blue, red takes on a yellow tinge. When contrasting or complementary colors in strong chroma with the same value are used against each other, they clash, producing a vibration that is fatiguing. When contrasting colors with strong differences in value are used

FIGURE 2.23 These diagrams illustrate the effect of adjacent colors: *A,* gray looks much darker against white than it does against black; *B,* a gray or neutral against a colored background appears to be tinted with the complement of the color; *C,* when placed side by side, complements of equal intensity create visual conflict. Complements of varying intensities enhance each other. (Courtesy of Large Lamp Department, General Electric Company.)

side by side or one against the other, the colors stand out but do not clash. Harmoniously blended colors of middle value used against each other tend to blend together, and at a distance the difference becomes almost indiscernible

FIGURE 2.24 Complementary afterimage. Stare at the black dot just below center in the image at left for 30 seconds, then look at the black dot in the white space at right. Prolonged concentration on any color reduces eye sensitivity to it, and the reverse (complementary) color, remaining unaffected, dominates the afterimage for a brief period until balance is restored.

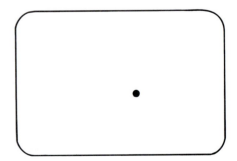

(see Figure 2.25). The latter combination is the basis for most shibui color schemes.

The juxtaposition of colors affects not only hue but also value. The change of value may be seen when a gray circle is placed on a white background. As black is added to the background, which becomes progressively darker, the gray circle appears progressively lighter, showing that colors may be made to appear either lighter or darker according to the tonal value of the adjoining or background color. When black and white are placed side by side, the white looks whiter and the black looks blacker. Colors closely blended conceal an object; contrasting colors emphasize an object. These facts about color have numerous applications in designing interiors.

The Effect of Natural and Artificial Light on Color

Without light, color does not exist. Both natural and artificial light are important elements in any room composition. Light can be used to make rugs look deeper, fabrics more luxurious, metals exotic, and woods softer. The mood of the room can become dramatic or warm and intimate.

The first consideration in planning the color scheme for a room should be the quantity and quality of natural light entering the room. The amount of natural light depends on the number, size, and placement of the windows. A room with few or small windows, and hence a small amount of light, is enhanced by light-reflecting colors. A room with large areas of glass may be more pleasant with a predominance of darker light-absorbing colors that reduce glare. The percentage of light reflected by some of the more common colors is as follows:

White	89%
Ivory	87%
Light gray	65%
Sky blue	65%
Intense yellow	62%
Light green	56%
Forest green	22%
Coconut brown	16%
Black	2%

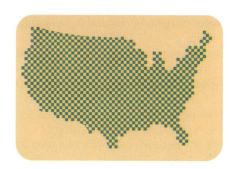

FIGURE 2.25 Additive spatial fusion. The green dot pattern in the shape of the United States merges into solid gray when viewed from a distance of 6 to 8 ft. At that distance the eye no longer distinguishes the individual colors. (Courtesy of Large Lamp Department, General Electric Company.)

To assure the necessary amount of natural light and still avoid glare, plan the color scheme for each room in relation to the *reflective characteristics* of the large elements in the room, particularly the backgrounds. For example, dark walls absorb most of the light and light walls reflect most of the light. The effect of the floor covering is the same. A dark carpet that has a **matte** finish makes a room much darker than a light-reflecting vinyl.

The quality of *natural light* depends on the direction from which it comes and the time of day. Light from the north is cool. Light from the east is warmer than northern light but cooler than the warm afternoon light from the south and west. Western light during early hours of the day is neutral, but in later afternoon it contains much red. Because of these differences, it can be wise to use warmer colors in rooms with cool light and cooler colors in sunny rooms with south and west exposures. Test colors by carefully observing them at different times. (See Figure 2.26.)

Metameric Colors

One concern for the designer is how various types of natural and artificial light can change the visual perception of a surface, a phenomenon known as **metamerism**. For example, two carpets that match in color during daylight may not match under incandescent artificial light at

FIGURE 2.26 Natural lighting floods the interior spaces of a large bank casting warm daylight hues on the tile floor, plants, and other background surfaces. When artificial light with its particular properties is reflected on these same surfaces, the colors will be somewhat altered. (Courtesy of American Olean Tile Co.)

night. All types of lighting (natural lighting during different times of the day and artificial lighting such as incandescent, fluorescent, halogen, etc.) produce unique effects. Therefore, it is important when selecting colors for backgrounds and furnishings to view each surface under all types of lighting conditions to ensure that the colors will match or be harmonious.

Understanding the interrelationship of color and artificial light is necessary to achieve beautiful color schemes. *The color of artificial light is determined by* (1) the source of light, (2) the surface reflecting it, (3) the type of diffusion, and (4) the amount of diffusion. *The color of an object is the result of* (1) the spectral qualities of the light source, (2) the reflective traits of surface materials, (3) the level of illumination, and (4) the method of lighting.

The Light Source

The sources of *artificial light—incandescence and fluorescence—*are discussed in Chapter 3, with an emphasis on methods of lighting. This chapter is concerned with the light source and its effect on color.

- Ordinary incandescent light casts a warm glow but can be varied by tinted globes.
- Fluorescent tubes come in white, warm, and cool tints. White light is the most natural and emphasizes cool colors.
- Warm light is most flattering to skin tones and is usually preferred in areas that have lower levels of illumination.
- Review of the color wheel demonstrates that to gray or neutralize a color, some of its complement must be added and to intensify a color, more of the basic hue must be added. Colored light produces the same effect. Warm light accentuates warm colors and neutralizes cool colors. Cool light intensifies cool colors and deadens warm colors. Warm light is friendly and tends to unify objects. Cool light expands space, produces a crisp atmosphere, and tends to make individual objects stand out.
- Both single and mixed colors take on a different look when subjected to artificial light. For example, a yellowish light brings out the yellow in yellow-green and yellow-orange. A cool light brings out the blue in blue-green and blue-violet. Under a warm light—regular incandescent or warm fluorescent—greens tend to be unified, but blues, which may be pleasantly harmonious in natural light, are thoroughly undependable.

The Surface That Reflects Light

As with natural light, absorptive and reflective surfaces of the room should be planned and observed under artificial light.

The Level of Illumination

The level of illumination also affects the appearance of color. Quantity of light is measured in **footcandles**: one footcandle equals the amount of light produced by one candle at a distance of 1 ft. Experts have established minimum standards of illumination for various purposes, and these standards can be measured with a light meter. The effect of color in a room when the light is bright can be stimulating, and a relaxing feeling can be experienced when the light is low. Color, however, may become dull, lifeless, and dreary with insufficient light. As illumination increases, color becomes more vibrant.

The Methods of Lighting

Color is also affected by the method of lighting. Light rays that fall directly from the source onto the surface are *direct lighting*. Light directed upwards and reflected from another surface, usually the ceiling or wall, is known as *indirect lighting*. The direct method, often used for task lighting, can also create a warm glow over any area. An indirect light reflecting from a cove onto the ceiling produces an overall light resembling the light of midday. This method of lighting is practical for kitchens and work areas, but can give living areas a feeling of flat monotony. Used alone, it can produce a commercial feeling. Portable lamps give direct light, indirect light, or both. With a diffused effect they can produce soft shadows that alter colors, adding interest and attractiveness to a room. Portable lamps can light any area and serve multiple purposes, creating a variety of decorative effects.

Artificial light, when understood and used with skill, may alter, subdue, highlight, or dramatize the colors of a room in a way that no other decorative medium can. (See Figure 2.27.) Because any situation has many variables, it is impractical to set down definite rules for the use of light and color. Therefore, before making a final choice, try each color in the environment in which it will be used and observe it during different hours of the day and after dark.

The Effect of Texture on Color

Color appears different when the texture is varied. Because smooth surfaces reflect light, fabrics with a deep, textured surface, such as pile carpet, velvet, and all manner of nubby weaves, cast tiny shadows. These materials appear darker than a smooth fabric that is dyed with the same hue and is of the same value and chroma. A rough-textured wall may appear grayed or soiled under artificial light because of shadows cast from the uneven surface. A smooth, shiny surface reflects light and provides the opposite effect of a rough texture. A dull or matte surface absorbs color, and if it is also dark, may absorb much of the color.

FIGURE 2.27 Rich royal blue fabrics appear cool and clear under artificial lighting conditions in this modern living space. The cool light further provides a formal feeling and highlights the glass, mirror, and metal materials employed in the room. (Courtesy of L. J. Graham Company, Inc./L. Lowenstein Inc.)

The Effect of Distance and Area on Color

Near colors appear darker and more brilliant than the same colors at a greater distance. Brighter and darker colors used in large rooms therefore seem less demanding than the same colors used in small rooms. Colors appear stronger in chroma when covering large areas. For example, a small color chip may be the exact color tone preferred for a room, but when that tone is painted on four walls, it looks much darker and brighter because the area of that color chip has been multiplied many thousands of times. When selecting a wall color from a small color chip, it is best to choose one several tints lighter than the color desired for the completed room. A good approach is to paint a sizable area of color on walls in opposite corners of the room and observe them in the light at different times of the day and night before making the complete application.

The Effect of Color on Temperature

Some evidence indicates that color can alter the apparent temperature of a room. When used in large amounts, colors such as red, orange, yellow, and brown tend to make a room feel warm. Colors such as blue, lavender, and gray tend to make a room feel cooler.

Some Uses of Color for the Interior

Off-White

A common notion among many untrained individuals is that off-white in itself is a specific color and complements any decor. This idea is far from the truth. Off-white is white tinted with a hue—any hue. To be compatible, however, off-whites must contain only the same hue. For example, off-white walls, ceilings, glass curtains, and fabrics work best in a room when tinted with the same hue. Value and intensity may vary, but the hue must be the same. Warm off-whites are more easily blended than cool off-whites, recalling a basic characteristic of warm and cool colors.

On the Ceiling

The ceiling is the largest unused area of a room, and its color is important to the general feeling. If the objective is to have the wall and ceiling look the same, the ceiling should be a tint of the wall, since the reflection from the walls and floor tends to make the ceiling look several shades darker than it actually is. If the walls are papered, the ceiling may be a tint of the background or the lightest color in the paper. If walls are paneled in dark wood, the ceiling can be effective when painted white or a light tint of the wood color. If the wood trim is painted white, a white ceiling is advisable. When the ceiling is too high, a darker shade or brighter hue makes it appear lower. If the ceiling is low, the opposite treatment can help make the ceiling appear higher. Often ceilings are painted white or off-white regardless of the respective wall treatment. (See Figure 2.28.)

When Selecting a Window Treatment

The success of any room largely depends on the window treatment and the color used for curtains, draperies,

A light ceiling expands space.

A dark ceiling feels lower.

FIGURE 2.28 Effects of color on a ceiling.

blinds, screens, shades, shutters, or other window decor (see Chapter 7). Windows can be the room's most conspicuous and decorative element or simply be treated as functional. If the objective is to have a completely blended background, the hard or soft treatment should be the same hue, value, and intensity as the wall. If a contrasting effect is desirable, a color that contrasts with the wall can be used, but it must relate well with other colors used throughout the room. Glass curtains are usually more pleasing when white or off-white. If the window treatment is of wood, metal, or materials other than fabrics, remember to consider the color of these materials in the room's total color effect.

For Wood Trim

The color of wood trim around doors, ceilings, floors, and other architectural features is important to the general color scheme of the room. When painted, it may be (1) the same hue, value, and intensity as the wall; (2) a darker shade of the wall hue; or (3) a color that contrasts with the wall, if it is related to some other major colors in the room. Many professional designers maintain the same wood trim color throughout the home—or at least on each floor—for an effective color transition from room to room.

When Walls Are Paneled

Where dark wood paneling is used, colors of intense chroma can be used in the room, since deep wood tones tend to absorb color. If paneled wood walls are light and a blended effect is desired, colors may be light and less intense. If wood paneling is more formal, colors employed for furnishings should complement this feeling. If wood paneling is informal in appearance, colors should enhance that casual effect.

In Altering Apparent Size and Proportion

An object that attracts the eye usually seems larger; therefore, items of furniture may be made to appear larger if painted or upholstered with colors in strong chroma. A small room may be made to seem even smaller if demanding colors, which are space-filling, are used on backgrounds and furniture. On the other hand, light, blended, and receding colors expand a room and seem to create more space. Through the skillful application of color a room's dimensions may be altered significantly, and architectural features and furnishings can be highlighted or minimized.

In Bringing Balance to a Room

Since that which attracts the eye seems larger and therefore appears heavier, a small area of bright color balances a large area of softly muted color, and a small area of dark color balances a larger area of light color. For example, a small bouquet of bright flowers placed near one end of a long table balances a large lamp of soft color placed near the other end. A small bright-blue chair balances a much larger gray-blue sofa. Entire areas of rooms may also be balanced through the use of color. A large end wall treated with bright or dark colors may be balanced on the other side of the room with a similar treatment.

In Transition from One Room to Another

Whenever two rooms adjoin, their colors should relate. One or more colors carried from one room to the other—but not necessarily used in the same manner—will make a pleasing transition. For example, the accent color in the wallpaper of an entrance hall may be neutralized and used on the walls of the adjoining living room or may be emphasized in a piece of upholstery fabric.

Where one room may be seen from another, like dining and living rooms, closely related colors establish color unity. Following are some of the most common and successful methods of achieving color transition.

- Many professional designers prefer to keep the *floor covering* consistent from room to room. For example, a gray carpet might be used for all rooms with the exception of hard floor surfaces for entries, bathrooms, and utility areas.
- Similar or matching *wall and ceiling colors* from room to room create a continuity of color transition.
- The consistent use of *moldings and architectural trim* throughout the home helps provide unity.
- Related colors employed on various pieces of *furniture* and for *window treatments* should be considered for effective color transition.
- *Accessories* that carry colors from one interior space to another aid in creating an effective flow of colors.

In Period Rooms

Particular styles and periods of furnishings have appropriate colors that reflect their character and set the feeling of authenticity (see Figures 2.2 and 9.1). Colors should be chosen with discrimination when designing period rooms. Many excellent sources provide full information on this subject.

In Hue Distribution

The distribution of color has already been discussed under hue, value, and intensity, but a brief reiteration is helpful. Color is the most unifying element available to the interior designer, and its skillful distribution is essential to the feeling of unity. Color distribution can be achieved in two major ways:

1. Planned value distribution is a necessary step. Each room can be enhanced with some light, some dark, and some medium tones used in varying amounts according to the effect desired. In most cases the darkest tones are used in the smallest amounts, although in special rooms the reverse may be employed with dramatic results. When applying the law of chromatic distribution to a room, backgrounds will be in the most neutralized tones, large pieces of furniture will have more intensity, and accents such as small chairs and accessories will be in the strongest chroma. This procedure in distributing color produces rooms with a feeling of serenity and lasting comfort.
2. Many successful rooms are planned around one dominant hue. This color need not be used on all major pieces of furniture, but it should be repeated at least once to give a feeling of unity. Unity may also be achieved by using colors containing one hue common to all. For example, hues on the color wheel going clockwise from orange to blue-green all contain yellow and combine well together. The color that is common to all—yellow—recedes and the other colors stand out.

Although the preceding guidelines describe the safest way to color scheme a room, deviating from them is possible and sometimes desirable. For example, dark walls can create a feeling of comfort, warmth, and security and unify the room's furnishings. A light floor visually expands space and when adjacent to dark walls creates a dramatic effect. Seldom, however, is a dark ceiling advisable. In the search for space, a common need today, a light ceiling seemingly provides space by visually extending the room's height. Under most conditions dark ceilings can decrease the feeling of space and be oppressive. On the other hand, depending on the architecture, a ceiling may be painted a dark value and provide a feeling of viewing the infinity of the night sky. This approach is often used effectively in commercial spaces like restaurants, museums, and exhibition areas.

It can be difficult to visualize how a room will look when completed; this ability develops through experience. Forming a mental picture of how colors appear when juxtaposed is not easy, and students and clients may need visual aid. This procedure requires preliminary planning. The following are three methods:

1. Make a chart using approximate proportions of various elements such as walls, floor, ceiling, furniture, and accents. Attach fabric, paint, and hard material samples to the chart. This method will not show exactly how the completed project will appear, but it will be helpful.
2. Assemble a setup with actual samples of all items to be used. Students often use this procedure in a design lab or in the classroom with an *A frame*. A designer can create this grouping of colors and materials for furnishings in a professional setting for the client. Samples are presented of all materials to be used in approximate proportions. This method most closely approximates the look of the completed room.
3. Professional designers can create a rendering of a particular space that indicates the planned color scheme. This allows the client to visualize the projected idea on a small scale.

Reflecting the Mood of the Room

More than any other element, color is capable of setting the general mood of a room. For example, various hues, values, and intensities can create a restful or stimulating feeling. Rich, muted tones most often produce a mood of tranquility, and lively, contrasting colors create an informal mood. General color moods can be evoked for specific areas of the house.

- The *entrance hall* introduces the home. The entrance area can effectively emphasize the theme chosen for major rooms. Color in this space can be somewhat dramatic and daring or simple and unobtrusive, depending on the occupant's taste.

- *Living areas* for more formal purposes generally have neutralized color schemes that tend to produce an atmosphere of tranquility. If a more lively mood is desired, colors of stronger intensity achieve this effect.
- *Informal living areas* such as family and recreation rooms are often treated with stimulating color schemes that create a cheerful and casual environment.
- *Dining rooms* are at their best when the color schemes are unobtrusive, permitting a variety of table decorations as well as a serene dining atmosphere.
- *Kitchens* and other work areas are usually more desirable when large areas of color are light, fresh, and clean looking. Bright accents of strong chroma can enhance these areas. Personal color preferences can help dictate a suitable color scheme for the occupant who will work in the space.
- *Bedrooms* are private areas, and personal preference should be the determining factor in the choice of colors. As a general rule, the master bedroom should be done in restful tones pleasing to the occupants. Children are often given the opportunity to select colors for their own rooms. These colors may only be employed for accents and small furnishings, but providing some color input can be very satisfying for a child.
- Color schemes for *bathrooms* are probably the most flexible. Colors may be stark white or dark in value, muted or intense, in any hue. The colors for this private area can reflect the style and mood of adjoining rooms.

Reflecting Personality

Color is a valuable design tool for reflecting the personality of the individual for whom it is chosen. Although there is little research to substantiate the theory that personal color preferences are related to certain personality characteristics, general associations are often suggested. For example, outgoing, informal, and friendly individuals are thought to prefer warm and bright colors, and more formal and private individuals, cool and more subdued colors.

The problem of selecting colors that reflect personality is compounded when a number of individuals are involved. Hopefully, input from all occupants will be considered before final color decisions are made. Current trends may be taken into account but need not be the determining factor. Regardless of what colors are in fashion, the personal preferences of the occupants should always be the main consideration.

Color in Wood

Since wood has color and each type of wood has a particular beauty, wood should not be overlooked when planning a color scheme. Heavily grained woods generally call for heavier textures and stronger colors than do fine-grained woods, as seen in Figure 2.29. Mixing woods can add interest to a room, but it is wise to use woods in close proximity that are similar in feeling. For example,

FIGURE 2.29 Each wood type has a particular color characteristic to be considered when color scheming a room. A room with all the same wood tends to be monotonous, and a room with too much variety of wood can be confusing. In this mountain residence the dark reddish tones of the wood used for architectural detailing nicely contrast with the light-colored lodgepole pine furniture. (Photograph by Lincoln Allen, Salt Lake City.)

FIGURE 2.30 Brilliant red used for panels, chairs, and lighting strips effectively enlivens the medium gray office space and workstations. (Photograph by Pam Singleton.)

rough-grained golden oak and formal reddish-brown mahogany are not particularly good companions, but finely grained light-brown maple and brownish walnut usually combine well. Of course, the style and design of a particular wood item must be considered when selecting various components for an interior space. Becoming familiar with the particular colors and characteristics of wood leads to success in selecting pleasing combinations for interiors. (See Chapter 8 for information on wood types, color, characteristics, and uses.)

COLOR CONSIDERATIONS FOR NONRESIDENTIAL SETTINGS

As outlined previously, human beings respond to color psychologically and physiologically. Color influences our moods, feelings, and emotional well-being as well as our associations with time, temperature, space, sounds, and smells. With this knowledge in mind, the designer can more successfully evaluate the functional needs for nonresidential projects such as industrial plants, business offices, medical offices, hospitals and care centers, retail concerns, hotels and inns, restaurants, transportation and government facilities. In an industrial setting, for example, colors can be planned to promote a positive environment, helping to alleviate negative responses, boredom, and lack of motivation. Successful color application can help reduce stress, contribute to safety through visual perception, and combat some of the uncomfortable environmental effects that might exist in a commercial or nonresidential setting. Particular colors may be specified for a restaurant, for example, that will help reduce the unpleasant effects of excessive noise, heat, odors, or cramped spaces. Numerous color systems, including some that are computer-aided, are available to the designer of nonresidential projects. Knowing what colors tend to make clients, customers, guests or patrons react in positive ways, the designer can specify colors that will be conducive to a comfortable, profitable, and aesthetically satisfying environment, as shown in Figure 2.30.

COLOR FORECASTS FOR THE 1990s

When reviewing color forecasts made by various professional sources, it is important to remember that there are no absolute color rules that can be applied at any particular time. It is good to be aware of color trends, but, ultimately, personal preferences for comfortable and pleasing colors are the most valuable consideration. The interior designer's responsibility is to help the client select colors that are right for a personal environment. The greatest challenge—and possibly the most satisfying reward—to any designer is to achieve beautiful and livable schemes for every room in a house through the knowledgeable use and distribution of color.

Organizations that help determine color preferences for American residential and nonresidential design include the Color Association of the United States, the Home Fashions League, the International Colour Authority, the National Decorating Products Association, and Colorcast. Color forecasts are drawn from the latest research conducted by color stylists and authorities, and they provide fairly accurate annual predictions that help consumers, professional designers, and merchandising experts.

Since color guides are only published annually, information on trend predictions for the 1990s is limited. However, research collected by color consultants and experts indicate the palette for the 1990s will be electric compared to the pastels of the 1980s. Colors will be rich and darker in value. Lively colors will be popular. The primary colors will be evident everywhere, whether in a tint, tone, or deep shade. Color forecasts are in general agreement that the following colors will prevail during the first half of the 1990s: yellows, yellowed tones, and gold in every cast and intensity as well as yellow-greens, mustards, bronzes, and copper; earthy deep reds, fresh reds, bright tints of red, blazing oranges, dark warm pinks and corals; clean and pure blues, electric blues, bluish-reds, blue-violets; forest greens, teal greens, rich emerald greens, olive greens, and fresh greens; turquoise; violets, orchids, deep plums, and wine hues. Neutral and neutralized colors will continue to be favorites.

As more consumers and professionals design with personal style in mind, the more difficult it becomes to make color forecasts for the future. It is likely that colors preferred during the next decade will be selected on the basis of individual taste preferences of the client and homeowner. However, research has shown professional color predictions to be quite accurate.

ASSIGNMENT

In the Student Work Packet are 10 color plates. By applying the principles discussed in this chapter, complete the 10 color plates according to the following directions and submit them to the instructor for evaluation.

Note: In doing all color plates, paint neatly and creatively using paint *only,* except for plate 8. In planning color schemes for the rooms in plates 6 through 10, first establish the dominant color you desire, then choose subordinate and accent colors. Keep the law of chromatic distribution and the criterion of livability in mind when planning each room.

Plate 1 (Process for Mixing True Tints)

After carefully studying the lesson material on mixing tints, proceed as follows:

1. Paint the six circles in the left-hand column with white.
2. Paint the second vertical group with the hue indicated.
3. Starting at the top, from left to right, add a *small* amount of red hue to white and paint the circle labeled "Result." Notice that the result is a bluish pink. This is because white is an imperfect pigment and contains blue. To correct this, add a *small* amount of yellow (paint the fourth circle yellow). The final result on the far right (which will be made up of white and red plus a touch of yellow) should be a clear light tint of the red in the second column.
4. Continue this procedure until all six tints are completed. To determine the proper hue to add for each correction, refer to the section on value. (*Note:* Access to Munsell color chips for comparisons is helpful.)
5. *Caution:* Be certain that the tint results at the far right are *clear* and *light* and that all final tints are as near the same value as possible.

Plate 2 (Process for Mixing Tones and Shades)

1. Begin with the top line and paint the first circle red.
2. Add a touch of black to the red to produce a *shade,* and fill in the middle circle.
3. Add a touch of white to the shade to produce a *tone,* and fill in the third circle. For a lighter tone, add a touch of the shade mixture to white.
4. Continue in this manner until a satisfactory shade and tone of each of the six hues in the left-hand column have been produced.
5. Each shade should contain the same amount of black and each tone the same amount of white for a consistent result.

Plate 3 (Value Distribution)

This is an exercise in the application of value distribution in creating two achromatic color schemes.

1. Fill in the circles on the left. Begin with black at the bottom and raise the value of each succeeding circle. The top circle should be white.
2. Using black, white, and values in between, paint the two identical pictures to illustrate the dissimilar effects created when value is varied. Distribute the values differently, keeping in mind that the darkest value works well when used in the least amount. Note the two sets of window drapery: sheers to the outside and drapery against the wall.

Plate 4 (Color Neutralization Process)

This is an exercise in neutralizing colors.

1. Paint the circles in the left-hand column in the hues indicated.
2. Paint the circles in the middle column with the complementary hue of each.
3. In the third column, make three degrees of neutralization by adding a *slight* touch of the complement to the first section,

a little more to the second section, and still a little more to the third section.

Caution: Be certain that all sections in the far-right column remain neutralized shades of the original hue in the far-left column, and *not* muddy browns.

Plates 5, 6, 7 (Monochromatic, Analogous or Complementary, and Shibui Color Schemes)

These are exercises in planning and executing color schemes.

1. Carefully examine Plates 5, 6, and 7. At the top of each one, the color scheme for the room to be painted is indicated: monochromatic, analogous or complementary, and shibui.
2. Plan each one carefully according to the scheme.
3. In planning the shibui color scheme, select an object from nature such as a leaf, piece of bark, seashell, or stone and use this as the basis for the color scheme. Evaluate the principles of shibui before completing Plate 7.
4. After planning the color schemes for Plates 5, 6, and 7, apply paint to the line drawings.

Plate 8 (Color Scheme from Wallpaper or Fabric)

This is an exercise in color scheming a room from wallpaper or fabric. Select a piece of patterned wallpaper or fabric and attach it to the entire wall area on Plate 8. Using this pattern as a basis, develop a color scheme for the room using the following procedure:

1. If the wallpaper or fabric will be used on all four walls, cover the entire area indicated. If it will be used on only one wall, cover about two-thirds of the area and paint the remaining area with a color that enhances the wallpaper or fabric.
2. Paint the ceiling a color (preferably a tint of the wall color) that complements the wall.
3. Finish the wood trim in one of the following ways: paint it the same hue as the wall, using the same value and intensity; use the same hue as the wall, but in a deeper value and intensity; use a contrasting color related to one of the room colors; use white (if it complements the fabric or wallpaper); or use a natural wood tone, in which case a picture of natural wood grain is acceptable.
4. Paint the floor a slightly darker shade of the wall hue for a blended effect or use an appropriate color taken from the patterned wallpaper or fabric.
5. If the goal is to blend curtains and drapery with the plain wall or with the wallpaper or fabric background, follow the procedure given for wood trim. If a contrasting effect is desired, select an appropriate color from the wallpaper or fabric. (Note that the drapery is the one against the wall. The glass curtain is the one to the outside.) If you select a hard window treatment (levelors, shutters, screens, vertical louvers, etc.), a picture of this treatment is acceptable.
6. For upholstery fabrics, pick up colors from the patterned wallpaper or fabric. One successful approach is to apply the law of chromatic distribution, in which the most intense colors are reserved for the smallest areas.

Plate 9 (Color Scheme from a Picture)

This is an exercise in using the colors in a picture to plan a scheme for a room.

1. Find a small picture appropriate for a living room wall.
2. Mount it on Plate 9 over the area indicated. Follow the same procedure for color planning a room as for Plate 8.
3. *Caution:* Examine the picture carefully and try to interpret the general feeling in the room.

Plate 10 (Color Transition)

This is an exercise in planning a color scheme for three adjoining rooms to provide a pleasant transition of color. Applying material found in this chapter, artistically paint the entrance, living room, and dining room in a related color scheme.

CHAPTER 3

Lighting

Natural Lighting

Combustion Lighting

Artificial Lighting

The Incandescent Filament Lamp

The Tungsten-Halogen Lamp

Fluorescent Lighting

The HID Lamp

Cold Cathode (neon)

Types of Lighting

General or Ambient Lighting

Task Lighting

Accent Lighting

Psychological Effects of Lighting

Lighting Fixtures

Architectural Lighting

Portable or Nonarchitectural Lighting

Switches and Outlets

Lighting for Areas and Activities

Economy and Energy Conservation

FIGURE 3.1 The famous Artichoke lamp was created by Danish lighting designer Poul Henningsen. The fixture has a layered design of projecting forms that allow the light to filter through in a fascinating manner. Two of these hanging fixtures are the principal sources of light in a public foyer. Other supportive lighting includes both wall and ceiling fixtures. A skylight lets daylight flood the space. (Courtesy of Louis Poulsen Lighting, Inc.)

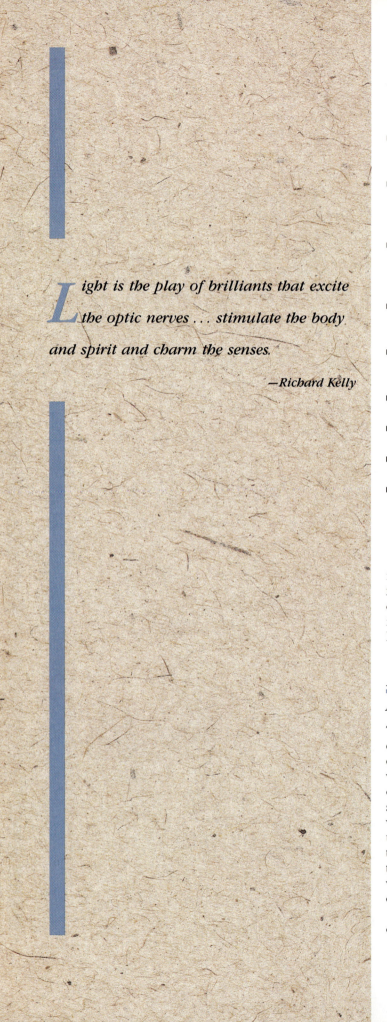

*T*hrough our sense of vision we perceive the world around us and function in our environment. Vision depends on both natural and artificial light; therefore, it is understandable that lighting is an essential element of interior design. A well-planned lighting system:

- Creates an environment that is comfortable and functional by providing adequate illumination for various activities.
- Provides a sense of safety and security. For example, stairways, hallways, basements, attics, porches, and garages all present hazards if not adequately and strategically lighted. Well-lit homes aid in preventing crime.
- Creates a mood or atmosphere. For example, low-level lighting gives a feeling of intimacy and relaxation, while brighter levels of lighting evoke a feeling of liveliness.
- Focuses attention on a specific object or draws attention to the room's focal point. Strong contrasts of light and shadow create dramatic effects.
- Helps change the apparent size and proportion of a space through skillful placement of fixtures and monitoring of the quality and quantity of light.
- Supports the style selected through the use of decorative or structural fixtures.
- Effectively shows the texture and form of an object or of an entire room.
- Aids in creating an environment that is both emotionally uplifting and aesthetically pleasing.
- Allows color to be perceived in various ways. The light source itself can project cool or warm colors in a manner that provides significant aesthetic and emotional effects. (See Chapter 2.)

Special consideration of lighting needs for both residential and commercial spaces is of utmost importance, from the initial planning stages until the last placement of accessories, as seen in Figure 3.1. Illumination falls into two broad categories: natural lighting and artificial lighting.

NATURAL LIGHTING

The principal source of natural light is the sun. Its properties, including ultraviolet light, warmth, and radiant energy, are of significant importance to people's health and well-being. Sunlight emits all visible wavelengths (the distance between two identical successive points of the spectrum) of radiant energy, as well as invisible infrared wavelengths (long rays felt as heat from the sun) and ultraviolet wavelengths (short rays at the end of the spectrum). White light is electromagnetic energy emitted in the visible portion of the spectrum, or in other words, white light results from combining different wavelengths of visible energy. (See Figure 3.2.)

The human eye sees the color of an object when light of mixed wavelengths is reflected into the eye from the

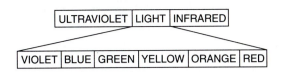

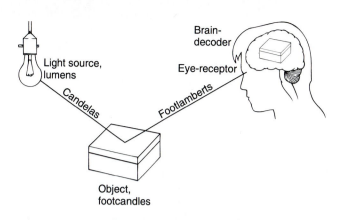

FIGURE 3.2 The visible spectrum. White light is composed of all the colors of the rainbow from red (the longest wavelength) to violet (the shortest wavelength).

object's surface. A particular surface absorbs or reflects a color of the spectrum depending on its composition. For example, if an object is yellow, the surface reflects wavelengths found in the yellow section of the spectrum and absorbs wavelengths of the other colors. Therefore, the process of vision depends on: (1) light, (2) an object to be seen, (3) a receptor, or our eyes, and (4), a decoder, or our brain. (See Figure 3.3.)

Light is measured in four different ways, which should be considered when planning lighting needs for a specific area. (See Figure 3.3.) The following definitions are abbreviated for clarity:

- **Footcandle:** The unit of measure for the amount of light falling on a surface.
- **Lumen:** A measure of light produced by one lamp. For example, a new 75-watt incandescent lamp produces 1,180 lumens (capacity of the light).
- **Footlambert:** The unit of measure for the amount of light reflected from a surface.
- **Candela:** The unit of measure for the intensity of light in a given direction.

FIGURE 3.3 The eye perceives the color of an object when light waves are reflected back to the eye after the other wavelengths are absorbed. The object must be sufficiently close to an adequate light source for the eye to be able to perceive it.

Often, the challenge for the designer is to control natural light within a living space to contribute to the occupant's comfort and aesthetic enjoyment. Natural light changes from morning to evening, with light shifting from soft to bright rays. A designer may therefore treat a south- and west-facing room with muted, cooler, and darker colors to counter the sun's afternoon warmth and glaring rays. Daylight also changes with the seasons and the weather. Admitting and controlling all types of natural light contributes to a pleasant and uplifting interior space, as seen in Figure 3.4.

FIGURE 3.4 Natural light floods this living space through a soaring bay window wall, creating a warm and comfortable atmosphere. (Courtesy of Andersen Windows, Inc.)

FIGURE 3.5 The window treatment of thin vertical louvers not only allows maximum natural light to enter this executive office space, but also permits the occupant and visitors an unobstructed view of the natural surroundings. (Photograph by Pam Singleton.)

The designer can also determine the most suitable window treatment for a particular structure after considering the position on the site, geographic location, and climate. Natural light can be allowed to enter a space in a manner that enhances the environment and minimizes glare, as seen in the commercial setting in Figure 3.5.

Combustion Lighting

Until the development of electric lighting, combustion was the only method of producing supplementary light. It still deserves consideration as a decorative element in residential design and for some commercial projects like

FIGURE 3.6 The Italian bistro in the Walt Disney World Swan Hotel was designed to create a warm and festive dining atmosphere for hotel and other guests. The wall sconces and hanging chandeliers effectively placed throughout the space help achieve that goal. (Photo courtesy of The Walt Disney Co.)

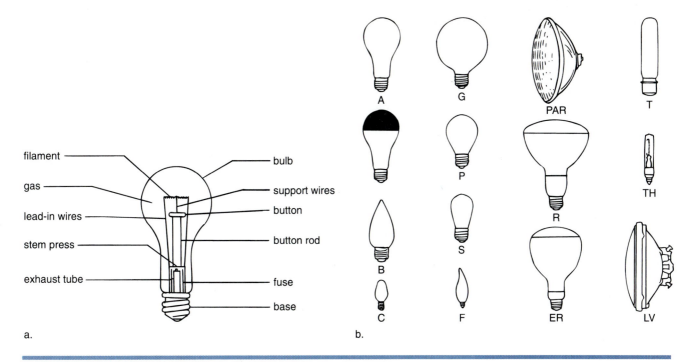

FIGURE 3.7 The incandescent filament lamp. A. Cross section. B. Common incandescent lamp styles. A: standard (arbitrary); B: oval or ovoid; C: candelabra; G: globe; P: pear; S: straight side; F: flare; PAR: parabolic reflector; R: reflector; ER: elliptical reflector; T: tubular; TH: tungsten-halogen; LV: low voltage.

restaurants. Fire, oil lamps, candles, and gaslights are all methods of combustion. Candles and a fire in a fireplace are still widely used, but as supplementary lighting. Their main value is in the soft glow that sheds a flattering light and bestows an atmosphere of warmth and intimacy.

ARTIFICIAL LIGHTING

Artificial lighting is a man-made source of illumination derived from electricity. The electrical energy is transformed into visible light and is identified as wattage. Using today's versatile artificial lighting sources created for function, comfort, and visual pleasure, designers can fully employ all aspects of their ingenuity in illumination.

Through the art of man-made lighting, space can be modified; structural elements can be emphasized or subordinated; color, texture, and form can be enhanced; plants, paintings, and other art objects can be brought into focus; and an atmosphere of cool formality or warm intimacy can be imparted to a room, as seen in Figure 3.6. To accomplish this, the designer needs to understand both the aesthetics and the techniques of lighting.

In most rooms a variety of lighting is desirable, because comfort, beauty, and mood are influenced by the source, color, amount, placement, and quality of illumination. Many students of design study the successful lighting techniques employed in theaters, restaurants, muse-

ums, stores, and offices, where effective and efficient lighting is a necessity.

Before selecting lighting fixtures for particular needs, the type of light source should be considered. The most familiar light sources are incandescent, tungsten-halogen, fluorescent, HID lighting, and neon. These sources use a bulb, called a **lamp** in the industry.

The Incandescent Filament Lamp

Incandescent lighting comes from the familiar light bulb invented by Thomas Edison in the latter half of the nineteenth century. Electricity flows through a tungsten **filament** sealed in a bulb, heating it and creating light. (See Figure 3.7a.) Incandescent light sources—the most common type employed for residential design—have the following attributes:

- Available in a wide variety of sizes, shapes, colors, and types as illustrated in Figure 3.7b.
- Small and adaptable. It is easy to control the quantity of light with dimmer switches.
- Do not flicker, hum, or cause significant interference with radio or television.
- Produce white light that casts a slight red and yellow hue.
- Are generally flattering to human skin coloring.
- Effectively highlight textures and forms.
- Are relatively inexpensive, although not as productive in terms of energy consumed.

- Permit precise optical control for effective accent and task lighting, although not the most efficient light source.

Incandescent light sources have some disadvantages. Exposing the lamp can cause an unpleasant glare. And warm incandescent light tends to neutralize cool colors.

The Tungsten-Halogen Lamp

A relatively new high-performance lighting source for both residential and commercial design is the **tungsten-halogen lamp** (also known as a quartz-halogen lamp). The halogen lamp is a type of incandescent lamp and operates on the same principle, although the shape of the lamp is different. Instead of a filament, the halogen lamp has a piece of hard quartz in a small enclosure that when heated attains higher temperatures and therefore produces a more intense light. When halogen gas is introduced into the enclosure the result is better performance output. Halogen lamps come in a variety of forms (see Figure 3.8) including the small popular series of low-voltage MR-16 and MR-11 reflector lamps. Following are some of the major advantages of halogen lamps:

- Although initially more expensive to buy and operate, these lamps last much longer than incandescent lamps—from 2,000 to 4,000 hours.
- They produce more intense light than incandescent lamps. For example, if the walls are white or light in value, one small 250-watt tungsten-halogen lamp could provide enough indirect background lighting for an entire average-size room. (However, it is not generally recommended that a room be lit only with one light source.)
- The light source is smaller, so it can be used with smaller fixtures and still provide an intense light.
- Halogen lamps can be used with a dimmer to provide a variety of lighting levels.
- Halogen lighting can be used in elegantly designed torcheres or uplighters suitable for a variety of styles, as shown in Figure 3.9.

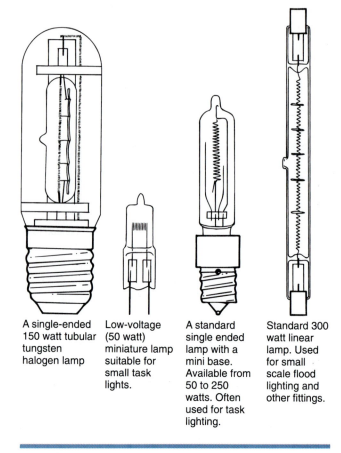

A single-ended 150 watt tubular tungsten halogen lamp

Low-voltage (50 watt) miniature lamp suitable for small task lights.

A standard single ended lamp with a mini base. Available from 50 to 250 watts. Often used for task lighting.

Standard 300 watt linear lamp. Used for small scale flood lighting and other fittings.

FIGURE 3.8 Styles of tungsten-halogen lamps.

- They are available in wall-mounted units that provide excellent background or spot lighting.
- Low-voltage halogen lamps are small and flexible enough to focus as a narrow beam suitable for task lighting.

One disadvantage of halogen lamps is that they are expensive. Also, they may require special sockets. These lamps require careful installation and if exposed should not be touched without gloves. Halogen lamps emit high

FIGURE 3.9 Tungsten-halogen lamps dramatically illuminate this contemporary living room. The brightness level is controlled by dimmers that can lower or raise the voltage, allowing the owners to control the mood. (Photograph by Peter Paige.)

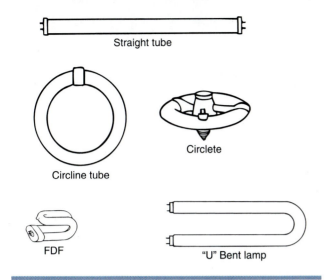

Straight tube

Circline tube

Circlete

FDF

"U" Bent lamp

FIGURE 3.10 Fluorescent lamps are available in straight, U-shaped, and circular shapes and in various diameters.

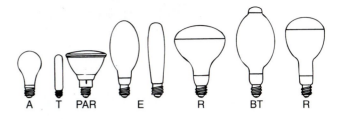

A   T   PAR   E   R   BT   R

FIGURE 3.11 Common HID lamp styles. A: standard (arbitrary); T: tubular; PAR: parabolic aluminized reflector; E: elliptical (conical or dimpled); R: reflector; BT: bulbous tubular.

levels of heat and tend to blacken when used with a dimmer. They must be carefully shielded, so they cannot be used as direct lighting.

Fluorescent Lighting

Fluorescent lighting, in wide use since World War II, is produced in a glass tube lined with a fluorescent coating, filled with mercury vapor and argon, and sealed at the ends with cathodes. When gases are activated by an electric current, ultraviolet rays stimulate the phosphorous bulb coating, which in turn emits visible light. Fluorescent lamps are made in straight, U-shaped, circline, and circlete shapes. (See Figure 3.10.) The most familiar type is the T12 tubular lamp that is about one and a half inches in diameter and comes in lengths from two to eight feet. Fluorescent lamps possess the following attributes:

- They emit less heat than incandescent lamps.
- Although the fixtures are expensive, they use less energy to produce a much greater amount of light so they are more economical to operate (the tubes last up to 15 times longer than incandescent lamps and require about one-third as much energy).
- A new family of small fluorescent straight lamps is being used in many applications where incandescent lamps were formerly used, especially for residential use.
- Fluorescent sources are larger and create broader areas of light than incandescents.
- They provide diffused, shadowless light.
- Fluorescents are particularly efficient for commercial lighting, especially in hospitals, schools, offices, stores, factories, and other large public spaces.

One disadvantage of fluorescent lamps is that initially, fixtures and lamps can be more expensive. Also, the light quality is somewhat flat and monotonous. Fluores-

cent light can distort colors and details. The most commonly used cool white lamp produces a cold light many people consider unflattering; however, this drawback has been partly solved by the introduction of cool white deluxe and warm white deluxe tubes. Fluorescent lamps have a tendency to hum and flicker. Fluorescent light is not as flexible and easy to control as incandescent light. Generally, care should be taken when combining these light types so that the color of the fluorescent light can be matched to the incandescent light.

Designers often mix both fluorescent and incandescent light in a space to combine the most desirable qualities of each lighting source.

The HID Lamp

Another source of light is **HID** (high-intensity discharge) lighting, which incorporates some of the desired qualities of both incandescent and fluorescent lighting. The lamp is similar to the incandescent bulb but is slightly larger. (See Figure 3.11.) HID is most commonly used for commercial and public spaces; however, with technology advances, this lighting source will eventually be used in the home.

There are three types of HID lamps: (1) mercury (tends to produce bluish light), (2) high-pressure sodium (tends to produce orange light and is the most efficient of the three types, and (3) metal halide (renders colors most accurately).

Some advantages and disadvantages include:

- HID light lasts from 16,000 to 24,000 hours. These lamps are highly efficient with about ten times the output of incandescent lighting.
- HID lamps are highly suitable for commercial and institutional demands for energy-saving lighting. However, poor color rendition and noise limit their use in small commercial and residential spaces at present.
- HID lamps require up to nine minutes to reach full light capacity from start-up. Because of their intense light, strong glare can occur if they are not shielded properly.

Scientists and researchers are currently addressing some of the problems of HID lamps.

FIGURE 3.12 Neon lighting in this public cafeteria adds a touch of drama as well as effective mood illumination. Yellow neon tubes zigzag through the space against a theatrical dark background. (Photograph by Pam Singleton.)

Cold Cathode (Neon)

The well-known neon tube is a **cold-cathode** lamp containing an inert gas at low pressure that emits a reddish glow when voltage is applied. Cold-cathode tubes can be fashioned in many decorative forms, especially curved, and are available in almost any color. This lighting source lasts for many years; however, it does require a transformer and is quite fragile. Neon lighting is most often employed for commercial projects, (see Figure 3.12), particularly for illuminated signs. Interesting effects can also be created for home use, especially if a certain mood or style is desired. For example, an Art Deco style can be supported with a neon lighting fixture.

Ambient or general lighting   Task or local lighting   Accent lighting

FIGURE 3.13 Three major types of artificial lighting.

TYPES OF LIGHTING

The three main types of lighting are (1) general or ambient, (2) task or local, and (3) accent (Figure 3.13).

General or Ambient Lighting

General or **ambient lighting** is background or fill light that spreads an even, overall luminosity and reduces harsh contrasts between pools of concentrated light. General lighting can be produced by large area light sources; by a number of small sources that illuminate ceilings, walls, and drapery brackets; by direct or indirect light; or by pendants, chandeliers, downlights, spotlights, and reflected light from portable fixtures. (See Figure 3.14.)

Direct Lighting

Direct lighting, often used for general lighting, is light thrown directly downward onto a particular area, result-ing in shadows and sharp contrast between dark and light. Downlights of all kinds yield direct lighting. They may cast an ambient glow over a large area or may be concentrated on a specific object.

Indirect Lighting

Indirect lighting, also often used for general lighting, is light that shines onto the ceiling or wall, as from a torchere, sconce, or hidden source, and is reflected back into the room. Indirect lighting tends to expand space visually and when reflected from the ceiling provides general illumination, resulting in few if any shadows. Like sunlight at midday, however, indirect lighting tends to be flat and in most cases needs to be supplemented by portable fixtures. Indirect lighting can also be used to dramatize a particular area or object and create a soft or exotic mood.

Direct and indirect lighting can be produced simultaneously by portable fixtures with open tops, particularly those with opaque shades that direct light both upward and downward. Some fixtures are specially

FIGURE 3.14 Ambient or general lighting is effectively provided from recessed ceiling fixtures and portable fixtures in this spacious living room. The fire in the fireplace creates an inviting, warm light. (Photograph by Mark Boisclair.)

FIGURE 3.15 Direct and indirect lighting.

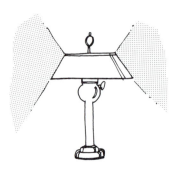

A portable fixture provides
direct and indirect light

Indirect lighting
provides visual interest

equipped to direct most of the light upward, some direct most of the light downward, and still others distribute the light more evenly. (See Figure 3.15.)

Task Lighting

Task lighting is functional and localized for a particular activity such as sewing, office work, reading, writing, pre-

paring food, or grooming. Task lighting is placed near the activity but is aimed to avoid glare and minimize shadows, as seen in Figure 3.16.

Most tasks of a concentrated nature, especially when prolonged, require a high level of illumination. This can be achieved by the use of pendants, recessed lights, track-mounted fixtures, and shielded fluorescent tubes either hanging, placed under shelves or cabinets, or wall

FIGURE 3.16 Task lighting for a study area in this contemporary home is architecturally built in above the work surface to provide adequate light for reading and clerical work. (Courtesy of General Electric.)

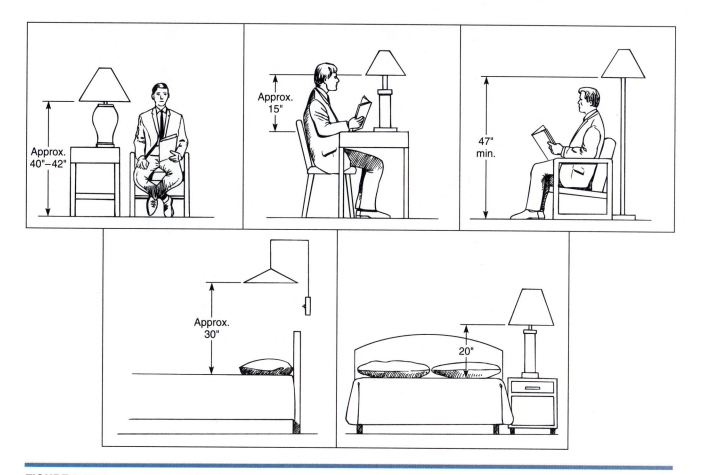

FIGURE 3.17 Lamps and shades for task lighting should be placed to minimize glare and shadows.

mounted above and on each side of a mirror. Placement, shade design, socket location, and shielding all contribute to controlling glare and supplying good light, as illustrated in Figure 3.17. Recessed or ceiling-mounted fixtures should have dimmers and be carefully placed to avoid glare. Additionally, the choice of lamps or tubes will determine the quantity of light (see Table 3.1).

Accent Lighting

Accent lighting employs a concentrated beam of light focusing on a particular object or area. A highly flexible lighting tool, accent lighting can be placed at any desired angle and be precisely controlled to provide the required amount of intensity and color to emphasize one area and

TABLE 3.1 Recommended ranges of light levels for some activities.

Activity	Prolonged Duration	Incandescent	Fluorescent
Craft work	Moderate to high	75–200 w	30–55 w
Dining	Low	40–60 w	16–22 w
Entertaining	Low to high	40–200 w	16–55 w
Grooming	High	150–200 w	40–55 w
Hand sewing	High	150–200 w	40–55 w
Ironing	High	150–200 w	40–55 w
Kitchen and laundry	High	150–200 w	40–55 w
Machine sewing	High	150–200 w	40–55 w
Reading musical scores	Moderate to high	75–200 w	30–55 w
Reading	High	150–200 w	40–55 w
Television viewing	Low to moderate	40–100 w	16–44 w
Writing	Moderate	75–100 w	30–44 w

FIGURE 3.18 Artistic placement of accent and ambient lighting in this Brooklyn, New York, apartment, designed by Stanley Jay Friedman, highlights the conversation area. Pools of light wash the walls, and art brings life to an achromatic gray scheme. (Courtesy of Stanley Jay Friedman. Photograph by Peter Vitale.)

subordinate others. This type of lighting can separate one area from another, highlight a treasured item, establish a focal point, or create a touch of drama, as illustrated in Figure 3.18. Accent lighting, which is often combined with general lighting, can be produced by recessed, surface-mounted, track-mounted, portable fixtures and other lighting fixtures.

PSYCHOLOGICAL EFFECTS OF LIGHTING

Successful lighting can provide a sense of emotional well-being in addition to satisfying physical requirements. With respect to human psychology, light has the following attributes:

- Light is associated with the exuberance of life itself and with human well-being.
- It can convey a sense of security, warmth, and comfort.
- It can evoke a mood, for example, low-level lighting can be intimate, cozy, and relaxing; bright light can be stimulating and active.
- Lack of light, or not enough light in the environment, may provoke feelings of depression, gloom, or even fear. (Light therapy is often used to treat feelings of depression.)
- Too much light or glaring light can be agitating, uncomfortable, and annoying, even resulting in physical ailments and an inability to function adequately.

It is essential, therefore, when planning light requirements for either residential or commercial interiors, to take into account the psychological impact of light to help satisfy both physical and emotional human needs.

LIGHTING FIXTURES

Fixtures, or **luminaires**, for artificial lighting sources can be divided into two groups: (1) architectural, or built-in, and (2) portable, or nonarchitectural.

Architectural Lighting

Architectural lighting, which includes wall-mounted and ceiling-mounted fixtures, is closely correlated with the structure of the room and should be included in the wiring plans of the original house as an integral part of the complete design. The flexibility of architectural lighting, however, can be fairly limited, considering the various functions that take place in a room. Many designers who prefer an uncluttered ceiling feel that ceiling-mounted recessed fixtures are more visually pleasing.

In terms of general types, *wall lighting* includes a variety of fixture styles that are permanently located on a wall surface. Other fixtures are mounted on the ceiling.

Wall-Mounted Fixtures

Several types of wall-mounted fixtures are shown in Figure 3.19. *Valance lighting* is positioned over a window. A horizontal fluorescent tube is placed behind a valance board and the light reflects off the ceiling and also shines on the drapery, thus producing both direct (downlight) and indirect (reflected) lighting.

Bracket lighting is similar to valance lighting, but the fixture is placed either high on the wall for general wall lighting or low for specific tasks such as washing dishes, cooking, or reading in bed. When used in living areas, the length of the bracket should relate to the furniture grouping it serves.

Cove lighting is placed near the ceiling, directing light upward and giving a feeling of height.

A *canopy* overhead provides general illumination. This lighting is used most in kitchens, baths, and dressing rooms, but it may be used elsewhere.

Wall sconces, or lighting fixtures permanently attached on the wall, may be modern or traditional in style and can be positioned to provide direct or indirect lighting. Sconces can substitute for portable fixtures that require floor or table space.

Ceiling-Mounted Fixtures

Figure 3.20 shows several kinds of ceiling-mounted fixtures. Recessed **downlighters** may focus on a definite object or produce general lighting when used in sufficient numbers (Figure 3.21). A recessed *wall-washer* is an adjustable unit that can be directed at any angle to "wash" the wall with light. A recessed **eyeball** is similar to a wall-washer but can swivel, allowing light to be angled where desired.

A *cornice* is usually built on the ceiling to direct the light downward only. This lighting can provide a dramatic effect for draperies, wall coverings, and art. When used over a window it can aid in eliminating the black mirror effect at night.

A *soffit* consists of enclosed light attached to the ceiling and designed to provide a high level of light directly below. Excellent for bathrooms, this light is also effective in niches, such as over built-in desks and sofas.

Track lighting consists of a track flush-mounted to the ceiling (it also may be mounted vertically or horizontally to a wall). It comes in a broad array of sizes, shapes, and finishes. Fixtures clip anywhere along the track to create a precisely designed optical system with a vast range of lighting effects. Layout configurations are infinite, and consumers can choose from an abundance of fixtures that are economical, easily installed, and highly energy efficient. Track lighting is a total lighting system that is virtually unlimited in flexibility to meet the needs of contemporary homes or commercial design projects (Figure 3.22).

Suspended fixtures or pendants, which are hung from the ceiling, are available in numerous designs. One example is the classic Artichoke lighting fixture seen in Figure 3.1. This lighting type is effective when ceilings are particularly high or can be designed simply for function and visual appeal. One popular type of suspended fixture is the **chandelier** (see Figure 3.23). When hung in an eight-foot-high dining room, a chandelier should be suspended approximately 30 inches above the table and raised three inches for each additional foot of ceiling height. Chandeliers must be high enough for clearance if they are hung in rooms in which people move about.

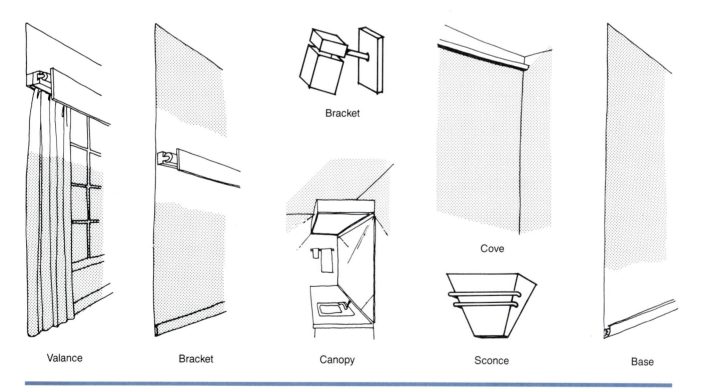

Valance   Bracket   Canopy   Sconce   Base

Bracket

Cove

FIGURE 3.19   Common types of wall-mounted fixtures.

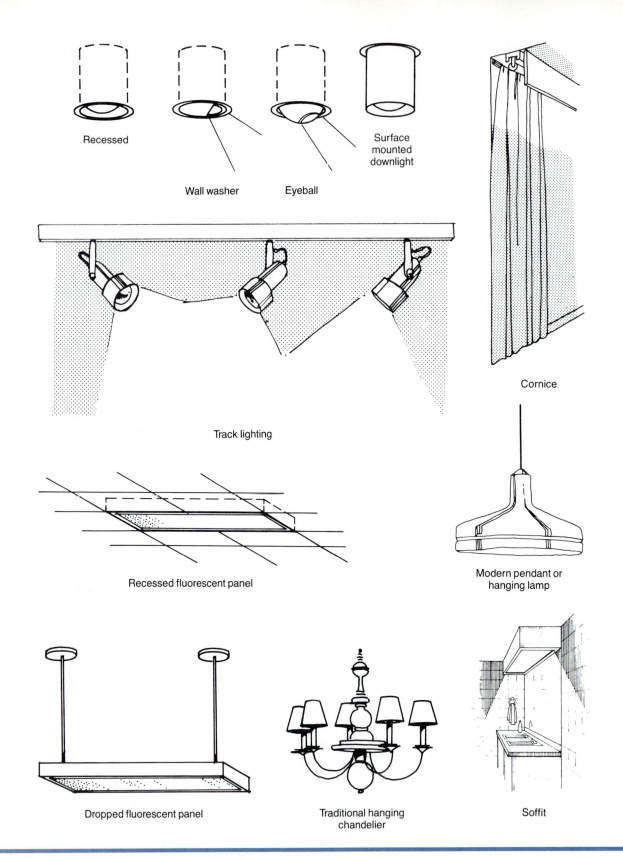

Recessed

Wall washer

Eyeball

Surface mounted downlight

Track lighting

Cornice

Recessed fluorescent panel

Modern pendant or hanging lamp

Dropped fluorescent panel

Traditional hanging chandelier

Soffit

FIGURE 3.20 Common types of ceiling-mounted fixtures.

FIGURE 3.21 Recessed
ceiling-mounted fixtures are often
used in office settings to provide
efficient overall general illumination.
In the entrance to this office,
recessed lights provide general
illumination for the receptionist's
desk. Cove and wall-mounted
fixtures highlight architectural
elements in the area beyond.
(Photograph by Pam Singleton.)

FIGURE 3.22 Track lighting,
attached to a wood strip ceiling, has
been placed at key points in this
office reception area to provide
flexible lighting where needed.
(Courtesy of Michael Jensen,
designer.)

Flush-mounted lighting, as opposed to recessed, refers to surface-mounted fixtures that may project a few inches into the room and reflect direct or indirect lighting, depending on the design and use. (Although treated as a separate lighting type previously, track lighting is a type of flush-mounted lighting.)

Luminous panels consist of recessed light diffused through ceiling panels. They are used primarily in kitchens, utility areas, bathrooms, offices, hospitals, schools, and other commercial and institutional spaces. (Refer to Figure 3.24.)

Custom-designed architectural lighting is lighting created for a particular purpose or design effect. Often this type is incorporated into built-in or stationary furniture and architectural features.

Floor lighting may be used in dark hallways and in the base of steps as a safety device.

Portable or Nonarchitectural Lighting

The term *portable lighting* indicates the ability to transport fixtures from location to location as desired, considering the purposes they serve and the area in which they are used. Portable fixtures (both table and floor models) are the oldest forms of electrical interior lighting. They provide flexible lighting in the residential or public environment and may be purely functional, decorative, or both. (Refer to Figures 3.25 through 3.28.)

Placement

Although portable fixtures often function as a secondary light source, their placement in the room is important. They generally should be positioned as part of a furniture grouping, near an electrical outlet, and out of the line of traffic.

FIGURE 3.23 A popular type of architectural fixture is the chandelier. A traditional wrought iron fixture with red shades contributes to the predominant Spanish style. It is hung sufficiently high that people working around the island will not bump into it. (Photograph by Pam Singleton.)

FIGURE 3.24 Luminous panels in a stepped ceiling not only define the boundaries of the reception area but also provide general illumination for completing applications or reviewing forms. (Courtesy of Lynn McGhie & Associates.)

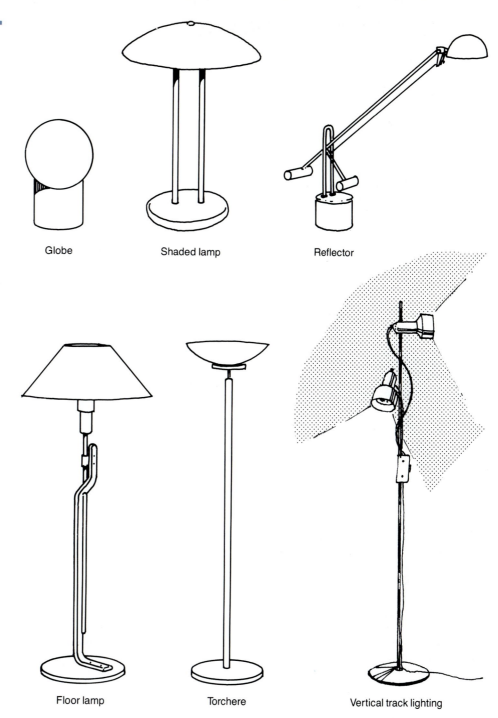

FIGURE 3.25 Typical portable or standing lamp styles.

Globe

Shaded lamp

Reflector

Floor lamp

Torchere

Vertical track lighting

Function

Functional fixtures should be chosen with their purpose in mind, for example, table lamps for reading, desk lamps for studying, or table and floor lamps to help direct light and provide general lighting. Usually a combination of both portable and ceiling- and wall-mounted fixtures satisfies lighting needs for function and visual interest within a space, as illustrated in Figure 3.29.

Shades

Most portable fixtures come with shades to help **diffuse** and direct the light. A table lamp used for reading is most effective when the bottom of the shade is at the eye level of the person seated — 38 in. to 42 in. above the floor. The shade works well when it is at least 16 in. across the bottom so that the lamp will shed light on more than just the reading area and thereby prevent eyestrain caused by

FIGURE 3.26 The large, adjustable curve of the Arco floor luminaire, designed by Achille Castiglioni in 1967, allows light to focus downward and gives a dramatic effect. (Courtesy of Atelier International.)

FIGURE 3.27 Another classic lamp is the Tizio, designed by Richard Sapper in Germany during the 1970s. The flexible lamp—which is available in a floor or table model—can be adjusted to a number of positions and is a popular choice for both contract and residential design. (Courtesy of Artemide.)

FIGURE 3.28 The Nesso lamp, sometimes called the "mushroom" because of its distinctive form, was designed in Italy. It is made of plastic and comes in a variety of colors and in two sizes. The graceful lamp sheds a soft light from four small interior bulbs. (Courtesy of Artemide. Photograph by Aldo Ballo.)

a sudden change from light to dark. When the shade is lined with white, maximum light is provided. Glare is eliminated when the shade covers the bulb and fixture.

Light Diffusion

A soft white bulb provides the best light diffusion. An opal glass diffuser bowl also improves the quality of light over standard glass because it helps reduce glare. A flat dishlike diffuser helps soften and mask direct light from horizontal bulbs.

Scale and Proportion

The scale and proportion of a fixture should be considered in relation to other furnishings and to the size of the room and the lamp itself. *Decorative fixtures* generally work best when the design is simple, unobtrusive, and suitable to the room's style and design. Some designs that are decorated on both the base and the shade may attract more attention than desired. Other designs, like those from a certain period, may be chosen to focus attention on the piece.

Structural fixtures devoid of ornamentation are popular with both professional designers and homeowners.

FIGURE 3.29 A variety of lighting sources in this room, including the wall sconces, hanging fixture, track, torchere, and portable lamp, show the light direction and effect of each type.

A room's success is enhanced when structural fixtures are simple, well proportioned and suitably scaled, and constructed of materials and textures that complement the room's style.

SWITCHES AND OUTLETS

The convenient location of switches and outlets is essential and must be indicated on the blueprint and electrical plan of the structure, as illustrated in Figure 3.30. Each room requires a light switch, which may or may not control both built-in and portable fixtures. Switches may be conveniently placed on the latch side of each access door to provide immediate illumination on entering and serve as a reminder to turn the lights off when leaving. Switches are also necessary at both ends of hallways and at the top and bottom of stairways. Where task lighting is necessary, switches should be placed within easy reach. Dimmers on switches allow great flexibility for various levels of lighting—ideal for creating a mood and also for conserving energy and the life of the lamp.

Throughout interior spaces, outlets should be plentiful and located for specific tasks. Outlets should be easily accessible for appliances in kitchens and utility areas and electrical equipment in bathrooms. When a room's function is determined, outlets can be conveniently located in accordance with local building codes. Outlets placed in regular intervals approximately 3 to 6 ft. apart between doorways and floor-length windows decrease the need for hazardous extension cords. Outlets

mounted 12 in. from the floor and wall switches located 50 in. from the floor are workable. Where heavy mechanical devices are power driven, special heavy-duty outlets should be provided. Outdoor outlets must be weather-proofed, made ground-fault interruptible, and situated safely.

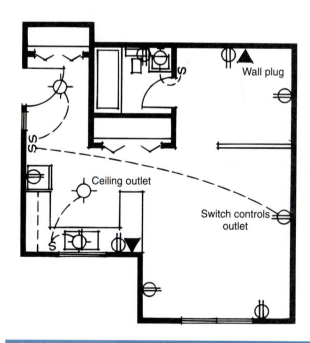

FIGURE 3.30 A floor plan indicating the wiring and location of electrical outlets and switches. This information aids the designer in determining a functional furniture arrangement.

FIGURE 3.31 Recessed ceiling lights, cove lighting placed high in wall niches, portable lamps, and firelight contribute to the cozy, warm atmoshpere of this Santa Fe style living room. (Photograph by Mark Boisclair.)

LIGHTING FOR AREAS AND ACTIVITIES

Since humans are psychologically and physically affected by light, it is an important factor when planning interior spaces. Glaring light is disturbing and hampers activities in an interior area, and bland or inefficient light can actually result in physical fatigue. Designers can alleviate lighting problems in both residential and commercial spaces by controlling the light source and causing the light to be reflected, absorbed, or redirected. This goal is achieved through careful choice of correct fixtures and lamps, coordination of placement, and consideration of colors and reflectants on surfaces to be lit. This section discusses lighting considerations for specific areas and activities in residential settings.

The *entrance area,* as the keynote to the decor of a home, can provide a cordial air of hospitality where lighting plays an important role. During the day the entry hall should be bright enough to allow a reasonable transition from the bright outdoors to the darker interior. Illumination need not be at a high level at night, but it should be strong enough to enable entering guests to see and be seen. Modern or traditional ceiling-mounted luminaires plus suitably placed wall sconces or portable fixtures that diffuse light can provide adequate illumination and a friendly atmosphere. Staircases should be well lit so treads and risers can be distinguished clearly. The entrance is an ideal place to try a dramatic lighting effect such as an accented art object or plant.

Living rooms need soft general background lighting supplemented by special area lighting, as shown in Figure 3.31. Both direct and indirect lighting sources are desirable, although an excess of indirect lighting may result in a washed-out appearance. Well-chosen lamps at necessary locations add a feeling of comfort and hospitality conducive to conversation. Built-in shelving, display cases, and art objects that are accented by downlights help to personalize a room and establish its focal point. For reading, studying, playing the piano, and similar activities, lighting should be direct and combined with general lighting to avoid strong contrast.

Dining areas deserve versatile lighting around the table area that can be adjusted for a variety of functions in addition to formal and casual dining, such as studying, sewing, and playing games. A low-level background can be provided by general lighting. A chandelier or pendant using incandescent globes and hung about 30 in. above the table adds sparkle to silver and glass at formal meals. Dimmer controls allow for a change of mood, and supplementary light from candles gives a flattering glow to skin tones. Creative use of accent light helps in avoiding flat downlight and adds interest, for example, highlighters on china closets or built-in niches, or uplighters spotting plants and art objects. If the dining space is part of or open to other areas, lighting can successfully set it apart.

Family and recreation rooms accommodate a variety of activities and thus require particularly flexible lighting. General lighting is essential, with area and task lighting supplied for specific activities. Television viewing is most comfortable when general lighting is at a low level with no strong contrasts or glare. The television screen itself reflects light and contributes to the total lighting effect. In a recreation area planned for table games, Ping-Pong, dancing, or other physical activities, a high level of illumination that does not interfere with these functions is preferable. Task and accent lighting can also be incorporated depending on style, function, and effect desired.

Kitchens and utility rooms function best when generous overall lighting for safety and efficiency is planned. Ceiling or close-to-ceiling fixtures such as recessed or flush downlights, track lighting, or illuminated ceiling panels can give adequate general light and eliminate shadows, although this is not the most favored way to provide light in a kitchen. More important are recessed or shielded fluorescent tubes over work areas and mounted under wall cabinets to illuminate counters, help prevent accidents, speed up food preparation, and enhance the decor. Task lighting is especially necessary in the mixing, cooking, and sink centers. Warm white deluxe tubes provide pleasing color to food and occupants. The table area should have inviting and adequate lighting for eating and possibly for studying. (See Figure 3.32.)

Bedrooms need comfortable general lighting with appropriate task lights for reading, desk work, grooming, and other activities, depending on the use of the space.

FIGURE 3.32 Lighting in a kitchen demands adequate light for such tasks as preparing and serving meals and cleaning up afterward. In this stimulating red, black, and natural wood kitchen, recessed lighting in the ceiling provides good overall lighting. (Photograph by Norman McGrath.)

Direct lighting is also efficient when placed over chests of drawers, in closets, close to seating, and over beds. Dim circulation lighting for safety at night is a basic requirement. Accent lighting can be effectively used to focus on a painting or wall unit at the head of the bed.

Bathrooms require shadowless lighting for shaving and grooming, which can be supplied by light from overhead and from both sides of a mirror and by light reflected upward from a light-colored basin or countertop. Mirror lighting is usually sufficient to illuminate an average-sized bath or powder room; however, general lighting overhead and over tub areas is also needed. (See Figure 3.33.)

Halls and stairways require overall illumination for safe passage. Fixtures may be recessed in or hung from the ceiling, attached to walls, or built in near the baseboard in hallways. Stairways should be well lit with treads and risers clearly defined. Well-shielded light fixtures that avoid blinding glare at the top and bottom of stairs is another safety factor.

Outdoor lighting at night enhances the exterior architecture, gardens, decks, patios, walkways, and other outdoor living areas and provides visual pleasure. This is true in residential, commercial, and institutional settings. Additionally, outdoor lighting helps alleviate the black

glass look inside by balancing and extending the lighting to the outside (refer to Figure 14.1). Weatherproof luminaires for outside use can be attached under the eaves and on exterior walls. Custom lighting often includes exposed and concealed fixtures placed at various important areas of the garden that throw light upward, downward, or in both directions on trees, plantings, a garden sculpture or fountain, a gazebo, and other garden features to create a visually exciting experience. The front door conveys the first impression of a home. Exterior lighting there can be set off by fixtures that have eye appeal and conform to the style of the house (refer to Figure 7.31).

ECONOMY AND ENERGY CONSERVATION

Knowledgeable planning and purchasing can give a space sufficient lighting and still save watts and dollars. The following guidelines can help conserve energy in lighting.

- Lighting should fit specific needs. Task areas such as kitchen counters require more light than nonworking areas such as circulation space. Sufficient light is important, but using more light than necessary wastes electrical energy.
- Dimmers are useful in adjusting light levels, increasing lamp life, and saving energy.
- Installing multiple switches makes it possible to use only the amount of light required in a specific area.
- Fixtures should be energy effective, allowing maximum light to be emitted instead of being trapped in the fixture.
- Fixtures that can be adjusted and placed where light is needed are a wise choice. For example, track lighting has great flexibility and permits the light to be directed where it is wanted.
- A reflectorized lamp is good for accent or task lighting. Low-voltage spotlights are especially effective where a tightly controlled beam is required.
- Light sources should be efficient. Light output varies in efficiency according to wattage and color. For example, fluorescent lamps use as much as 80 percent less energy, produce 5 to 30 times as much light, and last 20 times longer than incandescent lamps. For this reason they are often used in commercial spaces, as seen in Figure 3.34.
- Three-way incandescent lamps allow selectivity in the amount of light used.
- Where appearance is not a consideration, as in garages and some basements, industrial reflectors are an economical option.
- When ceilings, walls, floors, and furniture have light-colored finishes they reflect more light. Rooms designed in dark colors absorb light and require more lighting.

FIGURE 3.33 Efficient lighting for grooming and safety is provided by well-placed recessed lighting in this striking bathroom. The lighting also brings out the beauty of line and texture of the tile design. (Courtesy of Dal-Tile.)

FIGURE 3.34 Energy-efficient and cost-efficient fluorescent lighting has been used in this office space. (Courtesy of Kimball Office Furniture Co.)

- Keeping reflectors, diffusers, and lamps clean helps to maintain lighting equipment.
- Lights should be turned off when not needed to conserve energy and extend the hours of lighting before lamp replacement.

ASSIGNMENT

Find a picture in a design magazine that demonstrates good lighting in a residential or commercial interior. Mount the picture on construction paper or mat board. Analyze the room and answer the following lighting questions on separate sheets of paper. Submit your answers with the picture.

1. What functions take place in the space? Have the lighting needs of the customers, employees, or residents been met?

2. What mood has been created? Is it conducive to the activities that take place in the room?
3. Is the space overlit or underlit?
4. Is there any glare?
5. Is there visual interest?
6. What types of fixtures are used? (Ceiling mounted? Wall mounted? Portable?)
7. Are the fixtures attractive? Are the styles in harmony with the rest of the room?
8. What types of lamps were used? (Incandescent? Fluorescent? HID? Neon?)
9. Does the color of the lamp bring out the colors of the furniture and background elements?
10. Have the reflectances of the materials in the space been considered?
11. What are your personal feelings about the space? Do you have any suggestions for improving the lighting?

PART TWO

Space Planning

CHAPTER 4

Space Planning

FIGURE 4.1 Efficient open planning allows space to freely flow throughout the interior of this contemporary home. Spaces for various functions are defined by the arrangement of furniture and by a change in floor level rather than by walls. (Photograph by Mark Boisclair.)

85

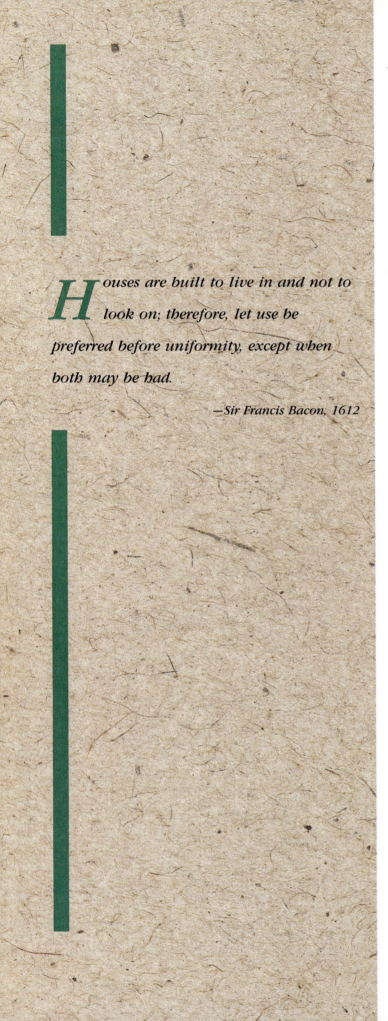

*H*ouses are built to live in and not to look on; therefore, let use be preferred before uniformity, except when both may be had.

—*Sir Francis Bacon, 1612*

*D*esigners today are aware of the impact of the physical interior environment on the occupant's life. The need for adequate shelter is only the beginning. Well-planned space should be given top priority to ensure an interior where human activities can be carried on with a minimum of frustration. The creation of an environment that promotes the comfort and convenience of the end **users**, both physically and psychologically, is a significant goal of the designer (Figure 4.1). Meeting human needs in specific environments, whether residential or nonresidential, requires intelligent study, insight, and knowledge of space planning.

THE BASIC GOALS OF DESIGN AND SPACE PLANNING

The designer's ultimate goal when planning a residence or commercial structure should be the integration of the basic requirements for an efficient and aesthetically pleasing space: functional needs, physical and psychological comfort, economic considerations, aesthetics, and individuality. Other criteria worth considering when planning space include conserving energy, incorporating ideas for "greening the environment," ensuring a healthy and safe environment, and addressing the needs of all users, including the physically challenged, children, or the elderly.

Functional Needs

To be livable, an interior should fulfill its intended function of satisfying the needs of the people for whom it is designed. Careful consideration of functional space should commence in the initial planning stage—before materials, components, and furnishings are specified. For a residential project, designers should ask numerous questions concerning the lifestyle, design preferences, and requirements of the end users. Part of the early planning phase, or program, involves completing a personal profile for each occupant, or in the case of a nonresidential project, spelling out the needs of the client in detail. Spatial requirements should be planned after carefully evaluating this information. Specific design requirements may be necessary for the special needs of users such as children, the elderly, or the physically challenged.

Physical and Psychological Comfort

The physical and psychological comfort of the occupants is an important aspect of the space planning process. For example, human beings should be physically and psychologically comfortable in relation to the scale and proportion of the architecture. The three-dimensional aspects of ceiling height as well as wall lengths of the space, or cubic footage, should be considered, since if the space is

FIGURE 4.2 A project oriented for special need users includes an entrance ramp with barrier-free access into the reception area, conference room, restroom, kitchenette, and offices. The 5 ft. turnabout required for wheelchairs is indicated. (Courtesy of Michael Jensen, Jonna Robison, and Chet Knight, designers.)

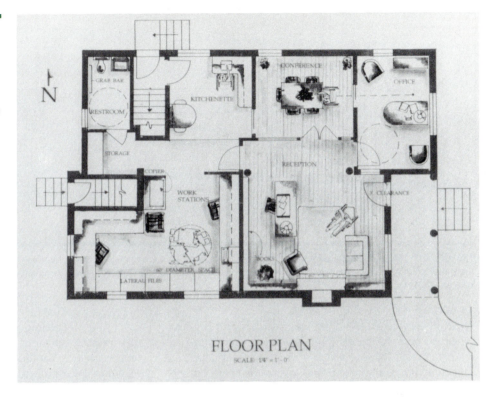

FLOOR PLAN
SCALE 1⁄4" = 1'-0"

too vast or too small, the occupants may feel uncomfortable or out of place. Satisfying human comfort entails many other design criteria as well, including selection and arrangement of line, color, form, lighting, and texture to create a sense of balance and harmony.

Furniture should be suitably scaled for comfort and arranged for purpose and efficiency. For example, a chair for relaxing should be comfortable and should fit the size of the occupant, with a table at the appropriate height close by to accommodate a lamp that produces adequate lighting with no glare.

Planning for the Physically Challenged

The needs of the physically challenged user are of utmost importance when planning a nonresidential space (see Figure 4.2); in addition, the designer must meet certain code and legal requirements. Even in residential design, physically challenged and elderly individuals are often members of a household or may be the only occupants. Some individuals may be temporarily or permanently confined to a wheelchair or be partially ambulatory. Some older persons, while not physically challenged or impaired, may want an environment that functions particularly well for convenience, safety, and security. Sensitive designers are aware of these requirements that contribute to an **accessible**, safe, and comfortable environment for those with special needs, as demonstrated in Figure 4.2. Some criteria include the following:

■ The home should be *free of architectural* **barriers** so that those who may be using a wheelchair, crutches, or a walker can easily circulate throughout various areas.

If possible, select a plan without stairs so all facilities are on one floor. Open planning is a wise choice. Traffic lanes should be kept clear and be well planned. Doors should be at least 32 in. wide with easy-to-turn knobs or lever handles.

■ *Bathrooms and fixtures* must be conveniently and safely located with ample room for manipulating a wheelchair. Grab bars conveniently positioned to walls by the tub and toilet provide added safety. Tubs should have flat, nonslip bottoms. Faucets should have temperature controls. Wall-hung toilets and showers without curbs are preferred.

■ **Clearances** between furnishings in all rooms of the house should be adequate to accommodate a wheelchair or walker. Traffic lanes must be kept free of clutter and be wide enough for easy movement.

■ *Easy access to garage and outdoor areas* is of utmost importance.

■ *Lighting* throughout the home should be located with access to switches, controls, and outlets. Switches should be located 3 ft above the floor and outlets 1 ft 3 in. above the floor. Pulldown lighting fixtures are an added convenience.

■ *Floor coverings* in hard, smooth surfaces that are slip resistant work most efficiently for safe and easy movement. If carpet is used, a dense, short pile is best. Generally, area and throw rugs should be avoided. Thresholds should be flat.

■ The *kitchen*, an area especially susceptible to accidents, should be arranged with heights, clearances, and other measurements planned for convenience and safety. Dishes, cooking utensils, and other items should be

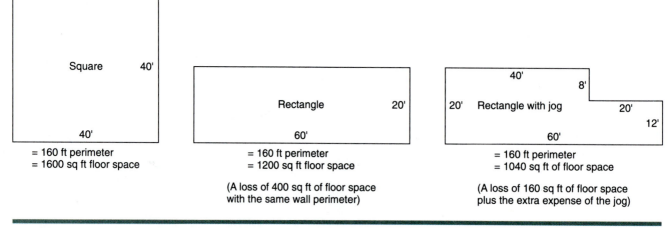

Square 40'

40'

= 160 ft perimeter
= 1600 sq ft floor space

Rectangle 20'

60'

= 160 ft perimeter
= 1200 sq ft floor space

(A loss of 400 sq ft of floor space
with the same wall perimeter)

40' 8'

20' Rectangle with jog 20'

12'

60'

= 160 ft perimeter
= 1040 sq ft of floor space

(A loss of 160 sq ft of floor space
plus the extra expense of the jog)

FIGURE 4.3 Price and square footage. The three enclosures, each requiring the same number of linear feet of exterior wall, illustrate how the price per square foot increases as the space deviates from the square.

within easy reach. Working surfaces that pull out and storage areas with open and revolving shelves are an asset. A front-loading dishwasher and washer/dryer, an upright refrigerator, and an oven with front controls are convenient. For those in wheelchairs, oven and dishwasher doors hinged at the side are most convenient. There should be easy access to the sink and faucets.

■ *Climate-control boxes* should be approximately 2 to 4 ft above the floor.

Economic Considerations

A home is probably the largest single investment a consumer will ever make. Receiving the best value possible for every dollar spent is, therefore, highly important. The designer should study costs on paper and look carefully at such criteria as available resources or allocated budget, client needs, materials and components required, time limits, building requirements and codes.

The cost of a structure is related to the amount of square footage within the space and varies depending on many factors, such as size, geographic location, materials specified, cubic square footage (the three-dimensional space or height, depth, and width of the space), special construction features (such as cathedral ceilings, angled spaces, and bay windows), and the cost of local labor. Average building costs per square foot, exclusive of the lot, depend on the region where the structure will be built. For example, costs are considerably higher in some areas of the nation like New York, California, Alaska, and Hawaii. Costs range from approximately $50 per square foot for a low-budget project to $75 and up for a luxury dwelling. For a commercial structure, the cost per square foot begins at about $75 and can soar much higher depending on the above criteria.

In residential projects the initial cost of buying a home is only the beginning; payments and upkeep must continue. According to most home-financing agencies, the monthly payment, including principal, interest, taxes, and insurance, should not exceed 28 percent of gross pay. A general formula that designers, builders, and clients use is that a monthly payment of approximately $500 is due for every $50,000 borrowed. Most clients have a limited budget for their project. As a result, intelligent decisions must be made to meet the needs of the user and remain within the limits of their budget.

Before the overall expense of the project is determined, the designer may be required to investigate ways of limiting building costs. The following suggestions concerning methods and materials can help minimize project costs:

■ *A well-designed floor plan:* The designer can work closely with the architect in creating the floor plan. A wide selection of excellent stock plans is also available. Often a designer will select a stock plan and make modifications to meet specific needs of the client.

■ *A basic plan:* Space can be maximized and costs minimized by employing a simple plan. Most residential plans are based on one of the six basic floor plan types: the rectangle or square, and the H, U, T, L, and E shapes. Of these plans, the rectangle, the L, and the U are most common. Regarding cost, the nearer to a square shape of the exterior walls, the less is the cost per square foot. Cost does not increase in direct proportion to a structure's square footage; jogs and angles drive the construction costs higher, as illustrated in Figure 4.3. Two stories cost proportionally less than a low, rambling plan, because the roof and foundation can serve twice the space, heating can be more centralized, and the second story provides extra insulation against summer heat and winter cold.

■ *A unified theme:* Unnecessary mixing of materials generally should be avoided. Any building material, no matter how old or new, works well when used appro-

FIGURE 4.4 A well-designed roof can permit the warm winter sun to flood the interior spaces in December and block out the hot summer sun in July.

priately. Simplicity is often the key to a well-designed residence.

- *Adequate insulation:* Adequate **insulation** reduces heating costs. Wood- or coal-burning stoves that meet strict EPA requirements can be used to efficiently cut down on heating costs.
- *Solar orientation:* Locating the structure to take the best advantage of the climate can save on heating and air-conditioning bills. The winter sun should strike long walls and large windows, but large areas of glass should not face the afternoon sun in the summer. (See Figure 4.4.) Passive solar energy systems might be incorporated. Positioning the house wisely can reduce

the cost of utilities. The cost of connecting water, gas, and electricity to the main lines depends on the distance from the house to the road.

- *Centralize:* Save money by using centralized plumbing. Bathrooms can be placed back to back as seen in Figure 4.5, or one above the other. Kitchen and utility room plumbing can be located to take advantage of the same major drains. Fireplaces can be planned to take advantage of a common chimney, shown in Figure 4.6.
- *Indigenous materials:* Materials found on-site in the construction area can offer great savings. Flawed ma-

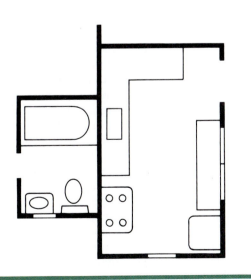

FIGURE 4.5 Back to back plumbing.

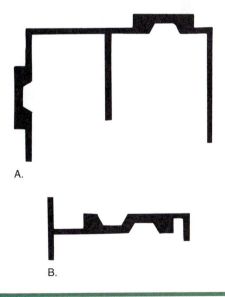

A.

B.

FIGURE 4.6 Two fireplaces can be combined to share the same chimney.

FIGURE 4.7 The lobby of the Western Medical Center in Anaheim, California, is designed with serene colors and a spacious feeling to decrease anxiety and communicate a calm, reassuring atmosphere. (Courtesy of Designedge, Inc., Peggy Honey, designer.)

terials may cost less and character can be gained by making a feature out of a fault.

■ *Standard milled items:* These include doors, window frames, cabinets, stairways, mantels, and wood trim. **Standard milled items** can be well designed and are readily available at factory-built prices. In some areas plastic plumbing pipe can be used instead of copper pipe.

■ *Consideration of long-term upkeep:* Before making the final decision on any item that goes into the completed house, the buyer might consider the upkeep over a long period of time. Some things that are more costly initially are the most economical in the long run. For example, the best heating plan for a particular house in its particular locality is the most economical. In some areas brick may cost more than frame construction or facades, but it never needs painting and the resale value is usually higher than that of wood. A lifetime roof costs considerably more than one of plain cedar shingles, but the latter may need repair through the years and is more of a fire hazard. Hardwood **balusters** are more costly than pine, but pine balusters are easily

broken and replacement may soon add up to more than the cost of the hardwood.

Aesthetics

Interior spaces should be pleasing to the users and ought to have a certain intrinsic appeal, as shown in Figure 4.7. It is essential that students of design develop awareness and sensitivity to the aesthetics of all interior environments, such as private dwellings, financial or educational institutions, offices, retail and hospitality spaces, health care centers, and other nonresidential interiors. A knowledgeable designer has a trained eye for discriminating between good and poor design. What is beauty, and what makes an interior environment appear beautiful?

Beauty has been described as that quality which pleases the senses and lifts the spirit and is most often a personal reaction. However, authorities in the interior design field generally agree that beauty in any object is achieved through the thoughtful application of the principles of design (scale, proportion, balance, emphasis, rhythm and harmony) and a skillful use of design elements (color, texture, form, space planning, lighting, pattern, and line), unified by a basic theme. A space design with these principles and elements in mind, regardless of style, should be satisfactory.

Individuality

Individuality is an elusive quality, particularly when considering its properties in a private dwelling. It often develops slowly and naturally, revealing the personality of the occupants. In custom-built structures this development is perhaps easier to achieve. In look-alike subdivisions and mobile home areas, for example, the challenge of expressing a personal statement is more difficult.

Often individuality or projecting a particular character is expressed in nonresidential projects. For example, the western theme of a restaurant, the old English style of a hotel, or the high-tech image of a specialty shop can be conveyed through the use of colors, furnishings, accessories and other elements.

PROGRAMMING AND THE DESIGN PROCESS

As the designer begins a residential or nonresidential project, it is essential to understand how the end users will function in the space and to collect all relevant background information. The designer must ask questions about the client's needs, the activities that will take place within the space, and special considerations unique to the project. After this information has been gathered, a **plan** or design process can be determined. This initial planning stage is called the **program**. The program is also a written or typed **design statement** summarizing all the requirements, goals, and objectives for one specific project and its users. In the case of a residential project, this is often referred to as a *client profile*. A nonresidential project may require a more extensive program. For example, designing spaces for a hotel would be more technical and complex than designing spaces for a private dwelling.

The written program outlines the client's expectations and the designer's commitment and responsibility. The program takes into consideration each occupant's needs and personality, the overall economic situation and budget restrictions of the project, safety, aesthetic expectations, space requirements, activities, and psychological and environmental considerations. It is an overall agreement on the goals and objectives to be met and the services to be provided. Satisfying a number of these goals simultaneously can be a complicated process and a challenge for the designer.

After the goals and requirements of the project have been defined and agreed on, the next step is to collect all pertinent information. This may involve additional client interviews, researching what is available, or examining the possibility of using certain materials and components. After gathering the information, the designer examines and analyzes the data.

Next, the designer explores possible solutions to the design problem. After generating a number of options, the designer evaluates which solution will best meet the needs, preferences, and budget of the client. In both residential and nonresidential projects, input from the client helps determine the most suitable solution. The designer identifies the best solution and communicates the ideas to the client through drawings and renderings of the project (Figure 4.8).

From the time the client agrees to the proposed solution of the design problem, the designer becomes involved in its implementation—specifying materials, working with contractors, and writing and signing contracts.

Following completion of the project, the designer should critically evaluate its outcome. The pivotal determinant of success is the reaction of the end users to the solutions of the initial problem. Have the goals of the design been achieved? Of course, a positive response is the desired goal. For example, if the occupant in a private residence or the end users in a nonresidential space feel comfortable and safe, can function effectively in the environment, are visually uplifted, and feel that their quality of life has been enriched, then the design project has been favorably evaluated—the human factor has been successfully considered, addressed, and satisfied.

Residential Projects

Residential projects involve designing spaces for single individuals or families in an environment that is often called a "home" and generally involves an entirely different design focus from planning nonresidential spaces. These private dwellings include detached houses, townhouses, condominiums, apartments, prefabricated houses, mobile homes, and dormitories.

Nonresidential Projects

The numerous types of commercial spaces on which a designer may work will have a variety of functions; therefore space planning involves a more complex procedure than for residential projects. To meet the needs of the client and end users, extensive study and research on the part of the designer are required. It is helpful for the student of design to be aware of the general categories of nonresidential design, each with unique functions and spaces, that convey the diversity of commercial design projects. These nonresidential projects include:

- *Business office design.* Includes planning for reception and entry areas, executive and management spaces, workstations or centers, clerical facilities, resource

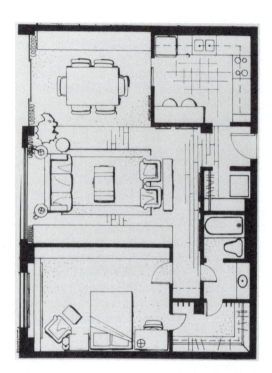
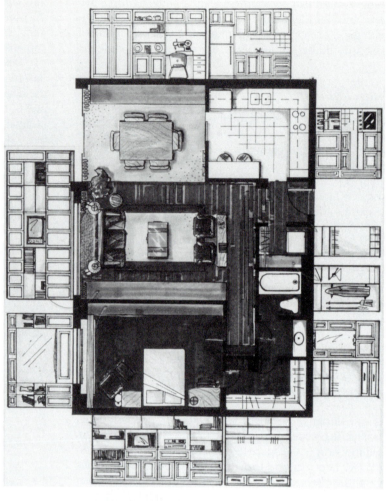

FIGURE 4.8 A space planning project may be presented to the client through renderings and a floor plan. The plan of this small one-bedroom apartment (left) indicates space allocation and furniture arrangement. The second version (right) gives more detail, including color schemes and a number of elevations. (Courtesy of Chet Knight, designer.)

spaces, conference rooms, restrooms.) (See Figures 4.9 and 4.10.)

- *Health care design.* Includes hospitals, medical offices, physical therapy centers, and mental institutions, each with different functional needs.
- *Industrial design.* Includes manufacturing factories, workshops, and warehouses.
- *Retail design.* Includes shopping malls, stores, shops, boutiques, galleries, and showrooms.
- *Financial institutions.* Includes banks, credit unions, stock exchanges, savings and loans.
- *Educational institutions.* Universities, colleges, and schools, including libraries, classrooms, faculty offices, studios, laboratories, lecture halls, eating facilities, and dormitories.
- *Government and public spaces.* Includes courthouses, municipal buildings, police and fire stations, post offices, museums, libraries, and other public buildings.

- *Hospitality planning.* Restaurants, hotels, resorts, inns and motels. (See Figure 4.11.)
- *Recreational spaces.* Sports clubs, health clubs, golf and tennis resorts, and other physical activities areas.
- *Transportation facilities.* Includes terminals and stations for airplanes, ships, buses, and trains.

Following the programming and design process specified for residential projects, the designer is particularly concerned with the following *space planning criteria* for specific nonresidential projects:

- *Functional requirements* of the client and/or end user. Consider the type of service or activity that will take place and the daily routines of employees, patrons, guests, patients, or clients.
- *Spatial organization.* Lay out the space by zoning and **diagramming** the various functions and needs required to determine a solution.

FIGURE 4.9 With the aid of a computer, space has been allocated for one floor of a skyscraper. Functional spaces required include executive offices, workstations, resource centers, conference rooms, restrooms, and adequate traffic patterns. The plan indicates such details as wall partitions, doors, stairways, windows, columns, lighting, and furnishings. (Courtesy of Valentiner Jones, architects. Drawn by Bill Hall.)

FIGURE 4.10 In this office building, seating for visitors is provided on two levels of the atrium/lobby. Granite planters subdivide the space into conversation areas framed by greenery. Outer walkways converge toward the elevators, located behind the tiled fountain. (Photograph courtesy of Tom Watson/Watson Photography.)

FIGURE 4.11 Hospitality design often includes projects such as hotels and restaurants. A lush lobby was designed by Michael Graves to welcome guests to the Walt Disney World Dolphin Hotel. Natural light filters through draped fabric that covers a domed ceiling in the rotunda. A fountain filled with statues of mythical sea creatures adds a charming note to this busy area. (Photo courtesy of The Walt Disney Co.)

- *Shape and size of the space.* The available cubic and square footage helps determine the total design of the space.
- *Traffic lanes or patterns.* Users should be able to travel effectively within all interior spaces with easy access to entrances and exits.
- *Building laws, codes, and restrictions.* **Codes** set by state and local government must be followed.
- *Interior systems.* Electrical, heating, and cooling systems, ventilation, plumbing, sanitary drainage, fire protection systems, elevators, escalators, ramps, acoustical control, and other systems must be carefully planned for efficiency and safety.
- *Specification of materials and components.* Lighting, style, colors, textures, and accessories that will contribute to the physical and psychological well-being of all users must be chosen.
- *Planning for the physically challenged.* The space must be made accessible for wheelchairs.

SITE SELECTION AND ORIENTATION

On certain projects, the designer may have input into selecting the site for a residential or nonresidential structure. Before making a selection, the designer should have the general plan of the structure in mind. Not until the site has been analyzed should the plan be finalized. For example, when selecting a site for a residence, many factors should be considered including such criteria as location of schools, transportation, availability of police and fire protection, quality of the neighborhood, utility availability (water, power, sewage disposal, garbage collection), taxes, and building codes and restrictions. Depending on the building's intended function, criteria when selecting a site for a nonresidential structure might include public convenience, efficiency, accessibility, and aesthetic appeal.

For a residence, a desirable topography is often a gently sloping lot that provides good natural drainage and allows sewer lines to be connected easily. A steep lot may cost less initially but may require expensive retaining walls and other hidden costs. Effective positioning of the structure on the site and orienting the structure to take advantage of solar properties are also important criteria.

THE FLOOR PLAN

The graphic details of a floor plan indicate the spatial boundaries of the structure that strongly influence the efficiency and comfort of interior spaces. Experience has proven that the intelligent application of basic design requirements to the general floor plan is conducive to the smooth working of an interior space. Styles have changed through the years, but certain desirable features have remained constant. For example, surveys indicate users appreciate well-planned **circulation** patterns whether in public or private spaces. In recent years, skyrocketing building costs and interest rates for private residences, along with dramatic changes in the family structure, have forced people to live in small spaces, making multipurpose areas a necessity.

Whether the designer is working directly with an architect or with a predesigned plan, it is essential to be able to read and understand an architect's working drawing of a floor plan. This graphic design is referred to as the **blueprint**, since the old printing method employed white lines on a bright blue ground. The standard today, however, is to use blue lines on a white ground. The floor plan is a two-dimensional drawing indicating the walls, floors, partitions, windows, stairs, cabinets, and other structural components that outline the available space. Floor plans are drawn precisely to *scale,* indicating size relationships. The most commonly used scale in a residential floor plan is 1/4 in. to 1 ft. In a nonresidential project, 1/8 in. to 1 ft. is often used. This scale reduces the size of the plan, allowing the designer to represent the outline of the structure and interior spaces on paper.

To understand the blueprint, it is necessary to become familiar with basic architectural drafting symbols as illustrated in Figure 4.12, which include room dimensions, closets, openings, stairways, bathroom fixtures, appliances, electrical outlets, and heating units. With this knowledge the designer can intelligently examine the

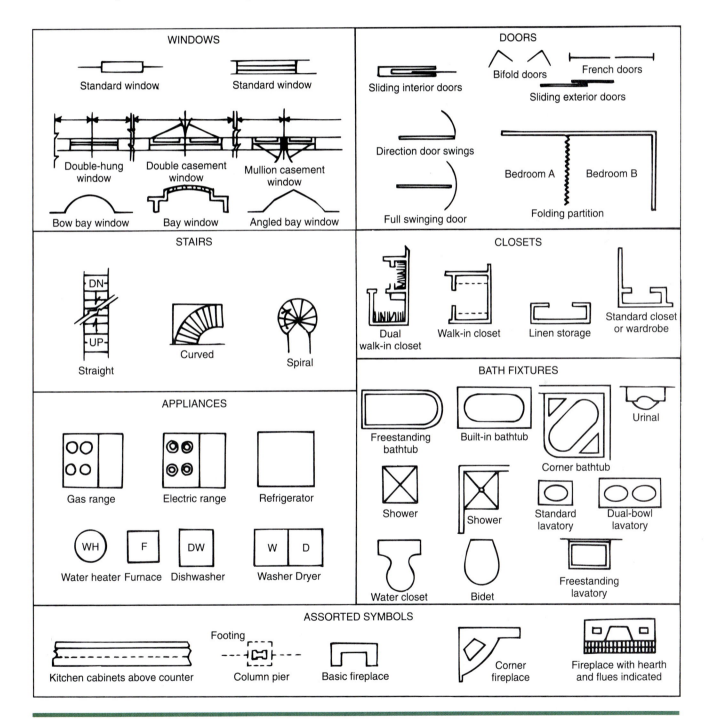

FIGURE 4.12 Architectural drafting symbols.

blueprint while "walking through" the spaces. Although the evaluation does not provide a three-dimensional understanding, it will reveal any objectionable features, which can be changed before the plan is finalized. Familiarization with a graphic floor, therefore, is an important step for the professional designer, builder, and often the client.

Interior Zoning

Defining basic areas in residential and nonresidential projects is helpful to the designer in the space planning process. Zoning interior spaces for a nonresidential project depends on the intended function. For example, zoning spaces for a restaurant would be considerably different from zoning spaces for a health care center or an office.

The functions or intended uses of space in a residential structure fall into three **zones** that combine related activities: (1) *service/work zones,* which include kitchen, utility, sewing, workshop, office, and other work-related areas; (2) *social zones,* which include living, dining, recreation, and entertaining areas; and (3) *private zones,* which include sleeping, dressing, and hygiene areas. These three zones should be viewed as a whole and have compatible spatial organization and interrelationships. Analyzing individual differences, lifestyles, and activities to take place within the space contributes to the smooth functioning of the residence.

Service or Work Zones

In the kitchen, utility room, sewing room, workshop, office, and other work-related areas the service or work zones function as support centers for the occupants and for accommodating various necessary activities for maintaining the household.

The Kitchen Area. Today's kitchens are no longer merely antiseptic centers for preparing meals. They have again become the hub of the home—an area where food preparation, serving, eating, and other activities take place. The kitchen is an area for socializing and relaxing with friends. Currently there is a demand for flexible kitchens geared both for those who hate to cook and might order food brought in, and for those who love to create culinary masterpieces. Architects and builders have responded to requests for more efficient and multipurpose kitchen spaces. Kitchen appliances, lighting, cabinets, and fixtures are constantly being improved and made more efficient because of the importance of this area to the consumer. Planning kitchen space includes the following considerations:

Shape or Arrangement. The arrangement of the kitchen should determine the location of work centers, accommodate physical limitations, and facilitate various every-day household activities that are carried out simultaneously. The basic kitchen arrangements or shapes are U-shape, L-shape, island, parallel, and one-wall, as illustrated in Figure 4.13.

The Work Centers. The kitchen is generally planned around the **work triangle**, three work centers forming a triangle:

> sink area (preparation and cleanup)
>
> cooking area (range and oven)
>
> refrigerator area

These work centers should be arranged for convenience and efficiency.

Placement of Work Centers. The walking distance between the three work centers should not be less than seven feet or more than twenty feet.

Physical Limitations of the User. Cabinet and countertop heights should be comfortably scaled to the person working in the space, and distances from one center to another should be comfortable. Standard countertop heights are usually 36 inches high but they can be custom designed for persons shorter or taller or for those who are physically challenged. Barrier-free spaces and clearances for wheelchair users should be planned.

Sufficient Cabinet and Countertop Space. Efficient and adequate cabinet and countertop space is necessary for a successful kitchen plan. There must be storage for:

> food (dry food, perishables, staples, and canned food)
>
> tableware (flatware, dishes, tablecloths, napkins, etc.)
>
> appliances (food processors, mixers, coffee maker, etc.)
>
> cleaning supplies (floor cleaners, soaps, paper products, towels, etc.)
>
> cooking utensils

A *pantry* space is a convenient addition to the kitchen area.

Food Preparation. Surfaces for mixing, washing, cutting, blending, and other activities of food preparation should be adequate and conveniently placed.

Eating. Countertop space or bars are popular for quick meals and snacks and can be logically incorporated into the kitchen design.

Appliances. Cabinets should be designed to accommodate such *permanently placed appliances* as refrigerators, ovens, cooking tops, ranges, sinks, garbage disposals, recycling bins, and trash compactors, and *portable appliances* such as microwaves, blenders, food proces-

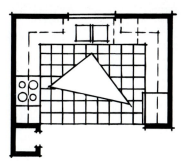

U-SHAPE KITCHEN
U-shape kitchens are generally considered the most comfortable and efficient. Work centers are out of the way of traffic and more conveniently located.

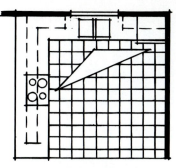

L-SHAPE KITCHEN
L-shape kitchens are a little more efficient than the parallel since traffic lanes do not intrude into the space. Work centers are conveniently located.

ISLAND KITCHEN
The island kitchen has similar qualities as the U-shape, but with the unwelcome addition of possible traffic through the space.

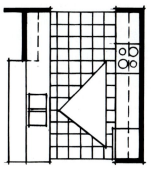

PARALLEL KITCHEN
Parallel kitchens provide undesirable traffic, especially when doors are located at each end. Work centers are more convenient than one-wall kitchens.

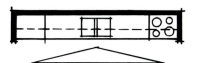

ONE-WALL KITCHEN
One-wall kitchens economically use one plumbing wall, can be concealed with folding doors and do not take up much space. They are usually most suitable for apartments and small living spaces. They have very little counterspace and work space pattern is long.

FIGURE 4.13 Basic kitchen arrangements.

sors, mixers, juicers, coffee grinders, electric knives, and other task-related appliances.

Lighting. Planning adequate lighting for various kitchen tasks is essential. Architecturally installed lighting is preferred and is most functional. For example, lighting may be placed around the perimeter of the countertops under the wall cabinets, on the ceiling, or in soffits. An abundance of lighting fixtures is available to meet every need and style preference. Artificial lighting should be positioned to avoid glare. Natural lighting depends on the size, number, and location of windows in the kitchen and the treatment of these windows depends on the amount of privacy desired, the style of the kitchen, and the personal preferences of the occupants.

Style. The style of the kitchen, whether modern or traditional, should reflect the tastes of the users. Colors, textures, materials, flooring, countertops, window treat-

ment, and accessories are the major elements to consider when designing the kitchen. (See Figure 4.14.)

Ready-made cabinets with a variety of colors and surfaces, such as plastic laminates or metal, are for those who prefer a kitchen with a sleek modern look. For those who enjoy a traditional style, finely crafted custom-made wood cabinets are available with new sealers and finishes that protect the wood. Wood cabinets can also be fashioned in contemporary designs. Whatever style of kitchen cabinets is selected, durability and cleanability of all materials should be considered.

The goal of the designer is to plan a kitchen that is efficient, durable, easily maintained, safe, well lit, and comfortable to work and live in.

Utility Areas. Function, convenience, and transition are major considerations with utility areas. *Laundry rooms* are often placed near the dressing and hygiene areas for convenience but may also be relegated to a

FIGURE 4.14 This kitchen work zone with an island arrangement is planned in a traditional style with ample cabinets and counterspace and durable and attractive surfaces of wood, tile, and marble. A window over the sink admits daylight and provides an outdoor view, and an informal eating space is conveniently close. (Photograph by Mark Boisclair.)

space close to the kitchen or garage. Convenient placement of the washer and dryer with easy access to water lines is necessary. A laundry tub or sink and adequate counter surfaces, space for the ironing board, sufficient storage, hanging space, and good lighting are also desirable.

Sewing, workshop, office, garden, and other work areas should be conveniently located with well-arranged space for required storage, furnishings, and equipment. Effective lighting is necessary to carry out these various activities.

Social Zones

The social zones (entry, living, dining, recreation, and entertainment areas) are where people meet for various activities. These zones include the entry area, the formal and informal living areas, the formal and informal eating areas, and the recreation and entertainment areas.

The Entrance Area. An entrance area, no matter how small, can introduce the home and direct traffic throughout the house. Whatever the general style or theme of the house, the entrance area is a good place to enhance it. (See Figures 4.15 and 4.16.) The entrance area can also leave a lasting impression on all who enter. Remember when selecting the floor covering that the entrance is a passageway and must take traffic. A hard-surface material such as wood, brick, tile, terrazzo, travertine, or other type of stone will provide a lifetime floor. A well-anchored area or throw rug adds warmth and serves as a color transition to adjoining rooms. The scale and amount of furniture used in the entrance area is deter-

FIGURE 4.15 A traditional entrance conveys a warm and welcoming introduction to the home. Cheerful yellow, apple green, and coral patterned fabrics and wallpaper contribute to this feeling, along with the table, stool, and comfortable wingback chair. (Courtesy of Schumacher.)

FIGURE 4.16 This contemporary entry makes a striking architectural impression with fenestration that allows natural light to flood the space. (Courtesy of Eduard Dreier, architect, and Guy Dreier Associates. Photograph by Richard Springgate.)

mined by the size of the room and available wall space. Both architectural and portable lighting should be adequate, welcoming, and glare free.

Formal Living Area. If the living room lives up to its name, it will provide for all household members and guests as well. Space may be relatively large or a cloistered parlor area, depending on requirements, preferences, and budget restrictions.

The formal living area works well when placed away from major traffic lanes and planned for both privacy and various functions such as conversation, listening to music, reading, relaxing and other activities. (See Figure 4.17.)

The transition from the entry to the living room is important. The entrance area should flow easily into the living room with a smooth transition of design elements.

Floors, Walls, Ceilings, and Other Backgrounds. These elements of the living room help determine the design approach. For example, walls may be simply painted or elaborately paneled and papered; floors can be hard, soft, or a combination; and ceilings may be structural or decorative. The designer should evaluate the clients' personal preferences for style, colors, furnishings, materials, and the general feeling of formality or informality desired.

Fireplace. If the living room has a fireplace, space can be planned to enhance this feature. A fireplace naturally becomes a focal point, depending on size, materials, and style. It can be emphasized through such elements as texture, color, lighting, and the arrangement of other furnishings.

FIGURE 4.17 In this formal living area, the fireplace serves as a focal point. It is flanked by mirrored walls, which visually expand the space. Comfortable seating is arranged for conversation or reading. (Photograph by Mark Boisclair.)

Window Type and Treatment. Particular attention to the window type and its treatment enhances the living space. The total architectural composition, natural lighting, location, furniture arrangement, the need for privacy, the window's view, and the room's style and mood should be considered before specifying the window treatment.

Furniture Selection and Arrangement. Seating, tables, storage pieces, and other furniture required for the living area must meet the needs and preferences of the users. The style can be traditional, modern, or eclectic—using pieces from a number of different periods. The arrangement of furnishings depends on existing space, the shape of the room, the placement of architectural features, the functions to serve, and visual satisfaction.

Lighting. Well-planned lighting, both natural and artificial, aesthetically and functionally supports the living room's design.

Accessories. Plants, flowers, art, pillows, ceramics, lamps, books, glass, and other items add the finishing touches to the living room and convey the personal taste and interests of the occupants.

Principles and Elements of Design. Throughout the design process, the principles (scale, proportion, balance, emphasis, rhythm, and harmony) and elements or tools of design (color, light, pattern, line, space, form, and texture) can be helpful references in achieving the desired goals for a functional, comfortable and beautiful living room.

Informal Living Areas. The *family room* came into being during the 1950s and has become one of the most important rooms in the home. To achieve a successful family room, the designer takes into account the tastes, interests, and activities of all household members. This room may take many forms, depending on the individual household, but the main objective of a successful family

FIGURE 4.18 An eclectic family room combines an informal plaid rug, comfortable overstuffed leather sofas, antiques, interesting accessories, and a soaring fireplace to offer the residents an inviting area for casual living. (Courtesy of Aldo Bussio. Photograph by John Rees.)

FIGURE 4.19 This family space is located in the social zone of the home and designed for private conversation and relaxing. Because the entertainment area is on the fireplace wall, the seating arrangement is well suited to different functions.

room is to provide a flexible area to serve many purposes, as seen in Figure 4.18, one that requires little upkeep.

The atmosphere of the family room should be one of comfortable intimacy. Activities vary according to the household, but most family rooms require suitable areas to snack, talk, watch television, read, and listen to music. A fireplace is an added attraction around which to gather with family and friends.

Floors, Walls, and Fabrics. If a household is active, the family room should have durable and easily cleaned backgrounds. For walls, wood paneling, scrubbable wallpapers, stone, and simple painted surfaces are practical. Flooring materials depend on the room's use, but generally hard or soft coverings are sensibly selected for comfort and easy maintenance (see Chapter 6). Fabrics are practical when they are durable, easy to clean, and stain resistant. Vinyl and leather upholstery are especially useful in family rooms and are available in a wide range of colors, patterns, and textures. Tightly woven fabrics are more durable than loosely woven pieces (see Chapter 5).

Furniture. Sturdy and comfortable furniture is practical, and easily movable pieces offer flexibility for rearranging on a moment's notice. Pieces of furniture that can serve a dual role are particularly serviceable. For example, a sofa can serve as a bed for an overnight guest, low tables can double as stools for seating, and tables that can be raised and lowered may serve for coffee tables, games, and eating.

Storage. Of all rooms in the house, the family room probably needs the most well-planned storage to take care of all items used in this area, such as a card table, folding chairs, games, records, videotapes, books, or a screen and projector. By using flexible storage units, otherwise dull rooms can be given new interest. Free-

standing walls, built-ins, or wall systems may be set up to provide floor-to-ceiling banks of drawers, cabinets, and shelves.

Entertainment. In today's family room, the television and VCR are generally standard equipment. Many of the new television designs provide a large screen and minimal cabinetry, resulting in greater flexibility for combining the television with other furnishings in the home environment. Locating the television in a central section of a wall of built-ins is an excellent way to incorporate this piece with other furnishings. It may be placed in a fireplace wall niche to take advantage of the furniture arrangement for convenient viewing. (See Figure 4.19.) In any case, the television should be placed to allow several individuals to view it comfortably.

Lighting. General lighting is usually desirable in the family room, as well as area lighting for specific activities. Carefully planned lighting will meet requirements for reading, television viewing, playing games, and conversation (see Chapter 3).

Other Activities. A current trend merges the family room and kitchen into one big room for cooking, informal dining, and many household activities. Family rooms function efficiently when located with easy access to the outside and the kitchen and away from the bedroom wing. Ideally, the room design can easily be changed as the household status changes.

Formal Dining Area. At the turn of the century the dining room was often a big and somber room with a massive table and sideboard, a chandelier, and heavily shrouded windows. Family members gathered here three times a day in a congenial atmosphere and learned manners and the art of conversation.

After World War I, dining rooms generally lost favor and were not considered a necessity. Open planning

FIGURE 4.20 The warmth of wood, architecturally fixed lighting, furniture placed for function, a few well-chosen accessories, and easy upkeep are features of this inviting modern dining room. (Courtesy of Ron Molen, architect.)

blended kitchen, dining, and living areas into one, and as a result family dining went out of fashion in many homes. A trend in the 1960s was a renewed interest in the dining room.

Planning the Space. An inviting formal dining area requires privacy from the front entrance area, and should be close to the food preparation area but shut off from the clutter of the kitchen. (See Figure 4.20.) In the dining room plan, unobtrusive colors or wallpapers facilitate the use of a variety of table settings. In a more traditional setting, a dado will protect the wall from chair bumps and finger marks.

Floor Coverings. As discussed in Chapter 6, carpets and rugs can be selected that shed dirt and clean well. Hard-surface materials are available for any decor. A combination of a hard-surface material with a rug under the dining table is an effective treatment.

Furniture. Keeping the dining room in the same basic theme and mood as the living room makes a pleasing transition. Furniture generally works best when suitably scaled to the room. The practical pedestal-base table

gives maximum knee room, and round and oval tables make it easier to squeeze in an extra person. If the dining room is spacious, a large cabinet with shelves for china and glass and drawers for linens and silver is a handsome addition. If space is limited, a shallow chest or a wall-hung shelf for serving can suffice.

Defining the Space. If the dining room is an alcove, part of a living room or multipurpose area, any number of treatments can set it apart. Walls may be papered or painted a different but coordinated color. Freestanding screens, a plant grouping, or an area rug can help define the space. Tables that convert to different sizes and heights and thus do double duty are useful here.

Lighting. Some type of artificial lighting over the table is needed for functional purposes. Traditionally, period chandeliers of all styles and materials are hung directly over the table. Modern treatments may incorporate unusual or other unique lighting methods, including architecturally built-in or custom-designed fixtures, as seen in Figure 4.20. The height from the table top to the bottom of the lighting fixture varies with taste, but a general trend is to hang the fixture lower than in the past. Additional lighting in the dining room includes lit china closets, uplighters in corners, spotlights on accessories, and other supportive lighting treatments. (See Chapter 3.)

Informal Dining Area. Informal eating areas for quick snacks and everyday family meals are most conveniently located in or near the kitchen. However, in today's home eating may take place in many areas of the home including the family room, entertainment room, bedrooms, or outside in the garden.

The eating area close to the kitchen can vary depending on the space and shape allocated. Some kitchens have eating areas at a bar or counter, often with bar stools or attached seats. Other kitchens may have the eating area in a bay window or alcove close by, as shown in Figure 4.14. Whatever the configuration, adequate space is necessary to accommodate furnishings such as tables, seating, serving surfaces, lighting, and supportive furnishings and accessories.

Generally, the style of the informal dining area is compatible with the kitchen's design. For example, if the kitchen conveys a casual country style, the eating area may carry out this theme.

Entertainment, Recreation, and Educational Centers. In a larger home additional space for entertainment, recreation, and education may be allocated. Indoor swimming pools; Ping-Pong, billiard and pool tables; a bar; space for dancing or television viewing; music centers, and computer and study centers are some of the functions included in these areas. (See Figure 4.21.) Accommodating these various activities requires careful consideration on the part of the designer when planning for convenience, safety, comfort, and aesthetics.

With the vast array of new electronic products for the home, new design problems have arisen and new design solutions are being explored. These products include the home computer with its many hardware and software components, videocassette recorders, video discs, videogame consoles, and satellite receivers. Integrating these products into the home so they will best serve the household and still preserve the domestic environment presents a challenge to the interior designer. A primary concern is securing adequate space to house this equipment efficiently.

Choosing the Space. The area in which the entertainment center is located should be planned with practicality in mind, since it will most likely have continual use. Combining it with space for other recreational activities is logical. Where can this space be found? A close examination may reveal underused space. The attic may have wasted space that can be put to good use. The basement may have possibilities, and noise is muffled in a downstairs location. The garage may be converted into a recreation center and the roof extended for a carport. An

FIGURE 4.21 In this spacious entertainment center, a pool table, comfortable furniture, a game table, and a bar are conveniently arranged with adequate lighting. (Courtesy of Gayl Baddeley/Associates.)

extra room that is already finished may be available after some minor shifting. Adding a new room is another, but more costly, possibility. Space problems involving a location for the educational center can be explored in a similar manner.

Floor and Wall Treatments. The background treatment for the entertainment center can make a big difference. Once the space is decided on, planning should start from the floor up. Since traffic and wear will be heavy, good-quality, heavy-duty flooring is practical. A carpet that can be rolled up for various activities gives versatility. Sturdy wall treatments with easy upkeep are a wise selection. (Refer to Chapter 6.)

Furnishings. A high priority is where to place the entertainment center; other furnishings can then be placed for function. Easily moved pieces are a good choice. To promote social interaction, lounge chairs and sofas should be comfortable and conveniently arranged. Covering them with vinyl or other durable and cleanable fabrics is a must.

Supportive furnishings—tables, especially cocktail and game tables—are functional additions to recreation and game centers. To avoid breakage and scratches, sturdy tables with durable finishes are practical. Comfortable, durable, and easily cleaned seating adds to the occupants' enjoyment, and a variety of possibilities are available (see Chapter 8).

Fireplace. A recreation or entertainment center can be enhanced by a fireplace with a wide hearth. If an architecturally fixed fireplace does not exist, freestanding models in many styles and materials are readily available.

FIGURE 4.22 Space has been arranged in this master bedroom to accommodate a king-size bed, two seating areas, end tables, adequate portable and architectural lighting and a large cabinet at the foot of the bed to conceal "his and hers" television sets. (Courtesy of Michael Rennick and Associates, Inc., Salt Lake City.)

Additional Furnishings. Additional items can add a great deal. A pull-down screen to show home movies and slides can be installed permanently at low cost. Extra folding chairs are often needed. For example, canvas director's chairs are inexpensive, colorful, and easily brought out of storage to handle a crowd. Large floor cushions can also invite informality and relaxation. A bar can be a popular gathering spot for family and friends.

Lighting. Choosing lighting that is inviting and functional is an important part of the planning process for a successful recreation and entertainment room. For example, lighting over a billiard table, around a bar, and close to the seating and entertainment center adds to the occupants' ability to use these facilities comfortably. Lighting in an educational center is primarily geared for function and should be efficient.

Private Zones

For maximum quiet and privacy, sleeping, dressing, and hygiene areas function best when away from the social and work zones of the residence. A bathroom, however, may be placed near both the social zones and the private zones for the convenience of guests.

Bedrooms for Adults. The master bedroom today has become a refuge from the pressures and stress of everyday living—a place where relaxation and activities other than sleeping may take place. Often the master bedroom is a luxurious part of the home. There may be space for a fireplace, a bar, a television set, a study, a conversation arrangement, an office, and even a physical fitness area.

Because the master bedroom is so personal and private, the process of designing it is different from that for any other room in the house. Traffic and wear and tear need not be of concern here. The main consideration should be twenty-four-hour comfort. Comfort does not require a large room, but it does require imagination and organization of space, as viewed in Figure 4.22. Keep in mind that the master bedroom is a room usually shared by a couple. Each occupant should have input as to personal preferences for furniture style, colors, fabrics, and general mood of the room.

The Bed. As the predominant feature of the room, the bed is the focal point and demands special attention. The choice may be a king, queen, standard, or twin size, a canopy bed, a sturdy four-poster, a sleek chrome or simple bamboo type, with a brass frame or no frame at all.

Other Functions. Before the actual interior design begins, the purposes the room will serve, other than repose, should be decided. For example, a bedroom and study can be a pleasant combination; bookshelves are convenient and lend warmth. Comfortable chairs invite relaxation. If space permits, a luxurious chaise may sub-

stitute for one of the chairs. Essential items are bedside tables or built-ins containing drawers or shelves with moisture-proof surfaces, large enough to provide spaces for necessary items such as a telephone, clock, or lamp (unless overhead architectural lighting is provided). Mirrors on the wall or on closet doors both expand space and function for dressing purposes.

Lighting. Lighting, both portable and architecturally fixed, needs to be adequate for dressing, reading, or relaxing. An abundance of lighting types—modern or traditional, informal or formal—is available to support the selected style (see lighting section in Chapter 3).

Window Treatments. The window treatment in the bedroom depends on a number of criteria, including the amount of natural light available and desired in the room and the size, style, type, and location of the window or windows. Draw draperies, window blinds, or shades keep morning light out when necessary.

Fabric. Fabric can add softness and color and set whatever mood is desired. For normal use, a delicate bedspread is not a wise choice. There are attractive bedspreads that are durable and do not wrinkle or show soil easily.

Style and Mood. Individual preferences and lifestyle can be guides for establishing the style and mood and for furnishing this most personal room. Generally, the goal is to achieve a pleasant and inviting mood of relaxation and comfort. Numerous furniture companies offer a wide range of both traditional and modern styles in many colors and finishes. Sometimes custom-made pieces or architecturally built-in furnishings are preferred. Furniture, colors, fabrics, and accessories can be chosen to support the desired style.

Bedrooms for Children and Young Adults. A child's room requires good storage, adequate lighting, a desk for study, a comfortable bed, and space for play. The design can be planned with the child's input so the room will reflect his or her personality. The smallest space, if skillfully planned and arranged, can meet these needs. For the young child, safety with simple, sturdy, small-scaled furniture is a paramount concern. If furniture for the nursery is wisely chosen, it can be converted to serve changing needs as the child grows. For example, a low chest of drawers can serve as a changing table for an infant and later be used for storage for a child of any age. An infant's wardrobe may become a bookcase later on.

Since the daily habits and interests of children during their developing years vary widely, their needs may be best served by letting them help to create the personal environments in which they spend their private lives (Figure 4.23). With long-range planning and frequent modifications, a child's room can serve from toddler to teenage years. As the child grows and changes, so should the

FIGURE 4.23 Space in a girl's room has been planned to accommodate a fanciful iron bed and a cupboard for storing dolls and quilts. A rocking horse adds to the charm. (Photograph by Pam Singleton.)

room. Individual needs can determine what changes should be made and when, but the maturing child requires ongoing alteration of the physical environment.

Almost any room can benefit from some type of bulletin board or display space where the child can exhibit schoolwork, photographs, and other prized possessions.

Durable and cleanable backgrounds—wallpaper, fabrics, floor coverings, and furniture—can be chosen with the child's individual taste in mind.

As the child grows older, his or her interests invariably change. An awareness of current trends, as well as a knowledge of traditional and contemporary styles, will enable the child to select furnishings that are particularly and personally appealing. The child will undoubtedly take pride in helping create a private environment that reflects his or her personality—an environment that can function at an optimum level.

Dressing and Clothes Storage. The dressing area may be in a separate space, in a closet, in the bedroom itself, or adjacent to or in the bathroom. Storage for clothing items should be close to the dressing area and bathroom and planned for convenience. A space for soiled clothing should be conveniently located. Adequate storage for clothing, jewelry, and other dressing items is generally limited, so using space to the best advantage is a challenge. Professional closet and storage planning has become a successful part of the building and housing industries.

Personal Hygiene. Bathrooms are usually placed between social and private areas for the convenience of the users. Since the beginning of the twentieth century, the bathroom has undergone many changes. From being one shared room at the end of the hall, it became a personal adjunct to the bedroom and as such became smaller and utilitarian. Then, in the 1940s and 1950s, color became the vogue. Appearing in so-called decorator colors were paint, wallpaper, floors, towels, and even plumbing fixtures. In the sixties white plumbing fixtures again became the fashion, but the bathroom itself took on an aura of elegance and became a glamour room in the American home.

No longer does the bathroom serve purely functional needs. Today, function and luxury are combined, and the room once hidden behind closed doors is frequently exposed to sky, garden, terrace, and in some instances to other rooms of the house. What was once a small, sterile room with three basic plumbing fixtures (sink, toilet, tub and shower) has become a powder room, dressing room, and even sitting room, often with additional luxury features such as whirlpool, sauna, spa, hot tub, television, or fireplace. Of course, these amenities require additional space.

Most homes have more than one bathroom. Some may have half or three-quarter baths as well. Major considerations for the designer are to determine the space available, the needs of the end users, and the most efficient arrangement of plumbing fixtures and supportive furnishings, storage, and lighting for each hygiene area in the residence.

Plumbing Fixtures. Tubs may be sunken and deep enough for standing. Larger tubs are also popular today, especially with water-massage elements. Tubs may be conveniently located in almost any place in the bathroom including the center of the room. They are available in all shapes, designs, colors, and sizes and with built-in seats. (See Figure 4.24.) Sometimes tubs are placed beside large windows to take advantage of a view. Beautiful manufactured or hand-carved basins are made of marble, onyx, china, or other materials. They may have baked-in or hand-painted traditional or contemporary motifs to set the theme of the room. Similar motifs are often coordinated for use on the toilet or bidet.

Accessories. Manufacturers have coordinated accessories in many materials and styles including shower curtains, towels, towel bars, soap dishes, mirrors, faucets, and other decorative and functional items. These accessories exhibit personal taste and help unify the bathroom and its relationship to other rooms.

FIGURE 4.24 This striking master bath has a section of glass block to admit additional light into the spacious shower. Ample storage and lighting are provided. (Courtesy of Dal-Tile.)

Upkeep. For the household bathroom, easy upkeep is important. Scrubbable vinyls, tile, and other background materials are available in numerous colors and patterns (see Chapter 6). If carpet is the choice, one that resists spots and cleans easily is a must. One of the most enduring materials for bathrooms through the years has been tile, which remains popular.

Storage. Ample storage in the bathroom for such items as towels, medicines, and grooming and cleaning aids is essential. A place for soiled clothing is also an advantage. Storage can be built-in shelves and cabinets or free-standing or wall-hung units placed for convenience. Storage can also be attractive, as, for example, when items like towels, soap, and other utilitarian items are nicely arranged on shelves.

Lighting. Good natural and artificial lighting is a requisite in the bathroom. Effective lighting around mirrors used for makeup and grooming needs is essential. Additionally, mirrors can double light and visually expand existing space. General lighting needs should also be planned.

Additional Considerations

Efficient Traffic Lanes
Well-planned traffic lanes are convenient and adequate in size without being wasteful. A central entrance hall should channel traffic to all areas of the house. From the kitchen, easy access to the front door, back door, utility room, service area, garage, and all areas of the home is desirable. Direct access to the outside service area from the utility area is also a convenient feature. At least one living area should have easy access to the outside living area. An access door—other than the large garage doors near the front of the house—leading directly into the kitchen is a valuable feature. All major traffic lanes should generally be routed to avoid going through any room to reach another.

Well-Placed Openings
Doors and windows should be conveniently located to preserve functional wall space. Well-designed windows and their placement within the wall area can make the task of window treatment more efficient. (See Figure 4.25.)

Doors wide enough to accommodate wheelchairs and walkers should be given special consideration. Doors that are placed for easy access in and out of all rooms contribute to smooth-functioning interior spaces.

Adequate Space
Allowing enough space for each member of the household is an essential requirement in planning interiors; however, a limited budget may preclude this necessity. Space preferences and needs vary for each individual and in some cases may be psychological rather than essential.

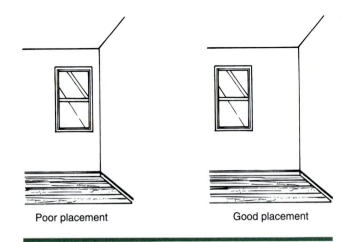

Poor placement   Good placement

FIGURE 4.25 Window placement.

Generally, 500 square feet per person provides sufficient space. Additionally, each room of the house requires special consideration for functional living space appropriate for all household activities.

Adequate wall and floor space is important to accommodate large pieces of furniture and other requirements such as sofas, dining tables, wall units, storage cabinets, pianos, entertainment centers, computers, desks, and beds. (See Figure 4.26.)

Sufficient storage space should be conveniently located throughout the house and garage. Attics and basements can provide added storage space. Needs may differ according to various lifestyles and household situations.

Legal and Environmental Concerns
Building codes established and enforced by the federal, state, and local governments help protect and promote safety, health, and the general well-being of occupants in various structures. Designers and architects adhere to

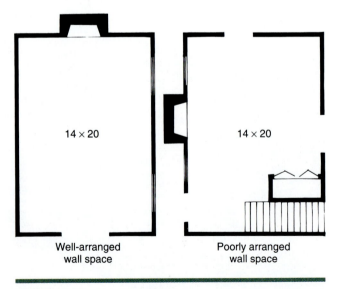

14 × 20   14 × 20

Well-arranged   Poorly arranged
wall space   wall space

FIGURE 4.26 Planning wall space.

FIGURE 4.27 Expanding a small house.

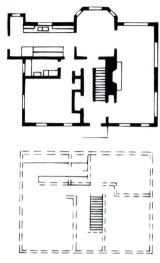

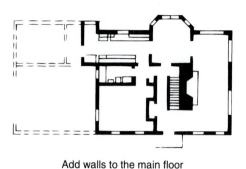

Add walls to the main floor   Add a second story

these codes during the design process as they consider fire resistance, protection, and safety.

Energy conservation is a primary concern of designers and the general public today. Wise planning involving such elements as heating and cooling systems, electrical systems, insulation, water use, mechanical systems and materials used can help conserve energy and contribute to this essential international effort.

Energy-efficient appliances are now available for use in service zones in the home and public places. Designers are also allocating space for recycling bins.

Projected Changes and Remodeling

Through the years household needs may fluctuate and remodeling may become necessary. A good plan can effectively accommodate projected revisions. For example, an initial kitchen plan may have a wall that could easily be expanded for added space or a family room window could be removed for additional living area. (See Figure 4.27.)

ANALYZING BASIC TYPES OF FLOOR PLANS

Spatial planning of interiors falls into two basic design approaches: closed and open planning.

The Closed Plan

The arrangement of floor space over the last century has fluctuated between closed and open planning. The **closed plan** provides separate and distinct rooms for specific activities and allows more individual privacy. Each room is enclosed by four walls with access through a door. The closed plan is particularly used for bathrooms

and bedrooms or where the inhabitants prefer this arrangement.

The Open Plan

In **opening planning** space for various activities flows from one area to another, broken by few or no wall barriers or partial divisions, as seen in Figure 4.28. One advantage of this plan is that it seems to expand space visually. Other advantages include more efficient heating and cooling and more flexibility within the living spaces. The open plan, promoted by architects such as Frank Lloyd Wright and Le Corbusier (see Chapter 13), has particular appeal to people with an informal lifestyle. Most residential plans incorporate both closed and open arrangements throughout the interior spaces, as illustrated in Figure 4.29.

FLOOR PLAN SHAPES

Most floor plans for residential design fall into nine basic shapes or styles, as illustrated in Figure 4.30. These floor plan shapes often have a few jogs, angles, or window extensions that do not change the basic shape of the structure. For example, it is difficult to find a good rectangular floor plan that does not have some jog to provide interest. The advantages and disadvantages associated with each shape can be evaluated by the following criteria:

■ Consider how the shape can be *positioned* on the site and the *landscaping potential*. For example, square and rectangle shapes can be more difficult to attractively position and landscape than shapes with more interesting angles.

FIGURE 4.28 Open planning allows the space to flow from area to area as demonstrated in this modern residence designed by architect Ralph Edwards. The living area is separated from the entry hall and dining area by a change in floor level, which clearly defines the space without limiting the view, as walls would do. The railing is a necessary safety feature. (Courtesy of Ralph Edwards, architect.)

FIGURE 4.29 Both open and closed planning have been incorporated into the first level of this floor plan. The family room, kitchen, and informal eating spaces are void of walls or partitions, allowing space to flow from one area to the other. The living, dining, and study areas have walls that enclose and define each room. (Courtesy of Knight and West Construction.)

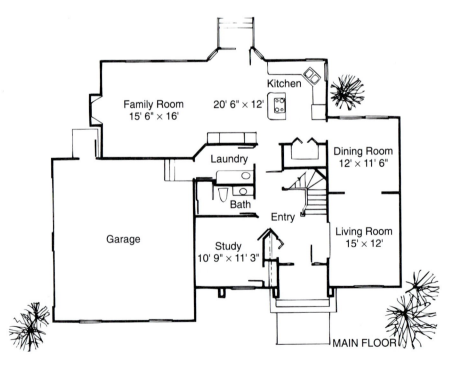

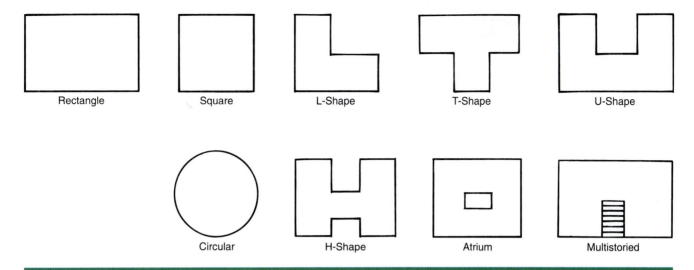

FIGURE 4.30 Basic floor plan shapes.

- Each angle and jog of a floor plan shape adds to the *expense* of the structure.
- Consider *zoning and interior arrangement* of activities within the structure. For example, it is more difficult to arrange various functions in a square because of the limited flexibility of the shape.
- *Traffic patterns* are usually more efficient in shapes with more angles than the square or rectangle offer.
- *Heating and cooling costs* are higher with added wings.
- Shapes with more wings or extensions allow additional *light and ventilation* in the residence.
- Keep in mind the *interest and individuality* of the shape and the potential for arranging furnishings within the space. The U, T, H, and atrium shapes, for example, are usually successful in meeting this criterion.
- *Private outdoor living space* is possible with shapes like the U, H, T, and atrium, but very difficult with the circle.

Following is a discussion of typical advantages and disadvantages of some of the most popular shapes employed in today's residential design.

Rectangle Plan

The simplest floor plan is the rectangle. The further the plan departs from this shape, the more complicated and costly it becomes. Each jog and additional roof angle mean added expense, and thus more dollars per square foot of floor space. The rectangle plan is readily adapted to both traditional and contemporary exteriors. (See Chapters 12 and 13.) Figure 4.31 illustrates an efficient rectangle plan with the following features:

- An entrance hall routes traffic to all areas of the house.
- Basic private, social, and work zones are well defined and conveniently located.

- Plumbing is back to back in the private zone.
- Windows and openings are somewhat limited but allow adequate ventilation and light.
- The family room has easy access to the outside and is convenient to the kitchen.
- Access from the kitchen and utility rooms to the outdoors and to the garage is convenient.
- An average amount of storage is provided.

Square Plan

The square plan is also a simple and inexpensive arrangement of space with distinct advantages and disadvantages similar to the rectangular plan. Many homes employing this basic shape were built after World War II to accommodate the need for efficient and low-budget housing. As a result, many subdivisions throughout America have rows of small homes built utilizing the square plan. Most designers try to minimize or even change this boxy shape—both for interiors and exteriors—through creative manipulation of the elements of design. Some considerations when employing the square plan include the following:

- The square plan is one of the least expensive to build because corners are limited to four. It requires only a basic and simple roof and foundation—generally the most costly elements of all house contruction.
- Care should be taken to arrange rooms so traffic can flow freely. Placement of an entrance and hallways can be a challenge in the square plan.
- Good planning should provide adequate light and air circulation—often a problem with the square plan. The center may be poorly lit. A centrally located skylight is one method of eliminating this condition.
- The square plan generally does not provide interesting and inviting outdoor living spaces; however, through skillful landscaping this problem can be eliminated.

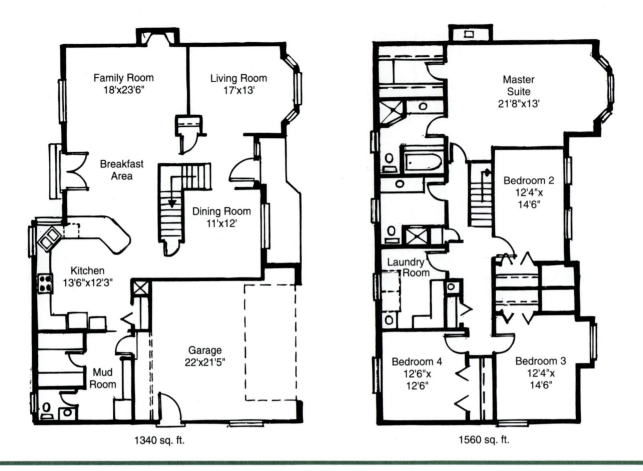

Family Room
18'x23'6"

Living Room
17'x13'

Breakfast
Area

Dining Room
11'x12'

Kitchen
13'6"x12'3"

Mud
Room

Garage
22'x21'5"

1340 sq. ft.

Master
Suite
21'8"x13'

Bedroom 2
12'4"x
14'6"

Laundry
Room

Bedroom 4
12'6"x
12'6"

Bedroom 3
12'4"x
14'6"

1560 sq. ft.

FIGURE 4.31   This plan, basically rectangular in shape, has a few jogs and window extensions to provide additional interest. (Courtesy of Knight and West Construction.)

Sometimes the square plan is turned on an angle to the lot, thus providing a diagonal or diamond shape.

- Good separation of interior living spaces is more difficult to arrange in the square plan (for example, with the sleeping and activities centers).

Multistoried Plan

Multistoried plans (Figure 4.32) provide living space on two or more levels, which allows versatile living. Desirable features of this plan include the following:

- A rectangular plan eliminates most unnecessary jogs.
- All basic areas are well defined on two levels.
- An entry hall channels traffic throughout the house.
- Traffic lanes are economical and permit easy access.
- Doors and windows are well placed.
- Plumbing is back to back on each floor, and second-story and basement plumbing is directly above and below the main-floor plumbing.
- The full basement may be roughed in and finished at a later date.
- An undesirable feature is that the front of the garage has no smaller access (entry) door.

L-Shaped Plan

The L-shaped plan (Figure 4.33) allows variety in space planning through an extension from the rectangular shape. Well-designed features of this simple L-shaped plan are the following:

- The plan incorporates the basic requirements for functional space allocation.
- A central entrance hall routes traffic directly to living, sleeping, and work areas without cross-circulation.
- Large glass doors open onto a private garden away from the street, giving an indoor-outdoor openness.
- The family room is conveniently combined with the kitchen for informal activities.
- The garage has an access door to the kitchen and others to the front and back lawns.
- The service area between the kitchen and half-bath is out of the main line of traffic yet convenient to the kitchen and the outside.
- The bedroom wing is away from the work and living areas.
- The family and private baths are back to back.
- The closet space is well placed in the bedrooms. Three closets open to the main entrance hall.

Second floor plan
1120 sq ft

Basement plan

FIGURE 4.32 A well-arranged two-story plan. (Courtesy of Home Building Plan Services.)

- The bar in the family room is handy for quick snacks. The separate dining room invites more formal meals.
- The rooms are well planned with well-placed openings and ample wall space. The corner bedroom has an added window for cross-ventilation.

T, U, and H Plans

These shapes allow additional space extensions, with advantages including more variety in room arrangement, easy division of noisy and quiet areas, effective traffic

---

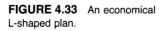

FIGURE 4.33 An economical L-shaped plan.

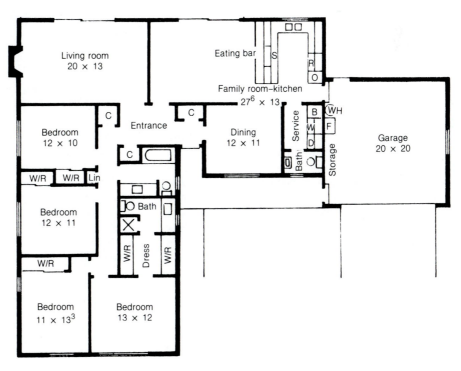

FIGURE 4.34 Atrium plan.

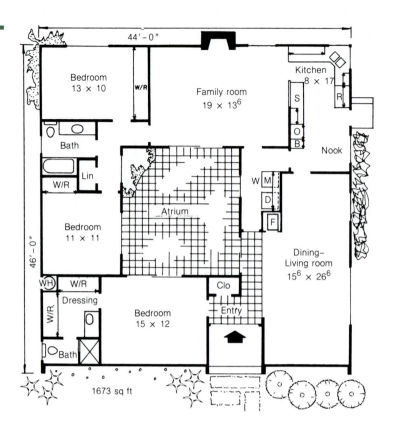

Bedroom
13 × 10

W/R

Family room
19 × 13⁶

Kitchen
8 × 17

S
O
B

R

Bath

Lin

W/R

Nook

Atrium

W M
D

Bedroom
11 × 11

F

Dining–
Living room
15⁶ × 26⁶

WH

W/R

Clo

Dressing

W/R.

Entry

Bedroom
15 × 12

Bath

46' – 0"

44' – 0"

1673 sq ft

lanes, opportunity for more efficient natural lighting and cross-ventilation, and more interesting landscaping possibilities. Disadvantages might include the cost involved for heating and cooling; added expense for foundation, roof, and jogs; and the need for a larger lot to accommodate the **T**, **U**, and **H** forms.

Atrium Plan

The **atrium plan** (Figures 4.34 and 4.35), an inner courtyard arrangement, was used by the ancient Romans and has become a desirable feature in many contemporary homes, particularly Spanish-style ones or where the geographic location or climate is conducive to this arrangement. This inner courtyard can be either completely enclosed as the central focus of the entire house or built within a **U** shape or to one side. The atrium can also be either open to the sky or topped with a skylight.

With the increasing importance of solar energy, the atrium can function as a sun room and be incorporated into a passive solar house design. The atrium plan has advantages and disadvantages similar to those for the other plans described thus far, but it has the added feature of the inviting interior private living space.

Circular Plan

The circular plan is often considered the least preferable shape because of problems involved with decorating and living in a circle. The lot is difficult to landscape and

FIGURE 4.35 An interior with an atrium plan brings privacy to the central area of the home. The glass ceiling covering this atrium in a private mountain residence designed by Walter Cowie allows light to flood the area and provides a pleasant living space. (Photograph by Lincoln Allen, Salt Lake City.)

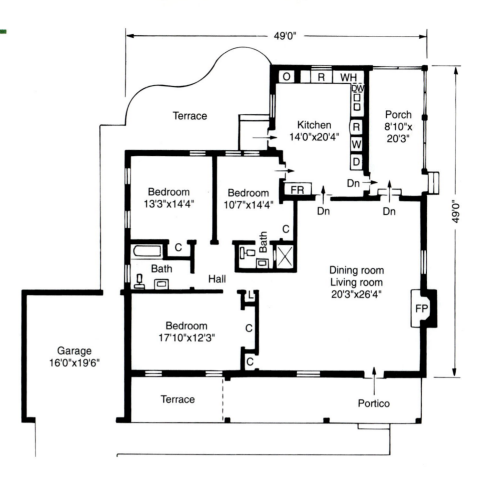

FIGURE 4.36 A poorly arranged floor plan.

Comparing Floor Plans

Careful examination and comparison of the floor plans in Figures 4.36 and 4.37 can help the student in reading and critically evaluating a plan.

A Poorly Arranged Floor Plan

Undesirable features of the poorly arranged plan (Figure 4.36) are as follows:

- Poor arrangement of space; square footage would be unnecessarily costly and living spaces inconvenient and frustrating; also, too many costly jogs
- Poorly planned traffic lanes
- Lack of an entranceway, making living room a major traffic lane
- Poorly located front door prevents a private conversation area around fireplace due to traffic-pattern problems
- No privacy in eating areas
- Inconvenient placement of garage makes transporting of groceries a chore

allows very little natural private living areas. An advantage is its unusual design, which can provide a unique living dimension when well planned.

- Necessity of crossing through a bedroom to reach half-bath from kitchen
- Uneconomical placement of plumbing
- Inconvenient location of washer and dryer in kitchen
- Window size and placement undesirable; window in small corner bedroom abutting the wall; windows in living room too small, providing inadequate light
- Insufficient storage in garage and throughout home
- Noisy and quiet areas not adequately separated
- Private informal living space ignored; for example, television set would have to be placed in living room

A Well-Arranged Floor Plan

The well-arranged plan in Figure 4.37, although expensive because of numerous shapes, angles, and jogs, meets many requirements for a successful and livable residential space. Some positive advantages of this plan include:

- Well-defined and spacious private, social, and work zones
- Creative and unusual arrangement of space to meet individual needs of occupants with the use of both open and closed planning
- Well-placed and convenient wall space and openings; adequate space for required furnishings
- Ample ventilation and lighting requirements

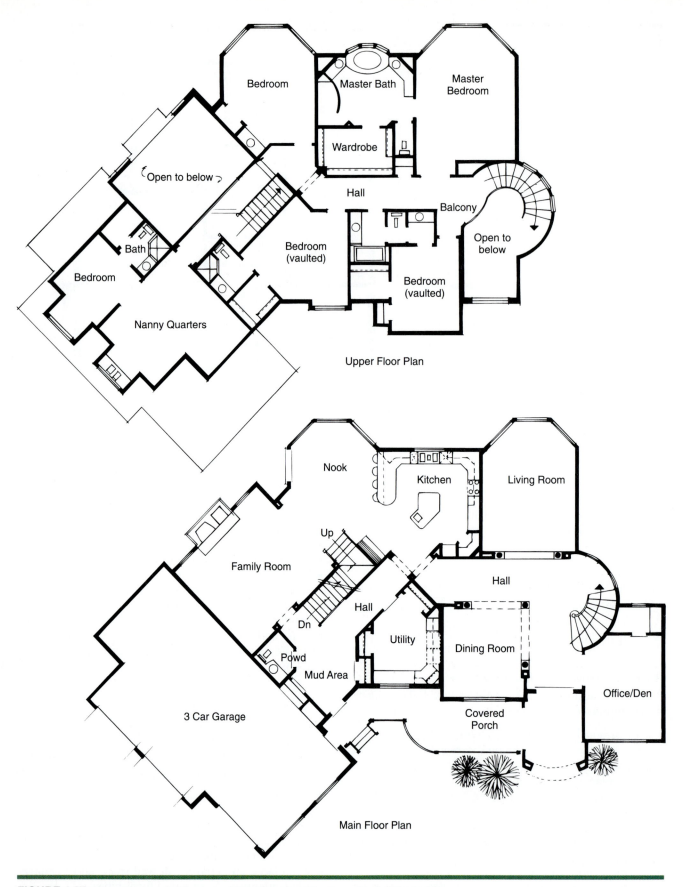

Upper Floor Plan

Main Floor Plan

FIGURE 4.37 A spacious and well-arranged two-story plan. (Courtesy of L & T Design, Orem, Utah. Gordon Jacobsen, architect.)

FIGURE 4.38 One-bedroom unit.

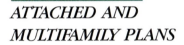

- Well-arranged traffic patterns; easy access to outdoors from social zones; spacious hallways throughout; large entry area
- Garage conveniently located to the kitchen; garage doors face away from the street side
- Efficient working space in the kitchen with an island for more counter space.
- Interesting landscaping possibilities because of plan shape.

ATTACHED AND MULTIFAMILY PLANS

Architects are currently designing high-density housing units accommodating a variety of lifestyles and tastes. In all cases, main concerns include efficient use of space, privacy, easy upkeep, security, and energy conservation. *Apartment houses, duplexes, garden apartments, clustered condominiums,* and *townhouses* are planned inside much like single detached houses. Floor plans for attached and multifamily housing may vary from large two-level multiroom units to compact one-room arrangements. For example, the following compact townhouse condominiums are designed for particular lifestyles.

The one-bedroom unit in Figure 4.38 has a conventional plan for a tandem buyer. Well-arranged space is convenient and adequate for a couple or for a single person. A *tandem arrangement* is one in which individual units are placed side by side or one behind the other.

The *compact studio* (Figure 4.39) shows how to make the most of limited space. The living room includes above-the-sofa storage, a dining room table that can be used for work or hobby space, a queen-sized bed that folds away during the day, and a compartmentalized bathroom.

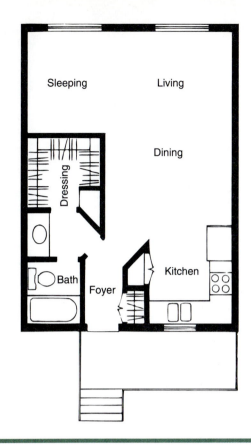

FIGURE 4.39 Compact studio.

ASSIGNMENT

The following assignment helps you demonstrate competency in selecting an economical and efficiently designed floor plan.

1. Select a floor plan that meets the requirements described in this text, keeping in mind that this plan must be for a *year-round family dwelling*. Do not attempt to draw a plan, because this requires special training and skill beyond the scope of this course.
2. Submit your plan, mounted on black, white, or gray paper, with an accompanying critique considering all features discussed under "Fundamental Requirements for the Completed Floor Plan."
3. In addition to the critique, compute the total cost of the chosen house by multiplying the total number of square feet by the *current* cost per square foot in your particular locale. If the plan has a basement or a second story or both, costs should be checked with a builder or architect. Building costs vary regionally and can even change from month to month.

PART THREE

Interior Materials and Components

CHAPTER 5

Textiles

FIGURE 5.1 A documentary pattern called "Godey's Roses and Ribbons" provides Victorian authenticity in this bedroom. The red/green complementary color scheme of rose, hunter green, aubergine, and mauve complements the style (Courtesy of Schumacher.)

Textiles for Interiors

Fibers

Natural Fibers

Man-Made Fibers

Construction of Fabrics

Woven Textiles

Nonwoven Textiles

Textile Coloring (Dyeing)

Dye Lots

Finishing

Prefinishes

Functional Finishes

Decorative Finishes

Decorative Textiles for Interiors

Sheers or Glass Curtains

Casements or Semisheers

Drapery

Upholstery

Slipcovers

Walls

Combining Fabrics

Pattern

Texture

Color

Solving Design Problems with Textiles

Textiles for Period and Contemporary Rooms

Textiles for Nonresidential Projects

Textile Specifications, Safety Codes, and Government Labeling

Environmental Concerns

Textile Presentation Layouts

Textile Terms

Textile Care and Maintenance

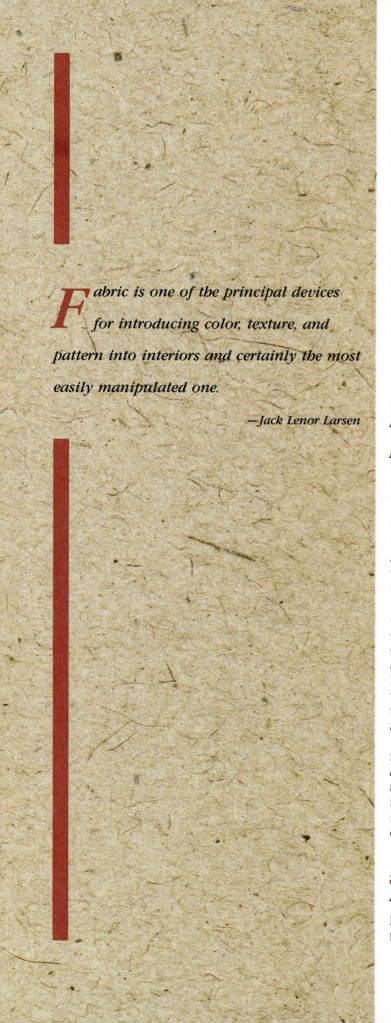

*F*abric is one of the principal devices for introducing color, texture, and pattern into interiors and certainly the most easily manipulated one.

—*Jack Lenor Larsen*

TEXTILES FOR INTERIORS

Authorities in the design field recognize that skillful use of fabric with the right color, texture, and design is a sure means of creating a successful room. For centuries fabric has been used to cover walls, drape windows and beds, and upholster chairs and sofas.

Textiles can enhance both residential and commercial interiors in many ways. They are *flexible and functional,* probably more versatile than any other element used for interior design. Textiles are pliable and easy to work with. They can be sewn, draped, bent, folded, wrapped, pleated, gathered, and stretched. Textiles can be used in every room in the house for such purposes as upholstery, window treatments, slipcovers, pillows and cushions, bedspreads, blankets and throws, towels, table linens, wall coverings, ceiling coverings, lamp shades, and trimmings.

Fabrics *humanize* living spaces. They provide a transition between architecture, furniture, and people and can lift our spirits and soothe our emotions by bringing *comfort, warmth, and softness* to homes and public places. (See Figures 5.1 and 5.2.) Fabrics are *visually appealing* when colors, patterns, and textures are skillfully selected (Figure 5.3). We can *express our lifestyles and personality* by selecting particular colors, textures, and styles. We can also set a mood of formality or informality in a room with textiles, *establish an authentic period,* or capture the feeling of a particular style.

Textiles are *acoustically absorbent.* They muffle the sounds of voices, music, appliances, mechanical devices, and other noises. Fabrics can be used to give *privacy and seclusion* in an interior. For example, draperies hung at a window provide privacy from the outside, and draperies can be hung around a bed for a feeling of seclusion.

Textiles are *readily available* to the designer and consumer. Fabrics in a variety of fibers, construction, colors, textures, and patterns are available through numerous retail and wholesale outlets. Since textiles are *relatively inexpensive,* they are affordable for all rooms of the house. Because of low cost, they can be replaced over the years as styles and personal preferences change. Finally, textiles are relatively *durable, easy to clean and maintain.*

The term *fabric* is applied to textiles or cloth manufactured by machine or by hand, which includes *weaving, knitting, twisting, felting,* and *lacing,* as well as the *fabrication of plastics.* The appearance and durability of a fabric are dependent on the type and qualities of materials used and the method of construction, as well as the color, pattern, finish, and other surface embellishment.

FIBERS

Fibers are the raw material of textiles, whether derived from nature or man-made. A perfect fiber that will ade-

FIGURE 5.2 For a nonresidential lounge and dining area, designer Carolyn Henry selected upholstery and drapery fabrics to add warmth and visual appeal. The colors and patterns complement the plush floral-patterned wall-to-wall carpet. (Photograph by Pam Singleton.)

FIGURE 5.3 Floral and plaid fabrics that share the same colors give a cheerful and welcoming feeling to this sitting area. Repeating the armchair's plaid fabric on the sofa's pillows serves to unite the pieces harmoniously. (Courtesy of Century Furniture Company.)

quately serve every general household purpose does not exist. Each fiber has its own desirable properties and limitations. Manufacturers have found that by blending certain fibers, the most desirable qualities of each can be incorporated into a fabric. With today's modern technology, new and better synthetic fibers are being created and old fibers improved.

Yarns are made by spinning various lengths of fibers (the raw material) into strands in preparation for fabric construction. Performance and appearance of the fabric are affected by the method and the amount of twisting of the fibers. A high twist produces more strength and durability but takes away some of the luster. Long filaments with little twist generally maintain a high luster but lose much of their stability. *Ply* is the result of twisting two or more single yarns together before weaving to give added strength or create a novel surface effect.

Natural Fibers

Fibers that come from nature fall into four classifications: protein, cellulosic, metallic, and mineral.

Protein Fibers

The *protein,* or *animal, fibers* of most importance are wool and silk.

Wool. *Wool* taken from the fleece of sheep or from Angora goat (mohair), camel, and other animal hairs has been used since the seventh or eighth century B.C. In early Egypt, Greece, Asia, and the Middle East it was used for clothing and some household articles. The advantages of wool are that it is resilient, resists abrasion, is a good insulator, is flame retardant, and can be used woven fine or coarse, loose or tight. It can be dyed from palest to deepest colors, cleans well, resists dirt, and can absorb moisture up to 20 percent of its weight without feeling damp. Its disadvantages include a tendency to yellow with age, shrink, and be damaged by moths and other insects. Wool can be expensive. It requires professional cleaning. It may cause allergies. Wool is used for both residential and nonresidential applications including upholstery, carpeting, draperies, and wall coverings.

Silk. *Silk* is an ancient fiber that, according to legend, was discovered in China about 2540 B.C. The process of producing it from the larvae of silkworms, known as *sericulture,* was kept secret for many years but gradually became known in countries around the world. The advantages of silk are that it is a beautiful long fiber, soft and luxurious, surpassed in strength only by nylon. It takes and holds dye well. Its disadvantages are that the sun's rays break down the fiber, necessitating its protection from direct sunlight. Silk is also susceptible to deterioration by soil, beetles, and moisture. It is expensive.

Raw silk, or uncultivated silk, is a shorter and coarser fiber with less luster. Both types of silk fibers are used for draperies, some upholstery applications, wall coverings, trimming, and fabric art.

Leather. *Leather,* although not a fiber, is an animal product (particularly the hides of cattle and swine) that has long been used for aesthetic and utilitarian household purposes. Its advantages are that it is pliable and durable, may be dyed or used in its natural color, and may be embossed or sueded. Genuine leather can be expensive, but it has been simulated to a remarkable degree and currently is available at reasonable prices. The disadvantage of leather is that it is susceptible to marks, holes, and tears. Leather is used for upholstery, wall coverings, and floor tiles.

Cellulosic Fibers

Cellulosic, or *vegetable,* fibers include stems, leaves, and seed hairs found in cotton, flax (linen), and some minor fibers.

Cotton. *Cotton,* a product of the cotton plant, is believed to have been grown in India during the fourth century B.C. and used in early Rome. Its advantages are that it is the most plentiful of the natural fibers. It takes and holds color well, washes easily, and can be woven any way—from sheer to heavyweight. Its flexibility allows it to be adapted for such functions as upholstery, floor coverings, and window treatments (see Figure 5.4). Its disadvantages are that it is not as durable as other fibers and it wrinkles. It can mildew and fade. The cost of cotton varies according to the quality of the fiber, weave, and finish.

Linen. *Linen,* made from flax fibers, is the most ancient of all the fibers. It was used for weaving in Egypt as early as 4000 B.C. Its advantages are that it is strong, pliable, lustrous, and washable, and it takes and holds color. It is absorbent. The disadvantages of linen are that it wrinkles readily unless chemically treated, which then reduces its wear potential; it fades and is stiff in nature; and it is difficult to clean. Linen is used for upholstery, drapery, table linens, and slipcovers.

Other Vegetable Fibers. Other miscellaneous vegetable fibers known and used since prehistoric times are *ramie* (China grass or grass linen, a fiber resembling linen), *yucca, milkweed, hemp, jute, kapok, palm leaves,* and *sisal.* These fibers are used in household materials such as floor coverings, wall fabrics, upholstery, padding, and place mats.

Metallic Fibers

Metallic fibers include strips of gold, silver, or copper that are used chiefly as accents in decorative fabrics. Metallic

FIGURE 5.4 Fabrics woven from natural fibers of cotton and linen have been attractively employed for spreads, pillows, upholstery, valance, and over-the-bed treatment. Natural fibers complement the rugged natural texture of the bundled reeds. (Photograph by Pam Singleton.)

fibers glitter without tarnishing and are washable if used in washable fabrics. Metallic fibers are a type of mineral fiber.

Mineral Fibers

Mineral fiber, found in *asbestos,* is difficult to spin without the addition of another fiber. Asbestos is best known for its fire-retardant quality, but it has been found to be unhealthy and unsafe.

Man-Made Fibers

Man-made fibers are derived either from chemicals or natural solutions chemically treated. The fabrics composed of man-made fibers have been improved in quality; durability; resistance to soil, mildew, and moths; ease of care; and other desirable properties. Although costs vary, these fabrics tend to be less expensive than those made from natural fibers. Man-made fibers fall into two categories: regenerated cellulosic and synthetic.

Regenerated Cellulosic Fibers

Regenerated cellulosic fibers are produced by changing the physical and chemical formation of natural ingredients. Some examples are rayon, **acetate**, and triacetate.

Synthetic Fibers

Synthetic fibers are produced from chemicals and carbon compounds. Some examples are nylon, acrylic, modacrylic polyester, olefin, and glass. To alleviate confusion among the huge array of manufactured fibers, the Federal Trade Commission (FTC) established rules and regulations under the Textile Products Identification Act. Under these regulations, each manufactured fiber is defined in specific terms and given a **generic** name, which along with the company's trade name must appear on the label attached to the fabric. The generic name is the term assigned to a chemical family of which all members exhibit certain traits. For example, all members of the nylon family are characterized by unusual strength and resistance to abrasion, but they will not hold up well under direct sunlight. The polyester family is known for its drip-dry quality and resistance to sun deterioration. The **trade name** identifies the manufacturer. Because manufacturers need to give specific names to their products, hundreds of trade names for man-made fibers exist, making it virtually impossible for the consumer to recognize them all. Familiarity with the general properties of each fiber family, however, and checking the label to make sure of the fabric content helps to select the fabric that best serves specific needs. The fiber alone, however, does not ensure good performance if the construction, dyes, and finishes are not properly handled.

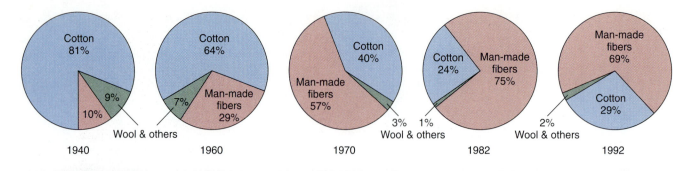

FIGURE 5.5 Change in fiber consumption.

During the past five decades, the production and consumption of man-made fibers has steadily increased. In 1940, man-made fibers accounted for only 10 percent of the fibers used; today, they account for approximately 75 percent of all fibers used by American textile mills, with polyester being the single most widely used fiber. The pie charts in Figure 5.5 show the change in fiber consumption from 1940 to 1992.

Table 5.1 lists the most common man-made fibers, their generic names, their qualities, their most important decorative uses, and recommendations for care to maintain appearance.

CONSTRUCTION OF FABRICS

The history of textile arts is almost as old as the history of humanity. The exact origin of the loom is not certain, but evidence suggests that it was used in Mesopotamia before 5000 B.C. Although modern mechanization has brought about great changes in textile production, weave structures are much the same as they were at the beginning of the Renaissance, and simple standard weaves are still basic to the industry. More intricate weaves that originated in Asia, such as damasks and brocades, are now produced on **Jacquard** looms.

Woven Textiles

This section discusses the most common weaves (illustrated in Figure 5.6), as well as some more intricate ones, used in today's decorative fabrics.

- *Plain weave* is made by the simple interweaving of warp (vertical or lengthwise) and weft or woof (horizontal or crosswise) threads, and may be single or double, regular or irregular.

  In the plain *single* weave, one weft thread passes over one warp thread and under the next. When the weave is balanced in sequence of over and under so that the warp and weft have the same yarn count per square inch, it is called *regular*. A plain regular weave is also called a *tabby* weave. When the warp and weft

differ because of different weights or textures of yarn, the weave is called *irregular* or *unbalanced*. Novelty yarns vary in appearance.

In the plain *double* (or *basket*) weave, two weft threads are interlaced with two warp threads. When the weave is regular, it is called *backed cloth*. This weave may also be irregular due to variations of weight or texture.

- *Twill weaves* are those in which two or more threads pass over or under another set of threads, skipping at regular intervals to produce a diagonal effect. Twill weaves may be regular or irregular. In the regular twill the long threads, or floats, pass over and under the same number of yarns. In the irregular twill the floats pass over and under a different number of threads. Irregular twills are used for many decorative fabrics such as denim, gabardine, and herringbone.

- *Satin weaves* have few interlacings or filling yarns with long floats. This combination produces a fabric with luster, softness, and drapability, especially when the fiber is smooth, as with satin and sateen.

- *Jacquard* is a loom machine system capable of creating multicolored fabrics of intricate patterns. It was invented in France in 1801 by Joseph-Marie Jacquard (1752–1834). Some of the most common woven fabrics created on the Jacquard loom include damasks, tapestries, and brocades.

- *Tapestry* weaving is a great art known since ancient times. This fabric was originally handwoven and made with bobbins. Tapestry can be woven on practically every type of loom, but the Jacquard is most commonly used. The weave is essentially plain but is made in a special way: across the warp in sections with the weft yarns interlocking around the same warp, into one another, or around adjacent warps, leaving a narrow slit. Tapestry has a rough feel. American Navajo rugs, French Aubusson rugs, and a wide range of upholstery fabrics are made of this type of weave.

- *Pile weaves* are produced by loops or tufts of yarn that stand out from the surface of the fabric. These loops may be cut, uncut, or a combination. The piles may be formed from the warp or the weft threads.

  A great many pile weaves are used in a wide variety of fabrics. The basic weave of the carpet industry is the

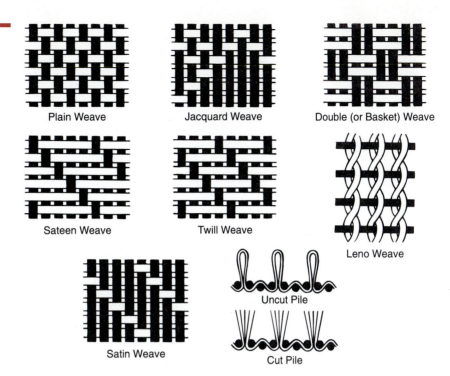

FIGURE 5.6 Common types of weaves.

Plain Weave   Jacquard Weave   Double (or Basket) Weave

Sateen Weave   Twill Weave   Leno Weave

Satin Weave   Uncut Pile / Cut Pile

raised-warp pile. Plush and velvet, originally woven by this method, are generally made today in a double cloth that is cut apart to produce the pile. Numerous household fabrics used for both utility and luxury are produced by one of the pile weaves, including terry cloth towels; corduroy, friezé, and velvet; and shag, velvet, and tufted carpets.

- *Extra warp and weft pattern weaves* are those in which extra warp and weft yarns are added to the fabric during weaving. Inlay pattern weaving was a well-known art in ancient Egypt, China, the Near East, and Peru. Some of the most beautiful decorative fabrics are made by this type of weaving. For commercial distribution, the Jacquard loom is used. Inlay weaves fall into several classifications but are all referred to as brocades.

- *Double-cloth weaves* are woven in two attached layers, often resulting in a quilted appearance. These fabrics, known to the ancient Peruvians, account for many of the durable and beautiful fabrics used today. When these fabrics are woven for commercial use, the Jacquard loom is required. Among the many varieties of this type, warp-faced pile weave and matelassé are two of the most common.

- *Open, lacelike weaves* can be obtained in a number of ways. One is the **leno,** a loose weave in which the warp threads are wound in half twists around each other, alternating in position on each row. The *gauze* weave is similar to leno but differs in that the warp threads maintain the same position in relation to the weft. Gauze weaves range from simple to complex. Sheers, semisheers, and novelty casements use these weaves.

- *Tension and texture-treated weaves* are those in which uneven tension in either weft or warp yarns produces an uneven surface effect. This may be accomplished in

a variety of ways and with multiple effects. Yarns of various twists, warp yarns held at different tension, floated yarns combined with tightly woven yarns, combinations of yarns that react differently to heat, irregular battening, irregular reeds, and combinations of unusual fibers are all used to produce a variety of surface effects. A commonly used decorative fabric of this type is *brocatelle,* in which floated and compactly woven yarns are combined to produce the raised effect.

- *Combination weaves* occur in many fabrics; they are produced by combining two or more weaves. The combined weaves are often suggested in the name of the fabric, such as brocaded satin and voided velvet.

Nonwoven Textiles

Knitting

Knitting is a process of interlocking a series of yarn loops by means of blunt needles. Through a variation of stitches, patterns are formed. Knitted fabrics, either hand- or machine-made, range from loose, open construction to close, fine weave. Finely knit fabrics are used for many home furnishing needs because of their wrinkle resistance, tight fit, and ease of care. The tendency of knitted fabrics to stretch is being overcome by new methods of production.

Twisting

Twisting, interlocking, and knotting of yarns account for various types of mesh construction, such as nets, laces, and macramé, the intricacies of which are unlimited. With the current revival of handcrafts, macramé has become particularly popular.

TABLE 5.1 Properties of man-made fibers

Generic Name	Appearance	Abrasion	Resilience	Heat Tolerance
Acetate (regenerated cellulose)	Smooth; silky; drapes well; holds shape well	Fair	Poor	Poor
Triacetate a subdivision of the acetate group	Crisp; smooth; silky; drapes well; strong colors	Fair	Good; resists wrinkling; retains pleats	Less sensitive than acetate
Acrylic	Wool-like; soft; bulky; warm; may squeak; rich colors; pilling depends on quality	Good; needs treatment for static	Good; holds heatset pleats	Sticks at 450°F
Modacrylic (modified acrylic)	Similar to acrylic; good color retention	Good	Fair to good	Does not melt
Aramid	Stiff and smooth	High; exceptional strength	Excellent; low stretchability	Not affected
Fiberglass	Soapy; lustrous; silky; color range fair; Beta Fiberglas has remarkable sheerness	Strongest of all fibers	Excellent	Fireproof
Nylon (polyamide)	Squeaky; silky; cold; natural luster; good color range; drapes well	Excellent	Very good; resists wrinkling; can be heat set to hold shape	High resistance
Olefin (propylene and ethylene)	Waxy; wool-like; color range fair	Good to excellent	Good; resists wrinkling	Poor; heat sensitive
Polyester	Silky, cotton, or wool-like; drapes well; color range fair	Good to excellent	Excellent; resists wrinkles	Sticks at 400°F
Rayon (regenerated cellulose)	Soft; drapes well; excellent color range; bright	Fair to good	Low to medium; crease retention poor	Excellent; does not melt
Saran	Soft; drapes well	Tough	Crease retentive	Shrinks in intense heat
Vinyl (thermoplastic resins)	Smooth; variety of weights; expanded vinyl closely resembles leather	Good	Low	Shrinks at 212–230°F in dry heat, less in moist heat

Notes: All man-made fibers are resistant to moths and mildew.
Insulation depends on construction and is primarily a function of thickness. Hollow polyester fibers provide particularly good insulation.
Costs are variable, depending on construction.

128 *Chapter 5*

Flammability	Light Tolerance	Decorative Uses	Care
Slow	Long exposure weakens fiber; colors fade unless protected by special finish	Curtains, drapery, upholstery, rugs; for shower curtains in blends with other fibers; moderate cost	Soil resistance fair; wash in lukewarm water or dry-clean, depending on dyes, finishes, decorative designs; quick drying; iron at moderate heat
Slowly combustible	More resistant than acetate	Same as acetate	Same as acetate
Resists fire; burns with yellow flame	Good	Rugs, carpets, blankets, curtains, drapery, upholstery	Keeps buoyancy when washed with warm water; machine dry; does not shrink, sag, or stretch; steam pressing reduces loft
Self-extinguishing	Excellent	Curtains, drapery, in carpet blends, furry rugs, blankets	Similar to acrylic; resists chemical stains; washable; use warm iron; shrinks unless stabilized; does not dry-clean well
Low flammability	Weakens with long exposure	Carpets	Not affected by moisture
Nonflammable	No loss	Curtains, drapery, bedspreads; Beta Fiberglas used for bedspreads	Impervious to moisture; hand wash; drip-dry; needs no ironing
Melts slowly	Poor	Upholstery, bedspreads, carpets	Washable; quick drying; use warm iron; resists soil; easy spot removal; static electricity unless treated
Slow to burn	Good	Rugs, blankets, upholstery, webbing, seat covers; low cost	Wash or dry-clean; iron at very low heat; good soil resistance
Burns slowly	Loses strength in prolonged exposure	Curtains, drapery, upholstery, carpets and rugs, pillow floss blankets	Soils easily; machine wash in warm water; dries quickly; use warm iron; resists stretching and shrinking
Burns quickly	Fades when not solution dyed	Curtains, upholstery, drapery, table linen, rugs; relatively inexpensive; probably most versatile fiber	Same as acetate; fair soil resistance
Nonflammable	Excellent	Outdoor furniture, upholstery and screening, curtains, drapery, wall coverings	Excellent ease of care; resists wrinkling and stains; water-repellent
Burns with difficulty	Weakens with long exposure	Shower curtains, wall coverings, upholstery when backed with fabric	Stain resistant; waterproof; wash and wipe clean

Felting

Felting is a nonwoven process of subjecting a mass of fibers to moisture, heat, and pressure, which produces a compact sheet that does not fray, absorbs sound, and provides good insulation against heat and cold. Felt was formerly made from wool and hair fibers. Through modern technology, new fibers and fusing methods are employed to produce a variety of nonwoven materials.

Bonding

A bonded fabric results when two fabrics are adhered (or bonded or laminated) together chemically or by heating methods. By bonding a layer of fabric to the underside, the face fabric can be stabilized. If care is not taken, however, cleaning may cause separation of the layers.

TEXTILE COLORING (DYEING)

Fibers and textiles are dyed or colored through various processes, providing an attractive visual element to the fabrics. These processes include (1) direct physical action, in which the structural elements of the fiber absorb the color; (2) chemical action, in which particular dyes have the ability to unite chemically with certain fibers; and (3) intermediate action, in which a **mordant** is used to unite the dye and fiber.

The various methods of dyeing yarns, fibers, and fabrics include (1) *solution* dyeing, in which the coloring agent is added to the viscous liquid of the synthetic before it is forced through the spinnerette to be formed into a fiber; (2) *stock* dyeing, in which the dye is applied to the fibers before they are processed into yarns; (3) *yarn* dyeing, in which the skeins or hanks of yarns are dyed before they are woven into fabrics; and (4) *piece* dyeing fabrics after they are woven. Piece dyeing, which usually produces a solid color in fabrics, can be done in several ways. *Jig* dyeing passes the open fabric back and forth through a stationary dye bath. *Pad* dyeing runs the fabric through the dye bath and then between rollers that squeeze the dye deeper into the yarns of the fabric. *Winch, reel,* or *beck* dyeing immerses the fabric continuously without strain to the fabric. *Continuous machine* dyeing has compartments for wetting out, dyeing, aftertreatments, washing, and rinsing. High-temperature processes are sometimes used for greater dye penetration. These processes are used especially for synthetic fibers.

Dye Lots

Each time a new dye solution or bath is mixed, the new solution may slightly change or vary from the previous bath. Each solution is called a **dye lot**. It is important, when using a fabric from more than one bolt for a certain project, to make sure they are from the same dye lot or that the colors still match.

FINISHING

The finish is a treatment that may be applied to the fiber or yarn before or after construction to change the appearance and performance. When the unfinished fabric comes from the loom it is referred to as **greige** or **gray goods**. Before the cloth is ready for the market it goes through a series of finishes: the preparation or prefinish, the functional finish, and the decorative finish.

Prefinishes

Prefinishes and preparation of the gray goods consist of a variety of treatments including (1) *bleaching* (to whiten), (2) *shrinking* (to prevent fiber contraction when exposed to moisture), (3) *heat setting* (to add stability especially for permanent pleating), (4) *beetling* or pounding (to give luster), (5) *gigging* or **napping** (to produce a flannel-like texture), (6) **calendering** (to provide a smooth finish and tighten the weave), (7) *durable* finishing (to strengthen the textile), (8) *preshrinking* (intense heat shrinks the textile to make it ready for finishing), (9) *boiling* (to rid the fabric of grease or other unwanted substances, and (10) *singeing* (to remove surface fuzz or lint). Following the preparatory finishing, the cloth is ready for the functional and decorative finishes.

Functional Finishes

Functional finishes are applied to improve performance. These standard textile finishes include: (1) *antibacterial* finishes (to help prevent mold and mildew), (2) *water-repellent* finishes (to resist stains), (3) *soil-repellent* finishes (to help resist soiling), (4) *flame-retardant* finishes (to help retard burning), (5) *mothproofing* finishes (to help prevent damage by insects), (6) *antistatic* finishes (to help guard against static), (7) *insulating* finishes (a coating bonded to the fabric to insulate against heat, cold, and noise), and (8) *carefree* finishes (to help resist creasing or wrinkles).

Decorative Finishes

Decorative finishes include printing and needlework.

Printing

Printing may be done by hand or by machine.

Hand Processes. With the exception of warp printing, fabrics are printed in the piece (after weaving). Hand processes require labor by the human hand. Some popular hand processes include (1) **batik**. Sections of the cloth that are not to be colored are blocked out in a design with wax; then the cloth is immersed in a dye solution. The wax is then removed to create a pattern. (2) *Hand block printing* requires a carved wooden or

FIGURE 5.7 This famous hand-blocked chintz design, "Victoria and Albert," was originally created in 1854 for Queen Victoria's first royal yacht, and it is still printed from the same wooden blocks. Vine tendrils outline profiles of Victoria (right) and Albert (left). (Courtesy of Stroheim & Romann, Inc.)

linoleum block that is then inked and stamped onto a piece of fabric to create the design, as seen in Figure 5.7. (3) *Tie-dye* is a hand-resist process that employs strings or knots tied on the fabric. The fabric is then immersed in dye, creating abstract patterns. (4) In the *silk-screen* process a specially prepared fabric screen resists the color penetration except in desired areas. Dye in paste form is forced through the screen onto the fabric below. A separate screen is prepared for each color used in the design. Only the silk-screen process produces hand-printed textiles on a large commercial scale. Some of these prints are so lovely that they rival fine paintings.

Mechanical Processes. Many prints are produced mechanically by the transfer of color from an engraved copper roller onto the fabric. This process is called *roller printing*. A separate copper roller must be engraved for each color of the design, but once prepared, the rollers can be used on a variety of color schemes for thousands of yards of fabric. Other types of roller printing include *embossing* (engraved rollers produce a pressed high-low design into the fabric), *moiré* (a type of embossed method that presses a watermark design into the fabric), and *warp* printing, (printing done on the warp yarns of a fabric before it is woven).

Other decorative finishes include *etching* (acid burns out one fiber, resulting in a design on a sheer fabric), *chemically treated textured* finishes (usually a puckered surface), *flocking* (small fibers are bonded to the fabric in a patterned design), *softening* finishes, and *brightening* finishes.

Printed fabrics come in designs of unlimited styles, including *documentaries*—designs copied from patterns of a particular historical period. These designs range

FIGURE 5.8 "Bainbridge" glazed cotton from Greeff's English Garden Collection features a Victorian floral bouquet design based on a documentary circa 1840. (Courtesy of Greeff Fabrics.)

from historic styles to modern and help establish an authentic feeling. (See Figure 5.8.)

Needlework

Needlework, the embellishing of fabrics with intricate stitchery, is an ancient art form. Today, a wide variety of needlework, such as embroidery, macramé, needlepoint, candlewicking, appliqué, and quilting, is again embellishing homes across the country.

DECORATIVE TEXTILES FOR INTERIORS

Today's interior designer has a wider choice of fabrics than ever before, with new fabrics appearing almost daily. The market abounds with fabrics suitable for every taste, style, and decorative purpose in every price range. Adding to the appeal of new and improved fibers is the seemingly unending variety of designs ranging from folk patterns from around the world to traditional and contemporary designs. Following is a discussion of the principal decorative uses of fabrics in the home.

FIGURE 5.9 A translucent sheer fabric was used for the treatment of large arched windows, allowing light to filter into the room. The fabric is swagged at the top to echo the shape of the arches, and gracefully tied back to unify the two windows. (Photograph by Pam Singleton.)

Sheers or Glass Curtains

Lightweight sheers or glass curtains may hang permanently over a glass window in either a commercial or residential setting. (All commercial textiles must comply with strict fire codes.) Sheers filter the light, thereby giving softness to the room and providing daytime privacy, as seen in Figure 5.9.

Fabric should be sheer enough to permit light, should be sunproof, and should wash or clean well without shrinkage. Any sheer fabric that has these qualities can be used for sheers or glass curtains. Batiste, voile, ninon, and chiffon are four popular examples.

Casements or Semisheers

Casements or semisheers are informal lightweight to mediumweight fabrics that serve as side drapery during the day and are drawn at night for privacy.

Fabric should be heavy enough for nighttime privacy but should permit some light. The fabric should be drapable, sun resistant, and nonsplitting and should wash or clean well without shrinkage. Leno weaves especially help control sagging. Fabric choice is unlimited. The style and functional requirements of the space, whether for residential or nonresidential projects, will help determine the type of weave desired.

Drapery

Fabrics for drapery should have a light to medium weight. They can serve as stationary side drapery or be designed to draw for privacy. In addition to function, drapery can add beauty, height, and dignity to a room. When the desired design, texture, weight, color, and method of hanging are employed, drapery can contribute to the style and help set the mood of the room (i.e., formal or informal; see Figure 5.2).

FIGURE 5.10 In a bedroom designed and executed by Tom Sheerer and Jeff Bilhuber, an abundance of white is used to unify and visually enlarge a small space. White upholstery conveys a sense of lightness and comfort. Fabric shades hung bottom-up at the slanted windows provide privacy while admitting light. A patterned rug and fur throw are luxurious touches. (Courtesy of F. J. Hakimian, Inc. and Bilhuber, Inc., N.Y. Photograph by Phillip H. Ennis.)

Fabric should drape gracefully, clean without shrinkage, and meet the particular needs of the room in which it is used. Any drapable fabric that is suitable for the style of furnishings, background, and window type can be used. Fabric types are silk, antique satin, chintz, damask, and other medium- to lightweight fabrics.

Upholstery

Upholstery is a medium- or lightweight fabric that covers furniture permanently, adds beauty and comfort, conceals or emphasizes furniture, and adds to or sets the theme or mood of the room. (See Figure 5.10.)

Fabric used for upholstery should have a tight weave, be durable and comfortable, and clean well. Common upholstery fabrics include heavyweight fabrics such as matelassé, tweed, tapestry, velvet, bouclé, friezé, and leather; mediumweight fabrics such as damask, brocatelle, and canvas; and lightweight fabrics such as antique satin, chintz, linen, homespun, and moiré. Upholstery fabrics for commercial treatments must meet rigid safety codes.

Slipcovers

Slipcovers may cover worn upholstered furniture, protect more expensive fabrics, and brighten or change a room's atmosphere.

Slipcovers are light- to mediumweight and should be durable, tightly woven, nonsnag, and nonstretch (unless they are of a stretch variety). There is a current trend toward looser fitting, informal-looking slipcovers. Some

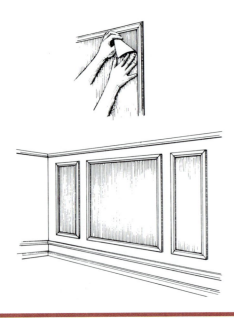

FIGURE 5.11 Framed fabric on a wall can add interest and style.

FIGURE 5.12 Bold patterns should be used with discretion. Too much pattern becomes overpowering.

manufacturers are offering furniture upholstered in muslin or other plain fabrics that can be purchased with several changes of slipcovers so that rooms can be dressed for seasonal changes. Indian Head, sailcloth, ticking, chintz, whipcord, and corduroy are all good choices for slipcovers.

Walls

Fabrics can be used on walls to add beauty or to solve a decorative problem as illustrated in Figure 5.11. (See Chapter 6 for uses of flexible wall coverings.) The fabric should have a tight weave with firm body. Canvas, burlap, moiré, ticking, heavy cotton or linen, velveteen, and damask are often used for wall coverings.

COMBINING FABRICS

Perhaps the most common question clients ask professional interior designers is, What fabric goes with what? This question has no absolute answer. Combining fabrics is a matter of training and skill. Some people seem to have an aptitude for acquiring this skill; others require much patient study and practice. Although an unexpected combination of materials may create a feeling of great interest and charm, some general principles will be helpful to the inexperienced designer when combining colors, textures, and patterns.

Pattern

Pattern indicates that the design has motifs sufficiently large in scale, or with enough contrast in color or tone, to permit the eye to distinguish them clearly. When the parts of the pattern are so subtle or are blended in such a way that they are indistinguishable, the design becomes one more of texture than of pattern.

Many people are afraid of patterned fabrics and avoid them entirely; others use them ineffectively, as illustrated in Figure 5.12. Although they are not a necessity, well-chosen patterned fabrics can enhance most rooms. The adroit use of pattern can camouflage defects, create beauty and glamour, and perform decorating miracles.

As with color, no absolute do's or don'ts govern the successful use of pattern. A few general guidelines, however, may be helpful.

- Patterns used within the same room should be *related*. Common elements such as color, texture, or motif tie them together and give an easy flow to the entire scheme. (See Figure 5.13.)
- The *principal pattern* need not be repeated in the room so long as one or more of the colors in that pattern are carried over into another area. The same pattern, however, may be repeated on furnishings or used at the windows or on the walls, depending on the overall effect desired. Odd pieces of furniture can be unified by covering them in the same fabric, and repetition of the fabric brings unity to a room.
- The use of no more than one *bold pattern* of the same type of design, such as a floral, is usually more effective.
- Once the dominant motif is established it can be interestingly supplemented by *small patterns, stripes, checks,* or *plaids* with complementary plain textures added. (See Figure 5.14.)
- When combining patterned fabrics, *scale or size* of the pattern should be considered. For example, if a bold floral print is combined with a plaid or a stripe or both, the continuation of the bold scale is often most effective. If an unobtrusive floral pattern is used, accompanying fabrics may blend well in scale and not overpower the principal pattern.
- *Unusual juxtaposition* of fabrics may create a dramatic effect, but this kind of carefree sophistication usually

FIGURE 5.13 In this grouping the ruby, forest green, and gold fabrics have a pleasing relationship to each other. The large pattern, reminiscent of the medieval period, is coordinated with a smaller pattern and a woven texture. (Courtesy of Kravet Fabrics, Inc.)

FIGURE 5.14 One bold pattern establishes the motif and is supplemented by a plaid and a plain fabric. The gardenlike colors of the floral design are echoed in the plaid of burgundy and green. The tassel tiebacks in gold and burgundy lend a rich effect. (Courtesy of Kravet Fabrics, Inc.)

develops from knowledge and practice that produce confidence to do the unexpected.

- Consider the *style and color* of the pattern. What is the period, look, or feeling desired? For example, does the pattern convey an informal country French style with a toile de Jouy pattern in deep red and cream? Or is the pattern a bold abstract with dramatic modern color combinations? Are these patterns *formal or informal* in nature?
- The pattern's *proportions and motifs* should be well designed. It should be a pattern that can be lived with for a long time.
- Success in combining patterns can be achieved with *practice, experience,* and consideration of basic guidelines. It is helpful to observe beautiful pattern combinations assembled by experienced professional designers as presented in design periodicals, design studios, showrooms, and home shows.

Texture

The surface quality of a textile is also an important element to consider when combining fabrics in a specific

project. Knowledge of what makes a fabric formal or informal is essential for successfully combining textiles.

Formal Fabrics

Formal fabrics are primarily those with smooth and often shiny textures, which often display elegant stylized and geometric patterns, as seen in Figure 5.15. Some examples of formal fabrics include velvet, damask, brocade, brocatelle, satin, shantung, and taffeta. Today, formal fabrics are often creatively used in both traditional and modern interiors in a wide range of colors and patterns.

Informal Fabrics

Informal fabrics are generally those with a rougher texture and matte finish, such as burlap, canvas, hopsacking, muslin, tweed, and bouclé. (See Figure 5.16.) Fabrics with a handcrafted quality often fall into this category. If the informal fabric employs pattern, the design may be bold, naturalistic, abstract, or geometric.

Many fabrics can be used in either category. For example, cottons and linens may have textures, colors, and

FIGURE 5.15 Smooth textures found on the antique satin, damask, and other elegant fabrics establish a formal mood in this small but luxurious living space. The soft textures of the pastel French rug contribute to the room's formality. (Courtesy of Bruce Stodola and the Design Studio at Barrows, Scottsdale, AZ. Photograph by Mark Boisclair.)

patterns that fit into a formal setting or are at home in an informal room. Traditionally, colors for informal fabrics have been bolder; but today white, pastels, and neutrals are also used informally. For example, pale pink canvas may cover seating units on informal wicker furniture frames.

The unique *surface quality* (rough, smooth, shiny, or dull) of each fabric should be considered and evaluated when coordinating them. The relationship should be supportive and appropriate for the room's style and mood. For example, informal dull monk's cloth is not at home in an elegant eighteenth-century English room with smooth and shiny damasks and satins but is more compatible on a wicker chair in an informal country style.

The *character* of the texture should be appropriate for its intended use or purpose. For example, if a comfortable fabric for a chair in a family room is required, a smooth, soft leather would be preferred over a rough burlap texture. Whatever the uses or functions of the

fabrics, the textures should be visually appealing, comfortable, and harmonious.

Color

When coordinating fabrics, another goal is to select colors that are compatible and harmonious. A few guidelines may be helpful.

Hue, Value, and Chroma

When selecting colors for fabrics, remember that color has three dimensions, as outlined in Chapter 2—hue, value, and chroma.

Hues fall into warm or cool color clans with neutral in between. One of these categories can be selected to dominate the scheme. What hues will best fit the needs and preferences of the occupants? Such criteria as cli-

FIGURE 5.16 Nubby wool textures and dull matte finishes on the upholstered furnishings, pillows, and throw enhance the effect of informality in this living space. The leaf-textured rug further supports the informal and artistic mood of the contemporary style. (Courtesy of Steve Chase and Associates. Photograph by Mary E. Nichols.)

mate, positioning of the space in relationship to the sun, and lifestyle should be considered.

Fabrics are either light, medium, or dark in value. Most fabric coordination is enhanced by including fabrics in all three levels of luminosity. For example, if the major fabrics in the room are light in value, the fabrics for smaller furnishings or accessories might be medium and dark in value. Many designers use darker values below, medium values in the middle areas, and lighter values on the upper portions of the space; of course, this method can be reversed for a more unusual effect. Using only dark and light values in a space creates drama; for example, a color scheme using black and white.

Fabrics are either muted or bright in chroma. A color scheme is usually successful when varying levels of chroma are selected. For example, if the major fabrics for the room are muted in chroma, some accents of bright

fabrics are visually interesting. A room with all muted colors can be dull and boring; a room with all intense colors can be tiring or even agitating.

Natural and Artificial Light
To be certain the colors of the fabrics are harmonious, compare them under all types of lighting in the space, both natural and artificial.

Style
Select a color scheme appropriate for the chosen style. For example, some colors used during the Victorian period were deep purples, mauves, greens, and reds. To provide an authentic combination of fabrics, these colors could be selected.

Mood

A feeling of formality or informality may be achieved through the selection of various colors. Generally, bright colors reflect a lively informal mood and muted and light colors produce a quieter, sedate mood.

Colors in a Pattern

Many designers draw on the colors in a patterned fabric or rug to skillfully coordinate other fabrics for a room, as seen in Figure 5.17. This method is fairly safe because the basic colors of the scheme are already coordinated. But take care that this approach does not become static or uninteresting.

New and Creative Color Combinations

Often, predictable color combinations and those that exactly match are not as interesting as those that are creative. Experience in training the eye while trying out fabric combinations, along with general guidelines, will help you develop a sense of what fabric selections are complementary and what groupings do not work well together.

SOLVING DESIGN PROBLEMS WITH TEXTILES

Problems can often be solved through the skillful use of fabric, with unlimited possibilities. Fabrics may serve many purposes. A well-chosen fabric can:

- *Lighten or darken a room.* Fabrics in high values can work wonders in visually lightening the room. If the room has too much light, fabrics in low values help darken the room.
- *Emphasize walls, windows, or furnishings* to attract desired attention. (See Figure 5.18.)
- *Conceal walls, windows, or furnishings.* A designer may want to draw attention away from a particular wall, window, or piece of furniture or conceal an unattractive feature. Fabrics can be employed in numerous ways to accomplish this goal.
- *Bring harmony and unity* to a room by repeated use of the same or complementary fabrics. (See Figure 5.19.)
- *Provide balance* to a room. For example, a bold-patterned fabric at a window or on a small piece of furniture balances a larger piece of plain furniture at

FIGURE 5.17 In this Greenwich Showhouse, the solid and paisley-patterned velvet upholstery fabrics were selected to harmonize with the colorful rug and enhance the effect of an Oriental pavilion. (Courtesy of F. J. Hakimian, Inc., N.Y. and Robert Metzger Interiors. Photograph by Phillip Ennis.)

FIGURE 5.18 Dramatically full bed draperies of sheer linen are attached to a framework suspended from the ceiling. Blue and white patterns enliven the draperies, rugs, and upholstery in this charming bedroom. (Mario Buatta, designer. Photograph courtesy Mario Buatta, Inc.)

FIGURE 5.19 Schumacher's "Treasure of the Forbidden City" features a sunflower yellow embroidery design on the walls, window, and pillows. A harmonious sense of balance is achieved through an onyx border that travels the top perimeter of the walls and the dark patterned rug on the floor. (Courtesy of Schumacher.)

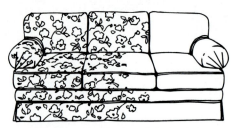

Large or conspicuous pattern tends to
make furniture appear larger.

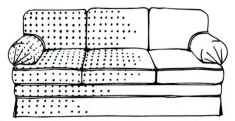

Small pattern diminishes size.

FIGURE 5.20 The effect of pattern and size.

the other side of the room. A spot of bright color balances a larger area of muted color.

- *Change the apparent size and proportion* of a piece of furniture or an entire room. For example, a sofa covered in a large pattern or bold-colored fabric appears larger than if it is covered in a light, plain color or a small unobtrusive pattern, as illustrated in Figure 5.20. A chair or love seat upholstered in a vertical stripe looks higher than the same piece covered in a plain fabric.
- *Establish the room's color scheme.* A successful method of color scheming a room is choosing a favorite patterned fabric as a starting point.
- *Establish the historic or modern style* of a room. If the room is based on a certain period, the fabric, more than any other item or furnishing, can set the desired feeling. Documentary fabrics can provide historically authentic styles.
- *Change the look of a room for different seasons.* For example, a couch and chairs in deep warm colors may be slipcovered in light-colored ticking for summer. Heavy winter drapery may be changed for light sheer glass curtains to create a cool atmosphere for summer.
- *Add softness and comfort,* providing a uniquely human factor. For example, fabrics for upholstery, linens, and draperies can provide comfort and warmth in a non-residential hospitality project, as seen in Figure 5.21.

TEXTILES FOR PERIOD AND CONTEMPORARY ROOMS

Design in textiles was used in ancient times as a symbolic medium for religious purposes. With the passage of time,

fabric became a significant medium for aesthetic expression. The design motifs used in the early rugs of East Turkistan are much the same as the designs used in the early rugs of the Inca and Navajo Indians, halfway around the world. This similarity is easily explainable. Primitive peoples represented the phenomena of nature in their early art forms. For example, the sun and stars were represented in identifiable form. The difference in early textile weaves is minimized because all were done on simple looms, and primitive cultures used natural fibers and dyes. Although each country developed characteristics peculiar to its origin, a common quality in their early crafts blends them together harmoniously.

A close relationship often existed among the designs of European, Near Eastern, and Eastern countries during the Middle Ages and the Renaissance. The explanation for this relationship is that the conqueror of a country imported artisans of all kinds to his homeland, where they continued to carry on their trades. In time they were influenced by the designs of their new environment, and the eventual blending of different methods and motifs produced art forms with distinct individuality. During the Renaissance and the seventeenth and eighteenth centuries fabrics from Far Eastern countries, with their unique motifs and colors, were in great demand and were imported to Europe and America.

With the increased sophistication in today's interiors, it is popular to draw on historic designs to establish an **authentic** feeling of a specific period or style. To accomplish this, documentary fabrics bearing designs from a wide range of historic periods are being produced by manufacturers. However, seldom does a client wish to create an entirely authentic period room; this is usually reserved for restoration projects.

To serve clients who prefer the modern look, an abundance of decorative and functional fabrics is also available. Current fabric selection trends in home design use contemporary fabrics that reflect today's techniques and innovations. Designers often use historic furnishings upholstered in the latest fabrics. For example, an eighteenth-century Queen Anne chair might be covered in a contemporary white wool fabric rather than the traditional damask of the earlier period. In other words, today's fabrics are flexible enough to be used for all types of furniture—modern or traditional.

The following is a list of historic styles and a brief outline of typical fabric types, colors, and patterns appropriate to each:

- **English Tudor** (in Colonial America: ca. 1608–1700). *Fabric types:* Crewel embroidery, linen, chintzes, velvets, cut velvets, tapestry, damasks, brocades, and leather. *Colors:* Deep rich reds, blues, greens, and golds. *Patterns:* Flamestitch, large floral sprays (often hand-blocked), and the pomegranate (motifs inspired by India).
- **Early American Colonial** (ca. 1608–1700). *Fabric types:* Simple homespun, broadcloth, and muslin. Hand em-

FIGURE 5.21 Fabrics can provide comfort and help soften a room in a nonresidential setting. The upholstery, linens, and draperies in this dining room selected by Carolyn Henry & Associates demonstrate the warmth and aesthetic appeal fabrics can provide in a public setting. (Photograph by Pam Singleton.)

broidery. Leather. *Colors:* Deep blue, rich red, pea soup green, white and neutral colors. *Patterns:* Small plaids, quaint prints, stripes, floral needlework designs.

■ **Early Georgian** (ca. 1700–1750). *Fabric types:* Elegant imported damasks, silks, brocades, taffetas, and velvets. Some leather. *Colors:* Muted Williamsburg blue and green, rich gold, and deep red. *Patterns:* Stylized floral bouquets. Stripes. Large all-over floral patterns.

■ **Late Georgian** (ca. 1750–1790). *Fabric types:* Elegant imported damasks, silks, brocades, and velvets. *Colors:* Rich reds, blues, gold, and turquoise. Some pastels introduced. *Patterns:* Large floral patterns, pineapples, stripes, Chinese motifs, and influence of rococo motifs from France.

■ **French Rococo (Louis XV)** (ca. 1730–1774). *Fabric types:* Damasks, moirés, silks, brocades, velvet, and taffeta. Elegant toile de Jouy printed cottons. *Colors:* Pale tints of green, yellow, peach, rose, and blue. *Patterns:* Small-scaled patterns, curving shells, scrolls, ribbons, and flowers. Introduction of toile de Jouy prints (especially pastoral scenes).

■ **French Neoclassic (Louis XVI)** (1760–1790). *Fabric types:* Same fabric types used as in the French Rococo period. Some chintz. *Colors:* Neutralized tints, especially soft blue, green, yellow, peach, and green. *Patterns:* Delicate sprays of flowers intertwined with stripes. Baskets of flowers, wreaths, ribbons, and bow knots with flowing ends. Chinese figures and motifs.

- **Country French** (ca. 1730–1760). *Fabric types:* Toile de Jouy. Ticking, tapestry, cottons and tweeds. *Colors:* Deep and muted blues, reds, greens, and yellows. White backgrounds. *Patterns:* Motifs copied from the court rococo style. Simple floral prints. Stripes. Toile de Jouy pastoral scenes, shepherdesses, folk scenes.
- **Neoclassic American Federal** (ca. 1790–1820). *Fabric types:* Formal brocades, damasks, velvets, chintz, satins, and moiré. *Colors:* Pale and muted tints, especially soft blue, green, yellow and peach. White or creamy backgrounds. *Patterns:* Urns and other motifs from ancient Greece and Rome. Pineapples. Oval motifs. Flowing ribbons with bows and delicate flowers, often on a stripe. Swags and garlands of flowers.
- **Neoclassic English.** Fabric types, colors, and patterns same as American Neoclassic.
- **French Empire** (ca. 1800–1820). *Fabric types:* Silks, taffetas, brocades, damasks, moiré. *Colors:* Strong colors. Emerald green, bright yellow, and gold. Rich reds and purples. Brilliant blues. Black and white. *Patterns:* Influence of Napoleon. Laurel wreath, honeybee, star, swan, military emblems. Motifs from ancient Greece and Egypt. Bold stripes.
- **American Empire** (ca. 1820–1850). Fabric types, colors, and patterns same as French Empire. (Similar colors used, but often muted, such as mauves, dull greens, and purples.)
- **Spanish Southwest** (ca. 1600s–present). **Santa Fe style** (ca. 1920s to present). *Fabric types:* Early period: Indian blankets, handwoven wools, cottons. Santa Fe style: Informal heavy cottons. Matelassé. Linens. *Colors:* Early period: Strong colors made with natural dyes. Santa Fe style: Desert colors: sand, soft purples, turquoise, and peach. *Patterns:* Geometrics. Stripes. Indian motifs.
- **Spanish Colonial.** *Fabric types:* Leather. Matelassé and heavy cotton weaves. Plain and cut velvets. *Colors:* Usually bold and bright. Vivid reds and pinks, cobalt blue, rich gold, black, white, and neutrals. *Patterns:* Strong floral patterns, usually large in scale. Bold geometrics and stripes.
- **Victorian** (1837– ca. 1910). *Fabric types:* Plain plush and cut velvets, damasks, lace, chintz, printed cottons, fringe and tassels. *Colors:* Mauves, purples, rich reds, tobacco brown, bottle green, mulberry, gold, and backgrounds of cream, white, and black. *Patterns:* Influences from many styles of the past. Large and small floral designs.
- **China and Japan.** *Fabric types:* Raw and fine silks, brocades, shantung, and damask. *Colors:* Jade green, white, medium blue, rich red, and peacock blue. Bright pink and yellow. Neutralized colors and white. Accents of black. *Patterns:* Figures, parasols, chrysanthemums, peonies, cherry blossoms, fret designs, bamboo, exotic birds, butterflies, floating clouds and mountains, dragons, curved bridges, pagodas, and herons.
- **Early Modern: Arts and Crafts** (ca. 1860–present). *Fabric types:* Linens, cottons, matelassé, other informal fabrics. *Colors:* Rich and dark greens, blues, and oranges.

Patterns: Influence of Gothic and Renaissance motifs but updated and stylized. Large and small floral prints. Flowing vines and stalks.
- **Early Modern: Art Nouveau.** (ca. 1885–present). *Fabric types:* Similar to Arts and Crafts. *Colors:* Soft muted golds, apricots, and greens. Rich stained glass colors inspired by Louis Comfort Tiffany, especially greens, blues, and purples. Soft pink, rose, lavender, black and white inspired by Charles Rennie Mackintosh. *Patterns:* Flowing vines, stalks, and flowers. Peacocks. Women with flowing hair and robes. Mackintosh rose design. Motifs inspired by nature.
- **Modern** (ca. 1920s–present). *Fabric types:* Many fabric types, both formal and informal. *Colors:* De Stijl movement from 1917 to 1933: red, yellow, blue, black, white, and grey. International Style of the 1920s: white especially used. Art Deco style from 1920s to 1940s to present: silver, white, black, red, chocolate brown, peach, muted blue and green, mauve, turquoise. Fabric designers today tend to use all hues, values, and chromas with no rules or limitations. White, grey, and neutrals continue to be popular. *Patterns:* Stylized motifs of all types, abstract and geometric designs. Many modern spaces have limited pattern use.

TEXTILES FOR NONRESIDENTIAL PROJECTS

Textile Specifications, Safety Codes, and Government Labeling

Selecting textiles for commercial projects requires steps similar to those outlined for residential projects. The interior designer plays a significant role in specifying fabrics that meet testing standards for high quality, required safety codes, and other criteria listed below. As the design process steps are followed, the functional needs of the client are determined, contracts are signed, and the specifications for installation of textiles are written. The designer and client must make sure that all costs involved are clear and agreed upon.

The textiles selected must meet standard tests for (1) *durability,* such as tests for strength and abrasion resistance, (2) *colorfastness* (tests the fabric's resistance to sun fading and losing color from various methods of cleaning), and (3) *flammability* (how quickly the fabric will ignite and spread, if it will extinguish on its own, and the quality of the fumes emitted by the burning fabric). Fabrics must meet strict fire codes enforced by state and local governments. Basically, this means the fabrics must be flame resistant and have a flame-retardant finish.

The textiles selected must be labeled to indicate their flammability and their fiber content (with percentages of natural and man-made fibers when applicable), and whether they have been treated with durable finishes such as Scotchgard or other protective treatments. The fabrics should be resistant to insects and static electricity and be easy to clean and maintain.

The designer should select colors, textures, and patterns that are attractive and suit the requirements of the client or end users (see Figure 5.22).

Environmental Concerns

Currently, many designers, manufacturers, and others involved in the design field are conscientiously dealing with environmental issues, such as pollution control, "greening" the earth, and recycling. Seminars, conferences, classes, and other means of communication are being held regularly and environmental organizations are helping to inform designers, consumers, and manufacturers on how to deal with these issues and become involved. For example, some textile and carpet mills are recycling and designers are creating "green environments" and "healthy houses" (see Chapter 13). The use of endangered species in manufacturing various products for residential and nonresidential design is being limited or eliminated. Additionally, the textile and carpet industries are involved in controlling toxics during the production process. Responsible designers are aware of these environmental issues and design accordingly.

TEXTILE PRESENTATION LAYOUTS

Presenting the specified textiles arranged in a professional layout is immensely helpful for the designer in

FIGURE 5.22 Brilliantly colored fabrics have been fashioned to hang and float in a fascinating composition in this dramatic atrium space in the Marriott Marquis Hotel in Atlanta, Georgia, designed by architect John Portman. (Courtesy of the Atlanta Marriott Marquis.)

FIGURE 5.23 Compatible colors, textures, and patterns are coordinated to produce a formal contemporary grouping of fabrics. This format is one typically adopted by professional designers. (Courtesy of Bengt Erlandsson.)

communicating to the client how the colors, textures, and patterns are coordinated and allocated for a particular space. Fabric samples are collected from various sources and cut to appropriate sizes indicating how each fabric will be used in a single room or in spaces in the project. The samples are then attached to a mat board, as shown in Figure 5.23. Students of design can benefit from following this professional hands-on procedure and gain knowledge of how to successfully combine and present fabrics.

TEXTILE TERMS

The information in this section can assist the designer in getting maximum service from popular fabrics in use today. The following are the most popular household fabrics, their qualities, and their uses. Fabrics are listed under their common decorative name.

Antique satin   A satin weave fabric with textured horizontal striations that imitate antique silk. Antique satin is light-

weight, usually a solid color, and is primarily used for drapery.

Batiste   A fine, soft, sheer fabric of plain weave made of various fibers. Glass curtains.

Bouclé   A French word meaning "curly." It indicates yarns are curled or looped in a flat or pile fabric. Heavyweight. Upholstery.

Bouclé marquisette   Sheer material of leno weave with a bouclé yarn. Glass curtains.

Broadcloth   A lightweight fabric in a plain or twill weave. Cotton, wool, or synthetic fibers popularly used. Draperies, bedspreads.

Brocade   A mediumweight fabric woven on a Jacquard loom. An embroidered multicolored pattern stands out in relief against a satin or ribbed background. Drapery and upholstery.

Brocatelle   A mediumweight Jacquard fabric with an extra set of wefts for backing, unevenly twisted, which results in a high-relief **repoussé** appearance on the surface. Upholstery and draperies.

Buckram   Stiffened material sized with glue. Reinforcement for draperies and valances.

Burlap   A mediumweight coarse fabric woven of jute in a plain, loose weave. Wall coverings, drapery, and lamp shades.

Calico   A lightweight plain cotton weave with a small all-over print.

Cambric   Plain weave cotton or linen. Called "handkerchief linen." Originally made in Cambrai, France. Very sheer to coarse. Used for linings.

Canvas   A mediumweight, closely woven cotton. A plain, diagonal weave in solids or prints. Upholstery, drapery, walls.

Casement   A broad term covering many drapery fabrics. Usually light, neutral colors in plain or novelty weaves.

Cashmere   Very soft wool textile derived from goat hair.

Challis   A lightweight wool, cotton, or synthetic soft fabric in a plain tight weave. Printed designs or plain. Drapery, upholstery.

Chenille   A heavyweight fabric woven with chenille yarns. When woven in a fabric, can create a pile similar to velvet; if woven on a Jacquard loom, can look similar to cut velvet. Upholstery, bedspreads.

Chiffon   A sheer fabric used for glass curtains. Tight weave, lightweight.

Chintz   A plain, tightly woven lightweight cotton fabric with fine yarns. Sometimes processed with a glazed finish. Can be either a solid color or printed. Draperies, slipcovers, bedspreads.

Color flag   The series of clippings attached to a purchased fabric sample to show the colorline.

Colorline   Refers to the complete color range of a given fabric series.

Colorway   Refers to the color of an individual fabric.

Corduroy   A heavyweight cotton or synthetic pile fabric, ribbed or corded lengthwise. Drapery, slipcovers, upholstery, bedspreads, and other uses.

Crepe   Crinkled or puckered fabrics of many types. Usually produced by twisting the yarn when weaving or by a chemical process. Cotton, silk, wool are typical. Plain weave.

Cretonne   First made in Creton, France. Similar to chintz but heavier. A cotton fabric with a printed design. Plain or rep weave.

Crewel embroidery A heavyweight plain-woven cotton, linen, or wool fabric embroidered with fine, loosely twisted, two-ply worsted yarns. Usually worked by hand in the Kashmir province of India. Drapery and upholstery.

Crocking Rubbing off color from dyed or printed fabrics.

Damask A Jacquard-woven mediumweight fabric with patterns providing unique weave effects. Can be woven self-tone, one-color warp, different-color filling, or multicolor in design. Distinguished from brocades because face of fabric is flatter. The color is reversed on the wrong side. Drapery and upholstery.

Denim A mediumweight, tightly woven cotton twill made of coarse yarns. Usually in a solid color, but can be patterned. Drapery, upholstery, bedspreads, walls, and numerous other uses.

Dotted swiss Sheer fabric woven with extra yarns forming dots when clipped. The effect may be produced by flocking. Curtains.

Duck Similar to canvas. Tightly woven and durable cotton textile. Often striped and used for awnings.

Embroidery Needle and thread art. Originally handwork designs. Today can also be machine produced.

Faille A lightweight, flat-ribbed fabric woven with fine yarns in the warp and heavier yarns in the filling using a plain weave. The ribbed effect is flatter than grosgrain and smaller than rep. Faille can be the base cloth for moiré. Drapery, upholstery.

Felt Wools or mixed fibers pressed into a compact sheet. A heavyweight fabric used for walls, table covers, and other uses.

Fiberglass Fibers and yarns produced from glass and woven into flexible lightweight fabrics. Noted for its fireproof qualities. Beta Fiberglas is a trademarked glass fiber. Curtains.

Film A lightweight thin or thick plastic sheet used for upholstery, shower curtains, or table coverings. Can be textured, patterned, or plain.

Flannel Twilled fabric made of wool or cotton. Soft yarns are brushed to produce a napped texture. Used for interlinings.

Friezé A strong heavyweight fabric with a fine, cut or uncut, low-loop surface woven on a wire loom to maintain an even size to the loops. Upholstery.

Gabardine Twill fabric with a distinct diagonal design. Durable, lightweight or mediumweight, made with natural or man-made fibers.

Gauze Sheer, thin textile constructed of leno or plain weave or both types. Originally silk, now also cotton, wool, linen, and synthetic fibers. Used for glass curtains.

Gimp Ornamental braid used to cover upholstery tacks.

Gingham Medium- or lightweight cotton or cottonlike fabric for informal use. Made of colored yarns forming checks, plaids, or stripes.

Grass cloth Coarse grasses glued to rice paper. Used for wall coverings.

Grenadine A leno weave textile that is similar to marquisette, but thinner. Often woven with dots or patterns. Used for glass curtains.

Gros point Heavyweight needlepoint embroidery. Upholstery.

Homespun Loosely woven lightweight fabric made to resemble handwoven material. Curtains or drapery.

Hopsacking A rough-surfaced mediumweight fabric loosely woven of various fibers in a plain basket weave. Mainly for drapery and slipcovers.

Insulating Fabrics processed with reflective metallic or foam plastic on one side to provide insulating qualities.

Jacquard Damasks, brocades, tapestries, and all fabrics requiring the Jacquard loom.

Khaki A coarse lightweight to mediumweight cotton twill weave dyed an earthy green color.

Lace Open needlework fabric originally handmade. Now produced by machine. Often has net background with floral and geometric designs. Used for curtains and tablecloths.

Lampas Fabric having a rep ground with satinlike figures formed of warp threads and contrasting figures formed of weft thread. Drapery and upholstery.

Lining A term applied to plain cotton or sateen fabrics that line or back support draperies or other decorative textiles.

Marquisette A sheer lightweight leno woven textile used for glass curtains. Made of natural or man-made fibers. Looks like gauze.

Matelassé A double-woven heavyweight fabric with a quilted appearance. Derived from the French word *matelasser,* meaning "to cushion" or "to pad." Upholstery.

Moiré A wavy, watery effect pressed into a ribbed surface such as taffeta or faille. A lightweight fabric suitable for drapery, upholstery, or bedspreads.

Monk's cloth A coarse mediumweight fabric in a loose weave of flax, jute, or hemp mixed with cotton, generally in neutral colors. May have sagging problems.

Muslin Bleached or unbleached plain, lightweight cotton weave. Has many uses in decorating, especially in Early American and modern rooms. Walls, drapery, slipcovers. Solid colors or printed patterns.

Needlepoint A heavyweight handmade or Jacquard fabric. Fine and delicate effect is known as *petit point;* larger needle-point is known as *gros point.*

Net A sheer lacelike fabric with a consistent mesh texture available in a variety of fibers. Suitable for glass curtains.

Ninon A sheer plain tight weave used for glass curtains. Has a smooth, crisp gossamer appearance.

Organdy A sheer crisp cotton fabric with good pleating qualities. Available plain, embroidered, or printed. Glass curtains.

Osnaburg A light- to mediumweight fabric similar to homespun. A loose, uneven, coarse cotton with solid color or printed motifs.

Oxford A plain-weave fabric. Large filling yarn goes over two warp yarns. An informal fabric with many uses.

Paisley A printed design inspired by original motifs from India and shawl motifs from Paisley, Scotland. Exaggerated curved raindrop or pear shape most typical design. Lightweight to mediumweight. Usually cotton.

Percale A tightly woven and durable lightweight textile. Can be plain or printed. Most often used for bed sheets.

Pilling Formation of fiber fuzz balls on fabric surface by wear or friction, encountered in spun nylon, polyester, acrylic, cashmere, or soft woolen yarns.

Pique A mediumweight to heavyweight cotton textile with raised cords or geometric designs running lengthwise. Often used for bedspreads and curtains. Many variations of this textile type.

Plissé A lightweight fabric with a crinkled or puckered effect created by chemical treatment. Curtains.

Plush A heavyweight pile fabric with greater depth than velvet. Usually has a high sheen. Upholstery.

Polished cotton A plain- or satin-weave cotton cloth characterized by a sheen ranging from dull to bright. Polish can be achieved either through the weave or by the addition of a resin finish.

Pongee Term derived from Chinese words for "natural color." Made from wild silk and left in its natural tan color. Lightweight and durable. Used for curtains.

Poplin Lightweight. Similar to rep. Has a lightly corded surface running through the fabric. Made of natural or man-made fibers. Often used for draperies.

Quilted fabrics A pattern stitched through a printed or plain fabric and through a layer of batting. Outline quilting traces around the pattern of a printed fabric. Loom quilting is a small repetitive design made by the quilting alone. Ultrasonic quilting produces thermally bonded welds in place of stitching threads.

Rep Plain-weave, lightweight fabric with narrow rounded ribs running the width or length of the fabric. Usually a fine warp with heavier filling yarns. Drapery, upholstery, slipcovers, bedspreads, and other informal uses.

Sailcloth A mediumweight fabric in a plain weave similar to canvas. Popular for informal indoor or outdoor upholstery.

Sateen A highly lustrous fabric usually made of mercerized cotton with a satin weave. Drapery lining.

Satin *Plain:* Fine yarns woven to give a more lustrous surface. May be lightweight or heavy enough for upholstery. Has many decorative uses when a formal style of decor is desired. *Antique:* A smooth satin face highlighted by slub (or twisted) yarn in a random pattern. Today it is an important fabric for drapery.

Seersucker A lightweight fabric employing a special weaving process producing a permanently wrinkled or puckered striped effect.

Serge Twill weave with a hard clear finish. Made from rayon, silk, cotton, or wool.

Shantung A heavy pongee. Usually made of wild silk and has a textured striated surface. Antique satin simulates shantung.

Sheer General term for thin, lightweight textiles most often used for glass curtains, bed curtains, or window treatments.

Suede Leather with a napped surface. Polyester suede washes and wears well. Upholstery.

Swiss A fine, thin cotton textile originally made in Switzerland and often used for glass curtains. May be plain, but usually is embroidered or designed with dots (**dotted swiss**), or figures that have been chemically applied. Man-made fibers also used.

Taffeta *Plain:* Tight and crisp smooth weave with slight horizontal ribbed effect. When woven of silk, it is a luxury fabric for drapery, bedspreads, and lamp shades. *Antique* or *shantung:* A smooth, soft weave with random slub yarn creating a textured effect. A lustrous fabric with many decorative uses, especially drapery and lamp shades.

Tapestry A figured multicolored fabric woven on a Jacquard loom made up of two sets of warp and weft. The design is formed by varying weave effects brought to the surface in combination with colored yarns. The surface has a rough texture. A heavyweight upholstery fabric.

Terry cloth A mediumweight cotton or linen pile fabric. May be cut or uncut. Loops may be on one side or both. Bedspreads, upholstery, and towels.

Ticking A mediumweight tightly woven cotton or linen fabric. A strong, usually striped fabric in a satin or twill weave. Mattresses, pillows, wall coverings, slipcovers, and drapery.

Toile de Jouy. A floral or scenic design usually printed on a plain cotton or linen ground. Originally printed in Jouy, France.

Trapunto Quilting that raises an area design on the surface of upholstery fabric.

Tweed Plain-weave, heavyweight upholstery fabric with a tweed texture because of flake (or knotted yarn) in multicolors. Upholstery.

Union cloth Half linen and half cotton fabric that is plain or patterned. Coarse weave. A variety of uses.

Velour A French term loosely applied to all types of fabrics with a nap or cut pile on one side. Specifically, it is a cut-pile fabric similar to regular velvet but with a higher pile. Heavyweight upholstery fabric.

Velvet A heavyweight fabric having a short, thick warp pile. May be of any fiber. *Crushed:* Most often the fabric is pulled through a narrow cylinder to create the crushed effect. *Cut:* Jacquard design, usually cut and uncut pile on a plain ground. *Antique:* Velvet that has an old look. Upholstery.

Velveteen A heavyweight weft-pile fabric with short pile, usually of cotton. Drapery, upholstery, bedspreads, and innumerable uses.

Vinyl A heavy nonwoven plastic fabric capable of being printed or embossed to produce any desired finish such as a leather, wood, floral, or textured design. Cloth backing prevents tearing. Walls and upholstery.

Voile A fine, soft, sheer fabric in a variety of textures used for glass curtains.

Webbing Heavyweight jute, cotton, or synthetic strips, generally 1 to 4 in. wide. Interwoven and plain or printed. Particularly used for modern seating units. Can also be used to support springs for an upholstered piece.

TEXTILE CARE AND MAINTENANCE

Although this is not required, after a design project is complete, interior designers can offer the client a valuable service by providing manufacturers' manuals, booklets, and other care instructions. Knowledge of the cleaning properties of particular fabrics is essential for upkeep. Following are some basic items to consider in textile care and maintenance:

- *Soil-resistant finishes.* Water-repellent, soil-resistant or soil-repellent, and soil-release finishes are all chemical processes that increase a fabric's resistance to soil and help make cleaning easier. For example, Scotchgard is a trade name for a finish that makes the surface of the fabric stain resistant. Manufacturers' labels or instructions accompanying the fabric inform the consumer about what to look for, how often to clean, and how effective the finish is. Often the finish is given to the fabric at the mill; however, it may be possible to purchase the soil-resistant or water-repellent finish and manually apply it. The designer can offer the client information regarding soil-resistant finishes.

■ *Protection from the sun.* Many fabrics are susceptible to sun damage, and window glass magnifies the destructive element in the sun's rays. Even the winter sun and reflection from the snow can be harmful. Lined and interlined draperies help protect fabrics from the sun, especially when fragile materials are used. Blinds drawn during the day and exterior awnings are practical. Trees or shrubbery can also help protect windows.

ASSIGNMENT

The following assignment will determine the student's ability to coordinate compatible materials for floors, walls, windows, and upholstery.

1. Select two neutral, colored, gray, or black mat boards approximately 9 in. by 12 in. that complement the fabrics selected.

2. Follow the format for arranging fabrics found in the Student Packet.

3. Coordinate background colors, materials, and fabrics for two rooms. Each completed layout should contain the following sample materials:

Ceiling:	Usually painted white or an off-white to blend with room
Floor	Sample of flooring or floor covering
Walls:	Select wall treatment (paint, paper, fabric, paneling, etc.)
Wood trim:	Indicate paint or natural wood sample
Windows:	Select and present window treatment
Upholstery:	Include upholstery fabrics for particular rooms chosen

4. Mount fabric and carpet samples on small scraps of mat board. If the fabric is heavy, crop it to fit the boards. If it is lightweight, it may be better to wrap the board. Mount the finished samples to the mat board in the appropriate space outlined.

5. Use professional lettering to indicate the room type (e.g., informal family room, formal living room). The project should be neatly presented.

CHAPTER 6

Floors, Walls, and Ceilings

FIGURE 6.1 This extravagant and witty drawing room in the Kip's Bay Showhouse of 1992 was designed by Juan Pablo Molyneux. The elegant backgrounds, including walls, ceiling, floors, windows, and fireplace, clearly establish a formal, eclectic French style and support the 18th- and 19th-century furnishings. (Courtesy of F. J. Hakimian, Inc., NY, and Juan Pablo Molyneux. Photograph by Peter Vitale).

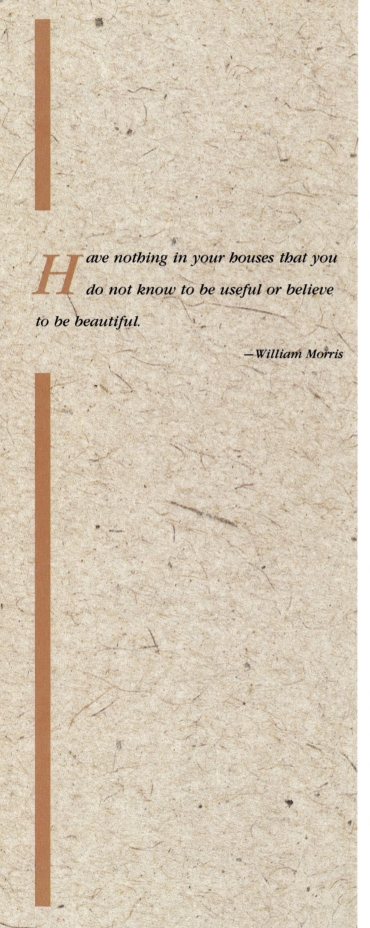

*T*he general scheme of any room is established by the architectural background: walls, floors, and ceilings, plus such items as fireplaces, doors, windows, paneling, and moldings. This is seen in Figure 6.1, where a theme of formality prevails. The decorative treatments added to these backgrounds, as well as to the movable objects in the room, should be in keeping with the overall feeling to give the room harmony and unity. Since backgrounds are for people, generally a wise choice is to make large areas—walls, floors, and ceilings—unobtrusive.

FLOORS AND FLOOR COVERINGS

Because of their function—primarily to be walked on and provide the foundation for other furnishings—floors, more than any other surface, take a great amount of abuse. After the floor's construction is complete, the task of covering this area is a major concern for the designer and client. The last decades have witnessed a renaissance in both hard-surface *nonresilient* and soft *resilient* floor coverings, with the market abounding in a variety of selections for every purpose and decor. Perhaps the most notable characteristic of today's materials is the merging of beauty and practicality due to improved technology, developments in old and new materials, and methods of production. Hard or soft flooring materials are no longer confined to particular areas of the house and may be used in any room. When deciding what type of floor covering is most suitable, the designer and the client need to determine whether the specific room (bedroom, entry, kitchen, family room, etc.) requires a hard or soft floor covering. Considerations include:

- The intended *function* (see Figure 6.2)
- The *number, age,* and *special needs of the occupants*
- The lifestyle of the occupants—*formal* or *informal*
- The *location* and *climate*
- Surface quality as a *safety factor* (stairways, nursery, rooms for elderly persons, etc.)
- *Code requirements,* including flame resistance, consideration for the physically challenged, and weight of materials
- *Acoustic properties* required for a specific area
- *Economic considerations*—initial expense plus long-term maintenance
- *Durability* required for a particular area
- *Style* qualities for a certain design direction
- *Personal preferences* of the occupants

HARD FLOORING

Nonresilient Flooring—Masonry

The term *resilient flooring* refers to the material's ability to spring back when pressed. *Nonresilient* flooring is not

FIGURE 6.2 Ceramic tile was selected for this nonresidential project because of its durable and aesthetic qualities. Light teal and peach tile arranged in repeated patterns visually divides the floor into measurable units, thus giving a sense of human scale to a very large space. (Courtesy of American Olean Tile Co.)

flexible. The initial cost of hard-surface nonresilient flooring is generally high. In long-range planning, however, this is more than compensated for by its extreme durability, versatility, ease of maintenance, and timeless usage. Hard-surface masonry flooring such as brick, stone, and tile remains popular. New setting methods for all types of masonry allow installation over most surfaces. The durable qualities of quarry, ceramic, and Mexican tile; stone; and wood allow these materials to be used throughout the home. They may flow from the inside entrance hall or family room out onto the porch or patio, thus expanding space, providing unity and beauty, and providing a practical surface requiring little upkeep.

Table 6.1 contains information on the most commonly used nonresilient hard floor coverings regarding

their characteristics and uses, plus some suggestions for treatment and care. (See Figures 6.3 through 6.7.)

Wood Flooring

Wood is considered the most versatile and is the most widely used of all flooring materials. It combines beauty, warmth, some resilience, resistance to indentation, durability, availability, and ease of installation. Wood floors provide a background for any style of furnishings, as seen in Figure 6.8. A standard flooring for centuries, wood waned in popularity during the first half of the twentieth century; currently, however, wood floors symbolize high fashion and are often chosen by designers and

TABLE 6.1 Hard-surface flooring: nonresilient

Material	Characteristics	Uses
Flagstone	Any flat stone that varies in size, thickness, quality, and color Versatile, durable, handsome Easy upkeep Colors range from soft grays through beiges and reddish browns May be cut or laid in natural shapes Surface slightly uneven Absorbs solar energy	Walks, patios, foyers, greenhouses, any heavy traffic area May be dressed up or down, making it appropriate for wide range of uses
Slate (specific type of stone)	More formal than flagstone Qualities similar to flagstone, except for color, which runs from gray to black Absorbs solar energy	May be used in traffic areas in formal rooms Appropriate for some period rooms—particularly sunrooms and dining rooms—and for greenhouses
Mexican tile or terra-cotta	Crude base made of unrefined clay Hand shaped and sun dried with smooth surface in limited range of colors Durable, informal, inexpensive Absorbs solar energy	Wherever a hard, cementlike surface is desired or wherever energy storage is desired
Concrete tile	May be solid or in squares, smooth or textured, polished or unpolished Color may be added before pouring or after Tile liner may be grouted to give a tile effect Absorbs and stores solar energy	Particularly desirable for some hardwear areas and for support of heavy equipment Tile patterns appropriate for foyers, penthouses, and any area where energy storage is required
Brick	Durable, little upkeep needed Comes in many textures, sizes, and colors Transmits moisture and cold readily and absorbs grease unless treated Absorbs and stores solar energy	Walks, patios, foyers, greenhouses, any room where a country look is desired
Exposed aggregate	Stones are laid in concrete and polished to smoothness, but surface remains uneven Absorbs and stores solar energy	Especially appropriate for walks and fireplace hearths
Quarry tile	Type of ceramic tile One of the hardest and most durable tiles May be glazed or unglazed Heat and frost resistant, easy upkeep, durable Both ceramic and quarry tile practically impervious to grease and chemicals Absorbs and stores solar energy	Suitable for many period rooms, especially Italian, early English, and rooms with Mediterranean feeling Can be used wherever hard surface is appropriate, such as in greenhouses Coolness makes it desirable in hot climates
Ceramic tile	Has unique aesthetic quality One of the hardest and most durable floor and wall coverings Common type using small squares is called mosaic May be glazed or unglazed; comes in many colors, patterns, and textures Glossy surface squares usually 4½ in. New developments producing handsome tiles 12-in. square with variety of designs, textures, and colors Pregrouted tile sheets up to 2 by 14 sq ft now available Absorbs and stores solar energy	Especially attractive for foyers, sunrooms, bathrooms, but may be suitable for any room depending on color, texture, and period of room

Treatment and Care	Advantages	Disadvantages
Careful waxing softens rugged effect and produces soft patina Coating of vinyl protects bricks from grease penetration Dust with dry mop, wash occasionally For stubborn stains, use trisodium phosphate	Easy upkeep May be cut or shaped in natural shapes Absorbs solar energy Versatile, durable, handsome	Expensive Difficult to repair if damaged Cold when not heated Does not absorb sound
May be polished or unpolished, but more often waxed and highly polished	Easy upkeep if sealed Same as for flagstone	Expensive Difficult to repair if damaged Cold when not heated Shows dust easily when polished
Care same as for terrazzo Surface seldom waxed	Durable Inexpensive Attractive for many styles of decor Absorbs solar energy Easy upkeep	Difficult to repair if damaged Cold when not heated Does not absorb sound
Heavy waxed surface necessary for maintenance Do not use lacquer, varnish, or shellac Special finishes available Wet before cleaning and use detergent Easy to maintain	Absorbs and stores solar energy Easy upkeep Inexpensive	Tends to give cold, industrial feeling when brought inside Does not absorb sound
Treatment and care same as for flagstone	Durable Little upkeep necessary Many uses Absorbs and stores solar energy Livable and interesting texture	Does not absorb sound Rough to touch Absorbs grease unless treated Transmits moisture and cold readily
Dust, wash occasionally	Same as for concrete	Rough to touch Same as for concrete
Unglazed: may be waxed to give soft sheen Glazed: dust with dry mop, wash when needed with soap and warm water	One of the hardest and most durable tiles Heat and frost resistant Easy upkeep, durable Flexible use for many styles Absorbs and stores solar energy Attractive appearance Variety of shapes to select Inexpensive	Similar to those for Mexican tile
Care same as for quarry tile	Very hard and durable A great variety of colors, textures, and patterns Absorbs and stores solar energy Can be used effectively in almost any space	Expensive Similar to those for quarry tile

TABLE 6.1, *continued*

Material	Characteristics	Uses
Marble	Hardest of nonresilient flooring materials Now available in many varieties Marble gives feeling of elegance More expensive than most other flooring materials, but is permanent New stone-cutting techniques have made marble lighter and less expensive Tiles are reinforced by epoxy–fiberglass coating	Wherever elegant durability is needed Especially appropriate with classic styles of furnishing
Granite	An igneous hard stone of cooled molten rock Has a fine- or coarse-grain (crystal or grain) texture Main colors are variations of gray, brown, black, pink, green, yellow, or combinations of these colors Has a coarse finish or can be polished until it shines Easy to cut for various uses Harder than marble	Floors, walls, tabletops, countertops, and steps Highly durable and excellent for heavy traffic areas Especially popular for nonresidential projects
Travertine	Porous limestone characterized by irregular cavities that should be filled with either clear or opaque epoxy resin Clear resin has three-dimensional appearance	In formal settings where durability is required
Terrazzo	Consists of cement mortar (matrix) into which marble chips (aggregate) are mixed Custom or precast; comes in large or small marble chips Larger chips give more formal appearance Available in limited range of colors Sanitary, durable, and easy to clean	Patios, foyers, halls, recreation rooms, bathrooms, or wherever traffic is heavy
Glass tile	Modules 1⅝ in. by 3/16 in. of impervious and homogenous glass Stable, inert, and nonporous with nonslip surface Unaffected by fire, heat, or frost Available in white and some earth tones May be custom colored Easy maintenance	Suitable for dark areas Adaptable for walls or floors
Glass block or vista-brick	Solid glass blocks 8 in. by 8 in. by 3 in. offer excellent light transmission, good visibility, and provide high-impact strength	Used as pavers, covers for light fixtures recessed in floor
Poured seamless vinyl	Plastic from a can Has glossy surface Nonslippery Easy to maintain	Kitchens, bathrooms, family rooms

homeowners. New methods of treatment have made wood a practical flooring for any area of the house.

Methods of Laying Wood Floors

The three basic methods of laying wood floors are in *strips, planks,* and **parquetry**. In the first method strips of wood, usually about 2½ in. wide with **tongue and groove**, are nailed in place. In the plank method, the planks may be uniform or **random**, varying in width from 3 in. to 7 in. Some have square edges; others are tongue and groove. The parquetry method makes use of short lengths of boards, arranging them in various designs such as checkerboard and herringbone. (See Figure 6.9.) For ease of installation and economy, 9- to 12-in. squares are assembled at the factory.

Wood Veneer

Sometimes a thin layer of hardwood is veneered to a less expensive wood, such as prefabricated parquet squares

Treatment and Care	Advantages	Disadvantages
Wash with soap and warm water	Good selection of colors and veining Elegant and luxurious Used for many formal styles Durable and permanent Easy maintenance	Very expensive Cold to touch Difficult to repair if damaged Does not absorb sound Slippery when wet
Easy maintenance: sweep clean; wipe with water when necessary	Same as for marble	Expensive Same as for marble
Wash with soap or detergent and warm water	Similar to those for marble	Similar to those for marble
Dust with dry mop, wash occasionally with detergent Some varieties need occasional waxing	Similar to those for marble	Similar to those for marble
Clean with detergent and warm water	Unaffected by fire, heat, or frost Easy maintenance Streamlined surface and "look" for modern settings Insulates Fairly durable	Can break Moderately expensive May give commercial look
Clean with detergent and warm water	Similar to those for glass tile	Similar to those for glass tile
Does not require waxing Clean with soap and warm water Avoid heavy detergents	Inexpensive Easy to clean Suitable where no seams are desired Safe, nonskid surface	Slippery when wet Hardness and texture not as pleasant as other materials

veneered and finished at the factory. These veneers are less expensive than solid wood, but they will not hold up as well under heavy wear. Sometimes thin layers of wood are laminated to a backing, making it durable and more resilient. Hardwood veneer is placed under a surface of vinyl sheeting to protect it from moisture, wear, and household chemicals. The veneer is backed with aluminum, vinyl, and asbestos to ensure a permanent, moisture-free bond to almost any subfloor. This veneer is available in a variety of woods and is generally maintained the same way as vinyl.

Plastic- (Acrylic-) Impregnated Wood Floors

Acrylic-wood flooring is a development in which real wood is impregnated with a liquid plastic hardened throughout the pore structure by irradiation. The result is a floor with the warmth of wood and remarkable durability tough enough to withstand the heaviest foot traffic. It is available in 12-in.-square prefinished parquet tiles, 5/16-in. thick, and comes in a variety of tones. Installation cost is comparable to that for other high-quality materials like terrazzo. Acrylic-wood flooring is an answer to the increasing demand for flooring with a

FIGURE 6.3 Dark slate arranged in a circular pattern provides a durable and attractive floor surface in this health spa in Atlantic City, New Jersey. (Courtesy of The Structural Slate Co.)

FIGURE 6.4 This handsome contemporary room is well planned, comfortable, and uncluttered. The deep-pile rug against the unglazed quarry tile floor and the undraped windows offset by well-placed plants are a fitting background for classic modern furniture. (Courtesy of American Olean Tile Company.)

FIGURE 6.5 This terrazzo floor with marble chips (aggregate) in a matrix (cement mortar) is used in a commercial setting and is an excellent flooring material for heavy use. It also provides an interesting floor texture that supports the dramatic design. (Courtesy of the National Terrazzo and Mosaic Association, Inc.)

FIGURE 6.6 Marble is one of the most elegant and luxurious surfacing stones. In this lavish bath the marble floor and walls are handsome and durable. (Photograph by Tim Street-Porter.)

FIGURE 6.7 A streamlined office design is enhanced by granite flooring providing an elegant and sophisticated atmosphere. (Photograph by Mark Boisclair.)

FIGURE 6.8 The warmth of a wood floor has timeless appeal. In this room the wood flooring creates a feeling of unity as well as beauty and becomes a durable and flexible background for other furnishings. The white band below the platform edge is a safety feature. (Courtesy of Bruce Hardwood Floors.)

natural mellow look that is durable and requires little maintenance. Because of its physical characteristics, acrylic-wood flooring is finding increased acceptance among designers as an alternative to natural untreated wood and other hard-surface flooring materials, particularly in high-traffic areas.

Particle Board

Particle board is made of pressed sawdust and small wood chips. It is most often used for subflooring.

Stained Wood Floors

Wood flooring need not be only in the familiar tones of natural wood but may also be as varied in color as fabric. Colored stain may be applied in basically the same way as a natural finish without obliterating the natural grain of the wood. Some color tones emphasize the pattern in the wood and may even produce a three-dimensional effect. This effect can be achieved by a *stain and sealer* method, in which only the surface is stained and then sealed with polyurethane, or the *stain wax* method, in which the

FIGURE 6.9 Patterns of wood floors.

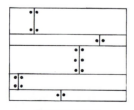

Random plank

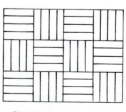

Checkerboard parquet

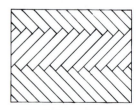

Herringbone parquet

stain penetrates into the wood, leaving a wax residue on the surface. When the latter process is repeated and the wood is thoroughly rubbed, the surface has a soft, protective **patina**. Preparation, application, and maintenance of wood with color stain is the same as for natural stain. Some currently popular stains like platinum give wood a *bleached* effect.

Stenciled and Painted Wood Floors

Stenciling, a process of applying paint through a stencil, was used historically as a substitute for expensive carpets. Today, stenciled floors are still an attractive alternative.

Resilient Flooring—Vinyl

The development of vinyl for floor use is in large measure responsible for the new interest in hard floor coverings. The effects that are being produced in vinyl are limitless (see Figure 6.10). Vinyl can be clear or vividly colored, translucent or opaque, textured or satin smooth. It comes in 6- and 12-ft *sheets* and *tiles,* or in a *can.* Vinyl is most often used in an informal scheme. Resilient hard-surface vinyl floors were once used only for kitchens, utility rooms, and bathrooms, but their present-day ele-

gance has admitted them into any room of the house. Small patterns mask tracking and spillage, pebble vinyls achieve a natural stone effect, and embossed patterns are reminiscent of Old World designs such as Moorish tile, travertine, and marble. An all-purpose vinyl in sheet or tile requires no adhesive. A conductive tile is made especially for hospitals and chemical and electronic laboratories as a safety measure to protect against the hazard of static electricity. A foam-cushion backing makes it possible to have a practical vinyl surface with the luxurious feel of carpet.

One drawback might include the negative appearance vinyl can have when simulating a natural material. Also, when the surface is textured with grooves, cleaning is a problem.

Table 6.2 lists characteristics, uses, and methods of care of resilient hard-surface floors.

SOFT FLOOR COVERINGS
History of Rugs and Carpets

As early as 3000 B.C., carpets were used in Egypt, and writers of the Bible and poets of early Greece and Rome

FIGURE 6.10 A midnight blue vinyl tile has been specified in this kitchen for its function as well as aesthetic qualities. The vinyl complements the patterned wallpaper and blue and white Delft floral ceramic tile. (Photograph by the makers of Armstrong vinyl flooring.)

TABLE 6.2 Hard-surface flooring: resilient

Material	Characteristics	Uses
Asphalt tile	Low in cost, durable Due to advanced technology, is being phased out	Wherever hard-surface, low-cost flooring is required
Cork tile	Provides maximum quiet and cushiony comfort underfoot Cork with vinyl or urethane surface highly resistant to wet and stains, but natural cork not suited for abuse of kitchen traffic, water damage, etc. Colors light to dark brown Dented by furniture	Especially appropriate for studies and other rooms with little traffic
Leather tile	Resilient, quiet, but expensive Natural or dyed colors	Studies and other limited areas with little traffic
Vinyl asbestos Vinyl composition or Reinforced vinyl	Excellent all-around low-cost flooring Available in tile or sheets Resists stains and wears well Hard and noisy Tiles may have self-adhesive backing Popularity has declined	May be used in any room
Vinyl cork	Has appearance of cork, but resists stain and easy to maintain Colors richer than natural cork	Wherever effect of real cork is desired
Vinyl tile	Tough, nonporous, resistant to stains, durable Comes in clear colors or special effects, including translucent and three-dimensional effects The more vinyl content, the higher the price Comes in great variety of patterns and colors	Extremely versatile, may be used in any room
Cushion-backed vinyl	Vinyl chips embedded in translucent vinyl base Has pebbly surface Shows no seams Goes on any floor Has cushion backing, making it resilient	Wherever desired
Sheet vinyl	Lies flat with adhesive only on sides Excellent do-it-yourself product	Wherever vinyl flooring is desired
Rubber tile	Tiles available 9 in. by 12 in., thickness ½ in. and ³⁄₁₆ in. Usually marble or travertine pattern laid at right angles to each other Sound absorbing, durable, nonskidding	Kitchens, bathrooms, utility rooms
Sheet rubber	Available in 36-by-¾ in. untrimmed widths Plain or marbleized Durable, nonskidding	Hard traffic areas Safe covering for stair treads
Vinylized fabric	Has appearance of vinyl Fabric bonded between layers of vinyl	Wherever specific pattern is desired

Treatment and Care	Advantages	Disadvantages
Coat of water-emulsion wax improves surface Use mild soap for cleaning	Inexpensive Fairly easy upkeep	Breaks easily Difficult to find Not as attractive or durable as other flooring
Maintenance not easy Dirt hard to dislodge from porous surface Wash with soap and water, coat with wax Vinyl coating protects surface	Easy to clean Rich color and texture Good insulation properties	Shows dust easily Not durable, dents easily Fairly expensive Not good when solar energy is desired
Warm water and mild soap	Quiet Luxurious look and feel Cleans well Rich colors, can be embossed	Very expensive Not durable Limited use
Exceptionally easy to maintain	Low-cost flooring Resists stains, wears well Very easy to maintain	Hard, does not absorb sound Not as attractive May be health hazard
Wash with soap and water; wax	Rich color and texture Resists stains More durable than real cork Easy to maintain	Not suitable where solar gain is needed Tendency to show dust and footprints
Easy care Some varieties have built-in luster and require no waxing	Tough, nonporous, stain-resistant, durable Wide variety of colors, textures, and patterns Versatile uses	Moderate cost The more vinyl, the higher the cost
Easy care, same as for other vinyl	More resilient Similar to those for vinyl tile	May tear or dent Similar to those for vinyl tile
Same as for other vinyl	Lies flat Similar to those for vinyl tile	If it has grooves, difficult to clean When strong pattern, may be tiresome Similar to those for vinyl tile
Wash with soap and water Avoid varnish or shellac	Easy to clean Durable, nonskidding Sound absorbing, good traction Safe when wet Raised surface knocks off dirt Excellent for nonresidential use	Relatively expensive
Same as for rubber tile	Same as those for rubber	Same as those for rubber
Same as for vinyl	Easy to clean Wide variety of colors and patterns	Cost may be high If patterned, may be visually tiring

mention carpets, although walking on such floor coverings was usually the prerogative of royalty. Colorful Oriental rugs have been produced in Persia, Turkey, China, and other Asiatic countries for centuries, where they were the principal item of home furnishing. In the Middle Ages, when the later Crusaders came into contact with the elegance and luxury of Constantinople, Antioch, and other Eastern cities, they carried back many of these fine rugs and created a great demand in the West, on which the Eastern trading companies capitalized from the fifteenth to the nineteenth centuries. These fine floor coverings soon became a symbol of status in Europe and America. Since the time when the first rug looms were established in Aubusson, France, weaving of fine floor coverings has been a continuously growing industry, with still greater volume predicted for the future.

Machine-Made Carpets

A number of factors have been responsible for the demand for machine-made carpets in the past few decades. Among them,

1. New and improved fibers, which have given consumers carpeting with the properties they have demanded at a reasonable cost
2. The fact that many Americans no longer view carpeting as a luxury, but as a necessity (it has been made standard equipment in most building projects and is often written into the contract)
3. The fact that carpeting is one of the few products offering more value per dollar than it did thirty years ago

Functional Values

A carpet insulates the floor against drafts, muffles noise, gives a feeling of comfort, and provides safety. A well-anchored carpet gives sure footing and helps prevent accidents. Additionally, carpets are easy to maintain with thorough vacuuming.

Decorative Values

A carpet can be the basis for the room's entire decor, as seen in Figure 6.11. It can bring furnishings into harmony, create personality and a feeling of luxury, and alter

FIGURE 6.11 In this comfortable living room designed by Michael R. LaRocca, the large patterned rug is the basis for the room's decor. The coral has been picked up from the rug for the wingback chair and lightened in value for the walls. Other colors in the rug have been used for accents to complement the total design. (Courtesy of F. J. Hakimian, Inc., NY and Michael R. LaRocca, Ltd. Photograph by Phillip Ennis.)

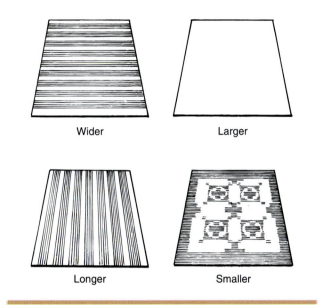

Wider

Larger

Longer

Smaller

FIGURE 6.12 Carpet can change the apparent size and proportion of a room.

the apparent size and proportion of a room (see Figure 6.12). The same carpet carried throughout the living areas of the home can serve as a transition from room to room, providing a feeling of unity. An art rug may be a room's focal point.

Quality of Soft Floor Coverings

Quality in carpeting depends on four ingredients: (1) the type and grade of fiber, (2) the depth of pile, (3) the density of pile, and (4) the construction.

Fiber. Over the years, virtually every fiber has been used in carpets. Today, however, about 90 percent of all carpeting sold in the United States is composed of synthetic fibers, principally nylon, acrylic, polyester, and olefin. Wool is the most-used natural fiber. Fibers are often blended to bring out the best characteristics of each. To affect quality, at least 20 percent of one fiber must be present. The carpet label provides the percentage by weight of the fibers.

Each company producing these fibers has developed variants adding to the fibers' practical and aesthetic qualities, such as better soil resistance, less static, more dyeing possibilities, more bulk, and more luster. Since each manufacturer needs to use a special name to designate its product in the carpet industry, a myriad of trade names are on the market. The generic name is therefore the key to determining fiber content.

Nylon. Nylon is the single most important synthetic fiber, accounting for about 90 percent of carpeting sold today. Nylon has excellent abrasion resistance; resists crushing and matting; and reduces static electricity, **pilling**, and fuzzing. It repels soil and cleans well, particularly in spot cleaning for stains. It is nonallergenic and is

mold-, mildew-, and mothproof. When combined with polyester, the two complementary fibers' specific strengths offset their respective weaknesses. Antron and Anso are new fourth-generation nylon fibers that have excellent performance features and exceptional soil and stain resistance.

Acrylic. Acrylic is much like wool in appearance. Its outstanding characteristic is solution dyeability. Resistance to abrasion and soiling is good. It cleans exceptionally well and has good crush resistance, but it is susceptible to some pilling. Orlon and Acrilan are popular trade names.

Polyester. Polyester is an exceptionally soft fiber offering good abrasion resistance. It combines the look and feel of wool with a durability approaching that of nylon. Stain and soil resistance are good, and it is easily cleaned. Although polyester has great bulk and bounce, it has a tendency to crush and pill. Trade names include Fortrel, Kodel, and Dacron.

Olefin. Olefin is another fiber of the 1960s. Polypropylene is a specific type of olefin and is the best known. It is predominant in needle-punch carpets, which are especially popular for kitchen and indoor-outdoor carpets. Ease of care and a nonabsorbent nature are its outstanding characteristics. Most stains lie on the surface, making it the easiest fiber to clean. Wearing qualities are comparable to nylon, and it is completely colorfast. Resilience can be controlled by construction. Polyethylene is also a specific olefin. Herculon is one popular trade name.

Wool. Wool is the luxury fiber and has long been regarded as the top carpet fiber. Other fibers express their aesthetic qualities in relation to how nearly they resemble wool. Great resilience accounts for the vital quality of wool in retaining its appearance. Wool has warmth, a dull matte look, durability, and soil resistance. It takes colors beautifully, cleans well, and when cared for, keeps its new look for years. Although relatively more expensive than synthetic fibers, natural wool maintains its prestigious position in the carpet field.

Cotton. Although not as durable or resilient as wool and synthetic fibers, *cotton* is soft, takes dye well, and is less expensive. It is used most often for flat woven area rugs like dhurries from India. Often, cotton strips are braided into rugs and used in informal settings.

Sisal, Jute, and Hemp. Sisal, jute, *hemp* and other grasses are inexpensive floor coverings generally limited to area or room-size rugs. These fibers can be woven into simple or intricate designs and are often made in sections and attached. Although they provide a natural look, they are not as comfortable underfoot. These cellulosic fibers are used most often in tropical climates. Japanese tatami mats are made from grasses; however, they are flammable and not durable.

Depth and Density of Pile. Pile depth and density affect carpet wear. Because deeper pile or a density of pile requires more yarn, it will be more durable. Density—the number of threads per square inch—can be examined by bending back a piece of carpet. If there are wide spaces between the threads or wide gaps between rows and large amounts of backing show, the carpet probably will not wear well. With shorter clipped carpets, density is especially important.

Construction Methods. Because of many new technical developments, the old and well-known weaves no longer account for the bulk of present-day carpets. Most carpets on the market today are tufted, with woven, needle-punched, knitted, and flocked carpets accounting for the remainder.

The performance of a carpet also depends on the *degree of twist* and the *heat setting of the fiber*. A tight twist helps the fiber spring back under crushing foot traffic, and proper heat setting prevents unraveling.

Tufting. Tufting accounts for approximately 90 percent of all carpet construction today. Based on the principle of the sewing machine, this method involves the insertion of thousands of threaded needles into a backing material. Heavy latex coating is applied to the backing to anchor the tufts permanently. Some have a double backing for greater strength. Although tufted carpets are generally made in solid colors, advances in dyeing technology make it possible to produce multicolor effects. Pattern attachments produce textural effects.

Weaving. Weaving once accounted for 90 percent of all broadloom produced. This amount was cut to less than 10 percent during the early seventies. The three types of woven carpets are Wilton, Axminster, and velvet, illustrated in Figure 6.13. The *Wilton* carpet takes its name from the town in England where it was first made in 1740. It is woven on a loom with a special Jacquard attachment. The yarns are carried along the background of the carpet until they are drawn to the surface to form loops. After more than 200 years, the Wilton carpet is still regarded as a standard of high quality.

The *Axminster* carpet also derives its name from the town in England where it was first manufactured in 1755. Originally a hand-knotted carpet, it is now made on a specialized American loom in which yarns are set in a crosswise row, permitting each tuft to be controlled individually. This process makes possible an almost unlimited combination of colors and patterns.

Velvet, the simplest form of carpet weaving, is traditionally a smooth-surface pile, cut or uncut in a solid color. The pile loops of velvet carpet are woven over long wires extending the full length of the carpet.

Needle-Punching. Needle-punch construction until recently has been used almost entirely for indoor–outdoor carpet. In this process an assembly of corded fiber webs is compacted and held together by felting needles that mechanically interlock the fibers. The back is coated with latex or other weather-resistant materials. This method can produce a wide variety of textures and the carpet sells at a low cost.

Flocking. Flocked carpets have short clipped fibers providing the appearance of velour. They may be produced by three basic methods: by beater bars, by spraying, and by an electrostatic method—the latter accounting for most flocked carpets. In this process, chopped fibers introduced into an electrostatic field become charged and then projected toward a backing fabric coated with adhesive, where they become vertically embedded.

Braiding. Braiding rugs by hand using small scraps of fabric—often from old clothing or bedding—dates back many centuries. The braids are sewn together to form a rug. Today braided rugs are both handcrafted and machine-made.

Hooking. Hooking also dates back many centuries and is still a method of construction often preferred by those who enjoy handcrafted products. Hooked rugs are made by forcing pile yarns through a backing (usually wool), allowing the craftsworker to create any design or color combination. Scandinavian rya rugs are one type of hooked rug.

FIGURE 6.13 Three types of woven carpets.

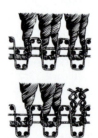

Axminster carpet. Top diagram shows differrent colored yarns. Bottom diagram shows use of curled down yarns for multilevel effect in face of carpet. (Courtesy of James Lees and Sons Company.)

Wilton carpet (loop pile). Pile is woven over strips of metal, which are removed during weaving process.

Velvet carpet (cut pile). Backing of jute and cotton holds pile yarn in place.

FIGURE 6.14 Surface characteristics of carpet.

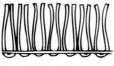
Cut or plush

Saxony

Random shear

Velour

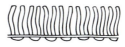
Frieze

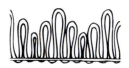
Multilevel loop

Shag

Level loop

Sculptured

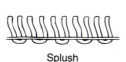
Splush

Level tip shear

Carpet Backings. The unseen part of a carpet—the backing—is important because a good foundation prevents stretching, buckling, and shrinking. The backing yarns should be firmly woven. Jute, the most widely used fiber, is strong but may mildew and is therefore not suitable where floors may be damp, such as in some basements or outdoors. Polypropylene resists mildew, is also strong, and may give better service where dampness is a problem. Tufted carpets should have a secondary backing applied for extra strength. It may be jute, polypropylene, rubber, or vinyl. All but jute and high-density rubber are placed on carpet for outdoor use.

Style Characteristics of Carpets

Definite style characteristics may be chosen within the categories of *cut pile* or *uncut loop pile,* with a variety of lengths determining the texture and design. The following are the surface characteristics produced in most fibers. (See Figure 6.14.)

- *Level-loop pile* has looped tufts all the same height. This low-cost carpet often has a foam or rubber backing and is usually used for kitchens and bathrooms, and in commercial settings.
- *Plush,* or velvet, has a dense upright and evenly cut pile under 1 in. in height. The luxurious carpet is enhanced by highlights and shadings, which provide an extra dimension. Plush carpets are generally more appropriate for formal areas.
- *Velour* is a style similar to cut velvet but is denser and has a much shorter pile. It is very durable.
- *Tip or random shear* has both cut and uncut pile. Random or tip shear is similar to multilevel loop, except the highest loops are sheared, providing a simple patterned effect.

- *Multilevel loop* surfaces have loops at several different heights. This carpet is practical, hides footprints, and masks spots and soiling. *Tweeds* are of this type—looped with a decided texture, often with a high–low pile of multicolored yarns.
- *Embossed* (also a type of sculptured) carpets are woven with high and low pile. The pile may be all loop, all cut, or a combination. This carpet style is one of the most popular.
- Custom-designed hand-*sculptured* carpet is one in which part of the surface has been cut away to form a pattern, or the pattern itself has been cut away from the background. This carpet style is often custom-made and more expensive.
- *Frieze* has a tightly twisted yarn, giving a rough, nubby appearance. Friezes are available in light and hard twists. Hard twists lie flat, keep a fresh appearance, and are less likely to show signs of wear.
- *Splush* is a term used to describe carpets with a pile height between shag and plush. It has a more textured surface compared to plush.
- *Shag* carpets have pile yarns that are more than 1 in. in height, may be looped or uncut, and provide an informal look. Many shags are generally low in density; however, during the past five years higher quality shags have been produced. The pile has a tendency to bend over or crush.
- *Saxony* is a combination of plush and short shag, twisted and heat set under high temperature and pressure, producing a deep, rich surface. It is wear resistant.
- *Flat-woven* cellulosic fiber rugs are machine-made of coarse flax fiber, paper pulp or "kraft" fiber, sisal, hemp, and various other grasses and rushes. They come in 1-ft squares to be sewn together or in full-

FIGURE 6.15 The flooring for the large lobby space in the KNIX country-western radio station had to be durable and wear resistant. A medium gray textured carpet was selected for the primary traffic pattern. A more luxurious rug defines a seating area for visitors. (Photograph by Pam Singleton.)

sized rugs. Fiber rugs are usually in natural colors but are sometimes dyed. Popular in warm climates, they also provide inexpensive year-round floor coverings in many contemporary settings. Other flat-woven styles include dhurries from India, Navajo rugs from America, and Rollikans from Scandinavia.

■ *Patterned* carpets of all kinds are gaining in popularity. A printing process, basically a screen-printing technique, has contributed to the interest in patterned floors. At first just simple geometrics, printed designs are now numerous and highly refined for any type of decor. Patterned carpets are also being produced by standard methods—particularly Axminster—and are becoming a fashion item in residential and commercial interiors.

Carpets for Specific Needs

■ *Room size* is important. Where space is limited, wall-to-wall carpets in solid colors or overall texture give a feeling of spaciousness. Large patterns tend to fill up space and are usually better reserved for more spacious areas.

■ For *heavy-traffic areas* such as family rooms, stairways, and passageways or in nonresidential settings, it is wise to select a good-quality carpet that wears well and is crush and soil resistant, as seen in Figure 6.15.

■ *Furniture style* is a consideration. The carpet can help express the character of the furniture, whether traditional or modern, formal or casual. Carefully chosen carpet can coordinate all furnishings of the room and provide unity.

FIGURE 6.16 The felted and uniquely textured carpet in natural shades flecked with color and blended with stretch wool, and the wool upholstery in fluid gem tones and classic designs, are equally appropriate for home or office. (Courtesy of the Wool Bureau.)

- A room's particular *lighting situation* must be evaluated. A sunny room may call for a carpet in cool colors or deep shades. For a northern exposure or dark room, one of the warm colors in lighter tones may be a better choice. Fibers, style characteristics, and textures of carpet absorb and reflect light differently.
- *Color* is important because the floor is the largest usable area of the room, the least often changed, and the background for all other furnishings. *Personal taste* can be the determining factor, but much thought and experimenting with samples will help make the decision a wiser one. A neutral, medium-colored carpet shows dirt less than a darker or a very light-colored one.
- Each carpet or rug type has a unique texture, for example, smooth, shiny, dull, rough, etc. (See Figure 6.16.) The surface quality of the carpet should be aesthetically *compatible* with other furnishings.
- If the carpet selected has a pronounced *pattern,* then walls, drapery, and upholstery tend to be complemented when plain colors or unobtrusive patterns are employed. (See Figure 6.17.) Carpets with a plain overall effect permit a wider choice of furnishings.
- *Upkeep and maintenance* are determining factors when selecting a carpet. Carpets that resist soil and are easy to clean cut down on labor and costs, thus keeping their attractive appearance longer.

Codes and Regulations

Federal, state, and local laws or codes and regulations set particular standards (particularly pertaining to flame resistance) regarding the performance and quality of a floor covering. The manufacturer is required to attach a label to the floor covering indicating (1) the name of the manufacturer with the Federal Trade Commission number, (2) the fiber content, (3) the weight of the fiber, and (4) flame-resistant qualities. Building codes vary in different areas; therefore, the designer must be knowledgeable about local codes and regulations before specifying a particular floor covering.

Rug and Carpet Sizes

Size is another consideration in selecting a carpet or rug. For convenience, the terms *rug* and *carpet* are often used interchangeably, although technically they are not the same. A *carpet* is a floor covering made in strips and often attached to the floor. Carpeting is woven in widths from 27 in.- to 18-ft-wide widths known as **broadloom.** Strips

FIGURE 6.17 A richly colored area rug in a contemporary eclectic setting in Connecticut is placed on a diagonal, defining the arrangement of furnishings. The placement of an exquisitely patterned Oriental rug in a clean structural background can enhance each by sheer contrast, bringing out the finest qualities of both. (Photograph by Norman McGrath.)

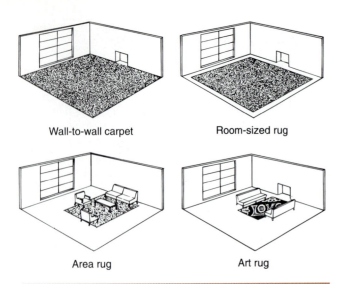

Wall-to-wall carpet

Room-sized rug

Area rug

Art rug

FIGURE 6.18 Rug sizes.

can be seamed or taped together and thus can cover great areas. A piece of carpet can be used as a rug.

A *rug* is a floor covering made in one piece, often with its own delineating border, and usually not intended to cover the entire floor. (Refer to Figure 6.18.)

Wall-to-wall carpeting has some distinct advantages: It creates continuity within a room or from room to room, makes rooms look larger, adds warmth and a feeling of luxury, requires only one cleaning process, and provides maximum safety from accidents. This carpeting treatment also has some disadvantages: It must be cleaned on the floor, it cannot be turned for even wear, and only part can be salvaged if moved.

A *room-sized rug* is one that comes within a few inches or even a foot or so of the walls, leaving a marginal strip of floor exposed. Standard-sized rugs will fit most rooms; the 9-by-12-ft rug is probably the most common. The room-sized rug has most of the advantages of wall-to-wall carpeting, plus some extra benefits. It can be turned for even distribution of wear and removed for cleaning. Two processes, however, are necessary for complete cleaning—one for the rug and the other for the exposed flooring material around it, usually wood.

An *area rug* does not cover the entire floor but is used to define an area of a room according to its function. The rug should, however, be large enough to accommodate all the furniture used in the area grouping. The appropriateness of the size depends on the room in which it is used. For example, in a large room a 9-by-12-ft rug might be considered an area rug. This type of rug is versatile and may easily be changed for different grouping arrangements or moved to a different room of the house.

An *art rug*, which is usually smaller than an area rug, is generally handcrafted and used as an accent or treated as a focal point. This rug is often placed so that furniture does not encroach on it, enabling it to be admired like a piece of art on the floor. Usually patterned, it may be

modern or traditional, such as a fine Oriental, an eighteenth-century needlepoint, an Indian dhurrie, or a custom-made modern design. Often an art rug functions as an area rug.

Scatter or *throw* rugs are smaller rugs often used as accents or as protection for a spot that receives hard wear.

Carpet Underlay

Before a carpet is laid, a pad or cushion is installed directly on the hard floor surface. Every carpet requires a good underlay, which provides tremendous value for the initial cost. Cushioning improves and helps to maintain the appearance of the carpet; enhances the resiliency, which helps prevent pile matting; and prolongs the life of the carpet from 50 to 75 percent. It also absorbs noise and creates a feeling of luxury. Even low and moderately priced carpet, when laid over a good pad, will take on the feeling of cushioned elegance.

There are six basic types of carpet underlay:

1. *Solid foam* underlays are made of prime urethane. They are firm, resilient, durable, and not affected by heat or moisture. Their cost is higher than bonded foam.
2. *Bonded foam* underlays are made of reconstituted urethane and are usually 9/16 in. thick. They are not affected by heat or cold, go on almost any surface, hold up well, and are moderately priced. This type of padding accounts for the highest percentage of underlay sold.
3. *Waffle sponge* is made of natural or synthetic rubber with a variety of fabric backings. This type of pad may deteriorate in the presence of heat or moisture.
4. *Flat sponge rubber* is made of natural or synthetic rubber with a variety of finishes and fabric backings. This type is used less than foam.
5. *Fiber* cushion underlays are made of jute, animal hair, rubber-coated jute, or combinations of plain or rubber-coated jute with animal hair. This type of pad is firm and extremely durable, but high cost limits its volume of sale.
6. *Carpet with attached cushioning* accounts for approximately 20 percent of all carpet sold today. This type of carpet can easily be picked up and relaid—a feature popular for those who move often or want to rotate a carpet to other areas of the home.

From this array of carpet cushioning, the choice should be based on individual needs, taking into consideration the condition of the floor, the amount of traffic, the function of the area to be covered, and the carpet being used.

Measuring and Installation

Before installing the selected floor covering it is necessary to figure the amount of material needed to complete the job. This process is almost always performed by a professional. To arrive at an estimate, however, determine the total area of the space to be covered and divide by 9 (the number of square feet in a yard). This will give the square yardage needed. Allow extra yardage for piecing the rug and for matching pattern repeats.

Installation Methods. When specifying carpet for a residential or nonresidential project the designer indicates installation methods and techniques. There are two basic installation methods. (1) The *stretch or tackless strip and pad method* employs a 1½-inch-wide plywood strip with small projecting metal pins. This strip is nailed around the perimeter of the room and the pad is nailed, glued, or stapled inside the strip. The carpet is stretched over the pad and then attached over the pins of the strip. (2) In the *glue-down method* glue or adhesive (either permanent or one that allows the release of the carpet when needed, such as double-faced tape) is applied to attach the carpet and pad to the floor. If no pad is used, the carpet is glued directly to the floor. No matter which method is used, the carpet should be laid so that the seams are smooth and the pile is uniform in direction to prevent light variations.

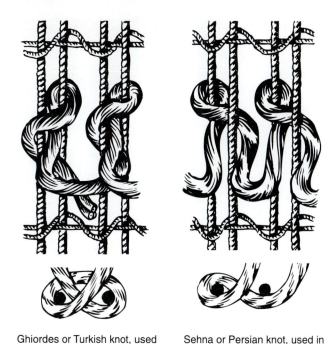

Ghiordes or Turkish knot, used in Turkey and elsewhere

Sehna or Persian knot, used in many parts of Iran

FIGURE 6.19 Principal knots used in making Oriental rugs.

Handmade Rugs

Oriental Rugs

The making of Oriental rugs is a great art, and the rugs have been coveted possessions for hundreds of years. During the eighteenth and nineteenth centuries, rugs from China and the Middle East were in great demand among well-to-do Americans who wanted such rugs to adorn their Georgian and Federal-period mansions. Not until late in the nineteenth century, however, were the rugs imported in great numbers.

With the advent of wall-to-wall carpeting, Oriental rugs went out of fashion in America, but during the past few decades they have been rediscovered and are again desirable for contemporary use, regardless of style. For example, Oriental rugs are at home in a seventeenth-century saltbox or a modern twentieth-century home. To meet the current demand, American manufacturers are duplicating authentic Oriental designs in loom-woven rugs retailing at a fraction of the cost of the handmade ones. These rugs are called "Oriental design rugs" to distinguish them from the hand-loomed rugs made in the Orient and called "Oriental rugs."

Oriental Rugs from Persia and Turkey. The great majority of Oriental rugs imported into America have come from Persia (Iran) and Turkey. These rugs are made by hand tying a knot in each weft thread as it crosses the warp. The knot is either the *Ghiordes,* or Turkish, or the *Sehna,* or Persian type, depending on the area in which it is made. Rugs are frequently made by members of a family who use the same pattern generation after generation. The name of the particular rug is usually that of the family or is taken from the name of the village or area in which it was made. (See Figure 6.19.)

The beauty of an Oriental rug depends on (1) the *quality of the wool fiber* (a few are made of silk), (2) the *fineness of the weave,* (3) the *intricacy of the design,* and (4) the *mellowness of color.* Design motifs range from simple geometrics to the most intricate of patterns combining flowers, trees, birds, and animals; sometimes they have become so stylized through the years that the original source is uncertain. The mellow patina and soft color of the early imports—so highly prized by Americans—were the result of years of constant use and often of exposure to light, sun, and sometimes sand and rain.

By the early part of the twentieth century, the supply of valuable old rugs was becoming scarce. New ones were being produced, but since Americans preferred the soft colors of the old ones to the vivid tones of fresh vegetable dyes, a way had to be found to produce the "old" look. To accomplish this, plants were set up around New York City for chemically bleaching new rugs after they arrived in this country. Rugs were bleached, retouched by a special painting process, and finally run through bar rollers that gave them a high glossy finish. This process damaged the rug and lessened the wearing quality. Fortunately, the high cost of the procedure soon made it prohibitive. Since about 1955, most Oriental rugs have been given only a light lime wash, either before they leave the country in which they are made or after they arrive in this country. This wash produces a mellow look and does little harm to the rug.

Oriental rugs are classified as *antique, semiantique,* or *modern.* A rug fifty years old is usually considered an

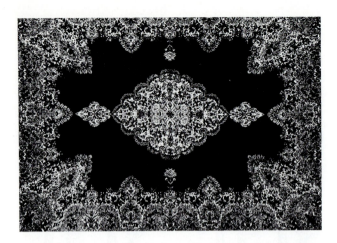

FIGURE 6.20 The most familiar of the Kiman designs: an open ground, a wide, uneven border, and a medallion center. (Courtesy of Karastan Rug Mills.)

FIGURE 6.21 This Sarouk rug was made in Iran. The all-over floral with rose or red ground is typical. (Courtesy of Chas. W. Jacobsen.)

antique. Semiantique rugs are slightly newer but have a natural patina acquired through gentle use. Modern Orientals, which may employ traditional or new designs, are those made in the Orient within the past 10 years. Age alone, however, does not make a rug valuable. Certain rugs that were originally coarse and poorly made generally are not valuable at any time, but good ones are always considered valuable.

Given the myriad types with distinct design origins from different areas, towns, tribes, and families, the study of Oriental rugs can be a lifelong pursuit. A logical beginning is to become familiar with the three Oriental rugs from the Near East that are particularly pleasing to American tastes—the Kirman, Sarouk, and Tekke, commonly called Bokhara.

- A top-grade *Kirman* is among the most costly of Oriental rugs. The most familiar type is one with a central medallion surrounded by a plain ground with a wide border of intricate design (Figure 6.20). Sometimes the entire ground is filled with delicate blooms. This rug is one of the few Orientals that is available with an ivory ground.
- The predominant colors in the *Sarouk* are exotic jewel tones of red, rose, and deep blue, with black and ivory as accent colors. Although the pattern is predominantly floral, it does feature some geometric devices. The Sarouk may also have a vibrant medallion outlined in dark colors. The pile is usually heavy. (See Figure 6.21.)
- *Bokhara (Tekke)* rugs, originally from Turkistan, are made in many Middle Eastern countries. The background of the Bokhara may be red, cream, or blue, but the predominant color is always red. The easily recognizable design is made up of octagons or polygons called *guls* (roses), which are repeated uniformly about the field. When the guls are quartered by narrow lines running the length and width of the field, the design is popularly called *Royal Bokhara*. (See Figure 6.22.)

Other well-known rugs from Iran include (1) the *Siraz,* which usually has a geometric pattern of red and blue; (2) the *Saraband,* with a field that is commonly red, covered with a palm-leaf design; (3) the *Isfahan,* one of the rarest and oldest of all antique rugs featuring a colorful floral pattern around a central medallion; (4) the *Hamadan* (the largest rug-producing section of Iran), usually featuring a stylized motif in the corners employing red, chestnut, and blue colors; (5) the *Kashan,* with intricate floral patterns, inspiring its name, "heavenly rug"; (6) the *Herez,* which has bold geometric designs with a medallion and ivory corners; (7) the *Nain,* probably the finest carpet woven in Iran today, with intricate floral designs; and (8) the *Qum,* an exceptionally fine rug, with the paisley motif most commonly employed.

Oriental Rugs from China.

The art of rug making has been practiced in China for over twelve centuries. The oldest known rugs were from the T'ang dynasty (A.D. 618–906). The oldest existing rug dates from the Ming dynasty (A.D. 1368–1644). Early designs were taken from ancient Chinese silk weaving and are symbolic of ancestor worship. Ancient symbols, of which there are over 100, fall into a number of categories. Chinese rugs can be recognized by the following characteristics:

- *Colors* of Chinese rugs are most typically blue and white (often used for the field), with yellow-orange, red-orange, gold, and cream also used in various combinations.
- *Geometric designs* are used primarily as border ornamentations. The Chinese T, key, or fret designs are the most familiar. The circle with a square in the center and two curved cells within a circle, symbolizing male and female, are common motifs.
- *Religious symbols* are commonly used, including the dragon, which symbolizes God and emperor, and waves and closed bands (eternity). Among the *mytho-*

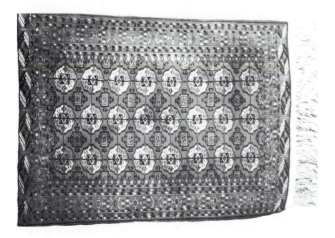

FIGURE 6.22 This Tekke-Turkoman (Bokhara) was made in central Asia. The straight line of geometric forms is typical. The ground is usually red. (Courtesy of Chas. W. Jacobsen.)

FIGURE 6.23 A Chinese design rug in the Bengali design. (Courtesy of Stark Carpet Corporation.)

logical symbols are the lion (authority), horse (strength), fish (abundance), and stag and crane (longevity).

- *Flowers* most commonly used are the lotus (purity), peony (prosperity), and chrysanthemum (fidelity).

Chinese rugs are made from complete paper models, and the design is outlined on a cotton warp. The pile is higher than on rugs made in the Middle East, and designs are sculptured by clipping the yarns along the contour of the pattern.

Rugs made in eastern China usually have all-over patterns reflecting the Middle Eastern influence. The two most familiar Chinese rugs are the *Mandarin,* which has no border, an open ground, and a different asymmetrical floral spray in each corner, and the *Peking,* which has a wide border, similar corner motifs, and a round central medallion. Peking design rugs made in India are called *Bengali.* (See Figure 6.23.)

Few rugs were made in China after the Second Sino-Japanese War (1937–1945), but after World War II production increased and some Chinese rugs were exported indirectly from the mainland. Since the opening of trade with China, rugs are once again being exported directly, but most Chinese-style rugs today come from Japan and India.

Oriental Rugs from India. Today many rugs of excellent quality are handmade in India for export to Europe and America. Rugs employing old and authentic designs from China, Iran, Turkey, and France are made from top-quality wool, mostly from New Zealand, and sell at moderate prices. Rugs imported into America from India come under several trade names.

- *Benares* rugs have a 100 percent wool nap, usually in natural colors with an ivory or cream ground.
- *Indo-Shahs* are some of the most common of the India-made rugs. The field is usually beige or pastel with

designs in deep royal blue, aquamarine, green, or gold. Indo-Shahs are made in French Aubusson or Savonnerie designs or in old Chinese patterns.

- *China* rugs are among the finest of the India rugs woven today. The designs are mostly French.
- *Bengali* is a Chinese design. A center medallion is typical, and blue usually predominates.
- *Pakistani* rugs are made in Pakistan. Designs are traditional Turkoman and come in a wide color range. The best known is the *Mari-Bukaro* (Bokhara, or Tekke).

In addition to these heavy deep-pile rugs, many finely woven Indian rugs are made in traditional Persian and Turkoman designs.

- *Kashmir Aubussons* are the flat-stitched tapestry Aubusson rugs employing authentic French designs.
- *Numdah* rugs (Figure 6.24), used in India for centuries, have been imported into the United States for many years and recently have had a revival in popularity. This

FIGURE 6.24 This Numdah rug is made of rough felt with wool embroidery in the "tree of life" design. (Photograph by Mark K. Allen.)

FIGURE 6.25 An Indian dhurrie rug, designed with the "tree of life" motif, provides a complementary background for Le Corbusier's classic leather and tubular steel Grand Confort chairs. (Courtesy of Patterson, Flynn & Martin/Jaime-Ardiles Arce.)

FIGURE 6.26 The French Savonnerie is a velvety pile carpet, typically with intricate French designs on a dark ground. (Courtesy of Stark Carpet Corporation.)

rug is an informal type made of felt, with the wool surface traditionally enriched with bird and floral motifs worked with a long, open stitch. The tree of life design is one of the most familiar being used; others have been modernized. Colors are in rich combinations of greens, blues, reds, and yellows on a natural ground. Numdahs are most often used for wall hangings or accent rugs and are effective in almost any informal room.

■ *Dhurries* are flat-weave rugs handwoven in India (see Figure 6.25). They are tightly woven in wool or cotton and incorporate both stylized and geometric designs. Colors are mostly pastels and medium tones on a natural field. **Dhurries** are currently much in vogue.

French Rugs

Two French-style carpets have been produced with little interruption since the seventeenth century: the Savonnerie and the Aubusson.

Savonnerie Rugs. **Savonnerie** is a pile carpet made by hand with knotted stitches in the manner of Orientals but with French patterns. (See Figure 6.26.) The Savonnerie factory, established in France in 1663 by Louis XIV, was an outgrowth of a workshop founded earlier in the Louvre. Although it was the first factory to produce tapestrylike carpets, it is best known for its velvety pile carpets, usually made in strong colors on a dark ground with elaborate designs sometimes taken from formal French gardens. Early Savonneries were made primarily for royal families of France and often bore the emblem of the king or prince for whom they were made. During the reign of kings Louis XIV, XV, and XVI, these rugs added warmth and splendor to the magnificent rooms of Versailles, Fontainebleau, and other great palaces and châteaux. Rugs of this type are still being produced.

Aubusson Rugs. **Aubusson rugs** are a distinctive type. The exact date and circumstances of the establishment of the Aubusson factory are uncertain. During the late sev-

FIGURE 6.27 Aubusson rugs are made of tapestry weave, usually with French designs in pastel colors. (Courtesy of Stark Carpet Corporation.)

FIGURE 6.28 North Africa is the source of this Moroccan rug commonly called Berber. (Courtesy of Ernest Tregavowan.)

enteenth century, however, when the upper classes of France became interested in beautifying their homes, long-established, privately owned workshops at Aubusson strove to imitate the weaving being done at Savonnerie and Gobelins to meet the new demand. Some of the oldest Aubusson rugs have an Oriental flavor, but later ones follow the French textile designs employing small-scaled stylized floral themes. Colors are usually soft, muted pastels, giving a faded effect. (See Figure 6.27.) These carpets are made in the tapestry weave but are somewhat less refined than the tapestries inspiring them. Although these rugs are no longer produced at

Aubusson, the name persists to designate the type of carpet rather than the name of the factory.

Moroccan Rugs

The Moroccan is a type of Oriental rug made primarily in northwest Africa. The character of the rug has changed little in 1,000 years. Its distinctive informality has made it a great favorite in contemporary decor. Moroccan rugs are of two basic types: the Berber and the Rabat.

- *Berber* rugs are the traditional types made primarily by Berber tribes in the Atlas Mountains. The designs are abstract and geometric. Some are primitive, often of natural wool color with simple black or brown design; others are vividly colored (Figure 6.28). Top-quality carpets referred to as Berbers are being made today by American companies. They are usually in natural colors and may be plain or have geometric designs. Berbers are particularly in demand for contemporary homes. (See Figure 6.29.)
- *Rabat* rugs are made mostly in factories in larger population centers. The designs show an oriental influence introduced into Morocco in the eighteenth century.

In 1938, a law was passed in Morocco prohibiting machine-made rugs. The law's intent was to safeguard employment for some 100,000 artisans and their families and to preserve the character of the handmade product. To ensure continuity in rug making, the government set

FIGURE 6.29 A textured Berber rug in natural earth tones is an attractive and functional floor covering for this living room setting. (Courtesy of Stark Carpet Corporation.)

FIGURE 6.30 This Navajo rug is characteristic of much of the art of the North American Indians and is similar to Peruvian rugs. (Photograph by Mark K. Allen.)

FIGURE 6.31 The Yeibechai (Yei) is a ceremonial rug made by the Navajo Indians of North America. Representations of animals and humans are found in folk art the world over. (Photograph by Mark K. Allen.)

up schools for girls between the ages of 9 and 15, in which the art of carpet weaving was taught. These *centres d'apprentissage* are located in the sultan's palace in Tangiers, a part of the picturesque Casbah.

The Spanish Matrimonia

The Spanish *matrimonia,* the traditional bridal gift in Spain, is the fringed, bold-figured *Manta* rug. Woven on the Jacquard loom, these rugs have subtle shadings, a handcrafted-like texture, and a three-dimensional quality. The Spaniards' legendary love of color is typified in the bright color combinations. Patterns are inspired by medieval motifs, classic Aubussons, Far East Orientals, mythical figures, the tree of life, and ornate **arabesques**. Adaptations of these rugs are being made today and are particularly appropriate for homes built in the Spanish tradition.

The Navajo Rug

The *Navajo* rug is a handwoven rug or blanket made by the Navajo Indians in the Southwest. Those of finest quality are made of wool and colored with vegetable dyes. Designs are usually geometric with frequent zigzag, **chevron**, and diamond motifs combined with stripes, as seen in Figure 6.30. Stylized representations of birds, animals, and human figures are sometimes used. (See Figure 6.31.) A remarkable similarity exists between the geometric designs of these rugs and designs of many rugs made in the Caucasus Mountains and in Peru. Navajo rugs do not have a pile and are usually only large enough for accent or art rugs. They are especially appropriate in houses with a Southwest look. Adobe houses are particularly enhanced by Navajo rugs.

Similarity in Folk Rugs

A striking similarity in appearance exists among **folk rugs** from most countries of the world because primitive peo-

ple most often use (1) simple geometric designs adapted from nature, (2) quaint representations of human and animal forms, (3) colors that are invariably those of natural wools or vegetable dyes, and (4) construction that is done by hand on simple looms. Whether the rugs are made by Berber tribes of North Africa, peasants in the highlands of Greece, Inca Indians in Peru, or Navajo Indians in North America, they have a feeling of kinship and may be used together to add charm to rooms with an informal atmosphere. (See Figure 6.32.)

Rya Rugs

Rya is a name derived from an old Norse word meaning "rough." This hand-hooked rug is a traditional import from Scandinavia, where it has been used for centuries. The **rya** is a high-pile shag rug combining a blend of multicolored yarns forced into a wool backing with a rug hook. The pile yarns are cut at an angle and at various heights, providing the "shaggy" appearance. Motifs are

FIGURE 6.32 A similarity is often present in folk rugs from remote areas. The Inca Indian influence that is evident in this rug from Peru bears a striking resemblance to rugs from eastern Turkey. (Courtesy of Ernest Tregavowan.)

FIGURE 6.33 A contemporary Danish rya rug with shaggy pile and a multicolored abstract design. (Photograph by August Anselon.)

drawn from nature, including the pine cone, tree, leaf, leaf skeleton, forest, ocean waves, raindrops, stylized flowers, animals including the reindeer, and birds including the turkey and pigeon. Geometric designs of all types are often combined with stylized nature themes. Rya rugs are ideally suited for use as area or art rugs in contemporary settings. (See Figure 6.33.)

Rag Rugs

Rag rugs were one of the first floor coverings made by American colonists. Scraps of cotton, linen, or wool were cut in narrow strips and then sewn together to form long strands woven in a plain weave on a cotton or linen warp. Through ingenious methods, rags were turned into colorful rugs—a craft still practiced.

Braided Rugs

Braided rugs were originally made in homes from scraps of clothing and blankets. They are still a favorite for rooms with a provincial atmosphere, especially in Early American and Country French rooms. Strips of rags are stitched together (on the bias), then braided into long ropes, which are either sewn or woven together in rounded or oval shapes (Figure 6.34). Varying bands of color can create colorful effects, adding warm informality to a room. Rugs of this type are also produced commercially at reasonable cost.

Hooked Rugs

Hooked rugs have been familiar to Americans since the late seventeenth century, and during the nineteenth century rug hooking became a highly developed art. Although generally thought of as native to America, hooked rugs were previously made in England, Scandinavia (rya rugs are a type of hooked rug), and other European countries. These rugs are made by hooking colored rags or yarns through a tightly stretched piece of burlap, can-

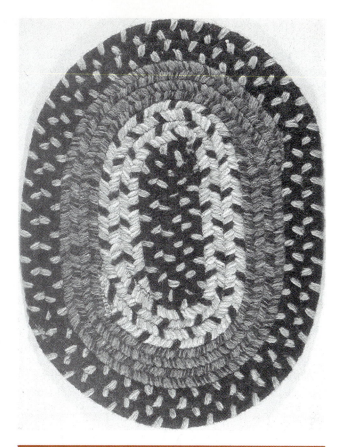

FIGURE 6.34 A braided rug can be used in any setting where a country look is desired.

vas, or wool to form a pile that may be cut or left in loops. The foundation fabric and the type of material used for filling determine the degree of durability. Designs and color combinations are limitless.

Needlepoint Rugs

Needlepoint rugs were originally made by embroidering with wool yarn on a heavy mesh canvas. Designs range from simple to highly complex floral motifs in a wide array of colors. A popular floor covering during the nineteenth century, needlepoint rugs (now mostly machine-made) are again finding favor.

WALLS AND WALL TREATMENTS

The background elements of a room are important factors in setting and maintaining the decorative scheme. Walls, floors, ceilings, windows, doors, and fireplaces are all part of the room's enclosure and are rarely hidden, except in small areas. Although these background elements provide a setting for furniture and fabrics, their most important function is to provide a background for people.

Walls occupy the largest area of a room, define its size and shape, and serve purposes of both function and beauty. Functionally, walls provide protection and privacy from the exterior surroundings and create interior areas of various shapes and sizes for particular activities. Walls also provide space for plumbing pipes and electrical and telephone wires, as well as insulation against heat and cold. Aesthetically, they contribute significantly not only to the success of a room but also to its general atmosphere and personality. Some walls emphasize openness and informality; others stress protection and formality.

Traditionally, walls were stationary ceiling supports and rooms were usually square or oblong. The design of today's walls not only includes traditional approaches but also other innovations, such as freestanding walls that are nonsupportive, allowing free placement within interior spaces. They may stop short of the ceiling, providing privacy but permitting the flow of air and light from one area to another.

Materials used on exterior walls carried into the interior and left exposed can form the room's architectural background. This arrangement accentuates the flow of space from the outside to the inside. Walls may be made of glass or plastic and slide into pockets or fold like accordions.

Walls can function as wall systems allowing storage or display space. Walls may also be integrated with attached built-in furniture. Or, walls may be cut out in various shapes and sizes, allowing a visual link to the next living space.

There are many materials available for wall treatments. Each type has advantages and disadvantages with regard to appearance, cost, upkeep, noise, insulation, and longevity. Some wall treatments are extremely versatile; others generally belong to certain moods and period styles. Materials for wall backgrounds should have appropriate textures and colors suitable for the occupant's lifestyle and the mood, theme, and style of the home.

When selecting wall materials, consider beauty, function, economy, and character—the goals of successful design. Before deciding what wall material is appropriate, answer some basic questions:

- Should walls be *emphasized or unobtrusive?* If active walls are planned, the treatment can be stronger—especially colors, textures, and patterns. If walls will take a passive role, a simple treatment is preferable.
- Will a *formal or informal* mood dominate? Walls can be elegant or casual. Rough or smooth textures and combinations of these should be considered.
- What is the *scale* of the room and furnishings? Wall treatment should relate in scale to enhance all interior components. For example, bold, rough concrete is not generally at home in a small-scaled space.
- Do walls need *insulating properties?* Certain materials may be more suitable for warm or cold climates.

- Is *light reflection or absorption* required of a particular wall treatment?
- Is the wall material supportive of the home's *style and character?*
- What are the *maintenance properties* of the wall material in terms of upkeep and cost?
- Does the wall material need to be *durable* for its particular function?

NONRESILIENT (OR RIGID) WALL COVERINGS

Table 6.3 lists the most frequently used nonresilient wall coverings, plus information on their general characteristics, fire ratings, insulation properties, uses, and care.

Plaster

Plaster is the simplest and most versatile of all wall treatments (see Figure 6.35). Plaster is a thick mixture of gypsum and water combined with lime and sand. This mixture is applied to a metal lattice, a special hardboard, or any rough masonry surface. Plaster has been used for centuries, but currently the cost is relatively high.

Wallboard

Wallboard may be a *gypsum plasterboard* or *pressed wood*. Gypsum plasterboard—called **drywall** construction—is the most common and is used extensively for walls in today's homes. Plasterboard and pressed wood are inexpensive wallboard treatments and come in 4-by-8-ft panels that are secured to the structure's vertical wood stud supports. Wallboard provides insulation against heat, cold, and noise and when painted produces a variety of effects from rough to smooth. Rough plasterlike walls are appropriate for informal rooms and some period rooms such as Spanish-style ones. Smooth plaster can be used in any style room and with any style furniture. Because of this, the plain wall is considered the safest background treatment to use in rooms in which furnishings may likely be changed from time to time. *Plastic laminate wallboards* are available in a wide range of colors and simulate a variety of textures.

Wood

Wood walls have been a favorite background treatment for centuries. Wood applied to walls may be boards, panels, or even shingles. (See Figures 6.36 and 6.37.) *Boards* can be of any wood type, cut in various widths, stained any color, and laid vertically, horizontally, or diagonally. They can be joined with tongue-in-groove, butted, or beveled edges. A wide variety of wood sheet *panels*, some with thin veneers, are also available with numerous fin-

TABLE 6.3 Nonresilient wall coverings

Material	General Characteristics and Cost	Finishes	Fire Rating	Insulation Properties	Uses and Care
Brick (fired clay)	Solid and durable Variety of sizes, shapes, and colors Old, natural brick has feeling of warmth May be laid in regular or varied patterns Pleasant texture High cost	No finish necessary May be painted or waxed	Fireproof	Reflects noise Conducts heat and cold	Interior and exterior walls Appropriate for large- or small-scaled rooms in a wide range of styles, and for fireplace facings and hearths Little or no upkeep
Concrete blocks (lightweight aggregate)	Substantial, cold, regular shape, large scale, textured Moderate cost	No finish necessary May be painted Waterproofing necessary for exterior	Fireproof	Fair insulator	Interior or exterior walls; fireplace facings Best when used in large-scaled rooms Lacks domestic warmth Little or no maintenance
Ceramic tile (clay)	Comes in variety of shapes, sizes, colors, and patterns, and in pregrouted sheets Desirable aesthetic quality Durable, resists water and stains, but may crack or break Moderately high cost	No finish necessary	Fireproof	Reflects noise Poor insulator	Bathrooms, kitchens, utility rooms Particularly appropriate for dados in Spanish and Mexican rooms Becoming more widely used Minimum upkeep
Fiberglass (panels)	Translucent panels of reinforced fiberglass Most often ribbed or corrugated Also available in flat sheets and in several thicknesses Comes translucent, white, or colored; may simulate brick, stone, or wood Moderate cost	No finish necessary	Fireproof	Good insulator	Room dividers, folding screens, tub enclosures, translucent lighting panels for ceilings, built-ins, and sliding doors Easy upkeep
Glass (architectural)	Can be clear, rubbed, corrugated, pebbled, frosted, colored, and curved Metal mesh core will prevent breakage and add to attractiveness May be tempered Moderately high cost	No finish necessary	Fireproof	Poor insulator	Sliding doors, screens, room dividers, clinical purposes, numerous other uses Mirror can usually expand space and add dramatic element to room One-way glass has many functional uses
Glass (block)	Excellent light transmission High-impact strength	No finish necessary	Fireproof	Solid glass blocks conduct heat Blocks with hollow air centers are good insulators	Suitable to lighten most dark areas Easy upkeep

Material	General Characteristics and Cost	Finishes	Fire Rating	Insulation Properties	Uses and Care
Metal (panels and tiles)	Stainless steel, plain, or grained—not reflective finish Serviceable, sturdy, not affected by acid, steam, or alkalies Solid copper: eye appeal May be plain, hammered, or antiqued Sealed to prevent tarnish or corrosion Aluminum glazes: solid aluminum coated with permanent vitreous glaze of porcelain, enamel, or epoxy enamel Sturdy, easy to maintain Lightweight and strong, but subject to dents that are difficult to repair Tends to have commercial effect Moderate cost	Factory finished with grain, or enameled in variety of colors	Fire resistant	Reflects heat	Kitchens, bathrooms, utility rooms, and wherever sturdy wall is desired Numerous functional and decorative uses Easy maintenance
Plaster and stucco	Smooth or textured, no seams or joints Easy to change Tends to chip and crack Moderately low cost	Paint, paper, or fabric	Fireproof	Special types have good insulation against noise	Most versatile of all wall treatments Appropriate for any room and any style Washable
Plastic (tiles)	Durable, rigid, thin, lightweight, variety of colors Simulates ceramic tile Decreasing in use Low cost	None	Poor	Poor insulator	Kitchens, bathrooms, utility rooms Excellent do-it-yourself item Easy upkeep
Plastic (sheets)	Durable, resilient Comes in variety of colors, patterns, and textures Moderately high cost	No finish necessary	Poor Some do not burn but emit noxious gas	Poor insulator	Wherever durable, resilient walls are needed Resists stains and cuts Easy maintenance
Stone	Great beauty If covering too large an area, may appear cold, depending on color Natural colors and textures Feeling of strength and durability Improves with age High cost	Waterproofing sometimes required (See Table 6.1 for specific stones)	Fireproof	Poor insulator Reflects sound	Fireplace surround or entire wall No upkeep
Wallboard (gypsum)	Surface may be finished in attractive colors and patterns, or imprinted with wood-grain appearance Lowest cost	Same as plaster: paint, paper, or fabric	Fire resistant	Excellent insulator	In any room in which low cost is primary consideration Care depends on finish

TABLE 6.3, *continued*

Material	General Characteristics and Cost	Finishes	Fire Rating	Insulation Properties	Uses and Care
Wallboard (plastic laminate)	Extremely durable Surface of laminate similar to plastic counter top Photo process can produce textured appearance, wood grains, colors, or patterns Matte or shiny surface High cost	Finished at factory Needs no additional finish	Smokes and melts	Reflects noise Fairly good insulator, depending on density and thickness	Hard-use areas of house (e.g., family rooms, children's rooms, basements) Resists stains and moisture Scratches are irreparable Wash with damp cloth
Wallboard hardboard (pressed wood)	Extremely durable, dent resistant, low cost, many wood grains and colors Wood grain applied via high-fidelity photo process Factory coated, virtually indestructible, easily installed Also available in embossed and textured surfaces simulating fabrics Moderate cost	May be stained, painted, or waxed	Surface melts Pressed wood burns	Reflects noise Insulation depends on thickness of pressed wood	In any area in which wood paneling of low cost and durability is required Wash with damp cloth
Wood (solid)	Natural grain throughout Comes in variety of natural grains from rough barn wood to rich grains for formal rooms Can be installed tongue and groove, plain edged, flush joint, or grooved Natural colors vary, but may be stained any color Subject to denting, but can be refinished indefinitely High cost	Needs protective finish to seal against stains and water	Susceptible to burning	Good insulator and noise reducer	Depending on type of wood and method of installation, will go in any room—period or modern Beauty improves with age and care Dust only
Wood (plywood)	Thin surface of wood veneer bonded to rugged and inexpensive panel backing Appears much like solid wood, but less expensive Comes in 4-ft-by-8-ft sheets for easy installation May or may not have vertical grooves Moderately high cost	Same as solid wood	Susceptible to burning	Good insulator and noise reducer	Same as solid wood

ishes, colors, and styles and are considerably less expensive. Exterior *shingles* are also available for interior use and are suitable for informal settings or places where moisture is a problem.

Wood **moldings** of all types, including those used for dados, wainscotting, window and door trims, cornices, and fireplace trims, are often used to enhance backgrounds. Stock moldings give the impression of a dado, cornice, **boiserie**, or complete period paneling. (See Figures 6.38, 6.39 and 6.40.)

Masonry

Masonry used for walls includes brick, tile, concrete block, and stone. *Brick*, which has been used since the time of the ancient Babylonians and pharaohs, has a timeless quality of warmth and adaptability. Its natural look is equally at home in traditional or modern settings and in residential or nonresidential spaces. *Ceramic tile*, available in many shapes, sizes, colors, patterns, and finishes, can be used for almost any style and room. It is especially

FIGURE 6.35 White textured plaster applied to the walls of this spacious living room supports the casual Southwestern style. (Courtesy of Kirkwood Shutters, Phoenix.)

FIGURE 6.36 In a modern home, wood planks are lined up vertically on the walls and also used for flooring and ceiling treatment, making an excellent background for furnishings and accessories. (Courtesy of Ron Molen, architect.)

FIGURE 6.37 For centuries, carved wood panelling was considered one of the most rich and elegant wall treatments. The wood wall in this room is typical of the English Tudor period and continues to be used to convey the style. (Courtesy of Stuart Designs, London.)

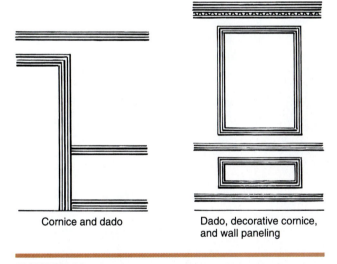

Cornice and dado   Dado, decorative cornice, and wall paneling

FIGURE 6.38 Architectural interest is added with stock moldings.

FIGURE 6.39 This traditional sunburst design can add formality to a front door. It is sturdy, lightweight, and easily installed. (Courtesy of Focal Point.)

FIGURE 6.40 This exquisite fretwork cornice, made of tough, lightweight modern material, is molded directly from notable wood or plaster originals. Through a precise process, architectural enrichment is produced in authentic detail for any style. (Courtesy of Focal Point.)

FIGURE 6.41 Ceramic tile is often selected for its aesthetic appeal and also for its durability. In this bath area, blue and white ceramic tiles have been laid in a dynamic wave pattern reminiscent of a motif used by the ancient Greeks. The glass block wall filters light and provides privacy. (Courtesy of Pittsburgh Corning Corporation.)

FIGURE 6.42 A stone wall laid in a horizontal pattern with random protruding pieces provides an informal and rugged background in this attractive California residence. The reflective ceiling creates the illusion of a much higher wall, and recessed lights dramatize its texture. (Courtesy of Steve Chase Associates. Photograph by Mary E. Nichols.)

FIGURE 6.43 The large wall-to-wall and ceiling-to-floor mirror in this dining room gives the illusion of twice the space and provides an engaging background. (Courtesy of Michael Rennick & Associates, Salt Lake City.)

popular for use in kitchens and bathrooms (see Figure 6.41).

Stone includes a vast variety of types, textures, and colors, including marble, travertine, slate, fieldstone, flagstone, and quartzite. Some stones, like marble, can provide a formal and elegant look, and some, like fieldstone, give an informal and casual feeling. Stone is popular for fireplaces, and in contemporary homes is widely used for walls (see Figure 6.42). For additional characteristics, see Table 6.1.

Other Wall Coverings

Mirrors can expand an area visually—an advantage in today's diminished living spaces (Figure 6.43). Mirrors are available in large sheets and precut panels ready to install, and they can cover an entire wall or be spaced on a wall for function or aesthetic appeal. Mirrors also have great light-reflecting qualities.

Metal such as stainless steel, copper, and aluminum is available in sheets and tiles. Finishes either are smooth and shiny or brushed. The latter has easier upkeep. Use of metal for interior walls should be planned with discretion because of its strong textural qualities.

Plastics are available in either sheets or tiles in a wide range of colors and styles. They are easy to clean and are completely waterproof, making them an excellent choice for bathrooms, kitchens, and utility rooms.

PAINTS AND FINISHES

To change the character of a room quickly and with a minimum of expense, nothing works like paint. Of all wall treatments, paint is the easiest to apply. It is made to adhere to any surface and is appropriate for any room or any style. Some paints resist rust, sun, and fire. Paints come in numerous colors, producing unlimited shades, tones, and tints. A painted wall surface can be smooth or given a variety of textures by use of a stiff brush, sponge, or special roller. A bonus with textured surfaces is a muffling of sound. Paints are made from a vast array of synthetic and natural materials.

Types of Paint

Alkyd Paint

Alkyd paint has virtually replaced oil paint. It is resin enamel that is fast drying, leaves no brush or roller marks, resists yellowing, and cleans better than latex. Depending on the color, one coat is generally sufficient. It is produced in high-gloss, semigloss, and matte finishes. Alkyd enamels must be thinned with solvent. They are recommended for plaster or plasterboard, woodwork, and wood siding and are probably the best for metal.

Acrylic Paint

Acrylic paint is a water-based synthetic resin paint. The more acrylic the paint contains, the higher the quality. Acrylic is extremely durable, odorless, easily applied, quick drying, and washable. Some acrylic paints resemble baked-on enamel and are almost impervious to damage.

Latex Paint

Latex is a type of acrylic. It is a water-mixed paint, so cleanup is easy. Latex leaves no overlap marks and dries quickly, and the characteristic odor fades quickly. Latex enamel, however, shows brush marks more readily than alkyd does. A difference between indoor and outdoor latex is that outdoor latex "breathes," thus allowing moisture to escape, which eliminates blistering. Latex paints are recommended for plaster or plasterboard, masonry, wood siding, **acoustical tile**, and metal.

Enamel Paint

Enamel is a special type of paint similar to oil paint and made with varnish or lacquer. Its finish is exceptionally hard and durable. It is available in high-gloss, semigloss, and matte types.

Epoxy Paint

Epoxy paint is prepared in two ways. The first is ready-mixed in a single can. The second type is a two-stage finish, or catalyzed epoxy, which, when used as directed, puts a tilelike coating on almost any surface. Once it hardens, this coating can be scratched, struck, or marked with crayon or pencil and still be washed back to a high gloss. Epoxies can be used on such surfaces as basement walls, shower stalls, and swimming pools.

Varnish

Varnish is a word sometimes used as a generic name for all clear resinous finishes. A resin is a natural or synthetic substance that, when dissolved in a suitable solvent, leaves a hard glossy film. Natural resins are the saps of certain trees or deposits of insects that feed on the sap. Synthetic resins are also available. Varnish is made from natural resins with alcohol or a drying oil and volatile thinners and dryers. It is usually a transparent coating and is commonly used on wood to protect the surface and allow the natural grain to show through. Some varnishes

have a colorant added to darken the wood, but the result is usually less satisfactory than when staining is done before applying clear varnish. Varnish comes in high-gloss or matte finishes.

Shellac

Shellac is a protective coating similar to varnish. It is made of a resinous substance called lac, which is deposited on trees in India and Asia. Its solvent is alcohol. Shellac dries more quickly than varnish but is less durable and is subject to water spots. Clear shellac does not discolor when applied to a light-colored surface.

Lacquer

Lacquer is a superior, quick-drying varnishlike finish made from resin from an Asiatic sumac (Chinese or Jap-

FIGURE 6.44 A variety of soft neutral tones were sponged on this wall to create a textured background for a contemporary Spanish style bedroom. (Photograph by Pam Singleton.)

anese lacquer) or from a synthetic nitro-cellulose resin. The finish ranges from high gloss to matte and comes in white, black, brown, or beige.

Polyurethane

Polyurethane is a varnishlike finish that provides an exceptionally tough plastic surface coating. It comes in high- or medium-gloss or matte finish. It is an excellent protective surface for hardwood floors in heavy-traffic areas and walls where moisture is a problem. Polyurethane is also used to protect furniture surfaces and wood paneling.

Stain

Stain penetrates wood pores and contains various colorants that can enhance the natural color or give the wood a different color. Be sure to make sample tests before staining begins, because woods react differently to the same stain.

Sealers and Fillers

Sealers and fillers are special substances used as preparatory bases for new surfaces to ensure a more professional finish.

Paint Textures and Decorative Finishes

There are several methods of providing unusual finishes with paint. The following techniques involve applying one or more colors of wet (often thinned) paint over a dry base coat of another color.

- *Sponging:* Paint is applied with a sponge over a base coat, giving a mottled or blotchy texture. (See Figure 6.44.)
- *Spattering:* Paint on a brush is flipped onto the base coat, giving a speckled appearance.
- *Stippling:* The look of sponging, but a more delicate effect is achieved by using a stippling brush to apply a colored paint lightly over the base color.
- *Ragging:* One or more colors are applied over the base coat, then partly removed by blotting or rolling with a rag to achieve a marbleized effect.
- *Color washing:* A coat of thinned paint or glaze is lightly applied over a base coat of another color.
- *Glazing:* Layers of one or more transparent colors are applied on top of a base coat, resulting in a progression of color effects.
- *Faux finishes:* **Faux** is French for "false." Faux finishes simulate the look of another material, such as stone or wood, by using various techniques to apply colored paints to a surface. Among the more popular effects are marble, granite, and woodgrains. More exotic faux finishes include tortoiseshell and malachite. In addition to being used on walls, faux finishes are used on moldings, doors, mantlepieces, and furniture.

In addition to these overall effects, paint can be used to create scenes, patterns, or borders.

- *Trompe l'oeil:* A delightful wall treatment, especially for those who desire an unusual effect or perhaps want to inject a note of humor. The French term literally means "fool the eye." **Trompe l'oeil** is a hand-painted wall or wallcovering, in almost any subject matter, giving a three-dimensional look. Very simple or extremely complicated designs can be used. (See the ceiling painting in Figure 6.1.)
- *Other effects:* Painted designs and borders that do not attempt the illusionistic effects of trompe l'oeil can be created either freehand or with stencils (see Figures 6.45 and 6.46). A stencil is a masking sheet with a pattern cut out of it, so that the pattern can be repeated. *Stenciling* is especially popular for rooms with an informal or country look. Stenciling designs can be purchased or personally created with countless possibilities.

RESILIENT (OR FLEXIBLE) WALL COVERINGS

Wallpaper

Using decorative paper as a wall covering has been important in enhancing interiors since the late sixteenth century in Europe and early colonial times in America. Although wallpapers have been more fashionable during some periods than others, they have always been esteemed as a valuable tool in transforming the visual aspect of interior space.

History of Wallpaper

Hand-painted wallpapers are known to have been made as early as 200 B.C. in China, where they were used for decorating tombs.

The first manufacture of wallpaper on an organized basis was in France toward the close of the sixteenth century. The first papers were painted in a marbleized effect—a design copied from imported Persian papers—and made for facing book covers and lining boxes. These were called *domino papers,* and the group of artisans who produced them were called *dominotiers.* Other groups in France were soon organized to fill the growing demand for decorative papers, and when Henry IV granted a charter in 1599 to the Guild of Paperhangers, the wallpaper industry had arrived.

The introduction of **flocked papers** during the early seventeenth century made it possible for people to simulate the elegant damasks used in homes of the wealthy. Two events in the latter half of the seventeenth century added momentum to the wallpaper industry: the establishment of trade with East India, bringing the Oriental influence into western Europe, and a new printing method developed by *Jean Papillon.* For the first time, a wallpaper

FIGURE 6.45 A hand-painted garden scene framed in an arch gives the sense of looking through a gateway into a secluded garden. (Photograph by Pam Singleton.)

was produced that could be matched to make the pattern continuous around the room. Jean Papillon became known as the father of wallpaper as we know it today. His skillful use of **chinoiserie** design, together with this new method of application, produced a style much in demand for the decoration of great houses all over Europe.

Through the works of *Baptiste Reveillon* in France and *John Baptiste Jackson* in England, *pictorial murals* became popular in these two countries during the latter half of the eighteenth century. During the eighteenth century in America, hand-painted papers from China were much in vogue for the great Georgian mansions being built along the Atlantic seacoast. *Carrington House* in Providence, Rhode Island, was one of the first firms in America to supply hand-painted papers. The high cost of imported papers—not only from China but also France and England—prohibited their common use.

In an attempt to make these highly prized wall coverings available to everyone, *Plunket Fleeson* in 1739 established his Philadelphia factory for printing wallpapers.

This endeavor met with only moderate success due to high operation costs.

During the second quarter of the nineteenth century, copper rollers turned by a rotary machine were invented in northern England. Although wallpaper was frequently used during the nineteenth century, it was not until the Industrial Revolution, when quantity replaced quality, that the wallpaper industry flourished in America.

With the advent of the modern style of architecture and home furnishings early in the twentieth century, wallpaper went out of fashion and plain walls were more in vogue. Late in the 1930s wallpaper again became fashionable, and when the industry developed a new method of silk-screen printing that produced papers of high quality at affordable prices, the demand multiplied.

Methods of Producing Wallpaper

The three most common methods of producing wall coverings are roller printing, hand blocking, and silk-screen

FIGURE 6.46 An original hand-painted fireplace makes an artistic focal point. The designs on the pillows repeat the motifs, providing a feeling of unity and freshness. (Photograph by Pam Singleton.)

printing. Embossed and flocked wall coverings are additional processes resulting in unique surface qualities. *Roller printing* is the most common process and the least expensive. This method is a cylinder process in which each color is applied in rapid succession. *Hand blocking* is a process in which each color is applied separately after the preceding one is dry. This method is slower and more costly than the roller method. *Silk-screen printing* is a more complicated process in which a wooden or metal frame tightly stretches a silk, nylon, or metal screen made for each color of the pattern. The frame is the full-sized pattern repeat. Portions of the pattern not to be printed are heavily varnished or bleached out. Each repeat is made by applying pigment, which seeps through the screens as it is pushed across by a squeegee implement edged with rubber. Each color is allowed to dry before the next frame is printed. This method produces a high-quality wall covering at reasonable cost.

Embossed paper is made by a machine process producing high and low surface effects. This method is used where texture and three-dimensional effects are desirable. Wall coverings of this type may simulate brick or stone with surprising realism. **Flocked** paper is produced by a method in which the design motif is outlined and

covered with a glue or an adhesive material. A fine wool-like fuzz is then blown onto it, producing a surface resembling cut velvet.

Common Wallpaper Terms

Following are the most commonly used wallpaper terms.

Washable   Usually refers to a wall covering that may be washed with lukewarm mild suds, but not scrubbed excessively.

Scrubbable   Refers to a wall covering more resistant to rubbing than washable types. Stains such as crayon marks can generally be removed from scrubbable wallpaper with cleaning agents recommended by the manufacturer or with soap and water.

Pretrimmed   Refers to rolls of wallpaper from which the selvage has been trimmed.

Semitrimmed   Means the selvage has been trimmed from only one edge of the wallpaper.

Prepasted   Paper that has had paste applied during the manufacturing process. Detailed instructions for hanging are usually included. Generally, prepasted paper is soaked in water and applied to the wall while wet.

Single roll   Wallpaper is always priced by the single roll, but usually is sold by the double or triple roll. Regardless of width, a single roll contains 36 sq. ft. Eurorolls (wall coverings produced in Europe and often used in the United States) contain 28 ft per single roll.

Double and triple roll   Regardless of width, a double roll (two single rolls) contains approximately 72 sq. ft., and a triple roll (three single rolls) contains 108 sq. ft. Generally, 18-in. and 20-in. wallpapers come in triple rolls. Double or triple rolls are used to minimize waste when cutting wallpaper into strips.

Dye lot   Original or first production of a color or colors. Each dye lot has a number. Because of color variations in different dye lots, a certain dye lot number can be specified when it is necessary to reorder a particular fabric or wallpaper.

Pattern repeat   When a wall covering has a pattern or motif, the patterns need to line up. The vertical and horizontal directions of the motif should match from the top to the bottom of the wall. If the pattern is large, there is more wall covering waste.

Sizing   A liquid that is painted on the wall before the wallpaper is applied. Sizing prevents the wallpaper from absorbing too much paste or adhesive and helps the wallpaper to adhere better to the wall.

Vinyl-Coated Coverings

For today's practical interior designer, numerous flexible wall coverings are available that have been treated with varying thicknesses of vinyl and made to simulate any type of wall covering—nonresilient or resilient. They may be washable or scrubbable; are waterproof, highly durable, and stain resistant; and can be used on nearly any type of wall and for any style. Vinyl wall coverings are applied using the same method appropriate for wallpaper.

The following are the most common vinyl wall coverings:

- *Vinyl-protected* wall covering is ordinary wallpaper with a coating of vinyl plastic to make it washable.
- *Vinyl-latex* wall covering is a paper impregnated with vinyl, laminated to lightweight fabric or paper, then vinyl coated. The thickness of the vinyl may vary. This process produces a durable wall covering that is scrubbable.
- *Coated fabric* is a wall covering with a woven cotton backing treated with an oil or plastic coating before the design is applied. This durable, tough, scrubbable material is ideal for kitchens and bathrooms.
- *Plastic foam* is a soft, flexible material available in rolls, squares, or rectangles. Its special properties are that it absorbs sound and insulates and is soil and stain resistant. It is easy to clean with soap and water. Although more expensive than some wall coverings, plastic foam is ideal for apartments with thin walls or television rooms and is particularly used in commercial and institutional settings. Foam coverings come in solid colors, embossed patterns, or large scenic designs.

Fabric Wall Coverings

Using fabric on walls is by no means a new idea. Fabric gave warmth to stone-walled rooms during the medieval and Renaissance periods. During the fifteenth and sixteenth centuries walls in wealthy Europeans' houses were covered with tapestries and leather. In the seventeenth century velvets, brocades, and damasks were used; and in many well-preserved palaces and châteaux, the fabric on the walls remains beautiful. Fabric-covered walls can provide rich pattern and a depth of texture, especially when upholstered.

Today, fabrics of many varieties are used on walls. The best choice, except when using the shirred method of application, is a medium-weight, closely woven fabric such as sailcloth, ticking, Indian head, or glazed chintz for an informal look and tapestry, brocade, and damask for a formal appearance. Some fabrics come prepared for pasting on walls and are laminated to a paper backing. All-over, nondirectional patterns are easy to use because they require no matching. A repeat pattern requires allowance for matching just as does wallpaper.

- The *shirring method* is the simplest way to cover a wall with fabric. The effect is attractive and the fabric is easy to take down and clean. Cut-to-fit rods are fastened just above the baseboard and near the ceiling. Single lengths of fabric are cut with a 4-in. allowance, top and bottom, for headings. The fabric is gathered the same as for sash curtains. Fabric can also be pleated or folded and installed on the wall.
- The *double-face masking tape* method is not permanent, because masking tape will dry out in time. Fabric is prepared by sewing together and pressing seams. The tape is placed around the edges of the wall, then the outer coat is peeled off. The fabric is applied first at the top and bottom, then at the sides. The straight grain of the fabric should be kept vertical.
- The *Velcro method* is similar to the masking tape method, except that one side of the Velcro tape is stitched along the edges of the fabric, then attached to the other side of the tape, which has been placed around the edges of the wall.
- In the *staple method* the fabric is prepared as in the masking tape method. The top is stapled first, then the bottom, and the sides last. Exposed staples may be concealed with braid or molding.
- The *paste method* is the most professional looking and most permanent method, but it requires special care and a set of wallpaper tools. The wall is prepared by a coat of liquid sealing or sizing to fill the pores in the wall surface. When the lengths of fabric are ready to be applied, a second coat of sealing is painted on the first section and the first strip of fabric is positioned like wallpaper. The same procedure is then followed for the remaining strips. When the job is completed, the fabric dries overnight and then is sprayed with a protective material.
- Fabric can be applied to *panels* and then installed on the wall. Edges are often concealed with moldings.

Other Resilient Wall Coverings

Japanese grass cloth or *hemp* is made from grass grown in Japan. Flexible, long-lasting, and easy to care for, grass cloth provides suitable backgrounds for a variety of styles. Colored grass cloth, however, does not hold color well. Other woven reeds such as *sisal* can provide handsome and practical wall coverings.

Wood veneer with fabric backing, another method of "papering" walls, produces a true wood surface and, once adhered to the wall, is difficult to distinguish from solid wood. One advantage over wood paneling is that this material can fit around corners or curves. It is available in sheets up to 24 in. wide and 12 ft long. The cost, however, is high.

Real leather tile, made of top-grain cowhide, provides a soft, warm, rich surface. It comes in a variety of fast colors to blend with traditional or modern decor. The leather is permanently bonded to an aluminum tile base with preapplied adhesive for easy installation. It is highly resistant to scuffing, and the only maintenance required is an occasional washing with mild soap and water. Leather can effectively be used above a dado, on walls in a family room or den, and wherever a durable leather-textured wall surface is desired. Leather tile in *suede* is also available on a custom-ordered basis. The depth of the brushed nap provides an interesting texture, but its high cost limits extensive use.

Cork is a moderately priced textured material producing a warm atmosphere in natural colors of brown. It is particularly adaptable for studies and rooms in which sound insulation is important. Unless plastic-impregnated, cork is not suitable for bathrooms, kitchens, and other hard-use areas.

Today's flexible wall coverings, both rigid and non-rigid, have much variety, beauty, and practicality. Patterns, colors, styles, and surface effects are unlimited for use in both residential and contract projects.

Decorative and Functional Values of Wall Coverings

Applying wall coverings is perhaps the surest means of completely changing the atmosphere of a room. They:

- Bring *beauty, charm,* and *interest* into an otherwise uninteresting room. (See Figure 6.47.)
- Add *architectural detail.* Many wallpapers simulate architectural features such as pilasters, cornices, dadoes, and latticework.
- Establish the *period or theme* for the room's design. (See Figure 6.48.) *Documentary* wallpapers and fabrics that authentically reproduce motifs and colors used during a particular period are available. (See Figure 6.49.)

- Set the mood of the room: formal, as seen in Figure 6.50, or informal.
- Supply an *effective background* for display with a blended or contrasting effect.
- Provide a *dramatic focus* by the use of a striking mural or pattern.
- Change the *visual aspect* of a room by the skillful use of *trompe l'oeil.* (See Figure 6.51.)
- Conceal *architectural defects or damaged walls.* A small all-over pattern works well for this purpose.
- Change the apparent *size and proportion* of a room (i.e., make it appear larger, smaller, higher, or lower). (See Figure 6.52.) A pattern with a three-dimensional effect can achieve spaciousness, and a bold pattern in advancing colors can make a room seem smaller. Using a vertical stripe or running the wall covering onto the ceiling about 12 to 18 in., especially if the ceiling is coved, can make a room look higher. Using horizontal lines or dropping the ceiling covering down onto the wall can make a ceiling look lower.
- Bring *harmony* into a room by unifying its different components, as seen in Figure 6.53
- Wallpaper is *low in cost, easy to apply,* and *relatively easy to clean.*

FIGURE 6.47 Sparsely and densely designed floral patterns in variations of blues, pinks, purples, and greens on a cream ground come together in Greeff's Pick-a-Flower Collection. The wallpaper and fabrics are well suited for a light country feeling. (Courtesy of Greeff Fabrics.)

FIGURE 6.48 Wall coverings can set the desired style of a room. "Nobuko" wall covering and coordinating fabric have a striking pattern of giant peonies, which are among the most popular flowers in Oriental design. (Courtesy of Van Luit).

FIGURE 6.49 A documentary wallpaper establishes an authentic feeling of the period and changes the visual aspect of the room. (From the Winterthur Museum Collection, courtesy of Van Luit and Company.)

FIGURE 6.50 An elegant wall covering with a rococo leaf and rose border frames a cream and white damask establishing a formal background for the room's furnishings. (Courtesy of Schumacher.)

FIGURE 6.51 A trompe l'oeil wallpaper border depicting swags of fabric held together at intervals by cords and tassels. (Courtesy of Scalamandré.)

Horizontal lines make a high room seem lower.

Vertical lines make a room appear higher.

A scenic paper with a third dimension can add perspective and create the illusion of space.

FIGURE 6.52 Wallpaper can change the apparent size and proportions of a room.

FIGURE 6.53 Wall coverings can tie together various furnishings in a room as demonstrated in this traditional dining area. Walls are covered with a lilies and vine motif in China blue, which is repeated for the window treatment and a few chairs, providing a unifying and harmonious effect. (Courtesy of Schumacher.)

■ Wall coverings are *flexible* and can be used in any room of the house.

As for carpets, federal, state, and local building codes and safety regulations pertain to wall coverings specified for nonresidential projects. For example, wall coverings must meet strict flammability regulations. The designer must specify wall coverings that satisfy building codes.

CEILINGS

The ceiling—the largest unused area of a room—has been given special attention for hundreds of years. The designs of ceilings in palatial interiors during the Renaissance were magnificently **coffered**, inlaid, **frescoed**, and adorned with decorative plaster. (A contemporary version of this treatment is seen in Figure 6.1.) Ceilings during the settlement period in America were usually low and plain with supportive beams. During the Georgian, Federal, Greek Revival, and Victorian periods, ceilings were generally not as ornately designed as in earlier periods in Europe; they ranged from simple applied decoration to elegantly adorned surfaces. For most of the twentieth century the design potential of the ceiling was generally neglected. Today, however, the ceiling is once again being brought into focus, as seen in Figure 6.54. Older, ornate ceilings are being restored, and new ones are often designed in dramatic and innovative ways.

The functions of the ceiling include providing (1) protection from the elements, (2) insulation for heating and cooling, (3) a source for artificial lighting (and in some cases, natural lighting when skylights are used), (4) an important element of the character and atmosphere of a room, (5) an acoustic barrier for absorbing or reflecting sound, and (6) a flame-resistant barrier that meets standard fire codes.

Ceiling Illusions

If a ceiling is much above or below the average main-floor height of 8 ft, it tends to alter the general feeling of the room. A high ceiling emphasizes space and tends to create a feeling of dignity and formality. A low ceiling, which decreases space, can produce a warm, informal atmosphere. Ceilings may be made to appear higher to

FIGURE 6.54 A pyramidal ceiling skylight runs the length of this private residence designed by architect Eduard Dreier, allowing light to flood all the major living and dining spaces, as well as providing powerful design interest. (Courtesy of Gayl Baddeley/Associates.)

FIGURE 6.55 Wallpaper extended beyond the walls and into coved ceilings gives the appearance of greater height.

suit an owner's preference for a more spacious feeling or lower to provide a cozy, intimate atmosphere. For height:

- Run the wall color or covering a short distance onto the ceiling, especially when the corners are **coved** (where walls and ceiling are joined by a curve instead of a right angle). This treatment causes the eye to move upward and makes the ceilings appear higher, as seen in Figure 6.55.
- Use a light color on a ceiling.
- Use a predominance of vertical lines in the architecture of the room and in the decorative elements, like a patterned wallpaper.
- Add a skylight to open up space.

FIGURE 6.56 Angled beams draw the eye upward and expand space.

- Use diagonal beams, which draw the eye upward, to make gabled ceilings appear even higher. (See Figures 6.56 and 6.57.)

For a lower ceiling effect:

- Paint it a darker color or use a patterned wall covering (see Figure 6.58).
- Extend the color or covering down onto the wall a short distance (**dropped ceilings**), where a border or a small molding may be used. As attention moves upward, it stops at the molding and the ceiling seems to begin at that point. In this way the ceiling can be psychologically lowered as much as 3 ft. Or, use a pattern on the ceiling. (See Figure 6.59.)
- Use a predominance of horizontal lines in the room's architecture and decorative elements.
- Use wood ceilings and horizontal beams, particularly in natural wood or a bold or dark color.

In recent years changing architectural styles have produced exhilarating ceiling designs, which add new dimensions to interior spaces, often by incorporating a variety of high and low ceilings within a private residence or commercial setting. A concern for energy efficiency has also determined the height of ceilings to some extent.

Types of Ceilings

Ceiling designs can be distinguished according to various structural forms and their placement or direction.

- The *flat* ceiling is usually plastered, painted, or covered with wood strips. The *flat-beamed* ceiling is one in which the structural beams are exposed or lightweight beams have been applied.
- The *shed* or *lean-to* ceiling rises diagonally to one side in a single slope. The furnishings in a room with this ceiling must be arranged carefully to achieve a comfortable balance.
- The *gabled, double-pitched,* or *cathedral* ceiling expands vertical space, especially when beams extend upward. If beams are placed horizontally, the room's length is emphasized. (See Figure 6.60.)
- The *sculptured,* custom-designed ceiling is usually not created as an unobtrusive background but may call attention to itself as the room's focal point. Sometimes designed in highly dramatic and unique ways, sculptured ceilings follow no set pattern and usually require ample space for construction and effect. (See Figure 6.61.)
- The *coved* ceiling is one in which the ceiling and wall flow into each other by means of a curved surface in place of right angles. Sometimes the perimeter is made to accommodate recessed lighting, allowing light to shine upward on the ceiling surface.
- *Vaulted and domed* ceilings are arched structures as opposed to flat planes—and, in a way, a complete extension of the coved ceiling.

FIGURE 6.57 Architect Ron Molen has created a triangular wood unit complete with lighting and suspended it from the ceiling over the bed. The strong form helps define the sleeping area and restates the lines of the triangular wood ceiling above. (Courtesy of Ron Molen, architect.)

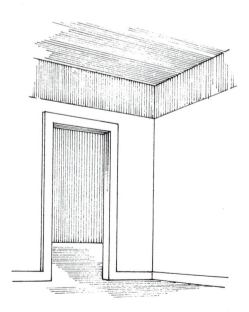

FIGURE 6.58 A dark paint on the ceiling or a wall covering coming down on the wall makes a ceiling appear lower.

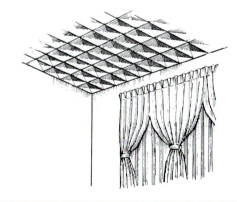

FIGURE 6.59 A patterned ceiling appears to advance and seems lower.

Floors, Walls, and Ceilings

FIGURE 6.60 To give the illusion of endless space, designer Harry Stein has painted the beams and part of the ceiling black and strategically placed numerous lamps. Other sections of the ceiling are mirrored, adding to the effect of depth in this New York penthouse. (Photograph by Norman McGrath.)

FIGURE 6.61 Sculptured ceiling.

- *Coffered* ceilings, popular in past centuries, are constructed of wooden members in a grid manner, often with moldings and sunken decorative panels.
- The *dropped* ceiling is one in which a portion or the entire area of a ceiling is lowered below the main structure. (See Figure 6.62.) This type of ceiling can define an area of a room (for example, a dining area in a dual-purpose living room), provide indirect lighting, and add interest to a living space.
- Architects often create *custom-designed* ceilings for specific residential or nonresidential projects. (See Figure 6.63.)

Types of Ceiling Materials

To satisfy the demands of contemporary architecture, new ceiling materials are being developed and old ones being revived. This section discusses some of the most common ceiling materials employed today.

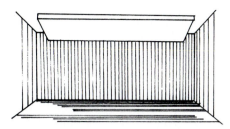

FIGURE 6.62 Dropped ceiling.

Plaster and Wallboard

Plaster and wallboard are the most common materials used for ceilings today. They are appropriate for any type of room, inexpensive, and easily applied, creating a unified background with the walls. The finished surface may be smooth, textured, wallpapered, or painted. Sometimes a plastered ceiling is stenciled or has applied decoration or moldings. Flat paint is usually preferable for ceilings, with high gloss reserved for special purposes.

Tiles

Tiles for ceilings come in a wide variety of materials, colors, and patterns. Many have acoustical properties for absorbing noise. Others have a foil backing, which cuts down on air-conditioning and heating costs. An easy method of installation for do-it-yourselfers uses metal tracks and clips, which have replaced the unwieldy furring wood strips previously used. Tiles can also be suspended from a supportive gridwork to create a three-dimensional effect.

Glass and Plastic

Glass or plastic panels, which can be translucent or transparent, are sometimes used in ceilings to provide overhead light—either natural daylight or recessed artificial

FIGURE 6.63 The Enchanted Lobby at the Walt Disney World Swan Hotel designed by Michael Graves was themed for fantasy and entertainment. The tropical illusion is reinforced by large palm-frond sconces and colorful parrot light fixtures. The high-pitched ceiling is painted with dramatic stripes resembling fabric. Handsome swan benches provide a warm touch. (Photo courtesy of The Walt Disney Co.)

light. Overall illumination may be provided, and striking lighting effects from high-up windows can be achieved. Skylight views add a new dimension.

Stamped Metal

Stamped metal ceilings were popular during the nineteenth century and are again being made today. These ceilings are used primarily in the restoration and construction of Victorian buildings. This treatment involves stamping or pressing designs onto metal panels, providing a unique embossed effect.

Fabric

Fabric, although not commonly used, can be stretched, shirred, or pasted (like wallpaper) to the ceiling surface. The softness of fabric provides a comfortable, warm feeling, and when used as a repeating fabric in the room can unify the interior.

Wood

Wood, either in strips, panels, beams, or planks, can provide a warm, inviting atmosphere. Wood ceilings, because of their visual weight, tend to lower the ceiling and may create a feeling of heaviness unless the ceiling is above average in height. Often wood is combined with plaster; for example, wood beams can stretch across a plastered ceiling. Wood can be left natural, stained, or painted. Where natural beams are not feasible, ceiling beams of polyurethane (which simulate hand-carved wood to a remarkable degree) can be glued to a regular ceiling.

INSULATING AGAINST NOISE AND HEAT LOSS

A major challenge facing architects and builders today is combating noise. Sound is being muffled by an increase in the mass and density of sound-deadening materials. In masonry construction the space between units is filled with insulation. Where formerly 2-by-4-in. studs were standard, 2-by-6-in. studs are now used to allow for more insulation. Where double studding is employed, an air space between the partitions is used in addition to insulating batts. Interior walls are often made by a series of slats, with spaces between filled with sound-absorbing materials. A finished wall material made of woven reeds, such as sisal, can be adhered to rigid insulation, thus providing a durable and attractive surface while adding to noise absorption.

In double ceilings, where one ceiling is above another, the lower one is suspended by means of clips so that the plasterboard is not attached directly to the joints, thus leaving a space for insulation materials. Floors are often given a deadening coat of plaster or a coat of lightweight concrete.

With energy conservation a major concern, the use of solar energy is increasing. In addition, architects and builders are using a variety of means to control heat loss. Windows are given double and triple **glazing**. Extra-thick insulating batts are used, and extra foam is blown between partitions and ceilings. Although used to deaden sounds, insulation also helps in avoiding heat loss. Thermobreak weather stripping is used around doors and windows, which separates the metal by nonconductive nylon or neoprene and prevents heat from escaping. Orienting a building to take the best advantage of the climate can save energy. Windows on the sunny side can absorb heat that can be stored for later use. Well-insulated walls on the cold side preserve heat.

CHAPTER 7

Windows, Doors, Stairways, and Fireplaces

FIGURE 7.1 A soaring two-story angled bay window is framed with softly swagged white fabric. The inviting neoclassic wood fireplace is flanked by an armoire and cabinets, providing concealed storage for an entertainment center. (Photograph by Mark Boisclair.)

Interior shapes and walls form a backdrop, setting the stage for the life that will be lived within. They also provide good designers with glorious backgrounds against which they can place furniture from many different periods and styles.

—*Norma Skurka*

Although glass walls were known to the ancient Egyptians and Romans, historically *windows* were merely small cutouts, known as the "wind's eye," in the walls of a house to permit smoke to escape, let in fresh air, and allow glimpses of the outside. Over the years, many types of windows have been planned as an integral part of the structural design of a building. Although window treatments change with style trends, they are enhanced when attuned to the architectural spirit of the structure, both exterior and interior.

Doors originally were purely functional, used only for necessary passage. In modern times they have assumed different forms with varying degrees of design importance and traffic control.

Stairways provide the practical function of transporting the user from floor to floor. They can also provide a striking visual experience. Their design, style, construction, and safety features are important considerations whether planning residential or nonresidential spaces.

Fireplaces relate to the interior backgrounds, such as walls, floors, and ceilings, as well as to the furnishings and general atmosphere planned for the space. Often a fireplace functions as the room's focal point. Fireplace design, type, construction, and location are considered in this chapter.

WINDOWS

The window is an important architectural and decorative element in a room. Traditionally, windows were often symmetrically placed in the facade of the house, with small panes the norm.

With the development of modern architecture and technology, new types of window openings were planned as integral parts of the basic design. Window placement and design, or **fenestration**, today can be either symmetrical or asymmetrical, and frequently openings of unusual shapes are used. The glass wall, the corner window, sliding glass doors, the straight or slanting clerestory, and the peaked two-story window are now as familiar as the double-hung or casement types standard for so many years.

The three primary functions of windows are (1) to admit *light*, (2) to provide *ventilation*, and (3) to enhance *visual communication*. Even though light and air can now be controlled, and windows are not absolutely necessary, planning a house without windows seems inconceivable. As efficient as modern technology is, there are no substitutes for fresh air, natural light, and an outdoor view to create a psychological association with the outdoors and provide a sense of well-being.

The window is a conspicuous element in both the exterior and interior design of a house. (See Figure 7.1.) As a source of interior light, the window is the first point to which the eye is drawn during the daytime, and at night a lighted window is the first thing seen from the outside.

Unfortunately, window openings are not always planned with indoor function in mind. Good planning can be ensured if an alert homeowner or interior designer works closely with the architect. For example, a window originally pushed into a corner—a placement that creates a problem for decorating—can easily be relocated on the plans of the house.

CONSIDERATIONS IN THE APPROACH TO WINDOW TREATMENT

It is helpful to approach the location, design, and treatment of any window by studying a number of primary considerations:

- Should the *architectural background* of the room against which the window will be seen and its placement in the wall in relation to the other architectural features of the room be emphasized, blended into the background, or camouflaged?
- The *type of window* can determine the treatment.
- Does the *outside view* need to be brought into focus or blocked out? For example, is the view that of a public thoroughfare, the neighbor's barbecue, a private garden, or a distant vista?
- Does *privacy* need to be created? Even if it does not, consider the cold, black appearance at night of a large expanse of glass.
- Is *light* excessive or insufficient? What is the exposure? Northern light is cool, but too much southern or western light can fade and damage furnishings.
- Window type and design can be a factor in the *furniture arrangement*. If there are many openings, for example, it may be difficult to arrange furnishings effectively.
- Is there a *wind problem*? If so, how can protection against wind be arranged?
- Is traffic or other *noise* a problem? Many window treatments can help muffle sounds.
- Window treatments can be an important factor in *conserving energy* and cutting heating and cooling bills.
- Is the window *stationary or movable*? The treatment needs to accommodate the window's function.

TYPES OF WINDOWS

The three general classifications of windows are (1) *movable*, (2) *stationary*, and (3) a *combination* of movable and stationary. All three types are available in standardized sizes. Glass panes may be supported by wood, metal, or plastic, each of which has particular advantages and disadvantages. Wood shrinks, swells, requires a protective finish, and is the most expensive. It discourages moisture

condensation, however, and emits less heat than metal. Metal is strong and does not shrink or swell perceptibly. Except for aluminum and stainless steel, however, it requires protective paint and causes moisture condensation in cold weather. Newer metal windows have a plastic thermal break built in to eliminate excessive heat loss and condensation. Plastic is stable and resists heat and cold.

Movable Windows

Movable windows are made to open to permit ventilation. Some of the most common are illustrated in Figure 7.2.

- **Double-hung windows** are made up of two **sashes** that may be raised or lowered to provide 50 percent ventilation. They are simple and inexpensive.
- The *corner window* consists of two windows that meet or almost meet in a corner. A corner window can be thought of as double windows and treated accordingly.
- **Casements** may swing inward or outward and permit up to 100 percent ventilation. Those that swing outward present no draping problem but can create a potential hazard outside. In-swinging casements must have special treatment. Valances must be hung high enough to clear the window. Side draperies should be out on the walls or hung on swinging-arm rods. Sheers on sash rods attached to top and bottom function well.
- *Ranch or strip windows* are wide and shallow. They are set far enough above the floor to allow furniture to be set against the wall, but they are not ceiling high.
- *Horizontal sliding windows* may be made up of two sliding panes or a large stationary central pane with a sliding pane on either side.
- *Fixed glazing with movable end sections (picture window)* refers to a window with a large stationary central section of small panes or one large pane, with double-hung windows at either end.
- **Awning** (or louvered) and **jalousie windows** consist of strips of glass, hinged at the top or bottom and opening outward or inward. Strips in jalousies are narrower than in the awning type. Both allow draft-free ventilation control.
- *Single-pivoting sash windows* are raised for ventilation by means of side mechanisms. These windows are most often used as skylights or in light wells.
- **Dormer windows** are vertical windows that project from an alcove in the roof, usually filling the entire space.
- **Palladian windows** feature a central arched window flanked by two smaller windows, often with movable sections. This window type is associated with the Georgian style and today is incorporated with numerous styles and given various interpretations.
- **French doors** are paired doors of glass. Since they are basically casement windows enlarged to walk through, they can be treated in the same manner. Draperies and cornices should clear the operating portion of the

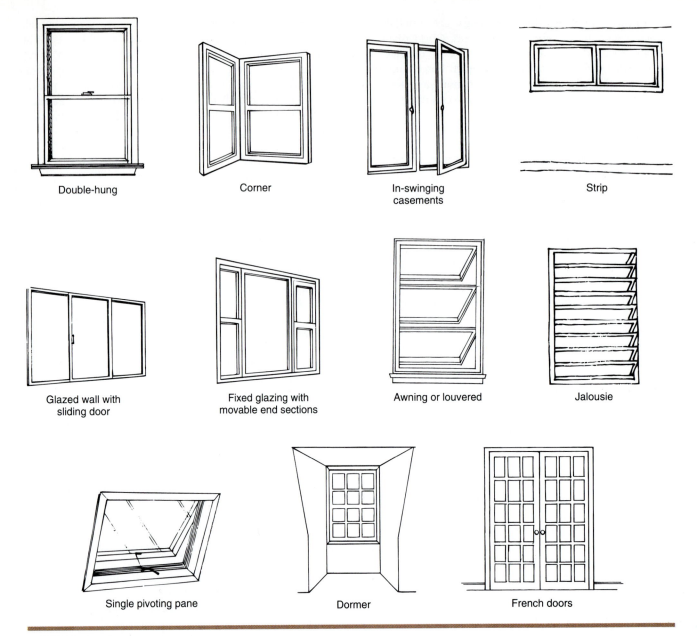

FIGURE 7.2 Types of movable windows.

Double-hung

Corner

In-swinging casements

Strip

Glazed wall with sliding door

Fixed glazing with movable end sections

Awning or louvered

Jalousie

Single pivoting pane

Dormer

French doors

door. **Louvers,** or slatted panels, are a popular alternative. Whatever the treatment, it should conform to the other windows in the room.

Stationary Windows

Stationary windows are built as an integral part of the wall construction and require no special framing. They may be made of plain or nonglare glass. Where large areas of glass are used, thermopanes or triple-glaze and nonshatter glass are advised. Some common stationary windows include fixed glazing, bay, bow, arch, Palladian, skylight, and clerestory. (See Figure 7.3.)

- *Fixed glazing* is a common feature of today's contemporary homes and may extend from floor to ceiling or begin a short distance above the floor. The window wall is expensive, requiring double or triple glaze for energy conservation. (See Figure 7.4.) Some disadvantages of the window wall are that (1) it may not allow enough privacy, (2) it may let in excessive light that can create glare and fade furnishings, and (3) the expanse of black area at night is uninviting.
- The *angle bay* can be made up of three or more windows that angle out of the room. The central pane may be stationary and the side ones movable.
- The **bay bow window** is a smooth, sweeping curve of multipanes.

- **Clerestory windows** may be straight or slanting windows set at the ceiling or high in a wall between two roof levels.
- *Arched windows* are those in which the upper part of a rectangular opening is topped by an arch (see Figure 5.9).
- *Skylights* may be single or grouped panels of clear or translucent glass or plastic, either flat or domed, and fixed or movable for ventilation. Entire skylight ceilings in kitchens, laundries, and bathrooms have the special advantage of providing adequate daylight for inside rooms. In small areas light from above can expand visual space and make the sky and trees part of a room. The skylight window has a number of disadvantages, however, including problems with water seepage, insulation, and cleaning. Also, it presents a security problem unless protected by safety-wired glass or other safety measures.

Combination of Movable and Stationary Windows

Window types often combine both movable and stationary sections. For example, a slanted clerestory window may be stationary on the top portion with a sliding glass door below, or an angled bay window may have movable sections flanking stationary center sections. With both movable and stationary parts, a window can provide more flexibility and ventilation capacity.

Other Window Types

The *single window* may be standard size, high and narrow, or a small cutout in the wall. *Double and multiple windows* are identical windows placed side by side. They may be separated by a strip of wall or only by their abutting window frames. Unifying them is usually the main objective of the designer.

Hexagons, circles, and other geometric shapes are occasionally used to provide a point of interest and additional light. These types may add variety to a room combined with other more common window types.

Architects and designers often find occasion to create *custom-designed windows* for clients, as shown in Figure 7.4. They can be of various sizes and shapes and may be movable, stationary, or combinations of both types.

TYPES OF WINDOW TREATMENTS

Deciding on an appropriate window treatment from the almost unlimited options available can be challenging. It is helpful to be familiar with the range of possibilities. All window treatments fall into two broad categories: soft and hard. This section discusses the most common types in use today, beginning with soft window treatments.

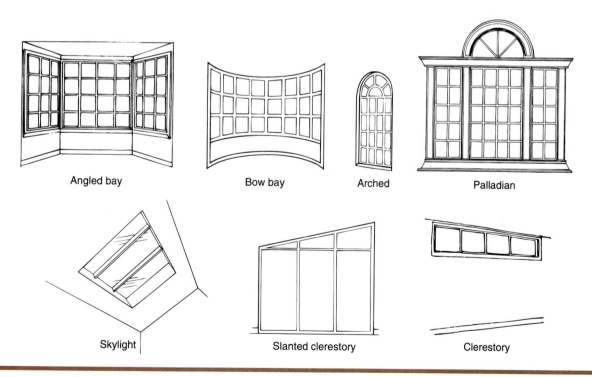

Angled bay   Bow bay   Arched   Palladian

Skylight   Slanted clerestory   Clerestory

FIGURE 7.3 Types of stationary windows.

FIGURE 7.4 A custom-designed two-story window wall allows a panoramic view of the spectacular setting. (Courtesy of Hurd Millwork Company, Inc.)

Figure 7.5 illustrates the parts of a window and several types of treatment.

Soft Window Treatments

Draperies

Draperies are usually made of a heavier fabric than curtains, but the terms are interchangeable. *Draw draperies* are made to draw over the window to control light, heat and cold, and provide privacy (see Figure 7.6). They hang straight and may be used alone or combined with other curtains, blinds, or shades. For example, with a combination of draw sheers and draw drapery—the most common usage—the view can be exposed and light, sound, heat, cold, and privacy can be controlled. Draperies that draw closed from both the right and left sides are called *two-way traverse.* Those that draw from one side only are called *one-way traverse.* Curtains and draperies are most often hung to one of three desirable lengths: (1) the sill, (2) the bottom of the **apron,** or (3) the floor. (See Figure 7.7.)

Side draperies are stationary at the sides of the window. Side draperies may be hung straight or tied back.

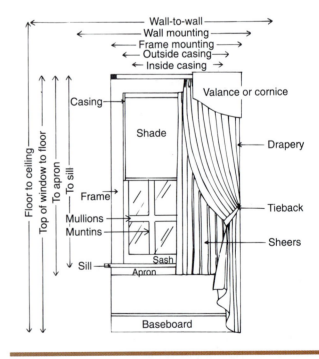

FIGURE 7.5 Window parts and treatment placement.

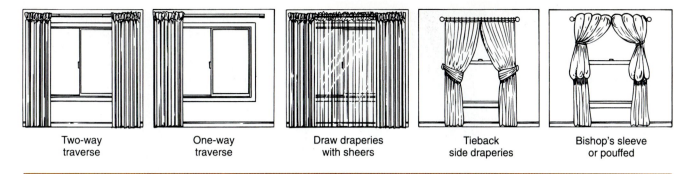

| Two-way traverse | One-way traverse | Draw draperies with sheers | Tieback side draperies | Bishop's sleeve or pouffed |

FIGURE 7.6 Types of draperies.

Their purpose is to bring beauty and style into the room. For daytime privacy sheers may be combined, and for nighttime privacy and warmth underdraws, louver blinds, or roller shades may be added (see Figure 7.8). *Bishop's sleeve or "pouffed" side draperies* are side draperies that are tied back at various levels in a "blossoming" or "pouffed" effect. This treatment is a soft, fresh alternative to the traditional side drapery type.

Glass curtains or sheers are used primarily to diffuse light and provide daytime privacy. They may be hung permanently against the glass or drawn back. Much of their beauty and efficiency depends on their fullness, most often three times the width of the window. When nighttime privacy is desired, sheers can be combined with draw draperies, blinds, or underdraws.

Semisheers or casements (the terms are sometimes used interchangeably with sheers) are generally made of a loosely woven fabric and are heavier than a sheer. They are most often used singly and drawn to control light and provide nighttime privacy. Semisheers that allow some light are the most common choice for large areas of glass.

Drapery lining serves several functions. Windows are viewed from two perspectives: outside and inside. Drapery lining provides a uniform and attractive view from the outside, covering patterns and colors seen most effectively from an interior perspective. A plain off-white lining usually will make windows unobtrusive. When several windows face the street, it is best to coordinate their appearance through the use of drapery lining, especially for windows on the same level. Drapery lining also provides additional insulation from heat and cold, protects the drapery, and adds a graceful draping quality.

Ready-mades are draperies and curtains made to standard lengths and available in most drapery depart-

FIGURE 7.7 Curtain and drapery lengths.

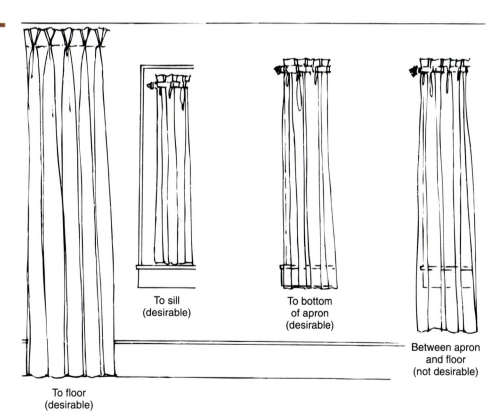

To sill (desirable)

To bottom of apron (desirable)

Between apron and floor (not desirable)

To floor (desirable)

FIGURE 7.8 Subtle custom hand-woven window coverings of natural flax enhance the lovely garden view while softly filtering the sunlight. The permanently fixed tieback draperies add definition and graceful lines in the Garden Pavilion Restaurant at the Century Plaza Hotel in Los Angeles. (Courtesy of Conrad Imports, Incorporated. Photograph by Fritz Taggart.)

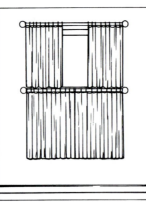

Center meet
Priscilla curtains

Crisscross
Priscilla
curtains

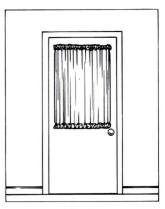

Shirred
curtains

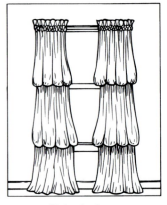

Sash
curtains

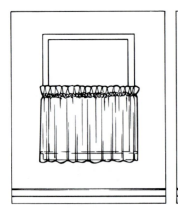

Cafe curtains,
one tier

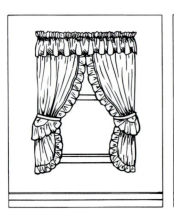

Cafe curtains,
two tiers

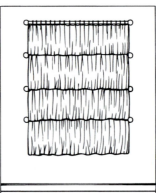

Tiered
curtains

Bishop's sleeve
or pouffed

FIGURE 7.9 Types of curtains.

ments. Although often less full than custom-made curtains and draperies, ready-mades often give quite satisfactory effects that belie their modest cost.

Curtains

The most common types of curtains are illustrated in Figure 7.9.

- *Priscilla curtains* are ruffled tiebacks most often used in traditional and informal settings. Traditionally they were used in kitchens, bathrooms, and bedrooms; however, because of the popularity of country style interiors in the 1980s, Priscilla curtains have been brought into many living, dining, and family rooms. They are usually made of light, sheer fabrics trimmed with a ruffle and shirred to a rod at the top of the window. One type of Priscilla curtain has the panels overlap in a crisscross fashion and another has a center meet arrangement.
- *Shirred curtains* are gathered on a rod and hung at the top of the window, letting the fabric drape softly. The amount of fabric used determines how full the effect of the curtains is.
- *Sash curtains* are usually sheer and are hung close to the glass. They are shirred at the top and often the bottom on sash rods. These curtains are used on many window types and doors with glass inserts.
- *Cafe curtains and tiers* are hung over the lower part of the window. (See Figure 7.10.) Usually used for privacy, they may draw or be stationary. Two or more tiers are often hung to cover the entire window, in which case the rods are concealed. Cafe curtains may be teamed with draw or side draperies, shades, blinds, or shutters. Cafe curtains are often embellished with a window top treatment.
- *Bishop's sleeve or "pouffed" curtains* are similar to the drapery type illustrated in Figure 7.6, but employ a sheerer fabric.

Fabric Shades

Some of the most common types of fabric shades are illustrated in Figures 7.11 and 7.12.

Roman shades have a flat surface when extended down (Figure 7.13). When drawn upward by a cord, the surface overlaps in horizontal folds made possible by a precreased rigid lining or by rings (or ring tape) and cords attached to the back of the shades. Roman shades come in six basic treatments: (1) shirred Roman, (2) shirred **balloon** (Figure 7.14), (3) flat Roman, (4) soft-pleated Roman, (5) balloon Roman, and (6) accordion-pleated Roman. Another type of balloon shade is the *cloud,* which is similar to the other balloons, but distinguished by an irregular puffed effect at the bottom of the shade.

Austrian shades consist of rows of lightweight fabric seamed to fall into deep scallops. The shade is operated

by a draw cord and is similar in design to the shirred balloon Roman.

Pleated fabric shades are also called "accordion shades" (because they are folded like the bellows of an accordion) and "soft shades." Pleated shades are factory manufactured, are available in a wide range of colors and finishes, and can be insulated. Fabrics can vary from opaque to translucent and can be patterned or plain. *Honeycomb shades* have smaller pleats and are usually made of a heavy polyester fabric. They operate on the same principle as the single pleated shade except two pleated shades are bonded together, resulting in a "honeycomb" cross section. This construction provides an energy-efficient insulation air space. The exterior side of the shade is white to reflect the sun's rays and provide uniformity on the outside. The stack-up return is relatively small for all pleated fabric shades, especially for honeycomb-pleated shades.

The *roller shade,* an old favorite, is an inexpensive window treatment. It may be installed between window casings or on the outside of the frame. The most common material is vinyl, which is available in a variety of weights. Traditionally, roller shades were white or off-white, but

FIGURE 7.10 A country kitchen is wrapped with documentary fabrics and wall coverings in light and dark greens on a white ground. A coordinated decorative fabric is used for the cafe curtain and cascading valance. (Courtesy of Greeff Fabrics.)

FIGURE 7.11 Types of Roman shades.

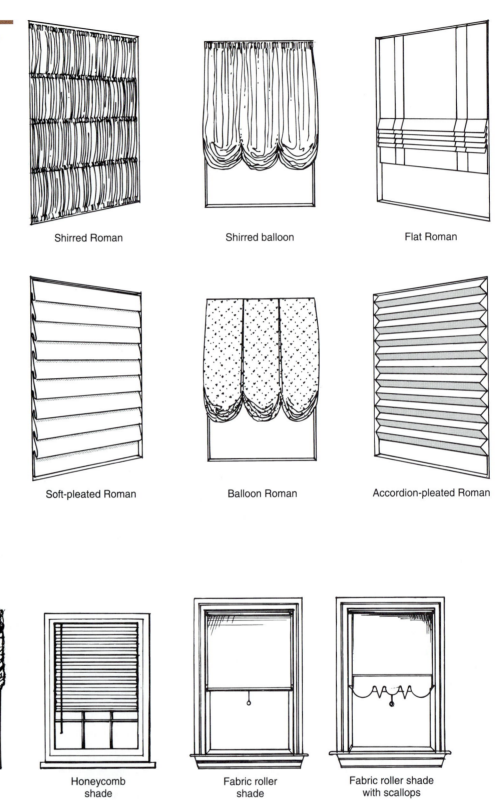

Shirred Roman

Shirred balloon

Flat Roman

Soft-pleated Roman

Balloon Roman

Accordion-pleated Roman

Austrian shade

Honeycomb shade

Fabric roller shade

Fabric roller shade with scallops

FIGURE 7.12 Other types of shades.

FIGURE 7.13 Roman shades have been custom designed to fit the angles of this window, allowing a sweeping view of the city. The simple tailored effect complements the architecture and the room's Southwest decor. (Photograph by Mark Boisclair.)

FIGURE 7.14 Balloon shade made of permanently pleated polyester has an ethereal appearance. (Photograph courtesy of Jack Lenor Larsen.)

are now available in the full spectrum of colors. Originally thought of as purely functional, the simple roller shade can be laminated with fabric and trimmed in a variety of ways and has assumed an important decorative role. When hung bottom-up, it is especially effective for privacy (see Figure 5.10). Roller shades may be light filtering or room darkening, depending on the thickness of the material. Shades are easy to maintain and insulate against heat and cold. *Window quilts or thermal shades* are made of additional layers of fabric, often have a decorative stitched pattern, and provide extra insulation.

Window Top Treatments

Many windows are embellished with treatments at the top or at the top and sides of the drapery or curtains. These treatments are of various designs and generally fall into two categories: those made of soft and those made of hard materials, shown in Figure 7.15.

Soft Materials: Valances

The **valance** is generally a shirred, pleated, or draped soft treatment across the window top (see Figure 7.16). It is used solely for appearance; it does not change the function of the drapery. The valance may match the side or draw draperies and is often shaped by a stiff interlining.

Windows, Doors, Stairways, and Fireplaces

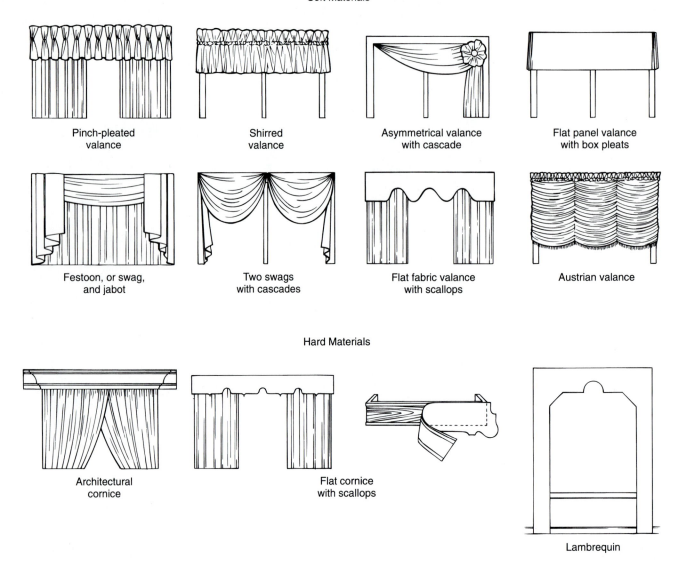

Pinch-pleated valance

Shirred valance

Asymmetrical valance with cascade

Flat panel valance with box pleats

Festoon, or swag, and jabot

Two swags with cascades

Flat fabric valance with scallops

Austrian valance

Hard Materials

Architectural cornice

Flat cornice with scallops

Lambrequin

FIGURE 7.15 Types of top treatments for windows.

If the fabric is patterned, the shape of the valance looks best when it conforms to that pattern. If the fabric is plain, the valance should run the same direction as the drapery. A valance screens hardware and gives the drapery a finished look. It can appear to extend the height and width of a window and unify windows of different sizes, thus altering the room's visual proportions.

A *swag* is a type of valance treatment wherein fabric is draped over the top of the window and tapered at the sides. A *festoon* is a single draped member of a swag. A *jabot* or *cascade* may drape down from the corners of the swag. The cascade has a vertical outside edge with an undulating edge closest to the swags. A jabot is a pair of cascades joined together with flowing outside edges. They are usually pleated and may be of varying lengths. Swags and jabots or cascades may be hung over sheers,

drapery, blinds, shutters or shades or at the top of bare windows. (See Figure 7.17.)

Hard Materials: Cornices and Lambrequins

Cornices are generally made of wood, metal, or another hard material and are placed at the top of the window treatment. Often cornices are a continuation of an architectural molding or cornice around the top perimeter of the wall extending outward to accommodate the window top. Cornices may be simple or decorative, such as a scalloped or pierced design. They may be stained, painted, or covered with fabric. A cornice with a fabric valance attached is an effective formal treatment.

Lambrequins are similar to cornices, but they also have a rigid treatment that extends vertically down both

FIGURE 7.16 Lengths of white fabric, wrapped around poles and tied back, form a simple but effective treatment for arched windows. (Courtesy of Scott Sandler, photographer, Phoenix, Arizona.)

FIGURE 7.17 Fringed and tasseled valances swagged over gilded poles complement the traditional furnishings at Blair House, Washington, D.C. The warm, cheerful colors welcome visiting heads-of-state. (Mario Buatta, designer. Courtesy of Mario Buatta, Incorporated.)

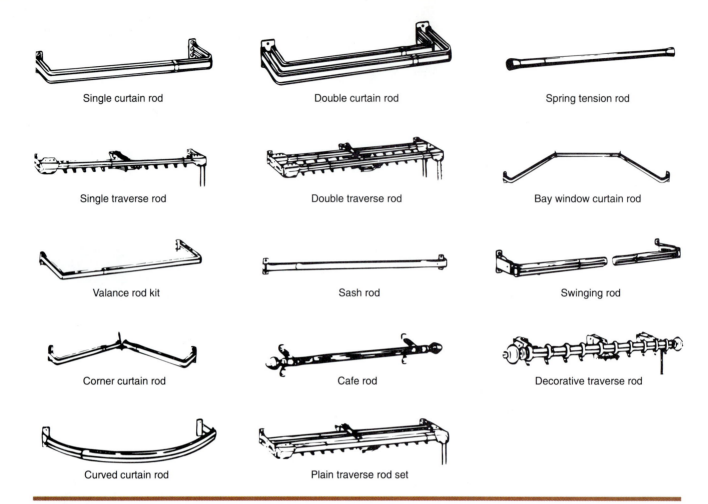

Single curtain rod

Double curtain rod

Spring tension rod

Single traverse rod

Double traverse rod

Bay window curtain rod

Valance rod kit

Sash rod

Swinging rod

Corner curtain rod

Cafe rod

Decorative traverse rod

Curved curtain rod

Plain traverse rod set

FIGURE 7.18 Curtain and drapery rods.

sides of the window. Lambrequins can be painted or covered with wallpaper or fabric and used with or without draperies, curtains, blinds, or shades. They provide a tailored look and can help unify a room.

Window Hardware

Functional

Figure 7.18 shows types of functional and decorative window hardware. Purely functional hardware is inconspicuous. *Sash rods* are flat rods attached close to the sash (often both top and bottom) on which curtains are shirred. *Extension rods* are used for stationary curtains and drapery. They extend to various lengths and are available in single and double sets. *Traverse rods* operate on a pulley system. Available as either one- or two-way traverse types, they are used for drawing curtains and drapery. *Spring tension rods* fit inside the casing. *Swinging rods* are mounted on a mechanism that permits the rod to swing backward. These rods are suitable for inswinging casements, dormers, and French doors. *Extender rods* extend outward to support stationary drapery beyond the window. *Ceiling tracks* with concealed draw-

ing mechanisms are especially popular in contemporary rooms. Small accessories such as hooks, rings, ring slides, brackets, and draw cords are all part of the unseen draw-drapery system.

Decorative

Decorative hardware is functional but also decorative. Rods may be wood (natural wood, stained, or painted) or metal (such as pewter, shiny or antique-finish brass, chrome, bronze, or wrought iron). Decorative hardware is equipped with a variety of *finials* or other decorative features to accommodate any style. Draperies are suspended on rings and may be cord operated or hand drawn. In the latter case, rings should be loose. Metal holdbacks that conform to the style of rods add a finishing touch.

Drapery and Curtain Headings

The *heading* is the pleating or gathering at the top of curtains and draperies that forms the fold (providing the beauty of fullness for drawing). Headings are made in a

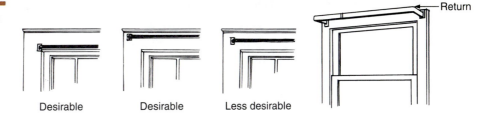

FIGURE 7.19 Rod placement on window frame.

Return

Desirable   Desirable   Less desirable

number of ways. *French or pinch pleats* are the most common type of heading. They are made by stitching together three small pleats about 3 in. from the top. The pleats, which are spaced 3½ to 4 in. apart, are held upright by an interlining of buckram. *Ripplefold* is a simple method of creating gentle, undulating folds by means of a compact track containing snap carriers. Folds are made from flat panels of fabric and are identical on both sides. *Accordion folds* are made by a combination of a compact track with snap carriers and a nylon heading tape. Trimly tailored pleats form architectural-like folds. *Easy pleats* are made with a special tape attached to the inside top of the drapery. When pleater hooks are inserted in ready-made pockets, folds are automatically formed.

In the past, *shirred headings* were most often used for kitchen, bedroom, and bathroom curtains, but today this type of heading is used for many styles and in any room. It is made by stitching a pocket approximately 1½ in. from the top, in which the rod is inserted. A series of additional pockets under the main rod pocket, gathered by inserting tape, gives a puffy look. Rod placement on windows is illustrated in Figure 7.19.

Tiebacks or *holdbacks* hold back stationary draperies. They come in a wide variety of materials and styles and may be cords, tassels, metal, wood, or matching or contrasting fabric. Designers often tie back drapery somewhere between one-half and one-third from the bottom—employing the proportions of the golden mean (see Chapter 1). *Trimmings* can give a finished look to draperies, cornices, and valances. Trimmings include a vast array of fringes, braids, edgings, cords, and tassels.

Hard Window Treatments

Blinds

Figure 7.20 shows several types of blinds. *Venetian blinds* were popular in ancient times, later in Colonial America, and then during the Art Deco period for purely functional purposes. Today, modern adaptations of the blind have again become popular window treatments in both traditional- and contemporary-style homes and nonresidential settings. In most cases, venetian blinds are constructed of aluminum, stainless steel, plastic, or wooden slats. The wooden slat blinds have been so popular that they are generally known just as *wooden blinds*. These horizontally or sometimes vertically arranged strips can be adjusted precisely for light and privacy. Venetian blinds can be mounted on the inside or outside of the window casing and provide a clean, streamlined look.

Miniblinds or louvers are made on the same principle as venetian blinds, but the metal or plastic slats are narrow (about 1 in.), creating a sleek, trim look, as shown in Figure 7.21. Miniblinds are strong, lightweight, and come complete, requiring no supplementary hardware. They can be mounted on the inside or outside of the casing. A wide range of colors is available. Miniblinds are treated on both sides. They can be adjusted to control light and privacy. Used alone they can add sophistication to the most formal interior or be at home in the most modest room. Miniblinds can be combined with a wide range of draw and side draperies for a more traditional look. The blinds are a little difficult to dust and clean; however, windows are made in which miniblinds are

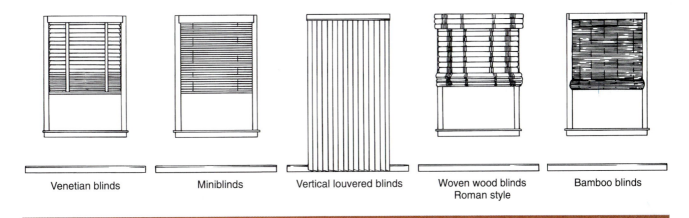

Venetian blinds   Miniblinds   Vertical louvered blinds   Woven wood blinds
Roman style   Bamboo blinds

FIGURE 7.20 Types of blinds.

Windows, Doors, Stairways, and Fireplaces

FIGURE 7.21 In this glass-walled seashore home, miniblinds control the light without obstructing the view. Skylights are left bare. (Photograph by Leland Lee, courtesy of Levalor Lorentzen Company.)

enclosed between two panes of glass to help eliminate dust problems. This style, although expensive, also provides better insulation. *Microminiblinds* have slats that measure about ½ in. They are not as durable as miniblinds.

Vertical blinds, also based on the design of venetian blinds, are made of vertical strips that pivot at the top or the top and bottom. (See Figure 7.22.) When drawn, the strips overlap to provide maximum privacy and light control. Usually made of plastic or metal, vertical blinds may have a different color on each side or may be covered with wallpaper or fabric. They are also available in wood. Vertical blinds provide a uniform, tailored appearance.

Woven split-wood and bamboo blinds are slats of wood interwoven with colored or plain yarn. Woven split-wood and bamboo blinds allow some light, and their warm natural texture is appropriate for many rooms and various styles. They may be used alone or combined with draperies and top treatments. This type of blind is raised by rolling or pleating.

Shutters

Figure 7.23 shows several types of shutters. *Louvered wood shutters* have been used since ancient times and continue to be a popular window treatment. They can substitute for drapery, be adjusted (by means of a vertical wooden support) for light and air, as seen in Figure 7.24, and are remarkably versatile. Shutters come in standard sizes and can be custom-made to fit any window. Light colors are more practical, because dark colors show dust more readily. Shutters can be used in tiers, have panels that are treated in the center with shirred fabric, have raised panel designs, or have vertical louvers. *Plantation shutters* have larger slats and are adaptable to many styles and window types. In Figure 7.25 one window is treated four ways with shutters as one possibility. Figure 7.26 shows a window designed with a soft window top (valance) and shutters.

Screens and Grills

Screens and grills can be effective window treatments. They can conceal an unsightly view, a group of poorly designed windows, an architectural defect, or a windowless wall. Two well known types are illustrated in Figure 7.27.

Shoji screens. The traditional Japanese *shoji* window or screen, with wood mullions and muntins supporting

FIGURE 7.22 Vertical blinds provide an efficient and simple window treatment that supports the modern style used in this bedroom. (Courtesy of Juan Montoya Design Corporation.)

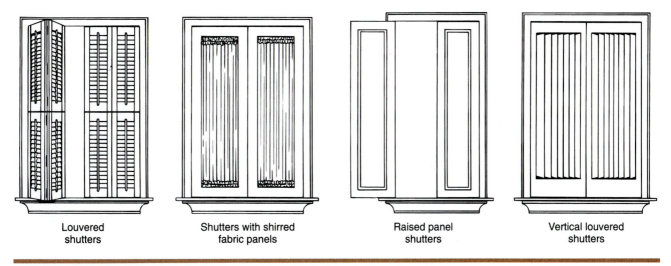

| Louvered shutters | Shutters with shirred fabric panels | Raised panel shutters | Vertical louvered shutters |

FIGURE 7.23 Types of shutters.

FIGURE 7.24 Shutters can also function as doors. In this private residence a wall of shutter doors opens onto a large terrace and view. These shutter doors can also be shut for privacy. (Courtesy of Gayl Baddeley/Associates.)

FIGURE 7.25 One window given four treatments.

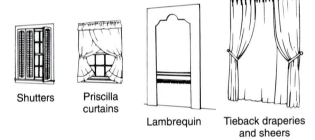

Shutters   Priscilla curtains   Lambrequin   Tieback draperies and sheers

FIGURE 7.26 French doors in this bedroom are treated with painted wood blinds that can be controlled for light and privacy or easily opened for access. The windows are topped with patterned flat balloon Roman valances that soften the straight lines of the blinds and add visual interest. (Courtesy of Charles Moore Associates, Austin, Texas. Photograph by Gabriel Bensur, Inc.)

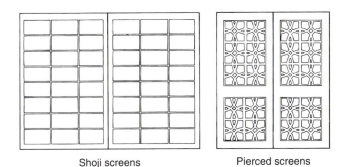

Shoji screens   Pierced screens

FIGURE 7.27 Types of screens.

rice-paper panes, can slide or be stationary, and may be used to establish an Oriental or contemporary theme. The translucent rice-paper panes do not allow a view, but do provide daytime privacy. Often shoji screens are fitted on a track to slide in front of a glass window.

Grills. Widely used in Spain and the Middle East for centuries, the pierced or grillwork screen can be an exotic window treatment and has become popular in America. Privacy can be secured while light filters through, creating an atmosphere of uncluttered appeal.

Glass Block, Leaded and Stained Glass

Glass block is a translucent block of irregular glass, widely used during the Art Deco period and International Style of the 1920s and 1930s. Today, glass block is again enjoying popularity, as seen in Figure 7.28. The block is made up of two hollow half pieces that are joined together and come in a variety of sizes and shapes. The surface quality of the glass can be plain, frosted, mottled, or textured. Currently, a few companies are producing glass block in triangular shapes to provide architects with more design options.

Beveled, leaded, and stained glass windows are being used in many homes today, both modern and tradi-

FIGURE 7.28 Translucent glass blocks in this large contemporary bath area allow additional light into the space without sacrificing privacy. (Courtesy of Pittsburgh Corning Corporation.)

tional, as seen in Figure 7.29. Beveled glass refers to the angle ground into the edge of plate glass, reflecting the light in colorful ways. It is joined with lead, usually in an intricate design. Stained glass is the art of arranging colorful pieces of glass into a pattern. Pieces of beveled or stained glass are joined by lead, zinc, or copper. Today, stock beveled and stained glass panels are available for doors, windows, sidelights, transoms (small windows over doorways or above larger windows), and skylights. Used for the latter, they bring a brilliant glow into a room. The private craftworker can provide custom designs for individual needs and style preferences.

Plants

Plants can be used successfully in lieu of other window treatments. Hung at varying heights and placed on pedestals or the floor, plants can form a bower of greenery that softens hard-edged architecture, filters the light, and affords privacy. A built-out window can become a greenhouse that uses passive solar energy.

Bare Windows

Bare windows are sometimes beautiful in themselves and if privacy is not a problem, concealing them in layers of drapery can be a mistake. Triple glazing can help control energy. For commercial or residential settings, a new development in window design is the use of liquid crystal.

Liquid Crystal

In the late 1980s a new glass technology was developed that allows for both vision and privacy. *Liquid crystal* is

FIGURE 7.29 Light filters through a stained glass window reflecting a design reminiscent of the Art Nouveau style. (Courtesy of Sonya Jacobs/The Stock Market.)

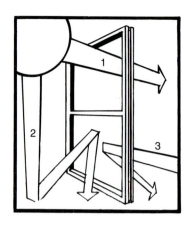

FIGURE 7.30 1. Coated low-E glass allows natural light and short-wave heat energy to enter freely. 2. In the summer, long-wave heat energy radiating from objects is reflected, lowering cooling costs. 3. In winter, internal long-wave heat energy is reflected, lowering heating costs. (Courtesy of PPG Industries.)

now available in window-size glass that can be changed from transparent to translucent and back again at the flick of a switch. This is accomplished with a thin film coated with liquid crystal droplets composed of molecules in a regular crystalline configuration. The film is bonded with polyvinyl interlayers and laminated between panels of heat-strengthened flat glass. When an electric current is sent through the panel, the liquid crystals, arrayed along the curved inner surfaces of each droplet, align to transmit light. The panel instantly becomes clear like a normal window. When the power is switched off, the liquid crystals realign randomly, scattering light, and the panel instantly becomes translucent.

These glass panels are marketed for use in corporate conference rooms, offices, and presentation facilities where the ability to see through glass normally is desired, but at certain times privacy is required. As the price of the panels decreases, use in residential applications should increase. Liquid crystal glass has made possible the multiple performance benefits of privacy, glare reduction, insulation, and solar control in a single product.

WINDOWS AND WINDOW TREATMENTS THAT CONSERVE ENERGY

Energy-Efficient Windows

Today, windows are available that can save energy without being bulky and heavy. Manufacturers are making multiple-glazed windows with a special antireflective coating and tinted glass to direct the sun's heating energy inward. The most popular are windows made with low-E (low emissivity) glass to help a home stay more comfortable.

Low-E glass was developed to take advantage of sunlight. The sun's energy spectrum is divided into three ranges of wavelengths: ultraviolet, visible light, and infrared, which can be felt as heat. The challenge is to let in most of the ultraviolet light and control infrared transmittance according to the season.

Low-E glass, with its low-emissivity pyrolytic coating, lets in approximately 95 percent as much sunlight as ordinary insulated glass, which allows the interior to look bright. Low-E glass blocks a significant part of the ultraviolet light that can fade rugs, fabrics, and curtains. It also blocks most of the long-wave infrared energy, helping to keep winter heat in and summer heat out. (See Figure 7.30.)

Performance can be even better with the addition of argon gas (a superinsulator) in the unit. As a result of these new energy-efficient developments, windows can be practical as well as beautiful.

Energy-Efficient Window Treatments

A window's treatment may also cut down on heating and cooling costs. Curtain and drapery manufacturers are producing a variety of insulators for windows to save energy, such as double-woven multilayered fabrics that trap warm air in the room and insulated shades, draperies, and linings that insulate against heat and cold, thus cutting down on utility bills.

Generally, natural materials do the finest job of insulating. The more yarn used in the fabric, the tighter the weave, the bulkier the material, and the fuller the drapery, the more air it will trap. Layered window treatments are effective insulators. One efficient combination is wooden blinds placed near the glass, with drawn sheers and lined draw draperies. To trap cold or hot air, the sides of the drapery may be anchored to the window frame or wall by two-faced fabric tape. Other effective energy-saving window treatments are quilted blinds, lambrequins and cornices sealed at the top and sides, and window shades equipped with side channels to seal the cracks, which can be operated by a mechanical device. Edge sealing is the most critical point for effective energy saving in window treatments.

DOORS

Although similar in function to windows, doors have distinctive qualities. For example, doors:

- Are an essential part of a room's architectural background.
- Allow passage into the house and from one room to another.
- By their location, control the flow of traffic.
- By their location, control the arrangement of furniture.
- Provide privacy or a two-way view, depending on their structural materials.
- Allow ventilation.
- Help control temperature.
- Provide sound barriers.
- Provide safety and security.

The main entrance door is generally the most important element and focal point in the facade, as shown in Figure 7.31. Traditional paneled period doors and leaded

FIGURE 7.31 Bold architectural curved forms are effectively repeated in this custom-designed entrance door for a single-family dwelling in California, creating a dynamic exterior focus. (Courtesy of Arthur Dyson, architect, AIA.)

FIGURE 7.32 Basic door types.

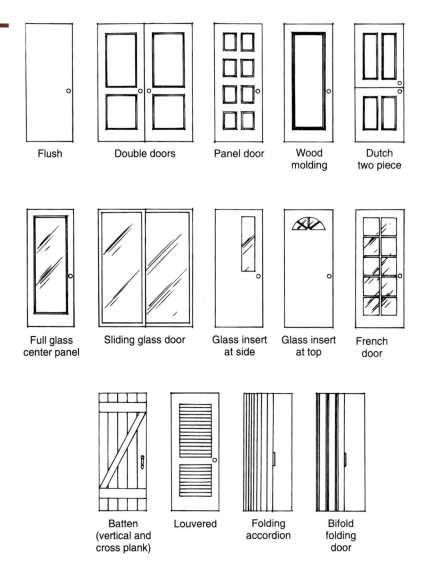

Flush | Double doors | Panel door | Wood molding | Dutch two piece

Full glass center panel | Sliding glass door | Glass insert at side | Glass insert at top | French door

Batten (vertical and cross plank) | Louvered | Folding accordion | Bifold folding door

glass panels continue to be popular. Many exterior and interior contemporary doors are plain and flush, sheathed on both sides with plywood. Metal interior doors with insulating cores are effective in saving energy.

Types of Doors

The three basic types of doors are (1) swinging, (2) folding, and (3) sliding. Figure 7.32 shows these basic types and stylistic variations. These doors may be constructed of wood, aluminum, plastic, and glass or a combination of these materials, depending on design, location, and function.

Swinging Doors

Swinging doors are easy to install and operate and are available in standard sizes. They may be single or double hinged at one side. Most doors are single-hinged and swing only one way; the double-hinged door swings both ways. The latter is convenient between kitchens and dining rooms. A swinging door placed near a corner, with the arc swinging toward the adjacent wall, preserves wall space and directs traffic along the side of the room. **French doors** are pairs of glass-paned single-hinged swinging doors that open the same way, leading to a private outside area or used between rooms. The **Dutch door** is a single-hinged door divided horizontally, making it possible to have ventilation and visual communication from the upper half while the lower half is closed.

Folding Doors

Folding doors are a practical solution to saving space. They are available in sizes from a single door to a full wall divider, and they may be attached at both top and bottom or at the top only. Made in a wide variety of styles (such as louvered) and materials (including plastic and fiberglass), they are flexible and relatively inexpensive.

Sliding Doors

Sliding doors used on the exterior may be part of a glass wall or installed in pairs that slide one behind the other. They are popular in contemporary houses to make the patio or garden a visual part of the living area. Sliding-glass doors should be made of safety glass.

Interior sliding doors usually slide into a pocket in the wall. Although not as flexible as folding doors, sliding doors are great space savers and can provide complete or partial privacy, depending on their material. The traditional Japanese shoji sliding panel is at home in both traditional and modern interiors, serving multiple uses.

Placement of Doors

If doors are well placed to preserve wall space and direct traffic efficiently, they present no problem. But if a room has a surplus of doors, it may be necessary to camouflage them. One possibility is to paint or paper the door the same as the wall. Another option is to remove the hinges and fill the opening with shelves for books and small art objects. Relocating a door is sometimes possible, and the expense may be worth it.

Treatment of Doors

The treatment of doors depends on the design and style of the room. Doors are often painted to blend with the walls, or wood doors may be stained or left natural. If a door has a particularly good design, painting it a contrasting color may augment the room's decoration. When walls are paneled, doors may conform to the walls or be painted in a contrasting color. Many of today's doors are dramatically tall, sometimes fitting into arched openings.

STAIRWAYS

Stairways may be free-standing or attached to one or two walls. Basically, stairways consist of the *tread* (horizontal

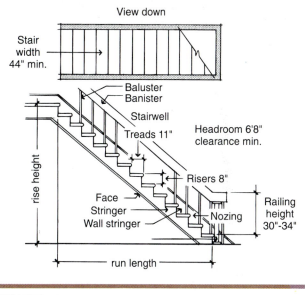

FIGURE 7.33 Stairway terminology.

member of the step), the *riser* (the vertical support), and a protective *railing*. Figure 7.33 illustrates steps and stairway terminology including common measurements for the elements of a stairway. In the past, stairways in simple homes were merely functional, allowing occupants to travel from one floor to another. In palatial settings stairways became extravagant features, often made of marble or wood with elaborately carved balustrades and columns (see Figure 7.34). Architects often exploit the stairway's sculptural potential, resulting in dramatic and often sweeping forms—especially when the stairway is a free-standing design as shown in Figure 7.35.

Not only are stairways visually important, but the designer needs to consider safety and functional aspects as well.

- The depth of a **tread** should accommodate the entire length of the foot, and a measurement of 11 in. is generally used. Often a tread is carpeted for additional safety, because hard surface materials can be a hazard. When treads are tapered on a curving staircase, take

FIGURE 7.34 A handsomely carved wood balustrade and staircase in an old traditional English style are designed in an L-shape. (Courtesy of Stuart Designs, England.)

FIGURE 7.35 This exquisite and welcoming curved staircase was custom made by expert craftspeople in the classical traditional style. Carved balusters are painted white and capped with a dark stained wood railing that matches the wood step. (Courtesy of Driwood Moulding Company.)

care to ensure that the small end of the tread is wide enough for safe use.

- The vertical distance between each tread is the **riser**, which should be no more than 8 in. high for comfort.
- A *handrail* is a necessary feature for occupants of all ages. Often a stairway has upright supports for the handrail (or banister) called *balusters*. A baluster can be designed in a variety of turned forms. A *balustrade* is the handrail together with its balusters.
- *Headroom clearance* should be planned for the top and bottom of the staircase; 6 ft 8 in. is considered a minimum clearance.
- Treads and risers should be *consistent in size.* Varying sizes on the same staircase is dangerous. A person expects and needs each step to be the same height and depth.
- The basic shapes or types of stairs include straight, L-shape, winder, U-shape, curved or circular, and spiral. The type of stair selected depends on the style of the home or commercial concern, the space available to accommodate the stairway, and the personal preference of the owners or occupants.
- Stairways in nonresidential settings can be bold and dramatic, introducing the client, patron, or customer to

the adjoining offices, shops, or other public spaces. Often the stairway functions as a focal point and can be aesthetically stimulating as well as serviceable, as demonstrated in Figure 7.36.

FIREPLACES

Fireplaces have served important functional roles through the centuries as a source of warmth and a place to cook meals. In simple homes the fireplace was the focus of the home and a place where the family congregated. In today's homes the fireplace is generally a visual luxury and may serve primarily as a room's focal point. Studies show that very few fireplaces are lit at all and then only when the climate is cool. When a fire is burning in the fireplace, the heat it generates is most often not adequate to warm an entire room unless planned with energy-efficiency features. Additionally, fireplaces are expensive and hard to clean after use, and they require space for fuel storage.

The fireplace, in spite of these drawbacks, remains a symbol of "hearth and home." American architect Frank Lloyd Wright felt that the fireplace was the "heart of the home" and built wings extending outwards from this point. Still considered a desirable and satisfying asset, fireplaces in residential living spaces can add to a home's market value. Fireplaces in public settings like restaurants, bars, hotels, and clubs can be particularly inviting, offering patrons a friendly and intimate atmosphere.

The *location* of a fireplace within the home and the room requires functional and visual planning. Most homes today have one fireplace, usually located either in the living or family room. Sometimes more than one fireplace may be featured in a single dwelling. Dining rooms, kitchens, recreation rooms, and master bedrooms are also popular spaces for a fireplace. *Placement* within a particular living space varies in the contemporary home, whether traditional or modern in design. A fireplace may be centered on a wall, placed in a corner (popular in the southwestern adobe home), situated asymmetrically, or made a freestanding unit away from the wall (typical in Scandinavian homes). A fireplace may even function as a wall divider between two living areas.

Regardless of their style, fireplaces have a basic placement and opening in relationship to the wall and room. Among the options are the one-way opening, the two-way opening of front and back, the two-way opening of front and side, the three-way opening of side, front, and back, and freestanding (Figure 7.37).

The *size* of the fireplace within a living space is flexible. Small fireplaces can have charm; an average- or medium-sized fireplace can be a focal point without overwhelming a room; and a very large fireplace can be a dramatic feature. The appropriate size of a fireplace is usually determined after considering the scale and proportion of a space.

The *style* of a fireplace generally falls into two categories: traditional or modern. Traditional styles for fireplace design provide charm and a feeling of authenticity. Great variety of design and style is prevalent in modern homes, and often fireplaces are custom designed for a particular space. Modern fireplaces may soar vertically or horizontally, or circular forms may be emphasized. The

FIGURE 7.36 The industrial-style stairway in this nonresidential setting is continued on the mezzanine level. The sweeping lines are emphasized by neon lights that repeat the shape of the railings and add a theatrical touch. (Courtesy of Gayl Baddeley/Associates.)

Windows, Doors, Stairways, and Fireplaces

FIGURE 7.37 The dynamic freestanding fireplace in this Cleveland home, designed by Stanley Jay Friedman, acts both as a principal focus in the space and as a major divider between the seating and dining spaces. (Courtesy of Stanley Jay Friedman. Photograph by Peter Vitale.)

fireplace may or may not have a mantel, the hearth may be on the floor or raised, and the fireplace may be set against the wall or project outward. The style of a fireplace is generally most successful when it complements the room's furnishings and background.

Wood-Burning Stoves

With the high cost of heating, the wood-burning stove has become popular and is available in a large range of styles. Faced with deteriorating air quality as well as wood-burning restrictions, however, many designers and homeowners are choosing alternatives to the wood-burning fireplace.

Wood-Burning Heaters

In 1988 the Environmental Protection Agency (EPA) established strict codes for wood-burning heaters or stoves. Today, only certified wood heaters that meet the emission limits may be sold. No person may install or operate a wood heater except in a manner consistent with the EPA's instructions.

A wood-burning heater or stove may no longer emit more than 8 grams of particulates per hour. An average wood-burning fireplace may emit up to 1,000 grams of particulates per hour. Therefore, heating homes with wood-burning heaters can drastically cut down on air pollutants.

Gas Fireplaces

Natural gas log sets, fireplaces, and fireplace inserts provide the ambience of wood-burning fireplaces and stoves with none of the inconveniences. Compared to wood burning, natural gas fireplace equipment is cleaner burning, simple to start, easy to keep clean, and costs a fraction of the price of wood to operate.

Tile Stoves

Tile stoves, descended from the beautiful alpine Kachelofen heaters of Europe, which can be traced back almost six centuries, are being manufactured today. They come in a variety of styles and provide economical ceramic radiant heat.

Fireplace Construction

Materials

The most common materials for fireplace construction include:

- *Brick,* available in many sizes, textures, and colors and laid in simple or intricate arrangements
- *Stone* of all types (marble, travertine, terrazzo, quartzite, fieldstone, granite, etc.)
- *Wood* of all varieties, either in strips (laid in numerous patterns and directions), panels, planks, or elaborately carved members
- Facings of *plaster* or *stucco,* painted or left plain
- *Concrete,* plain or with exposed aggregate accents
- *Tile* in a variety of colors, textures, and patterns.

Fireplace design often includes combinations of these materials. For example, a stone fireplace may have a handsome wood mantel, or a plastered fireplace may be outlined around the opening with colorfully patterned tile (see Figure 7.38).

FIGURE 7.38 An unusual fireplace in wood and tile becomes a center of interest in this cozy living space. (Courtesy of F. J. Hakimian, Inc., NY. Design by Tom O'Toole. Photograph, Phillip Ennis.)

Construction

Fireplaces should be constructed with adequate *safety, functional,* and *maintenance* features. A fireplace should draw properly, incorporate fireproof materials, and be constructed so that ashes can be conveniently removed. Firescreens—usually glass or wire mesh—can be built-in or freestanding and can help contain flying sparks from a burning fire. The concern for *energy conservation* has prompted new fireplace construction, allowing more efficient use of fuel and heat output. One popular choice is the freestanding metal stove.

Construction may incorporate the fireplace as part of the total wall composition by using shelves or built-in furnishings, extending the fireplace material the full length and height of the wall, or constructing it independently. Consideration of the scale and proportion of the room, the style, the materials to be employed, and the effect and function desired can help to determine the most appropriate construction for a particular living space.

ASSIGNMENT

Using Plate 11 in the Student Work Packet, carefully examine the window at the top of the page and design an appropriate treatment for each of the following three conditions:

1. The window has an unsightly view, but it must provide light during the daytime. Since the room is near a public highway, it must have day- and nighttime privacy as well as noise control.
2. The window has a pleasant view onto a private enclosed garden, but it needs nighttime privacy and energy control.
3. The window has a dramatic hilltop vista both night and day. Privacy is not a problem. Since the window faces west, however, faded furnishings and energy conservation are major considerations.

PART FOUR

Furniture and Furnishings

CHAPTER 8

Furniture Selection

FIGURE 8.1 In a reception area of a large office complex, a striking glass and metal coffee table and rich black leather sofas welcome clients. The modern furnishings are comfortably in scale with human proportions and are well placed to make the most of a small space. (Photograph by Mark Boisclair.)

Considering the Human Factor

Function

Aesthetics

Quality

Budget

Types of Furniture

Chairs

Sofas

Tables

Beds

Storage

Built-In, Wall, and Modular Units

Systems Furniture

Quality and Craftsmanship

Wood

Metal

Synthetic Materials

Rattan, Cane, Rush, and Wicker

Upholstered Furniture

Parts of Upholstered Furniture

Upholstery Fabrics

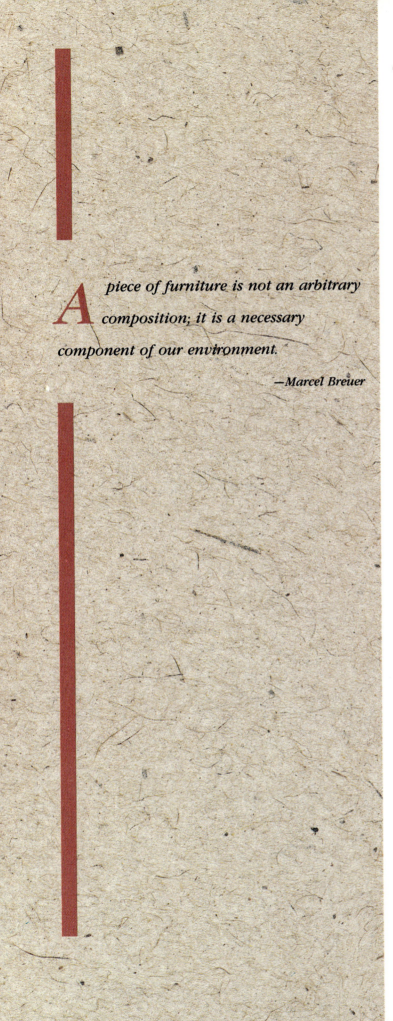

A piece of furniture is not an arbitrary composition; it is a necessary component of our environment.

—Marcel Breuer

Selecting furniture for residential and nonresidential projects is a major responsibility of the designer since furniture is required to meet a variety of human needs in a variety of spaces. Planning furniture for a space is an important part of the design process that ultimately must satisfy the needs of the end user. Furniture for residential and nonresidential spaces is often interchangeable. For example, in Figure 8.1, sofas and tables that could fit in a private living space have been selected to provide a comfortable environment for clients in this reception area of a large commercial concern.

Furnishing a space can be a rewarding experience and purchases can last a lifetime. Careful study and planning enable the designer and consumer to make wise decisions. This approach requires time and effort but pays long-term dividends. Knowledge of the principles and elements of design and understanding how a fine piece of furniture is made aid in the selection process.

Fashions in furnishings come and go. Being able to discriminate between long-lasting and faddish designs is worthwhile. If a piece of furniture is well designed initially, it will always be good.

CONSIDERING THE HUMAN FACTOR

When selecting furniture for either residential or nonresidential projects it is essential to consider the human factor. Most interiors require furniture that will satisfy specific functions within a space. Today the market abounds with furniture of many types, styles, materials, and prices, to satisfy particular lifestyles and fulfill particular needs. Wise furniture selections depend on a number of basic considerations that include function, aesthetics, quality, and budget.

Function

Furniture should serve a useful purpose. The designer and client must ask: (1) What furniture is needed? (2) Will the furniture be used in a residential or nonresidential setting? (3) Who will use it? (4) Where will the furniture be placed? (5) What purpose will it serve? Figure 8.2 shows an executive office with a desk surrounded by built-in storage and comfortable seating that functions efficiently for the user. In a private residence the requirements are entirely different. For instance, an informal family room designed for two adults and two children might require a sofa, chairs, and tables that function as durable, practical, and comfortable pieces for relaxation.

Space Allocation and Function

How much space is available to accommodate the furniture? Space is generally limited in today's structures. The size of the furniture is determined by the space available.

FIGURE 8.2 Furnishings for an executive office are well planned for its function. A desk designed to fit within a windowed bay is surrounded with built-in storage. A leather upholstered desk chair and a seating group close by for consultations contribute to an attractive and efficient environment. (Photograph by Mark Boisclair.)

In a small space, for example, lightly scaled furniture with superfluous designs eliminated and built-in units help conserve space. In a larger space, a hotel lobby for example, the number of pieces and size of the furniture may be increased.

What furniture types will be required to satisfy the functional needs of a particular project: seating units, tables, beds, storage units, built-ins, custom-designed or systems furniture? How many of each, what specific type, what finishes, materials, and fabrics will best suit the activities that will take place? Each furniture type is designed to fulfill certain functions.

Comfort and Convenience

To function adequately, furniture should be comfortable for the users and convenient for the various activities it must serve. Seating pieces, for example, should provide good back support and be in scale with human dimensions. The study of human dimensions, called *anthropometrics,* is a science that measures such criteria as a person's height, weight, and shape. It is closely related to **ergonomics**, a science whose goal is to provide a comfortable relationship between human beings and their environment (especially the working environment) through the study of body mechanics and sensory performance. These efforts have had great impact on human comfort and convenience. (See Figure 8.3.)

Physically Challenged

Suitable furniture may be required to meet the functional needs of users who are physically challenged. This task is particularly relevant to many nonresidential projects like

FIGURE 8.3 A classic example of an ergonomic chair is the Jefferson, designed by Niels Diffrient in 1986. The chair is accompanied by an ottoman, and a computer workstation for a computer keyboard and monitor. The grouping was designed for human comfort based on scientific studies of the human anatomy. (Courtesy of Domore Corporation.)

health care, transportation, and hospitality facilities. Furniture placement and clearances to accommodate the physically challenged are covered in Chapter 10.

Aesthetics

Often the initial impression of a furniture piece is a matter of subjective personal taste. What is beautiful to one individual may not be so to another. An acquaintance with the principles of design, however, helps provide a knowledgeable background. This ability to discriminate between fine furniture and faddish, elaborate, or overly ornate furniture involves training the eye. In a nonresidential space furniture generally reflects the tastes of the owners or the designer, or the company image.

The design or style of furniture should be compatible with the intended function and complement the overall theme and architectural background. The designer should have a thorough knowledge of furniture styles, and it is helpful for the consumer to be able to distinguish one style from another, what mood is created by each, and which styles are compatible. The mood should be visually appealing for the end users, as reflected in Figure 8.4.

Individuality and character are the unique aspects that draw the user to a particular piece or style. This is especially evident in private living spaces, where owners want to express their personality, lifestyle, values, and tastes.

Quality

How a piece of furniture is made and the quality of the materials used are of vital concern to the designer and end user for both residential and nonresidential projects. The quality of construction, materials, and finishes ranges from poor to excellent and often depends on the integrity of the manufacturer and the word of a salesperson. A good manufacturer takes great pride in the skilled workmanship that goes into the product, because the company's reputation depends on it.

Budget

The client's budget is a necessary consideration when planning and furnishing a space. What is the cost of the furniture in relation to the budget allocation? Almost all design projects have a certain budget limit that must be respected.

In addition to the initial cost of furniture, the lifetime costs must also be considered, such as maintenance, repairs, and replacements of parts. Fine quality and good design are always wise investments and, if carefully selected, furniture can be obtained at reasonable cost. In other words, furniture that is well designed is not necessarily expensive. Since purchasing furniture for residential spaces involves a long-term investment, take the time necessary to select the best—one furniture piece at a time.

TYPES OF FURNITURE

Human beings first created crude but somewhat functional pieces of furniture. As time passed the process was refined, and furniture became an important art form. By the time of the ancient civilizations of Egypt,

Mesopotamia, Greece, and Rome, furniture was elegantly formed and decorated, satisfying the need for both function and beauty. After the development of these early cultures, various styles evolved that proved to have a lasting influence on following generations, especially the English and French designs. However, basic furniture types remained fairly constant with the exception of built-ins and modular units that would emerge on a grand scale during the twentieth century. Figure 8.5 shows some furniture types found in today's homes.

Chairs

For centuries people have been fascinated by the design potential of the seating unit. Human beings use chairs every day for a variety of functions; they are essential pieces of furniture. Figures 8.6 through 8.11 show some examples of different types of chairs.

Some considerations when choosing chairs include the following: (1) The height, depth, and width should comfortably accommodate the human form. (2) An adjustable chair can give flexible service. (3) Ergonomic designs, based on extensive anthropometric studies, provide maximum comfort. (4) Chairs of varying sizes are available, ranging from simple and lightly scaled side chairs to oversized upholstered lounge chairs. (5) Materials generally include wood, metal, plastic, leather, and textiles. (6) Styles from all periods are available to suit any taste. (7) There are chairs to satisfy every possible function—whether for relaxation or work. Generally, a variety of chair sizes and designs are required for numerous functions within a home.

FIGURE 8.4 The upholstered French chair and contemporary sofas, along with tables and a casepiece (French armoire), have been selected to suit the personal taste of the occupants. The seating units provide comfort for conversation and relaxation. Note the modern adaptation of an early French Renaissance fireplace. (Courtesy of Bruce Stodola and The Design Studio at Barrows.)

Side chair   Open arm chair   Wing chair   Channelback chair   Tub chair   Ladderback chair

Spoonback chair   Skirted club chair   Windsor   Lawson lounge   Recliner

Camelback   Lawson   Tuxedo

Studio couch   Chesterfield   Love seat

Studio couch opened to bed

Rollaway bed

Convertible sofa

Convertible sofa open to bed

Chaise longue

FIGURE 8.5 Furniture types: Seating pieces and beds (above); tables, case furniture, desks, beds, and pianos (opposite).

Nested tables   Tea table   Harvest table   Pedestal table   Tilt-top pedestal

Tier table   Butterfly table   Console   Pembroke   Gateleg   Lamp table

Hutch   Secretary   Breakfront   Armoire   China cabinet

Double chest   Chest on chest   Chest of drawers   Kneehole desk

Buffet   Student desk

Four-poster bed   Canopy bed   Ottoman   Grand piano   Console piano

FIGURE 8.7 This Queen Anne "wing chair," so named for the curved half-sides that rise to the height of the high back, originally offered protection from the drafts and chills of poorly heated rooms. The arms are made up of two scrolls, one vertical and one horizontal, which meet to outline a graceful flat C-shaped scroll. (Courtesy of Kindel.)

FIGURE 8.6 This popular traditional Provincial French chair is based on the Louis XV style. (Courtesy of Century Furniture Co.)

FIGURE 8.8 This reproduction of a Philadelphia Chippendale side chair, originally made between 1760 and 1780, features heavily carved acanthus leaf clusters with cabriole front legs that terminate in claw-and-ball feet. (Courtesy of Kindel.)

FIGURE 8.9 Charles and Ray Eames experimented with various wood forms. The Eames® DCW chair (1943–1953) is an early example of a molded plywood chair design. (Courtesy of Herman Miller, Inc., archives.)

FIGURE 8.10 The "Ribbon" Chair 582, created by French designer Pierre Paulin in 1965, is constructed of a tubular metal frame that is covered with a tension-held rubber sheet and then upholstered. (Courtesy of Artifort.)

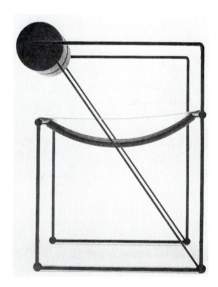

FIGURE 8.11 The Seconda armchair (1982), designed by Swiss architect Mario Botta, is constructed of perforated sheet metal with a backrest of polyurethane. (Courtesy of ICF.)

Sofas

Sofas are long upholstered seating units accommodating two or more persons (see Figures 8.12 and 8.13). Through the ages particular terms have been associated with certain designs. *Lawson* is a popular type with armrests lower than the back support. The most common *sofas*, a familiar term for most seating of this type, include the following: (1) The *couch* is a long upholstered unit with a low back and one endpiece. (2) The *davenport*, originally a small writing desk named after its designer, is often used today to define a convertible sofa. (3) The *tuxedo* is a completely upholstered piece with armrests the same height as the back. (4) The *chesterfield* is an upholstered sofa with upholstered ends. (5) The *divan*, a low couch without arms or back units, derived from stacked rugs used in Turkey for seating purposes. (6) The *love seat* is a smaller sofa for seating two persons. (7) The *settee* is a lightly scaled piece, often with some upholstered sections. (8) *Settles*, completely constructed of wood with very high backs, originally were used in early American homes to retain heat from fireplaces. (9) *Dual-*

FIGURE 8.12 Matching sofas backed up to a tall sofa table divide a large room into separate seating areas. (Courtesy of Gayl Baddeley Associates.)

FIGURE 8.13 When Le Corbusier designed the Grand Confort Collection in 1928, he eliminated the traditional construction of an upholstered piece and used a light support of tubular steel with loose cushions. (Courtesy of Atelier International.)

purpose sofas can be used for both sleeping and seating. *Studios, sofa-beds,* and *convertible sofas* fall into this category. (10) *Modular and sectional sofas* have become popular in recent years. (See Figure 8.14.)

Tables

(1) Dining and kitchen tables (see Figure 8.15), (2) coffee tables (see Figure 8.16), (3) end or occasional tables, (4) game tables, and (5) desks are all functional furniture pieces used in the home to serve various needs. Tables should be sturdy, strong, and durable and of a usable size and shape. The height should be adequate and comfortable for the intended function.

Beds

A bed may be (1) built-in, (2) composed of modular units, (3) freestanding (see Figure 8.17), (4) a dual-

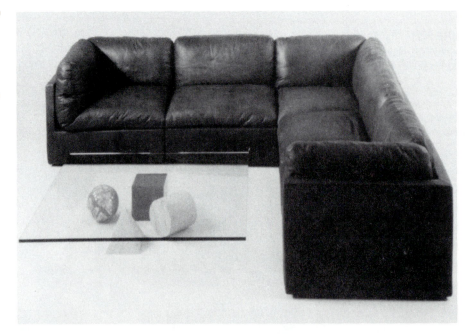

FIGURE 8.14 Ottawa Modular Seating, creating by Italian designers DePas, D'Urbino, and Lomazzi in 1974, is luxuriously comfortable with soft Dacron cushions. It is easily maintained with Velcro®-edged removable, cleanable upholstery. (Courtesy of ICF.)

FIGURE 8.15 An example of a traditional style table is seen in this French dining room. The table in the Louis XV style is compatible with the accompanying furnishings and backgrounds. (Courtesy of Century Furniture Company.)

FIGURE 8.16 The classic Barcelona table, designed by Mies van der Rohe in 1929, has a chrome X-shaped base topped with a slab of glass and is used as a coffee table in a formal or informal setting. (Courtesy of Knoll International.)

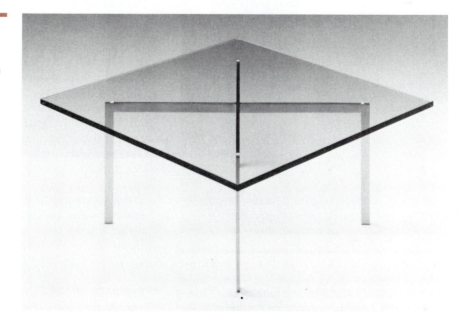

FIGURE 8.17 In designer Montie Simmon's home, a four-poster bed of brushed metal is the central focus in the eclectic master suite. Sheer fabrics hung at the corners soften the effect. (Photograph by Pam Singleton.)

purpose piece, (5) a fold-down-from-the-wall type, (6) a bunk bed, (7) a waterbed, or (8) a trundle bed.

Storage

Many innovative pieces designed for functional storage are available to help alleviate the problems of small living spaces. Convenient and efficient storage can be provided in many rooms of the house with *chests, cupboards, hutches, china cabinets, shelves,* and *armoires* (see Figures 8.4 and 8.18).

Built-In Wall and Modular Units

Built-in furnishings may function as seating, tables, beds, and storage space and are an integral part of the wall

FIGURE 8.18 A modern casepiece, Sideboard 2, designed by Charles Rennie Mackintosh at the turn of the century, was put in production in 1974. The piece, made of ebonized wood and contrasted with pearlized and stained glass, can be used for a variety of functions. (Courtesy of Atelier International.)

construction. They have the advantage of providing architectural unity and a more spacious feeling. A drawback can be the inability to move the components. **Modular** units can be arranged in a variety of compositions, providing great flexibility.

Systems Furniture

Systems furniture are modular pieces used for office design projects. They consist of work surfaces, storage units, and vertical panels that make up a workstation (these may be private, semiprivate, or a combination of the two). These flexible pieces can be set up in a variety of configurations to fit the space available. They can serve the needs of executive, management, secretarial, clerical, and word processing workstations. (Refer to Figures 2.30 and 10.2.)

QUALITY AND CRAFTSMANSHIP

The quality of construction and craftsmanship of a piece of furniture are often readily apparent. By knowing what constitutes quality in these areas, one can be assured of

getting well-made furniture. Following are some construction features to look for:

- All sections of furniture must be *firmly joined* and secure.
- Furniture should be *well proportioned and comfortable.* Sit on a chair or sofa to test its comfort. Check the depth of the seat and height of the back and arms. If a lounge chair is being chosen for a particular person, it is wise to have that person try it out.
- A well-constructed chest, chair, or table remains *rigid and sturdy* when one tries to rock it.
- A fine-quality *finish* is smooth and evenly applied, with no spotting, sticky areas, running, or buildup of coats. Good wood furniture has a mellow patina resulting only from much rubbing, a practice requiring time and effort and therefore adding to the total cost. Finishes make woods highly resistant to marks from glasses, spills, scratches, and abrasions. Even cigarette burns are no longer the catastrophe they once were. These wonder-working finishes are often completely invisible and let the beauty of the wood grain and color shine through. Poorly constructed furniture often has a hard shine produced by varnish, which may cover inferior wood but will quickly reveal scratches.
- *Back panels* should be recessed and smoothly finished.
- *Movable units* like drawers and door panels must be durable and easily operated. (See Figure 8.19.) Drawer runners are best when made of metal, plastic, or durable hardwood. Well-made drawers have solid sides, three-ply nonwarp bottoms that are sanded and sealed

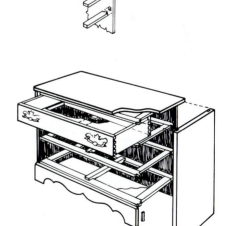

FIGURE 8.19 Inner characteristics of furniture determine durability: selected hardwoods; mortise and tenon joints; heavy-duty center drawer guides; drawers dovetailed front and back; durable dust panels between drawers; durable drawer bottoms held rigidly in grooves; strong casebacks recessed into ends; well-mounted top and sides; drawer interiors sanded and sealed. (Courtesy of Stanley Furniture.)

against snags, dovetail joints, and are separated by dust barriers.

- *Leg and base supports* should be particularly sturdy with a durable finish because they take much abuse.
- Furniture with *flat areas* like tables, cabinets, and desk tops should be constructed of durable material in order to maintain its function and appearance. Although some materials are practical, each may have a particular hazard; for example, marble may stain, glass may break, plastic may chip, and hardwood may scratch.
- The *edges* of tables and other pieces are especially susceptible to damage and wear. Rounded edges, reinforced strips, and edges made of solid hardwood are more practical.

Wood

Wood is the major material used for furniture construction. A piece of furniture marked *solid* is made from solid hardwood. The label *genuine* shows that the furniture is made of a single hardwood, with veneer on flat surfaces and solid structural parts such as the legs. **Veneer** is a thin layer of finishing wood applied to the body of a less refined wood. (See Figure 8.20.) Although it was once believed that furniture with veneer was of inferior quality, the contrary is true. With advanced methods of cutting and **laminating** veneers, a piece of veneered furniture can be stronger and more resistant to warping than a solid piece. Only veneering permits the beautiful effects achieved by the different methods of matching wood grains. The wood **grain** is determined by its natural growth. The method in which the wood is cut into lumber (sawed) produces a variety of grains.

Furniture is made from both hard and soft woods. *Hardwoods* come from *deciduous trees* (those that drop their leaves), such as oak and maple. Hardwoods are more durable and dent resistant than softwoods, and they are more costly. Hardwoods are generally more attractive than softwoods and often are preferred for fine furniture. *Softwoods* come from *coniferous trees* (those with needles that are mostly green the year round), such as pine and spruce. Softwoods are used for less expensive furniture and are also used in combination with hardwoods. The woods most widely used in furniture construction today are pine, birch, maple, oak, cherry, walnut, mahogany, beech, pecan, and teak (see "Color in Wood," Chapter 2). Labels describing the finish such as "fruit wood finish" or "walnut finish" refer to the color only, not to the species of wood used. Each wood has its own special properties. Wood selected for a particular furniture piece should be properly dried; well suited for its intended construction, purpose, finish, size, and style; and resistant to warping, splitting, swelling, and shrinking. Table 8.1 lists the most common woods and their uses.

Considering the Environment

Currently, a strong feeling of responsibility exists among designers, manufacturers, and consumers to do their part to preserve the environment. Many furniture companies have strict policies regarding environmental issues and the use of wood from threatened or endangered species of trees, especially from rain forests. Woods are chosen from reforestable trees like maple and oak instead of rosewood, for example, which is not easily replenished. In some cases the use of certain woods for furniture construction is restricted by federal and state laws.

Construction Methods

The quality and type of wood joinings indicate the durability and aesthetic quality of a piece. The most common construction methods for joining wood are the following (also refer to Figure 8.21):

- **Mortise and tenon**: The mortise (hole) joins with a piece that has a projecting piece (tenon). This forms a strong joint used to secure parts for furniture frames.
- **Dowel**: Rounded dowels (pegs) join into corresponding holes. Widely used for casepieces.
- **Miter**: Edges are cut at a 45-degree angle and may have a supportive strip straddling the joint.
- **Dovetail**: A splaying dovetail form fits into grooves of the same size and form. This type of joint is found on fine furniture, especially to join drawer fronts and sides.
- **Tongue and groove**: Tongue and groove forms extend the entire width of the piece.
- *Rabbeted or rebated:* One edge has a groove cut the entire width to accommodate a straight-edged piece.
- *Butt:* This type is not used for fine furniture. It is sometimes found on inexpensive furniture, but it must have cross-supports or corner blocks.

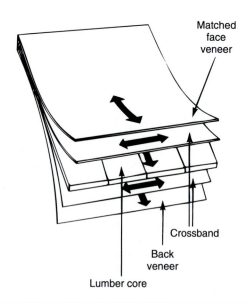

FIGURE 8.20 Veneering.

TABLE 8.1 Most common wood types

Wood Type	Characteristics	Uses in Home
Acacia	Hardwood. Light brown.	Furniture. Woodwork. Often used for religious decorations.
Alder	A light, weak wood. White to light browns.	Furniture. Framing.
Ash	A blond hardwood. Texture resembles oak. Relatively inexpensive.	Cabinetry and furniture. Furniture framing. Flooring.
Bamboo	A tropical tubular woody plant with a raised joint.	Oriental-style furniture. Decorative accessories.
Beech	A blond hardwood. Fine grain texture. Strong.	Informal furniture. Popular in Scandinavia. Flooring.
Birch	Subtle wavy grain. Hard and durable. Takes stains well, or beautiful in natural finish.	Furniture. Popular in Scandinavia. Flooring, doors, cabinetry.
Cedar	Reddish-brown, often with yellow streaks. Soft. Lightweight. Strong odor. Moth repellent.	Closet lining, chests. Informal furniture. Shingles. Siding. Paneling.
Cherry	Reddish-brown hardwood. Resembles mahogany. Durable. Strong.	Used in small quantities. Inlay and marquetry work. Popular for Early American furniture.
Cypress	Color varies. Usually from light yellow to darkish-brown. Soft. Warp resistant. Inexpensive. Weathers silver gray.	Particularly used as a finish wood. Outside finish work. Doors, shingles, siding. Some informal furniture.
Ebony	Exquisite dark heartwood with brownish-black streaks. Ebony, sometimes red or green. Hard and heavy.	Modern and Oriental furniture. Inlay and marquetry designs.
Elm	Light brown with gray overtones. Takes stain well. Slight undulating grain. Hard and heavy.	Particularly used for veneers. Furniture. Interior finish work.
Fir	Strong and durable. Wavy grain. Takes stain well. Resembles pine.	Plywood and laminated sheets. Cabinetry. Trim pieces. Inexpensive furniture.
Gum	Reddish-brown. Medium hard. Resembles mahogany. Interesting grains.	Veneers. Doors. Interior trim. Furniture parts.
Mahogany	Reddish or reddish-golden brown with fine grain. Can be beautifully finished.	Fine expensive furniture. Especially popular for Queen Anne, Chippendale, and other 18th century furniture. Paneling and cabinetwork.
Maple	White to pale yellowish-brown. Fine grain. Hard and heavy. Resembles birch. Relatively inexpensive.	Informal furniture. Popular for Early American style. Flooring. Cabinetwork.
Oak	White oak is light to golden brown. Red oak has pinkish tones. Straight to strong wavy grain. Hard and durable.	Most important wood for furniture, trim, and cabinetwork. Quarter sawn (straight grain) usually preferred for fine furniture and paneling.
Pecan	White to reddish brown. Refined grain, often with darkish streaks. Hard, strong, and heavy.	Fine furniture. Furniture parts. Cabinetwork, paneling, and trim.
Pine	Off-white to pale yellow. Soft. Not strong. Lightweight. Inexpensive. Close grain with occasional wavy grain.	Flooring, doors, trim. Early American or provincial furniture and paneling. Cabinetwork.
Poplar	Off-white to yellowish brown. Softwood. Lightweight. Subtle straight grain. Inexpensive.	Informal furniture. Works well painted. Trim, cabinetwork, and exterior siding.
Rattan	A jungle vine from the Orient. Pale yellow to light brown. Soft and pliable.	Informal furniture with Oriental feeling. Can be nicely painted and stained.
Redwood	Uniform red color. Grays when exposed to weather. Available in large planks.	Exterior finishes. Beams, paneling, etc. Cabinetwork. Outdoor furniture.
Rosewood	Fine textured reddish-brown hardwood with black streaks. Beautiful when highly polished.	Popular for fine 18th century furniture. Inlay designs. Danish Modern furniture.
Satinwood	Pale blond color with smooth satin finish. Unique grain. Expensive.	Fine furniture and finish work. Inlay and parquetry designs.
Teak	Yellow to reddish-brown with fine black streaks. Strong and durable. Beautiful with oiled finish.	Popularly used for Oriental and Danish designed furniture. Decorative and functional accessories.
Walnut	Light to dark golden brown. A variety of beautiful grains. Hard, strong, and durable. Expensive.	Used for fine furniture in many styles. Especially used during 18th century Queen Anne period, called the "Age of Walnut." Paneling.
Yew	Dark reddish-brown hardwood particularly found in England. Close grained.	Cabinetwork and some furniture.

FIGURE 8.21 Types of wood joining.

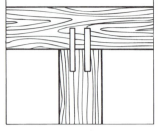

Mortise and tenon

Dowel

Miter

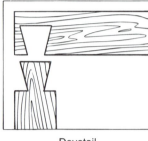
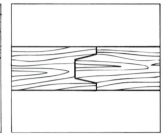

Dovetail

Tongue and groove

Types of Finishes

Principal types of finishes applied to wood furniture include staining, paint, oil, varnish, shellac, lacquer, and polyurethane. Special or unusual finishes include stenciling, faux (simulating other materials such as marble and granite), spattering, stippling, glazing, sponging, and handpainted designs (such as ribbons, flowers, foliage, figures, butterflies, geometrics, or trompe l'oeil, etc.).

Metal

Metal was used as a material for furniture in ancient civilizations. Bronze and iron were particularly used by the Egyptians, Assyrians, Greeks, and Romans for chairs, lamps, accent pieces on furniture, table bases, and other small furnishings. During the Middle Ages and Renaissance, exquisitely **wrought iron** and other metals were used for many furnishings and also for ornamental supports, hinges, bands, handles, and locks. In the eighteenth century metals were especially employed for accenting fine furniture. By the Victorian and Industrial Revolution periods, iron and brass beds (particularly popular) and iron furniture of all types were produced for indoor and outdoor use. With the advent of the Bauhaus and other modern movements since the turn of the century, new methods of working metal have been developed, like tubular steel (see Figure 8.22), sheet metal, chrome-plated steel, wire, steel with baked-on enamel, and small and large metal rods and pipes for furniture construction.

Metal can be shaped in many forms. It can be riveted, bolted, and welded, providing great flexibility of design. The most common metals used for furniture construction include brass, bronze, iron, steel, and aluminum. A wide range of finishes are available today including chromium plating, shiny, dull, striated, and textured in numerous ways. Steel with baked-on enamel in many colors is popular.

Metal is relatively inexpensive, strong, durable, and cool to the touch. Some metal furniture is lightweight and transportable. Be sure that the metal is rustproof. If metal furniture is damaged, repairs can be costly.

Synthetic Materials

Man-made products for furniture construction have revolutionized the design field. Now synthetic materials, such as acrylics, vinyls, polyurethanes, and laminates, are used for almost all furniture types and in numerous ways. Basically, synthetic materials are employed in six ways:

1. *Lamination and bonding agents;* for example, adhering plywoods, veneers, and wood chips.
2. *Molded furniture,* either as a part of or as an entire piece.
3. *Functional hardwood parts* and *decorative accent pieces.*
4. *Finishes* of all types like paints and lacquers.
5. *Upholstery* fabrics including vinyls, nylons, polyesters, **acrylics,** and so on (see Chapter 5).
6. *Upholstery fillers* (see next section on Upholstered Furniture).

Synthetics can be molded, sprayed, foamed, blown, or rolled into many sizes and forms, and their use for residential and contract furnishings is unlimited. (See Figure 8.23.) Foamed plastics have revolutionized furniture construction, allowing more lightly scaled furniture designs.

Synthetic materials are available in a wide range of colors, textures, and patterns. Lucite and Plexiglas have

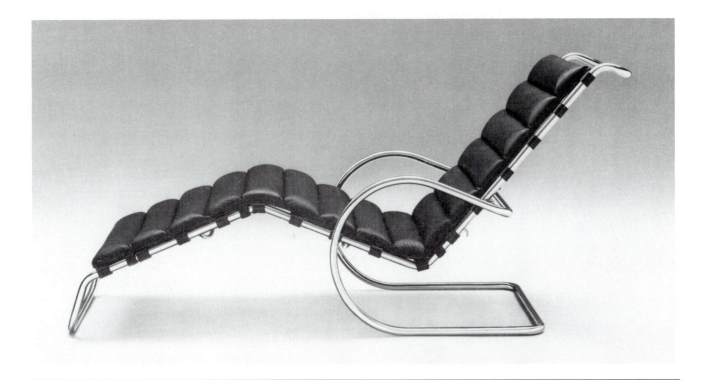

FIGURE 8.22 Mies van der Rohe, the world-renowned modern architect and furniture designer, created this adjustable chaise lounge in the 1920s, using tubular steel for the supporting frame. (Courtesy of Knoll International.)

FIGURE 8.23 Danish designer Vernor Panton created his classic stacking chair in the 1960s. Now made of polyurethane, this graceful cantilever design is the first example of a single-form molded fiberglass chair. (Courtesy of Vitra.)

transparent and translucent properties. Synthetics are durable and easy to keep clean. However, some synthetics may dull over time, break, or scratch and are very difficult to repair. Also, some synthetic materials are flammable.

When well designed, synthetics mix well with other furnishings and can be successfully combined with other materials for furniture pieces.

Rattan, Cane, Rush, and Wicker

Rattan, cane, rush, and wicker are materials that come from natural sources such as palms and grasses. Because of their nature, rattan, wicker, cane and rush are compatible in an informal setting; in an eclectic formal room, they can add interest to the decor. These materials can be used effectively in both inside and outside spaces.

- *Rattan poles* are cut from the rattan palm and can be bent to form a variety of designs. They are particularly used for chairs, tables, and beds.
- **Cane** is split rattan from the rattan palm and is interwoven (known as mesh). Cane was introduced into England about 1660. It was used for chair seats and backs and some outdoor table tops. Today, all-cane chairs, tables, bedheads, and other pieces are made for inside use as well as for outdoor living spaces. (See Figures 8.24 and 8.25.)
- *Rush* is tightly twisted long grass (often paper is used as a substitute) that is made into a cord. The cord is then

FIGURE 8.24 Marcel Breuer combined cane with tubular steel (he was the first designer to use tubular steel for furniture construction) for his famous Cesca chair while he was a faculty member at the Bauhaus design school during the 1920s. (Courtesy of Thonet Industries, Inc.)

woven and mainly used for the seat and back of chairs. This country craft has been known since medieval times.

■ *Wicker (or basketwork)* is more accurately a method (rather than a specific material) of chair construction using rushes, twigs, and reeds that has been used since ancient times. Wickerwork or basketwork continues to be popular today and wicker is a common term for this type of furniture.

UPHOLSTERED FURNITURE

Upholstered furniture was known in ancient civilizations when fabric—especially animal skins, rush, or leather—was simply stretched over a sturdy frame. Seats and backs with fabric stretched over a frame are still used for lightweight pieces today. During the Renaissance simple padding or cushions were placed on top of the stretched fabric. Later, fabrics were used to cover the cushion and stretched fabric. By the sixteenth century padding made of horsehair, feathers, wool, and down made cushions even deeper and more comfortable. In the eighteenth century springs were introduced and modern upholstery had arrived. Little change occurred in upholstery construction until the introduction of synthetics during the 1930s, which had a tremendous impact on the furniture industry. Upholstered furniture today is basically of two types: (1) *overstuffed*—referring to furniture that has padding or stuffing attached over the frame—and (2) an *exposed frame with partially exposed sections.*

FIGURE 8.25 Rattan chairs give visual interest and help unify a mix of natural materials and textures in this family room. The unusual wall treatment of vertical poles fits well with the informal Southwestern-style setting. (Photograph by Mark Boisclair.)

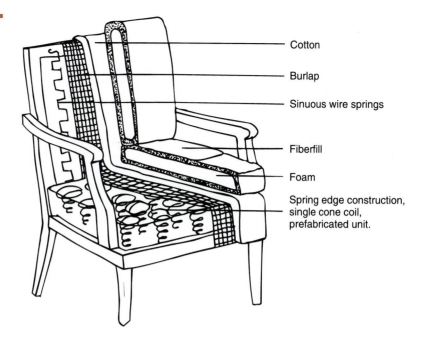

FIGURE 8.26 Upholstery construction. (After Stanley Furniture, by permission of Stanley Furniture Company.)

Cotton

Burlap

Sinuous wire springs

Fiberfill

Foam

Spring edge construction, single cone coil, prefabricated unit.

Parts of Upholstered Furniture

Hidden beneath the cover of upholstered furniture are the elements that should produce durability, comfort, and quality (refer to Figure 8.26).

Frame

A good *frame* is constructed of kiln-dried hardwood such as maple, poplar, oak, ash, birch, or elm. (Softwoods tend to split.) The wood frame should be firmly assembled and usually joined by double dowels that are spiral grooved and then glued. Reinforcement braces of metal or wood blocks should be glued and screwed to the corners. Nails are never used for good-quality furniture. Frames may also be of synthetics, metals, wicker, or rattan.

Webbing

Generally of linen, jute, plastic, or rubber, the *webbing* is arranged in a basketweave and used on the frame to provide support for the springs and cushioning. Good-quality webbing measures 3 to 4 in. in width.

Springs

The *spring* construction may be of either sinuous wire or coils. The sinuous wire is simpler and by some criteria better. It is particularly desirable for slimline modern furniture and light-seated occasional chairs. The cone coil comes in both single and double cone (see Figure 8.27). The *single-cone coil* is a prefabricated unit for standard styles. It is an all-wire unit with coils tied to each other and attached to top and bottom border wires. *Double-cone coils* are mounted and affixed on a resilient base such as strips of webbing or metal, and are hand tied

at the top to prevent slipping. This construction provides maximum comfort and is used in more expensive deep-seated upholstery. Fine-quality springs have individual coil springs contained in a muslin. *Burlap* is used to protect and cover springs.

Filling, Stuffing, and Padding

Filling, stuffing, or *padding* materials of various types and qualities are used for cushioning, either alone or in combination. These materials—but not the qualities—are listed on the label. In the past, long curled hair, cotton, moss, or kapok was used. Today, the most commonly used fillings include the following:

1. *Polyester* is lightweight, resilient, and odorless, and it resists mildew and moths. It may be used alone or combined with cores of foam or innersprings. Polyester fillings are often wrapped with Dacron.
2. *Foam rubber* or *latex* (looks like well-beaten egg whites with tiny holes close together) is used in solid sections. It is durable and resilient and holds its shape well. It may deteriorate over time if it is not of good quality.
3. *Polyurethane foam* is more suitably used today than foam rubber and is highly resilient. Along with polyester, it is the most used filler. Polyurethane is often

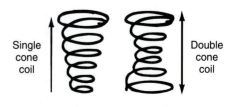

Single cone coil

Double cone coil

FIGURE 8.27 Single- and double-cone coils.

wrapped with polyester for use on fine furniture. It resists liquids, moths, and mildew.

4. *Down* or *feathers* are soft but because they are not resilient, require frequent plumping up to maintain shape. This filling is generally reserved for back cushions only. Because of its high cost, its use is somewhat limited.

5. *Rubberized fibers* such as sisal, which have less resiliency than the previously mentioned filling materials, are used in moderately priced furniture.

6. *Shredded fibers* from natural sources such as some leaves are generally used in low-priced furniture.

7. *Cotton* is occasionally used for small pieces.

Muslin used as covering over the filling material is always employed on fine-quality furniture to prevent seepage and facilitate movement. *Cotton felt* is used to protect springs and other filling materials, and it is used alone on inexpensive furniture.

Fabric

Fabric is used to cover all the construction of the piece, and it should be professionally finished. Seat and back *cushions and pillows,* filled with the materials just mentioned, may be added to complement the furniture's style. They may be fastened or movable, depending on the style and preferred degree of flexibility. Cushioning should be comfortable, resilient, and able to take hard usage, and it should stay in place. Since new materials are being added continually and older ones being improved, some important questions are, What kind of cushioning does the chair or sofa have? (Three types are seen in Figure 8.28.) Will it retain its shape? Can it be cleaned? Is it odorless and nonallergenic?

Upholstery Fabrics

In the purchase of upholstered furniture, fabric is a primary consideration, because it is an expression of personality and individual taste (see Figure 8.29). In selecting the fabric, use is generally the determining factor. Selecting suitable upholstery fabric involves answering questions such as the following:

1. What type of *fiber and weave* are employed, and how *durable* is the fabric? An upholstery fabric, for exam-

ple, will last longer if the warp and fill are the same weight and tightly woven (see Chapter 5 for fiber information).

2. Is the fabric *attractive* and *comfortable* to the touch?

3. Is a *pattern or plain* fabric preferred? Fabrics with small overall patterns tend to show soil less than solid colors. If a pattern is used, is it in scale with the room, and does it support the style?

4. Is the fabric *suitable for its intended function*? For example, will the upholstery be used by active children in a family room or by a single professional in a seldom-used area?

5. Is the fabric the best quality the *budget* will allow, considering long-term wear and maintenance? It is usually inadvisable to buy expensive fabric for cheap furniture and fabric of lesser quality for fine furniture. Fabric and furniture should generally be in the same price category.

6. What *maintenance* process is necessary? Does the particular upholstery fabric require a *water- and soil-repellent finish* like Scotchgard or Zepel? This process is best applied when the fabric is treated at the factory rather than after it has been cut.

7. Does the upholstery fabric fit the *style, mood,* and *character* of the room? Is the fabric formal or informal? Does it seem to conform to the lifestyle of the occupants and complement its environment?

Additionally, the quality of upholstery construction is readily apparent, because the consumer can inspect the finished product firsthand. In selecting a piece of upholstered furniture, consider the following criteria:

■ *Precise tailoring* is necessary for a well-finished appearance. Seams, welts, and cording should be smooth, straight, and firmly sewn. Hems and pleats should hang evenly, with no loose threads.

■ Large *patterns* should be carefully centered and matched on each cushion and skirt.

■ When fabrics are *quilted,* close, secure stitching prevents snagging.

■ *Cushions* should fit snugly.

■ If *zippers* are used, they must be sewn straight with no puckering and they must operate easily.

■ When fabric has a *nap,* it should only run in one direction.

■ Fabric should be *smoothly stretched* over the frame with no buckling.

FIGURE 8.28 Types of cushions.

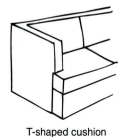

T-shaped cushion

Square cushion

Slip seat

FIGURE 8.29 This unique modern sofa upholstered in bright-colored fabrics reflects the Memphis style, a style originated by Austrian-born Italian designer Ettore Sottsass in 1981, advocating freedom of expression, especially when combining color and form. (Courtesy of Thayer Coggin, Inc. and designer Milo Baughman.)

- *Back panels* should be firmly and neatly tacked or stitched.
- *Exposed wood parts* should be of hardwood and be well finished.

Government Labels
Federal and state laws require labels to be attached to furnishings to provide specific information about the piece. Reputable manufacturers guarantee or warranty the materials used, or that the furniture's performance will meet the specifications outlined on the label. This "promise" gives the designer and client assurance that the merchandise will be satisfactory.

CHAPTER 9

Furniture Styles

FIGURE 9.1 To create the look and feel of an eighteenth-century dining room it is important to know about the furniture of the period and to appreciate historic use of color, fabrics, and wall and floor coverings. (Courtesy of Henredon Furniture Industries, Inc.)

Basic Furniture Styles

The Spanish Styles

Seventeenth- and Eighteenth-Century Country Style (Early American Furnishings)

Early and Late Georgian (circa 1700–1790)

The Neoclassic Period (circa 1790–1845)

The French Styles in America (Late Eighteenth Century to Present)

Victorian Furniture (circa 1840–1900)

General Classification of Furniture Styles

Contemporary and Modern Furnishings

American Oriental Style

Style Selection

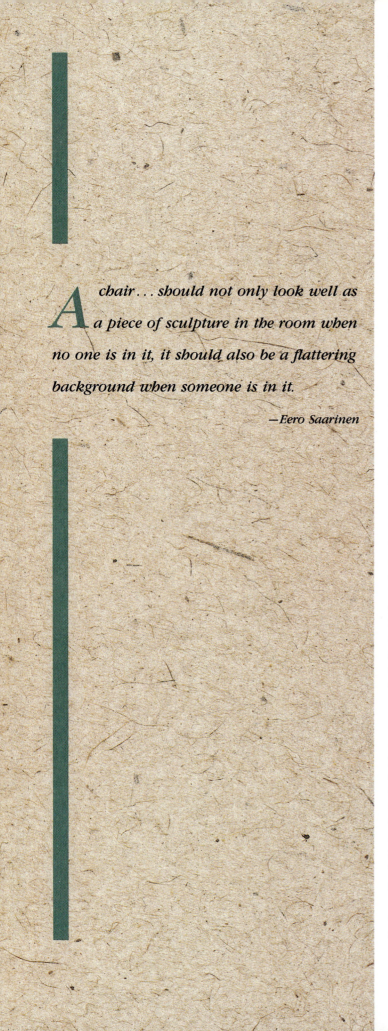

BASIC FURNITURE STYLES

Throughout history, the diversity of world cultures has found expression in many directions, including the way people have lived in their homes and the furnishings with which they surrounded themselves. Invariably the most basic piece of furniture in all Western countries has been the "seat." Differences in designs for seating pieces and other items of furniture, as well as the decorative arts, were the result of a number of factors including climate, politics, religion, and customs, which varied from one country to another.

Interest in America's cultural heritage has grown in recent years, and furniture is an important element of a concern for historic homes. Today few restraints are imposed on how furniture is combined. Effectively integrating the past with the present, however, requires pertinent information (see Figure 9.1). Although a complete understanding of period styles is not necessary to create an attractive home, basic knowledge of historic furnishings can deepen the aesthetic appreciation of our design heritage and foster creative energies. A working knowledge of the most commonly used styles of furniture, both traditional and modern, is essential to the interior designer.

A detailed consideration of furniture styles is beyond the scope of a beginning course in interior design. This chapter briefly characterizes the furniture styles that have had the greatest impact on Americans.

The Spanish Styles

The Spanish settlers built their private and public buildings primarily in what is now New Mexico and California during the seventeenth to nineteenth centuries. The Spanish Mission or Colonial, Southwest Adobe, Monterey, and California ranch architectural styles reflect the basic Spanish heritage in the United States, with each having distinctive regional differences in construction, style, and furniture design. The Spanish adapted their homes and other buildings to existing cultural and geographical conditions but still retained their own unique background.

The California Mission/Colonial Style
(circa Eighteenth Century to the Present)
During the eighteenth century, when the Spanish were colonizing what is now the state of California, a string of Catholic missions was built along the California coast, introducing characteristics of architecture based on prototypes in Spain. Furniture brought to America from Spain was highly treasured. Other furniture was copied from original Spanish designs. The Mexican influence was also incorporated into the Spanish Mission or Colonial style. (See Figure 9.2.)

General Characteristics. Heavily proportioned, strong, and sturdy furnishings reflecting the cultures of Spain and

Ladderback

Leather seated chair

Shepherd's chair

Highback chair

Spanish foot

Leather upholstered bench

Trestle table

Vargueno

Brass nailhead

Nailhead

Cupboard or Trastero

Panelled door

Moorish arch

Spanish tile

Headboard with finials

Filigree pineapple sconce

Bull's-eye mirror (Moorish)

FIGURE 9.2 Spanish (Colonial/Mission style).

Furniture Styles

Mexico. Moorish influence from Spain. Furnishings often painted. Strong use of geometric designs. Use of spindles, finials, and grilles. Walnut and oak were popular—usually stained dark. Scrolled Spanish foot. Nails and joinings frankly exposed. (Some nailheads of brass and iron often had patterns.) Furniture often ornamented with silver and other metals.

PRINCIPAL FURNITURE TYPES—MOST TYPICAL PIECES

- *Seating:* Chairs often accented with heavy metal nailheads and ironwork. Ladderback chairs topped with hoods and finials. Tooled leather chairs. Vigorous use of geometric designs, lattice, and **turned** spindles. *Shepherd's chair.* Leather upholstered bench.
- *Casepieces:* The *vargueno* (a cabinet-desk with a fall front), an essential Spanish piece. Cupboard or *trastero* with grille doors and geometric carvings.
- *Tables:* Heavily carved *trestle* table with iron **stretchers**. Legs straight or splayed outwards.
- *Beds:* Carved spindle arrangement topped with finials were typical.

Fabrics. Leather, often embossed or painted. Velvets and tapestries for formal look. Wool, leather, and rush for informal furnishings. Colors in strong chroma (see Chapter 2). Motifs drawn from Spain and Mexico.

Accessories. Wrought-iron chandeliers, candlesticks, and sconces. Tinware, often with a perforated design. Hand-painted Mexican tile and pottery. Christian religious relics. Mirrors with ironwork or heavily carved wooden frames.

The Southwest Adobe
(circa Seventeenth to Twentieth Century)
and the Santa Fe Styles (circa 1920s to present)

When the Spanish settled in the area that is now New Mexico and parts of Arizona, they based their home designs on pueblo dwellings of the native Indians living in these regions. However, they incorporated Spanish furniture designs that were familiar and more practical for their lifestyle. The result of blending the Spanish and Indian cultures was a unique and influential design direction known as the Southwest Adobe style. Furnishings for Southwest Adobe homes were basically the same as in the Spanish Mission and Colonial homes—furnishings reflecting Spanish and Mexican influences. A strong Indian influence was also incorporated. Later, when settlers arrived in the area from the eastern colonies, they brought English furniture for use in the Southwest Adobe home. In the 1920s, 1930s, and 1940s a fresh style based on original Southwest Adobe interiors and furnishings was developed primarily by easterners vacationing or living in Santa Fe, which had become a popular tourist resort. These two design directions contributed characteristics that gradually developed into a distinctive and highly

sophisticated style. This popular updated interior treatment, known as the Santa Fe style, utilizes modern interpretations of furnishings, colors, fabrics, and accessories and has been a popular design approach during the past several decades. (See Figure 9.3.)

General Characteristics. Simple and functional pieces, often crudely fashioned. (General characteristics similar to Spanish Mission and Colonial style furnishings.) Furnishings set against irregular and molded adobe stuccoed walls. Santa Fe style features eclectic look that includes European antiques with Southwestern American handicrafts and art, providing a fresh, contemporary look.

PRINCIPAL FURNITURE TYPES—MOST TYPICAL PIECES

- *Seating:* Chairs with spindle backs, rush-bottom seats. Simple lodgepole pine furniture currently popular in the Santa Fe style. Equipale leather and wood chair. (Equipale is a Mexican term for a type of rattan chair made of palm leaves or pigskin.) Carved colonial bench.
- *Casepieces:* Storage pieces with perforated tin design insets. Large cupboard, *trastero,* often painted and with lattice design. Stars-and-stripes cupboard. Mexican cupboard. Geometrically carved grain chest. High cupboard with spindle forms. Chest on curved legs.
- *Tables:* Equipale leather and wood drum table (leather stretched and laced over a circular form). Trestle table. Simple table with carved apron.
- *Beds:* Carved colonial bed. Lodgepole pine bed often used for the Santa Fe style.

Fabrics. Informal fabrics. Wool and cotton textiles. Geometric designs. Indian influence. Embroidery. Southwest Adobe interiors may feature brilliant colors. Santa Fe style most often utilizes warm desert colors, including sage greens, peaches, pinks, blue-greens, tans, corals, and purples. White. Black in small amounts.

Accessories. Handcrafted Spanish, Indian, and Mexican arts, especially geometrically designed Navajo rugs and blankets. Tinware. Indian pottery and baskets. Hand-painted Mexican pottery, mirrors, sconces, and tile. Indian, Mexican, and Spanish religious relics. Iron, wood, or clay candlesticks. Cactus plants. Accessories displayed in *nichos* (**niches** built into the wall). Handcrafted stylized animals. Kachina (Indian) dolls. Any accessory reflecting the New Mexican lifestyle (i.e., boots, skulls of animals, wagon wheels, farm tools, and cooking utensils). Items fashioned of silver. Colorfully painted undulating wooden snakes. Accessories highly individualistic, with unexpected combinations of items.

Spanish Monterey and California Ranch Styles

Typical furnishings for these two styles (see Chapter 12) are similar to those found in the Spanish Mission or

Carved wooden armchair

Lodge pole pine chair

Carved wooden armchair

Equipale leather
and wood chair

Carved geometric
design bench

Carved bench
with Southwest motifs

Drum table

Equipale leather
and wood table

Carved table
with splayed legs

Cabinet with
wood lattice and
carved geometric
design (trastero)

Cabinet with
perforated tin
panels

Cabinet with hood
and spindles

Hutch with hood
and spindles

Carved chest

Carved and painted
headboard

Lodge pole
pine bed

Mirror with
perforated
tin frame

Indian basket
and wool rug

Iron candlestand

Religious relic

FIGURE 9.3 Spanish (Santa Fe style).

Colonial style. The Spanish Monterey style typically includes eighteenth-century English furniture blending with the Spanish influences, which often produces a more formal look.

Seventeenth- and Eighteenth-Century Country Style (Early American Furnishings)

An informal provincial style emerged in America during the settlement period in the seventeenth and eighteenth centuries and became popularly known as Early American. Architecture and furnishings reflected the colonists' English, Dutch, Swedish, and German heritage. (See Chapter 12 for additional information on seventeenth-century homes in America.)

Many furnishings were brought on ships from the native country or authentically reproduced in the new land. The English colonies were dominant, and their furniture clearly expresses its Gothic, Elizabethan, Jacobean, or William and Mary heritage. Some of these original furnishings have had a continued appeal for Americans through the centuries. (See Figures 9.4 and 9.5.)

General Characteristics

Informal country or village look. Simple handcrafted furnishings. Pine, maple, oak, cherry, and hickory wood used most often. Utilitarian pieces.

PRINCIPAL FURNITURE TYPES — MOST TYPICAL PIECES

- *Seating: Brewster chair:* Developed by early Pilgrims. Has numerous turned spindles, a wood seat, and heavily turned posts. *Bannister-back chairs* similar in design, most often with split spindles. *Wainscot chair:* A wood paneled chair of English and French influence during the sixteenth and seventeenth centuries; originally an addition of a seat to the wooden wall paneling or wainscot. **Ladderback chairs** have a back with horizontal slats in a ladder arrangement; popular since time of the Pilgrims. *Carver chair* (circa 1660), like one owned by the first governor of Plymouth colony; three or five turned spindles in back, rush seat, finials, and a variety of turnings. *Jacobean chair* (circa 1660): High back, finials, and wide, carved front stretcher; back panel and seat usually leather; later version had a cane back. *William and Mary wing back:* First luxurious upholstered chair in colonies; crested top rail and gracefully rolled arms. Early **cabriole leg** joined by turned **stretchers**. Spanish (paintbrush) feet. *Windsor chairs* have a wood frame with a turned spindle back, a thick saddle-shaped seat, and splayed legs. Originated in England during the early eighteenth century. **Hitchcock chair:** Although of a later period (early 1800s), this chair, with a unique gold stencil of fruit and flowers, is often used in contemporary homes to provide an early American look. *Joint stool* wood seating; baluster-turned legs joined by stretchers;

some had wide overhang tops that doubled as tables. *Benches,* called forms, made in varying lengths for different functions. *Settles:* Benches with high backs, usually plain and made of pine; helped shield against drafts. *Jacobean day bed,* with typical turnings, was a prized possession. Simple and utilitarian wood furniture was handcrafted by the Shakers and reflected their strict religious beliefs.

- *Casepieces: Court cupboard:* Influenced by English Tudor designs; a large and handsomely carved cupboard, often with large, bulbous forms showing the Elizabethan influence. *Hadley chest:* First discovered in Hadley, Massachusetts; displays tulips carved over front rails. (Chests were given regional forms.) *Sunflower chest* common in colonial Connecticut, with either carved or painted sunflower motifs and split spindles showing Jacobean influences. **Hutch:** An open cabinet for china storage. *Corner cupboard* fits into a corner and is curved or diagonal; prominent in eighteenth-century America. *Slant-top desk:* Shape derived from early Bible boxes; slant top served for reading and writing; a forerunner of future desks. *William and Mary highboy and lowboy:* **highboy** is a chest of drawers supported on various number of legs following Flemish forms; **lowboy** is a table with two to four drawers. *William and Mary double-hooded desk:* High desk topped with two hoods symbolizing the joint reign of King William and Queen Mary of England at the end of the seventeenth century. *Dry sink:* A cabinet to hold a pitcher and wash basin. The German and Swiss colonists developed a delightful peasant art in Pennsylvania. Painted chests and other handcrafted items were typical.

- *Tables: Trestle table:* A medieval table characterized by trestle or splayed leg supports; various styles based on this original type emerged in America. *Gateleg table:* Large or small table with hinged legs supporting the drop leaves. *Butterfly gateleg:* Hinged legs in the shape of butterfly wings. *Candle stand:* Small pedestal table, often with three legs. *Table chair* could be manipulated for use as a table or chair.

- *Beds:* Simple frame. Often large and hand carved. *Trundle bed:* A low bed made to slip under the regular bed during the day. *Cradles:* Handcrafted of pine or oak with deep sides and often a hood for warmth.

Fabrics. Fabrics made on looms. Homespun wool. Some cotton. Natural dyes employed. Coverlets for beds. Needlework of all types. Rugs made from fabric scraps. Imported printed cottons with quaint motifs.

Accessories. Quaint pictures, often of family members. Utilitarian items of silver, pewter, iron, tin, brass, and copper. Simple pottery, often handpainted. Items of wood including churns, bowls, buckets, kegs, dippers, boxes for spices, spoons, doughboxes, and other household articles. Candles and holders. Freestanding and wall clocks

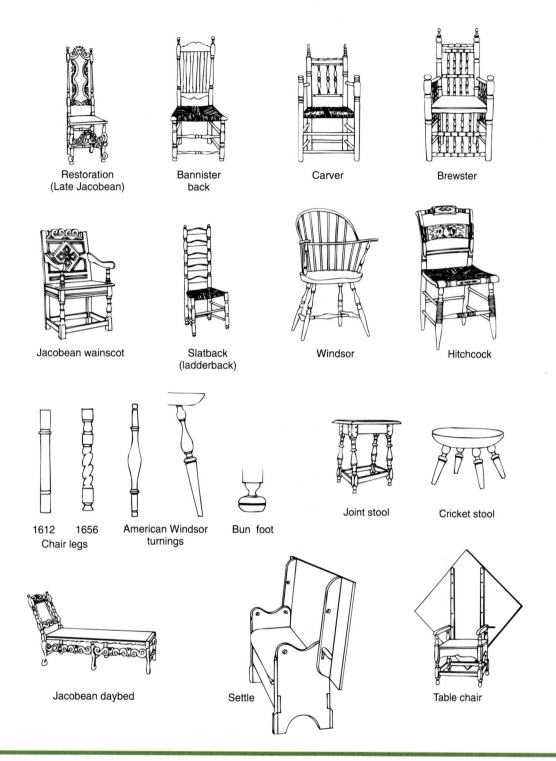

Restoration
(Late Jacobean)

Bannister
back

Carver

Brewster

Jacobean wainscot

Slatback
(ladderback)

Windsor

Hitchcock

1612   1656
Chair legs

American Windsor
turnings

Bun foot

Joint stool

Cricket stool

Jacobean daybed

Settle

Table chair

FIGURE 9.4   Early American (17th and 18th century country style).

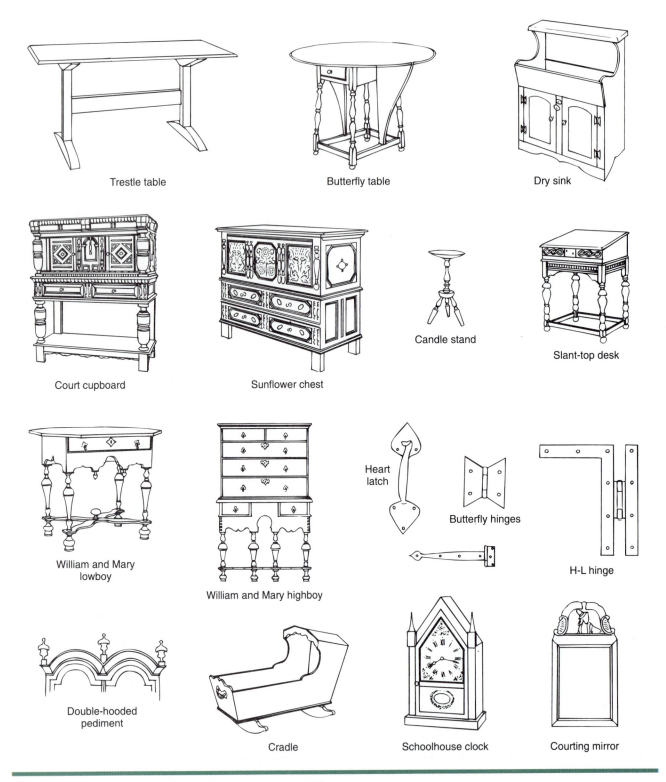

Trestle table

Butterfly table

Dry sink

Court cupboard

Sunflower chest

Candle stand

Slant-top desk

William and Mary lowboy

William and Mary highboy

Heart latch

Butterfly hinges

H-L hinge

Double-hooded pediment

Cradle

Schoolhouse clock

Courting mirror

FIGURE 9.5 Early American (17th and 18th century country style).

after about 1720. Schoolhouse clock a favorite. The courting mirror was presented to a prospective bride. Square mirrors, often with William and Mary–type cresting.

Early and Late Georgian (circa 1700–1790)

As Americans prospered and began to live a more leisurely lifestyle, homes and furnishings reflected eighteenth-century England and became more formal and refined than those of the earlier settlement period. Commonly known as Georgian, the style was named after Kings George I, II, and III of England, whose reigns dated from 1714 to 1820 (see Chapter 12). The style known as **Queen Anne**, named after the queen who reigned from 1702 to 1714, was introduced around 1700 and marked the beginning of a new, elegant style in American furniture design. It was based on the curve and displayed a grace and refinement formerly unknown in English furniture. The Early Georgian period began in the early 1700s and continued until about 1745, the year that introduced on a grand scale Thomas Chippendale's more heavy and masculine furniture. The Queen Anne style had an immediate and lasting influence on Americans, who found in its timeless and versatile design a practicality that combined well with most styles. Early Queen Anne was less formal and ornate, using simpler forms. Later, the Queen Anne style became more decorative and elegant and was used in a more dignified setting.

Chippendale furniture (produced in England in the eighteenth century during the "Golden Age" of great cabinetmakers) graced the Georgian mansions of a new affluent society in America during the mid- and late eighteenth century. **Thomas Chippendale** (1718–1779) wrote *The Gentleman and Cabinet-Makers Director* in 1754, which had a tremendous influence on other cabinetmakers, who widely copied his designs. Chippendale furniture, therefore, was a product of a "school" rather than the work of a single man. It incorporates designs from Queen Anne, Gothic, French, Adam, and Chinese styles. It uses both straight and curved lines and is large in scale, sturdy, and elegant. The use of Chippendale furniture generally marks the introduction of the Late Georgian style, although Queen Anne furniture designs continued to be popular. Both Queen Anne and Chippendale furniture took on distinct regional differences in the colonies. Today, both styles are often appropriately combined when designing the Georgian style.

Queen Anne Furniture (circa Early 1700s–1745)

General Characteristics. Queen Anne furniture (see Figure 9.6) is based on the **cyma (S)** curve. Graceful and dainty. May be formal and elegant or informal and simple, depending on upholstery employed. Use of mahogany. Introduction of lacquering an important innovation. The *scallop-shell motif* most typical and particularly employed for chairs, tables, secretaries, mirrors, and other pieces. Simple butterfly-shaped metal hardware.

PRINCIPAL FURNITURE TYPES — MOST TYPICAL PIECES

- *Seating:* The *fiddleback side chair* is the most popular piece, distinguished by its unique fiddleback slat with the cyma-curve top rail and *cabriole leg* design (a leg shaped in a double curve with a swelling of the upper part). Use of the *pad* or **club foot**. *Claw and ball foot* employed late in Queen Anne period. *Wing chair,* an upholstered lounge chair with upper side units or "wings," developed about 1750. The *round-about chair* much in vogue. *Sofa* with high curved back.
- *Casepieces:* The *highboy* is a tall chest of drawers arranged in two sections supported by turned or cabriole legs; *lowboy* is a low table with small drawers supported by turned or cabriole legs.
- *Tables:* Tea table is a delicate, small table supported on slender cabriole legs. *Tilt-top table* with a central pedestal and the **dropleaf table** were popular pieces.

Fabrics. Elegant formal damasks, velvets, taffetas, and brocades. For a less formal effect, a light background chintz with flower motifs was popular. Also, simple cotton and wool fabrics. Colors: red, gold, muted green, and blue most common.

Accessories. Oriental rugs. Oriental porcelain vases. Baroque brass or bronze chandeliers. Mirrors had tall vertical frame with characteristic S-curved top, often lacquered. Tallcase clock (c. 1720) often lacquered.

Chippendale Furniture (circa 1745–1790)

General Characteristics. Chippendale furniture (see Figure 9.7) is sturdy and elegant, with vigorous carving in high relief. More masculine in form than Queen Anne. Mahogany almost exclusively used, with secondary woods utilized for accents. Ornate metal butterfly, stirrup, and ring hardware.

PRINCIPAL FURNITURE TYPES — MOST TYPICAL PIECES

- *Seating:* Yokeback chair construction with upturned "shoulder" ends typical. Side chairs employ influence of rococo, Gothic, Chinese, and Adam designs. Modified and more ornate versions of Queen Anne. *Pierced ladderback chair.* Claw-and-ball foot. Cabriole leg with acanthus leaf or shell motif. Straight **Marlborough leg** often employed. *Camelback sofa* with distinctive hump or humps on backrest unit. *Wing chair* similar to Queen Anne wing chair, but more masculine form; wings larger and flared. Marlborough leg most typical.
- *Casepieces:* Highboys, lowboys, and *chest on chest* important casepieces. *Secretary* with *bracket* supports. Elaborate carvings. **Breakfront** cabinet with a projecting center section flanked with two side panels. *Knee-*

Wingback
Armchair

Fiddleback
Side Chair c. 1705

Fiddleback
Side Chair c. 1710

Stool

Late Queen Anne
Settee c. 1715

Drake   Pad   Club   Spanish

Claw & Ball   Slipper   Bracket

Tea Table

Highboy

Lowboy

Butterfly Hardware

Mirror
c. 1700

Mirror
c. 1720

Tall Case Clock

FIGURE 9.6   Queen Anne (Georgian period).

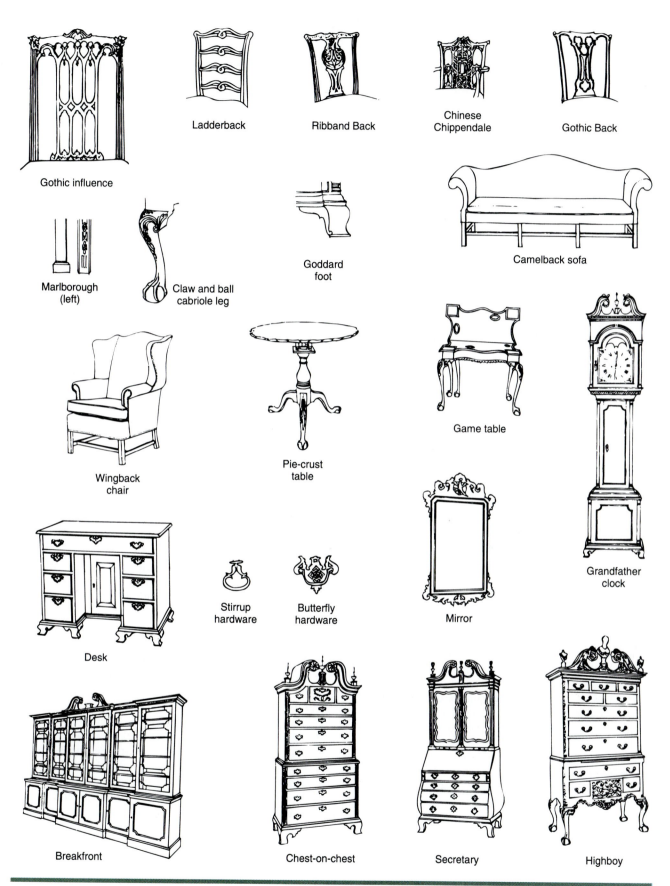

Gothic influence

Ladderback

Ribband Back

Chinese
Chippendale

Gothic Back

Marlborough
(left)

Claw and ball
cabriole leg

Goddard
foot

Camelback sofa

Wingback
chair

Pie-crust
table

Game table

Grandfather
clock

Desk

Stirrup
hardware

Butterfly
hardware

Mirror

Breakfront

Chest-on-chest

Secretary

Highboy

FIGURE 9.7 Chippendale (Georgian period).

hole desk an important piece—sometimes massive. Casepieces often topped with carved **finials** and *broken* and *scrolled pediments.* Bracket supports, often with **fret** designs.

- *Tables: Piecrust tilt-top table* a favorite piece. *Folding card table.*
- *Beds:* The *Chinese Chippendale* style, with dramatic use of fret motif, was one of the most favored bed designs.

Fabrics. Formal damasks particularly used; also brocades, taffetas, and velvets. Rich gold, yellow, deep red, blue, and "Williamsburg green" typical colors.

Accessories. Chippendale-styled mirrors. Baroque brass or bronze chandeliers. Oriental rugs and porcelain. Wall sconces. Tall, elegantly carved case clocks.

The Neoclassic Period (circa 1790–1845)

The last decade of the eighteenth century and the first four decades of the nineteenth century were characterized by Neoclassicism. The Neoclassic period is divided into three overlapping but identifiable subperiods: (1) the Early Federal Period (circa 1790–1804); (2) the Late Federal, Early American Empire, and Regency period (circa 1804–1825); and (3) the Greek Revival or Late American Empire period (circa 1825–1845).

Early Federal Period (circa 1790–1804)

Furniture in America from about 1790 to 1804, known as Federal, was distinguished by light forms and straight lines, with some semicircular and elliptical curves. After the Revolutionary War Americans were weary of English domination in architecture and furnishings. They looked to France, Italy, and Greece for inspiration. Ironically, the Federal period was dominated by the styles of English cabinetmakers **George Hepplewhite** (d. 1786), Thomas Sheraton (1751–1806), and the **Adam** brothers (Robert, 1728–1792, and James, 1730–1794), whose designs grew out of classicism and the Louis XVI taste. The Adam influence in America, however, was seen more in interior architecture than in furnishings. These new styles were more delicate than Queen Anne and Chippendale, and the emphasis was on color and surface decoration rather than form. Dining room furniture in the new style was particularly popular because the smaller scale made it suitable for most homes. During the Early Federal period America produced its most famous cabinetmaker, Duncan Phyfe (1768–1854).

In the Early Federal period monumental casepieces of the Chippendale period were replaced by lighter forms. The highboy, lowboy, and cabriole leg went out of style. There were a number of innovations: the buffet; the china cabinet; the dining-room extension table; the **tambour front** secretary or desk, with a flexible shutter made of thin wood strips on canvas or linen; the *Martha Washington chair,* called a "Lolling chair"; and numerous small tables for a variety of functions—the sewing-bag table being a notable example.

The designs of Hepplewhite and Sheraton were freely exchanged, and frequently a furniture item would incorporate designs of both. For example, a chair may have had a Sheraton-styled back and Hepplewhite-styled legs and been labeled either Sheraton, Hepplewhite, or both—Hepplewhite/Sheraton. Some features were consistently employed by both styles such as the *French bracket foot,* oval and round hardware, and *crossbanding* (the practice of veneering small sections of lighter wood opposite to the grain of the wood surface). Stretchers were rarely used.

In spite of the similarities and overlapping designs, Hepplewhite and Sheraton furniture had distinctive characteristics.

Hepplewhite Furniture

General Characteristics. Hepplewhite furniture (see Figure 9.8) was a bridge between the Chippendale style and the Neoclassic style. This can be seen in the use of a modified Chippendale scroll on casepieces and mirrors, the camelback sofa, and the serpentine front. The typical Hepplewhite leg is straight, square, tapered, and either plain or fluted, and it terminates with or without a *spade foot.* Inlay—especially the eagle, **paterae,** and bellflower motifs—was popular. Brass ring hardware was used on furniture; glass and china knobs were a later feature.

PRINCIPAL FURNITURE TYPES—MOST TYPICAL PIECES

- *Seating:* Chair backs in the form of shields, hearts, or ovals, with the honeysuckle, shell of flowers, and *Prince of Wales plume* favored motifs. Sofas have upholstered curved or camel backs with arms that flare back from the seat. The *Windsor chair* was modified, and the *rocking chair* came into favor during the first quarter of the eighteenth century. (The Windsor chair today is more associated with the Early Settlement period.)
- *Casepieces: Sideboard* among most important pieces, supported on six legs with concave front ends. *Tambour secretaries* an innovation, often displaying scroll pediments. *China cabinets* and *bookcases* popular. *Chests* had straight or serpentine fronts. (Hepplewhite employed crossbanding in straight lines on casepieces.)
- *Tables: Dining tables* given special importance. Usually oval with typical straight supports. **Pembroke tables** with drop leaves, either oval or serpentine. *Pier table* and *sewing-bag table* with typical legs.
- *Beds: Four-poster bed* with high, slender, fluted, or spiralled posts.

Fabrics. Formal and elegant damasks, velvets, brocades, and taffetas. Fabrics and wallpapers with French and classical themes in pastel colors, particularly soft blues and greens.

Bellflower &
Eagle motifs

Tapered

Hepplewhite legs
fluted leg with
thimble foot

Tapered leg
with
thimble foot

Heart Back

Shield Back
Chair

Martha Washington
Chair

Paterae

Hepplewhite
Table

Camelback Sofa

Inlay

Sideboard

Sewing Bag

Serpentine
Front

Extension Dining Table

Pembroke Table

Mirror

FIGURE 9.8   Hepplewhite (Federal/Neoclassic period).

Accessories. Mirrors strongly influenced by Robert Adam and Chippendale. Mirrors often convex, with the eagle motif. (The eagle, America's new official national emblem, was a favorite motif.) Elegant **crystal** chandeliers. Wedgwood china and medallions. Oriental or French rugs. Intricate stitchery crafts. Tall, slender clock cases. Two especially popular clocks were the "pillar and scroll" shelf clock and the Willard banjo clock. Fine silver and glass accessories.

Sheraton Furniture

General Characteristics. Sheraton furniture (see Figure 9.9) shows the dominance of straight lines and simplicity of design. Graceful and well proportioned. Influenced primarily by the Adam brothers, Hepplewhite, and Louis XVI style in France. Employed classical motifs such as the urn, festoons, swags, scrolls, pendant flowers, rosettes, and oval paterae. Arabesques and other motifs painted on furniture were a later feature. Typical Sheraton leg is straight, tapered, and reeded and terminates in a thimble foot.

PRINCIPAL FURNITURE TYPES — MOST TYPICAL PIECES

- *Seating:* Chair backs square, but in a variety of designs with or without arms. Sofas have carved wood railing across the back and armrest extends straight above the leg, leaving an opening between the armrest and upholstery. Sofas sometimes extremely long.
- *Casepieces: Chests* have bowed fronts. *Buffets* have convex front ends. *Secretaries* have finials, often in the form of an urn. (Sheraton used oval crossbanding on his casepieces.)
- *Tables: Dining tables* typically supported on two or more columns with three or four splayed reeded legs. Numerous *small tables* with straight or pedestal supports. *Sofa table* an innovation. Many *dual-purpose tables.*
- *Beds: Four poster* topped by a canopy or terminating in a carved vase. Sheraton was first to design *twin beds.*

Fabrics. See Hepplewhite.

Accessories. Mirrors architectural in form with gilt frame consisting of side colonnette supports. Some were horizontal, made in three sections to hang over the mantel. Some combined features of Hepplewhite and Sheraton. (See Hepplewhite.)

Duncan Phyfe

Among the many fine cabinetmakers of whom New York and other design centers boasted, the most famous was Duncan Phyfe. Phyfe maintained his New York workshop from 1795 to 1847. The enormous furniture output of those years falls into two periods: (1) his early (and many critics considered his best) work inspired by Robert Adam, Hepplewhite, and Sheraton, with some Regency features and (2) his later work influenced by French Empire styles. Phyfe more than any other is credited with having established the Empire style in America. His designs during the Greek Revival period followed the current fashion and were heavy and massive but usually had a monumental grace.

Although Phyfe's work covered a wide range of styles, his name is associated more with Regency than any other, and his furniture was called New York Regency (see Figure 9.10). He is the only American to whom is attributed a "period furniture style."

General Characteristics (Early Duncan Phyfe Furniture). Strikingly fine proportions. Clean, simple lines with freehand curves. Structural soundness. Restraint in the use of ornamentation, which consists of turning, fluting, reeding, and *foliate carving.* Principal motifs were the lyre, palm leaves, holly, laurel, small acanthus, lion's head, medallions, wheat, and swags. Some early pieces so similar to Sheraton's that they could be mistaken for reproductions.

PRINCIPAL FURNITURE TYPES — MOST TYPICAL PIECES

- *Seating:* Low backs rolled over top rail. Back panels have cross splat or cane. The lyre is distinctive. Seats are of the *slip type.* Legs are straight and reeded, or *saber-shaped,* ending in animal paws. Some chairs have *curule-shaped* supports reminiscent of Pompeii. Early sofas followed Sheraton design. Phyfe sofas have a reeded front rail in sleigh form, often with the lyre motif. Feet are reeded, curule, or *cornucopia. Récamier sofa* followed lines of the French Empire style.
- *Tables:* Numerous tables designed for a variety of functions. Most popular were the **console,** a simple pedestal supported on splayed legs; *card table,* with a folding top; *library table,* long and narrow with drop leaves supported on ends by lyres or columns; and the *dining table.* (Phyfe is credited with having invented the accordion extension table.)

Fabrics. Similar to Hepplewhite and Sheraton.

Accessories. One of the best known Phyfe accessories is the *cheval,* a full-figure-length mirror mounted on trestles swinging from vertical posts.

Late Federal, Early American Empire, and Regency Period (circa 1804–1825)

Furniture of the second phase of the Neoclassic period in America, from about 1804 to 1825, is referred to as Late Federal, Early Empire, or **Regency** style, because it was marked by the continuing Federal period in America, the Napoleonic period in France, and the Regency period in England (see Figure 9.11). Furniture manufacturing was dominated in America by Duncan Phyfe, who developed furniture along the lines of the English Regency and French Empire styles. Other notable cabinetmakers of

Chair Back

French Bracket Foot

Sheraton/
Hepplewhite
Side Chair

Sheraton Leg

Martha Washington
Chair

Armchair

Sofa

Chest with
French Bracket

Tambour
Table

Pembroke Table

Pedestal Table

Splayed leg

Architectural
Mirror

Sheraton Sideboard

Extension Table

FIGURE 9.9 Sheraton (Federal/Neoclassic period).

Curule
form chair

Ancient Grecian
sabre leg chair

Side chair
with sabre leg

Lyre back
chair

Sofa with
cornucopia legs

Window bench

Card table

Library table

Accordion extension
table

Cheval glass with
column supports

Lyre motif

Cornucopia legs

Lion's paw foot
with caster

Lion's head pull

FIGURE 9.10 Duncan Phyfe (Federal, American Empire, and Regency period).

Klismos Chair

Scroll Chair
(animal legs)

Recamier
(Cornucopia leg)

Settee

Pier Table

Table
(falcon support)

Caryatid
Support

Buffet
(Paw foot)

Sleigh Bed
(Egyptian column)

Girandole Mirror
(Bull's eye)

Banjo Clock

Acanthus leaf carving

FIGURE 9.11 American Empire.

the period included Charles-Honore Lannuier and Joseph Meeks of New York, Samuel McIntire in Salem, and John Seymour in Boston.

Ancient motifs from Rome, Greece, and Egypt, particularly favored by Napoleon, were combined to create a new style. Napoleon actually dictated the new style to classic artist Jacques-Louis David (1748–1825) and decorators Percier and Fontaine.

A renewed interest in the "Golden Age" of ancient Grecian and Roman architecture influenced designers to build magnificent temple-style mansions employing the "Three Orders of Architecture." The English Regency period (the time of George IV's Regency) flourished during this period, with furniture interpreted in more delicate terms. Leaders in England were Thomas Hope (1770–1831) and Thomas Sheraton. *Biedermeier furniture* in Germany was an extreme simplification of the style.

General Characteristics. Concepts of the French Empire and English Regency styles were transplanted to America through periodicals published abroad and sent to the new republic and by imported pieces that were copied. Furnishings were generally heavy, massive, and masculine. Supports included lion-paw feet and figural elements of swans and dolphins. Large areas of plain veneer appeared. Many surfaces were enhanced with classical ormolu mounts and brass **inlay**. Typical motifs: the lyre, honeysuckle, cornucopia, honey bee, laurel wreaths, swags, **festoons**, crowns, torches, animal forms, and *caryatids*.

Furniture made early in the period was well designed and expertly finished; but after the second decade of the nineteenth century both design and workmanship deteriorated, and heavy, ostentatious furniture became the vogue. Dominant woods: rosewood, mahogany, and ebony.

PRINCIPAL FURNITURE TYPES—MOST TYPICAL PIECES

- *Seating:* Grecian Klismos chair, Roman curule, or X-based chairs dominant. Some chairs had heavy scrolls with winged or caryatid supports. Popular Boston rocker became higher, with broad top rail. Window bench in vogue. Many interpretations of the Grecian couch. Récamier similar to the Roman couch.
- *Casepieces:* Heavy sideboards supported on short legs with brass lion-paw feet and lion-mask pulls. Wardrobe introduced.
- *Tables:* French-styled *pier table* (a side table with mirror backdrop) assumed extraordinary designs. Small tables designed to serve multiple purposes.
- *Beds:* Sleigh bed was introduced.

Fabrics. Elegant damasks, brocades, and velvets. Green, yellow, red, gold, and blue in strong chroma, also white and black. Motifs drawn from ancient Egypt, Greece, and Rome.

Accessories. The well-known "banjo" clock. The "bull's-eye" rounded mirror with convex or concave glass, often surmounted by an eagle, continued to be popular. **Torchère lamps.** Harp and lyre. Crystal and oil-vessel chandeliers. Ceiling fan (*punkah*) used in southern United States. Ormolu decorations applied to furnishings. Pier mirrors with column frames. Bowls supported by a columned base. Other accessories reflecting Egyptian, Roman, and Grecian themes.

The Greek Revival Period (circa 1825–1845)

The third phase of the Neoclassic Style in America is known as Greek Revival or Late American Empire (see Figure 9.12). Duncan Phyfe, who continued to produce furniture until 1847, followed the fashion trends but was more restrained than most cabinetmakers of the day, among whom were Forbes & Son, Thomas Astens, and Joseph Meeks of New York; Antoine Gabriel Quervelle and the Loud brothers of Philadelphia (the latter made pianos); and William Hancock of Boston. All these designers worked in distinct regional styles during the 1820s and 1830s.

General Characteristics. Furniture of the Greek Revival style was bold and monumental in character, following the taste of England and France. Many pieces were heavier versions of the Empire Style. After 1820, furniture showed definite American divergence from English tradition. Supports became large animal-paw feet with hairy shanks combined with a profusion of deep, heavy carving of **acanthus** leaves, cornucopias, plumes, and diamond-patterned pineapple motifs and ormolu. Legs had ornate turnings and twisted reeding. Swan and dolphin were favorite decorations.

In the late 1830s carving was superseded by plain surfaces and simple lines known as "pillar and scroll." Highly figured veneers were standard as surface features. Darkened mahogany surfaces were lavishly gilded, painted, and stenciled with abstract linear patterns, Greek **anthemia**, and large fruit and floral motifs. (*Anthemion,* the Greek term for "flower," refers to a stylized honeysuckle or palm leaf decoration.)

PRINCIPAL FURNITURE TYPES—MOST TYPICAL PIECES

- *Seating:* Gondola reflecting the French Restoration style. Heavily scrolled and profusely carved sofas.
- *Casepieces:* Enormous *wardrobe* with plain wood doors and stencil trim a typical piece.
- *Tables: Pier table* of extraordinary design. **Pedestal** or pillar table of plain design. Table with pineapple-motif pedestal and splayed, hairy legs with bold acanthus design. Pillar pedestal *card table.*

Fabrics. Increased use of cotton. Continued popularity of elegant fabrics. Horsehair often used for seat upholstery. Stripes became broader, in contrasting colors.

Gondola

Carved sofa

Volute scroll

Scrolls

Pillar pedestal
card table

Table with
hairy shank

Pillar table

Pier table

Stenciled wardrobe

Greek fret

Animal paw foot
with hairy shank

Anthemion

Stylized anthemion

Acanthus leaf

Lighthouse clock

FIGURE 9.12 Greek Revival (Neoclassic period).

Fabrics printed with bold medallions on an open ground with borders of anthemia and Greek key patterns popular. Colors strong, with golden yellow and crimson red being favorites.

Accessories. American manufacturers at Boston and Sandwich, Massachusetts, produced fine glass that was pierced, cut, and colored. Silver tea sets, porcelain, and stoneware also of American make. Oil-burning lighting devices decorated in classical or rococo designs. Dolphin-shaped glass candlesticks and hurricane glass over candles. Brass fireplace and lighting fixtures.

The French Styles in America (Late Eighteenth Century to Present)

Eighteenth-century French settlers in America had a particular influence on domestic architecture and furnishings that has continued into the twentieth century.

When Louis XIV (1643–1715) finished his magnificent palace of Versailles outside of Paris, European designers began imitating the grandeur of its interiors and furnishings. But the extravagant style of Louis XIV had little impact on America. It was under the reign of his grandson, Louis XV (1715–1774), that the rococo style emerged—a style enthusiastically embraced in America and still widely imitated. This ornately curved style was influenced by Madame du Pompadour and then Madame du Barry, who lived at the palace of Versailles and helped promote the feminine, delicate style. After Louis XV's death, the reign of Louis XVI (1774–1793) marked a significant change in French design. With the discovery of Pompeii and a renewed interest in classicism, the new style employed the use of straight lines and classical motifs. Both the Louis XV and XVI styles reflected the love of luxury, extravagance, beauty, and frivolity that paved the way for the French Revolution.

The Empire style (1804–1815) was so called because of the association with the French emperor Napoleon. The Empire style was a return to the classic lines of the ancient Greek, Roman, and Egyptian prototypes. This style had an important influence on American furniture design in the early and late American Empire periods (circa 1804–1845).

Furniture of the Louis XV period was later simplified by those who did not live at the court. They produced an extremely popular and versatile style that Europeans and Americans have termed Provincial French, which may be successfully dressed up or down. The choice of fabrics often determines the degree of formality. Excellent reproductions of these exquisite styles, along with more informal interpretations, are currently being produced by manufacturers, sometimes with a surprising degree of authenticity.

Country French is the most rustic and informal style. Its charm results from incorporating handcrafted furniture and accessories reflecting the distinctive flavor of the French countryside.

Italian Provincial is a style originated by American furniture companies after World War II. Italian Provincial has much in common with the Louis XVI style but is much more restrained and characterized by dignified simplicity. This style has had limited use in the United States.

Louis XV Style (1715–1774)

General Characteristics. Furniture of the Louis XV style (see Figure 9.13) is elegant, graceful, and elaborately carved, with a strong feminine influence, dainty and more lightly scaled than Louis XIV. The style is free-form and asymmetrical decoration is typical. Court French Louis XV features gilded, painted, and *chinoiserie* lacquered surfaces. A variety of local and imported woods are used, with exotic woods especially popular for **marquetry**. There is lavish use of ormolu mounts.

PRINCIPAL FURNITURE TYPES—MOST TYPICAL PIECES

- *Seating: Fauteuil* (open-arm chair) and **bergère** (closed-arm chair), with or without wings, are classic pieces. Both employ the curved *cabriole leg* and up-turned *dolphin nose foot*. Extended **chaise longue** is luxurious piece. Fashionable *marquise* was an extrawide bergère. Chairs typically made for variety of functions. *Sofas* and *day beds* assumed various forms. *Canape sofa* had unbroken back and inward-curving ends. *Stools* followed typical curved lines.
- *Casepieces:* **Commode** (chest of drawers)—often with a marble top—most characteristic piece. Chinese themes and gilded, lacquered, and painted finishes typical. **Armoire** (large upright storage piece) with flowing carved decoration an essential item. *Secretaire* and *console* are also well-known casepieces. Small *lady's writing desk* one of most appealing innovations of eighteenth century.
- *Tables:* Tables to meet all needs designed employing typical curved lines, treatments, and motifs popular in the Louis XV style. One of most important was the *bureau plat* (a large table-desk).
- *Beds:* Lavishly carved and draped canopy bed of the Louis XIV period remained fashionable in palaces, but began to be replaced by the *alcove bed.*

Fabrics. Formal and elegant. Tapestries, cut velvets, brocatelles. Brocades and silks often with small patterns. Asymmetrically arranged flowers and flowing ribbons popular motifs. Colors in soft pastels, gold, green, Venetian blue, and peach.

Accessories. Aubusson, Savonnerie, or Oriental rugs (see Chapter 6). Elaborate crystal chandeliers. Asymmetrical candle holders and wall *sconces*. Clocks with swirling metal designs in the Louis XV expression. Mirrors small with ornate frames. Perforated metal and other elaborately treated firescreens. Oil paintings in ornate

Fauteuil

Stool

Marquise

Cabriole legs

Tête-à-tête

Canapé

Hardware

Pedestal secretaire

Drop front
writing desk

Bureau plat

Commode

Alcove bed

Ormolu

Shelf clock

Console
and mirror

FIGURE 9.13 Louis XV (French style).

gold frames. French and Oriental porcelains. Busts of royalty and nobility.

Louis XVI Style (1774–1793)

General Characteristics. Distinguished by renewed interest in architectural forms and ornament of ancient Greece and Rome—in particular, discovery of the ancient city of Pompeii, which had been covered by volcanic ash for centuries—furniture of the Louis XVI style shows strict adherence to rectangular forms (see Figure 9.14). Straight lines replaced flowing free forms of the previous style. The feminine influence at court continued with Louis XVI's queen, Marie Antoinette, who supported Neoclassicism. Furnishings had finishes often painted and gilded in pale colors. Exquisitely finished wood was popular, especially mahogany, rosewood, and exotic woods for expanded marquetry. Ormolu continued in use with designs assuming classical forms. Laurel and acanthus, rosettes, wreaths, festoons, lyres, swans, urns, ribbons (the love knot), egg and dart, bound arrows, and animals were important motifs. Carving was simple and more delicate. Inset of porcelain plaques became popular in fine furniture. *Gesso* work (a plaster made of chalk and white lead that is carved into various designs) was applied to furniture, then painted.

PRINCIPAL FURNITURE TYPES—MOST TYPICAL PIECES

- *Seating:* **Fauteuil** and *bergère* chairs characterized by use of straight lines. Most distinguishing feature of Louis XVI furniture: the supports, which are clearly seen in seating pieces. Legs straight and tapered—either square or round with vertical or spiral reeding or fluting terminating in a slender thimblelike shape—often surmounted by a square block enclosing a carved rosette. Sofas or *canapes* followed form of chairs. Backs of chairs and sofas straight or oval. Innovation called the *confident* was large canape with seat added at each end. *Day beds* popular. *Benches* long and narrow. *Stools* followed form of chairs.
- *Casepieces: Desks, commodes, cabinets,* and *secretaries* with floral decorations; stone, wood, and porcelain inlays; ormolu mounts; **galleries**; and brass or gilt moldings. *Armoire* with straight forms. Roll-top desk very popular. Small drop-leaf desks made in great numbers.
- *Tables: Bureau plat* remained a favorite. The *console,* a decorative table to go against the wall, and the *console-buffet,* used as a serving table for the dining room, both well-known pieces. *Dining table* became a necessity because, for first time, rooms specified for dining. Numerous small tables designed; among most important was the *bouillotte*—a small circular gaming table with a metal gallery edge—and the *gueridon* for candles and small articles. Marble tops typical.
- *Beds:* For most beds, head and foot boards of the same height, following the characteristic designs of chair backs. These were frequently placed in alcoves with the long side against the wall. Favored bed of Marie Antoi-

nette was the *"angel" bed,* with a much shortened canopy or *lambrequin* that supported lavish hangings.

Fabrics. Formal silks, damasks, velvets, and tapestries. Colors in soft pale colors. Motifs drawn from classical Greece and Rome. Bouquets and baskets of flowers and the love knot with flowing ribbon motif especially popular. Small floral prints alternating with stripes. **Toile de Jouy** (cotton or linen with pastoral and ancient classical scenes) used for a less formal feeling.

Accessories. Elegant and formal accessories of gold gilt. Mirrors architectural and rectangular. Frames painted and gilded. *Trumeau* mirror usually had upper section painted with Sèvres vases and delicate scrolls. Sconces and candelabra with urns, festoons, columns, and other classical motifs. Ormolu clocks for mantels and hanging clocks of gilt bronze surmounted by a fluttering bow fashionable. Elaborate fireplace accessories. Exquisite crystal chandeliers. Aubusson, Savonnerie, and Oriental rugs. Oil paintings in ornate gold frames. Busts of royalty and nobility often sculpted in marble.

Provincial French and Country French

General Characteristics. Furnishings were influenced by the Court styles of Louis XIV, XV, and XVI but were simpler, more affordable (see Figure 9.15) with simple, unadorned surfaces. Furniture was designed for family functions rather than court life. Pieces ranged from expensive furnishings (mostly associated with the Provincial French style, which flourished primarily in Paris) to inexpensive furnishings (mostly associated with the Country French style popular in the country provinces), with regional and social-economic differences. Oak, walnut, and fruitwood were popular. Louis XV style emerged as the most prominent influence for Provincial French furniture. Country French was distinguished by homemade crafted pieces, distinctively charming and homey. Sturdy **distressed** furniture was influenced by Louis XIV with a rural and rustic feeling and both straight and curved lines.

PRINCIPAL FURNITURE TYPES—MOST TYPICAL PIECES

- *Seating:* Ladderback chair with a rush seat and **salamander** back. Simplified version of the Louis XV *fauteuil* typical of the Provincial French style. Stool with a rush seat popular in the Country French style.
- *Casepieces:* Simplified Louis XV *commode, buffet,* and *armoire* most important pieces. *Hutch* (open cupboard) and *cupboards* with "chicken wire" grilles.
- *Tables:* Long, end, and other functional tables in Louis XV style. Small *breading table* for bread making an important item.
- *Beds:* Closed bed or *lit clos* (with draw curtains for warmth) an essential piece in the Country French home.

FIGURE 9.14 Louis XVI (French style).

Fauteuil

Bergère

Gilded stool

Reeded legs

Confident settee

Chaise longue

Canapé

Commode

Bureau plat

Ormolu

Escutcheon

Secretaire

Console server

Gueridon

Bouillotte

Angel bed

Trumeau

Clock with fluttering ribbon

Salamander Back

Open Arm Chair

Wing Chair

Stool

Settee with Straw Seat

Table

Long Narrow Table

Armoire

Commode

Detail of Chicken Wire

Hutch

Panetiere

Kneading Trough

Bed–Lit Clos

Clock

FIGURE 9.15 Provincial French.

Fabrics. Formal Provincial French fabrics include velvets, tapestries, damasks, and silks often employing motifs popular at court. Cottons, wool, and linen used for informal Provincial French and Country French. Toile de Jouy one of the most distinctive fabrics of either style approach. Plaids, checks, stripes, and small, quaint prints. Colors: red, blue, white, and apple green especially dominant.

Accessories. For a formal Provincial French direction, accessories similar to the Louis XV and XVI styles. Among informal accessories, both decorative and utilitarian items including the *panetière* (bread box) and items of pewter, copper, wood, and painted tin. **Primitive paintings,** *silhouettes,* brightly painted pottery, and pictures of song birds. *Tole lamps.*

French Empire (circa 1804–1815)

General Characteristics. French Empire furniture (see Figure 9.16) is characterized by massiveness, bisymmetry, and rectangularity emphasized by rigid edges and right angles, with function and comfort sacrificed for show. Most furniture was an adaptation of preexisting types. Mahogany was most preferred, with ebony, rosewood, and other exotic woods also highly prized. Large veneered surfaces replaced marquetry and lacquer. Most furniture supports were caryatids, but other common props were sphinxes and Egyptian busts. Elaborate ormolu mounts were used in profusion. The dominant motif was the capital letter *N* enclosed in a laurel wreath tied with a bow of ribbon. Other motifs were the imperial eagle, military symbols, and Egyptian and classical Grecian and Roman themes.

PRINCIPAL FURNITURE TYPES—MOST TYPICAL PIECES

- *Seating:* Chairs marked by broad, simple lines, both straight and curved. Back legs usually straight, with front legs straight, saber, or in form of a winged lion. *Gondola chair,* with back curved downward to form the arm, a great favorite. *Side chair* made without arms to accommodate soldier's saber. *Meridienne,* a small sofa or day bed with one end higher than the other. *Reclining couch* with flaring swan-neck end pieces named for the famous Madame Récamier. *X-stool* in great demand, since only those of rank permitted to sit on chairs before the emperor.
- *Casepieces:* Casepieces massive and elaborately decorated with ormolu. Fashionable *commode* had oblong marble top resting on a square or octagonal base (plinth) and was flanked by caryatids enriched with ormolu. *Sideboard* with cupboard below. *Bookcases* enormous. *Fall-front secretary* and *roll-top desk* followed prevailing style but had a number of adaptations.
- *Tables: Circular or octagonal tables* made in wide diversity of types to serve particular needs. *Dining tables* round and massive, supported by columns, classical figures, or animals. *Bureau plat* continued to be pop-

ular. Most essential piece of Empire furniture was *console*—placed against wall, had a rectangular or semicircular top, and was supported by a variety of typical supports; back panel was often a mirror. Numerous side tables and center tables of varying sizes. Three-legged *tripod* popular. *Lavabo*—a tripod with a porcelain wash basin—was an innovation. *Bouillotte* and *gueridon* common. Tall *pedestals* to support statues and vases popular. *Toilet tables* came into use.

- *Beds:* Heavy, majestic beds designed to be placed lengthwise against the wall. *Boat-bed,* with head and foot the same height and connected by a segmental line, was characteristic. *Tent* or *field bed* (a tribute to Napoleon) was a four-poster with a canopy resembling a tent.

Fabrics. Silks lavishly employed for furnishings. (The silk industry was revolutionized in 1801 by the invention of the Jacquard loom.) Taffetas, damasks, satins, brocades, and velvets in high demand. Fabrics typically had open ground with Empire motifs of contrasting colors. Brilliant green (Empire green) was favored color, along with gold, red, crimson, blue, black, and white. Popular motifs were letter *N* in a laurel wreath, bees, stars, swans, and eagles. Also, motifs drawn from ancient Egypt, Greece, and Rome, including the fret, honeysuckle, vase forms, anthemion, caryatids, heads of Apollo, and heads of horses and rams.

Accessories. For the most part accessories represented adjuncts of the Napoleonic reign or items of classical or Egyptian origin. Psyche was a large swinging mirror enclosed in a rectangular frame supported by two columns, always richly decorated. Dressing-table mirrors and portable mirrors were designed especially for ladies. Clocks of the pendulum type produced in abundance. Clocks usually rested on marble bases incorporated into a group of mythological figures, often covered by a glass dome. Sèvres porcelain pieces bearing Empire designs, Greek vases, bronze table lamps, busts, statues, and engravings of Napoleon's family and officers were displayed in profusion.

Victorian Furniture (circa 1840–1900)

Queen Victoria reigned in England from 1837 to 1901, and during this period a variety of architectural styles and furnishings were designed bearing her name (see Chapter 12). During the **Victorian era** imitations of furniture styles of the past were interpreted in various manifestations in America. These primarily included Gothic, rococo, and a concurrent concept called Renaissance Revival style, which was typified by massive forms and deeply carved ornamentation. Merging into the Renaissance Revival style was the regeneration of the Louis XVI style. This trend was introduced into America by the Paris–New York firms of Rinquet Le Prince and Marsotte.

Bergère chair

Side chair

Fauteuil

Meridienne Sofa

X-Stool

Mahogany Commode

Secretary with
figure supports

Dressing Table

Lavabo with
swan supports

Console with
Egyptian heads

Psyche mirror

French Empire Bed

Pedestal

Swan motif

Anthemion

Laurel wreath

Lion's Head
Pull

Table support

Cornucopia leg

Honey bee
motif

Lion's paw
foot

FIGURE 9.16 French Empire.

Their furniture followed late eighteenth-century French precedents in both form and ornament and reached the height of American popularity in the 1860s.

Two names that stand out in America during the Victorian era are New York–based John Belter (1804–1863), whose rococo style dominated the mid-nineteenth century, and the English designer Charles Eastlake (1836–1906), whose "Reform" furniture was popular from the 1870s through the 1890s. Eastlake's furniture was principally drawn from Gothic and Renaissance themes. He wrote his influential *Hints on Household Taste* in 1868.

Much Victorian furniture, which in this century was long maligned as no better than junk, is now sought as valuable antiques. Many Victorian furniture admirers are enthusiastically restoring, refinishing, and reintroducing these treasured pieces. After moving from the parlor to attic to junkyard to antique shops, Victorian furniture has returned to use in contemporary homes. Designers are finding that nineteenth-century furniture is a good mixer and, to the surprise of many, is often at its best in a modern structural setting.

Belter Rococo, Eastlake Gothic/Renaissance, and Classic Victorian (circa 1840–1900)

General Characteristics. Elaborate adaptations of French Rococo, Second Empire, Neoclassic, Gothic, Renaissance, Oriental, Elizabethan, and Jacobean prototypes were designed during the Victorian era. Usually, particular styles of furnishings were fashioned to complement their Victorian architectural counterparts. However, drawing from the numerous furniture styles of the Victorian era, which varied from region to region, three styles can be consistently identified as those most popularly associated with the period and considered collector's pieces today:

1. *Belter Rococo.* Although Victorian furniture was a mix of many stylistic influences, the image most commonly evoked by Americans is the lavish Belter or Victorian Rococo parlor with its florid walls and carpets, marble-topped tables, and excessively carved suites adapted from the Louis XV style (see Figure 9.17). Lest the room seem bare, accessories of all types were placed on every surface and hung on all available wall space. Woods most commonly used for Victorian Rococo furniture were walnut, rosewood, and mahogany.
2. The *Eastlake* or *Gothic/Renaissance* (see Figure 9.18) parlor laden with furniture and accessories recalling Renaissance and Gothic forms was also one of the most popular Victorian styles. This direction employed more lightly scaled and simplified machine-made furniture having basically rectilinear forms with incised, carved, and turned design applications. Many American cabinetmakers adapted and modified Eastlake's designs for use in American Victorian homes. Oak was the most typical wood used for Eastlake furniture.

3. Regeneration of the *Louis XVI* or *Classic Victorian* style followed the other two styles in popularity. Furniture was simple in expression, delicately scaled and decorated, borrowing themes from the French Louis XVI period.

PRINCIPAL FURNITURE TYPES—MOST TYPICAL PIECES

- *Seating: Belter "lady's and gentleman's"* chairs showing rococo influence. Elaborately carved *high-back* side chair. *Balloon-back* chair in Louis XV style. *Vis-à-vis* sofa allowing occupants to face each other to talk. Carved rosewood *crested* sofa. Classic Victorian chair. *Renaissance Revival* sofa with gilt incised lines, cresting, and turned legs. Walnut Eastlake *settee* and chair. *Gothic "rose window"* chair.
- *Casepieces:* Laminated round *bureau* (dresser). Belter rosewood *console* with **étagère**. Eastlake dresser with simple chest of drawers and rectangular mirror design. *Wooten patent desk* displaying Eastlake's influence with incising, short spindles, and characteristic cresting.
- *Tables:* Rococo rosewood and Eastlake center tables. Eastlake side table with incised decoration. Tall Eastlake-style pedestal stand.
- *Beds:* Carved and laminated Belter rosewood bed. Massive and lavishly carved Eastlake Renaissance bed. Iron or brass bed with Gothic arch design.

Fabrics. Formal brocades, plush velvet, lace, and damasks. Use of black horsehair upholstery. Large and small patterns profusely employed, with flower, foliage, and fruit motifs most common. Use of gold fringe. Colors: deep red, dark pinks, mauves, purples, golds, browns, and dark greens.

Accessories. Gilt pier mirror. Whatnot shelves laden with bric-à-brac. Small bronze statuary. Dried flowers under glass domes. Patterned rugs and carpets. Collections of all types displayed. Electrified gasolier chandeliers (often formed of brass or wrought iron). Tinted and painted glass lamps. Silhouette and charcoal portraits. Currier and Ives prints. Blackamoor statuettes. Picture viewer for stereoscopic photographs prominently displayed on a tabletop.

GENERAL CLASSIFICATION OF FURNITURE STYLES

Furniture styles typically fall into two general categories: (1) period or traditional and (2) modern or contemporary. Designers should be familiar with the terms used to describe period or traditional furniture:

Antique A piece of furniture or work of art that, according to United States law, must be at least 100 years old.

Reproduction A copy of an original. Some reproductions are done so meticulously that only the well-trained eye can

Highback Chair

Lady's Chair

Gentleman's Chair

Balloon Chair

Console with "whatnot" shelves

Tête-à-tête

Rosewood Carved Sofa

Bureau (Dresser) Concave front

Carved Rosewood Bed

Rococo Rosewood Center Table

Gilt Pier Mirror

FIGURE 9.17 Victorian (Belter Rococo).

Tufted Side Chair
Turned straight leg

Eastlake Chair

Walnut Settee

Renaissance Revival
sofa with cresting

Pedestal

Side Table
Incised decoration

Dresser

Wooten Patent Desk
Eastlake influence

Detail

Eastlake Bed

FIGURE 9.18 Victorian (Eastlake–Renaissance).

detect the difference, yet some modern reproductions are far from exact copies.

Adaptation A piece in which only some elements from the original have been adapted to a contemporary design.

Period style A term used to designate a single item or a complete interior, including the architectural background, furniture, and decorative arts prevalent in a specific country or a particular time in history. This style is often referred to as *traditional*.

Having discussed the most important traditional styles, we now look at contemporary and modern furniture.

Contemporary and Modern Furnishings

Contemporary

Current styles are called **contemporary**, often referring to eclectic designs that to some degree have been adapted from historical or modern influences. For example, "classic contemporary" is a modified historical style marked by a fresh interpretation suitable for today's home. Many manufacturers of contemporary furniture use authentic motifs and carvings. The grace and dignity of Old World artistry is combined with contemporary originality to produce fine furniture that has timeless beauty and appeal. Additionally, these furnishings are produced employing the latest advancements in technology and materials, making them sturdy and durable.

Modern

At any time in history when a new art form emerges that breaks all ties with previous design forms—whether in music, architecture, or furniture—it is referred to as *modern*. Today's modern furniture design is principally an expression of the twentieth century and aptly suggests the tempo of modern Americans. The roots of modernism can be traced to the Industrial Revolution in Europe. With the invention of new materials and technology, a fresh approach to furnishings gradually emerged. (See Chapter 13 for an outline of the development of modern architecture and design.) Since the early twentieth century, modern design has gone through many stages, each contributing something of lasting value. Some furniture designs of the modern period have become twentieth-century classics. Since a complete study of the development of modern furniture is beyond the scope of this introductory text, only a brief outline of the major design directions and contributors is presented. The following discussion complements the discussion of modern architecture in Chapter 13.

Earliest Modern Furniture. As early as 1840, Michael Thonet developed a process for bending wood—a process still employed by manufacturers today. His **bentwood rocker** and *Vienna café chair* remain classic pieces. (See Figure 9.19.)

The Arts and Crafts Movement. In England and America in the latter half of the nineteenth century, the Arts and Crafts Movement revolted against machine-made products and advocated a return to handcrafted furnishings. Inspiration was drawn from medieval and Gothic prototypes. Oak was the most common wood used. Furniture was simple, sturdy, and structural. (See Figure 9.19.) Leading furniture designers included:

England: William Morris was the founder of the movement. Charles Eastlake, Edward W. Godwin, Philip Webb, Ernest Gimson, and Charles F. A. Voysey created simple handcrafted furniture considered early expressions of modernism.

America: Gustav Stickley, Frank Lloyd Wright, Henry Hobson Richardson, and Charles and Henry Greene designed handcrafted structural furniture based on their own distinctive interpretations of the movement.

Furniture of the Arts and Crafts Movement in the United States is also known as Mission style.

Art Nouveau (circa 1890–1910). Art Nouveau is a decorative style based on natural forms that flourished primarily in Europe and America. Art Nouveau motifs include flowers, meandering vines, the female form, reptiles, waves of the ocean, the sinuous whiplash line, and flowing forms of all types. (See Figures 9.19 and 9.20.) Leading contributors included:

France: When Samuel Bing opened his Paris studio, La Maison de l'Art Nouveau, in 1895, the style was officially named. Hector Guimard, Emile Gallé, and Louis Majorelle were known for their exquisite and elegant furniture.

Belgium: Henri van de Velde, considered the spokesman for the style, opened his own furniture studio in Brussels.

England: Arthur Heygate Mackmurdo and Charles F. A. Voysey created furniture in a more conservative and symmetrical manner, typical of the English approach.

Spain: Antonio Gaudi, considered the most "wild and imaginative" of all the Art Nouveau designers, was known for his sculptural and expressive furnishings.

Germany: Richard Riemerschmid designed simple interpretations of the new style. In Germany and Austria the style was known as *Jugendstijl.*

Finland: Eliel Saarinen, whose White Collection is well known, is considered the father of modern architecture in Finland.

Scotland: One of the most outstanding designers of the period was Charles Rennie Mackintosh in Glasgow. His designs took two different approaches: one, Art Nouveau style; the other, strong, angular, and geometric. His creations included pink and white Art Nouveau furniture and extraordinary "perpendicular" furniture. The latter furnishings were geometric compositions with tall, straight chair backs—significant contributions to the modern movement. Classic pieces include the *Argyle, Hill House,* and *Willow chairs.*

America: Prominent New York designer Louis Comfort Tiffany designed superb stained-glass lamps and other furnishings considered collector's items today.

The Secession (circa 1897–1903). The Secession was an artistic movement that "seceded" from historical styles. The movement's focus was primarily in Vienna, Austria. Leaders included Otto Wagner, Adolf Loos, Josef Maria Olbrich, and **Josef Hoffmann**. Hoffmann's furniture has had a long-lasting influence on the design world. His classic pieces include the *Fledermaus, Prague,* and *Haus Koller chairs* designed during the first decade of the century (see Figure 9.20). The *Wiener Werkstatte* (studio), formed by Hoffmann in 1903, was an offshoot of the Secession and provided a setting where a more geometric and structural design approach was fostered.

De Stijl (1917–circa 1932). De Stijl was a radical style that emerged in Holland in 1917. The group adhered to strict design principles they called *neoplasti-*

Bentwood Rocker
Michael Thonet

Vienna Cafe
Michael Thonet

Morris Chair
Phillip Webb

Eastlake Chest

Godwin cabinet

Voysey Chair

Stickley Chair

Robie Chair
Frank Lloyd Wright

Cathedra Chair
H.H. Richardson

Greene & Greene
Armchair

Adirondack Chair
Am. Arts & Crafts

Art Nouveau Chair
Hector Guimard

Art Nouveau Chair
Emile Gallé

FIGURE 9.19 Early modern furniture (Thonet, Arts & Crafts, and Art Nouveau).

Art Nouveau Chair
Louis Majorelle

Art Nouveau Chair
Henri Van de Velde

Art Nouveau Chair
Arthur Mackmurdo

Art Nouveau Chair
Antonio Gaudi

White Collection
Eliel Saarinen

Argyle Chair
C.R. Mackintosh

Hill Chair
C.R. Mackintosh

Secession Stool
Otto Wagner

Fledermaus Chair
Josef Hoffmann

Prague Chair
Josef Hoffmann

Haus Koller Chair
Josef Hoffmann

Red/Blue Chair
Gerrit Rietveld

Zig-Zag Chair
Gerrit Rietveld

FIGURE 9.20 Early modern furniture (Art Nouveau, Secession, and De Stijl).

cism: (1) only red, yellow, blue, white, gray, and black were used; and all creations (2) had to be *abstract*; (3) have smooth, shiny surfaces; and (4) be composed only of right angles. Leaders included the painter Piet Mondrian; Theo van Doesburg, the founder; and Gerrit Rietveld, whose furniture pieces are well-known classics. Two outstanding pieces are the *Red/Blue* (1918) and *Zigzag* (1934) *chairs* (see Figure 9.20).

The Bauhaus (1919–1933) and International Style.

The focal point of modern design from 1919 to 1933 was the *Bauhaus* in Weimar, Germany. Its philosophy was that aesthetically pleasing objects could be created by mechanical means. At this experimental design school, two great furniture pioneers, **Marcel Breuer** and Ludwig Mies van der Rohe, developed the cantilever chair and the use of tubular steel for furniture construction. Classics include Marcel Breuer's *Wassily lounge* (1925) and *Cesca chair* (1928) and Mies van der Rohe's *Barcelona Collection* (1929) and *Brno chair* (1930) (see Figure 9.21).

Le Corbusier, who worked out of his studio in Paris, is considered a master of the International Style. His classics include the *Petit* and *Grand Confort* (1928) and *Pony chaise lounge* (1929). Other designers of note in Paris were Eileen Gray, who designed the *Transat chair* (1927), and Robert Mallet-Stevens, whose *Mallet-Stevens stacking chair* (1928) is particularly popular.

Art Deco (circa 1909–1940).

Art Deco was a decorative style that flourished in Europe and America principally between World War I and World War II. The term *Art Deco* was derived from the great Paris Exposition in 1925—the *Exposition des Arts Decoratifs*. Inspiration for the new style was drawn from many sources, including the glamour of the movies and stage, jazz music, African art, ancient Egyptian, Assyrian and Aztec Indian cultures, new technology, the Bauhaus and International Style, the skyscraper, a sophisticated new society, and the fashion world. Motifs include the zigzag; lightning flash; pyramid; Egyptian themes, including the sunburst and palm tree; the peacock; stylized flowers and animals; and numerous geometric shapes. For furniture design many types of new materials were employed, and old materials were used in refreshing new ways (see Figures 9.21 and 9.22). Some outstanding designers and classics of the period are:

France: Jacques-Emile Ruhlmann, whose elegant and expensive furniture was widely imitated.

America: Frank Lloyd Wright's *Imperial chair* (1920) is a classic. **Paul Frankl**, known for his *skyscraper furniture*, and Donald Deskey, designer of the furnishings for Radio City Music Hall in New York, are influential furniture designers of the style. Eliel Saarinen, the prominent Finnish designer, moved to America in 1922 and soon became director of the prestigious design school Cranbrook Academy, in Michigan. His best-known classics of this period include the *Cranbrook sidechair* (1929) and the *Blue Collection* (1929).

The 1930s.

The decade of the 1930s witnessed the contribution of a number of designers from various countries whose classics are still widely recognized. These include (1) Spain's Salvador Dali, designer of the surrealistic *Mae West Lips chair* (1936, revived by the Italians as the *Marilyn* in 1972); (2) Denmark's Kaare Klint, who designed the *Deck chair* (1933); (3) England's T. H. Robsjohn-Gibbings, critic, historian, and designer, who revived the classic *Klismos chair* (1936) of ancient Greece; and (4) Argentina's design team of Bonet, Kurchan, and Hardoy, creators of the famous *Butterfly chair* (1938). (See Figure 9.22.)

Postwar Scandinavia.

After World War II, the Scandinavian countries developed furniture of exceptional quality and design. (See Figure 9.23.) Classic pieces and designers include:

Finland: **Alvar Aalto** designed a series of lightly scaled laminated bentwood designs. Eero Aarnio exploited new forms and materials, as expressed in his *Globe* (1966) and *Gyro* (1968) *chairs*.

Denmark: Hans Wegner is known for his expert craftsmanship and beauty of form and materials. His outstanding classics include *"The chair"* (1949), *Peacock chair* (1947), and *Chair 24* (1950). Arne Jacobsen is known for his sculptural *Egg* and *Swan chairs* (1958) and his *Series 7 Group* (1955). Poul Kjaerholm preferred combining natural materials with metal. His outstanding classics are *Chair 22* (1956) and *Chair 20* (1968). Vernor Panton, who currently works out of Switzerland, is renowned for his work in molded plastic. His *Panton Stacking Chair* (1960–1968) is a landmark piece. Currently, a new generation of Scandinavian designers continues to uphold the high standards of design, craftsmanship, and technology set by previous masters.

Postwar America.

After World War II, America emerged as a world leader in furniture design, led by **Charles Eames** and Eero Saarinen. Eames and Saarinen were responsible for many innovations in furniture design, including molded fiberglass and plywood creations. Eames's classic pieces include the *Eames Lounge Chair 670* (1956), *DAR Shell chair* (1950), and the *Aluminum Group* (1958). The *Tulip Pedestal Group* (1957) is considered Saarinen's most important furniture design. Other important designers are **Harry Bertoia**, known for his *Wire Collection* (1951); Warren Platner, who also developed an important *Wire Collection* (1966); and George Nelson, who created the *Coconut chair* (1956). (See Figure 9.23.)

Cesca Chair
Marcel Breuer

Wassily Lounge
Marcel Breuer

Barcelona
Mies van der Rohe

Brno Chair
Mies van der Rohe

MR Chair
Mies van der Rohe

Grand Confort
Le Corbusier

Basculant Chair
Le Corbusier

"Pony" Chaise
Le Corbusier

Smoking Table
Eileen Gray

Transat Lounge
Eileen Gray

Stacking Chair
Robert Maillet-Stevens

FIGURE 9.21 Modern furniture (Bauhaus/International style).

Art Deco Cabinet
Jacques-Emile Ruhlmann

Imperial Chair
Frank Lloyd Wright

Taliesin Lounge
Frank Lloyd Wright

Art Deco Table
Donald Deskey

Cranbrook Chair
Eliel Saarinen

Blue Collection
Eliel Saarinen

"Lips" or "Marilyn" Lounge
Salvador Dali/Studio 65

Deck Chair
Kaare Klint

Klismos Chair
T.H. Robsjohn-Gibbings

Butterfly Chair
Bonet, Kurchan & Hardoy

Paimio (Scroll) Chair
Alvar Aalto

FIGURE 9.22 Modern furniture (Art Deco and 1930s).

Aalto stool
Scandinavia

Globe chair
Eero Aarnio
Scandinavia

Gyro
Eero Aarnio
Scandinavia

"The Chair"
Hans Wegner
Scandinavia

Peacock chair
Hans Wegner
Scandinavia

Egg chair
Arne Jacobsen
Scandinavia

Chair 22
Poul Kjaerholm
Scandinavia

Panton Stacking Chair
Vernor Panton
Scandinavia

Eames Lounge
Charles Eames
U.S.A.

Tulip/Pedestal
Eero Saarinen
U.S.A.

Wire chair
Warren Platner
U.S.A.

Diamond chair
Harry Bertoia
U.S.A.

Coconut chair
George Nelson
U.S.A.

FIGURE 9.23   Classic modern furniture (postwar period–1950s).

Italian Design. Influenced by the Bauhaus and International Style, Italian designers attracted world attention after World War II for their innovative use of materials and technology. Pioneer designer Gio Ponti created his classic *Superleggera chair* in 1957. Joe Colombo was particularly noted for his plastic designs including the *Elda chair* (1965) and *Colombo chair* (1967). Vico Magistretti is another prominent Italian designer responsible for numerous classics. Two of his best known are the *Selene* (1961) and *Maralunga* (1973). Other outstanding classics from Italy include the *Plia chair* (1969) by Giancarlo Piretti; the *Soriana Collection* (1970) by Tobia and Afra Scarpa; the *Sacco* (1969) by Design Studio; and the *Cab chair* (1977) by Mario Bellini. (See Figure 9.24.)

Other Postwar Contributions. This period saw the development of the sculptural furniture of Pierre Paulin in France and Pedro Freideberg in Mexico. Paulin's best-known classic is the *Ribbon Chair* (1965). *Pop furniture* was created by numerous designers, especially during the 1960s. Representative of this style is the *Hand chair* (1963) designed by Pedro Freideberg. (See Figure 9.24.)

The Handcraft Revival. At the end of the 1970s in England and America, inspired by the ideals of William Morris and the Arts and Crafts Movement in England during the latter half of the nineteenth century, some designers returned to the handcraft movement. This furniture is beautifully handcrafted and finished. Some classic pieces and designers are the *Ebony Gothic chair* (1978) by John Makepeace in England; *Rocking Chairs* (1970s and 1980s) by Sam Maloof in California; and *Bench with Horses* (1979) by Judy Kensley McKie in Boston. Currently the Handcraft Revival is a strong design direction. (See Figure 9.24.)

Furniture of the 1980s. During the 1980s various design directions emerged, many of them extensions or reinterpretations of previous modern styles. (See Figure 9.25.) Of particular note are the following:

- *Handcraft revival* (just described).
- *High-tech* furniture employs the most advanced scientific and industrial techniques and materials.
- *Post-Modern* is a prominent direction in both architecture and furniture design distinguished by a freer spirit of expression. Primarily rejecting the austere International style, Post-Modern designers are both historically aware and sensitive to new modern concepts expressed through strong form and subtle colors. Outstanding leaders of this style are Michael Graves, whose *Graves armchair* (1982) is a classic example, and Robert Venturi, designer of the popular *Venturi Collection* (1980s)—a series of chairs borrowing styles of the past interpreted in extraordinary ways.
- *Classic modern* brings styles of the past into the twentieth century, adapted in elegant and simplified terms. The *Grande Flute* chairs (1985) by the late New York

interior designer Angelo Donghia are based on eighteenth-century Louis XVI chairs and are typical of this trend.

- *Ergonomic* furniture is created with a concern for human comfort and efficiency. Niels Diffrient's *Jefferson chair* (1985) is a superb example. It has adjustable angles for maximum comfort and function and is named after one of President Thomas Jefferson's chairs of similar design.
- *Memphis* is an avant-garde group of about 20 international designers assembled in 1981 by Italian-based Ettore Sottsass, Jr. Named after Memphis, the home of Elvis Presley, and the ancient city of Memphis in Egypt, the **Memphis** design group was encouraged by Sottsass to employ complete freedom of expression with an emphasis on style, color, and form. Sottsass's colorful *Carlton bookshelf/room divider* (1981) is a much publicized piece. Michele de Lucchi's *First chair* (1983), with its circular composition, is another piece that has received international recognition.
- *Art furniture* is furniture created by artists as a piece for "art's sake." This new design approach is expressed individualistically by various artists, each creating a unique piece or collection. These pieces may or may not be functional or comfortable. Some pieces of furniture that have received national acclaim are *Queen Anne, Queen Anne* (1981) by Terence and Laura Main, and *Nothing Continues to Happen* (1981) by Howard Meister.
- *Individualists.* A number of individualistic designers have created outstanding classic furnishings during the past decade that have gained international recognition. Although this list is extensive, a few are particularly outstanding. Philippe Starck in France has created unusual pieces of furniture derived from many sources. His *Richard III chair* (1980s) is representative. Swiss architect and furniture designer Mario Botta has designed a series of unique furniture pieces. The *87 Seconda* (1982) is one of his best-known works. Italian designers Vico Magistretti and Gaetano Pesce continue as leaders in the design field in Italy today. Magistretti's *Sindbad chair* (1980s), and Pesce's *Sunset in New York* (1980) are good examples.

Classics of the 1990s. It will take a few years to determine the classics of the 1990s; however, a few new creations are representative of some of the design directions of this decade. (See Figure 9.26.) Italian Massimo Iosa-Ghini's *Bolidista chair* represents the strong and unusual Boldissimo style. Milo Baughman's *Mac II* shows a design that draws inspiration from the past modern style of Charles Rennie Mackintosh. Architect Frank Gehry has designed an innovative collection called *Cross Check* for Knoll International inspired by hockey sticks. Peter Danko calls his new seating designs *Chairs for the Electronic Cottage,* combining simple, folksy decoration with high-tech composite wood and stressed-skin seat construction. California's Modernist master, Paul Tuttle,

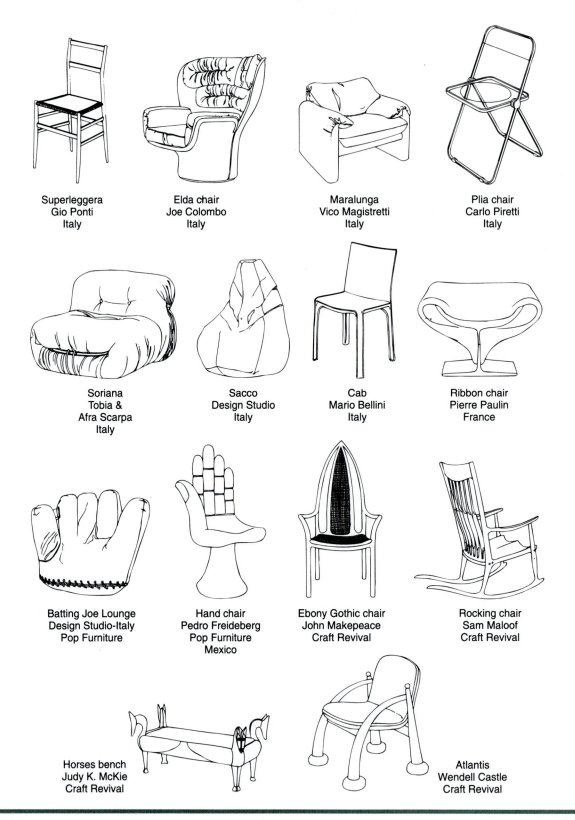

Superleggera
Gio Ponti
Italy

Elda chair
Joe Colombo
Italy

Maralunga
Vico Magistretti
Italy

Plia chair
Carlo Piretti
Italy

Soriana
Tobia &
Afra Scarpa
Italy

Sacco
Design Studio
Italy

Cab
Mario Bellini
Italy

Ribbon chair
Pierre Paulin
France

Batting Joe Lounge
Design Studio-Italy
Pop Furniture

Hand chair
Pedro Freideberg
Pop Furniture
Mexico

Ebony Gothic chair
John Makepeace
Craft Revival

Rocking chair
Sam Maloof
Craft Revival

Horses bench
Judy K. McKie
Craft Revival

Atlantis
Wendell Castle
Craft Revival

FIGURE 9.24 Classic modern furniture (1950s to 1970s).

Graves chair
Post-modern

Venturi chair
Post-modern

Grand Flute
Angelo Donghia
Classic Modern

Jefferson chair
Niels Diffrient
Ergonomic

Carlton Bookcase
Ettore Sottsass, Jr.
Memphis style

First chair
Michele de Lucci
Memphis style

Queen Anne, Queen Anne
Terence & Laura Main
Art Furniture

Nothing Continues
to Happen Chair
Howard Meister
Art Furniture

Richard III Chair
Philippe Starck
France

Seconda chair
Mario Botta
Italy

Sindbad
Vico Magistretti
Italy

Sunset in New York
Gaetano Pesce
Italy

FIGURE 9.25 Classic modern furniture (1980s).

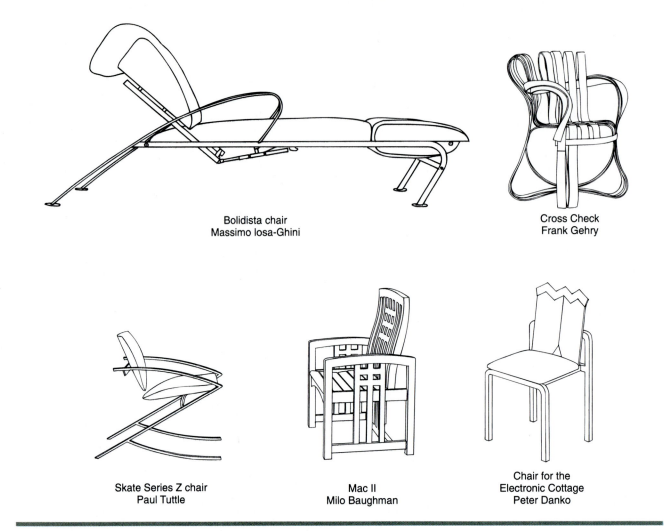

Bolidista chair
Massimo Iosa-Ghini

Cross Check
Frank Gehry

Skate Series Z chair
Paul Tuttle

Mac II
Milo Baughman

Chair for the
Electronic Cottage
Peter Danko

FIGURE 9.26 *Classic modern furniture (1990s).*

continues to design progressive creations including his *Skate Series-"Z" chair*. The Crafts Revival, Memphis, Pop Furniture, and Art Furniture are all enduring styles in the 1990s. Substantial contributions to modern furniture design are currently being made by Scandinavian, German, Italian, American, and Japanese designers.

American Oriental Style

The Oriental influence, particularly from China and Japan, is part of America's early tradition. Furnishings and accessories inspired by Oriental motifs were enjoyed in Europe and have remained popular in the twentieth century. Principles and elements of Japanese architecture, which include the predominance of the horizontal line, the use of natural materials, asymmetry, open planning, simplicity, and the absence of ornamentation, were used by Frank Lloyd Wright in his buildings and are an integral part of the Japanese and Organic Modern-style houses in America today.

The interior of the Japanese house is open and uncluttered; wood floors have tatami mats; ceilings are beamed or modular; walls are plain; and shoji screens, often used for both walls and windows, open onto gardens. Furniture is sparse, usually in a natural finish, and built low. Basic pieces include a low table, a chest, and *zabuton* (pillows) for seating.

Design influences from China have had their greatest impact for American designers in the field of furniture and accessories. Manufacturers in the United States have borrowed freely from both Japan and China to create "Oriental" furniture collections. Following are some of the most recognizable features of Oriental furnishings found in American homes. (See Figure 9.27.)

FROM JAPAN

- Simple unembellished furniture, usually in a natural finish
- Low tables
- Zabuton or pillows often stacked on floor
- *Tansu* (Oriental chest) with brass hardware typical

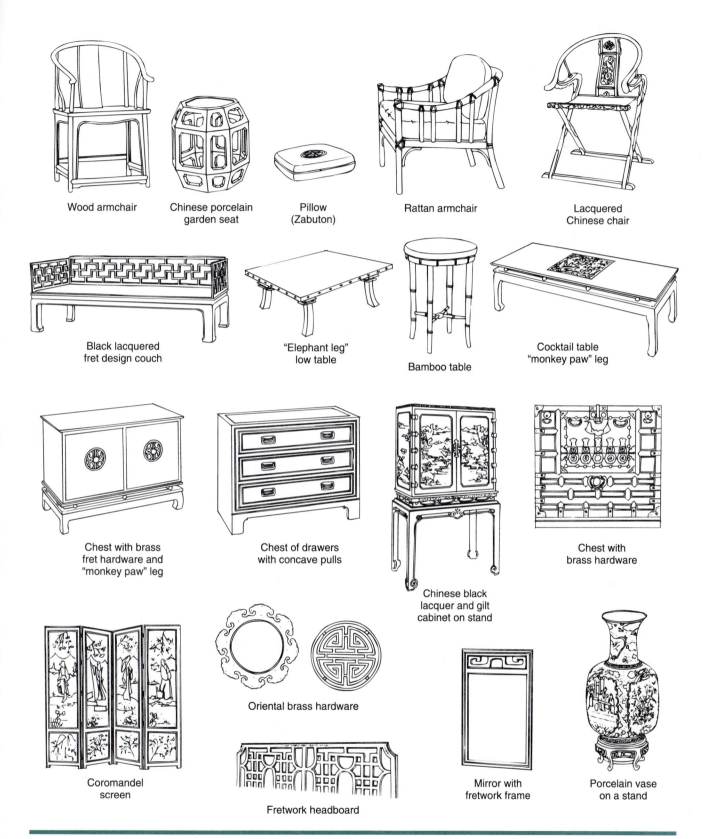

Wood armchair

Chinese porcelain
garden seat

Pillow
(Zabuton)

Rattan armchair

Lacquered
Chinese chair

Black lacquered
fret design couch

"Elephant leg"
low table

Bamboo table

Cocktail table
"monkey paw" leg

Chest with brass
fret hardware and
"monkey paw" leg

Chest of drawers
with concave pulls

Chinese black
lacquer and gilt
cabinet on stand

Chest with
brass hardware

Coromandel
screen

Oriental brass hardware

Fretwork headboard

Mirror with
fretwork frame

Porcelain vase
on a stand

FIGURE 9.27 Far Eastern furniture.

- Incorporation of shibui color schemes and philosophies (see Chapter 2)
- Only a few treasured items displayed (see following list)

FROM CHINA

- More decorative furnishings employing certain motifs (to be described). A vast selection of pieces for many functions are manufactured.
- *Finishes:* Lacquered finishes in black, red-orange, gold, and green. *Tortoise shell* (a mottled effect). Painted Oriental scenes, motifs, and figures on furniture surfaces. Highly polished natural finishes.
- *Colors:* Those from China are brighter. Blue, white, red, red-orange, gold, yellow-gold, and jade green.

TYPICAL FORMS, MOTIFS, AND ACCESSORIES FROM JAPAN AND CHINA

- *Forms:* "Monkey paw" legs (slight turning inwards). "Elephant leg" (slight swelling and splaying outwards). *Pagoda* forms. *Fret design. Chest-on-chest* arrangements with a slight separation between pieces.
- *Motifs:* Bamboo, chrysanthemum (most popular flower), and cherry blossoms; asymmetrical pine branch; fret design; mandarin duck and heron; the horse, tiger, dragon, and fish; Oriental figures, parasols, and pagodas; Mt. Fuji and floating clouds. Many motifs associated with the Japanese and Chinese cultures.
- *Accessories: Bonsai* plants, Oriental figures, *calligraphy,* **coromandel screen** (freestanding decorative multipaneled screen), wall-hung multipaneled screen, Chinese porcelain vases (particularly *"Ginger jar"* vases), Chinese rugs (usually employing combinations of blue, white, red-orange, and gold), *temple foo dogs,* brass hardware, statues of Oriental gods and goddesses and animals (mentioned under motifs), simple flower arrangements called **ikebana**, pieces made of jade and ivory, the hanging scroll (often with calligraphy forms), wood carvings, lacquerware, and, occasionally, Oriental fans and kimonos.

Style Selection

Considering the numerous styles of interior furnishings available, making a selection can be simplified by determining the general feeling desired. The approaches fall into five basic categories: informal provincial, formal traditional, informal modern, formal modern, and eclectic. The designer can help the client to choose one of these style directions to achieve a compatible, functional, and aesthetically satisfying environment.

Informal Provincial

This is generally a handcrafted, simple, and casual look. To achieve this informality, one ethnic style or combined furnishings from many country sources may be used, as long as the feeling is one of unpretentious homeyness. Whether part of the architectural background, movable furniture, or arts and crafts, informal provincial furnishings from the same country or many countries generally share a natural affinity and combine well. The term *country look* became popular during the early sixties. Shortly thereafter it became a catchall term for almost anything from rustic to manor. Today, however, it has become a viable style. The look is cloistered, comfortable, and rustic and may incorporate furniture from a number of countries as long as designs are rooted in the past and have an aura of charm and informality. Styles most commonly employed in America providing this feeling are Early American (seventeenth and eighteenth century), Country English (often simplified Georgian), Country Provincial French, and Spanish. Also appropriate are Dutch, Swedish, and German furnishings.

Formal Traditional

The term *traditional* may refer to interior furnishings from any country so long as they are of the more formal styles. Many of the favorite traditional designs come from the eighteenth century, an age of great prosperity during which the arts flourished in the Western world. The furniture styles of this period from both France and England have been great favorites with many Americans who enjoy their warmth, grace, and elegance. Some of these styles have been adapted and scaled to meet present-day requirements without losing their character. Styles appropriate for a formal traditional look include Early and Late Georgian (Queen Anne and Chippendale furniture), Federal (Hepplewhite, Sheraton, and Adam furniture), Court French (Louis XV and XVI), Empire and Greek Revival (Duncan Phyfe furniture), English Regency (Hope and Sheraton furniture), and Victorian (Belter and Eastlake).

Informal Modern

Numerous types and styles of "modern" furniture are available on the market, drawing principally from European, Oriental, and American designers. When an informal modern setting is preferred, generally casual fabrics with a matte finish, simple materials, and unpretentious accessories will provide the result. Almost all modern styles can be incorporated into an informal look depending on these qualities. Informal modern furniture styles particularly suitable for this direction include the Santa Fe style, Scandinavian, modern furniture inspired by Japanese prototypes, and the Handcraft Revival. Other modern styles including the Secession, De Stijl, Bauhaus and International style, Post-Modern, and Italian can generally be designed in either an informal or formal manner, depending on the supportive treatment.

Formal Modern

A formal modern environment can be created by employing elegant, sophisticated, and refined architectural backgrounds, accessories, and fabrics (often with a shiny surface). Art Nouveau, Art Deco, classic modern, and Post-Modern furniture are particularly well suited for a formal setting. Italian, Secession, Wiener Werkstatte, De Stijl, Bauhaus and International style furniture may be very formal and sophisticated, depending on supportive elements. Modern Oriental is often used in a formal manner.

Eclectic or Mixing Styles

Today, fewer consumers than before buy matched items of furniture, and do not wish to maintain the same style of furniture throughout the house or even throughout the same room. The **eclectic** look—which is a mixing rather than a matching one—is in vogue. (See Figures 9.28 and 9.29.) Eclectic does not mean a hodge-podge, however. Pieces should be related in scale and chosen with a final goal in mind. There should be a common theme—some element that ties the pieces together. For example, to achieve the provincial look, informality is the key and all country furniture, regardless of the source, is generally compatible. For a formal traditional look, dignity is the key, and refined pieces of almost any style can be combined with pleasant results. The modern look often allows for more daring and imagination.

Whatever the general theme of a room, it ought not dominate and thereby create a feeling of monotony. Interest is aroused by the unexpected. For example, a pair of Victorian chairs placed in a modern setting brings something special to a room. A modern sofa gives a period room a fresh, updated look. The clean sweep of modern decor may serve as the most effective background for a highly prized antique.

Today, more than ever before, designers and their clients are taking a sophisticated look at furnishings of the past and present and finding new ways to use them. Furnishings of the past enrich present-day living and add new life to the old. As new domestic and foreign influences come along, they can be adapted to meet current needs.

ASSIGNMENT

Visit a wide range of furniture stores, from the economy-priced factory outlets to the most prestigious showrooms, and make the following observations:

1. Compare the quality of design and craftsmanship and the prices. Note your findings at different price levels.

FIGURE 9.28 The eclectic approach is achieved in this living room by combining French Louis XV chairs and a French rug with an Oriental end table and modern twentieth-century furnishings. (Courtesy of Esto Photographics Inc.)

FIGURE 9.29 The visual impact of a coromandel screen is demonstrated in this law firm's reception area. Sofas covered in bright glazed cotton flank a coffee table in a Chinese style. The use of furnishings associated with a residence implies to visitors that in this office, clients are welcomed like guests. (Courtesy of Norman Day, designer.)

2. Observe room setups for the overall effect, then make a detailed examination of the floor coverings, wall and window treatments, individual pieces of furniture, and accessories. Identify various furniture styles.

3. Feel the wood and inspect the upholstery and drapery fabrics. Note the furnishings that appeal repeatedly to you to determine your personal preferences.

4. Submit a paper discussing the information you learned from your visits.

CHAPTER **10**

Furniture Arrangement and Wall Composition

FIGURE 10.1 A contemporary Greek Revival interior designed by Robert Metzger is reminiscent of this early nineteenth-century style, including the use of gold and blue, a patterned rug, torcheres, and asymmetrical couches with the distinctive lion's paw foot. (Courtesy of F. J. Hakimian, Inc., N.Y. and Robert Metzger Interiors. Photograph by Phillip Ennis.)

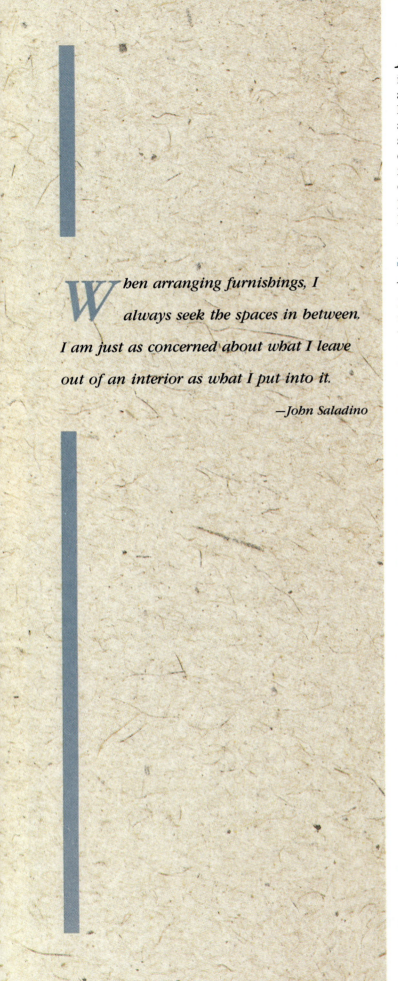

When arranging furnishings, I always seek the spaces in between. I am just as concerned about what I leave out of an interior as what I put into it.

—*John Saladino*

Planning for furniture is an important part of the design process, from the early stages of formulating ideas to the actual placement of furniture, furnishings, and equipment (known in the design profession as FF&E) within a space. The arrangement of furnishings in a room constitutes a composition in spatial design and, if successful, incorporates certain artistic principles and elements, as seen in Figure 10.1. Since a room is planned for particular people and their unique way of living, however, furnishing a room should be approached from a practical, commonsense point of view, employing the principles of design as guidelines.

DESIGNING SPACE WITH FURNITURE

New economic standards, contemporary trends in architecture, changing lifestyles, new furniture styles, and a variety of functions and needs, all influence the use of space in both residential and nonresidential design. With the increase in building costs, space is at a premium, and its distribution has changed to meet today's needs. For example, in residential design, during the early years of the century, the parlor was a small, often austere room used only for special occasions. The dining room was the gathering place for families three times a day, and the kitchen was big and homey—the heart of the home. In the late twenties, open planning became the vogue, with the entranceway, living room, dining room, and often the kitchen constructed as one open space, with areas of activity defined by rugs and furniture placement and through the use of color and fabric. The past decades have seen a return to more privacy but with an easy feeling of flexibility. Little need exists for the parlor today, although a living room off bounds to household activities is once again in demand. The dining room is back, but it is smaller and generally used as a dual-purpose space, since three-times-a-day togetherness is seldom possible. The kitchen, expanded into a family room, has again taken on the main burden of household living.

The key word today in furniture arrangement for both homes and public spaces is *efficiency,* as shown in Figure 10.2. Strict adherence to any set of rules is most likely inappropriate. When arranging furniture in any room of a residence, first priority should be given to *the household and its lifestyle.* Beauty and good design are important, but comfort and convenience are the most essential. A room can be pleasant in appearance but impractical for living.

In spite of differences in lifestyles, room-furnishing procedures and guidelines can provide assistance.

PROGRAMMING FURNITURE NEEDS

As mentioned in Chapter 4, programming is the initial planning stage of the design process. In this phase the

FIGURE 10.2 For this nonresidential project, a furniture system was specified for an open-plan office space. This functional furniture system provides a private work area and convenient storage for each employee, while conserving floor space. As the company's needs change, the modular units can be rearranged or added to at reasonable cost. (Courtesy of Kimball Office Furniture Co.)

designer gathers information to determine the needs of the end users. Activities, special considerations, and other criteria relevant to the project are analyzed and goals are established to solve the project's particular problems. A well-organized plan or program aids the designer in creating a space that is efficient and successful, as demonstrated in the residential project seen in Figure 10.3. Whether the space is being furnished for the first time or undergoing some minor modifications, it is essential to keep in mind the function the furniture must serve and the mood and style desired. Generally, no room must adhere so rigidly to a theme or style that it is monotonous or does not allow for new expressions.

Function

The *function* or functions that will take place within a space dictate what furniture, furnishings, and equipment (FF&E) will satisfy the end users whether in a residential or nonresidential setting. The program indicates what pieces are needed, how many, and what types, such as seating, tables, beds, desks, and storage units. Types of furniture might also include furniture systems, modular units, built-ins, or custom-designed pieces. Rarely is a piece of furniture complete in itself because related pieces are needed for function, comfort, or both. For example, a desk needs a chair, a piano needs a bench,

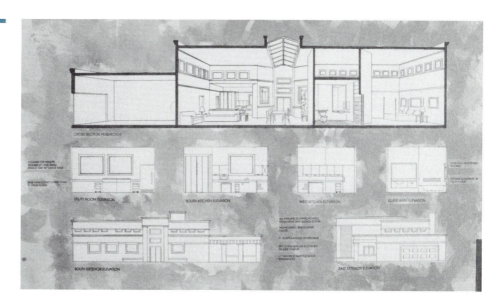

FIGURE 10.3 A cross section perspective with accompanying elevations helps communicate the proposed project to the client. (Courtesy of Paul Tew, designer.)

FIGURE 10.4 The large living space in this Palm Springs, California, residence has been functionally divided. Two L-shaped sofas, each with its own coffee table, form the conversational group that is centered on the fireplace. Four chairs flank a round table away from the major conversation area. (Courtesy of Michael Rennick and Associates, Inc., Salt Lake City.)

and a lounge chair and sofa require a table to accommodate items such as glasses, ash trays, magazines, and lighting. After determining what furnishings will best meet functional needs for a particular space, the designer must consider other criteria closely related to function, including human comfort.

Human Comfort

An important function furniture must serve is providing *comfort* for the end users. Comfort is directly related to how effectively the human body is accommodated, as seen in the arrangement of furniture in Figure 10.4. Since people vary in size and proportion, a piece of furniture may be comfortable for one occupant but not for another. For example, a small chair may be comfortable for a small person but uncomfortable for a larger person. Furniture should also be easy to use and operate. For instance, a desk and desk chair should be convenient for the tasks they must support, and a storage cabinet should have shelves the user can reach. Other attributes of "user-friendly" furniture are how easily it can be moved or rearranged and how efficiently it can be cleaned. Some

terms related to design and human comfort include ergonomics, proxemics, anthropometrics, and territoriality.

- **Ergonomics** is the study of human beings and their responses to various working conditions and environments. The goal is to produce furnishings that are comfortable to use for particular functions and tasks. (See Chapter 8 and Figure 8.3.)
- **Proxemics** involves a study of the use of space by human beings in a particular culture. Research reveals that everyone has an invisible comfort zone or area of surrounding space called a "space bubble." Discomfort may result when a person with a smaller space bubble gets too close to the space of a person with a larger space bubble. Our individual comfort zones vary in relationship to our culture and background experiences. Knowing this information, the designer can more effectively create environments with furniture that will meet particular needs for comfort and space, especially in a nonresidential setting.
- **Anthropometrics** is a study that measures the size and proportion of the human body. The results of these studies provide valuable information for designers when specifying furnishings for human comfort and

well-being. The average human being weighs between 100 and 200 pounds and is between 5 and 6 feet in height. These measurements are the criteria for designing and positioning furnishings for functional and comfortable interiors.

- **Territoriality** is a term used to describe human needs for personal space. Most individuals want a space that belongs to them—like a bedroom, a certain chair in the family room or at the kitchen table, or even a particular bench or pew in their church. Observing children who share a bedroom often reveals this need for private space. For example, children may make it clear what side of the room is theirs, or what part of the closet is for their belongings only. This need for a space of our own usually carries over into our adult lives and a sensitive designer will plan furnishings accordingly.

Special Need Users

The elderly, infants, or the physically challenged have special needs and problems that designers must consider. In planning spaces for both residential and non-residential design designers must adequately satisfy these needs for safety, convenience, comfort, and well being, as discussed in Chapter 4 (see Figure 4.2).

Barrier-free access for physically challenged users in a public space is not only necessary, but required by law. For example, furniture should be placed so that a person in a wheelchair can easily access all facilities. This means that passageways or hallways should be from 36 to 42 inches wide to accommodate a wheelchair. A wheelchair requires a 5-foot radius to turn around.

Analyzing and Evaluating the Space

The designer should assess the room's *size, shape, assets, and possibilities.* Next, the following questions may be asked: (1) Are the dimensions of the room pleasing, or will altering the apparent height, width, or length be necessary? (2) Are the openings well placed for balance and convenience? (3) Are there jogs, niches, or other features to be minimized or emphasized, or would the addition of some architectural feature add interest? (4) Would built-in furniture be effective? (5) Will it be necessary to redirect traffic? (6) What is the light exposure? (7) How much will the quality and quantity of light affect the choice of colors and furnishings?

Arranging Furniture on a Floor Plan

A *floor plan drawn to scale* can aid in determining furniture placement within a space. Generally, graph paper using a measurement of $\frac{1}{4}$ in. equaling 1 ft is preferable for use in residential design (see Figure 10.5). Commercial space planning usually requires a smaller scale to accommodate larger spaces. The drawn plan indicates the exact position of all architectural features and mechanical systems such as doors, windows, radiators, heat

vents, and electrical outlets. *Circulation* or *traffic lanes* (lanes in which traffic must pass from one door to another, one room to another, and around furnishings and activity centers) should be clearly marked. Experiments with different furniture arrangements can be made on the plan. *Furniture templates* can be moved around until the desired functional and decorative effects are achieved. Although this procedure may not produce the final solution to furniture arrangement, moving templates around on paper is much simpler than pushing heavy pieces around the room, and it saves time and energy.

Computer-Aided Design

When planning furniture for particular spaces, many designers have access to computer-aided design (CAD) programs. Furniture of various types, colors, and textures can be called up on the computer screen and an infinite number of solutions for arranging the furniture for a specific project can be explored, as demonstrated in Figure 10.6. Once the desired furniture arrangement is created, pieces can be specified with confidence.

GUIDELINES FOR FURNITURE ARRANGEMENT

When the programming and design process has arrived at the stage when the actual arrangement of furniture, furnishings, and equipment is to take place, consider these guidelines:

- For both residences and public spaces, decide who will use the room and for what purposes. Keep the *functions and multifunctions* of the room in mind and group furniture for those functions. For example, arrange a principal living room area with comfortable sofas, chairs, tables, and convenient lamps, providing a pleasant area for conversation. Generally, furniture pieces arranged for conversation are placed within 8 to 10 ft and arranged to encourage eye contact.
- Arrange furniture to accommodate necessary major and minor *traffic lanes.* Allocate space for occupants to *circulate* or move about easily from room to room and within the space itself. Doorways should be free. Major traffic lanes, unobstructed by furniture, allow occupants to circulate freely within a space. Generally, major traffic lanes require 6 ft and minor lanes 4 ft. Redirecting traffic is sometimes necessary. This can be accomplished by skillful furniture placement and the use of screens, dividers, and plants. (See Figures 10.7, 10.8, and 10.9.)
- Adequate *clearance* between furnishings is essential; for example, occupants need leg room and enough space to conveniently get into and out of dining chairs around a table. Sensibly placed furnishings will help

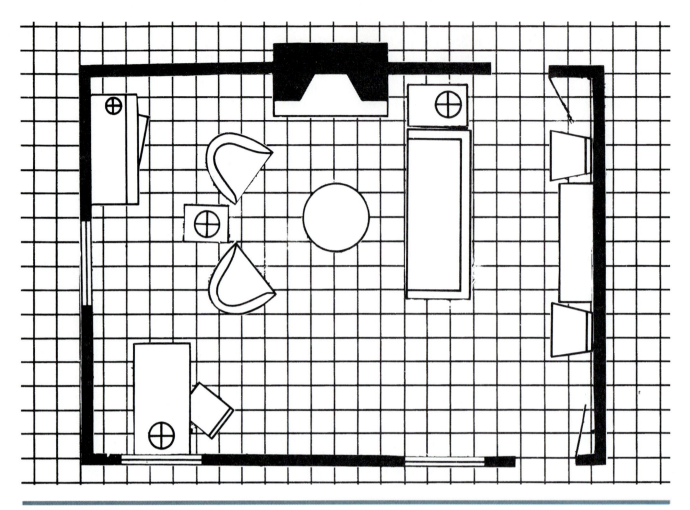

FIGURE 10.5 Furniture drawn to scale is arranged on graph paper using a measurement of $\frac{1}{4}$ in., equaling 1 ft.

FIGURE 10.6 Computer-graphic techniques provide numerous opportunities for the interior designer to manipulate forms within a space until a desirable solution is created. (Courtesy of Henry Christiansen, civil engineer.)

FIGURE 10.7 Designer Bruce Stodola created a comfortable and inviting living space by pulling the main furniture grouping away from the wall and near the fireplace. This not only encourages conversation but moves the traffic pattern behind and around the grouping rather than through it. (Photograph by Mark Boisclair.)

FIGURE 10.8 Arranging traffic lanes.

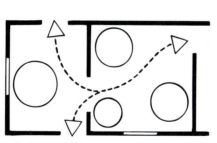

Indicate traffic lanes and areas of activity.

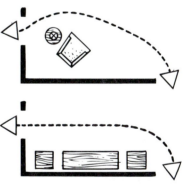

Avoid blocking doorways.

FIGURE 10.9 Redirect traffic if necessary.

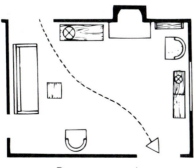

Poor arrangement.

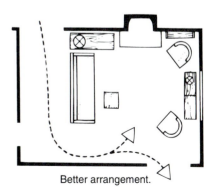

Better arrangement.

TABLE 10.1 Efficient clearance spaces

Living Room	
Traffic path—major	4 ft to 6 ft
Traffic path—minor	1 ft, 4 in. to 4 ft
Foot room between sofa or chair and edge of coffee table top	1 ft to 15 in.
Floor space in front of chair for feet and legs	1 ft, 6 in. to 2 ft, 6 in.
Chair or bench space in front of desk or piano	3 ft
Dining Room	
Space for occupied chairs	1 ft, 6 in. to 1 ft, 10 in.
Space to get into chairs	1 ft, 10 in. to 3 ft
Space for person to assist in seating	4 ft, 6 in.
Traffic path around table and occupied chairs	1 ft, 6 in. to 2 ft
Kitchen	
Working space in front of cabinets	2 ft to 6 ft
Counter space between equipment	3 ft to 5 ft
Ventilation for attachments in back of some appliances	3 in. to 5 in.
Bedroom	
Space for making bed	1 ft, 6 in. to 2 ft
Space between twin beds	1 ft, 6 in. to 2 ft, 4 in.
Space in front of chest of drawers	3 ft
Space in front of dresser	3 ft to 4 ft (both directions)
Bathroom	
Space between front of tub and opposite wall	2 ft, 6 in. to 3 ft, 6 in.
Space in front of toilet	1 ft, 6 in. to 2 ft
Space at sides of toilet	1 ft to 1 ft, 6 in.
Space between fronts of fixtures	2 ft to 3 ft

people avoid bumping into corners or barriers and provide efficient movement and access to furnishings. (See Table 10.1.)

- Determine the room's *focal point*. The center of interest may be a painting, a large piece of furniture, a panoramic view from the window, or a fireplace. Once this decision is made, emphasize the center of interest by arranging other furnishings in a supportive manner. (See Figure 10.10.)
- *Large furnishings* usually work best when placed parallel to the wall, except when a room lends itself to a diagonal arrangement. A large reclining chair can be inviting when placed at an angle. Avoid pushing large pieces tightly into a corner or close against floor-to-ceiling windows.
- Keep furnishings in *scale* with the room. The overall dimensions and architectural background can determine the size and general feeling of the furnishings so that they complement the room.
- Arrange furnishings to give the room a sense of *equilibrium*. Opposite walls, when balanced, help provide harmony and a feeling of rest. Consider the size, color, texture, and form of furniture. For example, placing all heavy pieces of furniture at one end of the room would create an unharmonious feeling of imbalance. When neither architectural features nor furniture distribution can create balance, it may be achieved through the knowledgeable use of color, fabrics, and accessories. Arrange the heaviest furniture along the highest wall in rooms with slanting ceilings to help obtain balance (see Figure 10.11).

- A good balance of *high and low and angular and rounded furniture* helps establish interest and variety. When furniture is all or predominantly low, create the feeling of height by incorporating shelves, mirrors, pictures, and hangings into a grouping.
- *Architectural features and mechanical systems* are an important concern when planning furnishings. Nothing should interfere with the opening of windows, swinging of doors, or functioning of heating or air conditioning devices. Lamps should be placed near electrical outlets.
- Create a feeling of space and form by placing furniture pieces with regard to the **positive areas** (the actual furniture pieces) and the **negative spaces** (the spaces between the furniture pieces).
- *Avoid crowding.* Underfurnishing a room is often more attractive than overcrowding. Studies reveal that overcrowding a space can actually have a negative psychological effect. Some empty spaces between groupings helps give an uncluttered effect. An occasional open space or empty corner enhances a room and gives the occupants breathing space. On the other hand, an underfurnished room may be stark and uninviting. Try to avoid either extreme.
- Since most groupings need *lighting,* choose appropriate lamps or lighting fixtures to provide adequate light for the particular purpose. Lighting fixtures and electrical outlets should be indicated on the floor plan.
- Achieving *rhythm,* the principle of design that allows the eye to move easily about the room, is a worthwhile goal when arranging furniture. A room is usually more

engaging when some pieces contrast in texture. For example, upholstered pieces are complemented by placing wood or metal tables close by. Placing furniture with alternating colors, forms, and height adds interest and rhythm.

■ The placement of *accessories* usually comes last and can pull other furnishings together, establish the mood and style of the room, and reflect the occupant's personal taste. Considerable flexibility is possible here, and it is generally necessary to experiment with placement after major and minor furnishings are in position to determine the most satisfying arrangement.

Planning a room that is functional, comfortable, conveniently arranged, and aesthetically appealing is the ultimate goal in spatial planning.

Spatial Planning for Rooms of Various Shapes

The *square or nearly square* room is considered one of the least pleasing in proportion. To give the room a new dimension, apply the principles and elements of design. Some suggestions: (1) Expand two opposite walls by using a light, receding color. Use a darker tone on the two remaining walls to pull them in (see Chapter 2). (2) "Extend" one wall by running bookshelves the entire length. (3) Place an area rug the full length of the room, but less than the width, with the long side parallel to the bookshelves. (4) Arrange furniture to create a rectangular effect. The wall opposite the bookshelves should have some interest to provide weight and pull it in. These are only a few of the ways to alter the proportions of a square room (see Figure 10.12).

A well proportioned *rectangular room* is the easiest to arrange. Comfort, convenience, and beauty should be the main concerns.

The *long, narrow room* may present a problem, but knowledgeable use of a few principles of optical illusion can modify the apparent proportions of the room. First,

FIGURE 10.11 In a room with a slanted ceiling the heaviest furniture grouping should be against the highest wall. This arrangement creates a focal point.

FIGURE 10.12 Furniture can be arranged to visually alter the proportions of a square room.

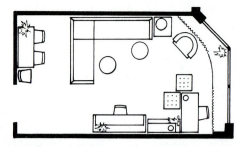

FIGURE 10.13 Principles of optical illusion alter the apparent proportions of a long, narrow room. The curved line of drapery, the angled sofa, and the desk placed at a right angle to the long wall make the room seem wider.

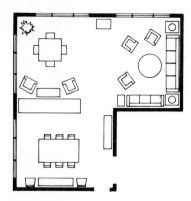

FIGURE 10.14 A divider provides storage and privacy in an L-shaped room.

determine the activity centers. Then, if the goal is to maintain the visual appearance of one large, flexible room, the furniture that stands out from the wall can be kept low. If the goal is to make separate compartments, some high pieces can be used as dividers. Furniture at right angles to the long wall will cut the length (refer to Figure 8.12). Sectional furniture may turn a corner to create a cross-room grouping (see Figure 10.13). Rugs can be used to define areas and preferably are placed at right angles to the long wall. Dividers and screens can create activity centers that cut the length of the room. Ceiling fixtures hung low will draw groupings together. A platform partition that creates a new level at one end of the room can shorten the room's appearance. Skillful use of color can work magic. Light colors expand space, and dark colors reduce space. Distinct changes of color for large areas such as a dining area will further alter the apparent room dimensions.

The *L-shaped room* lends itself naturally to a division of activities, particularly living and dining. Area rugs, dividers, and furniture placement can easily create livable space in the L-shaped room. (See Figure 10.14.)

The *room with a jog* need not be a problem. The offset area can be used in such a way that it becomes a feature of and asset to the room.

Space Planning for Specific Residential Spaces

Each room of the house presents a unique problem according to its function. Since the functions of different rooms vary greatly, each room should be considered separately.

Entrance Hall

An entry is a passageway and should not be cluttered. Empty space permitting an *easy flow of traffic* is essential. The size of the room necessarily determines the amount and scale of the furniture that should be placed against the wall. If space permits, an entrance can accommodate

all or some of the following pieces: a bench, a console or narrow table, a mirror, lighting, a coat rack, and accessories.

Where the front door opens directly into the living room, a desirable plan is to create an unobstructed entrance to redirect traffic and provide some privacy. This arrangement may be accomplished in a number of ways, depending on the space available, the placement of the door, and the arrangement of the other rooms.

A successful way to set off an entrance is by use of a built-in or freestanding storage wall. This wall requires slightly more room than a screen or a single wall divider, but it has important advantages. If space is available, a deeper storage wall may provide closet space for outer garments on one side and open shelves for books or display on all or part of the opposite side. The storage divider can be planned with numerous combinations, depending on personal needs, and it may be a decorative as well as functional element.

Where space does not permit a heavy divider, a screen (as seen in Figure 10.15), either freestanding, with a track, or with a panel attached to the wall and the remaining panels free-swinging, may serve as a partial

FIGURE 10.15 A standing screen creates a foyer and a backdrop for a desk.

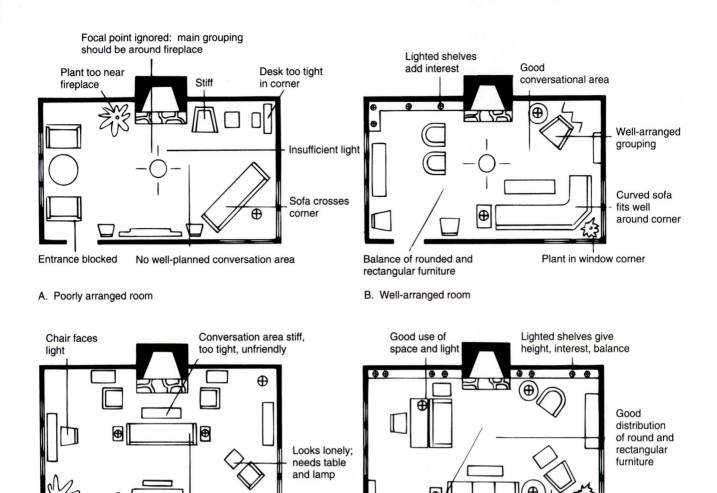

FIGURE 10.16 Four arrangements of a 14 × 24 ft living room.

divider. In a small room where any type of divider would cut needed space, the furniture may be arranged to redirect traffic by turning a sofa, a piano, or chairs toward the room and at right angles to the door, leaving a passageway for traffic. Such devices can provide limited privacy and create the feeling of an entranceway.

Living Room

The *conversation area* is the most important group in the living room and usually enhances and is combined with the focal point. In some cases the conversation area itself is the focal point of the room. Most important to keep in mind when planning the conversation area is its function—to provide an intimate grouping, out of the line of traffic, in which people can hear and be heard in a relaxed atmosphere. The optimum distance across this area is between 8 and 10 ft. A conversation area can be enlarged by including occasional chairs. (See Figure 10.16.)

Built-in seating is usually not as comfortable or flexible as movable sofas and chairs, which may be regrouped for more intimate occasions or opened out to invite more participants. The *sunken conversation "pit"* has had some popularity, but it can be restrictive. It may serve nicely as a supplementary area where space will allow, but it is usually not preferred for the principal conversation area of a living room.

Bringing furniture *out and away from the walls* in a room is more conducive to intimate conversation than placing it directly against the walls. (See Figure 10.17.) An *angled or slightly curved sofa* lends itself to easy conversation more than a long, straight one does, and a comfortable corner is satisfying. The curve of a sectional sofa is invariably occupied first, just as the corner table in a restaurant is the most popular.

FIGURE 10.17 A corner arrangement need not be placed against the wall.

A current solution to providing a flexible seating arrangement is movable *modular furniture*. Two or three separate pieces that fit together may be purchased at once; others can be added later. Modular furniture can be arranged in a variety of placements depending on space and the number of pieces. (See Figure 10.18.)

The Basic Conversation Groupings. Figure 10.19 illustrates six basic conversation groupings:

1. The *straight-line grouping* is ideal for public places but is not conducive to intimate conversation.
2. The *L-shaped grouping* is good for conversation and lends itself to both large and small areas.
3. The *U-shaped grouping* is comfortable and attractive but requires considerable space.
4. The *box-shaped grouping* is popular where space is ample. Allow space for a sufficient opening to present an inviting aspect.

FIGURE 10.18 The International Style of architecture makes a striking background for an L-shaped black banquette, mirror-imaged by white modular seating units. Additional modules form a secondary seating area that follows the angled wall. Drama is added by the colorful geometric painting over the fireplace and a bold abstract sculpture by the window. The home, designed by Douglas Sydnor, AIA, was the recipient of the *Phoenix Home and Garden* "Home of the Year Award." Interior by Barbara Arkules, ASID. (Photograph by Mark Boisclair.)

FIGURE 10.19 Six basic conversation groupings.

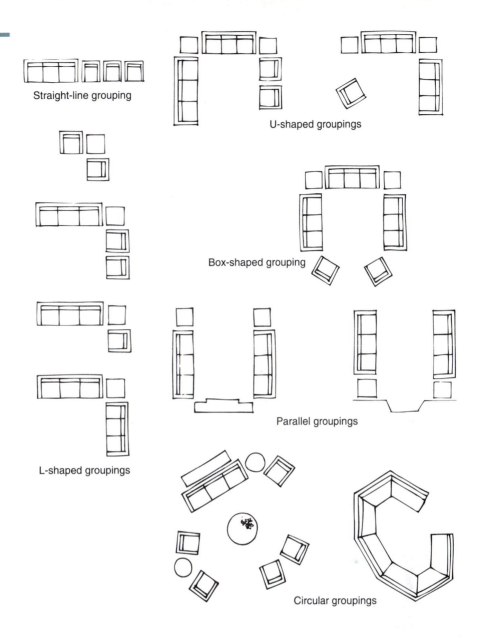

Straight-line grouping

U-shaped groupings

Box-shaped grouping

L-shaped groupings

Parallel groupings

Circular groupings

5. The *parallel grouping* emphasizes an existing focal point such as a fireplace or a special wall feature and provides a pleasant arrangement for conversation.

6. The *circular grouping* may encompass an entire room or an area of a large room. This arrangement can be intimate and inviting, because it provides an enveloping seating element.

To ensure that household members and guests enjoy good conversation, provide the best possible environment. Soft, low-level *lighting* adds a feeling of intimacy to a conversation area; however, this does not mean the area should be in semidarkness. People need to see the features of those with whom they are talking. A low-hanging light can pull a grouping together and serve for reading when turned to its maximum power. *Mirrors* hung where people talking can look up and see themselves, however, are distracting and may be annoying.

Rigidly placed chairs can make the guest believe that moving them would be a major calamity, so provide comfortable *living room chairs* of various types and sizes for flexibility. Suitable tables placed conveniently near lounge chairs and sofas hold lamps and small items such as books, magazines, and refreshments.

The *use of pairs* can enhance a living room in many ways. Identical items can be a unifying factor; they can give balance and pull together unrelated furniture. A pair of chairs can create a conversation grouping in a number of ways: angled about a table to give an intimate corner feeling, as seen in Figure 10.20; placed on either side of a fireplace; or placed side by side to balance a sofa on the opposite side. Where space is adequate, a pair of love seats or sofas may be used in place of single chairs. Identical tables placed at each end of a sofa have always been a popular arrangement in American homes. Placing them in front of a sofa is a flexible substitute for a standard

FIGURE 10.20 Chairs in a corner for privacy encourage conversation.

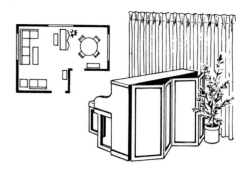

FIGURE 10.21 An upright piano may serve as a partial room divider.

coffee table. Two similar chests placed on either side of a doorway or a fireplace will enhance almost any room. Pairs of lamps, candelabra, or wall accessories can have a pleasing effect. When carried to an extreme, however, the use of pairs can be boring.

Finding the right wall space for a *piano* is often a problem. Direct sunlight and changes in climate can have a damaging effect on a piano, limiting possible placement within the room. An upright piano can be placed against a wall or at right angles to the wall with other appropriate furnishings concealing the backside. A piano placed at right angles to the wall may also function as a room divider, as seen in Figure 10.21. A grand piano may be more difficult to place in the average room because of its size. The curved side should be toward the listeners, not facing a wall or corner, so that when the lid is raised the sound will be projected toward the audience. In addition, the pianist and the listeners should be able to see one

FIGURE 10.22 Designer Laurence Lake placed the grand piano on the diagonal with the room's architecture and in relation to the other furnishings in this living room, so the occupants can better hear the music and watch the pianist. (Photograph by Pam Singleton.)

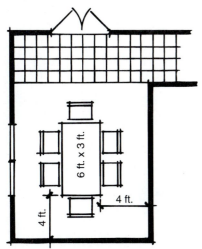
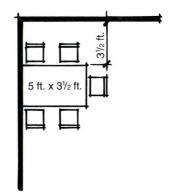
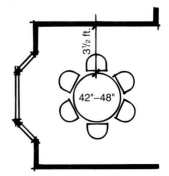

A rectangular table with six chairs placed in the room's center requires 2 ft. to 4 ft. space for clearance. Occupied chair requires 1½ ft. to 2 ft. clearance.

A rectangular table with one end placed against the wall accommodates five chairs with less space required.

A round table placed in the room's center accommodates six chairs with less space requirements.

FIGURE 10.23 Typical dining table arrangements.

another, as shown in Figure 10.22. A bay window furnishes a beautiful setting for a grand piano if temperature and light conditions permit. In a large room a grand piano may be placed to form a room divider.

In the living room, most tables are placed where a functional need exists, including *end tables* and *coffee tables.* The scale, shape, and height of each table should be right for the purpose and size of the chair or sofa it accompanies. Generally a good height for a coffee table is 16 in. **Console tables** can be decorative as well as functional and when combined with a mirror or picture are an asset to almost any room. The *writing table* or *desk* may be placed flush or with its short end against the wall. When the desk is placed in front of a window, the chair should be placed behind it, facing away from the light.

Large case or wall pieces are usually located to lend a feeling of balance. If the area is small, careful planning is necessary to place the large piece where it will be most functional and will complement the wall space.

Dining Room

The scale of the room can help determine the size of the furniture for use in the dining room. Furniture arrangement seldom presents much choice in this room. The *table* is usually placed in the center of the room under an architecturally fixed *lighting source* with a *chest* or *buffet* for storage against the longest wall and a *small serving piece* near the kitchen door. If the room is large enough, a high piece such as a *breakfront* or *china cabinet* can provide space for display and add dignity as well (refer to Figures 8.15 and 9.1). *Corner cupboards* are often the answer for storage and display in smaller rooms.

Chairs generally work best when not too wide across the front so they do not take up too much room around the table. Where space is limited, a *round or oval table* allows more room for passage and seats occupants more easily than a *rectangular table* of the same width and length (see Figure 10.23). If the dining area is small, one option is to use a dropleaf table that, when not in use, may be closed and placed against the wall along with a wall-hung shelf for serving.

Occupants need adequate space for a pleasurable and convenient dining experience. Getting into a chair at the table requires about 2 ft. Assisting someone in seating requires about 4½ ft.

Family Room

The family room is probably the most used room of the house. Here family members congregate around an entertainment center, read, converse, play games, and often entertain. More than in any other area of the house, the arrangement of furniture is of utmost importance to accommodate easy adjustment for various activities. Use, convenience, and practicality are guiding principles in arranging furnishings, as shown in Figure 10.24.

- *Seating* for conversation incorporates similar solutions discussed for the living room. When television viewing is an important activity, plan seating for easy viewing. Include additional flexible seating for various activities where space permits.
- A number of *tables* can add to the occupants' comfort, including a large coffee table to accommodate beverages and food and side tables for lighting and other necessary items.

FIGURE 10.24 Arranging furnishings for a good sense of balance throughout the interior space is a prime consideration. This family living area demonstrates balance between high and low pieces as well as balance in relationship to form and floor space. The sofa serves to divide this space from the eating area. The bookcases and cabinets are located on one wall for efficiency and to conserve space. (Courtesy of Barrow Design Studio. Photograph by Richard Embery, Scottsdale, AZ.)

- Convenient and adequate *lighting* is essential in a family room and must be comfortable and flexible enough to accommodate all activities (see Chapter 3).
- An *audiovisual entertainment system* has become an important addition to the family room in recent decades. Special planning is necessary for placing a television set, movie screen, stereo, or complete entertainment center to take best advantage of possible space.
- Family rooms may also serve as an area for quiet games. A *game table* can be incorporated into the space, when available. When space is limited, games can be played on kitchen or dining tables in other areas of the home.

Bedrooms

Since furniture arrangement in a bedroom is usually more limited than in other rooms, carefully planned space is especially important. Before furniture placement begins, decide which purposes the room will serve in addition to sleeping.

- Because of its size, the *bed* will occupy the dominant place in the room, and seldom is there more than one wall large enough to accommodate it. Once the bed is established, plan traffic lanes with careful attention to nighttime walking. The foot of the bed is often a good place for a *storage chest* or *narrow bench*. In children's rooms bunk beds or trundle beds can often solve a space problem when a room must serve two or more occupants.
- *Built-in units or tables* placed at the sides of a bed are essential to accommodate necessary items.
- *Lighting* should be conveniently located next to the bed and by additional functional areas.
- Windows should be kept free of furnishings to facilitate *ventilation* and *light*.

FIGURE 10.25 A spacious traditionally designed master bedroom offers a pleasant retreat for the inhabitants. A comfortable four-poster bed, large windows, and fireplace add to the room's warmth. (Photograph by Tim Street-Porter.)

- Space permitting, *seating,* such as a small bench, side chair, lounge chair, or chaise longue, is a practical and comfortable addition in a bedroom (see Figure 10.25). The foot of the bed is often a good place for a long, narrow bench.
- *Chests, built-ins, chests of drawers,* and other *casepieces* are essential furnishings in a bedroom for clothing *storage.* Built-in under-the-bed drawers can convert unused space into storage.
- A *mirror* is a necessary furnishing. It can either be attached to sliding closet doors, be freestanding, or be mounted on walls or furniture.

Nonresidential Furniture Planning

As mentioned in Chapter 4, nonresidential projects include transportation, medical, retail, hospitality, entertainment, business, museum, government, education, and industrial facilities. Each of these public places has unique functions. When programming the arrangement of furniture for a nonresidential project, the designer must determine the activities that will take place and the furniture needed to adequately serve these purposes.

Arranging furniture in a nonresidential space may require solving special placement problems unique to the particular setting. For example, furniture systems or workstations need to be conveniently arranged within an office space; attached multiseating units require special placement in an airport. Often furnishings employed for residential spaces are suitable for use in a nonresidential space, but may require alternative arrangement because of the diverse functions unique to the commercial facility.

The design process for arranging furniture in a nonresidential setting follows many of the principles outlined for residences. Organization of space, circulation, clearances, comfort, lighting, balance, rhythm, and other criteria are also considerations when placing furniture to achieve a public space that is attractive, comfortable, and efficient, as seen in Figure 10.26

Arranging furniture for the physically challenged is an important task for the designer. Passageways must be kept barrier-free with furniture arranged for convenience and safety as required by federal, state, and local laws. Special consideration should be given to provide easy access to dining tables, theater seats, airport seats, toilets, sinks, vending machines, workstations, hotel beds and storage, public counters, and a myriad of other public furnishings. (See Table 10.2.)

Arranging furniture for aesthetics and atmosphere can add to users' enjoyment of a particular nonresidential space. For example, a health-care facility can be made more cozy and homey by artfully arranging the seating in the lounge area, as seen in Figure 10.27, or an intimate and romantic mood can be achieved in a restaurant by arranging chairs and tables around a large fireplace.

Making the Most of Space with Furniture

Making a Small Room Appear Larger

Through the adroit use of the principles and elements of design, a small room can be made to appear much larger than it is. First, examine the room carefully and define the traffic lanes. Then, beginning with the backgrounds, apply space-making principles to expand the room. The results of studied efforts in creating the feeling of space can be amazing (see Figure 10.28).

BACKGROUND

- Plain, light walls and coordinated wall-to-wall and floor-to-ceiling drapery expand space.

FIGURE 10.26 For this reception area within a large public space, designer Laurence Lake used a custom area rug to define the space and separate it from the surrounding traffic patterns. The contemporary glass and metal coffee table echoes the L-shape of the seating and the angle of the rug. Dramatic chairs almost appear to float. An Oriental vase harmonizes in its color and geometric shape and contrasts in its intricacy of design. (Photograph by Pam Singleton.)

TABLE 10.2 Accessibility for the physically challenged

Doorways: 32″ minimum
One-way passage: 36″ minimum
Two-way passage: 64″ minimum
Corner turn: 42″ minimum
Wheelchair turnabout 360 degrees: 60″ diameter
Toilet stall: 60″ × 60″ with 32″ outward swinging door

Specifications standards for the physically challenged are available from: American National Standards Institute, Inc. *Specifications for Making Buildings and Facilities Accessible to and Usable by Physically Handicapped People.* ANSI A1117.1 New York: American National Standards Institute, Inc., 1986.

FIGURE 10.27 At the waiting area of the Dixie Medical Center, comfortable yet firm seating is arranged to welcome visitors. Soft colors, interesting textures, and plants give a homelike warmth. (Courtesy of Designedge, Inc., Peggy Honey, designer.)

FIGURE 10.28 In this small sitting area, vertical paneling in a pale color, along with the mirrored wall (left), helps expand the space. The shutters don't take up floor space, so the sofa can be positioned flush against the wall. The sofa and upholstered armchair are large enough to appear comfortable but don't seem crowded. A glass coffee table and lightly scaled side chairs have little visual weight. The dramatic sculpture at right occupies what would otherwise be unused space. An interesting assortment of fabrics and an area rug add color and texture. (Courtesy of Bill E. Coleman and J. H. Armer Company.)

Desirable

Less desirable

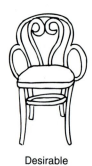
Desirable

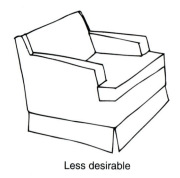
Less desirable

Desirable

Less desirable

FIGURE 10.29 Lightly scaled furniture helps provide a more spacious appearance.

- Patterned walls and full, ruffled curtains seem to fill up a room.

FURNITURE

- *Small-scaled furniture* can be accommodated more readily in a small space than large-scaled pieces—but a dollhouse effect should be avoided. (See Figure 10.29.)
- *Casepieces supported on legs* rather than those flush to the floor allow additional space.
- *High, shallow pieces* for storage and display lead the eye upward.
- Tables and other furnishings with *rounded corners* take up less space.
- *Clear glass or plastic tops* on tables allow the eye to see additional space.
- Chairs and other furnishings with *see-through backs* or backs and sides of *caning* or of *clear plastic* help to provide a sense of more space.
- *Furnishings with no arms* free space.
- Upholstered pieces covered in a *plain or small all-over patterned fabric* blended to the room's background provide visual space. Repeating the same fabric on other pieces helps unify furniture and has a space-making effect.
- Upholstery that is neatly *tailored* and *without skirts* gives an uncluttered look.
- *Furniture aligned against walls* leaves the center of the room free.
- Extended to the ceiling, *shelves and high storage units attached to walls* visually add height and if terminated approximately 1 ft from the floor, allow the perimeter of the room to be seen, adding to the sense of space. Smaller units such as serving tables, consoles, **buffets**, and desks can also be wall hung, eliminating the need for space-using legs (Figure 10.30).

LIGHTING

- Light cast on *ceilings* or on the *upper part of the wall or drapery* directs the eye upward.
- Lamps with *inconspicuous shades* that provide indirect lighting help conserve space.

- *Uplighters* placed at key points on the floor around the perimeter of the room add to the illusion of height and space.
- Lighting the *corners* of the room adds to a spacious feeling as the eye moves out to the light. If the corners are dark, the eye stops at the light's edge.

ACCESSORIES

- Avoid *clutter.* Rather than being scattered about the room, items used sparingly and in a well-organized way will enhance the space.
- *A few bold accessories* can give a sophisticated feeling without visually eliminating space.
- *Mirrors* strategically placed can reflect a wall, the outdoors, or a particular area, thus multiplying space.
- A few *plants,* preferably small-leaved ones, can give an airy feeling.

For additional space-saving techniques, see the section in Chapter 1 on space.

Making a Large Room Appear Smaller

The challenge of making a big room livable is not a common one, but it does occur. Following are some

FIGURE 10.30 A wall-hung shelf with rounded corners takes little space.

FIGURE 10.31 In this large living area designed by architect Charles Gwathmey, the space is visually divided by marble tiles inset into the wood floor and the sweep of a dropped section of the ceiling. Separate furniture groupings encourage conversation. (Photograph © Paul Warchol; courtesy Charles Gwathmey.)

suggestions for selecting and arranging furniture to provide a comfortable human dimension.

- The most important consideration is *scale*. Massive furniture, overscaled patterns, and large pictures can be chosen.
- All furnishings, however, need not be massive. After large pieces have established the broad outlines of the room, lighter pieces can be used to complete the groupings.
- Too little furniture in a big room can result in a cold, uninviting interior, and too much furniture may give a feeling of clutter. More important than quantity, however, is the *arrangement*. The best technique is to plan separate areas of different sizes. Some may be small and intimate; others, more open (see Figure 10.31).

Occasional chairs may be moved from one group to another, thus forming a link between groupings.
- All furniture used in the middle of a room should look attractive from all angles. A *sofa-back table* is a versatile and attractive piece to serve two areas.
- A few empty spaces in a large room can be pleasant. A room that looks as though it could use one more item has a certain appeal. One writer referred to this as "the charm of the incomplete."

WALL COMPOSITION

A floor is on a horizontal plane, and its composition is primarily one of furniture arrangement, which also

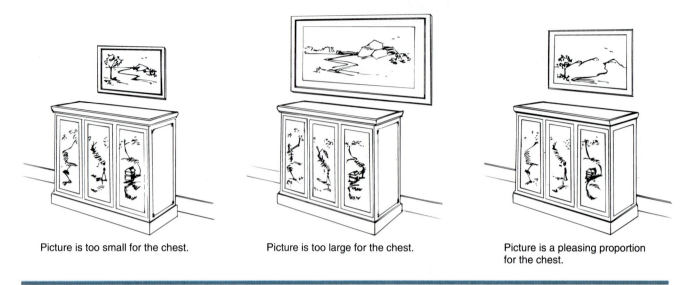

Picture is too small for the chest.

Picture is too large for the chest.

Picture is a pleasing proportion for the chest.

FIGURE 10.32 Scale relationships.

affects wall elevation. The floor plan, whether for a residential or nonresidential space, is always designed with this third dimension in mind. A wall is on a *vertical plane* limited by ceiling, floor, corners, and other permanent *architectural features* such as doors, windows, mantels, and paneling. Because the wall is viewed from a different angle, *movable items* such as hanging and portable lamps and pieces of furniture seen in relationship to the wall are part of the complete composition. If architectural features are not well planned, a designer can disguise or emphasize whatever will enhance the total wall composition. If *ceilings* are below standard height (8 ft), avoid any horizontal division of the wall, since this tends to make the ceiling seem lower. Instead, emphasize vertical lines to add height. If ceilings are too high, emphasize horizontal lines to make the ceilings appear lower. Consider *wall elevation in a room* individually. Each composition should present a pleasing effect suitable to the style and mood of the room.

Application of the principles and elements of design is helpful when selecting and arranging items for a wall composition.

- The *scale relationship* among the individual items, and between the overall composition and the room, should seem right. The placement of items against the wall and the *proportion of the wall* to be covered should be carefully planned in a manner complementary to the complete composition. (See Figure 10.32.)
- Try to achieve a feeling of *balance* (see Chapter 1). An asymmetrical composition remains interesting longer than a bisymmetrical one. Some formal balance, however, can bring unity to the arrangement. (See Figure 10.33.)
- *Straight lines* are enhanced when *curved lines* are introduced. A composition can be enhanced by a pleasing *juxtaposition* of rectangular, square, circular, and oval shapes. Variety with a sense of unity is an

important goal when combining various lines and shapes.
- *Uneven numbers* often make a more interesting composition than even numbers.

No specific rules of measurement are available by which to produce a perfect composition. That intangible quality of taste or judgment must therefore be relied on to achieve a wall composition that is easy to live with, complementary to the architectural background and style, and visually satisfying.

Two-Dimensional Art

The need to add some form of visual interest to the walls of a dwelling has existed for centuries. From elaborately painted walls uncovered in the ancient Roman towns of Pompeii and Herculaneum to arrangements of pictures in homes of the twentieth century, artwork selected for a home reveals much about the owner's personality and individual taste. Watercolors, paintings, prints, posters, and other two-dimensional artworks are favorite items employed for wall compositions. Following are considerations for selecting and arranging two-dimensional art for a wall composition.

- The *frame* is extremely important. A picture worth displaying is worth framing appropriately. (Some pictures do not call for a frame and are complete without one.) Frames are available in many materials, including wood of all types, metals, enamels, paints, and gilded surfaces, and they may also be structurally or decoratively designed. A frame should not dominate the artwork but should complement the subject, style, and feeling of the picture. Often traditional oil paintings are framed in heavy, ornately carved frames, and simple etchings and watercolors in lighter, narrower frames. Many two-dimensional artworks are enhanced by a

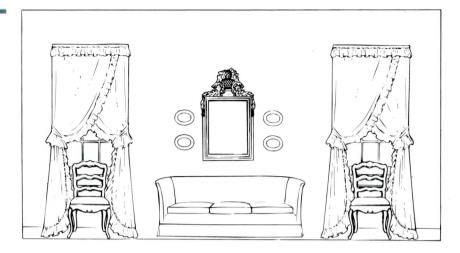

FIGURE 10.33 Achieving balance in a wall composition. (A) Bisymmetrical balance may become monotonous. (B) Asymmetrical balance remains interesting longer.

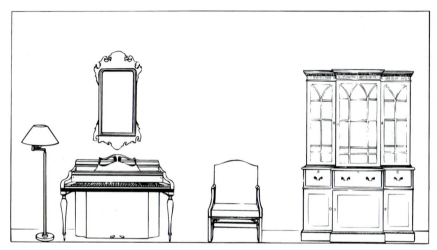

mat, which will make the picture larger and can make a nice transition between the picture and the wall. (See Chapter 11.)

- When a picture is selected for a composition, the *texture* of the wall should be compatible with the art piece.
- Pictures can be hung *individually or in groupings,* but whatever alternative is selected, it should relate to the sofa, chairs, tables, or other furnishings that constitute part of the *total wall composition.* Usually a picture relates best to the composition when not "floating" alone on the wall. A table, console, or other furnishing beneath the picture can stabilize the artwork.

- *Positive areas* are the actual spaces filled with the two-dimensional artwork; *negative spaces* are the areas in between these pieces. Regardless of shape and size, each picture hung should have a pleasing space surrounding it in relationship to the adjoining picture. (See Figure 10.34.)
- When a single picture is used on a wall, it may work best when hung at *eye level,* or hung at *unusual levels* for a sophisticated treatment.
- Wall art can provide the room's *focal point,* with furnishings arranged to support this emphasis.
- A picture hung above a chair or sofa should be placed high enough so the head of the seated person does not

FIGURE 10.34 Symmetrical and asymmetrical arrangements of art are hung with careful attention to the relationship of positive spaces (the art itself) and negative spaces (spaces between the art pieces).

Asymmetrical

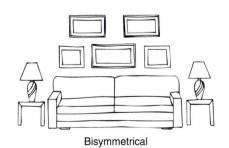

Bisymmetrical

Furniture Arrangement and Wall Composition

touch the frame: approximately 6 to 8 in. provides sufficient *clearance*. Additionally, pictures are seen and appreciated when not obstructed by lamps, flower arrangements, or other accessories.

■ To assemble an arrangement of a two-dimensional art composition, lay a large sheet of brown paper the size of the area to be covered on the floor. Arrange pictures and other objects on the paper until the final composition is created. Trace each object around the perimeter, and mark a point where it will be hung on the wall. Then hold the paper up against the wall with marks made where nails or hooks will go. The pictures can be hung easily in the planned arrangement.

■ Pictures look best when hung *flat against the wall* with nails and hooks securely attached and cords and wires concealed.

Storage Units

A storage unit partially or completely covering a wall and extending from floor to ceiling, containing both open shelves and closed units, will occupy little space, provide abundant storage, and be an important architectural feature in the room. The unit can incorporate books, pictures, mirrors, and other objects, as well as the television.

FIGURE 10.35 Storage wall planning and organization are combined in creating a center for storage display and versatile use. The drop-down table folds up when not in use to provide extra floor space and to mask unsightly storage. (Courtesy of Interliebke.)

When artfully planned and arranged into a harmonious composition, the storage wall can be a masterpiece of design and color and may even form the room's focal point.

Since walls of a room form the background not only for furniture but for people, the final effect usually works best when not an obstructive one. With this in mind, and with an acute awareness of the importance of the relationship of form, space, line, texture, and color, a successful wall composition can be achieved. (See Figure 10.35.)

ASSIGNMENT 1

Carefully observe and analyze wall arrangements in magazines, studio setups, homes, and public spaces. On graph paper, do some experimenting with various wall compositions until you believe that you have developed some skill. Then arrange the walls in a room of your choosing.

The specific class assignment is left to the discretion of the instructor.

ASSIGNMENT 2

In the following assignment, you are given an opportunity to apply the principles and guidelines of floor composition discussed in the chapter. Study the four living room arrangements in the Student Work Packet.

This assignment includes plans for five rooms, templates, and graph paper. Examine each of the empty rooms to determine its assets and defects. Rooms 1 and 2 present particular problems that need to be resolved. Decide on the functions of each room and the areas of activity. Experiment on the graph paper until you have found a satisfactory arrangement for each room. Then arrange the templates to take the best advantage of space in creating pleasant, functional rooms. Follow the procedures outlined in the chapter.

The completed rooms should be checked with the 12 items on the following checklist. Room arrangements will be evaluated according to this list.

Refer to Table 10.1 for a list of the minimum clearances for placement of furniture.

Checklist for Arranging Furniture

1. Are traffic or circulation lanes neatly marked and left free? Mark the major traffic lanes in red. (These are the lanes that lead from one door to another.)
2. Where the outside door opens directly into the living room, has an entranceway been created that provides some privacy, particularly for the main conversation area?
3. Has one well-chosen center of interest been made the important, yet not completely dominating, focal point in the room? Is this grouping comfortably and conveniently arranged, out of the line of traffic, yet open enough to be inviting?
4. Are other areas of activity clearly defined, conveniently located, and artistically arranged with all necessary items?
5. In dual-purpose living–dining rooms, is there a screen, a divider, or an effective furniture arrangement to provide some privacy or adequate division of space?
6. Large pieces of furniture:

   - Is each piece placed to take the best advantage of space and not pushed tightly into a corner?
   - Is each piece placed parallel to the wall (with the possible exception of a lounge chair), unless the major seating arrangement is based on a diagonal plan?
   - Does a large piece block a window?
   - Where windows are near the floor, are large pieces placed out far enough to allow passage behind?

7. Does the room have a sense of balance?

   - Do opposite walls seem the same?
   - Are high and low pieces pleasingly distributed?
   - Are round and rectangular pieces pleasingly distributed?

8. Are occasional chairs placed at convenient points to be moved easily into various groupings?
9. Is lighting adequate and conveniently located? Are all electrical outlets indicated?
10. Does each living room have a feeling of comfort and interest, with a variety of activity areas for music, reading, writing, and conversation, without being crowded or cluttered? Are dining areas arranged for convenience? Are bedrooms furnished to make the best use of space, with room for nighttime walking?
11. Is there a feeling of unity?
12. Is each room's composition done with professional neatness?

CHAPTER 11

Accessories

FIGURE 11.1 The warm reds and rich blues of the area rug are picked up in the painting over the fireplace, the chair upholstery and the accent pillows. Use of a clear plexiglass table allows the rug to be seen from all angles. A fascinating mix of African tribal pieces and objects from the American Southwest testifies to the personal interests of the owners. (Photograph by Mark Boisclair.)

Functional Accessories

Decorative Accessories

Art
Screens
Lamps
Books
Mirrors
Clocks
Flowers, Foliage, and Plants
Finishing Touches

Accessory Checklist

Selecting and Placing Accessories

Selecting Accessories
Placing Accessories

Nonresidential Accessories

It is never the value of objects or pictures placed together in the same room or the quality of furniture which is used that gives style and which shows taste. It is their selection and the way they are put together. It is the contrast of color and texture: it is one object in unexpected juxtaposition with another.

—David Hicks

The process of selecting and arranging accessories for both residential and nonresidential settings deserves thoughtful consideration. When the project is successfully completed, accessories will most certainly enhance the setting, as demonstrated in Figure 11.1.

Accessories may be described as a wide variety of objects, usually smaller in scale than other basic furnishings, that may be functional, decorative, or both. Accessories add the finishing touches to a room, more surely reflecting the *personal taste and individuality* of the user than any other element. Personally selected accessories provide occupants and visitors with an interesting and visually pleasurable experience (see Figure 11.2). These items may be almost anything from a decorative screen or sculpture to a functional lamp or door knocker, and they can be a powerful tool in *establishing the design theme*. Accessories can either be authentic to a certain historic style or be mixed to support a variety of styles. The latter approach is often considered more creative; for example, an antique picture and frame in a stark modern interior can provide an interesting impact by pure contrast. Accessories can also be *supportive of the architectural background*. For example, an informal arrangement of flowers in a basket enhances a rustic wood wall, and an elegant porcelain vase enhances a formal French panelled wall.

Accessories are highly *flexible* in terms of their use in the environment. They can be placed in a variety of areas within a space, relocated or rotated when desired, or even replaced when necessary without disrupting the total design impact. For example, a small, treasured antique box could be placed on a bookshelf, coffee table, end table, or even relegated to another room and still be visually effective.

Additionally, a *focal point* may be established through the use of accessories. For instance, a large painting in an elegant frame placed over the fireplace mantel commands immediate attention. A group of paintings arranged on a prominent wall also creates emphasis in a room. Most homes are enriched by the addition of both decorative and functional accessories.

FUNCTIONAL ACCESSORIES

Functional accessories serve a utilitarian purpose but may also become an interesting display item. Some items, such as towel racks, drapery rods, door knobs, or plumbing fixtures, may be attached to the architectural background. Other practical accessories may be moved from room to room or from one place to another within the space, such as a mirror, lamp, clock, or tray.

The purpose or use of the room should be the prime consideration when selecting functional accessories. (See Figure 11.3.) For example, if lighting is required beside a lounge chair in a living room, choose an appropriate lamp that will meet the needs of the user. Making a list of

FIGURE 11.2 Attention to details in the selection and placement of accessories, from large floral arrangements to small tabletop lamps, creates a memorable experience for diners in the luxurious Orchids restaurant at the Omni Netherland Plaza Hotel. (Courtesy of White House Publishing, Cincinnati, Ohio.)

FIGURE 11.3 Functional accessories in this kitchen include cooking utensils and containers, trays, dishes, and fixtures. Decorative accessories include the plant, wall plaques, and candlesticks. The warm tones of brass and copper complement the dark green walls, maple cabinets, and white tile countertops. (Courtesy of Dal-Tile.)

functional accessories, including built-in, attached, or portable, that will be necessary in each room helps to determine the successful selection and placement of each item.

DECORATIVE ACCESSORIES

Decorative accessories generally provide no other value than the pleasure derived from their aesthetic qualities. Decorative items abound in furniture and antique stores, galleries, design studios, art and craft exhibitions or shows, and numerous other sources. Accessories are available in every traditional or modern style and may be handcrafted or machine-made—old or new.

Whether functional or purely decorative, each accessory can contribute to the enhancement of an interior if chosen with care and discrimination. Following is an outline of the basic accessories that complete a room and give a desirable, lived-in feeling.

Art

Paintings, drawings, original prints, photographs, sculpture, and other types of art are some of the most personal items in a home and when effectively displayed contribute to a room's appeal and distinctiveness. Two-dimensional art consists of a variety of works in many different media.

Paintings

Original paintings in *oil, acrylic, watercolor,* or *tempera* are usually the most expensive type of art. They range

FIGURE 11.4 An oil painting over the fireplace and another on the side wall contribute to the visual interest in this living area. A tall folding screen draws attention to the corner grouping. (Courtesy of Lynn McGhie & Associates.)

from the works of famous painters to those of local artists, as shown in Figure 11.4. Much satisfaction comes from owning an original work of art. Designers should suggest using original art when the client's budget allows.

Drawings

Original drawings are usually executed in *ink, charcoal, pencil,* or *crayon.* Drawings can provide a welcome variety of art in a space and like original paintings are satisfying because they are one of a kind.

Prints and Photographs

Original prints include *etchings, lithographs, woodcuts, steel engravings,* and *drypoint.* They are designed by an artist and usually produced by him or under his supervision. *Limited edition prints* are numbered and signed by the artist. A piece numbered 27/100, for example, indicates that the print is the twenty-seventh of a total of 100. The fewer prints produced, the rarer the piece, although limited prints are usually less expensive than one-of-a-kind paintings and drawings.

Posters, originally called "poor man's art" at the turn of the century, are available at minimal cost. They are usually considered a low-budget accessory but are often seen in fine contemporary settings. Photographic *reproductions* of original paintings, drawings, or prints are also widely available and inexpensive.

Family or artistic *photographs,* by professionals or nonprofessionals, add variety and interest as accessories. Many interiors are enhanced by good photographs.

Importance of Frames and Mats

Displaying two-dimensional art is a sure way to express individual taste and personality. Naturally the art itself is important, but the way it is framed also attracts attention. The frame and mat can either enhance or detract from the art. Most homes today are eclectic (a mix of styles), and any look can be incorporated. The market abounds in frames of all types, from elegant wood and gilded frames to simple enamel and chrome frames.

Mats are generally used for original drawings, prints, photographs, and watercolors to protect them from direct contact with the glass and from any condensation than can occur with temperature changes. Quality mats are acid-free to protect the displayed work from discoloration and serious damage. A mat is most effective when it does not detract from the work but complements the medium, colors, and subject. Today, framing professionals are creating unusual and interesting effects with cut mat designs. Following are some considerations for determining how to frame and mat art work:

- Consider the *colors* in the art piece and the room where it will be displayed. What frame and mat colors will accent or blend with the art?

- Consider the *style* of the room. If the style is informal country, formal traditional, or sophisticated modern, the frames that best support the style will enhance the entire decor. Many people prefer an eclectic style, providing a more flexible selection of frames and mats.
- The architectural background *textures* help determine what frame and mat will complement the art. Consider the effect of smooth, shiny, rough, dull, or combinations of these basic textures.
- Will the picture be enhanced with a *decorative* (with applied ornamentation) or *structural* (devoid of ornamentation) frame?
- Consider the *frame materials* available to determine the types that will suit the style and mood desired. The most typical materials used for picture frames include wood, metal, ceramics, leather, laminates, fabrics, glass, and **cloisonné** (enamelware with various colors arranged in a design and separated by a slender metal filament).
- Consider *line and form.* Will the picture require a horizonal, vertical, oval, diagonal, or circular frame and mat?
- Consider the *size of the frame.* How large must the frame measure in order to enhance the art? Is the space where it will be displayed compatible with the size?
- Drawings, etchings, watercolors, and prints of all types are usually complemented by including a mat. How many mats, in what color or colors, how wide, and what type? (Oils may or may not have a liner such as linen, velvet, or leather, but are almost never placed within a mat.)
- *Glass* is usually used over prints, watercolors, and etchings but is almost never used over an oil painting. Regular or nonglare glass is available. Nonglare glass tends to give a clouded appearance but does cut down on sunlight damage.

Sculpture

Three-dimensional works of art can be treasured accessories in residential or nonresidential settings. Sculpture is fashioned in many media, including metals, marble and other stone, wood, glass, and ceramics, and can be modern or traditional in style. The subject matter can be expressed in either naturalistic, stylistic, abstract, or geometric directions or a combination.

Placement often depends on the size of the piece. If small, the piece may be best displayed on a shelf, mantel, or tabletop. If the sculpture is large, it can dominate an area or provide a focal point. A pedestal may be used for either a small or large sculpture to give it greater prominence. Lighting that spotlights the art can add visual interest, as seen in Figures 11.5 and 11.6.

Other Types of Art and Crafts

Ceramics. Accessories made of clay include sculpture, dishes, bowls, platters, pots, and tiles. Clay comes in a

FIGURE 11.5 The flowing shape of the abstract sculpture on the coffee table complements the rounded edges of the architecture, which are echoed in the sofa. Even the coffee table base gives the appearance of having been shaped by nature rather than geometry. (Gail Adams and Nancy Kitchell, designers; photograph by Pam Singleton.)

variety of types ranging from coarse to fine and in a wide variety of colors that affect the final product. In addition, the artisan may create a unique ceramic piece by applying different types of ornamentation, colors, textures, and shapes. The resulting piece may be formal, informal, decorative, structural, modern, or traditional. **Ceramics** fall into four basic categories: (1) porcelain, (2) china, (3) earthenware, and (4) stoneware.

Mosaics. A **mosaic** is made up of small, usually square pieces (tesserae) of ceramic, stone, or glass arranged in an artistic design and set in cement. Used for floors and murals in ancient times, today mosaics are used for a

variety of small decorative objects including trays, boxes, pictures, and small tables.

Glass Art. Accessories formed of glass include vases, dishes, bowls, and sculpture. *Hand-blown glass* has been a popular art for centuries, and exquisite pieces from many countries, each with its own design approach, have been widely appreciated in America. Modern designs have been pioneered, most notably by the Italians and Scandinavians, who fashion beautiful and unique pieces. Glass can be *etched, colored, enameled, pressed, gilded, cut,* and *engraved. Leaded stained glass,* an artistic composition of small pieces of colored glass held together by lead, has also been known through the ages, particularly during the Gothic period when stained glass was used to create extraordinary windows. Today, stained glass can be made into window and door panels, hung at a window, or designed as a freestanding piece of art. (Refer to Figure 7.29.)

Weaving and Textile Art. The art of weaving has been known in almost every country of the world, and each has developed distinctive cultural designs. Most weavers through the centuries have employed a simple hand loom, wool yarns, natural dyes, and simple designs. During the twentieth century, and especially at the Bauhaus in Germany during the 1920s, new designs and approaches were fostered in this medium. Today, weaving and other art compositions employing fabrics and fibers are regarded as highly valued works of art and make beautiful accessories in both private and public settings. Combined with imagination, new yarns, colors, and other innovations make weaving and fabric-art designs limitless.

Another type of textile design used for both functional and decorative purposes is *quilting*. This traditional process involves arranging small pieces of colored plain or patterned fabrics into a simple or intricate design. Quilts are enjoying renewed appreciation today and are appropriately used in both traditional and modern interiors. (See Figure 11.7.)

Tapestry is an intricate (usually pictorial) multicolored handwoven textile design with a ribbed surface. Today, most tapestries used as accessories are machine-made. Some copy patterns used in previous times and some are more modern in design. Tapestries can be used as accessories in a similar manner as paintings.

Pillows and Cushions. As accessories, pillows and cushions add a touch of warmth and human comfort, helping to soften the straight lines of architecture and furnishings. They are available in a wide variety of colors and may be patterned or plain, as seen in Figures 11.1 and 11.5. Handcrafted pillows may be intricately stitched, woven, or created by other forms of fabric art. Pillows are often placed on sofas, beds, and chairs and sometimes on the floor.

Rugs and Blankets. Handcrafted and custom-designed rugs are widely used as accessories, often as a

FIGURE 11.6 In another view of the room shown in Figure 11.5, a row of sculpted heads on the fireplace wall is emphasized by pools of light. The dramatic lighted table behind the sofa provides harmony of shape with contrast of texture. (Photograph by Pam Singleton.)

FIGURE 11.7 A quilt used as a table covering and folk art in the armoire are compatible with the caned chairs and gazebo-like setting of this charming dining area. (Photograph courtesy of Lynn McGhie Associates.)

focal point in a room or as the basis for a room's color scheme, as seen in Figure 11.8. (Refer to Chapter 6.) Blankets such as the Navajo Indians and Finnish make add a pleasant decorative touch in a room.

Baskets. The art of basket weaving has changed little since ancient times. Today's designers have further developed this art by introducing new approaches in color, form, pattern, and style. Traditional baskets created by particular cultures display distinctive characteristics and styles that are highly valued. Almost any home, especially an informal environment, can be enhanced by the use of baskets, whether displayed alone, as part of a grouping, or as containers for flowers and plants (see Figure 11.1).

Wood Crafts. Wood carving is another art that has survived through the ages and continues today as a medium for highly prized decorative and structural accessories. Items carved of wood and used as accessories include sculpture and statuary, either traditional or modern; bowls, vases, picture and mirror frames, lamp bases, clocks, kitchen utensils, and candle holders. Wooden accessories are a practical choice for commercial design, as shown in Figure 11.9.

Metal Works. Bronze, brass, gold, silver, pewter, iron, aluminum, steel, stainless steel, chromium, tin, and copper are some of the most popular metals employed for accessories. Sculpture, statuary, pots, bowls, vases, plates,

FIGURE 11.8 The architectural treatment of wood, brick, and pebble concrete is an effective background for display of books, pottery, paintings, weavings, and rugs. The items are arranged for maximum enjoyment in this informal modern decor. (Courtesy of Ron Molen, architect.)

FIGURE 11.9 An eye-catching arrangement of wooden objects against a diagonally paneled wall makes an effective display in this casual restaurant setting. (Courtesy of Lynn McGhie & Associates.)

platters, candle holders, fire tools, decorative and functional hardware, and other items can be beautifully fashioned from metal, often providing the right textural touch and variety to a space (see Figure 11.3).

Candles. Originally used for purely functional purposes, handcrafted candles today are a highly intricate art form. Candles are created in many colors and in a wide range of textures and forms suitable for both traditional and modern settings. Candles are often used for decorative accents in the interior and, when lit, provide a warm, inviting element in the private or public environment.

Screens

One graceful means of individualizing an environment is through the use of a freestanding screen. A wide variety of screens in numerous styles and materials are on the market. The versatile shutter screen with movable lou-

FIGURE 11.10   (left and below) Floor lamps with Ionic scrolls and opaque shades flank the seating areas in this large living space designed by Michael de Santis. Uplighting comes from an unexpected source—tall, fluted pilasters that appear to be peeled open to release the light within. Seating groups angled out from the walls encourage cross-communication and circulation. (Courtesy of Michael de Santis, ASID, Michael de Santis, Inc. Photograph by Phillip Ennis.)

vers and mirror screens may be used almost anywhere. Wood frames affixed with light-filtering materials such as caning, pierced metal, or filigree come in a wide assortment of designs from geometric to exotic arabesques. A decorative screen gives an architectural quality to a room, enhances the room's decor, provides a backdrop for a furniture grouping (see Figure 11.4), substitutes for side drapery, or serves as the room's focal point.

In addition to its decorative values, a screen may serve many functional purposes. It can be the primary multipurpose item in the home, easily moved from one room to another. It can (1) set off an entrance where the front door opens directly into the living area, (2) act as a divider between living and dining areas, (3) close off a kitchen, (4) set off a private area by making a room within a room, (5) redirect traffic when strategically placed, (6) extend the apparent size of a room by replacing a door with an airy see-through effect, (7) control the flow of air and the direction of light, (8) camouflage an old-fashioned radiator or air-conditioning unit, and (9) conceal storage. Whatever the theme of the room, a well-designed screen used in the right place is a valuable asset.

Lamps

The lamp is an important element of beauty and purpose both during the daytime and at night, providing light when needed and functioning as an accessory at all times. A lighting fixture that is carefully chosen for a specific room, style, mood, location or purpose can be an important contributing element, as shown in Figure 11.6. Lamps are available in a wide range of styles—traditional or modern, decorative or structural, with or without a shade. Figure 11.10 shows the impact a designer can create with a decorative lamp. Some popular base materials include ceramics, metal of all types, wood, glass, plastics, and stone. Portable lamps, floor lamps, sconces, torchères, and pendants (chandeliers) are particularly favored as lighting accessories. Lamp shades also act as accessories when they are matched to curtains, bedspreads, or wall coverings.

When selecting lamps for the interior, (1) select lamps that are well proportioned and are in scale with other furnishings, (2) make sure the colors and materials of the lamp are compatible with other colors and textures in the room, (3) select lamps that complement the room's decor, (4) consider the functional as well as the decorative requirements the lamp must serve. Generally, lamps work well when their design is simple and unobtrusive. (Refer to Chapter 3 for further information on lamps and lighting considerations.)

Books

Books can do more than anything—except people—to add friendliness to a home. Cicero said, "A room without books is a body without a soul." Usually no room has a mood that would preclude books nor a color scheme so complete it could not benefit from the warm tones and textures of books. Bookshelves can go in almost any room in the home, require little space, and create a warm, friendly atmosphere, as illustrated in Figure 11.11. They can be planned in the initial design of the house or added later. The living room, family room, and study are excellent areas to hold a multiplying collection of books

FIGURE 11.11 Two built-in niches flanking the fireplace are filled with books. Other accessories including paintings, candles, porcelain, pillows, and lamps reflect the owner's interests and taste. French doors open into a garden with whimsical animal statues placed on the lawn. (Photograph by Alex Groves.)

FIGURE 11.12 Options for displaying books.

A doorway framed with books is a
valuable addition to a room.

Create an entranceway
with bookshelves.

for the entire household. Children need bookshelves in their rooms at a height they can easily reach. Other bedrooms can accommodate shelves where space permits—usually close to the bed for nighttime reading. Kitchens need handy shelves for reference books and cookbooks. Bookshelves often can be fitted into numerous unused spaces in the house such as niches, odd corners, around or over doors and windows, or used as a space divider. A room divider can hold books on one or both sides. (See Figure 11.12.) Additionally, books can add a decorative quality to a room with their textures, colors, and shapes. They also mix well with other accessories; for example, a few books flanked with interesting bookends, placed by a plant and small sculpture, or placed on a coffee table with other items add interest to a room.

Mirrors

Since the fourteenth century, mirrors have been a decorative and functional object in homes and public places and a helpful tool for the interior designer. Mirrors are available in almost any size and in frames to fit any decor. Mirrors can (1) add beauty, (2) multiply space, (3) conceal unattractive structural features, (4) distribute and double light, (5) brighten dark areas, and (6) bring life into an otherwise drab room. (See Figure 11.13.) Because of their myriad uses, mirrors have steadily increased in popularity through the years and today play an indispensable role in all styles of interiors.

Clocks

Clocks have long been important accessories in the home. From the handsome antique grandfather clock encased in an elegantly carved case to the high-tech clocks of the late twentieth century, they not only serve a necessary function but also add an important decorative touch to any room because by their very nature they attract attention. Clocks are available in numerous styles and sizes and in a variety of textures such as wood, metal, porcelain, and glass. Style preference, available space,

and function are important considerations when selecting a clock. Depending on their size, clocks may be mounted on the wall, placed on the floor, a shelf, a table top, a mantel, or grouped with other accessories. Naturally, a clock must be placed where it can be seen easily.

Flowers, Foliage, and Plants

Fresh Flowers

Of all accessories making up the final touches of a residence or commercial space, almost nothing can duplicate the effect of fresh flowers. A bouquet of live foliage and flowers greatly enhances a room, adding a special warmth and appeal. The extra effort that fresh arrangements require reflects the personal taste of the occupants. Whatever the season, flowers and foliage of some type are available. With a little imagination they can be arranged and displayed in a way that adds life, interest, and beauty to an interior space (see Figure 11.14).

The art of flower arrangement can be learned in the classroom or acquired by observation and experience. Three popular flower arranging styles are (1) Oriental *(ikebana)*, (2) traditional, and (3) contemporary freestyle. The flowers' container contributes to the total success of the arrangement and generally works best when the texture, pattern, and size are complementary. Glass, metal, porcelain, pottery, and baskets are often used because they can be effectively combined with traditional or modern furnishings.

Plants

Living plants generously placed around living spaces contribute to the total design scheme and help to bring something of the outdoors into the interior. Personal preference for texture, form, color, and size is a consideration in selecting plants, as well as special care requirements for light, water, and temperature. A plant may function as part of a focal point, soften rigid architectural features, complement an arrangement of other accesso-

FIGURE 11.13 An imposing mirror adds a strong vertical element and anchors a tall wall in this cathedral-ceilinged living room. The intricate carving of the mirror frame harmonizes in spirit with other decorative elements in the room, from the delicate leaded windows over the doors and the needlework pillows to the tracery of the coffee table and the displayed coral and seashells. (Courtesy of The Barrows Design Studio. Photograph by Richard Embery.)

FIGURE 11.14 Large and small floral arrangements and potted topiaries add a festive air to this contemporary French dining room. Because the walls, window treatment, and upholstery are off-white, flowers, table settings, and other accessories can be used to establish a color scheme for special occasions. (Courtesy of Bruce Stodola, ASID, and The Design Studio at Barrows. Photograph by Mark Boisclair.)

ries, or be an inviting addition in itself. A plant can also be set off by its container.

Dried Arrangements

Dried flowers, weeds, branches, pods, and other foliage types are often arranged as alternatives to fresh plants and flowers. They have the advantage of being permanent and require no upkeep other than dusting. Dried arrangements are particularly attractive when placed in a well-designed container. For example, tall branches of corkscrew willow are complemented when placed in a handsomely thrown piece of pottery. Although many designers select living plants and flowers, an artful arrangement of dried flowers, weeds, and other foliage can function as a well-appreciated accessory.

Silk Flowers and Foliage

Today there is a growing demand for flowers, foliage, and plants made of silk and other fibers. Like dried arrangements, they are permanent and require only occasional dusting. Well-made silk flowers, foliage, and plants look amazingly natural. Many commercial and institutional organizations use these arrangements because of the easy upkeep and one-time investment. Some designers arrange dried flowers and foliage with silk flowers for a more natural effect.

Finishing Touches

The finishing touches to an interior scheme, like pieces of fine jewelry, give a personal stamp.

Hardware

A contemporary room can be made strikingly modern and a traditional room can take on an authentic feeling through the discriminating use of small details such as door knockers, doorknobs, switch plates, curtain rods, and tiebacks. Drawer pulls, **escutcheons**, and hinges can give a piece of furniture a definite feeling of any period. Whether the style is Early American, Georgian, French, classical, Spanish, Oriental, or modern, the right hardware can convey the appropriate mood. (See Figure 11.15.)

ACCESSORY CHECKLIST

When determining what accessories are suitable for a particular space, it is helpful to consider a wide range of possibilities. Reviewing an outline of numerous items often sparks an idea of the accessory or accessories that tie an entire grouping together. Table 11.1 lists the most commonly selected accessories for both residential and nonresidential settings.

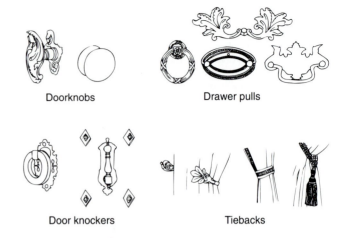

Doorknobs Drawer pulls

Door knockers Tiebacks

FIGURE 11.15 Finishing touches.

SELECTING AND PLACING ACCESSORIES

Selecting Accessories

Selecting items that will enrich the total design of a room can be a challenging and rewarding process. A first step is to determine what functional and decorative accessories are required to meet the needs of the owner. Will the accessories be utilitarian or displayed for aesthetic pleasure? Will the items be incorporated into the scheme to enhance the background or function primarily as a point of interest? Always keep in mind the principles and elements of design. For example, will the item be suitable in texture, color, and form to complement the style, background, and other accessories and furnishings in the room? Is the item in scale with the other furnishings and the space allocated? Will it help bring balance and harmony to the room? These are only a few of the questions that arise when applying the basic theories of design.

Some of the most common sources for both decorative and functional accessories are art galleries, auction houses, museums, antique dealers, specialty shops, art and craft shows, exhibitions, greenhouses, flower shops, design studios, retail stores, and tourist shops. Although selecting accessories can be a conscious effort, finding that unexpected "treasure" that appeals instantly adds a feeling of spontaneity to the home.

The process of selecting accessories is often more rewarding when they are collected over a long period of time and accumulated from a variety of sources. Items that reflect personal taste and individuality are usually the most interesting and appealing. (See Figure 11.16.) If a room lacks character, search for the right accessories—ones that are in keeping with the quality of the interior and either strengthen the chosen theme or, by contrast, add excitement. Leaving a little empty space need not be of concern—there is often a "charm in the incomplete."

TABLE 11.1 Accessory checklist

Animal skins	Kitchen and cooking utensils
Aquariums and fish	Kites
Arms and armor	Lamps
Art (two-dimensional)	Maps, charts, and documents
Ashtrays	Mirrors
Baskets	Models (airplanes, ships, etc.)
Bath accessories (soap dish, toothbrush container, towel racks, towels, washcloths, scales, toilet-paper holder)	Mosaics
	Musical items (instruments, music stands, sheet music, etc.)
Birdcages	Music boxes
Books and magazines	Needlework
Blankets	Pedestals (for displays)
Bottles	Pillows
Bowls	Pitchers
Boxes	Plants
Brassware	Plates and platters (decorative)
Calendars	Photo albums
Candles	Pottery
Candlesticks	Puzzles
Canisters	Quilts
Ceramics	Rugs
Coat racks	Screens
Clocks	Sculpture
Collections (coins, guns, stamps, antique items, etc.)	Serving carts
	Shells and rocks
Cushions	Shelves (a small, decorative, carved wood shelf, for example)
Desk accessories (pen and pencil holders, letter holders, desk pad, address book, small clock, etc.)	Silk flower and foliage arrangements
	Silverware
Dishes	Stools
Dolls	Tablecloths, mats, and napkins
Doll houses	Tapestries
Figurines	Telephones
Fireplace tools and firescreen	Tools (antique rake, for example)
Flowers	Toys
Flower and plant containers	Toy furniture
Foliage	Trays
Frames (for art, photos, etc.)	Trophies
Games	Umbrella stands
Glassware	Vases
Hardware (door knobs, hinges, racks, pulls, tiebacks, hooks, escutcheons, rods, etc.)	Wastebaskets
	Weavings
	Wreaths

Placing Accessories

The desire to display prized possessions is universal; the challenge is to arrange these treasured objects into an appealing composition. If the collected items are worth acquiring, they are worth displaying. Successful placement of accessories lies in training the eye to see beauty in color, texture, form, and spatial relationships. Application of the principles and elements of design is helpful when planning the best location for each item. For example, when positioning a large oil painting on the wall, the principles of harmony, balance, emphasis, and scale are particularly important as design goals, and the elements of color, texture, line, space, form, and picture content are essential considerations.

Grouping Accessories

Grouping items in an artistic arrangement can be an effective means of creating an interesting display in the room. By themselves small things may be insignificant, but through skillful arrangement even the simplest items can take on special meaning. (See Figure 11.17.) When grouping small objects, keep in mind that they are seen against a background of walls and furniture, which can be considered part of the arrangement. Be aware of the relationship of the items to each other. Perhaps a grouping of round objects of varying sizes is pleasing, but adding a rectangle can provide a different perspective. In an arrangement with three elements—a horizontal piece, a higher intermediate piece, and a tall vertical piece—the

FIGURE 11.16 Accessories with an animal theme and a profusion of plants not only give personality to this living area but also unify the indoor and outdoor spaces. Needlepoint dogs on a chair and a terra cotta rabbit on the floor look alert, while a blue ceramic cat naps on the sofa. Another gaily colored cat waits outside for someone to open the door. A potted flower outside is the mate to others inside. Vines spilling from baskets atop the armoire lead the eye to others climbing the patio wall. (Photograph by Mark Boisclair.)

FIGURE 11.17 A diverse collection of accessory objects, including paintings, photographs, plants, ceramics, and pillows, is displayed on virtually every available surface in this eclectic living room. Collections like this not only give pleasure to the owners but also interest visitors. (Photograph by Mark Boisclair.)

eye moves from the low horizontal to the high vertical, providing a sense of transition. This rhythm is seen in nature when the eye observes the earth, flowering plants, and towering trees. A common color subtly running through each element can add unity to an arrangement; varying colors and textures can create a sense of interest and variety.

Experiment

Experimentation with accessories can help create the desired outcome. Items for functional or decorative use in all areas of the home add visual pleasure when displayed alone or grouped with an aesthetic eye. Books can be combined with an occasional figurine, a small painting, a trophy, or any small article. A plant sprawling over the edge of a shelf to a lower level provides an interesting

effect. Experimenting with combinations of accessories and their placement is a valuable learning process.

NONRESIDENTIAL ACCESSORIES

Designers often play an important role in selecting accessories for commercial and institutional spaces. Art and accessories should be placed so as not to interfere with the function of the facility, but still contribute an aesthetic quality to the interior. Most often, nonresidential spaces do not incorporate personal items that express the tastes of individuals, except private offices, for example. However, adding accessories to a nonresidential setting can provide an inviting, warm character in an otherwise sparse setting. (See Figure 11.18.)

FIGURE 11.18 Framed prints, a striking floral arrangement, and a potted palm add individuality to the sleek contemporary furnishings of this office setting. (Photograph by Mark Boisclair.)

Often the designer is limited in purchasing fine-quality items for the nonresidential setting because of budget restrictions. The challenge is to obtain accessories that project an aesthetic appeal that will last through the years. Such items as plants and art work—often large in scale—are often chosen for schools, offices, hospitals, libraries, hotels, retail stores, restaurants, and other public settings. Also, accessories that relate to the function of the facility itself can add character to the space; for example, prints in a restaurant might pertain to the history or theme of the eating establishment. Whatever accessories are selected for the nonresidential setting, the result should be an enhancement of the environment and the addition of a humanizing element.

PART FIVE

Interior and Exterior Styles

CHAPTER 12
Historic Heritage of Architecture and Design

CHAPTER 13
Modern Architecture and Design

CHAPTER 12

Historic Heritage of Architecture and Design

FIGURE 12.1 Monticello (1769–1809), Palladian-style home of Thomas Jefferson, Charlottesville, Virginia, reflects the Federal-Roman influence. (Photograph courtesy of Richard Gunn.)

Classic Influences

The Classic Orders of Architecture

The Spanish Influence

Spanish Colonial/Mission Style

Southwestern Style

California Ranch House

Monterey House

The English Heritage—Medieval and Renaissance Influence (1607–Eighteenth Century)

Early Half-Timber, Brick, and Stone Houses

Elizabethan Manor House

Cotswold House

New England Saltbox, Garrison, Gambrel, and Cape Cod

Half-House

Two-Room or Double House

Saltbox

Garrison (Jetty)

Gambrel

Cape Cod (Transitional)

The English Heritage—The Georgian Period

Early Georgian or Wren-Georgian Style

Late Georgian or Gibbs-Palladian Style

Neoclassicism in America (circa 1790–1845)

Federal Period

Greek Revival Period

Other International Influences

French Style (1714–1789)

The French House in America

Dutch Influences

German Style

Swedish Style

The Victorian Era (circa 1837–1900)

Gothic Revival (1840s–1880s)

Italianate Style (1830–1890s/1920s)

Mansard or General Grant Style (1850s–1880s)

Queen Anne Style (1870s–1880s)

Octagonal (1850s–1870s)

Exotic Revival (1835–1890)

Stick Style (1860–1890)

Romanesque Revival

Shingle Style (1880–1900)

Victorian Interiors

Beaux Arts Mansions

Traditional Styles Revived

Preserving Our Architectural Heritage

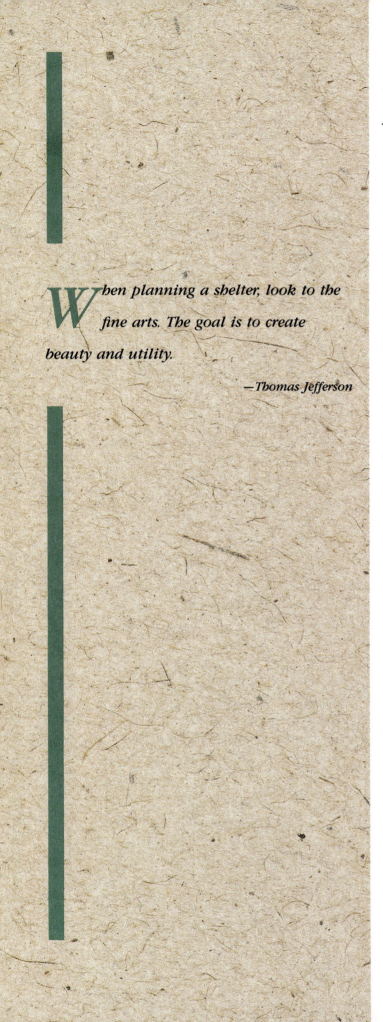

When planning a shelter, look to the fine arts. The goal is to create beauty and utility.

—*Thomas Jefferson*

The history of American architecture is the history of our nation. Where did that history begin? The general agreement is that the mainstream of American culture stems from those English colonists who founded Jamestown in 1607 and landed in Plymouth in 1620.

The dwellings of the earliest colonists were merely crude shelters against the elements. Soon, however, settlers in divergent areas ranging from New England to Louisiana, living under particular circumstances and using **indigenous** materials, constructed buildings that filled their individual needs and expressed their distinctive characteristics. Through this process a variety of architectural styles evolved gradually and naturally. Because speed was necessary in providing all settlers a suitable shelter, it helped determine a principal characteristic common to early **colonial** architecture—simplicity.

An understanding of the traditional styles of American architecture is necessary to the interior designer. This knowledge can deepen an appreciation of our architectural heritage and provide a foundation for better understanding the present. (See Figure 12.1.) Rarely are the period styles copied precisely today, but many individual elements such as roofs, doors, windows, and other architectural details are often used to give a feeling of a historical style. Exteriors of a particular period may be adapted to fit today's floor plans and yet retain the desired traditional appearance. One advantage of a well-designed historical style, whether residential or nonresidential, is that as current trends come and go, classic traditional styles are always appreciated.

Of equal necessity to the interior designer is an appreciation for the background of modern architecture, with its roots beginning as early as the late nineteenth century. Just as the well-designed period style will endure, so also will the well-designed modern structure. (See Chapter 13.) Following is an outline of the major historical styles or periods that have had an impact on the field of architecture and design.

CLASSIC INFLUENCES

The ancient Greeks (fifth century B.C.–first century B.C.) made significant contributions in art and architecture, especially during what is known as the Golden Age. For centuries, architects and designers have drawn inspiration from the forms and motifs created during this period. In the U.S. and Europe, the Grecian influence was especially evident during the eighteenth- and nineteenth-century Neoclassic period. Some details of Greek architecture and design that continue to influence today's designers are depicted in Figure 12.2.

The Classic Orders of Architecture

The Greeks developed a system of coding the design and details of columns, capitals, and **architraves**. The coding

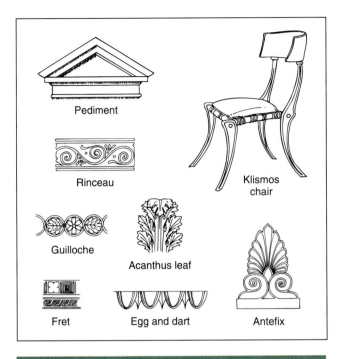

FIGURE 12.2 Ancient classical Greece: architectural details.

system is known as the three classic orders of architecture: Doric, Ionic, and Corinthian, named after the regions where they originated (see Figure 12.3).

1. The Doric order is the simplest and thought by some to be the most beautiful and stately of the three orders. The Doric column has a plain square block (abacus) capital. The column itself is fluted (has recurring concave vertical carvings). The masterpiece of Greek temples, The Parthenon in Athens, is an example of the Doric order of architecture.
2. The Ionic order displays small motifs combined with a large scroll or spiral design called a volute (thought to be inspired by the curve of a ram's horns, a shell, or a parchment scroll). The fluted column is slender in proportion and rests on a circular base.
3. The Corinthian order is the most elaborate of the three. It is distinguished by two rows of intricately carved acanthus leaf designs and other smaller motifs and a slender fluted column. The Corinthian order

was developed late in the fifth century B.C. but was used most by the Romans.

The Romans adapted the Greek orders and added two more, the Tuscan and Composite. In architecture, the Roman arch, in combination with the barrel vault or arched roof, allowed domed construction. The Pantheon (Figure 12.4), one of the world's most important examples of this type of construction, was one inspiration for Thomas Jefferson's home, Monticello, shown at the beginning of the chapter.

Other influential periods in interior design and architecture include the Romanesque, Gothic, Renaissance and Baroque periods (see Table 12.1). In the U.S., however, the earliest influence may be credited to the Spanish.

THE SPANISH INFLUENCE
(circa 1565–twentieth century)

The Spaniards established the first permanent European settlement in the U.S. in Florida. As early as 1565 the Spaniards built a military garrison in St. Augustine. Soon, early settlers introduced the Spanish style of architecture into the South. Of homes from this period, practically none remains. The damp climate, frequent hurricanes, persistent fires, and the ravages of war have destroyed these first dwellings. One house in St. Augustine, Florida, however, still stands on its original foundation. It was built in the late 1500s and was restored in 1888 and again in 1959. This house is claimed by some to be the oldest in the United States and is called *Oldest House*. (See Figure 12.5.) By the first part of the eighteenth century, a style known as the "St. Augustine look" emerged with homes featuring a definite Spanish feeling including balconies, **loggias** (a room or hallway with an arcade or colonnade opening on one side), and wooden gratings over the windows. The Spanish tradition further spread when explorers, politicians, the Catholic clergy, and others settled in what is now New Mexico, Texas, Arizona, and California. The Spanish home as we know it today falls into four distinct categories: the Spanish

FIGURE 12.3 Classic Greek orders.

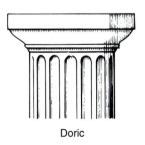

Doric

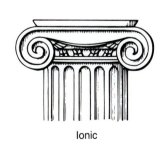

Ionic

Corinthian

FIGURE 12.4 Interior of the Pantheon in Rome.

Colonial/Mission, Southwest Adobe, California Ranch, and Monterey styles.

Spanish Colonial/Mission Style

In the sixteenth century Cortez introduced the Spanish influence into Mexico, where it took on a colonial atmo-sphere unique to the area. The early Spanish Colonial style was simple because of unskilled Indian labor and crude materials. The style was further influenced by the chain of Catholic missions built along the California coast from 1769 to 1823. Spanish architecture has had a romantic appeal for Americans, and when well designed, this type of home has a definite charm. It is especially favored in warm, dry climates, restricting its practical use to the southern and western areas of the United States. From time to time—during the 1920s and 1960s, for instance—the Spanish Colonial and Mission styles have been actively revived, and characteristics of the two styles have often been combined. Numerous examples of this style are found in southern California, especially in the Santa Barbara area, where many Spanish-style buildings, both residential and commercial, have been authentically restored and opened to the public. (An example is *Casa Covarrubias.*)

The following are general characteristics of the Spanish Colonial and Mission house. (Refer to Figure 12.6.)

EXTERIOR

- Blending of the Mexican, Indian, and Spanish cultures
- Stucco-covered walls, whitewashed or tinted, often with a crude finish
- Low-pitched tile roof with broad overhang
- Heavily carved doors in geometric patterns used throughout
- **Arcaded** porches surrounding an inner court

TABLE 12.1

Style (Period)	Principal Countries	Characteristics	Principal Building Types
Romanesque (Middle Ages) ca. 800–1150	Italy, France, England	Simple, massive. Use of horizontal line. Rusticated stone. Semicircular arch and vault. Thick, short columns. Thick walls, small window openings, dimly lit interiors.	Churches, monasteries, castles, fortifications. (Revival in 19th c.: city halls, libraries, churches, town houses.)
Gothic (Middle Ages) ca. 1150–1500	Italy, France, England, Germany	Symbolized wealth and power. Pointed Gothic arch and vault. Use of vertical line. Slender, clustered columns. Tracery. Buttress and flying buttress.	Churches, palaces. Outstanding example: Notre Dame in Paris. (Revival in 19th c.: houses, churches, public buildings.
Renaissance (or "rebirth") ca. 1400–early 17th c.	Italy, France, England, Germany, Spain	Intense interest in classical antiquity. Adapted classic forms: columns, pediments, domes, pilasters, cornices, entablatures. Symmetrical design. Bold scale. Highly decorated surfaces.	Palaces, churches, public buildings. Outstanding example: Andrea Palladio's Villa Rotonda in Italy (1567).
Baroque ca. 16th c.–mid-18th c.	Italy, France, Germany, Austria, Spain, England	Dramatic, elaborate, decorative. Bold scale. Concave and convex walls. Dramatic lighting effects. Flamboyant curved forms, strong sense of movement. Asymmetrical forms.	Churches, palaces, public buildings. Outstanding examples: Bernini's Piazza at St. Peter's in Rome; palace of Versailles in France.

FIGURE 12.5 Oldest House (1565), St. Augustine, Florida. This Spanish house rests on its original foundation. Some historians claim this is the oldest house in the United States. (Courtesy of the St. Augustine Historical Society.)

- Intricate wrought-iron designs employed for interior and exterior
- *Reja,* or wooden grating, typical on windows of original houses

- Balconies and terraces occasionally built

INTERIOR

- Floors of plain wood or paved with Mexican tile or brick
- Whitewashed stucco walls, often with a crude finish
- Colorful painted tile trim around doors and on stair risers
- Chandeliers of handwrought black iron
- Heavy masculine furnishings with deep geometric carvings
- Accessories and artifacts depicting religious themes, especially in Catholic and Indian relics (see Figure 12.7)

Southwestern Style

In 1605 Southern colonists traveled to the area that is now New Mexico, where they found Indians living in **pueblos.** Taos Pueblo, first visited by Captain Pedro de Alvarado in 1540, is considered the oldest and perhaps the largest continuously occupied apartment dwelling in the United States. Today it houses about 1,500 Pueblo Indians, whose way of life has changed little in 800 years.

Dominated for about 300 years by Spain or Spanish Mexico, a unique vernacular architecture evolved incorporating elements of the native Indian, Spanish, and Mexican cultures. In 1610 Santa Fe became the capital for Spain, later for Mexico, and finally for New Mexico. In that same year *Palace of the Governors,* which is the

FIGURE 12.6 Spanish Mission/Colonial style.

Low-pitch roof

Loggia

Wrought iron

Reja

Geometric carved door

Tile risers

Atrium (courtyard)

FIGURE 12.7 A contemporary interior with Spanish features includes frescoed walls, a bright red and gold scheme with handmade fabric for the sofa, a table with splayed legs, a wrought iron candelabra, and Spanish colonial antiques and accessories. (Photograph by Pam Singleton.)

FIGURE 12.8 Palace of the Governors (1610), Santa Fe, New Mexico. The oldest public building in the United States. (Courtesy of the New Mexico Department of Development.)

oldest public building in the United States, was built on the site of an old Indian pueblo (see Figure 12.8). An ancient **adobe** structure known as *Old House,* near the San Miguel Mission in Santa Fe, is claimed by some historians to be the oldest house in the United States. Whether the structure is older than Oldest House in St. Augustine has not been definitely established. The adobe houses built today, mainly in Arizona and New Mexico, follow the same basic style as the early adobes. Santa Fe, more than any other city in the Southwest, has admirably preserved the heritage of the early adobe dwelling, with structures in this style dominating both residential and public buildings. From the 1920s to the present, a unique style based on the Southwest Adobe style, known as the *Santa Fe style,* has emerged and remains popular. This style incorporates many of the original concepts of the early exterior and interior features. Some characteristics of the Southwestern style are illustrated in Figure 12.9.

General characteristics of the Southwest Adobe house are as follows.

EXTERIOR

- Thick adobe brick construction providing good insulation against heat
- Flat roof and deeply set windows and doors, often painted blue or turquoise
- Exterior finished with a thin coating of mud
- Sculptured contoured exterior and interior corners

- Rough-hewn pole **beams** called *vigas* projecting through walls
- Rectangular plan with one or more stories
- Pole ladders on exterior in place of interior stairs
- A courtyard-centered arrangement surrounded by a Greek Revival colonnade (row of columns) was a typical later feature; posts have a carved **corbel** or bracket top called a *zapata*

INTERIOR

- Informal feeling
- Backgrounds of plastered surfaces with exposed ceiling beams *(vigas)* and brackets *(zapatas)*
- *Latillas,* or sticks, arranged on ceiling between *vigas*
- Rounded, molded, plastered fireplace, often in corner, with a round arched opening; often a long seating ledge flanking fireplace
- Tile or wood plank floors
- Small recessed niche in wall, often used for displaying religious artifacts
- Furniture and accessories are a blend of Spanish, Indian, and Mexican pieces; Santa Fe style furnishings are eclectic (see Figure 12.10)
- Colors reflect the desert landscape

Adobe structures of particular interest are Old House, Santa Fe, New Mexico; S. Parson's House, Santa Fe, New Mexico; Palace of the Governors, Santa Fe, New Mexico; and the University of New Mexico, Albuquerque, New Mexico.

FIGURE 12.9 Spanish Southwestern style.

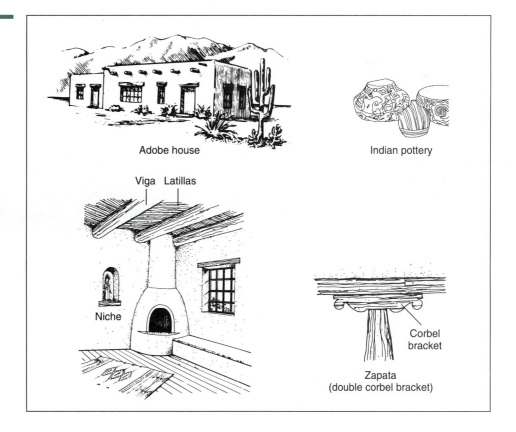

Adobe house

Indian pottery

Viga   Latillas

Niche

Corbel bracket

Zapata (double corbel bracket)

FIGURE 12.10 An interior reflecting the Santa Fe style features an architectural background of white plastered walls, recessed niches over the fireplace, Mexican tile, and dramatic lodgepole beams. The style is further expressed by the use of Mexican, Indian, Spanish, and contemporary furnishings and accessories. (Photograph by Pam Singleton.)

California Ranch House

The California ranch house is a mixture of the Spanish style and the old western farmhouse built circa 1800 to the present. The low, rambling structure was suited to an informal lifestyle (see Figure 12.11). This style originally emerged from the old adobe home with its flat roof; but considering the rainy California climate, a pitched roof was more practical and was added to the structure in the early 1800s. Often a three-sided fence enclosed and defined the outdoor living space—the beginnings of what we now regard as the **patio**. This type of house is currently popular in the West. The term **ranch style** has been used so freely that individuals tend to believe it means merely a long, low house. An authentic California ranch house, however, has several identifying characteristics.

EXTERIOR

- Structure hugging a relatively flat terrain
- Long, low roofline; roof originally of tar, then tile; today tile or shingles used
- Wide, low overhangs supported by posts cover a porch
- Indigenous materials used for construction, such as adobe, wood, stucco, or brick
- Wing-sheltered patio easily accessible from most rooms

INTERIOR

- Similar to interior details of Spanish Colonial (today, great freedom of style is incorporated)

Monterey House

The Monterey house is a blending of the Spanish, French, and New England architecture that had its birth in California when that state was a colony of Spain and Monterey was the most important seaport on the West Coast.

FIGURE 12.11 California ranch house.

Since lumber was plentiful but workers scarce, builders employed Indians, skilled in the use of adobe, for constructing the thick walls. The Spanish influence was seen primarily in the red tile roofs. The overhanging **balconies** with their wrought-iron railings reflected the French houses of New Orleans. The basic style had already been established when the settlers arrived from New England with their English ideas; but they contributed doors, windows, and moldings, some of which they brought with them. *Thomas Larkin*, of Boston, Massachusetts, contributed significantly to the original Monterey style when he combined these various cultural details in his home in Monterey (which was completed in 1837 and is now open to the public). He even introduced the use of wallpaper and applied it to the plastered walls. In fact, many historians believe Larkin built the first Monterey home and thus influenced others to build their homes based on the same principles. After more than 100 years the Monterey house continues to be a popular style of architecture in some areas of the country, particularly in California.

The following are general characteristics of the Monterey house. (Also see Figure 12.12.)

EXTERIOR

- Adobe, stucco, or whitewashed brick walls, sometimes tinted
- Flat-pitched tile roofs
- Wide overhangs to shade windows
- Long second-story balcony supported with posts (French *galerie* influence)
- Woodwork showing New England influence

INTERIOR

- Walls, floors, and other backgrounds incorporate English and Spanish influences, as does the exterior

FIGURE 12.12 Monterey house.

- Furnishings and accessories are either elegant or simple English, Spanish, or a combination; however, one style generally dominates

THE ENGLISH HERITAGE— MEDIEVAL AND RENAISSANCE INFLUENCE
(1607–eighteenth century)

The mainstream of American culture began at Jamestown, Virginia, and Plymouth, Massachusetts, in the seventeenth century. The culture English colonists brought to the new land when they settled along the Atlantic seaboard had a greater influence on America than all other cultures combined. Technically, American houses built during the seventeenth century and based on historic English prototypes fall under the category of English Medieval. However, styles that have emerged from this period, although displaying many overlapping characteristics, are quite distinctive and are popularly known under particular names. The most prominent of these English Medieval styles include the half-timber, stone, or brick Tudor house, the Elizabethan or Jacobean manor, the Cotswold, the saltbox, the garrison, the gambrel, and the Cape Cod.

Early Half-Timber, Brick, and Stone Houses

The first permanent dwellings constructed by English settlers who landed in *Jamestown* in 1607 were initially little more than caves dug in the earth or crude thatched huts. Some huts were copied from native Americans. As soon as initial hardships were overcome, however, settlers began building more substantial houses based on those they had known in England. Early structures were patterned after the **half-timbered** one-room Tudor and Elizabethan "hall" familiar in England at the time. These simple one-room spaces were quite small, with a high **pitched roof** of thatch and a side chimney. The half-timber house was constructed of massive wooden frames, with sections in between filled with plaster or masonry. An early filling material was called **wattle and daub**—interlaced boughs covered with clay and mud. (When used in America today, half-timber construction is usually simulated by placing boards on the surface, which gives the appearance of the original construction.) Another popular filling material of the period was brick **nogging**—bricks arranged in a pattern in between the half-timber exterior framing. Of the many thatched half-timber English cottages, the charming *Anne Hathaway's Cottage* (home of William Shakespeare's wife) outside of Stratford-upon-Avon, England, is perhaps the most famous. One picturesque half-timber house built in England in the sixteenth century and relocated in America in 1925 is *Agecroft Hall* in Windsor Farms, Virginia. Often the half-timber stone or brick medieval English house is referred to as **Tudor**, but in fact the English Tudor period officially ended with the death of Elizabeth I in 1603, a few years before Jamestown was settled. The influence, however, of the Tudor style continued during the seventeenth century in both England and America. (Although the earliest homes of the colonists employed this building technique, the real influence of the Tudor home in America has been from the Beaux Arts period to current times.)

Having come primarily from the upper classes, the Jamestown colonists preferred brick, the material to which they were accustomed, and there was an abundance of clay in the Jamestown area. Although almost nothing remains of the earliest dwellings around Jamestown, one extant brick structure, the *Adam Thoroughgood House* (circa 1636) in Norfolk, Virginia, reflects its English prototype (see Figure 12.13). It features brick construction, sharp gables, massive buttressed chimneys, small diamond-paned windows, and a simple doorway typical of the **medieval** tradition of English houses. Many historians believe that the Adam Thoroughgood House is the oldest brick residence in America.

The Medieval English Tudor house is characterized by the following features. (Also refer to Figure 12.14.)

EXTERIOR

- Two to three stories
- Rambling design
- Half-timber most common construction (stone or brick optional), with **wattle and daub** or brick **nogging** (**clapboard** used in New England often covered half-timber because of severe climate); stone or brick construction optional and often simplified versions of the style
- Use of the **Tudor arch** over doorways and fireplaces
- Second-story overhang or *jetty* frequently used
- Sharp **gables**
- **Clustered** or **columned chimneys: buttressed**, stone-end, or simple unembellished
- **Bay windows** (optional)
- Small-paned leaded windows, often diamond shaped, casement windows
- Projecting porch or doorway (optional)

Elizabethan Manor House

During the reign of Elizabeth I (who was a Tudor), the Gothic and Medieval English design in architecture merged with the new Dutch influence, resulting in the great ornate-gabled house known as the *Elizabethan.*

FIGURE 12.13 Adam Thoroughgood House (ca. 1636), Norfolk, Virginia. The oldest brick house in America, with a style reminiscent of its English ancestry. (Courtesy of Haycox Photoramic, Inc., Norfolk, Virginia.)

FIGURE 12.14 Tudor/Elizabethan style.

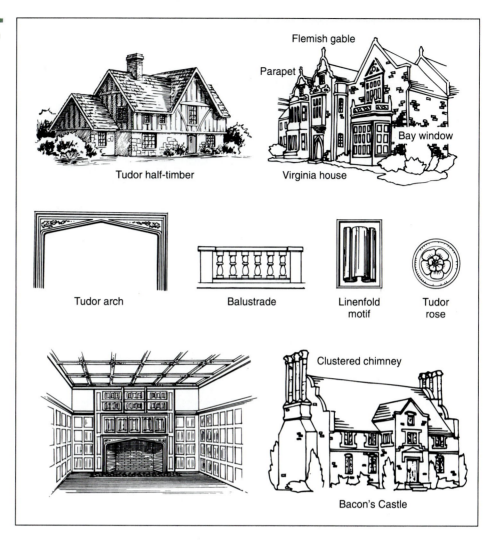

Flemish gable
Parapet
Bay window
Tudor half-timber
Virginia house
Tudor arch
Balustrade
Linenfold motif
Tudor rose
Clustered chimney
Bacon's Castle

Although elements of the Elizabethan style continued to be popular through the following centuries in England, especially during the **Jacobean period** (the reigns of James I, Charles I, Charles II, and James II in the seventeenth century), the style had little long-lasting influence in America. A fine example of medieval architecture in the Elizabethan style is *Virginia House* in Richmond, Virginia, a majestic structure once the county seat of Warwick, England. Virginia House was moved to America in 1925 and now stands reassembled at Windsor Farms near Richmond, Virginia. Another excellent example of the English manor house reflecting both Elizabethan and Jacobean influence in America is *Bacon's Castle* (1665) in Surrey County, Virginia, with its typical *cross-plan* (plan in the shape of a cross). The English manor house built in the colonies follows the same general style as its prototype in England, with the following features.

EXTERIOR

- Rambling design, often **E**-shaped or employing the English cross-plan, with the two-story projecting entrance
- Large house with two or three stories
- Stone or brick structures most typical (half-timber construction, a carryover from the earlier Tudor period, optional)
- **Flemish gables** and **parapets** reflecting Dutch influence; especially popular in Jacobean England
- **Balustrades** often used on roofline or above windows and edging balconies and terraces
- Bay and oriel windows with small leaded panes
- Doorways recessed; round or Tudor arch framing; Tudor arch, also Gothic arch (optional)
- Numerous clustered chimneys and exterior chimneys common

INTERIOR

- *Simple Tudor homes:* plain plastered walls, sometimes with simple vertical wood paneling; half-timbering often exposed inside
- Large fireplace with heavy wood mantel or Tudor arch and brick interior
- Wide plank wood floors; Tudor arch over doorways optional
- Heavy wood-beam ceilings

FIGURE 12.15 Interior with rich wood paneling, carved chairs, chandelier, and fireplace typical of the English Tudor home. (Courtesy of Stuart Interiors, England.)

- Furniture often handcrafted and simple; some pieces brought from England with typical English carvings
- Simple informal fabrics, typically homespun, cottons, and wools
- *Elizabethan and Jacobean manor homes:* more elegant interior details; wood paneling, bay windows, leaded panes; Tudor arch over doorways
- Wood or stone fireplaces with Tudor arch
- Gothic detailing (optional)
- Wood or stone floors
- Elizabethan and Jacobean furniture and fabrics; some Gothic furniture
- Fabrics: tapestry, crewel embroidery, chintz, leather; rich colors; flame stitch and large flower motifs popular

Figure 12.15 shows an interior of a typical English Tudor home.

Cotswold House

A sixteenth-century English cottage typical of houses in the **Cotswold** area can be seen in Dearborn, Michigan, where it was relocated (see Figure 12.16). These stone houses are often characterized by a front attached chimney, an asymmetrical arrangement, dormer windows, and a low cottage look. Construction of stone in gray and gold tones is typical, although some houses have a light-colored stucco applied over the stone walls. The Cotswold house is a simplified interpretation of the

Tudor and Elizabethan styles. Houses of this type and others of English origin have had an important influence on American domestic architecture from its beginning and from time to time have had a resurgence.

NEW ENGLAND SALTBOX, GARRISON, GAMBREL, AND CAPE COD

The Pilgrims who first landed at Massachusetts Bay for the most part came from a low economic class and were seeking political and religious freedom. Although ill-equipped to meet the hardships that awaited them, they were courageous, vigorous, and devout zealots who responded to the challenge of establishing a home in a harsh and unknown land. The Pilgrims' first shelters were similar to those of the Jamestown settlers—little more than dugouts or crude huts of boughs covered with clay (wattle and daub). Yet by the middle of the seventeenth century their homes had a surprising degree of comfort.

Because the land was heavily wooded and had to be cleared for dwellings, wood was the logical choice for construction material. In addition, adequate tools were in short supply, and speed in construction was a necessity. These two factors accounted for distinctive characteristics of the seventeenth-century New England house: *wood construction* and *simplicity*. Early houses, which were built from memory, were derived from English folk architecture of the late Medieval and Elizabethan periods. Through the forthright use of local materials and necessary **adaptations**, the result was a unique provincialism expressing the vigor of the early colonists. Fortunately, the sharp gables, steep roofs, large chimneys, and small-paned windows, to which the colonists had been accustomed, were practical for the severe New England climate.

The strong Tudor and Elizabethan influences in early New England architecture can be seen in many of the seventeenth-century houses that are still standing. A New England parsonage in Springfield, Massachusetts, built in 1639 of half-timber construction and with a projecting tower, reveals its English ancestry.

A unique example of a stone house in the medieval tradition is *Old Stone House* in Guilford, Connecticut. Built in 1639, its 2-ft-thick walls are made of local stone and mortar mixed with yellow clay and pulverized oyster shells. The simple facade with its tiny windows and large exterior chimneys is typical of the English Medieval influence. Stone construction was rare in the area due to a lack of materials. This house remains the oldest stone house in New England and is open to the public.

Important seventeenth-century New England houses reflecting the English Medieval tradition are *Witch House* (1642), *House of Seven Gables* (1668), and *John Ward House* (1684), Salem, Massachusetts; *Whipple House* (1638), and *Strawberry Hill,* or Proctor House (circa 1670), Ipswich, Massachusetts; *Fairbanks House* (1636), Dedham, Massachusetts; and *Ironmaster's House* (1636), Saugus, Massachusetts.

Because of the circumstances peculiar to the environment, homes of the New England settlers, although still retaining medieval features, took on characteristics that became uniquely American.

Half-House

The first houses were but a single room (half-house) with the chimney on the side wall. The door opened into a tiny entrance that abutted the chimney; from there, steep stairs rose to an attic.

Two-Room or Double House

Soon a second room was added on the other side, and the fireplace became the central core of the house. *John Howland House,* built in 1666 in Plymouth, Massachusetts, the only extant house in which Pilgrims once lived, shows the original medieval-like half-house and the 1750 addition, as seen in Figure 12.17. *John Alden House,* built in 1653 (now restored), is an example of a two-room house in the medieval tradition.

The four most common seventeenth-century homes are the saltbox, garrison, gambrel, and Cape Cod. (See Figure 12.18.)

Saltbox

To provide additional space, a *lean-to* that usually became the kitchen was added to the two-room house. Late

FIGURE 12.16 Old Cotswold Cottage, sixteenth-century English Medieval. Reassembled in Dearborn, Michigan. (Courtesy of the Henry Ford Museum, Dearborn, Michigan.)

Historic Heritage of Architecture and Design ▬▬▬▬▬▬▬▬▬▬▬▬▬▬▬▬▬▬▬▬▬▬▬▬ 357

FIGURE 12.17 Howland House (1666), Plymouth, Massachusetts. The only house still standing in Plymouth in which Pilgrims once lived. (Courtesy of the Pilgrim John Howland Society, Plymouth, Massachusetts.)

in the century the lean-to was often part of the original plan. This type of house, called a *saltbox* because the shape resembled the boxes in which settlers stored their salt, became the most characteristic silhouette of many early colonial houses. Three noteworthy examples extant today are *John Quincy Adams House* (1675), Quincy, Massachusetts; *Jethro Coffin House* (1686), Nantucket Island; and *Ogden House* (1690), Fairfield, Connecticut.

Garrison (Jetty)

In many houses the second story extended beyond the first floor, a carryover from medieval England. The overhang, or *jetty*, had end brackets with hand-carved **pendants**. This house is commonly called a *garrison*. The garrison-styled *Parson Capen House* in Topsfield, Massachusetts, built in 1683, is a superb example of medieval framing in America. Three garrison houses of particular interest are *Paul Revere House*, 1650, Boston's oldest house; *John Ward House* (1684), Salem, Massachusetts; and *Scotch-Boardman House* (1651), Saugus, Massachusetts.

FIGURE 12.18 Four seventeenth-century New England houses.

Gambrel

Another modification had a *double-pitched roof* made of two sections of rafters. This roof style was inexpensive to build and permitted more headroom in the attic. The **gambrel roof** is often incorrectly called Dutch colonial. Seventeenth-century examples of the gambrel-roof house are *Fairbanks House* (1636), Dedham, near Boston; *Harlow-Holmes House* (1649), Plymouth, Massachusetts; and *Glebe House* (1690), Woodbury, Connecticut.

Cape Cod (Transitional)

During the final decade of the seventeenth century one of America's best-loved houses made its appearance. This style was an outgrowth of the half-house and the two-room or double house. What has come to be known as the *Cape Cod* was a humble cottage that retained much medieval character. Covered with *clapboards* or shingles, the structure had a *central chimney*, a simple *plank doorway*, and *small-paned windows*—often two on one side of the entrance and one on the other. The Cape Cod derived its name from the great number of these houses built on Cape Cod.

Early in the eighteenth century, the Cape Cod house took on some of the features of early **Georgian** architecture, such as *dormers, dentil-trim, cornices,* impressive end-chimneys, and symmetrically arranged *double-hung windows*. A paneled central doorway had a *transom* (small window above a door or window) of small glass panes topped by a flat cornice. Later in the century, a **pedimented** doorway was sometimes added. The Cape Cod has been one of the most widely copied and adapted houses in America and has proven appropriate for almost any area in the country. Although the style often took on a more formal aspect in the eighteenth century, the quaint seventeenth-century form with the low roofline has persisted virtually unchanged to the present. Two seventeenth-century Cape Cod houses of particular interest are *Jabez Wilder House* (circa 1690), Hingham, Massachusetts, and *Jonathon Kendrick House* (late seven-

FIGURE 12.19   Jonathon Kendrick House (late seventeenth century), South Orleans, Massachusetts, an early Cape Cod style. (Photograph by Arthur Haskell, courtesy of the Library of Congress.)

teenth century), South Orleans, Massachusetts (see Figure 12.19). Two transitional structures built early in the eighteenth century showing the Georgian influence that followed are *Brush-Everard House* and *Raleigh Tavern,* both in Colonial Williamsburg, Virginia. (See Figure 12.20.)

Along with their own distinguishing characteristics, the four seventeenth-century New England houses share a number of features. (See Figure 12.21.)

EXTERIOR

- Rectangular plan
- Wood or shingle construction
- Central chimney
- Small casement windows
- Asymmetrical and symmetrical arrangement
- Simple English medieval character

FIGURE 12.20   Brush-Everard House (1717), an early eighteenth-century transitional style. Tall windows, dormers, and dentil trim show Georgian influence. (Courtesy of the Colonial Williamsburg Foundation.)

FIGURE 12.21 The Oyster Bay Room at the Winterthur Museum reflects a typical 17th century interior: wood plank floors with an Oriental rug, plastered walls, a low beam ceiling, a large fireplace, and simple wood furniture. (Courtesy of Winterthur Museum.)

INTERIOR

- Plain plaster walls or **palisade** (vertical) wood paneling common; **wainscoting** employed
- Exposed beamed ceiling
- Small-paned casement windows with diamond panes or double-hung sash windows
- Wide plank floors (later, Oriental rugs popular)
- Large brick fireplace with cooking utensils
- Furniture often homemade; Windsor chairs; furniture with Elizabethan and Jacobean influences, including the Elizabethan court cupboard, the Carver chair, and the Hadley chest; later, furniture became more elegant
- Fabrics similar to those in Elizabethan and Jacobean manor home typical

THE ENGLISH HERITAGE— THE GEORGIAN PERIOD
(circa 1700–1790)

The period when England was ruled by the Stuarts, roughly the seventeenth century, is divided into three subperiods: (1) Jacobean (1603–1689), (2) William and Mary (1689–1702), and (3) Queen Anne (1702–1714). For the first forty years in the seventeenth century there was little change in English architecture inside or out. Many houses that were started during the Elizabethan period were not completed until well into the seventeenth century and incorporated Jacobean influences.

Then **Inigo Jones** (1573–1652), the prominent English architect of the early seventeenth century, revolutionized English architecture when he introduced the **Renaissance** and **Palladian influence** to England. When Inigo Jones built his *Queen's House* in Greenwich, England, with its unique square plan (the English had been used to the rambling design), a new style evolved. *Sir Christopher Wren* (1632–1723), the great English architect responsible for rebuilding much of London after the Great Fire of 1666, became its foremost exponent. In Wren's capable hands the ideas of Inigo Jones developed into a gracious architectural style (called Queen Anne style in England) adaptable to both manor house and modest dwelling. Because this style flourished during the reigns of the English kings George I, George II, and George III, it became known as *Georgian*. Although Sir Christopher Wren never came to America, his influence was the dominant force in American architecture during the early Georgian period (circa 1700–1750). The later part of the Georgian period was dominated by the *Palladianism* of another eminent English architect, *James Gibbs* (1683–1754).

By the second decade of the eighteenth century, the colonies had grown and the people prospered largely because of the expansion of shipping and commerce. English craftspeople and builders, laden with tools and architectural drawings, arrived in the colonies. There they worked with local craftspeople, and the rugged simplicity of the earlier houses soon gave way to the new and grander Georgian style. (See Figure 12.22.) At the time of the American Revolution, the new style had become familiar in American cities from Jamestown to Portsmouth.

Early Georgian or Wren-Georgian Style (circa 1720–1750)

The Early Georgian house in America retained the basic elements, fine proportions, and symmetry of its English **prototype**, but it took on local differences.

The following are general characteristics of the early Georgian–Wren baroque style. (Also refer to Figure 12.23.)

EXTERIOR

- Influence of English Baroque and Sir Christopher Wren
- Symmetrical **facade** with a general feeling of dignity and formality
- Two to three stories—rectangular block
- Symmetrically placed double-hung (sash) windows with small panes
- Central doorway flanked by **pilasters** and crowned by one of the four pediment forms (see Figure 12.24) reflecting the classical styles of Greece and Rome
- **Hipped roof**, often with a balustrade protecting a **captain's** or **widow's walk**; dormer windows typical, often with shutters
- Tall end chimneys

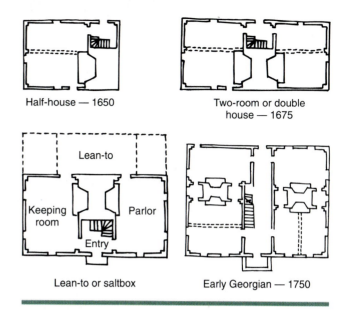

FIGURE 12.22 Development of the New England house.

- Brick, clapboard, or stone construction
- Cornice with dentils or **modillions**
- **Stringcourse** (bands of stone or brick between stories) (optional)
- Corner **quoins** (optional)
- **Cupola** or **belvedere** (optional)
- Gabled or gambrel roof (optional); gambrel roof typical in New England

English craftspeople who arrived in the colonies in the eighteenth century brought with them handbooks for builders, filled with uniform structural information and carefully drawn decorative detail. The widespread dissemination of these manuals accounts in large measure for the similarity seen in the architecture of the period. This style of architecture, commonly known as Georgian, was first seen in the colonies in Virginia, and the earliest structure was the *Wren Building* at William and Mary College in Williamsburg. (According to some, it was designed by Wren himself or by someone in his office, but this has not been documented.) The Wren-Georgian style, however, reached its greatest refinement in the gracious mansions plantation owners built along the lower James River in Virginia. Three splendid and thoroughly English examples of these early eighteenth-century houses, all extant and in a remarkable state of preservation, are *Westover* (1730–1740) and *Carter's Grove* (1750–1753; see Figure 12.25), both of which have side wings that were later additions, and *Berkeley* (1726). Another notable example is the *Governor's Palace* in Williamsburg, Virginia (1706–1720).

As the new style spread, great brick and wood mansions were built in the new Georgian manner, but with regional differences. Rooflines varied from the hipped style to sharp gables and gambrel. Since wood was plentiful, it was the common building material in New

FIGURE 12.23 Early Georgian
(Wren).

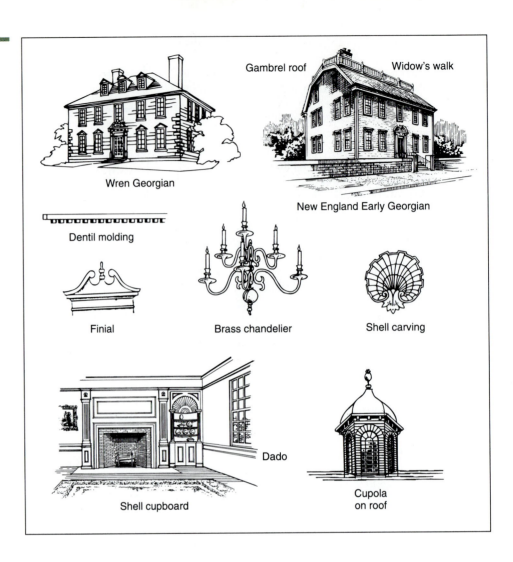

Wren Georgian

Gambrel roof   Widow's walk

New England Early Georgian

Dentil molding

Finial   Brass chandelier   Shell carving

Shell cupboard   Dado   Cupola
on roof

FIGURE 12.24 Pediment forms.

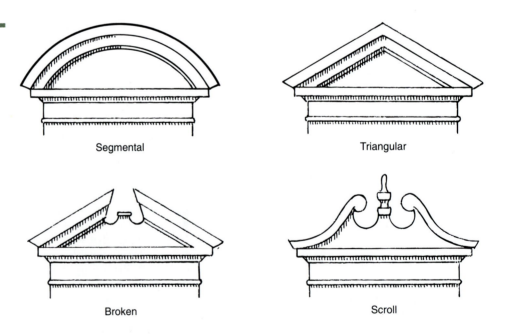

Segmental   Triangular

Broken   Scroll

FIGURE 12.25 Carter's Grove (1750–1783). One of the most beautiful Early Georgian houses in America. The side dependencies, built at a later date, show the Palladian influence. (Courtesy of the Colonial Williamsburg Foundation.)

FIGURE 12.26 Hunter House (1746), Newport, Rhode Island. Typical of the Wren-Georgian style in the North, it ranks among the ten best examples of colonial residential architecture in America. (Photograph by John T. Hopf, courtesy of the Newport County Chamber of Commerce.)

England. Although Georgian houses in the North lacked some of the formal elegance of Southern mansions, they reflected the formal grandeur of the Wren-Georgian style. New Englanders also favored the gambrel roof. Some examples of Wren-Georgian architecture in the North are *MacPheadris-Warner House* (1718–1723), Portsmouth, New Hampshire; *Ropes Memorial* (1719), Salem, Massachusetts; *Hunter House* (1746), Newport, Rhode Island (Figure 12.26); and *Wentworth-Gardner House* (1760), Portsmouth, New Hampshire.

Late Georgian or Gibbs-Palladian Style (circa 1750–1790)

The Roman Palladian style (developed by *Andrea Palladio* (1518–1580), an Italian Renaissance architect), which became popular with the English aristocracy in the early eighteenth century, was introduced to America near the middle of that century, primarily through books. Among the many builders' manuals that made their way to the colonies, perhaps most important was *James Gibbs's A Book of Architecture,* first published in England in 1728 and believed to have reached the new land in 1751. Intended as a pattern book, its simple and conservative style had an immediate appeal to the colonists and exerted a powerful influence on American architecture. Although buildings retained the basic Wren-Georgian style, Gibbs's new Palladianism offered a more monumental quality and greater degree of formality than did earlier buildings.

The following are general characteristics of the late Georgian Palladian style in America.

EXTERIOR

- Features of basic structure essentially Wren-Georgian
- Classical details such as pilasters and pediments
- Central section of facade emphasized by pedimented **pavilion** or breakfront extending above the roofline
- Pavilion sometimes flat, sometimes projecting **portico** form
- Side dependencies or wings connected to the main block, often by open **colonnades**
- **Palladian window** prevalent
- Quoining on corners (optional)
- Pilasters on corners (optional)

In the South the Palladian influence was seen in the symmetrical villalike plan with its central block and side dependencies. Early Georgian structures like Carter's Grove in Virginia often featured wings added when the Wren or Palladian style was in vogue. Some outstanding Palladian houses in the South are *Tyron Palace* (1760), New Bern, North Carolina; *Hammond-Harwood House* (1773–1774), Annapolis, Maryland; and *Miles Brewton House* (1765–1769), Charleston, South Carolina.

In the Middle Atlantic states, side dependencies (when used) were usually detached from the central block. *Mount Pleasant,* built in 1761 in Fairmount Park, Philadelphia, was the most imposing house of the area (see Figure 12.27). Another great mansion with a formal Gibbs facade in Fairmount Park is *Woodford* (1742–1756).

In the North after 1750, wood continued to be the principal material used for construction and side dependencies were rarely added. Only the facades revealed Gibbs's Palladianism with their triangular-topped pavil-

FIGURE 12.27 Mount Pleasant (1761), Fairmount Park, Philadelphia, Pennsylvania. The imposing mansion with its formal Gibbs-style facade was considered one of the grandest in the colonies. (Courtesy of the Convention and Tourist Bureau, Philadelphia, Pennsylvania.)

FIGURE 12.28 Longfellow House (1750), Cambridge, Massachusetts. Its classical detail with the triangular-topped pavilion reveals Gibbs's Palladianism. (Courtesy of the U.S. Department of the Interior, National Park Service.)

ions, the **classical** detail of which was more authentically done than anywhere else in the colonies. Examples of particular merit are *Longfellow House* (1750), Cambridge, Massachusetts (see Figure 12.28); *Lady Pepperell Mansion* (circa 1760), Kittery Point, Maine; *Shelton's Tavern* (1760), Litchfield, Connecticut; and *Jeremiah Lee House* (1768), Marblehead, Massachusetts.

INTERIOR—EARLY WREN AND LATE GEORGIAN PALLADIAN

- Cornices with dentil trim
- Pediments over doorways and mantels
- Painted wood paneling or plaster; stained wood panelling; late Georgian featured more Palladian interior details
- Wallpaper above a **dado**; late Georgian favored continental or Chinese wallpaper
- Wood plank floors with Oriental rugs
- Fireplaces with wood panels and classic details; late Georgian fireplace often has pediment mantel; fireplace has **ears** or square projections at top corners
- Brass or bronze baroque chandeliers
- William and Mary, Queen Anne, and Chippendale furniture; Chippendale especially popular in late Georgian interior (see Figure 12.29)
- Elegant and formal fabrics: damasks, velvets, brocades, etc.
- Prominent colors: rich golds and reds, Williamsburg green, deep gray-blue

NEOCLASSICISM IN AMERICA
(circa 1790–1845)

Neoclassicism in America, which covered the last decade of the eighteenth century and the first four decades of the nineteenth century, is made up of two periods: Federal and **Greek Revival**. Between Georgian Palladianism, Federal, and Greek Revival, however, no clear lines of demarcation exist. Rather, one style gradually blends into the next. Much neoclassicism was communicated to the colonies through books, but also, young men were encouraged to go abroad and study classical architecture. This effort resulted in a group of trained and highly motivated American-born architects. In the early nineteenth century British and French architects began arriving on the scene—among whom English-born *Benjamin Latrobe* (1764–1820) was the first—and European ideas were further infused into American architecture.

Federal Period (circa 1790–1825)

The decades following the revolutionary war were eventful for America. The tendency was to break with anything reflecting English dominance, and interest in French modes grew. Consequently, when the excavation of **Pompeii** captured the interest of French designers during the reign of Louis XVI, as well as the interest of the brothers Robert and James Adam in England, the new classical style rapidly superseded the Georgian. Although America was reluctant to adopt this style from England, the neoclassic designs of English architects and cabinetmakers exerted great influence during the period following the adoption of the Declaration of Independence. The architectural style of the early Federal period, influenced primarily by the designs of the Adam brothers, was concentrated in the North; but the later phase, dominated by *Thomas Jefferson,* occurred in the South.

Two main factors brought about this change in America: (1) the need for an official architecture and (2) Thomas Jefferson's enthusiasm for the new classicism, together with his distaste for English-Georgian architecture.

FIGURE 12.29 The Port Royal Parlor at the Winterthur Museum displays Georgian features including Chippendale furniture with a few Queen Anne pieces, typical wood floors with Oriental rugs, dadoes, cornices with dentil trim, and a chimneypiece with the broken pediment design. (Courtesy of Winterthur Museum.)

Jefferson was a scholar and skillful architect, and his designs for the new *Capitol of Virginia* at Richmond, inspired by the Maison Carré in France, established the columned portico as the essential motif of American official architecture. His home, *Monticello,* inspired by the ancient Pantheon in Rome (refer to Figure 12.4), strongly influenced the design of domestic buildings. Jefferson's support of architects such as Latrobe, who was trained in the new classicism, enabled the classical revival to attain a greater vogue in America than it did in England. Young architects traveled to Greece and Rome, where they took exact measurements of Greek temples and adapted them to American buildings. Throughout America buildings had columns capped with one of the three famous Greek orders (i.e., Doric, Ionic, or Corinthian; refer to Fig-

ure 12.3). Columns also appeared inside, separating rooms and supporting mantels. Triangular pediments were placed over doorways, windows, and fireplaces; **reeding, bead-and-reel, egg-and-dart,** the urn, and all manner of classical decorations were employed both inside and out. Around 1820, Jeffersonian classicism had developed into a full-blown Greek revival. The Wren-Georgian style was not immediately discarded, however. The basic style of the Georgian house continued to be used, and only the details, particularly the addition of the pillared portico, indicated the postrevolutionary date.

In residential work of the Federal period, four names stand out as representing the best American architectural design: *Samuel McIntire* (1757–1811) of Salem, *Charles Bulfinch* (1763–1844) of Boston, *John McComb* of New

FIGURE 12.30 Pingree House (1804), Salem, Massachusetts. A dignified Federal-period mansion designed by Samuel McIntire. (Courtesy of the Chamber of Commerce, Salem, Massachusetts.)

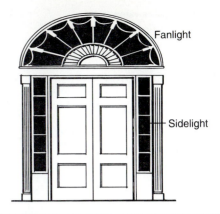

FIGURE 12.31 A doorway in the Neoclassic-Federal style, with sidelights and an elliptical fanlight.

York, and *Benjamin Latrobe* in the South. Among these architects, the first is probably the best known. McIntire planned three-story, square, dignified mansions with exquisite detail and simplicity. McIntire's influence was largely responsible for transforming the small seaport town of Salem, Massachusetts, into the city that became known as the New World Venice. The elegant three-story porticoed homes he designed for well-to-do citizens are considered representative of one of the purest styles of architecture ever developed. (See Figure 12.30.) Salem remains today the most typical example of an American city of the Federal period.

The following are typical characteristics of the Federal-English and Federal-Roman period house.

EXTERIOR — FEDERAL-ENGLISH INFLUENCE

- Influence of Robert Adam and English Georgian architecture
- Influence of Samuel McIntire and Charles Bulfinch
- Influence of ancient Grecian and Roman architecture and detailing
- Three stories high, with smaller third story
- A columned portico in front
- Doorway sidelights (frequently); entrance topped by **elliptical fanlight** (Figure 12.31)
- Delicate classical detail
- Windows crowned by pediments or **jack arch lintels** (optional)
- Stringcourse (optional)
- Flattened hipped roof with balustrade above cornice concealing roof (optional)

EXTERIOR — FEDERAL-ROMAN INFLUENCE

- A rejection of the mannered delicacy of the Adam style associated with the English Georgian architecture
- Expresses qualities of strength and dignity based on architecture of Republican Rome
- Influence of Andrea Palladio and Thomas Jefferson

INTERIOR

- Classical detailing from ancient Greece, Rome, and Pompeii; Adamesque motifs; plaster ceilings with Adam motifs an important feature
- Woodwork usually painted white; wallpaper, often scenic, above a dado (optional)
- Adam mantels
- Crystal chandeliers
- Parquet or wood plank floors; Oriental rugs
- Hepplewhite and Sheraton furniture; Martha Washington chair
- Fabrics: formal and elegant; damasks, silks, velvets, brocades; motifs from ancient Greece and Pompeii and from Democratic America
- Colors: muted blues and greens; soft pinks, yellows, and peaches popular

Excellent residential examples of the Federal period extant today are the *Pierce-Nichols House* (1782) and *Pingree House* (1804), Salem, Massachusetts; *Harrison Gray Otis House* (1796), Boston, Massachusetts; *Monticello* (completed 1769–1809); Charlottesville, Virginia; *Homewood* (circa 1800), Baltimore, Maryland; *Nathaniel Russell House* (1809), Charleston, South Carolina; and the *White House* (present structure completed 1829), Washington, D.C. Figure 12.32 shows details of the Federal style as they appear in the dining room at Monticello.

Greek Revival Period (circa 1825–1845)

Although the Neoclassic style reached the South later than the North, the style of the Greek Revival period—the final phase of neoclassicism—became more predominant in the South than anywhere else. The size and elegance of the plantation mansion, the ample space for expansion, and the luxurious manner of living lent themselves well to the new style (Figure 12.33). The architects in the South did not merely build **replicas** of Grecian temples, but adapted the **classic** style to meet the needs of the hot climate. Two-story columns framed the cool **verandas**, often encircling the entire house. The

FIGURE 12.32 The dining room at Monticello in the Federal style, featuring Hepplewhite furniture and typical woodwork of the period. (Courtesy of the Thomas Jefferson Memorial Foundation, Inc. Photograph by James Tkatch.)

FIGURE 12.33 The Jefferson Davis home in Richmond, Virginia, with its stately two-story columned porch, was one of the first Southern Greek Revival mansions. (Photograph by Richard Gunn.)

magnificent columns were replicas of the classic orders of architecture (see Figure 12.3).

On a more modest scale, the Greek Revival house was a simple pitched-roof structure much like earlier houses, but the short end faced the street (such houses are especially found in Charleston, South Carolina). Authentic Greek details were applied to the front corners. The house had Doric pilasters topped with a flat entablature and pediment displaying a full entablature around the cornice. The door was usually asymmetrically placed, and the entire structure was painted white.

The Greek Revival house is characterized by the following features.

EXTERIOR

- Continued use of Georgian, Federal, and French forms
- Precise adherence to Greek proportions, orders, and ornaments
- Isolated temple form
- Profuse use of two-story columns on more pretentious houses; columns often continue on all sides; second story balcony (optional)
- White exterior typical
- Many or a few steps leading up to the veranda or porch; in damp climates, house raised to accommodate a high basement
- House often built with gable end to street, with or without proper colonnaded portico attachment

- In absence of a portico, placement of pilasters, frieze, and classically framed doorway
- French doors and shutters often used, especially in South
- Sidelights and fanlights continue

INTERIOR

- Grand treatment of classical orders (columns and pilasters)
- Elegant crystal or oil-vessel-type chandeliers; ceiling fan (punkah) used in South
- Fireplace of black or white marble
- Continuation of scenic wallpaper above a dado
- Bold patterned rugs
- Dominant masculine feeling; Empire and Duncan Phyfe furniture; harp a favorite piece; some use of English Regency
- White plaster walls
- White ivory button on newel post signifying paid mortgage
- Colors: Empire green, gold, black and white, rich reds and blues; colors and motifs popular with Napoleon copied
- Fabrics: elegant and formal; velvets, damasks, and brocades

A period room in the Greek Revival style is shown in Figure 12.34. (Refer to Figure 10.1. for a contemporary application of the style.)

FIGURE 12.34 This parlor, from the Empire period, reflects the Greek revival in architecture and furniture. (Winterthur Museum, Wilmington, Delaware.)

FIGURE 12.35 A room from the Palais Paar in Vienna, Austria, displays the influence of the decorative Louis XV rococo style. (The Metropolitan Museum of Art. Purchase, 1963. Funds given by the Charles B. Wrightman Foundation. [63.229.1].)

Some examples of Greek Revival houses are *Andalusia* (1836), Bucks County, Pennsylvania; *Wilcox-Cutts House* (1843), Orwell, Vermont; *Alvin T. Smith House* (1850s), Forest Grove, Oregon; *Stanton Hall* (1852–1857), Natchez, Mississippi; the *Mississippi Governor's Mansion* (1841), Jackson, Mississippi; and *Dunlieth* (1847), Natchez, Mississippi.

OTHER INTERNATIONAL INFLUENCES

French Style (1714–1789)

Rococo Style, Louis XV (circa 1714–1774)

Rococo (a term meaning *rocks and shells*) is a style of art, architecture, and decoration that developed mainly in France during the reign of Louis XV, then spread to the palaces, churches, and residences of the wealthy in Italy, Germany, Austria, and other European countries. The new style was a reaction against the excesses of baroque and classicism in interior decoration more than in architecture. The rococo style reflected the tastes of women at the French court, particularly Madame du Pompadour, a woman of class and refinement. Human comfort and convenience were a concern and an intimate and inviting atmosphere prevailed (Figure 12.35). The following are major characteristics of the rococo style:

- Formal, elegant, intimate, comfortable, visually charming, graceful, feminine, and somewhat frivolous
- Use of delicate decorative details; many surfaces decorated; profuse use of curves, scrolls, and foliage asymmetrically arranged
- Prominent motifs: the shell and Venus; fireplace with shell motif especially popular

- Wooden panels with curved moldings; classical orders used sparingly on both exterior and interior surfaces
- Compared to baroque, lightly scaled furnishings and ornamentation
- Chinese motifs and wallpapers popular
- Pastel colors prevalent
- Rectangular parquet floors with French Aubusson or Savonnerie rugs or Oriental rugs
- Long French doors that allow light to flood the room

French Neoclassic Style, Louis XVI (1760–1789)

The neoclassic court style in France (see Figure 12.36) flourished during the reign of Louis XVI and Marie Antoinette. The principal design influences were ancient Greece, Pompeii, and the work of Robert Adam in England. The design principles of classical Greece and Rome were revived, but applied in more delicate terms. In 1755 the ancient city of Pompeii was discovered and excavations began that excited the design world. The Petite Trianon at Versailles is one of the most important examples of the French neoclassic style along with various rooms at the palace of Versailles. The development of the Louis XVI court style came to a halt with the onslaught of the French Revolution in 1789.

The French neoclassic style is characterized by the following features:

- Formal, delicate, and elegant
- More restraint in ornamentation than rococo style
- Use of straight lines and rectangular forms; curves, when used, precisely formed by the compass; rectangular wood paneled walls often painted with gold or silver finishes

FIGURE 12.36   A room from the Hotel in the cours d'Albret, Bordeaux, with painted oak paneling, reflects the formal and elegant neoclassic Louis XVI style. (The Metropolitan Museum of Art, gift of Mrs. Herbert N. Straus, 1943 [43.158.1].)

FIGURE 12.37 Characteristics of the French country style can be seen in the French ladderback chairs (called *chaise à capucine*) with typical informal plaid fabric, the simple white plastered walls, clay tile floor, French doors, and simplified Louis XV china cabinet. (Courtesy of Century Furniture Company.)

- Classical details and motifs particularly influenced by the decorations of the ancient city of Pompeii and the works of Robert Adam, such as arabesques, urns, and garlands
- Symmetrical balance dominates
- Parquet wood floors and French rugs typical
- Use of pastel colors
- Carved marble fireplace most common
- Tall French windows and double doors

Provincial French or Country French (Eighteenth century–present)

Throughout France the lesser nobility and wealthy merchants copied or adopted the styles of Louis XV and XVI but in an effort to economize, simplified the interiors and furnishings. The emphasis of the country French style focused on comfort, livability, and family life. The rococo style was particularly embraced by the provinces (similar to counties in the United States). American designers have been inspired by the provincial French style, which has recently been popular with clients (see Figure 12.37).

The French House in America

The heartland of America—the area between the Allegheny and the Rocky mountains, from Canada to the Gulf of Mexico—was controlled by France for over a hundred years; yet during this time, little of the area was colonized.

The Norman Cottage

French colonists who came to America in the seventeenth century settled mainly along the St. Lawrence River and in the South along the Mississippi River. The houses they built in the North often had high hipped roofs and rounded corner towers with whitewashed exteriors,

FIGURE 12.38 Abraham Hasbrouck House (1692–1712). One of the original stone houses still standing along Huguenot Street in New Paltz, New York. (Courtesy of the Huguenot Historical Society, New Paltz, New York.)

reminiscent of the **châteaux** and manor houses the colonists had known in France, but greatly simplified. In 1678 French Huguenots founded a settlement in New Paltz, New York. Five of the original stone houses built there are standing today, along what is called Huguenot Street. One of these houses is the *Abraham Hasbrouck House* (1692–1712). (See Figure 12.38.)

The French Plantation House

In the South the basic structure of the northern cottage was retained and adapted to the climate by the addition of an encircling **galerie** or porch covered by a broad **bonnet roof** (see Figure 12.39). The roof provided shelter from frequent rains and gave a pavilionlike appear-

ance. Another practical adaptation was raising the house to allow an air passage underneath, which helped to keep the house dry and cool. Because of the high water table, use of basements was impossible. A further variation was the raised cottage, in which the ground floor was built of brick or stone, topped by a white plastered wooden pavilion. *French doors* opened on all sides onto the porch, which served as a hallway.

With the passage of time, new architectural influences could be seen in the evolution of the French house. The masonry wall of the lower floor was replaced by posts that supported an encircling balcony. When neoclassicism swept the country, posts gave way to classical columns on both upper and lower stories and windows were surmounted by pediments.

FIGURE 12.39 French plantation house styles.

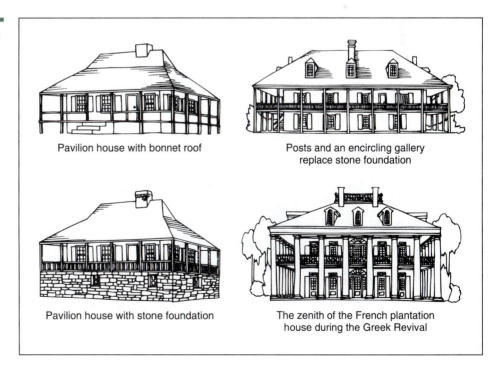

Pavilion house with bonnet roof

Posts and an encircling gallery replace stone foundation

Pavilion house with stone foundation

The zenith of the French plantation house during the Greek Revival

During the prosperous decades that preceded the Civil War, the Greek Revival period reached its zenith in the great plantation mansions of the South. Two-story Greek columns swept from ground to roofline. Delicate wooden balustrades enclosed upper galleries and rooftops. Graceful fanlights crowned the doors. What had begun as a modest French farmhouse had blossomed into the **antebellum** mansion of exquisite beauty and grandeur.

The Gallery House

The tiny French Cajun cottage, with its front porch protected by an overhanging roof, was the original gallery house. As the Cajun cottage evolved, it was enlarged and a second-story gallery was added on the front. As it was further embellished, it developed into the full-blown Greek Revival style characterizing many southern mansions. Some of the magnificent antebellum mansions that have survived are *Shadows-on-the-Teche* (1830), New Iberia, Louisiana (see Figure 12.40); *Oak Alley* (1836), St. James Parish, Louisiana; *San Francisco* (1849), Lower Mississippi, Louisiana; *Dunlieth* (1847), Natchez, Mississippi; and *Houmas* (circa 1840s), north of New Orleans, Louisiana.

The French Town House

The galleries of the French town house faced away from the street onto a private courtyard. The ground floor was used for shops or utilitarian purposes; the family quarters were above. Lacy cast-iron balconies facing the street were added in the nineteenth century, which gave the *Old French Quarter* of New Orleans a flavor of French architecture found nowhere else in America.

Over the years, houses recalling original French city houses, manors, and cottages have been built in America

FIGURE 12.40 Shadows-on-the-Teche (1830), New Iberia, Louisiana. A fabled and beautiful southern Greek Revival mansion with the typical French gallery. (Photograph by Gleason, courtesy of the National Trust for Historic Preservation, Washington, D.C.)

adopting various prominent features and even combining characteristics from the originals to suit contemporary needs and tastes. In more recent years many distinctive American modifications of the French house have been developed, and this style direction continues to be popular. (See Figure 12.41.)

Four general French exterior styles based on original prototypes have emerged and are known under the following names:

LOUISIANA FRENCH

- High raised basement to protect from floods and dampness
- High steep-hipped roof with or without dormers
- Tall decorative chimney on each end
- French windows and shutters
- Porch with one-story columns
- Lacy ironwork (originally added during the Victorian era)

FRENCH CITY HOUSE

- Formal, dignified, bisymmetrical design
- High hipped roof
- Windows breaking line of **eaves**
- Delicate stucco or painted brick
- Lacy ironwork (frequently)
- Central doorway, often recessed
- Quoining (frequently)

FRENCH MANOR HOUSE

- Style a combination of simple chateau and glorified farmhouse, usually built like shallow horseshoe around three sides of courtyard
- **Dovecote** roofs on wings
- Mansard roof with dormers on central structure
- French windows on main floor; use of shutters
- Beautifully symmetrical
- Brick painted in delicate colors
- Quoining (optional)

FRENCH COTTAGE

- Low hipped or dovecote roof (or both)
- Asymmetrical design
- Recessed double doors (frequently)
- French windows and shutters
- Small **U**-shaped courtyard at entrance
- Quoining (frequently)
- Lacy wrought-iron work (optional)

Some interior treatment characteristics that are typical of the various French styles are known in America as French provincial, provincial French, or country French (see Figure 12.37).

INTERIORS — COUNTRY OR PROVINCIAL FRENCH STYLES

- Adaptation of Court French, but in simpler terms
- Painted or wood paneling for wall treatment—not as ornate as Court French; plain plaster walls for a typical country feeling

FIGURE 12.41 American 20th Century adaptations of the French house.

Louisiana French—raised basement

French city house

French manor

French cottage

- French doors
- Fireplace similar to Court French (rococo), but not as decorated, or a hooded fireplace
- Floor treatment same as Court French; also terra-cotta tile and braided rugs typical for a country look
- Use of simplified Louis XV furniture; wood finishes; armoire was important piece; salamander ladderback chairs
- Cottons, linens, and informal textiles; motifs associated with French themes; checks and stripes; small quaint prints; toile de Jouy

Currently there is great flexibility and freedom in designing American homes employing French styles. The characteristics just listed can be incorporated into today's French-style home to provide an authentic feeling of original treatments. Contemporary French homes often employ only a suggestion of authentic French structures, interior backgrounds, and furnishings to reflect the owner's personal preferences and living style.

Dutch Influences

In 1650 Dutch settlements were well established throughout the regions of Manhattan Island (which Dutch settlers named New Amsterdam), New Jersey, and Delaware. Although Dutch domination was brief, Albany, New York, still reflects Flemish influence in the few remaining houses with **stepped gables** (or crow-stepped gables) and **Flemish gables**. Some early Dutch homes had distinctive patterned brickwork on one or both sides of the structure. Dutch houses built in the countryside were usually constructed of fieldstone, shingle, or clapboard

and typically had high gable ends with a long sweeping roofline extending over a full-length porch (the flowing eave). The early Dutch gambrel, or **bell gambrel**, had a high breaking point just below the ridgeline; later it was dropped to its final position.

Four notable examples of the Dutch house in America are *Van Cortlandt Manor*, Croton-on-Hudson, New York, begun in 1665, now authentically restored (see Figure 12.42); *Van Rensselaer Manor* (1650), Hudson River, opposite Albany; *Dyckman House* (1783), New York, New York; and *Richard Vreeland House*, Leonia, New Jersey, built circa 1786.

German Style

German colonists who settled in Pennsylvania built a variety of homes reflecting medieval features, ranging from simple log cabins to half-timbered homes (called *Fachwerkbau*) to large stone manors. Structures most identified with the German contribution during the eighteenth century are homes built of local fieldstone with 2-ft-thick walls. The typical roof was steeply pitched, but the gambrel was sometimes used. A distinguishing feature found in some German houses was a sheltering hood between the first and second stories, known as a **pent roof**. Often the owner's place of business or the barn was integrated into the home. Examples of stone houses built by the Pennsylvania Germans, mistakenly referred to as Pennsylvania Dutch (Deutsch), are *Ingham Manor* (circa 1750), Bucks County, Pennsylvania; *Thompson-Neeley House* (1701), Washington Crossing, Pennsylvania; *Squire Boone House* (home of Daniel Boone), Baumstown, Pennsylva-

FIGURE 12.42 Van Cortlandt Manor, a restored Revolutionary War estate in Croton-on-Hudson, New York. Built of fieldstone with characteristic long, sweeping Dutch roofline extending over full-length porch. (Courtesy of Sleepy Hollow Restorations, Tarrytown, New York.)

nia (circa 1735); and *Georg Mueller House,* Milbach, Pennsylvania (1752).

Swedish Style

Swedish colonists who settled in the Delaware Valley in 1638 introduced the *log cabin* to America, although it was also familiar to the German settlers. Log construction, however, was borrowed to only a limited extent on the eastern seaboard. With the opening of new wilderness areas for colonization, particularly with the westward movement, the log cabin, with its numerous adaptations, became the standard dwelling. Swedish colonists also built stone houses, often with gambrel roofs, large endchimneys, and dormers. Three of the few authenticated early Swedish houses extant are *John Morton Homestead* (log; 1654), New Prospect Park, Pennsylvania;

Hendrickson House (1690), Delaware Valley, Pennsylvania; and *Keith House* (1722), Graeme Park, Pennsylvania (see Figure 12.43).

In the twentieth century the log cabin has enjoyed a revival. This method of log construction has been employed for everything from simple vacation homes to millionaires' cabins. One example of an extravagant log cabin is *Sagamore Lodge,* vacation home of Alfred Gwynne Vanderbilt, Adirondack Mountains, New York (1893).

Interiors of Dutch, German, and Swedish Houses

Dutch, German, and Scandinavian settlers' crafts contributions were perhaps more influential than the various homes they built. Handcrafted furniture was often painted with delightful and colorful motifs from the

FIGURE 12.43 Keith House (1722), Graeme Park, Montgomery County, Pennsylvania. Representative of the work of Swedish artisans, who built this structure from native fieldstone. (Courtesy of the Pennsylvania Historical and Museum Commission.)

homeland. Tole painting, handmade quilts, stenciling, glass design, pottery, and other decorative crafts were beautifully designed and today have become an important inspiration for the current Crafts Revival in America.

THE VICTORIAN ERA
(circa 1837–1900)

Architecture of the Industrial Age coincided with the reign of *Queen Victoria* and bears her name. Nostalgia for buildings of the past pervaded America during this time, expressing itself in an unprecedented monopoly over other architectural styles. The revival of interest in Victorian architecture led to years of harsh criticism. The style has long been maligned and held in disrepute, having been referred to as the "battle of the styles," among other derogatory terms.

In recent years, however, many authorities have regarded Victorian architecture as inventive, full of vigor and diversity, and representative of a coherent and unified course of development. Today many individuals believe architecture of the nineteenth century is particularly American and represents the most significant style in our nation's history. Americans have rediscovered these picturesque yet long-neglected Victorian dwellings and have remodeled or restored them for private or commercial use. Numerous Victorian homes have also been restored and opened to the public. The heritage of Victorian houses has again gained nationwide appreciation.

During the second half of the nineteenth century, through, a rapid succession of overlapping modes, four major architectural styles emerged: Gothic, Italianate, Mansardic (Second Empire), and Queen Anne. Five additional Victorian designs popular during the period were the Octagonal, Exotic, Stick, Romanesque Revival, and Shingle styles.

Gothic Revival (1840s–1880s)

Andrew Jackson Downing (1803–1892) is considered the father of the Gothic Revival in America. Since stone, the material used in English Gothic, was costly and stonemasons were few, Downing translated the English stone Gothic into wood, and the style became known as *Carpenter Gothic.* (See Figure 12.44.) Thousands of these houses, many of which are still standing, were built throughout the country from the 1840s to 1860s. The Gothic Revival also includes houses built of stone employing Gothic detailing.

The following are general characteristics of the Gothic Revival and Carpenter Gothic styles.

- Use of Gothic arch; Tudor arch (optional)
- Broken, picturesque exterior, planned from inside out
- Steep gables; finials on roof (optional)

FIGURE 12.44 Carpenter Gothic.

- Porches leading to informal gardens
- Lofty windows, often pointed; leaded windows
- Carpenter Gothic: wood sheathing, often **board and batten** (vertical boards)
- Carpenter Gothic: *bargeboard* or *vergeboard* (shaped wooden edging) under gables
- Carpenter Gothic: "**gingerbread**" decoration in gables (from stone **tracery**, which consisted of ornate patterns in the pointed arches of Gothic architecture)

One famous Gothic Revival structure from the period is *Lyndhurst,* built from 1838 to 1841 in Tarrytown, New York, overlooking the Hudson River (see Figure 12.45). A well-known Carpenter Gothic structure is now a bed-and-breakfast establishment: *The Abbey* in Cape May, New Jersey.

Italianate Style (1830–1890s/1920s)

In the 1830s America's admiration for the Italian arts resulted in popularity for the modified Italian **villa.** Used for both urban and suburban dwellings, including town houses, the Italianate style remained popular for 100 years and left a lasting imprint on American architecture. A later development was a cube-shaped house, but the tower—called a cupola, belvedere, or observatory—continued as the most distinctive feature. A wealth of Italianate dwellings are found in northern California, the Midwest, and the Northwest.

The following are general characteristics of the Italianate style. (Also refer to Figure 12.46.)

- Stately structures with vertical emphasis
- Low-pitched or low-hipped overhanging roof supported with large decorative brackets
- Free arrangement of bold square or rectangular blocks; structure topped by a square tower (belvedere or cupola) built for pleasure rather than utility
- Easy access to outdoor terraces
- Windows topped with pediments, fanciful crowns, hoods, or "eyebrows"
- Small entry porches (optional)
- Use of the Italian arch and columns
- Bay windows

FIGURE 12.45 Dining room at Lyndhurst with carved Gothic style furniture and detailing. (Courtesy of the National Trust for Historic Preservation, Washington, D.C.)

Mansard or General Grant Style (1850s–1880s)

The **mansard roof**, which François Mansart introduced in France in the 1600s, was the answer to many architectural problems. The roof was adaptable, took a variety of shapes and sizes, and provided more efficient use of space. The style is also known as the General Grant style after President Ulysses S. Grant. An excellent example of the French Mansard style is the *Governor's Mansion,* 1871, in Jefferson City, Missouri.

The Mansard house is characterized by the following. (Also refer to Figure 12.47.)

- Stately structure, rectangular or square form, towers (optional)
- Tall French windows opening onto deep porches; windows often topped with decorative pediments or crowns

FIGURE 12.46 Italianate Victorian.

- Dormer windows break the roofline (optional)
- Crowned by a steep sloping mansard roof; massive cornices with brackets smaller than Italianate; roofline frequently topped by iron cresting (wrought iron railing) and finials; colored-tile patterns (optional)
- Quoining on corners and stringcourse (belt course) typical

Queen Anne Style (1870s–1880s)

The most whimsical of the Victorian era's eclectic styles was the so-called Queen Anne. This style had no relationship to Queen Anne of England and was a deliberate imitation of many defunct architectural styles.

The Queen Anne style, with its full range of architectural detailing, has some identifying features.

- All manner of decorative wood and plaster detailings, including gingerbread, festoons, spindles, brackets, vergeboards, patterned shingles, and belt courses
- Variable heights and shapes; sometimes built on grand scale
- **Fish-scale shingles** common (in the form of overlapping fish scales)
- Numerous steps leading up to porch; porches often circular with **colonnettes** and turned railings
- Windows grouped in banks, with upper panes often colored
- Most distinctive feature is circular or square tower extending from ground level to all floors, topped with a cone-shaped roof; many other projections including bay windows, balconies, porches, and turrets

Two examples are the *Clevenger-McConaha House* (circa 1887) in Centerville, Indiana, and the *Whitmore*

FIGURE 12.47 Mansard Victorian.

Mansion (1898), in Nephi, Utah. A famous nonresidential Queen Anne structure is the Hotel del Coronado in Coronado, California (see Figure 12.48).

In addition to the four major Victorian styles, another five design directions were prevalent during the period: the Octagonal, Exotic, Stick, Romanesque Revival, and Shingle styles.

Octagonal (1850s– 1870s)

Only a few hundred homes remain standing today that exhibit the octagonal plan. The *Orson Squire Fowler House* (1848–1858), Fishkill, New York and the *Dewey-*

Jenkins House (1855), Milwaukee, Wisconsin are two good examples of the Octagonal style. Outstanding features of the Octagonal style are:

■ An eight-sided architectural form (sometimes either fewer or more sides used)
■ Topped with a cupola
■ Accompanying features: a high basement, a low-hipped roof topping the octagonal, quoining, porches, balustrades, and decorative features found on other Victorian styles

Exotic Revival (1835–1890)

In the 1830s to 1890s some architects and builders were fascinated with "exotic" styles from "exotic" places. The most prevalent revivals in America include the Middle-Eastern influence and Swiss Chalet. One of the best known of Exotic-style Victorian mansions is *Alana* (1872), a majestic Persian castle on the Hudson River in New York, and the *Vedanta Society Headquarters* (turn of the century) in San Francisco, California. Features include the following:

■ *Swiss Chalet:* Extravagant use of gingerbread; porches; balustrades; steeply pitched roof (Swiss style often used for resort homes on the eastern seacoast)

FIGURE 12.48 The Hotel del Coronado is an example of Queen Anne Victorian. (Courtesy of the Hotel del Coronado, Coronado, California.)

- *Middle-Eastern:* Particularly Turkish and Moorish themes; onion domes; mosque arches; intricate oriental detailing

Stick Style (1860–1890)

The Stick style is easily recognizable by the decorative stickwork applied to the walls of the structure. With its half-timbered effect, the Stick style comes close to being identified as a Tudor style. This type of house was built particularly in the northeastern and northwestern parts of the United States. The *J. N. A. Griswold House* (1863), in Newport, Rhode Island, is a fine example of the Stick style. Often the *William Carson House* (1885), in Eureka, California, is labeled by historians as the Stick style and sometimes as Queen Anne and High Victorian Eclectic. Regardless of its label, the Carson House is one of the most delightful Victorian homes in the nation. Typical distinctive features of the Stick style include the following:

- Horizontal, vertical, or diagonal wood strips applied on top of exterior walls of plaster, shingles, or clapboard
- Porch, often with Y-shaped supports; turned column supports (frequently)
- Steeply gabled roof with clustered chimneys
- Brackets, balustrades, pendants, dormers, and decorative trusses
- Towers (optional)

Romanesque Revival

The Romanesque Revival style was introduced by *Henry Hobson Richardson* (1838–1886), who is considered one of the most important early modern architects in America (see Chapter 13). He borrowed features from the Medieval Romanesque period and incorporated them into his clean structural (simple, devoid of historic details) buildings. One of his finest residential works is the *John J. Glessner House* (1885–1887) in Chicago, Illinois, recently restored and opened to the public. Richardson's Romanesque designs, widely copied during the Victorian period by numerous architects, have the following features:

- Massive stone masonry with a rusticated surface
- Use of the heavy Roman arch, especially over the doorway
- Emphasis on the horizontal line
- Strong, solid, and simple structure with no ornamentation

Shingle Style (1880–1900)

The Shingle style is considered to be the last of the Victorian styles and is recognized by shingles everywhere on the exterior. The style originated in New England, but soon the approach was used across the nation. Henry Hobson Richardson also was a prominent exponent of the Shingle style. Three outstanding examples are the *John Bryant House* (1880), Cohasset, Massachusetts; *Kragsyde* (1884), Manchester-by-the-Sea, Massachusetts; and the *William Low House* (1887), Bristol, Rhode Island. Features of the Shingle style include:

- Exterior of shingles, usually found on all wall surfaces and either stained dark brown, painted white, or weathered gray
- Simple structure with little or no decoration
- Roofs include hipped, steep-pitched, turrets, and other styles
- Porches extend across front and often wrap around sides
- Romanesque arches, bays, towers, dormers, and balustrades (optional)

Victorian Interiors

Interiors during the Victorian period varied from region to region in the United States, but generally the feeling was similar and included the following characteristics. (See Figure 12.49 for a contemporary interpretation of a Victorian interior.)

- A variety and profusion of patterned wallpaper, fabrics, carpets, and rugs; flower motifs particularly favored; velvets, damasks, brocades, and other formal fabrics; rich gold, mauve, red, and purple especially popular
- Window treatments included lace casements, elegant tied-back side draperies; topped with an ornate metal crown or valance
- Fireplaces ornately designed; marble and round-headed fireplaces popular; mirrors with gilded or large carved wooden frames over fireplace
- Furniture massive and heavily carved, drawing themes from Gothic, French, Italian, and other styles of the past; marble tops on casepieces; Belter and Eastlake designs
- Accessories everywhere; wax flowers under glass, stereo viewers, family portraits and other pictures (often hung on long cords), knickknacks and personal collections of all kinds displayed
- Lighting: heavy chandeliers of crystal, brass, colorful tinted glass, and white opaline glass balls typical; electrified gasolier in many designs

Beaux Arts Mansions

Beginning in the early 1880s, a revival of Old World styles left a legacy of Victorian extravagance in many areas of the country, concentrated especially in New York State; Newport, Rhode Island; and Florida. *William Kissam Vanderbilt's* elegant château on Fifth Avenue in New York City, built in 1881, triggered the building of extravagant architecture by a few powerful, wealthy American families.

The name *Beaux Arts* was applied to this style after the world-famous design school *L'École des Beaux Arts* in Paris, a school dedicated to promoting architectural styles of the past. *Richard Morris Hunt* (1827–95), one of the first American architects to train at L'École des Beaux Arts, was the most prominent designer of this opulent style. The architectural firm of *McKim, Mead & White* soon followed Hunt as popular designers in this direction, creating fabulous mansions employing magnificent use of past styles. The rage for palatial mansions was also inspired by flamboyant Victorian architecture and supported by world-traveling Americans who wanted to imitate the castle-lined Rhine River in Germany and the Loire River in France. On every eminence was erected a Greek temple, an Italian villa, a medieval fortress, a Tudor manor house, a French château, or a dwelling with Near Eastern influence. Soon the Beaux Arts mansions inspired further building in other metropolitan areas of the United States, especially in Chicago, Philadelphia, Washington, D.C., and southern California.

The style remained popular in America during the jazz age but generally died out with the stock market crash and Great Depression in the 1930s. Many structures in this style have been victims of twentieth-century "progress." Others, through the concerned efforts of dedicated individuals and organizations, remain as monu-

FIGURE 12.49 A contemporary Victorian interior, designed by Michael R. LaRocca, demonstrates the eclectic look so popular during the latter half of the 19th century. Tudor, Moorish, French, and Greek Revival are the principal styles employed. The patterned rug, numerous accessories, and the chandelier further convey the Victorian feeling. (Courtesy of F. J. Hakimian, Inc., N.Y. and Michael R. LaRocca, Ltd. Photograph by Phillip Ennis.)

FIGURE 12.50 Lavishly decorated dining room at The Breakers, the summer "cottage" of the Vanderbilt family in Newport, Rhode Island. (Courtesy of The Preservation Society of Newport County, Newport, R.I. Photograph by John T. Hopf.)

ments to Beaux Arts architecture. A few of the best-known Beaux Arts palaces are:

- *The Breakers* (1892–1895), Newport, Rhode Island; Richard Morris Hunt, architect; an enormous Italian villa known as the "summer cottage," the palatial home of Cornelius Vanderbilt II (see Figure 12.50)
- *Marble House* (1892), Newport, Rhode Island; Richard Morris Hunt, architect; a French neoclassically designed "summer cottage" patterned after the Petit Trianon at the Palace of Versailles; the residence of William Kissam Vanderbilt (see Figure 12.51)
- *Elms* (1901), Newport, Rhode Island; one of the finest examples of an eighteenth-century French château in the United States; summer home of coal magnate Edward Berwind
- *Viz-Caya,* Miami, Florida; a splendid Italian mansion built of some pieces from original Italian villas; residence of James Deering
- *Ringling Mansion,* Sarasota, Florida; a pink mansion for the owner of the Ringling Circus, patterned after the Doges' Palace in Venice
- *Biltmore House* (1888–1895), Asheville, North Carolina; Richard Morris Hunt, architect; an extraordinary French château built for George Washington Vanderbilt (Figures 12.52 and 12.53)
- *Hearst Castle* (1919), San Simeon, California; home of publishing magnate William Randolph Hearst; a Hispano-Moresque palace filled with European treasures

All of the Beaux Arts mansions just listed are open to the public.

Traditional Styles Revived

Although the palatial Beaux Arts homes were suitable for the very wealthy, they were hardly affordable for the rest of America. Many beautiful traditionally styled homes were also built during the Beaux Arts period capturing styles of the past interpreted in simpler terms. These smaller and more affordable homes were introduced in 1886 when McKim, Mead & White designed a formal Georgian Revival home for H. A. C. Taylor. Traditional styles particularly popular were Spanish Colonial, Georgian Colonial, Greek Revival, English Tudor, French Colonial, and Italian Renaissance. The preference for traditional styles continues today throughout the country, interpreted in countless variations. For example, since the years when colonial architecture was developed and refined, its popularity has never ceased throughout the United States, especially with respect to the small home. Although building materials may vary in different areas, this need not alter the inherent charm found in the original styles. Because colonial styles depend so little on ornamentation and so much on proportion and scale for their beauty, they must be expertly designed and built.

When confronted with designing contemporary traditional homes, the architect today is generally influenced by features of original prototypes but will often reinterpret and adapt a style in numerous ways suitable for current living conditions. Well-designed homes based on styles of the past are appropriate for many areas of the country and never seem to become outdated.

PRESERVING OUR ARCHITECTURAL HERITAGE

Only during the past 20 to 30 years has the preservation of our architectural heritage generated widespread interest. Some earlier reconstructed villages—notably *Colonial Williamsburg* in Virginia, *Sturbridge Village* in Massachusetts, and *Strawberry Banke* in Portsmouth, New Hampshire—have for some Americans created a nostalgic curiosity about the legacy of our nation. Many houses, some of which are featured in this chapter, have been

FIGURE 12.51 Marble House (1892), Newport, Rhode Island. A lavish Beaux Arts mansion modeled after the Petit Trianon in Versailles, France. (Photograph by John T. Hopf, courtesy of the Newport County Chamber of Commerce.)

authentically restored and opened to the public. Hundreds of homes have been preserved, but thousands have been destroyed. Magnificent structures built to stand for hundreds of years have fallen before the bulldozer.

Perhaps the most important towns surviving today with much of their early architecture extant are Ipswich and Salem, Massachusetts; Portsmouth, New Hampshire; Newport, Rhode Island; Williamsburg, Virginia; Charleston, South Carolina; Savannah, Georgia; Natchez, Mississippi; and New Orleans, Louisiana. *Ipswich*, Massachusetts, probably has the most seventeenth-century houses. *Salem* is well known for its imposing Federal-period mansions. Many designed by McIntire border famed Chestnut Street, once reputed to be the "handsomest street in America." *Newport*, once known as the "Athens of the New World," claims the distinction of having more

prerevolutionary buildings (about 300) than any other community in the United States. In *Portsmouth*, however, the most complete and well-preserved record remains. The houses range from simple structures with weathered siding and shingles to large elaborately designed and decorated houses of the Georgian and early Federal periods. *Charleston* has preserved more of the beauty of its rich historical background than perhaps any other colonial city on the continent. In no other city in the United States are there so many superbly built and exquisitely decorated southern-style homes. Once every year the Charleston Historic Foundation sponsors Open-House Days, during which many private homes are open to the public. Every March, *Natchez*, a romantic antebellum city, recreates the charm of plantation living by opening some 30 of its great houses to the public.

FIGURE 12.52 Biltmore House (1888–1895), the Beaux Arts mansion built by architect Richard Morris Hunt for George W. Vanderbilt and patterned after a French Renaissance château. (Courtesy of Biltmore House and Gardens.)

FIGURE 12.53 In the opulent banquet hall at Biltmore House, the ceiling arches rise 70 ft above the 72′ × 42′ room. (Courtesy of Biltmore House and Gardens.)

In the past, individuals interested in old structures were sometimes looked on as eccentric. This attitude is changing, however. Throughout the country, organizations have been established to locate, research, and preserve old buildings in local communities. The concern of these organizations is not limited to impressive public buildings and distinguished mansions; their interest extends to all structures—old mills, candy factories, even whole neighborhoods—provided that these buildings have documented historic value. Many of these organized groups are made up of young people who are finding in their architectural heritage a sense of permanency and a connection to the past.

The *National Trust for Historic Preservation* in Washington, D.C., founded in 1949, is the largest organization in the country devoted to the preservation of historic buildings, districts, and neighborhoods. A private entity sustained by public and private contributions, the National Trust maintains historic buildings as museums, disseminates information about preservation to property owners and to the public at large, and assists in a variety of preservation, restoration, and rehabilitation efforts around the country. Local chapters have been organized in cities and counties throughout the country. Many sites continue to be designated as historic landmarks for preservation and restoration.

The *Victorian Society of America,* founded in the late 1960s, has local chapters from coast to coast. Members of this organization are dedicated to preservation of the architecture and decorative arts of the nineteenth and early twentieth centuries. Their efforts are predicated on the belief that the Victorian era was the most typically American era in our country's history.

The present trend of preserving America's past continues to gain momentum. Although thousands of impressive historical buildings have needlessly been destroyed, many others can and have been saved. Restoration involves experts in many areas including research, history, design, and craftsmanship. Of course, adequate funding is necessary to execute each project.

Enthusiasts of American architectural history, those interested in America's cultural heritage, and casual observers can view houses from every period today thanks to the efforts of many organizations and individuals. A considerable number of these houses are in their original form, and others have been restored. Many are furnished in the authentic style of the time in which they were built and are open to the public.

CHAPTER 13

Modern Architecture and Design

FIGURE 13.1 Frank Lloyd Wright's modern residential design, Falling Water (1936), in Mill Run, PA, was built over a waterfall and demonstrates the architect's philosophy: "A house should grow out of the land." (Courtesy of the Western Pennsylvania Conservancy.)

Beginnings of Modernism

The Industrial Revolution and the Beginnings of Modernism

Michael Thonet

Principal Early Modern Movements (Latter Half of Nineteenth Century)

Arts and Crafts Movement

Arts and Crafts Movement in America

Art Nouveau

The Chicago School

Principal Modern Movements (Early Twentieth Century)

Organic Architecture (circa 1894 to present)

The International Style (Turn of Century to Present)

Art Deco (circa 1920s–1940)

Post–World War II Modernism

The Traditional Japanese House

Chinese Influence in Western Interiors

Current Trends

Trends in Residential and Nonresidential Design

Options for Prospective Home Owners in the 1990s

The Custom-Designed House

The Predesigned Home Plan

The Factory-Built (Prefabricated) House

Shell Framing

The Tract Home

The Condominium

Remodeling and Restoring a House

The Energy-Efficient House

The Solar House

The Earth-Sheltered House

Looking to the Future

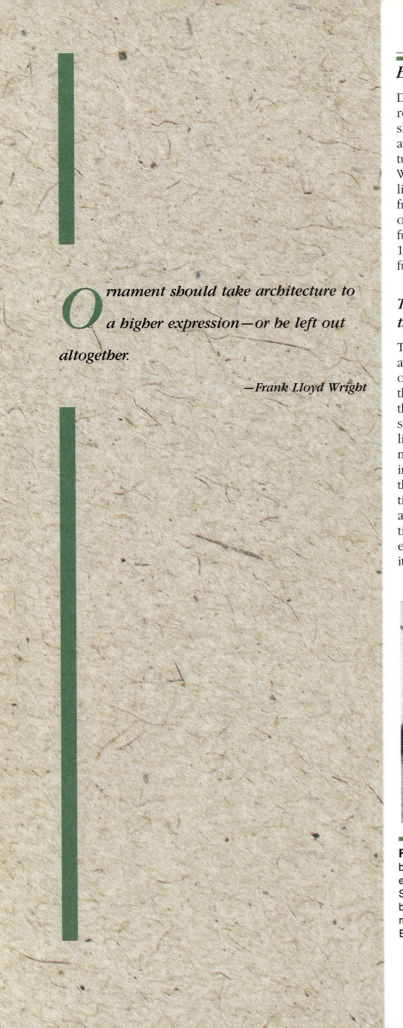

*O*rnament should take architecture to a higher expression—or be left out altogether.

—*Frank Lloyd Wright*

BEGINNINGS OF MODERNISM

During the 1880s, many designers in the United States rebelled against nineteenth-century eclecticism and enslavement to the past—a reaction first seen in Europe—and a completely new house form evolved (leading eventually to such classics of modern design as Frank Lloyd Wright's Falling Water house, shown in Figure 13.1). Earlier, however, the Shakers, a religious order in America from the last quarter of the eighteenth century, felt decoration was wicked. Their structurally simple houses and furnishings reflected this philosophy, as seen in Figure 13.2. But the clean lines of functionalism would not be fully developed until the twentieth century.

The Industrial Revolution and the Beginnings of Modernism

The influential roots of modernism in the United States and Europe can primarily be traced to the Industrial Revolution, a period that continued from the late 1700s until the early twentieth century. This era introduced the use of the machine for manufacturing furniture and other essentials for living, helping to change the way people lived. New advancements in technology and the development of new materials led to extraordinary architectural innovations. For example, iron grid construction allowed the architect to enclose vast spaces such as railroad stations, exhibition halls, libraries, stock exchanges, theaters, and other public buildings. The Industrial Revolution also paved the way for new design philosophies and expressions that slowly led to modern design as we know it today.

FIGURE 13.2 "Less is more" and "form follows function" were battle cries of pioneer modernists of the twentieth century. The extremely simple and unadorned homes and furniture of the Shakers were developed through a sense of religious obligation, but the result was clean and finely crafted design still admired by modernists today. (Courtesy of The Metropolitan Museum of Art, Emily C. Chadbourne Fund, 1972.)

FIGURE 13.3 The early modern classic bentwood rocker (1860), manufactured by the Thonet Company, has a sinuous frame of bent wood, a process invented by Michael Thonet, and a natural cane seat and back. (Courtesy of Thonet Industries.)

Michael Thonet

As early as 1830, Austrian designer *Michael Thonet* (1796–1871) developed a process for bending thin strips of wood into fanciful curved forms for furniture construction. Thonet also conceived a method of mass producing these designs and opened his own manufacturing plant that still produces these original designs today. The pieces he designed became immensely popular throughout Europe and the United States for use in schools, cafes, public buildings, and private homes. One of his most famous designs, the bentwood rocker shown in Figure 13.3, is lightweight, strong, and still considered a classic of early modern furniture design.

The study of the modern movement in Europe and America is extensive, and many significant contributions were made on both continents. For the intent of this introductory text, however, only major developments in the evolution of modern architecture and design can be highlighted.

PRINCIPAL EARLY MODERN MOVEMENTS

(Latter Half of Nineteenth Century)

Arts and Crafts Movement

The Arts and Crafts Movement (circa 1860s to 1890s), founded by *William Morris* (1834–1896) in England, re-

jected the machine and modern society. The design group found the ideals of the Middle Ages a perfect model for their own handcrafted furniture and decorative objects. This philosophy was reflected in simple unadorned architecture and furnishings that ironically are considered early beginnings of modernism. The influence of the Arts and Crafts Movement can be seen in Figure 13.4. Other Arts and Crafts leaders in England

FIGURE 13.4 Timberpeg has created a living room inspired by the Arts and Crafts Movement of the late 19th century but interpreted in contemporary terms. Simple handcrafted oak furniture and pattern details drawn from original motifs add to the authenticity. (Courtesy of Timberpeg. Photograph by Keith Scott Morton.)

FIGURE 13.5 An oak casepiece designed by Charles F. A. Voysey in 1896 demonstrates the simple, well-crafted approach typical of the Arts and Crafts philosophy. The addition of the contrasting copper hardware adds visual interest. Decoration could be applied if it was "for art's sake and not pretentious show." (Courtesy of the Victoria & Albert Museum, London, Crown Copyright.)

FIGURE 13.6 The Gamble House in Pasadena, California, is now the headquarters for the Greene & Greene Foundation and remains the finest example of their craftsman approach to architecture. (Courtesy of Esto Photographics; © Peter Aaron.)

included *Charles Francis Annesley Voysey* (see Figure 13.5) (1857–1941) and *Philip Webb* (1831–1915), who designed simple and well-planned houses.

Arts and Crafts Movement in America

The Arts and Crafts Movement in America (circa 1860s–1920s) was the counterpart of the English movement. The foremost exponents were *Gustav Stickley* (1848–1942) in New Jersey and the brothers *Charles Greene* (1868–1957) and *Henry Greene* (1870–1954) in Pasadena, California. Stickley published his advanced design ideas in a periodical called *The Craftsman*. Greene and Greene designed handsome handcrafted furnishings for their new residential architecture. They helped develop the *bungalow* and *shingle-styled* homes in southern California that, in turn, influenced the nation. These homes featured wood construction with handcrafted finishing, wide overhanging roofs, stained glass, shutters, and low horizontal lines. Greene and Greene's masterpiece is the Gamble House (1907) in Pasadena, California (see Figures 13.6 and 13.7). The fresh "modern" approach of all these craftsmen-designers had a tremendous impact on the design world.

Boston-based designer *Henry Hobson Richardson* (1838–1886) is considered America's father of modern

FIGURE 13.7 This interior view of the Gamble House reveals exquisitely handcrafted wooden architectural members and handcrafted furnishings. (Courtesy of Esto Photographics; © Peter Aaron.)

FIGURE 13.8 Henry Hobson Richardson employed rusticated stone, horizontal lines, and heavy Romanesque arches and columns, which are evident in his last work—the Glessner House in Chicago. (Courtesy of the Chicago Architecture Foundation.)

FIGURE 13.9 An interior by Henry Hobson Richardson conveys the elements of the Romanesque approach preferred by the architect through the use of wood paneling, beams, and horizontal emphasis. (Courtesy of Esto Photographics; © Wayne Andrews.)

architecture. He looked to the Romanesque churches of the Middle Ages for inspiration, using heavy rusticated stone, round arches, towers, and horizontal lines in his work. The structural and simple aspects of his architecture were combined with the latest advancements in technology. Richardson's vigorous Romanesque-styled homes are early examples of "modernism." (See Figures 13.8 and 13.9.)

Art Nouveau

Art Nouveau (circa 1890–1910) was a completely new decorative style considered modern at the time. It was based on nature and employed organic and animal motifs of all types, including flowing vines, flowers, stalks, reptiles, peacocks, and the female form. In 1893 in Brussels, Belgian architect *Victor Horta* (1861–1947) built his exquisite Tassel House, which has become a symbol of Art Nouveau architecture. (See Figure 13.10.) The sinuous curves of Art Nouveau were found in his architecture, furniture, and accessories. The style was popular throughout Europe and America, with various designers

FIGURE 13.10 The Tassel House in Brussels, Belgium (1892–1893), is one of Victor Horta's best-known town houses and one of the earliest private residences designed in the Art Nouveau style. Swirling organic forms decorate the interior of the entry. The graceful stair railings and supports are fashioned in iron. (Photograph courtesy of the Museum of Modern Art, New York.)

FIGURE 13.11 The white studio drawing room in the Mackintosh House (1900) at the Hunterian Art Gallery at the University of Glasgow. All furnishings were designed by Charles Rennie Mackintosh and his wife, Margaret, at the turn of the century. The Mackintosh rose motif is found on the back of the chair in the foreground and on the doors of the bookcase on the right of the fireplace. (Courtesy of the Hunterian Art Gallery, University of Glasgow.)

interpreting the style in their own manner. Other important contributors were the French architect and furniture designer *Hector Guimard* (1867–1942) and the whimsical and imaginative designer *Antonio Gaudi* (1852–1926) in Spain.

A titan of the modern movement, active during the Art Nouveau period, was *Charles Rennie Mackintosh* (1868–1928) in Glasgow, Scotland. He combined aspects of Art Nouveau with a new direction he developed called the *perpendicular style*. His houses and furniture displayed graceful Art Nouveau motifs side by side with strong geometric forms, as seen in Figure 13.11. Mackintosh exerted tremendous influence on other architects on the continent and in America.

Louis Sullivan (1856–1924), of the Chicago School in America, is considered one of the foremost exponents of Art Nouveau in America. He employed organic motifs for architectural detailing on his buildings.

Another designer, *Louis Comfort Tiffany* (1848–1933), is considered one of America's greatest designers in the Art Nouveau style and is especially known for his exquisite stained-glass windows and lamps. (See Figure 13.12.)

The Chicago School

The Chicago School (1870s–circa 1910) claimed as its principal members early modern architects *Louis Sullivan* and *Frank Lloyd Wright* (1867–1959), two leaders among a group of innovative designers who introduced new ideas for home and commercial design that were extraordinary for the time. The most important member of the Chicago School in the development of the modern American home was Wright, who worked for a few years as a draftsman for Sullivan.

PRINCIPAL MODERN MOVEMENTS
(Early Twentieth Century)
Organic Architecture
(Circa 1894 to Present)

In 1892 Frank Lloyd Wright broke with Sullivan and set up his own practice in Oak Park, Illinois, where he designed over 35 homes in his *prairie style* employing **organic architecture**, a term he formulated. His revolutionary work was soon recognized in Europe and by the turn

FIGURE 13.12 Louis Comfort Tiffany was both an interior designer and industrial designer. His best known works are his beautiful stained glass pieces. This Tiffany lamp (c. 1900) shows organic motifs, a favorite of the Art Nouveau period. (Courtesy of The Metropolitan Museum of Art, Gift of Hugh Grant, 1974.)

of the century was well known in the Chicago area. His innovative techniques eventually won acclaim throughout the United States, and in 1936 Wright won the American Institute of Architects (AIA) Gold Medal Award for the Kaufmann residence, *Falling Water,* built in Bear Run, Pennsylvania, and considered his residential masterpiece (see Figure 13.1). A Frank Lloyd Wright interior is shown in Figure 13.13. The fundamental principles of organic architecture continue to be a prominent modern design direction and include the following characteristics.

- House and site coexist harmoniously; "a house should grow out of the land"; natural materials compatible with site are used
- Frankly revealed structural members; simple geometric ornamentation, if any
- Planning arranged from inside to outside with spatial flexibility (**open planning**); fireplace functions as heart of home
- Large spacious balconies and terraces with wide overhanging eaves incorporated into design
- Horizontal emphasis and asymmetrical composition

The International Style (Turn of Century to Present)

At the turn of the century, roots of the International Style—a style entirely contrary to Wright's organic architecture—were evidenced primarily through the efforts of a few major design groups in Europe. The

FIGURE 13.13 A reconstructed Frank Lloyd Wright room at the Metropolitan Museum of Art. (Courtesy of The Metropolitan Museum of Art, Purchase, Bequest of Emily Crane Chadbourne, 1972. [1972.60.1] Installation through the generosity of Saul P. Steinberg and Reliance Group Holdings, Inc.)

FIGURE 13.14 Dining room of the Palais Stoclet (1905–1911) in Brussels, Belgium, with all furnishings executed by Josef Hoffmann and the Secessionists. This private home is a hallmark of this design direction. (Photograph courtesy of The Museum of Modern Art, New York.)

FIGURE 13.15 The inventive Fledermaus chair (1907) by Josef Hoffmann is an excellent example of the Secession design approach in Vienna, Austria. The chair, with its distinctive carved ball forms under the arms and seat, was created for use in a Viennese theater bar. (Courtesy of ICF.)

Secession in Austria and Germany and De Stijl in Holland made contributions to the style early in the century. During the 1920s, design concepts put forth by Bauhaus members in Germany, Le Corbusier in France, and various designers particularly in Scandinavia and America led to the fully developed International Style.

The Secession

The **Secession** (circa 1897–1903) was a radical design movement founded by *Otto Wagner* (1841–1918), *Josef Maria Olbrich* (1867–1908), *Josef Hoffmann* (1870–1956) and others in Vienna, Munich, and Berlin at the turn of the century. Their motto was "to each time its art, and to each art its freedom." In 1903 Hoffmann and others set up a more formal workshop named the *Wiener Werkstatte* in Vienna. The structural and geometrical architecture and furnishings of this group highly influenced the International Style. The most important work by this group was the *Palais Stoclet* (1911) in Brussels. (See Figures 13.14 and 13.15.)

De Stijl

De Stijl (1917–1931) in Holland was a group of extremists who felt all design should be reduced to basic design elements: the use of only red, blue, yellow, black, gray, and white; total abstraction; smooth shiny surfaces; and compositions at right angles—ideas that would help establish the International Style. Leaders included *Theo van Doesburg* (1883–1931), the founder; *Piet Mondrian;* and *Gerrit Rietveld* (1888–1964), whose *Schroeder House* (1924) in Utrecht is a landmark. (See Figure 13.16.) Rietveld applied De Stijl theories of design when he designed the Red/Blue chair in 1918 (Figure 13.17).

FIGURE 13.16 The angular interior of the Schroeder House in Utrecht, Holland (1924), designed by Gerrit Rietveld, exemplifies the theories of the De Stijl movement. (Photograph courtesy of The Museum of Modern Art, New York.)

FIGURE 13.17 One of the finest examples of furniture from De Stijl is the Red/Blue chair (1918), designed in Holland by Gerrit Rietveld. It is constructed of wood in an abstract arrangement and painted red, blue, yellow, and black. (Courtesy of Atelier International.)

The Bauhaus

The **Bauhaus** (1919–1933) was an experimental design school founded by architect and designer **Walter Gropius** (1883–1969) in 1919 in Weimar, Germany, for the purpose of unifying art and technology. The Bauhaus concentrated on applying practical artisanship to solve industrial problems characterized by an economy of design and geometric proportion. The school, however, met with vigorous opposition from the German government. It was moved twice, and finally Hitler's stormtroopers closed the Bauhaus in 1933. In the meantime, Gropius, *Marcel Breuer* (1902–1981), *Ludwig Mies van der Rohe* (1886–1969), and other great Bauhaus faculty members fled to America, where they gave impetus to the new movement. Mies's *Farnsworth House* (1947) in Plano, Illinois, became an important prototype of the International Style (Figure 13.18). Marcel Breuer's furniture remain classics of the International Style (Figure 13.19).

FIGURE 13.18 The Farnsworth House, Plano, Illinois by Mies van der Rohe (1946–1950). The architect's philosophy of "less is more" is expressed in this glass and metal domestic project in the International Style—designed after he became the director at Illinois Institute of Technology. (Photograph by Bill Hedrich, Hedrich-Blessing.)

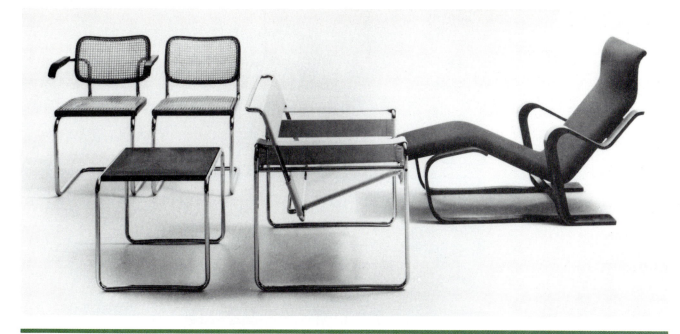

FIGURE 13.19 Classic Bauhaus furniture designed by master architect and furniture designer Marcel Breuer. From *left to right,* the Cesca chairs, Laccio table, and Wassily lounge, designed by Breuer while he taught at the Bauhaus. The Isokon lounge, *far right,* was designed in 1935 in England. (Courtesy of Knoll International.)

Le Corbusier

Le Corbusier (Charles-Edouard Jeanneret-Gris) (1887–1965) worked out of his Paris studio during the 1920s until his death. Considered a giant of modern architecture, he built in Poissy, France, his famous *Villa Savoye* (1930), a home that has become an important residential example of the International Style.

Features of the International Style

The **International Style**, a term coined by *Philip Johnson* (b. 1906), one of America's best-known modern architects, and architect and writer *Henry-Russell Hitchcock* in the 1930s, firmly established a discipline based on functionalism and purity of line for a new generation of architects. After the Bauhaus closed in 1933, Mies van der Rohe, Walter Gropius, and Marcel Breuer, in particular, further developed their ideas on modern architecture in the United States. Gropius and Breuer assumed teaching positions at Harvard University, and Mies van der Rohe became the director of the Illinois Institute of Technology in Chicago. The formula set down for the new International Style had features conflicting with Frank Lloyd Wright's organic architecture, although some features were similar. Today, the style, developed by many individuals and design groups through the years, continues to be interpreted and reinterpreted. Major features include:

- Basically simple design; ornamentation, if employed, generally geometric or abstract
- Flat roof; emphasis on the horizontal line; today, vertical, curved, and diagonal lines often used
- Common materials: reinforced concrete, stucco, steel, and glass; exterior and interior walls usually have stark white finish
- House designed to contrast with nature rather than blend with surroundings
- Asymmetrical composition usually dominant
- Continuous wall surfaces, often combined with large openings and panes of glass
- Open floor plan
- Clearly expressed function

Some notable homes in America designed in the International Style are the *Lovell House* (1929) in Los Angeles by *Richard Neutra* (1892–1970) (Figure 13.20), the *Farnsworth House* (1949–1951) by Ludwig Mies van der Rohe in Plano, Illinois; the *Walter Gropius House* (1938), in Lincoln, Massachusetts; and the *Glass House* (1949) by

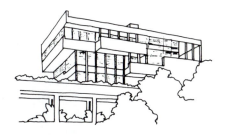

FIGURE 13.20 The International Style. The Lovell House (1929), Los Angeles, California, by architect Richard Neutra.

FIGURE 13.21 Architect Philip Johnson's "Glass House" in New Canaan, Connecticut (1949), with glass walls and Barcelona furniture by Mies van der Rohe. Johnson was an early follower of Mies van der Rohe. (Courtesy of Ezra Stoller.)

FIGURE 13.22 Richard Meier's Douglas House, set on a steep wooded site, makes a striking contrast with its natural surroundings. The clean white planes and structural design are a good example of current expression of the International Style as developed during the 1920s and 1930s. (Photograph by Ezra Stoller.)

Philip Johnson in New Canaan, Connecticut (Figure 13.21). The *Douglas House* (1975), designed by prominent American architect *Richard Meier* (b. 1934), is a good example of the International Style applied in a contemporary manner (Figure 13.22).

Art Deco (circa 1920s–1940)

During the 1920s and 1930s in America, a new decorative style flourished based on numerous design influences including the International Style, the ancient Egyptian and Aztec cultures, the jazz age, the glamorous cinema, the fashion world, the new industrial age, and other aspects of modern society. Architecture reflected motifs from many of these influences while incorporating the latest materials and techniques.

The Art Deco style, introduced on a grand scale at the Paris Exhibition in 1925, especially influenced American designers. A few outstanding architects and furniture designers of the Art Deco style are Finnish-born American architect *Eliel Saarinen* (1873–1950) (see his Blue chair in Figure 13.23); *Paul Frankl,* known for his skyscraper furniture (see Figure 13.24); and French designer *Jacques-Emile Ruhlmann* (1879–1933), who created extravagant and expensive furniture designs. In New York, two significant examples are Radio City Music Hall with furnishings by *Donald Deskey* and the Chrysler building. Major features of the Art Deco style include:

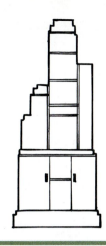

FIGURE 13.24 Paul Frankl helped promote modern American furniture during the 1920s and 1930s and was inspired in his own approach to furniture design by the uniquely American skyscraper—an Art Deco theme he employed for numerous pieces.

- Romantic, glamorous, sleek, exotic, and whimsical in expression, with strong contrasts; sophisticated, yet naive
- Unusual and luxurious materials, often with shiny surfaces
- Influence of industry, technology, and International Style
- Use of red, black, gray, white, silver, pink, mauve, and many grayed colors
- Strong geometric forms including the pyramid, ziggurat (stepped pyramid), zigzag, and sunburst motifs (Figure 13.25)

FIGURE 13.23 The Blue chair, designed by Eliel Saarinen in 1929, was designed at the Cranbrook Academy of Art. The Art Deco piece has a blue lacquered frame accented with gold leaf. (Courtesy of ICF.)

FIGURE 13.25 A contemporary interior reflecting the Art Deco period. The room's design combines a tiered fireplace (a favorite Art Deco treatment), uplighting, and Le Corbusier's tubular steel Grand Confort furniture collection. (Photograph by Norman McGrath.)

FIGURE 13.26 Charles and Ray Eames designed their Case Study House in Santa Monica in 1949. With its prefabricated components and modular arrangement, the house is now considered to be an early example of the High Tech architectural style. (Photograph by Julius Shulman.)

- Palm tree, Egyptian figures, and motifs borrowed from ancient cultures
- Influence of the glamorous cinema and Broadway theater
- Men and women wearing the latest fashions used as motifs

Post–World War II Modernism

After World War II, although the Organic and International styles continued to be popular, new architectural directions emerged as a number of individualists in America and Europe inspired new designs. Some primary directions and current expressions are discussed here.

Charles and Ray Eames

Charles Eames (1907–1978) and his wife *Ray* were two of the most influential post–World War II designers because of their revolutionary innovations in chair forms. They pioneered chairs constructed of molded plywood that were put into production by Herman Miller. The Eames's lounge chair remains one of the world's favorite modern classics. They also developed structures using industrial components made of steel that are considered early examples of what is now known as High Tech architecture. One important example of this type is the Eames's own *Case Study House* designed in 1949 in Santa Monica, California, shown in Figure 13.27.

Eero Saarinen

Eero Saarinen (1910–1961) migrated from Finland to the United States with his father, Eliel, when the latter assumed the directorship at Cranbrook Academy of Art in Bloomfield, Michigan. After World War II Saarinen quickly gained an international reputation for his sculptural furniture and structures. He often collaborated in his designs with his friend Charles Eames, particularly with molded furniture forms. Saarinen's outstanding designs include his *Womb chair, Pedestal chair,* the *TWA Terminal* in New York, the *St. Louis Memorial Arch,* and *Dulles Airport* in Virginia.

Brutalism

Brutalism developed during the '50s and '60s as a reaction to the International Style. It is characterized by massive structures that are often sculptural, with raw concrete surfaces. The rough textures are often accented with panels of strong color.

Paul Rudolph (born 1918), who studied with Walter Gropius at Harvard, is a well-known early exponent of Brutalism. In 1958 he was appointed chairman of the Department of Architecture at Yale University where he had an opportunity to design the department's building (Figure 13.27). His houses and public buildings constructed during this time demonstrated his bold use of raw concrete, often in a striated pattern, which his contemporaries found controversial. Rudolph has also designed extraordinary buildings sheathed with glass, including the *Bond Center* in Hong Kong.

Louis Kahn (1901–1974) designed a series of dramatic examples of Brutalistic architectural forms that have had a significant impact on modern design. His *Kimball Art Museum* in Ft. Worth, Texas, the *Salk Institute* in La Jolla, California, and the *Richards Memorial* at the University of Pennsylvania are outstanding works.

Buckminster Fuller

Buckminster Fuller (1895–1983) was an important engineer, architect, and educator who contributed revolutionary theories to modern design. Fuller developed the **geodesic dome**, as seen in his *U.S. Pavilion* at the 1967 Montreal World's Fair (Figure 13.28). His mathematically precise structures have greatly influenced other architects and designers whose projects may require enclosing large areas of space economically.

Classic Modernism

This style incorporates simplified and elegant structural designs influenced by ancient Greece and Rome and interpreted in modern terms. The approach is usually delicate and "pretty," often with lacy concrete blocks, slender

FIGURE 13.27 Paul Rudolph's controversial Art and Architecture Building, Yale University, designed in 1963, is an outstanding example of Brutalism with its ribbed concrete texture used for exterior and interior surfaces. (Courtesy Yale University Office of Public Affairs.)

FIGURE 13.28 The spherelike U.S. Pavilion at the Montreal World's Fair Expo '67, designed by Buckminster Fuller, is a good example of the architect's patented method of construction known as the geodesic dome. (Photograph by Miriam Stimpson.)

FIGURE 13.29 Finnish designer Alvar Aalto designed the cantilevered Pension chair in 1946 using laminated birch with a seat and back of webbing. The birch table is also by Aalto. They are excellent examples of Scandinavian modern furniture design. (Courtesy of ICF.)

columns, and a white finish. American architect *Edward Durell Stone* (1902–1978) spearheaded this direction. His *John F. Kennedy Center* is an excellent example of Classic Modernism.

Scandinavian Style

Alvar Aalto (1898–1976), Finland's master architect and furniture designer, was particularly influential in spreading modern ideas from Scandinavia to the United States. (See Figure 13.29.) This style is a compatible blend of Organic and International styles. Simple structural white surfaces complemented with the use of natural materials are typical. (See Figure 13.30.)

Post-Modern Style

By the late 1960s, Post-Modern architecture began to borrow from the early modernists, whose principles were combined with new creative designs and modern technology. In many respects Post-Modern architecture rejects the International Style and borrows freely from the past, but in extreme contemporary terms. The style continued to be popular during the 1980s. Some historians feel that the Post-Modern style today is simply an update of the old Art Deco style; and, indeed, many similar motifs are used. Major exponents of this style are **Michael Graves** (b. 1934), designer of the *Portland Building* in Portland, Oregon, the *Swan* and *Dolphin* hotels at Disneyworld in Florida, (see Figures 13.31, 4.11, and 6.63),

FIGURE 13.30 The Scandinavian influence in the American home shows a congenial combination of the Organic and International styles. Clean white walls with wood detailing are typical. The classic modern Scandinavian chairs on the right were designed by Poul Kjaerholm of Denmark in 1956. (Photograph © Ezra Stoller Associates/ESTO.)

and numerous residential projects (see Figure 13.32); *Robert Stern* (b. 1938), whose structures are reminiscent of historic buildings, but interpreted in his own unique style; and **Philip Johnson**, responsible for Post-Modern buildings in cities across the nation. Their works have sparked numerous architects to follow similar design principles for both residential and commercial projects.

FIGURE 13.31 The Post-Modern Walt Disney World Dolphin Hotel in Florida stretches 27 stories tall. The hotel features unusual architecture by award-winning Michael Graves, such as six-story-tall dolphin statues, monkeys in the chandeliers, and even a stair-step waterfall cascading nine stories into a 56-foot clam shell. The building has been described as "entertainment architecture." (Photograph courtesy of The Walt Disney Co.)

FIGURE 13.32 Michael Graves designed this Post-Modern residence in New Jersey in 1986. In the entry (below), tall lighting fixtures are capped with Egyptian-like capitals. In the living room (right), the fireplace wall dominates the space. The placement of classic Villa Gallia chairs, designed by the Secessionist Josef Hoffmann at the turn of the century, complements the fireplace wall. (Photograph by William Taylor.)

Freestyle Movement (1980 to present)

Freestyle, one of the most significant recent trends in residential architecture, emerged in California during the 1980s. Architects with diverse—and often contradictory—approaches are involved in the movement, all expressing their own personal interpretations. The basic elements of Freestyle seek (1) to combine American and European architectural styles with local California design to create a livable environment and (2) to enrich the routine of daily living through various textures, colors, and expressive form, as seen in Figure 13.33. One outstanding leader of this design direction is Frank O. Gehry. (See Figure 13.34.)

High Tech Style

The High Tech style of architecture became popular during the 1970s, although earlier efforts had been demonstrated in the work of Charles and Ray Eames and others. The High Tech approach utilizes frankly exposed industrial units, construction elements, and mechanical systems. These architectural structures are often punctuated with bright primary colors. Utility and function are evident in the use of the latest materials (especially metal) and technology. Two key examples of High Tech architecture are *Lloyds of London* by *Richard Rodgers* (b. 1933), and the *Pompidou Center* in Paris by Rodgers and *Renzo Piano* (b. 1937).

Modern Italian Design

After World War II, Italy emerged as a world leader in the field of modern design, bringing fresh new ideas and uses of materials and technology to the international arena. The Italians are particularly noted for exploring the potential of plastics for furniture design coupled with creative and imaginative use of form, color, and texture. *Gio Ponti* and *Luigi Nervi* were two architects who pioneered modern architectural expressions. *Joe Columbo* (1930–1971), *Vico Magistretti* (b. 1920), and numerous others contributed much to the advancement of modern furniture design. The Milan Furniture Fair and Milan Triennale are two of the world's most important product exhibitions.

FIGURE 13.33 A powerful use of art by Frank Stella, Ellsworth Kelly, Donald Judd, and Robert Rauschenberg in this gallerylike living room mixes with an antique table and comfortable sofas. Use of the Freestyle expression is evident. (Photograph by Tim Street-Porter.)

Crafts Revival

The Crafts Revival (1970s to present), a movement based on the Arts and Crafts ideals of the late nineteenth century, demonstrates the revitalization of handcraft skills. The current Crafts Revival rejects industrialization and instead regards furniture as fine pieces of art. English designer *John Makepeace* and American designer *Wendell Castle* are major contributors.

Memphis Style

Memphis, a name borrowed from both Elvis Presley's home town and the ancient city of Memphis in Egypt, is a style that arose primarily in Italy, spearheaded by *Ettore*

FIGURE 13.34 Frank O. Gehry's own house in Santa Monica, California. The architect has embellished an old 1930s house with chain link, glass, corrugated metal, and other materials in a design reflecting the controversial Freestyle direction. (Photograph by Tim Street-Porter.)

Sottsass. The style has been called a mix of "fifties funk" with "Surrealist punk." The Sottsass design in Figure 13.35 exemplifies the philosophy, including complete freedom in the use of color, texture, and form. In 1981 Sottsass invited many internationally known designers to join him in generating fresh and imaginative furnishings expressing a new outlook on life (see Figure 8.29).

Deconstructivism

Deconstructivism is an architectural direction that emerged in the late '80s to express an extreme reaction to the negative aspects of current society such as crime, poverty, devastation, and war. Architecture and design are depicted with irregular, unpredictable, and even partly demolished forms.

Looking to the Future

Currently, architects around the nation and in other parts of the world are exploring new concepts and philosophies in an attempt to design buildings that meet the needs of a changing society. Along with inventive new directions and a continuation of current styles, historic styles continue to fascinate architects. They often borrow freely from past artistic movements but reinterpret these designs in fresh new expressions.

The Traditional Japanese House

Interestingly, the traditional Japanese house has contributed much to the modern style of architecture in America, especially to the mass-produced **prefabricated** house. Frank Lloyd Wright, who greatly admired the Japanese house and design philosophy, was instrumental in introducing this style to the United States. The classic Japanese house was constructed of wood; and although many of the houses built today use concrete, steel, masonry, and stucco, the classic Japanese form is very prominent. In

FIGURE 13.35 The Carlton, designed in 1981 by Ettore Sottsass, Jr., is a signature piece representing the Italian-based Memphis design group. This inventive approach uses brilliant colors and unusual shapes to create furniture with humor and style. (Photograph courtesy of Memphis Milano and Grace Designs.)

recent years, many architects, particularly in California, have adapted Japanese ideas to meet American needs. (See Figures 13.36 and 13.37.)

The following are general characteristics of the traditional Japanese house.

- Simplicity in line and form
- Most often constructed of wood and other natural materials
- Close connection to outdoors; garden (often several small gardens) is an integral part of the house

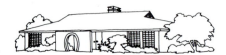

FIGURE 13.36 Japanese house.

- Open planning with **fusuma screen** partitions
- Materials left in natural state; little, if any, ornamentation
- Predominance of horizontal lines
- Unpretentious facade with frequent retaining walls
- Sloping, protective overhangs with hipped and gabled roof
- Natural stone foundation supporting post and roof
- Avoidance of bilateral symmetry
- Honest expression of basic structure
- Feeling of serenity and refinement
- Universal use of a uniform module and the 3-by-6-foot **tatami mat**
- **Tokonoma**—a recessed sacred area in the room that functions as a focal point; a place for special accessories
- Window treatment is the **shoji screen**
- Both house and garden elements symbolic, incorporating basic Japanese philosophies

FIGURE 13.37 The Jack Lenor Larsen apartment is an excellent example of the Japanese influence in the American home. A rock steps up to a Japanese-styled dining area complete with low table and legless chairs. In the living room area *fusuma* screens with a subtle pattern are the focus. A simple treatment of textures and a *shubui* color scheme add to the feeling. (Photograph by Norman McGrath.)

Chinese Influence in Western Interiors

For centuries the Western world has been captivated with designs from China. Many designers have drawn inspiration from Chinese motifs, colors, furnishings, and accessories to create interiors that reflect aspects of China's unique style and culture. For example, an interior can convey a Chinese feeling by simply adding authentic accessories and design motifs, as illustrated in Figure 13.38. A few features and items of Chinese design that are particularly favored by Western designers include:

- Motifs such as fret designs, exotic flowers and birds, pagodas, dragons, and human figures, used for fabrics, wallpapers, and details on furniture and accessories
- Accessories such as the coromandel screen, porcelain, jade, brass, ivory, and religious statues
- Colors of black, gold, red-orange, jade, and peacock blue
- Shiny lacquered finishes
- Brass hardware with distinctively Chinese designs

CURRENT TRENDS

Because of inflation, high interest rates, the need for energy conservation, smaller families, and changes in lifestyles, a number of significant changes in the demands of the building market have occurred. For example,

FIGURE 13.38 The Chinese influence is seen in this dining area designed by Michael de Santis using fret design, Chinese characters, black lacquer, and Chinese porcelain. (Courtesy of F. J. Hakimian, Inc., NY. Design by Michael de Santis, Inc., NY. Photograph by Phillip Ennis.)

- Buyers are better educated than in the past and are asking more questions.
- Buyers want optimum balance of value and cost—a concept known in the building market as "value effectiveness." In other words, people want their money's worth when buying a home.
- Buyers are interested in saving energy.
- Buyers place a high value on prestigious locations.
- Living units must suit a variety of lifestyles.
- Buyers place a high priority on security.
- Buyers want homes with low maintenance, labor-saving devices, and water-saving appliances, especially dishwashers, toilets, and shower heads.

Trends in Residential and Nonresidential Design

Environmentally Responsible Interior Spaces

Interior design is a profession concerned with today's serious environmental issues. The materials and furnishings of an interior can have an immediate effect on the health and welfare of the occupants. For example, when considering air pollution, people generally think of outdoor air pollution and its causes. However, we must also think about the quality of the air we breathe indoors. Since human beings live and work so much indoors, it is essential that designers be aware of possible health hazards and plan interiors that are conducive to the health and well-being of the occupants.

The causes of interior air pollution are toxic emissions from building materials and furnishings, such as the fumes of (1) formaldehyde (found in plywood, household cleaners, carpeting, synthetic fibers, paper goods, etc.); (2) benzene (found in cigarette smoke, plastics, inks, rubber, detergents, etc.); and (3) trichloroethylene (found in inks, varnishes, paints, adhesives, lacquers, etc.). These fumes in the workplace and at home, and even the carbon dioxide that we exhale, accumulate and pollute our air. When interiors have poor air quality that is harmful to the occupants, the term used to describe this condition is an "unhealthy environment."

Materials used in an interior can even be fatal. For example, many fire disasters have been caused by the interior treatments such as draperies and carpeting catching fire, which can cause more deaths than the burning of the building itself. Specifying flame-retardant materials can help prevent this situation.

Many organizations have been researching ways of purifying the air in a sealed environment. For example, bringing plants into living areas can contribute to cleaner air. One study found that within 24 hours, plants had removed 87 percent of the toxic pollutants in the air. The plants' leaves and roots absorb the pollutants and convert them to food, and then release fresh, clean oxygen. Figure 13.39 shows lush green plants used in a public interior space to aid in **greening the environment**.

Greening of Interiors

Addressing environmental issues in interior design and applying solutions is called the "greening of interiors." Some major concerns in addition to air quality include waste management, dealing with climate changes, preserving the rain forests, and recycling. Some solutions involve air conditioning systems that cycle cleaner, better controlled air, specifying the use of nontropical woods, and even recycling carpets and textiles.

The field of interior design demands professionals who are environmentally conscious. Currently, designers may spend as much time increasing their knowledge about "greening" factors as choosing which shade of one color goes with another. This demanding field holds professionals responsible for the mental and physical well-being of those who will occupy the interiors they create.

The Smart House

A buzzword of the '90s is the term "cocooning." Wishing to spend more time at home, people are choosing to enhance their homes and family lifestyles by investing substantial resources in home furnishings, accessories, entertainment, and other elements that contribute to a safer and more enjoyable environment. One current trend that demonstrates this point is the development of the "Smart House," a term that refers to an electronically controlled environment. For example, the amount of light for either nighttime or daytime illumination can easily be programmed to suit the particular needs of the occupants. The custom-designed Smart House is planned to provide the latest developments in technology, including security systems, lighting, intercoms, central vacuums, entertainment systems, and even equipment that can monitor children's activities within the home. In other words, the Smart House is "intelligent" because of its electronic devices that are capable of serving a myriad of needs.

Housing Forecasts

To anticipate market needs, architects and builders are forecasting the following trends for the near future.

- Fewer single-family homes will be built in conventional subdivisions.
- Living spaces in both attached and detached housing will be smaller than those to which Americans have become accustomed.
- The enclosed architectural area (or volume) will be utilized to make spaces more flexible and give them a larger appearance.
- Although rooms will be fewer, they will be larger and have more flexibility.
- Floor plans will be influenced by changing lifestyles and will be more expandable.

- More industrialization and factory-made parts will be used, with on-site building techniques joining with pre-fabrications.
- Buyers will have more options, such as the capacity to add or subtract walls and choose or refuse luxury appliances.
- Security will be given a high priority.
- New product advances will be used to save labor, cut down on maintenance, promote luxury and convenience, save energy, and save space while retaining the appearance of spaciousness.

OPTIONS FOR PROSPECTIVE HOME OWNERS IN THE 1990s

A wide variety of options are available for the prospective home owner today. Consumers can choose a custom-designed, predesigned, shell, mobile, factory-built, or tract home; a condominium; an apartment; or an older home to remodel. Each option has advantages and disadvantages. The buyer's household size, lifestyle, and economic capability will determine the choice.

Although increasingly fewer buyers are able to build the home of their dreams, some are able to plan and build single-family detached houses. Three building options are available: (1) the custom-designed plan, (2) the predesigned plan, and (3) the factory-built (prefabricated) package and shell home (factory-built with no interior fittings). Buyers must carefully examine each option to determine which one most closely meets the household's physical and economic needs.

The Custom-Designed House

The buyer who selects a custom-designed plan hires an architect, who generally first works out a personalized style. The architect also designs a floor plan that indicates room arrangement, traffic lanes, storage, wall space, doors, and windows. When the design and plan have been finalized, the architect makes rough drawings for the buyer's approval, then prepares final working drawings and helps the buyer select materials. The architect also obtains contract bids, acts as a liaison between buyer and builder, and oversees construction to ensure that the home is built according to the buyer's specifications. A

FIGURE 13.39 The greening of the environment is a concern of most designers today. In this large public atrium space, lush green plants in abundance are not only pleasant for the users but also healthy accessories to the environment. (Courtesy of American Olean Tile Co.)

custom-designed plan is the most expensive procedure for the prospective home owner.

The Predesigned Home Plan

Some buyers consider the cost of an architect's services prohibitive and choose a predesigned plan instead. Thousands of plans are available, and a set of complete working drawings is moderately priced, depending on the designer and the size of the home. These drawings can be purchased directly from the plan service, from the individual designer, or through building magazines.

After selecting a plan, the buyer hires a contractor and discusses any minor changes desired. Modifications can usually be incorporated with little or no expense during the initial planning stage. When the details have been worked out, the project should proceed much the same as with a custom-designed plan, except that an architect will not be supervising unless the buyer makes special arrangements for this service.

The Factory-Built (Prefabricated) House

The use of industrialized building techniques is not new in the United States. Many of the early settlers built their homes from panelized parts shipped from England. Since the colonial period, technology has greatly advanced, and today a well-constructed factory-produced house can hardly be distinguished from its traditionally constructed counterpart. Unfortunately, the term *prefab* has long carried the stigma of inexpensive inferior housing, but public resistance to factory-built homes has changed because of improvements in design, materials, and construction. Currently, many consumers are purchasing and enjoying the benefits of the prefab house.

Factory-built houses come in three basic types: (1) the **modular** house, consisting of various elements made and put together at the factory and shipped for immediate assembly on a permanent site; (2) the *component unit,* a precut house in which all materials are cut, sized, and labeled in sequence for fast erection; and (3) the *mobile home,* also a modular house, but put together at the factory and shipped in one or two units to be placed on a temporary foundation. Today, however, mobile homes are being placed in permanent communities planned and landscaped only for this home type.

Buying a factory-built house has a number of benefits. Because these homes are built in quantity, less waste occurs, quality can be controlled (which many manufacturers claim produces a higher quality home), and inspection is less expensive. All these factors add up to a quality home for less money. Another item to be considered is time. Building a custom home can take months—even years—to plan and execute. The factory-built home can be ready for occupancy in a fraction of the time it takes to construct a house by traditional methods. Also, factory-built homes can be just as energy efficient as their site-built counterparts.

Mobile homes began as makeshift shelters in the housing-shortage days of the 1940s. The term *mobile home* is a misnomer, because these homes usually spend only a short time on the move. When mobile homes were first put on the market, they were looked on as a poor relation of conventional housing, and mobile-home parks (trailer courts) were a dreaded neighborhood liability. Today, their role in the housing market is of increased importance. With skyrocketing prices, the need for manufactured housing has grown, with the greatest demand coming from the young and old.

Shell Framing

One concept enjoying moderate success is shell framing, in which the builder constructs, on the owner's foundation, a bare frame with doors and windows. Finishing of the roof, interior walls, plumbing, electricity, and all interior fittings is left to the owner. Shell-framing components are also available from various manufacturing concerns.

The Tract Home

The term *tract home* refers to a house that is one of a group of dwellings in which only a few alternative plans are used. Mass production allows the builder to offer such a house at a price considerably lower than for a custom-built one. A completed tract home is offered at a set price "as is." If the buyer contracts with the builder before construction has begun, however, minor changes can be made at little or no extra cost. The buyer is also permitted to select paint colors and have some choice in the selection of floor coverings and appliances.

The Condominium

Another alternative in the choice of a home is the **condominium** or town-house apartment. *Condominium* is a Latin word dating back to the sixth century, meaning "joint dominion" or "joint ownership." Such an arrangement does not specify a type of housing; instead, it is a financial governance commitment that may involve any type of housing. The occupant is the sole owner of an apartment or housing unit in a multifamily project, but shares with other co-owners common areas and elements of the property, such as gardens, swimming pools, recreation rooms, and lobbies. All owners share in making the rules and governing the project, and in many places they also share responsibility for enforcing the rules.

The *co-op* is a variation of the condominium. In the co-op the resident owns a share in the corporation that owns the building. Co-op residents have a long-term proprietary lease on their units but often must get approval of a would-be buyer from the board of directors. Condominium owners may sell to whomever they wish and

FIGURE 13.40 Reston, Virginia (1960s), was one of the first clustered housing townships of its kind in the United States. A variety of styles are pleasantly arranged around a lake, shops, and other facilities. (Courtesy of Ron Molen, architect.)

have their own mortgage on their individual unit. Co-op tenants might share the mortgage of the entire project.

Condominiums are designed in two basic styles: (1) the conventional row house or town house and (2) the cluster (Figure 13.40). Town-house condominiums are usually two or three stories and are made up of similar attached units. **Cluster planning** has more the appearance of the single-family dwelling; detached and attached single-family houses are clustered around culs-de-sac with a central recreation area and are separated from each other by green belts.

Remodeling and Restoring a House

Two trends in the United States are to buy a "fixer upper" or to stay in a dwelling and make modifications to suit personal needs or desires. With soaring housing costs, families and individuals are seeking more affordable alternatives, and finding an older or used home to remodel can be both challenging and rewarding. Victorian homes, for example, are particularly popular. These homes cannot be reproduced today without incurring great expense; but many Victorian homes built during the latter half of the nineteenth century are being purchased at a lower price, saved from destruction, and lovingly restored. In some areas of the United States entire deteriorated neighborhoods are being revived. In most cases the homes in these areas are exceptionally inexpensive. Additionally, older neighborhoods are drawing younger families and singles who are revitalizing the homes and the area. Whether restoring a period home, fixing up a run-down home, or staying in a current home and

FIGURE 13.41 A passive solar energy exterior. The lean-to greenhouse is designed to fit against the house, extend living space, and serve as a passive solar collector to help reduce fuel bills. (Photograph by Robert Perron, courtesy of Lord and Burnham.)

FIGURE 13.42 A passive solar energy interior. The solarium is weather tight, totally insulated, and ideally suited to serve as an energy-efficient collector. (Photograph by Robert Perron, courtesy of Lord and Burnham.)

remodeling, it is wise to consider advantages and disadvantages. Low cost, the individuality of an older home (especially in the case of a period home), and the satisfaction that comes from creating and restoring a home are some advantages.

Disadvantages include the possibility of considerable repair work, including new wiring, plumbing, roofing, and other interior and exterior replacements; termite problems; and unexpected and considerable costs for restoration and remodeling.

THE ENERGY-EFFICIENT HOUSE

A principal challenge that architects and builders will continue to face in the 1990s is the conservation of energy. In meeting this challenge the heat from the sun, or solar energy, is being harnessed successfully and used to supplement dwindling and progressively more expensive energy supplies.

The Solar House

Solar houses come in a variety of guises and may be large or small, but all have one common attribute: they are built to capture the sun's energy and conserve conventional fuel. Solar energy is used by way of two major systems: **passive** and **active**.

The Passive Solar Energy System

The passive system is a nonmechanical method relying on the house itself to absorb and store the sun's heat, as seen in Figures 13.41 and 13.42. The system uses indoor thermal masses of air, as found in garden rooms, greenhouses, and indoor pools, and masses of masonry, such as walls and floors, that are directly penetrated by the sun's heat. In each case heat is absorbed during the day and radiated at night.

The *envelope* house, a self-cooling and self-heating unit, is a unique concept in passive thermal regulation. By this method the house is encircled by a continuously circulated envelope of air. Excess heat is stored in a layer of insulated earth beneath the house. An integral part of the envelope house is the greenhouse, which acts as the solar collector. This system works in any climate and can be adapted to any style of house.

Waterwall space heating is a passive method in which a water-filled panel installed between the wall studs acts as a solar-powered radiator storing and releasing the sun's heat. Many innovations are being tried in which simple applications that do not require any moving parts work very well. The passive solar energy system has a number of advantages over the active system: (1) it allows more design freedom, (2) it is simpler to operate, (3) it is silent, and (4) it is more economical.

The Active Solar Energy System

The active system relies entirely on mechanical means—collector panels, fans, pumps, and a storage area—to trap the heat and distribute it throughout the house. Some disadvantages of active solar systems are that (1) the collector panels are expensive, (2) the panels limit the house design, and (3) the indispensable photovoltaic cells, used to generate electricity from solar energy, are in a semiexperimental stage and need perfecting for the residential market.

The Earth-Sheltered House

The idea of homes inside the earth dates back to prehistoric times when earth dwellings protected humans from the elements. The earth is a natural temperature moderator that keeps temperatures fairly constant, and the darkness and dampness formerly associated with earth-sheltered living have been overcome by today's sophisticated weatherproofing and lighting. Although the earth-sheltered house has many possibilities and holds great promise, it has some definite disadvantages. This type of dwelling needs a large tract of land, the floor plan requires particular attention, and at present its use is severely hampered by building code restrictions.

LOOKING TO THE FUTURE

Housing alternatives during the past few decades have encompassed many new design expressions, building materials, technological advances, and creative solutions to housing requirements. Many architects and designers foresee a number of trends in housing during the 1990s, including (1) a continuing preference for authentic historical styles; (2) new materials, technology, and adaptations incorporated into period home styles; (3) a demand for homes with more open and livable spaces; (4) a decrease in the popularity of solar homes (however, better materials will be utilized for this home type); (5) new expressions of the modern style in form, color, and materials, but continuing popularity and development of the basic directions of Organic or International styles; (6) an increase in home restoration and renovation; (7) a challenge to architects to design more affordable homes; (8) smaller but more efficiently planned homes; (9) incorporation of better insulation elements; (10) more two-, three-, and four-plex houses massed together to give the image of semidetached houses; (11) a larger condominium market; and (12) a strong move to suburban areas, although regional differences may alter this trend, and some metropolitan centers will encourage development of new housing or restoration and renovation in urban areas.

PART SIX

The Profession of Interior Design

CHAPTER 14

Interior Design as a Career

FIGURE 14.1 In this elegant dining room of a private residence in Florida the gently curving shapes of the chandelier and furniture are an effective contrast to the straight-line geometry of the setting. The outdoor area becomes part of the indoor space by the artful lighting of a hanging architectural fragment on the existing privacy wall. (Courtesy of Michael de Santis, ASID, Michael de Santis, Inc. Photograph by Phillip Ennis.)

*I*nterior designers are the experts who can help us collect our thoughts, express our tastes, stretch our imaginations, weigh the pleasures and practicalities, and take the best possible advantage of the great legacy of design that is at our doorstep.

—*Showcase of Interior Design*

*T*he following definition of an interior designer was formulated by the National Council for Interior Design Qualifications (NCIDQ) and has been endorsed by the American Society of Interior Designers (ASID), the Foundation for Interior Design Education Research (FIDER), and the Interior Design Educators Council, Inc. (IDEC).

The professional interior designer is a person qualified by education, experience, and examination, who

1. identifies, researches, and creatively solves problems pertaining to the function and quality of the interior environment
2. performs services relative to interior spaces, including programming, design analysis, space planning, and aesthetics using specialized knowledge of interior construction, building codes, equipment, materials, and furnishings, and
3. prepares all drawings and documents relative to the design of interior spaces in order to enhance and protect the health, safety, and welfare of the public.

HISTORY OF THE INTERIOR DESIGN PROFESSION

The profession of interior design, the separate and distinctive career direction just described, is a relatively new profession that evolved primarily during the latter half of the nineteenth century and the early decades of the twentieth century, then fully emerged in the decades following World War II. Interiors designed prior to the establishment of the profession as we know it today were executed primarily by furniture designers, painters, sculptors, architects, and others active in the decorative arts. Some major developments instrumental in establishing the profession of interior design are discussed in this section.

Early Development of Interior Design

Authors, moralists, and other early advocates of good design were deeply interested in the relationship of human comfort and well-being incorporated with the effective use of sound principles of design. The development of interior design in America was influenced by the writings and sermons of many individuals and by various publications.

William Morris and the Arts and Crafts Movement (1860s) in England advocated "good design for everyone." English author and moralist Charles Eastlake in 1868 wrote *Hints on Household Taste,* one of the first books on interior decoration. In the U.S., American Arts and Crafts Movement leader Gustav Stickley published *The Craftsman* at the turn of the century, illustrating numerous articles on home design. In the late nineteenth

FIGURE 14.2 Elsie de Wolfe, considered America's first professional interior designer, believed the home should express the good taste of the owner. In her own dining room in New York City, 1896, traditional furnishings (which she preferred) have been carefully selected and coordinated. (Photograph from the Byron Collection, The Museum of the City of New York.)

century, various publications such as *Godey's Lady's Book, Harper's New Monthly, Harper's Bazaar,* and *Ladies Home Journal,* advocated more tasteful interiors. In the 1890s, Edith Wharton and Ogden Codman wrote *The Decoration of Houses,* which was intended to show that the purpose of interior decoration was to bring out the proportions of a well-designed room. This book was reluctantly published in 1907—the publishers were not certain the public would be interested in such a topic. As early as 1890, Candace Wheeler published an article entitled "Interior Decoration as a Profession for Women." Then, W. C. Gannet wrote a privately printed series of essays called *"The House Beautiful,"* from which the publication of a magazine of the same title derived its impetus and was first published in 1896. Soon, other home-decorating periodicals appeared on the market.

At the turn of the century and on into the next decades, architects like Frank Lloyd Wright, Greene & Greene, and other progressive designers both in America and Europe saw the need to integrate the exterior of a structure with the interior spaces and furnishings. Most often the architects themselves assumed this responsibility.

The impact of social and economic growth on interior design was an important factor for the development of the profession. As the U.S. became one of the most prosperous nations in the world, the profession of interior design found a prominent place in society. Americans demanded more efficient and aesthetically pleasing private and public environments—and were willing to

support a new profession that would implement that desire.

Elsie de Wolfe

Although there were many relatively unknown decorating shops and private decorators in America and Europe at the turn of the century, one of the most famous individuals to offer interior decorating services to the public was New York actress Elsie de Wolfe. With her expert knowledge of French furniture and antiques, she felt confident that she had a unique, marketable service to offer the public (see Figure 14.2). In 1901 Elsie de Wolfe set herself up in business as "America's first interior decorator." Through her efforts, along with the work of others during this period, including Nancy McClelland; Syrie Maugham, known for her "white" interiors; Dorothy Draper, who wrote a decorating advice column; Rose Cummings; and later Billy Baldwin, who was known as the "Dean of Decorators," the profession of interior decorating was established. The female interior decorators became known as "the ladies of good taste." Other well-known pioneer interior decorators followed—both women and men who promoted the new profession.

The establishment of professional interior design societies began in the 1930s and gave credibility to the new vocation. For decades, the accepted term for the profession was *interior decorator,* a term the professional societies felt implied dealing only with the superficial

FIGURE 14.3 An English country-style room, designed by well-known New York interior designer Mario Buatta, has pale glazed walls, striped festoon curtains at the windows, and wall-to-wall trellis-patterned carpeting with a 19th century Bessarabian rug. Cushions in rainbow colors on a chintz-covered sofa welcome the visitor. The mix of patterns, colors, and styles, as if individual pieces had been slowly accumulated over a long period, is typical of English country style. (Courtesy of Mario Buatta, Incorporated.)

FIGURE 14.4 In this large living area designer Steve Chase emphasized neutral colors and natural textures and used boldly patterned carpeting to unify the space. Cove lighting highlights the rich tones of the paneled ceiling and casts a warm glow throughout the living space. (Courtesy of Steve Chase and Associates. Photograph by Mary E. Nichols.)

FIGURE 14.5 Prominent designer John Saladino combined period and modern furniture and accessories for this eclectic living area. (Photograph by Peter Margonelli.)

embellishment of the interior. The term *interior designer* soon replaced the old term and implied a well-trained professional who understands and applies highly technical skills.

Some of the prominent professional interior designers of today include Michael de Santis (see Figures 14.1 and 11.10), Mario Buatta (Figures 14.3 and 7.17), Jay Spectre, Steve Chase (Figure 14.4), John Saladino (see Figure 14.5), Mark Hampton, Juan Montoya (Figure 7.22), Robert Metzger (Figure 10.1), and Mimi London. Their projects are often featured in popular design periodicals.

RESPONSIBILITIES OF AN INTERIOR DESIGNER

The professional interior designer is:

- Required to be proficient in the planning, designing, and implementing of residential and nonresidential design.
- Qualified to coordinate all elements of design to create functional and aesthetically pleasing living and working environments that fulfill the total needs of the client or user.
- Trained to make the most of space. Living and working space is diminishing in size because of increased building costs, and the designer therefore is challenged to use every square foot to the best advantage.

- Qualified to work with an architect from the initial planning stages of an environment to completion, working from empty space until the last interior detail is in place and the client is satisfied.
- Knowledgeable about and able to appropriately integrate period and contemporary styles of architecture, furniture, and decorative arts.
- Knowledgeable about furniture materials and construction, and has the creative ability to custom design furnishings such as case goods and redesign or add architectural elements such as wood trim, doors, and mantels.
- Concerned not only with the immediate effect but also with the construction, durability, and maintenance of fabrics and finishes. A designer is also well qualified to select and employ fabrics and textiles for the best performance and appearance as applied to all aspects of an interior, including floor, wall, window, and upholstery treatments.
- Knowledgeable about lighting and its effect on interior colors, finishes, and spaces.
- Familiar with a broad range of products and services, and must have a good working relationship with those professionals who provide the products and services to ensure that ordering, shipping, delivery, and installations go smoothly.
- Able to draw upon reliable sources to complete a design project, including manufacturers, cabinetmakers, artisans such as upholsterers and refinishers, and professionals in workrooms, antique shops, showrooms, and auction rooms. These sources can be invaluable to

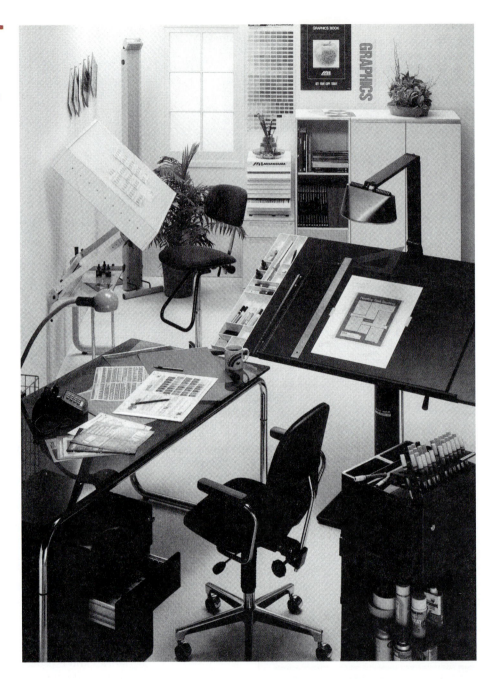

the client, because access to some high-quality merchandise, labor, and services is available only through professionals.

- Responsible for the completed project and willing to see that any flaws in quality or craftsmanship are corrected.
- A good visual and oral communicator. One of the many requisites of a successful design is a sound designer-client-resource relationship.
- Able to incorporate artistry and expertise with the client's purposes and objectives within the bounds of good taste.
- An effective salesperson, for without this element, the interior design profession would not exist.

- A person with attributes including enthusiasm, imagination, curiosity, perceptual skills, sociability, keen insight regarding people, respect for time commitments, and organizational and record-keeping skills.

WORKING PROCEDURES FOR THE PROFESSIONAL INTERIOR DESIGNER

Establishment of a successful working procedure, combined with creative design solutions and the satisfaction of the client, is the goal of a professional interior designer. Although it is not the intent of this book to cover the designer's entire working procedure, the following outlines the basic elements involved:

- *Workspace.* To successfully carry out their responsibilities, designers need a suitable workplace with a desk and chair set up for drawing and planning. Good lighting and storage are also essential, along with all necessary equipment to accomplish these tasks, as seen in Figure 14.6.
- *Contract of agreement.* The interior designer and client must agree on the responsibilities expected of each party. A contract of agreement or letter of agreement is a legal and binding document that outlines these responsibilities and is signed by all parties involved. Some items summarized involve a definition of the project and the services to be provided, fees, and specific conditions and terms of various responsibilities.
- *Programming.* After the designer and client have a project agreement with common goals in mind, the design process commences. (See chapter 4.) The program helps determine this designer/client understanding. A program may be set up for a small residential job or a large commercial project. It involves developing a step-by-step working procedure, taking into account all needs of the client. Information is obtained concerning such criteria as space allocation, intended function, furnishings, and special requirements. The goals and

objectives are set, and the budget is considered. All information is reviewed and evaluated.
- *Presentation to the client.* After the program information has been collected and evaluated, it is presented to the client for approval. At this point projected budget and design solutions may be agreed upon.
- *First-step drawings.* In this initial stage the designer makes preliminary sketches and drawings indicating space allocations, interior architecture, and furnishings. Involving clients in this process is usually optional, but the client's final approval is necessary.
- *Final detailed drawings.* These are completed during this stage. Renderings, elevations, and often perspectives are professionally executed. (See Figures 14.7 through 14.10.)
- *Presentation to the client for final approval.* Finished professional drawings and specifications are presented to the client. Specifications are itemized outlines of furnishings and materials needed to complete a particular project. Each required item is listed with the name of the manufacturer or company, stock numbers, quantity, color, and any additional information required for ordering and purchasing. Also indicated is the location where the installation will take place. For nonresidential design, details on safety requirements of each finish, costs, and other necessary information regarding the merchandise are also shown.
- *Blueprints or "construction drawings."* These are made to determine the actual working procedures and

FIGURE 14.7 In this floor plan for a condominium, the furniture placement and color scheme are indicated to help the client visualize the end result. (Courtesy of Nina Lewis.)

D.E. CONDOMINIUM
SCALE ¼"=1'-0"

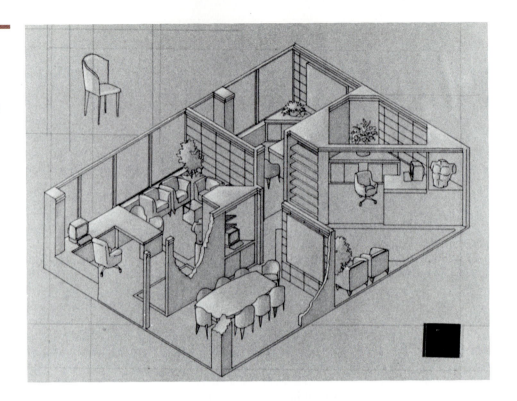

FIGURE 14.8 A three-dimensional isometric rendering, which is based on a 30° angle, is useful in depicting interior spaces and furnishings and how they will function for the client. (Courtesy of Paul David Tew, designer.)

MASTER SUITE

PLAN: ¼"=1'-0"

CHET KNIGHT

FIGURE 14.9 This rendering and floor plan for a master bedroom helps to convey to the client how the space will be allocated and how the room will appear when finished. (Courtesy of Chet Knight.)

FIGURE 14.10 Architects and designers often build working models of a project to present to the client and aid in the designing and building process. This model by architect Arthur Dyson was built to scale to identify all details of the project including integration to the site. (Courtesy of Arthur Dyson, architect.)

cost. At this stage the designer works with architects, contractors, electricians, plumbers, and all those connected with the construction and technical aspects such as air conditioning, heating, wiring, safety, and acoustics.

■ *Estimates and bids.* After blueprints or construction drawings are completed, the designer submits them to contractors for estimates and bids. Usually the job is awarded to the lowest bidder. Sometimes the project is completed on a cost-plus basis rather than on a predetermined price agreement.

■ *Scheduling the project.* The designer now schedules the final project with the contractor and others involved in the actual working process.

■ *Purchase of necessary materials.* The designer acquires all materials needed for the completion of the project—a process requiring a sound professional business background. Selections must be made, purchase orders filled out, and delivery dates determined. Coordinating these aspects of the design process is necessary to ensure project completion.

■ *Supervision of all major aspects of the design project.* Supervision is a necessary step in which the designer checks to see that all specifications are accurate and well executed.

■ *Supervision of the final details.* Arranging furniture, pictures, lamps, and other accessories until all furnish-

ings are in place is the last stage of the working procedure. It is an essential step in the satisfactory completion of the job.

■ *Evaluation.* Often the professional designer follows up or evaluates the project at a later date to determine the success of the design solutions.

Fee Systems

Interior designers are compensated for their services in a number of ways. Each designer or firm establishes a system of fee structuring that is most efficient for their business. It is important that the interior designer and client are in agreement on the terms of payment. Following are the most common fee systems:

1. A designer who receives a *flat or fixed fee* determines the time and expense involved for the particular project and charges the client this specified amount.
2. An *hourly fee* is a set rate for each hour of time spent on the project. This fee varies depending on many factors including customary fees in a particular area or region, the competence and status of the designer, and the demand for his or her services.
3. A *cost plus fee* involves a designer buying merchandise at wholesale prices and selling the goods to clients for an additional 20 percent charge.

4. A *fee based on the total square feet of the project* is generally used by experienced designers who are fairly knowledgeable in estimating costs involved in completing a space. The fee is charged for each square foot based on the cost appraisal for the whole project.

5. A designer may be compensated by receiving a *percentage of the total project expenditure*. This system provides a guaranteed fee regardless of what the project may cost. If the completed project has additional costs, the designer is financially protected.

PREPARING FOR A CAREER IN INTERIOR DESIGN

Deciding on a career is a search process that requires careful examination and evaluation of one's interests and capabilities as well as one's inadequacies. Creativity, sensitivity to the environment, and interest in America's cultural heritage and ancestral homes as well as today's contemporary design are all necessary traits for an individual who is seriously pursuing a career in interior design. A designer is also concerned with improving the quality of personal environments, work spaces, and institutional and recreational environments.

One of the initial steps toward becoming a professional interior designer is to successfully complete an interior design program at a college, university, or design school (preferably a FIDER-accredited educational facility) (see Table 14.1) where students are educated and trained in such areas as:

- Visual, written, verbal, and graphic communication skills, as well as drafting skills and preparation of a portfolio
- Theory, elements, and principles of design

TABLE 14.1 The Foundation for Interior Design Education Research recognizes three types of undergraduate programs

Baccalaureate Degree	Certificate or Diploma Programs	Certificate Programs
four years intensive training	three years intensive training	two years emphasis is technical for interior design aides
interior design major	usually specialized design schools that require prerequisite training in liberal arts	usually offered at community, junior, or technical colleges
see curriculum outlined in text		

- Development of knowledge about building and interior support systems and building codes, textiles, lighting, materials, and barrier-free design
- Programming and planning, interior component selection, furniture layout, space planning, and cost estimates
- History of art, architecture, interiors, and furnishings
- Business practices and principles
- Human factors and ergonomics
- Product design and construction

Most interior design programs require students to participate in an internship or in work-study courses as part of the requirements for graduation. Internship programs vary somewhat in different schools, but all have the same objective, which is to enable the student to experience firsthand the professional business world prior to graduation by combining classroom theory with practice. Students work in the interior design area of a reputable business establishment during the summer months, part-time during the school year, or both. Some schools give college credits. The monetary agreement, if any, is arranged between the student and the firm.

Internship experience is invaluable to the student. By becoming actively involved in the real world of interior design, students

- Experience operational procedures, policies, and various phases of design, such as client-designer relationships; learn about interactions of designers within a firm; and observe and participate in design from concept to implementation.
- Learn to be open to new and different attitudes and perspectives in all aspects of design.
- Learn more about themselves in terms of potential future desires and goals as a professional interior designer.
- Acquire valuable experience that can be entered on a job resumé for use after graduation.

Licensing and Registering

A number of states have a licensing program that tests professional interior designers to protect the well-being of the public. The licensing program deals with safety and health issues. States also set standards for educational requirements, experience, and ethics. Basically, there are two types of licensing acts:

1. A *title act* protects those who are competent to use particular "titles" that pertain to the profession of interior design. Because of the title act, clients can be reassured that persons using these titles are qualified professional interior designers.

2. A *practice act* requires those who qualify as professional interior designers and plan to practice this occupation to register with a state board.

The title act and practice act guarantee the public that an interior designer has met certain requirements involving ethics, education, competence, experience, and the successful completion of the NCIDQ exams.

National Council for Interior Design Qualifications

The **National Council for Interior Design Qualifications (NCIDQ)** organization was formed in 1972 to establish a professional level of competence for interior designers. Level of competence is determined through an examination. Another purpose of NCIDQ is to investigate the advantages and disadvantages of pursuing legal registration or certification of the profession.

The incorporation charter of the council provides membership for professional design organizations only; it offers no provisions for membership to individuals. All council member organizations require the NCIDQ exam as a prerequisite for professional membership. Nonaffiliated interior designers who have the required education and experience may apply directly to NCIDQ to take the exam.

The examination, offered twice a year at various locations around the country, consists of two parts given on two consecutive days. The first part—the academic section—tests the candidate's knowledge in such areas as history, modern design, technical information, business practices, and ethics. The second part is a ten-hour exam testing the candidate's ability to arrive at a conceptual solution to a realistic design problem. The problem requires a design concept statement, space planning, furniture selection and arrangement, interior surfaces, interior systems, presentation skills, and project specifications. Information about the council can be obtained by writing to NCIDQ, 118 East 25th Street, New York, NY 10010.

Information on and locations of schools offering interior design programs can be obtained from local libraries or from the **Foundation for Interior Design Education Research (FIDER)**, Room 1501, 322 8th Avenue, New York, NY 10001.

The interior design profession offers a rewarding career for well-trained, dedicated individuals.

OPPORTUNITIES FOR INTERIOR DESIGNERS

As the demand for quality housing and commercial facilities rises, interior designers are finding more and more opportunities for creative job possibilities. They are now perceived as important in the design process and are employed by many offices and businesses in architecture-related fields. Interior designers are being sought by industry, which has become aware of interior designers' buying power, and manufacturers are turning to the design community for advice in product development.

Major design trade centers are found in New York, Texas, California, and Illinois. One of the most notable trade centers for residential furniture is in High Point, North Carolina.

Career opportunities open to professional interior designers fall into two general categories: residential and nonresidential design.

Residential Design

Residential design involves the designing of private living quarters or homes, including detached houses, apartments, condominiums, town houses, dormitories, and mobile homes. (See Figure 14.11.)

Nonresidential Design

Nonresidential design, also known as contract or commercial design, is not related to private living spaces. General categories of nonresidential design include:

- *Office design.* Ranging from a small office space to a large corporation.
- *Government and public buildings.* City halls, courthouses, post offices, police and fire stations, libraries, and museums.
- *Retail design.* Shopping malls, stores, shows, galleries, and showrooms.
- *Health care.* Hospitals, clinics, nursing homes, and doctors' offices (see Figure 14.12).
- *Entertainment design.* Theaters, concert halls, auditoriums, and convention centers.
- *Hospitality design.* Hotels, motels, resorts, inns, and clubs.
- *Financial institutions.* Banks, stock exchanges, credit unions, and savings and loan facilities.
- *Recreation.* Health and spa centers, swimming pools, bowling alleys, and other sports facilities.
- *Industrial design.* Warehouses, factories, laboratories, workshops, and manufacturing plants.
- *Institutional design.* Public and private universities, colleges, and schools.
- *Transportation.* Airports, train stations, terminals, motor homes, boats and ships, and other transportation vehicles and facilities.

Specialized Design

A designer may focus on specific design-related projects:

Rendering designer prepares realistic, three-dimensional drawings and illustrations of a designer's concept for an interior.

Set designer works on television, theater, and movie productions or creates complete room displays for

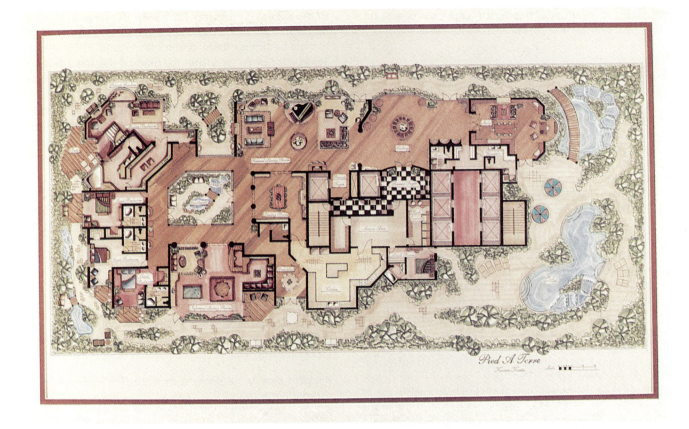

FIGURE 14.11 For this residential design project the designer has drawn the floor plan to reflect the use of space and furnishings and help communicate this information to the clients. (Courtesy of Karen Korte, designer.)

FIGURE 14.12 A project for a children's support center required that the effect be calming, one that would decrease anxiety and communicate reassurance. A rendering, an isometric drawing, and materials used are presented for communicating the proposal to the client. (Courtesy of Michael Jensen, Jonna Robison and Chet Knight, designers.)

department stores, furniture companies, and manufacturers for advertising.

Adaptive reuse designer works on the restoration or remodeling of historic buildings for a new function.

Historic preservation and restoration designer restores and preserves a historic structure as it was in the past.

Kitchen designer helps clients create the most efficient and functional kitchen space to fulfill particular needs.

Lighting specialist designs lighting plans essential in the design process.

Color consultant aids clients in both residential and nonresidential programs.

Interior design educator is generally employed at a secondary, college, or university level.

Design journalist or photographer completes work for newspapers, magazines, or publishers on a variety of timely aspects of interior design.

Drafting designer prepares precise mechanical drawings, often on the computer, for architects, designers, builders, and furnishing manufacturers.

Buyer buys merchandise for furniture or department stores and studios.

Additional design specialist areas are found in storage, cabinet, and closet design; window treatments; hard floor materials (tile, wood, stone, etc.); exhibition design; marketing consultant or representative; wholesale representative or "rep"; communication design; textile design; design specialist for physically challenged users; model home design; energy conservation; solar home design; and environmental safety design.

Other challenging opportunities are developing in government, business, and industry, where the diverse skills of design professionals are considered essential to long-range planning and product development. Experienced professional interior designers are currently serving in key positions with large corporations in industry, manufacturing, transportation, communications, recreation, computer-aided design, and many other areas. Designers are now members of state and federal governments.

COMPUTER APPLICATIONS FOR INTERIOR DESIGN

Interior designers deal with many elements to present a pleasing and precise solution. Many hours are spent consulting plans, sketches, fabrics, and materials. The use of the computer has made this communication time more effective, thorough, and efficient.

Available to the interior designer are computer-generated representations of exteriors and interiors of the project, showing shape, realistic surface textures, light and shadow, mass or plane, and lighting models. With a palette of several hundred colors, the computer allows the user to create and manipulate the design in numerous ways, to create multiple views, and to experiment with color schemes and structural changes. Such a "walk-through" can be invaluable in evaluating the design and pinpointing problem areas. (See Figures 14.13 and 14.14.) Some major tasks computers are capable of handling include:

1. *Expediting routine office tasks* such as filing, bookkeeping, billing, purchase orders, and other clerical duties.
2. *Drafting and perspective drawing.* **Computer-aided design (CAD)** programs completely eliminate the need for manual drawing, although most architectural firms use the CAD systems for redrawing and ideation. Floor plans, perspectives, elevations, and full-color renderings of furniture and architecture can be produced in a fraction of the time it takes to produce them by hand. A normal job requiring 160 drawing hours for a draftsman can be completed in 4.5 hours by a trained CAD operator.
3. *Aiding in the planning process with data banks of information readily available.* Because all information used in the design process is filed in the computer's memory system, it is retrievable. Specification lists and facilities reports can be accessed as detailed printouts, which accurately list all the components in any design on file. The program keeps track of all data, drawing figures and point allocations automatically so that the user does not have to keep records of items. When the data are retrieved, the computer can display on the screen or page an area as large as the floor plan of an entire building or as minute as a single pencil on a desktop—or any area in between.
4. *Estimating costs.* With cost information stored in the computer's memory, the task of projecting plan proposals into cost estimates is relatively simple.
5. *Preparing specifications,* which can be an effortless task. The computer is capable of storing suppliers' catalog data including prices and other valuable information, facilitating efficient preparation for project specifications. Manufacturers can supply electronic images of their products that can be introduced in plans and perspective drawings.
6. *Communicating.* Computers can rapidly and accurately communicate information between architects, builders, and designers through an efficient **computer network** system.
7. *Ordering.* Orders for required furnishings can be placed directly through the computer to the manufacturer.

Computer programs typically come to the user with a basic working capacity. The user may augment a particular program by purchasing specialty packages that adapt the system to the efficient processing of a specific area,

FIGURE 14.13 Computer technology has been used to create the exterior of a multilevel structure with ease and efficiency, eliminating the numerous hours required when rendered by hand at a drafting table. (Courtesy of Kevin MacCabe, Pre-Arc Design Lab.)

such as interior design. In time, the designer can create a personalized library of software programs intended for his or her discipline. Standard graphic items include typical floor-plan symbols such as wall types, windows, doors, cabinetry, and popular furniture types.

As the computer becomes more adapted to usage in the design world, many innovations are being developed to make the work of the designer and architect more efficient. One such invention has been developed by the architectural firm of Skidmore, Owings, and Merrill. The architects have devised a CAD-CAM (computer-aided design and computer-aided manufacturing) program to create models of buildings already designed and recorded in the computer. They use a laser cutter to cut out parts needed to construct a model for presentation to clients. Because of the cutting ability and exactness of the laser, the models are more accurate in scale and more cost efficient. The investment for the development of the laser cutter was approximately $35,000, whereas the price for each model cut by hand would be approximately

$70,000. It reduces the time for model making from days of tedious work to hours. To the interior designer, a CAD system can be what the bulldozer is to the user of a shovel. It permits each user to get the job done more quickly and efficiently and less expensively. It strips tedium away and allows the computer and designer to work in concert, with each doing what it does best.

Being relatively new to the design realm, computers have both pros and cons for use in architecture and interior design. Although the computer reduces labor costs, enhances efficiencies, expands visualization, and eliminates repetitive work for draftsmen and designers, initial expenses in investment, training time for employees, and software management are sometimes problem areas. Although computer application has generally been most efficient in major firms that have literally hundreds of projects at a time, smaller computers with higher capabilities are now available for use in smaller firms. Many small firms are also taking advantage of opportunities to connect into centralized equipment systems, which are often offered by larger manufacturing firms or by other individual services. With constant advancements in computer equipment and techniques, training design students is an ongoing process, and it is often necessary for the new employee to receive updated training for the first few weeks on the job. Currently, there are few well-qualified and proficient CAD operators. The student of design could place himself or herself at the head of the competition by becoming trained in the use of computer-aided design.

PROFESSIONAL INTERIOR DESIGN SOCIETIES

American Society of Interior Designers

The **American Society of Interior Designers (ASID)** is a professional international organization established to en-

act and maintain standards of excellence to enhance the growing recognition of interior design as a profession. It was formed in 1975 through the consolidation of the American Institute of Interior Designers (AID) and the National Society of Interior Designers (NSID), but its roots date back half a century to the founding of AID in 1931. ASID is the largest organization of interior designers in the world, representing over 33,000 members in the United States as well as abroad. It represents interior design as a profession dedicated to serving people, and it provides a forum for its thousands of talented members to bring their differing points of view into harmony to promote unified action. ASID fosters the development and improvement of interior design practice through a variety of activities and programs that reflect a broad spectrum of professional concerns, ranging from interior design to community service workshops. During the 1990s, ASID plans to take a leadership role in historic interior design to take advantage of the boom in restoration of historic buildings.

FIGURE 14.14 With the use of CAD (computer-aided design), an interior can be manipulated by the designer in various ways, such as changing colors, textures, lighting, and furniture placement to arrive at the desired solution of a problem. A "walk-through" of the finished space allows the designer to further investigate all possible solutions. (Courtesy of Kevin MacCabe, Pre-Arc Design Lab.)

Over 150 *student chapters* of ASID are in colleges across the country, and current student membership is over 8,000. The society's educational program includes seminars, show house tours, lectures, access to designers and restricted design centers, and opportunities to participate in national student competitions. Of particular importance to members is the fact that upon graduation they are eligible to advance automatically to associate membership in the society.

The advancement to professional membership is earned after an applicant fulfills the practical experience requirements and completes the National Council for Interior Design Qualification (NCIDQ) exam. Professional members are distinguished by the letters *ASID* beside their name, which serve as a symbol of professional excellence. The national ASID headquarters is located at 608 Massachusetts Ave., N.E., Washington, DC 20002.

Institute of Business Designers

The *Institute of Business Designers* (IBD) is an internationally established organization dedicated to the professional designer whose major field is commercial and institutional interiors and products. This includes designers responsible for offices; hotels; hospitals and health care facilities; and other institutions such as stores, schools, theaters, and banks.

The institute is dedicated to exploring new directions in design, expanding the influence of the designer and supplementing the formal education of its members. To accomplish this, IBD is actively involved in design research, continuing education, and student design education programs. The institute also sponsors major design competitions.

As with ASID, IBD has various membership categories and requirements for membership, including education, experience, and the NCIDQ examination. Information regarding this organization can be obtained by writing to the IBD national office, 341 Merchandise Mart, Chicago, IL 60654.

Interior Design Society

The *Interior Design Society (IDS),* another national organization, is a relative newcomer to the profession. Organized in 1973, IDS is steadily growing across the country. The society, which is an arm of the *National Home Furnishings Association,* provides its members with a variety of sales aids and educational programs, as well as the professional recognition they deserve as retail designers. The headquarters is at P. O. Box 2396, High Point, NC 27261.

Interior Design Educators Council

The **Interior Design Educators Council, Inc. (IDEC),** incorporated in 1967, is dedicated to the development of interior design education. Its purpose is to strive to improve the teaching of interior design and, through this, the professional level of interior design practice. The IDEC program is concerned with establishing and strengthening the lines of communication among individual educators, educational institutes, and organizations concerned with interior design. It is an international organization and an associate member of the *International Federation of Interior Designers (IFID).* During its brief history, IDEC has been a catalyst for change and a strong contributor to most of the major accomplishments that have made the profession of interior design what it is today. Every teacher of interior design can benefit from membership in this organization. Information about IDEC can be obtained by writing to IDEC, 14252 Culver Dr., Suite A-311, Irvine, CA 92714.

National Council for Interior Design Qualifications (NCIDQ)

For information on **NCIDQ**, see p. 427.

Other Professional Organizations

Other professional design-related organizations are the following:

American Association of Housing Educators (AAHE)
Box 3AE, New Mexico State University
Las Cruces, NM 88003

American Home Lighting Institute (AHLI)
435 North Michigan Ave.
Chicago, IL 60611

American Institute of Architects (AIA)
1735 New York Ave.
Washington, DC 20006

Business & Inst. Furniture Manufacturers' Assoc. (BIFMA)
2335 Burton S.E.
Grand Rapids, MI 49506

Color Association of the United States
24 East 48th St.
New York, NY 10016

Color Marketing Group
1134 Fifteenth Street, NW
Washington, DC 20005

Council of Federal Interior Designers (CFID)
P.O. Box 27565
Washington, DC 20038

Designers' Lighting Forum (DLF)
IESNA, 345 East 47th St.
New York, NY 10017

Environmental Design Research
Association, Inc. (EDRA)
L'Enfant Plaza Station

P.O. Box 23129
Washington, DC 20024

Foundation for Interior Design
Education Research (FIDER)
60 Monroe Center
Grand Rapids, MI 49503

Illumineering Engineering Society
of North America (IESNA)
345 East 47th St.
New York, NY 10017

Interior Designers of Canada (IDC)
Ontario Design Centre
260 King St. East, #506
Toronto, Ontario, Canada M5A 1K3

International Association of Lighting Designers
(IALD)
c/o Wheel Gersztof Associates
30 West 22nd St.
New York, NY 10010

International Colour Authority
c/o Benjamin Dent & Company
33 Bedford Place
London WC1B 5JX, England

International Federation of Interior Designers (IFI)
P.O. Box 19126
1000 CG Amsterdam, Nederland

International Furnishings and Design Associates
(IFDA)
107 World Trade Center
P.O. Box 58045
Dallas, TX 75258

The International Society of Interior Designers
(ISID)
433 South Spring St., Suite 6-D
Los Angeles, CA 90013

National Association of Home Builders (NAHB)
15th and M Streets, NW
Washington, DC 20005-2892

National Association of Schools of Art and Design
(NASAD)
11250 Roger Bacon Drive #21
Reston, VA 22090

National Lighting Bureau (NLB)
2101 L. Street, NW
Washington, DC 20037

GETTING THAT FIRST JOB

How is that important first job obtained? Carefully designing and planning strategies for obtaining a job are often a full-time project. Reading trade journals, newsletters, and periodicals dealing with the field of interior design is a good start. Every available source of information, including visits to offices of agencies and professional organizations, can be explored.

Before going to the first interview, the prospective professional interior designer should examine personal needs, assets, and weaknesses. Determine salary requirements and corresponding responsibilities for that salary. Is the resumé a full and honest representation? Does it say too little or too much? Is the **portfolio** a true reflection of the best professional and creative work?

Next, examine your personal appearance carefully and objectively. The importance of personal appearance and presentation cannot be overemphasized. Being well groomed and appropriately dressed, standing straight, and sitting properly are all important. First impressions are lasting.

Approach the potential employer in a positive state of mind. The applicant should be polite, articulate, straightforward, honest, and self-confident, but without arrogance. It is helpful to point out one's training, skills, and genuine desire to be of service to the company.

ATTAINING VISIBILITY

A question facing every new interior designer is, How am I going to become known in the design field? To answer this question, a few suggestions may be helpful:

- Be proud of and enthusiastic about the profession. Let others be aware of this. Believe in yourself and in what you are doing. Before asking the public to believe in you, you must believe in yourself.
- Put your profession within reach of everyone in the community. Offer to give lectures for your firm. Contact local societies, clubs, and charities who may be interested in a lecture or slide presentation. Set up an adult education class through local high schools or colleges.
- Write articles for local newspapers. Express stimulating ideas. A good place to start might be an article on children's rooms, because these rooms quickly capture the public's interest.
- Contact local radio stations. They may be interested in presenting a series of daytime lectures on practical interior design problems.
- Show courtesy and concern for every client encountered, regardless of whether or not a contract is secured.
- Become involved in preservation and restoration efforts. If no preservation society exists in the community, the opportunity may be there to organize one. Nearly every town has some building worth preserving. Being responsible for putting a structure on the National Register of Historic Places can bring prestige, visibility, and a sense of pride to the community.
- Participate in national and local professional interior design or related organizations.

THE INTERIOR DESIGNER'S CHALLENGE FOR THE FUTURE

In light of the impact professional design and designers have on the economic, social, cultural, and environmental life of our nation, the challenge for the interior designer as a protector of the human environment in the final decade of the twentieth century is significant. Perhaps the first challenge and major responsibility is to design for people. Many designers are concerned primarily with the big commercial jobs that offer visible recognition. These types of jobs are most assuredly desirable and essential, but until people take precedence over buildings, the interior design profession will not have met its most important obligation: *to improve the quality of life for everyone.* To accomplish this, the interior designer must heighten the awareness on all levels of society of the many ways in which interior designers can affect the living and working environment.

In today's cost-inflated world, profound *social and economic changes* are occurring that present new challenges requiring immediate attention. Energy was once inexpensive and abundant, and home owners took it for granted. Today, *energy conservation* must be a part of design consciousness in all aspects of housing, both the exterior and the interior. Ever-rising costs and the changes in the size and composition of families, along with their increasing mobility, present a whole new range of problems, of which one of the most crucial is space. Many home owners are redesigning current facilities rather than building larger quarters. A shift from the group-oriented society of the 1960s to a concern for personal fulfillment is seen in the enlargement of home entertainment centers such as wet bars, hot tubs, wide video screens, and health and fitness centers.

Designers today and in the future will be challenged with addressing crucial environmental issues such as air quality, waste management, endangered rain forests, and recycling. Applying solutions to these concerns requires careful consideration and planning of environments that contribute to the emotional and physical well-being of the occupants in both residential and nonresidential projects. (See Chapter 13.) A considerable amount of time during the design process is spent evaluating *responsible solutions to environmental issues.* For example, "greening the environment or interior" is one means of providing better air quality since plants have been found to absorb pollutants and convert them to food, and then release fresh, clean oxygen. (See Figure 14.15.)

Technology is rapidly making inroads in residential designs. The burgeoning computer market and its corresponding technologies such as home computers, along with modified use of media equipment, specialized sound systems, and television apparatus, are making a direct impact on the interior design industry. For example, the "Smart House," as it is known today, incorporates the latest technological developments in home design that can regulate and perform daily tasks for the convenience and safety of the occupants. These technologies also present new problems to the designers, who must integrate the necessary machinery into personal living spaces without sacrificing the essential character of the home environment.

Another challenge to the interior designer is *preservation and restoration.* Awakening to the preservation of America's cultural heritage has prompted many people to buy and restore older homes. Long-standing but well-constructed buildings of all styles are being recycled to serve a wide range of commercial and public needs.

Despite the accomplishments of the preservation movement in America in recent years, the focus has been on exterior architecture rather than on interiors, which imposes a responsibility on the interior designer to broaden understanding and appreciation of the homes in which American ancestors lived. These homes provide a living record of social and cultural history and afford a base for authentic restoration and preservation. To bring about a fuller knowledge and understanding of the living past, the Educational Foundation of ASID is undertaking a research task with a "Significant Interiors" survey, which reaches across the country.

The requirement that today's interior designer stay up to date in the profession is no small order. In our rapidly changing world, some estimate that the amount of information doubles every four years, putting excessive demands on professionals in every field. As design has become more demanding and technical, specialists have emerged to take over in areas where the interior designer requires particular expertise, such as in lighting, drafting, and computer design.

As a practicing professional, the interior designer is compelled to *keep abreast of the field through a continuing educational process* in order to serve clients adequately. The interior designer must also remember that each job and client is unique. It is imperative to be careful and responsible with the client's funds, maintain integrity, and conscientiously lead and educate—not dictate. Although the ultimate goal is to support human values, family life, and society as a whole, the designer also has a responsibility to industry and the quality of life in a working environment.

The future will present many new conditions demanding innovative design solutions. Constant recycling and renovation of the environment are necessary to meet changing human needs. The shifting of population centers will bring about growth in some existing towns and communities and the development of new ones, which will require new ecological designs. By the turn of the century, it is predicted that artificial space habitats for human beings may exist. It is possible that technology may already be in place to implement such dramatic changes, but will interior designers be creatively and psychologically prepared?

All of this does not mean designers need to submit unquestioningly to the trends and fashions of the future.

FIGURE 14.15 Greening the environment in this master bedroom through the generous use of large plants provides a healthy atmosphere for the inhabitants. (Courtesy of Michael Rennick and Associates, Inc., Salt Lake City.)

Designers must be masters of change, not blind followers. The future can be built on the appreciation of and dedication to preserving the best of the past and combining it with the finest of the present. Designers should constantly and consistently reexamine old and eternal values. Environments may change, but the human needs, desires, and aspirations that have endured since the beginning of civilization will most likely remain the same.

The challenge for the designers of the future is to meet the demands of current and future technological advances while addressing functional and aesthetic needs of society. In view of current and future challenges in residential and nonresidential design, the services of interior designers are invaluable now and will be in demand even more in the future.

Interior Design as a Career

GLOSSARY

AAHE   American Association of Housing Educators.

Aalto, Alvar (1899–1976)   Internationally known Finnish pioneer of modern architecture and furnishings.

abacus   Small slab found on top of the capital of a column.

abstract   A type of decorative design that tends to draw away from nature. The design is modified so that the subject may not be recognizable.

acanthus leaves   A stylized design motif inspired by the acanthus plant and especially favored by the ancient Greeks and Romans.

accent lighting   Artistic lighting used to focus and emphasize particular objects or features.

accessible   An unobstructive passage into and throughout a structure making it negotiable for wheelchair users and others with physical limitations.

acetate   A man-made fiber derived from reconstituted cellulose and acetic acid.

achromatic   Hues "without color"; specifically, gray, black, and white.

acoustics   In design, the study of sound, including its properties and successful adaptation in a human environment.

acrylics   Strong, flexible, and transparent plastics that can be formed into any shape; used for many types of furnishings. Lucite and Plexiglas are common trade names.

active solar energy system   Architectural systems particularly designed to collect and distribute solar heat, often requiring additional supportive energy.

Adam, Robert (1728–1792)   Most important English designer and architect in the Neoclassic style. His work was inspired by the excavations of ancient Pompeii and Herculaneum in Italy.

adaptation   The modification of an item to make it fit more perfectly under conditions of its current environment. In furniture design, an adaptation indicates that only some elements of the original have been adapted to the present design.

adaptive reuse   Historical structures recycled for current use.

additive color   Mixing or adding primary hues through the use of either dyes and pigments or lighting.

adobe brick   A brick of sun-dried earth and straw; most often used in the Southwest adobe–style dwelling.

aesthetic   Pertaining to the beauty found in nature or an artistic composition.

affinity   Relationship, attraction, kinship.

afterimage   When the human eye focuses on a strong hue, the eye becomes saturated with that hue and an afterimage of that hue's complement can be seen when the eye focuses on a neutral surface.

air-exchange unit   A unit that allows fresh outside air to be drawn into a structure and discharges stale air. Contributes to a "healthy environment."

aisle   A hallway that runs parallel to the nave of a church and is separated from it by an arcade.

Albers, Josef (1888–1976)   A teacher at the Bauhaus in Germany and later at Yale University. Known for his theories on color.

A lamp   Term designated for the familiar arbitrary-shaped standard light globe or lamp.

alternation   A method of creating rhythm by changing or alternating the various elements of design. For example, thin stripe, fat stripe, thin stripe, etc., on a fabric.

ambient light A term interchangeable with *general lighting*; lighting that provides overall illumination.

amenities Certain areas or facilities for employees, owners, or renters that are commonly shared, such as social or recreational areas.

American Society of Interior Designers (ASID) The principal professional international organization of interior designers established to enact and maintain standards of excellence in the field.

amp (or ampere) The measurement of electrical current in a particular circuit.

analogous colors Hues adjacent on the color wheel.

analysis A step of the programming process in which information concerning each part is evaluated and decisions established.

anodize The application of a protective oxide covering on metal.

antebellum Existing before the Civil War.

anthemion A radiating stylized honeysuckle flower motif used by the ancient Greeks and in Neoclassic design.

anthropometrics The science of measuring the dimensions and functions of the human body and applying the results to the total design approach, ultimately providing human comfort and well-being.

antique A work of art, piece of furniture, or decorative object made at a much earlier period than the present, often at least 100 years old; according to U.S. customs laws, an item made before 1830.

apron The horizontal section beneath a table top, a chair seat, a chest of drawers, or window sill.

apse A semicircular or polygonal recess found at the end of a church plan.

arabesque A leaf-and-scroll pattern with stems rising from a root or other motif branching in spiral form; usually in a vertical panel.

arcade A series of adjoining arches with their supporting columns on piers.

arcaded panel A panel with a field depicting two dwarf columns supporting an arch.

architrave A horizontal member located above the column and capital in classical architecture.

architectural lighting Permanently wired and architecturally fixed luminaires.

armoire The French term for a tall cupboard or wardrobe with doors.

Art Deco A term derived from the 1925 Paris exhibition called "Les Expositions des Arts Decoratifs"; known during the period as Moderne or Modernistic. This stylistic movement emerged during the pre–World War I era and generally ended before the outbreak of World War II. It encompassed architecture, furniture, and the decorative arts.

artificial lighting Manufactured lighting produced by incandescence or fluorescence.

Art Nouveau A modern stylistic movement based on the flowing lines of nature that flourished principally in Europe and the United States circa 1890–1910.

Arts and Crafts Movement Founded by William Morris and others in England (circa 1860), this artistic movement was inspired by the pre-industrial craftsmanship of the medieval and Renaissance periods whose purpose was to create good design in all mediums. Known as one of the first important modern movements, its influence in hand-crafted items is still prevalent today.

ashlar Square or rectangular blocks of stone masonry used in the construction of a building.

ASID American Society of Interior Designers.

asymmetrical balance Placement of various objects or furnishings to create a sense of equilibrium.

atrium plan A floor plan in which all major rooms open onto a central atrium or court that may be open or roofed in glass.

Aubusson rug A flat tapestry rug woven in Aubusson, France, starting in the 16th century. Depicts various figures, scenes, and floral motifs.

Austrian shades A type of window shade scalloped at the bottom and shirred at the top.

authentic Conforming to an original so as to reproduce essential features.

awning window Windows with a hinge at the top allowing the window to swing outwards. (Occasionally the window is hinged at the bottom.)

Axminster Named after a town in England, this carpet construction has a cut wool pile and jute back. Now made on a special American loom, the yarns are set in a crosswise row, permitting each tuft to be controlled individually and allowing almost unlimited combinations of colors and patterns.

baffle A mechanism for deflecting light or directing it to reduce glare.

balance The placement of objects or furnishings in either a bisymmetrical, asymmetrical, or radial approach to create a sense of equilibrium.

balcony A projecting platform from the exterior or interior wall of a structure enclosed by a railing.

ballast An electrical transformer that converts current necessary for fluorescent lighting.

balloon-frame construction A type of construction employing a simple and economical skeletal frame and used most often for small wood houses with closely placed supportive elements with spaces in between for wiring, plumbing, and insulation.

balloon shades Term applied to shade window treatments that draw up from the bottom and display a shirred top with billowing gathered panels and a softly scalloped bottom.

baluster A turned, upright support of a rail, as in the railing of a staircase.

balustrade A row of balusters topped by a rail.

banquette Architecturally built-in seating units sometimes used in modern residential design or public settings.

baroque A powerful and imaginative art and design direction circa seventeenth and eighteenth centuries characterized by elaborate and massive decorative elements; a reaction against the severe classic style.

barrel vault An arched roof known since 4,000 B.C. and perfected by the ancient Romans.

barrier-free design Passageways designed so no physical obstacles prevent access for wheelchair users to various facilities throughout a space.

baseboard A strip of molding attached at the bottom of the wall along the floor's edge.

bas-relief A type of decoration in which the design is slightly raised from the surface or background.

batik A process of decorating fabric by wax coating the parts not to be dyed. After the fabric is dyed, the wax is removed.

batten A long strip of wood employed to cover the joint between two larger wood strips.

Bauhaus A school of art and architecture in Weimar (and later Dessau), Germany, from 1919–1933, founded by Walter Gropius for the purpose of uniting art and industry; considered the most influential element in the promotion of modern design and the International Style of architecture.

bay window An angled window that projects outwards from the wall surface.

bead-and-reel A convex classical Greek molding, with disks singly or in pairs, alternating with oblong beads.

beam A horizontal timber or metal bar supported on vertical posts, used to support a roof or ceiling.

bell gambrel A type of gambrel roof associated with the early Dutch settlers. The lower section splays outward to give the roof a "bell-shaped" appearance.

beltcourse See *stringcourse*.

Belter, John Henry (d. 1865) Popular New York cabinetmaker during the Victorian era known especially for his ornate Rococo Revival rosewood furniture.

belvedere See *cupola*.

bentwood A process of bending narrow strips of wood into various artistic forms; developed primarily by Austrian designer Michael Thonet during the latter half of the eighteenth century.

bergère A French armchair featuring a wood frame with upholstered arm panels, seat and back.

Bertoia, Harry (1915–1978) Important Italian-born American modern artist and furniture designer.

bevel The edge of any flat surface that has been cut at a slant to the main surface.

bidet A water-cleansing fixture used by adults after the toilet facility.

biodegradable The ability of a material to decompose naturally.

biotechnology The use of new advancements in engineering and technology in product design and the environment.

bisymmetrical design The arrangement of objects and furnishings so that they mirror each other. Sometimes called symmetrical, formal, or passive balance.

B lamp A term applied to a torpedo-shaped oval or candelabra lamp.

blueprint A photographic print, formerly white lines on a bright blue ground, used for copying architectural plans. The standard today is blue lines on a white ground.

board-and-batten construction Construction employing wide upright boards placed side by side with joints covered by *battens*.

boiserie A French word generally used to designate carved wood paneling.

bolection molding A projecting molding with a rounded edge.

bonnet roof A type of French hipped roof with a bottom that covers a surrounding porch. The shape resembles a bonnet.

bow window A semicurved window that projects outwards from the wall surface.

breakfront A large cabinet or bookcase, with a center section projecting beyond the flanking end sections.

Breuer, Marcel (1902–1981) Well-known teacher at the Bauhaus in Germany and later at Harvard University. Important architect and furniture designer. His classic modern chairs include the Cesca and Wassily.

Brewster color theory Another term for the Standard Color Wheel theory.

broadloom Carpet woven in 12-foot widths.

Brutalism A term first coined in the 1950s for a type of modern architecture that usually emphasizes raw concrete surfaces and bold form. Paul Rudolph and Louis Kahn were leading exponents of the design.

buffet A cabinet for holding dining room accessories and from which food may be served.

bullnose A 180-degree rounded wooden edge on a table, step, or top of a cabinet.

burl A strong irregularity in the wood grain providing an interesting design and color; often used for veneering in furniture.

burnish To make shiny or lustrous by rubbing.

buttress A supportive structure first used on the Gothic cathedral that splays from a wall to make it stable.

cabriole leg A furniture leg support designed in the form of a conventionalized animal leg with knee, ankle, and foot creating a double curve or **S** shape.

CAD (CADD) Computer-aided design (and drafting).

calendering A finishing process employed for fabrics where the textile is pressed between rollers.

candela In lighting, the unit of measure of *candlepower*.

candlepower A measurement of light intensity equal to the luminosity of a candle.

caning Flexible rattan or cane woven in open mesh for chairbacks, seats, and other furniture members.

canister A small box or case used for holding tea, coffee, flour, salt, or sugar. Early imported canisters were prized household items.

cantilever A projecting beam or furniture member supported at one end only.

capital The top treatment of a column. In classical Greek architecture, the capitals were Doric, Ionic, or Corinthian in style.

captain's walk A balustraded observation platform built atop the roof of a coastal dwelling, providing an unobstructed view of the sea; also called a widow's walk (most often found on Georgian and Federal homes).

casement window A window hinged on one side only, allowing it to swing inward or outward.

casepiece A general term applied to furniture storage pieces that have no upholstered components.

cella The interior space (or cell) of an ancient Roman temple especially copied during the Greek Revival period.

cellulosic fibers Term applied to natural fibers that come from plants such as cotton and linen.

ceramics Decorative or functional items fashioned from clay and fired (or baked) in a kiln.

chair rail See *dado*.

chaise longue A French term for a lounge chair (with or without arms) with an extended seat providing leg support for the occupant.

chandelier A lighting fixture suspended from the ceiling with branches to support candles or electric lamps.

château A castle or large country house in France.

chevron A repeating **V** shape or "zigzag" motif consisting of diagonal bars meeting at a point.

chimneypiece The architectural design that sheathes the firebox and flue.

chinoiserie (French) Refers to Chinese designs, which were popularly employed during the eighteenth century on European furniture.

Chippendale, Thomas (1718–1779) One of the most famous British furniture designers and cabinetmakers. Published his furniture designs in *The Gentleman and Cabinet-Maker's Director*, 1754.

chroma The purity or saturation of a color.

circa Approximately.

circulation The traffic patterns of occupants within an interior space—particularly important when planning rooms, stairways, hallways, etc.

C lamp A term to identify a cone-shaped lamp bulb.

clapboard A horizontal overlapping of thin wood boards used for the exterior sheathing of structures; popularly employed for seventeenth- and eighteenth-century Colonial style homes.

classic A term generally applied to design of timeless quality that transcends changes in taste and fashion.

classical A term relating to the arts of ancient Greece or Rome—especially designs created during the "Golden Age."

Classic Modernism A modern style of architecture that borrows design features from classical Greece and Rome. Edward Durell Stone was one of the leaders of this approach.

clearance The planning of space required by building codes to clear combustible heating units such as fireplaces, stoves, or furnaces. Also, adequate clearance space between furnishings for the convenience of users.

clerestory Windows placed at the top of a structure's wall allowing extra light; first built by the ancient Romans for churches and palaces.

closed plan An architectural floor plan in which interior space is divided into separate rooms.

club foot A club-shaped or rounded foot on a cabriole leg. Especially associated with Queen Anne furniture.

cluster planning A method of arranging concentrated dwelling units, usually low-rise and either separate or attached, to take advantage of communal open spaces.

code Federal, state, or local laws applied to the design of buildings in relation to safety and health standards.

coffered ceiling Ornamental sunken panels between beams employed for a flat, vaulted, or domed ceiling providing a three-dimensional effect.

cold cathode lighting Technical term for neon lighting.

Colonial A term loosely used in referring to the 200-year period that includes the settlement of the early colonies in America through the Federal period (circa 1607–1835). According to some authorities, however, nothing after 1776 is properly called Colonial.

colonnade Columns arranged in a straight or curved row, often supporting an entablature.

colonnette A miniature colonnade used for decoration.

columned chimney (clustered chimney) A cluster or arrangement of a number of chimneys together, associated with the English Medieval style.

C.O.M. Customer's own material. The customer purchases fabric for a job from another source.

commode A French term referring to a low chest supported on legs with drawers.

complementary colors Two colors directly across the color wheel from each other. Also various combinations of cool and warm colors.

computer network Computer terminals within an office that are connected by cables, permitting access to the same data.

computer-aided design (CAD) Designing and drafting are developed on a computer screen where a variety of perspective views can be created and printed. CAD techniques are now in general use by many design offices.

conceptual drawings The design concept or idea is sketched or illustrated.

condominium A multiunit structure, such as an apartment house, in which each unit is individually owned. Maintenance and services are provided but are paid for by the residents.

conduction heater A method of heating employing a radiator that circulates hot water or steam, providing warm air within a space.

console table A table designed to be fixed on a wall; sometimes supported by two front legs.

contemporary design Living or occurring at the same period of time. In furniture the term commonly refers to a modified type of modern or updated traditional design.

conventional design A type of applied ornamentation or decorative design that stylizes or modifies nature.

corbel A bracket or projection from a wall used to support a molding or beam.

Corinthian The most ornate of the three Greek orders, characterized by its capital of small volutes (spiral, scroll-shaped ornaments) and acanthus leaves.

cornice A horizontal and projecting member that crowns an architectural composition; a molding on a wall near the ceiling or under the eaves of the roof. Cornice board is a molding used with drapery instead of a valance.

coromandel screen A large free-standing paneled lacquered screen with incised designs, made in China but originally imported from the Coromandel Coast of India.

corridor Term used for a hallway, generally in a public building.

Cotswold An area of rolling green hills and limestone outcroppings, mainly in Gloucestershire, England. The region is famous for picturesque stone houses called Cotswolds.

coved ceiling A ceiling that meets the wall by means of a concave curve rather than a right angle.

cove lighting A lamp or lighting placed near the ceiling with a deflector that directs the light upward.

Crafts Revival A modern style popular since the 1960s that draws inspiration from the ideals of the Arts and Crafts Movement during the latter half of the 19th century.

credenza A long, table-height cupboard with drawers and doors. Popular during the Italian Renaissance; today, a low storage unit with doors and often drawers.

crown lintel An architectural detail used above windows, particularly in the late 18th and early 19th centuries. The lintel, often called a jack-arch lintel, features a crown-shaped keystone.

crown molding The uppermost molding.

cruciform A cross-shaped form.

crystal The finest quality of lead glass.

cupola A small structure built on top of a roof for a lookout or to provide interior lighting; commonly used in Georgian, Federal, and Victorian structures.

cyma curve A double curve formed by the union of a concave and convex line.

dado The lower part of an interior wall when treated in a different manner from the wall above; usually defined by a molding called a dado cap or chair railing.

daub A sticky or heavy mud or plaster infill between half-timber construction on the medieval English house.

day-bed An extended type of couch or chair that can be used as a bed.

deconstructivism A modern style of architecture developed by a few architects in the late 1980s that employs broken, warped, overlapping, unexpected, or disturbing forms.

demographics A term relating to statistics concerning a specific population.

design process A progression of steps involved in addressing and solving design problems.

design statement A simple statement outlining the goals and needs of the end users for a specific design project.

De Stijl A Dutch art and design movement from 1917–1929 characterized by abstract forms, right angles, smooth shiny surfaces, and the use of primary colors plus black, white, and gray; helped pioneer Modernism.

dhurrie rug A cotton or wool flat tapestry woven rug from India. Designs usually depict stylized or abstract flowers or animals combined with geometric forms.

diagramming The process of planning space on paper.

diffuse To soften and disperse or spread light over a surface by covering the lamp with a glass or plastic covering.

distressed Refers to a surface treatment found on antique reproductions when the furniture is intentionally damaged to provide an aged appearance.

Doric Pertaining to the simplest of the three orders of ancient Greek architecture.

dormer A window in a small gablelike projection built out from a sloping roof.

double glazing A process of hermetically sealing two sheets of glass together with air trapped between. This type of glass provides efficient insulation against heat and cold.

double-hung window A window divided into two sections, one lowering from the top, and the other rising from the bottom.

dovecote Originally, a small, compartmented, raised house or box, used for housing domestic pigeons; eventually became a roof type.

dovetail joint A type of wood joint used in furniture construction consisting of two slotted fan-shaped pieces that interlock.

dowel A round wood peg. Often used for furniture joinery, the peg is inserted into a cavity of the same size.

dower chest A chest to hold items for a prospective bride; used by most civilizations. In early Pennsylvania it took on distinctive characteristics.

downlight Recessed or ceiling-mounted architectural lighting with lamps that direct the light downwards.

Dresden Fine porcelain made in Meissen, near Dresden, Germany. Established 1710–1720, the factory produced some of the most famous china in Europe.

drop-leaf table A table with one or two hinged members that can drop to the sides or be supported to provide a larger tabletop surface.

dropped ceiling A ceiling that is suspended below the original ceiling. Often ceilings are dropped when too high for personal preference or function.

drywall A structural wall also known as Sheetrock or plasterboard.

Dutch door A single-hinged door divided horizontally so each section can be opened independently.

dye lot Fabric or wallpaper from one batch of a specific dye mixture.

Eames, Charles (1907–1979) Internationally known post–World War II modern designer along with his wife, Ray. The Eames Lounge is an important classic chair.

Early Georgian (1700–1750) A stately and elegant architectural and decorative style in America reflecting the English Renaissance.

ears Small squares or rectangles outlined with moldings. Found on the edges of some chimneypieces, doors, or other architectural details.

eave A protecting lower edge of a roof which overhangs the walls of a building.

eclecticism Mixing furnishings or borrowing styles from various sources and periods with an eye to compatibility.

egg-and-dart A classical Greek molding consisting of ovoid (egg-shaped) forms alternating with dartlike designs.

electromagnet A core of magnetic material surrounded by a coil of wire through which an electric current is passed to magnetize the core.

elements of design The "tools" used by the designer to create an environment and achieve the goals or principles of design. The elements are texture, line, pattern, space, form or shape, light, and color.

ell A wing or extension placed at a right angle to the structure.

elliptical fanlight A fan-shaped window that topped the central doorways of Federal-period houses in America.

embossing A treatment used for fabrics and wallpapers that imprints a three-dimensional pattern on the surface.

Empire (1804–1820) A grand decorative style influenced by the reign of Napoleon I of France.

entablature The upper part of a wall, usually supported by columns or pilasters and in classical orders consisting of the *architrave, frieze,* and *cornice.*

epergne A tiered centerpiece.

ergonomics A relatively new science with a goal to provide a comfortable relationship between human beings and their environment (especially the working environment), through the study of body mechanics and sensory performance.

escutcheon In hardware, it refers to a shaped plate for a keyhole or a metal fitting to which a handle or knob is attached.

étagère A series of shelves supported by vertical supports; used chiefly for display.

eyeball In lighting, a ceiling-mounted or recessed incandescent fixture with a pivoting spherical lamp that can be maneuvered to direct the light where desired.

facade Refers to the exterior front of a building, either decorative or structural.

fanlight See *elliptical fanlight.*

fauteuil   The French term for an open armchair.

faux finish   A "false" impression of a natural material. For example, to finish a surface so it looks like wood, marble, or granite.

Federal period   The political, social, and decorative formation era in America following the Revolutionary War (circa 1790–1825).

fenestration   The placement, type, and design of windows and other openings found on a building.

festoon   A carved, molded, or painted classical ornament representing a decorative chain, swag, or strip.

fiber   A natural or synthetic substance processed into a thread or yarn of continuous length.

fiberglass   Glass fibers used for fabric or molded for furniture, furniture parts, or skylights.

filament   A threadlike conductor (as of carbon or metal) that is rendered incandescent (brilliant) by the passage of an electric current.

finial   An upright ornament that forms the upper extremity of an architectural detail, a piece of furniture, or an accessory.

fish-scale shingles   Small pointed or rounded shingles that provide decorative interest on the exterior of the Queen Anne Victorian house.

F lamp   A flame-shaped lamp or bulb, often with a striated flame design. Used particularly for chandeliers.

Flemish   Relating to or characteristic of the Low Countries, now Belgium and the Netherlands.

Flemish gable   A gable composed of graceful curves or steps. An architectural detail especially used by the Dutch settlers.

flocking   A process employed for duplicating the effect of velvet fabrics on wallpaper in which fibers are applied to an adhesive. A type of carpet also involves this process.

flokati rug (or floccati)   A rug woven from goat's hair that has been soaked in cold water to give it a thick texture. Generally imported from Greece.

fluorescent lighting   Artificial light produced when a gaseous mixture of mercury and argon, sealed within a glass tube that is lined with a fluorescent coating, is activated by an electrical current.

fluting   Parallel concave grooves commonly used on the shafts of columns.

foil   Anything that serves, by contrast of color, pattern, texture, or other elements, to adorn or set off another thing to advantage; also a wallpaper with the appearance of a thin sheet of metal; a background.

folk rugs   Handwoven flat rugs made by various ethnic groups depicting native designs and using natural dyes.

footcandle   An international unit of light measurement. It is the illumination at a 1-ft distance from the light of one candle. The intensity of light is calculated in footcandles.

footlambert   In lighting, the unit of measure for reflected light.

Foundation for Interior Design Education Research (FIDER)   The national accrediting organization for interior design educational programs.

Frankl, Paul (1887–1958)   Austrian-born American furniture and interior designer. Particularly known for his "skyscraper" furniture and contribution to the Art Deco style.

Freestyle   A modern design direction employed by some architects and interior designers expressing free use of color, form, texture, and other elements to create an unexpected design.

French doors   Paired, single-hinged doors of paned glass—a walk-through window—which swings either inward or outward.

French Empire   See *Empire*.

fresco   The art of painting on moist lime plaster with water-based pigments.

fretwork   Interlaced ornamental work either perforated or cut in low relief, usually in geometric patterns; also, tracery of glazed doors and windows.

frieze   The horizontal decorative section found between the *architrave* and the *cornice* in classical architecture.

Fuller, Buckminster (1895–1983)   American engineer, architect, designer, and educator. Developed the revolutionary "geodesic dome" construction.

fusuma screen   A sliding movable screen used in Japanese houses as a partition to define space.

gable   The triangular-shaped end portion of a building formed by a pitched roof.

galerie   A term for a covered porch found on the French home.

gallery   A miniature railing placed along the edge of a tabletop or shelf.

gambrel roof   A roof made from two lengths of lumber, the upper one being flatter and the lower one a steeper slope.

generic   A term pertaining to the characteristics of a particular type or class of fibers.

geodesic dome   A dome of interlocking polygons held together by a self-supporting network of rods and covered with a variety of materials—usually a plastic membrane or glass. The geodesic dome was developed by Buckminster Fuller, an American architect and engineer.

Georgian   An English architectural and furniture style popular during the reigns of George I, II, and III in England (circa 1714–1790) and copied by Americans; furniture included the styles of Queen Anne, Chippendale, Hepplewhite, and Sheraton.

gingerbread   Lacy architectural detail on a Victorian house.

G lamp   A globe-shaped lamp or bulb.

glass block   Hollow glass forms in a variety of sizes and textures used in building construction to emit light.

glazing (paint treatment)   A type of painted surface treatment achieved by applying layers of colored transparent paint to produce a striated effect.

glazing (windows)   Placement of window glass in an architectural opening.

golden mean   The division of a line somewhere between 1/2 and 1/3 its length. Can be applied when planning any wall composition.

golden section   The division of a line or form in such a way that the ratio of the smaller portion to the larger is the same as that of the larger portion to the whole.

Gothic   Refers to the period from approximately 1160 to 1530 A.D., in which the ecclesiastical architecture dominated all the arts. The Gothic arch and vault were the most significant design contributions.

gradation   A type of rhythm produced by the succession of the size of an object from large to small or of a color from dark to light.

grain   Refers to the vertical configurations or textural (coarse or fine) features of wood.

Graves, Michael (b. 1934) American architect who has played a significant role in the development of the Post-Modern style.

graygoods or greige Woven fabrics that have not been dyed, treated, or changed from their natural state.

Greek Revival The third and final phase (circa 1825–1845) of the Neoclassic style in America in which bold and monumental characteristics were related to the early forms of Greece and Rome.

greening the environment A popular term used by designers to refer to creating a healthy environment through the use of live plants and foliage.

Gropius, Walter (1883–1969) German architect who was one of the key figures in the development of modernism. Founder of the Bauhaus.

grout A mortar (generally of cement), used to set tiles or fill in cavities.

half-timber construction Construction of timber frame, with the spaces filled with masonry or lath and plaster.

hand or handle The feel or drape of fabric.

hardware Metal fittings used for furniture such as keyholes, drawer and cupboard pulls.

healthy environment A term applied to an environment that has clean air free of pollutants.

Hepplewhite, George (d. 1786) Important 18th century English furniture designer and cabinetmaker whose furniture drawings were the inspiration for the Hepplewhite style of furniture.

HID High-intensity discharge lighting.

highboy A tall chest of drawers supported on tall legs and divided horizontally into two sections; particularly popular during the Georgian period.

High Tech A current design expression developed during the late 1970s employing industrial components and the latest technology, providing a streamlined and mechanical appearance.

hip roof A roof with sloping ends and sloping sides.

Hitchcock chair An American chair (1820–1850) named for Lambert Hitchcock of Connecticut. It derives from a Sheraton "fancy" chair and is often black with stenciled fruit and flower motifs.

Hoffmann, Josef (1870–1956) Important early modern Austrian architect and designer and leader of the Secession and Wiener Werkstatte.

hue The distinct name of a color such as blue, orange, or yellow. One of the three dimensions of color in the Munsell color system.

hutch An informal chest or cabinet common to many countries, which came to America from England. The type most commonly used has bottom doors and open upper shelves.

HVAC Indication for heating, ventilating, and air-conditioning systems.

ikebana The Japanese term for the art of arranging flowers according to precise rules.

incandescent lighting Light produced by heating a tungsten filament sealed in a light bulb.

indigenous Inherent; native to or living naturally in a country.

ingress A term referring to the entrance into a building.

inlay Pieces of stone, wood, shell, metal, or ivory arranged in a design composition and set into another piece of wood or other material for a decorative effect.

insulation The use of nonconductors between the inside and outside of a structure or between materials to prevent the transfer of sound, heat, cold, or electricity.

intensity A dimension of color that denotes the dullness or brightness of a hue. Also referred to as *chroma*.

Interior Design Educators Council (IDEC) A society formed for interior design educators.

International Style A style of architecture based on the Bauhaus and principles of other leading modernists. Developed during the 1920s, the style is simple, structural, and functional.

Ionic The second Greek order designated by the spiral volutes of its capital.

Italianate Name given to one of the main styles of American Victorian architecture. It embodied many features of the Italian villa and remained in vogue for almost 100 years (circa 1830s–1920s).

jack-arch lintel See *crown lintel*.

Jacobean From the Latin *Jacobus* (James); the general term for English furniture styles from circa 1603–1688. Jacobean was the prototype of most furniture made by the early colonists in New England during the seventeenth and early eighteenth centuries.

Jacquard A loom apparatus for weaving fabrics of intricate weaves and patterns; invented in France in 1801 by Joseph Marie Jacquard.

jalousie window A window made of narrow horizontal and adjustable glass louvers that control ventilation and light.

jamb The vertical side sections of a window or door.

Johnson, Phillip (b. 1906) Often referred to as the "dean of modern American architecture." Leading figure in the development of modern architecture.

Jones, Inigo (1573–1652) English architect largely responsible for introducing Renaissance and classical architecture in England.

knot Wood with a distinctive oval or round feature in the grain. Knots, which were originally avoided, are often chosen today for their effect.

ladderback A term describing a chair with a back composed of horizontal slats resembling a ladder.

lambrequin An ornamental window treatment, usually in the form of a wooden frame across the top and down the sides of the window, either painted or covered with fabric. Common in French country houses.

laminate The binding of layers of wood together. In paneling, several layers are laid alternately across the grain for strength and durability. For decorative purposes, a thin layer of fine wood (veneer) is glued to the surface of the basic wood; a process also used for plastics.

lamp The light source (base and bulb or tube) of artificial lighting.

late Georgian (1750–1790) An American style especially popular during the reigns of George II and III of England. Strong influence of architects James Gibbs in America and Andrea Palladio in Italy.

latex A rubberlike substance found in paint, most often water-based.

lath Thin strips of wood or a metal mesh attached to the structural frame of a building to support plaster, tile, reinforced concrete, or other material.

lathe A machine used to turn wood or metal into various shapes.

latillas Crude sticks laid between the *vigas* (pole beams) in the Southwest Adobe-style home.

law of chromatic distribution "The large areas should be covered in the most neutralized colors of the scheme. As the areas reduce in size, the chromatic intensity may be proportionally increased."

Le Corbusier (1887–1965) (Charles Edouard Jenneret) One of the most significant leaders in the development of modernism and the International Style.

leno A loose, open weave with warp yarns wound in half twists around each other, alternating in position on each row.

linenfold A Gothic decorative detail depicting a stylized folded linen fabric.

lintel The horizontal beam or component that spans the area between openings such as columns, windows, and doors.

Louis XV style (1723–1774) French period also known as rococo. Marked by elaborate asymmetrical curvilinear designs.

Louis XVI style (1770–1790) French Neoclassic period inspired by the excavations of ancient Pompeii and Herculaneum.

louver A slatted panel (usually wood) for controlling the flow of air and the radiation of light; most often used as a window treatment.

lowboy A low chest of drawers supported on legs; particularly associated with the Georgian style.

lumen A quantitative unit for measuring light output.

luminaire A complete light fixture including the lamp and all supportive elements.

luminescence Commonly referred to as fluorescence.

mantel The shelf that projects from a chimneypiece.

mansard roof A roof having two slopes on all sides, the lower one steeper than the upper one.

marbleizing A painted surface treatment that imitates the texture of polished marble.

Marlborough leg A square straight leg with a square foot most often associated with Chippendale furniture.

marquetry A decorative inlay design glued into furniture and floors employing a variety of woods or other materials.

matte A dull finish.

medieval Refers to the Middle Ages—a turbulent time that followed the decline of the Roman Empire and extended to the Renaissance, covering roughly 1,000 years (circa 500 to 1500 A.D.).

melamine An extremely durable opaque or translucent plastic used most often for dinnerware and counter tops; well-known trade names include Formica and Melmac.

Memphis A radical modern style that originated in 1981 with the Austrian designer Ettore Sottsass. Characterized by free use of color, form, and texture.

metamerism The effect of various types of light in changing the appearance of a color.

metope In classic architecture, the square panels between the triglyphs found on the entablature of the Doric order.

miter Joining two members of material at a 45-degree angle to form a corner.

modillion An ornamental bracket (usually console shaped) that often supports a cornice or soffit.

modular Constructed with standardized units or modules.

module One in a series of standardized units to be integrated together, such as building construction units or a set of furniture.

molding An architectural wood strip, usually decorative, that projects from the ceiling or wall surface; may also be of metal, plaster, or plastic.

monochromatic A color scheme that uses one color with varying value and chroma.

mordant Any substance that serves to produce a fixed color in a textile fiber, leather, or other similar material.

mortise and tenon A type of joint used in furniture construction with a projecting tenon that fits into the mortise or cavity.

mosaic A floor or wall decoration made up of small pieces of stone or glass arranged in a design.

mottle A dripped or irregular color.

mullion A horizontal member dividing glazed doors, windows, or bookcases.

Munsell color theory A popular color theory based on three dimensions of color: hue, value, and chroma. Each color has a number notation.

muntin A vertical bar dividing the panes of a window, door, or bookcase. *Muntin* is often used interchangeably with *mullion.*

nap A fuzzy surface found on fabrics composed of short fibers or hairs.

National Council for Interior Design Qualification (NCIDQ) An official body for testing professional interior design competencies and establishing guidelines for legal licensing.

nave The principal section of a church, usually flanked by the aisles and extending from the entrance to the altar or chancel.

negative space A term that refers to the area around forms in a two- or three-dimensional composition.

Neoclassic Revivals simulating the ancient classical designs of Greece and Rome, such as Louix XVI, Adam, Directoire, and Empire styles.

neutralized color A hue that has been neutralized or dulled in its intensity or chroma.

newel post The main post at the foot of a stairway.

niche A shallow recess in an exterior or interior wall; usually with a rounded head.

nogging The brickwork (or infill) found between half-timber construction.

nonarchitectural lighting Any type of luminaire that is portable.

nosing The projecting edge at the top of a stair's riser.

occult balance Another term for asymmetrical or informal balance.

open office planning A large office space where divisions are made by modular furnishings to create workstations.

open plan A floor plan with a minimum of fixed partitions, allowing space to flow from one area to another.

opposition A type of rhythm found in a room wherever right angles meet.

orders of architecture In classical Grecian architecture: the Doric, Ionic, and Corinthian styles of columns.

organic architecture Modern architectural approach put forth by Frank Lloyd Wright. The house should "grow out of the land."

orientation Placement or arrangement of various elements such as buildings, windows, rooms, or furnishings in relation to points on the compass or other elements.

Ostwald color theory A color theory based on the amount of black and white added to a hue.

ottoman A general term for a large upholstered footstool.

palisade wall A wall constructed of boards and battens (vertical paneling).

Palladianism Relating to a classical style in architecture based on the works of Andrea Palladio (1518–1580), the most copied of all Italian architects.

Palladian window A window consisting of three vertical parts with the central section higher than the flanking ones and surmounted by a fanlight. This window was a popular feature in the Palladian style of architecture in England in the seventeenth century and in America in the eighteenth century.

parapet A low wall or protective railing at the edge of a roof or platform.

PAR lamp Reflective parabolic aluminized reflector lamp.

parquetry A mosaic of wood laid in geometric patterns.

passive solar energy system A system of collecting, storing, and distributing solar heat by employing elements of the structure such as glassed-in porches oriented to the sun.

paterae Oval or round decorative details particularly used during the Federal period.

patina A mellow surface often developed with age.

patio (Spanish) A courtyard.

pavilion A part of a building projecting from the main structure.

pedestal A support at the base of a column; any base or foundation on which to display an art object.

pediment A triangular architectural structure above a portico, window, or door.

pembroke table A small table with one drawer and drop leaves.

pendant An object suspended from above.

pendant chandelier A light suspended from the ceiling with a single fixture.

pent roof A roof type used on the Pennsylvania German house. A small projected eave found above the first story.

perimeter lighting Lighting that follows the outer boundary of a room.

period style A term used to designate a single item or a complete interior including the architectural background, furniture, and decorative arts prevalent in a specific country at a particular time in history.

peristyle A series of columns surrounding a structure. Also a garden surrounded by columns at the back of an ancient Roman house.

pier A rectangular pillar devoid of detail.

pilaster An upright rectangular projection or partial column fixed to a wall, architecturally treated as a column.

pilling Describes fiber that works out of the yarn structure and makes little balls on the surface of a carpet or fabric.

pitched roof A sloping roof—either a low or high pitch.

plan A drawn arrangement of elements in a structure indicating walls, rooms, spaces, and so forth shown from floor level.

PL lamp A twin fluorescent bulb.

plywood A process of laminating layers of wood with alternating grain direction. Usually the top layer or *veneer* is of a finer quality; used for furniture and paneling.

POE Postoccupancy evaluation.

polyurethane A group of plastics characterized by light weight and flexibility and varying in density, hardness, and resilience.

Pompeii An Italian city buried in 79 A.D. by the ash of Mount Vesuvius and excavated in the eighteenth century. The great interest it aroused in the classical arts inaugurated the classic revival.

portfolio A flexible case used by designers containing renderings, pictures, and other design-related projects.

portico A projection from the main structure of a building over the front entrance supported by columns and often capped by a pediment.

positive space The two- or three-dimensional shapes or forms within a space.

Post-Modernism A new direction of modern architecture that for the most part rejects the philosophies of the Bauhaus; freely borrows from the past, but extremely reinterpreted and updated.

Prang color wheel Another term for the standard color wheel.

prefabricated (prefab) Mass produced in standardized modules or parts for later assembly at the factory or building site.

primitive painting Refers to many American paintings done in the late seventeenth and early eighteenth centuries by untrained artists. The style is peculiar and unlifelike, and all such works have a remarkable similarity that is easily distinguishable.

principles of design The goals of a design composition consisting of scale, proportion, balance, rhythm, emphasis, and harmony.

program The first step in a design project, involving a verbal outline of goals, requirements, and plans.

prototype An original from which another item is modeled.

proxemics A study developed especially during the 1980s concerned with the relationship of human psychological aspects to personal space needs.

PS lamp A reference to the pear-shaped incandescent lamp or bulb.

Pueblo One of the Indian tribes of New Mexico; an Indian village built in the form of apartment houses.

Queen Anne period The reign of Queen Anne of England from 1702 to 1714. Also associated with a type of 18th century furniture.

quoin A solid exterior angle on a building distinguished from the adjoining surface by material, color, size, or projection.

ragging and rag rolling A wall surface treatment where paint is partially wiped or rolled off with a rag.

rail The horizontal member of a door frame or panel.

rainbow roof A gently curved gable particularly seen on a Cape Cod house.

ranch style Also known as a California ranch or rambler home; a ground-hugging single-level plan with a low-pitched overhanging roof supported by posts.

random plank Wood planks laid in a manner disregarding the width of individual boards.

reeding A small convex molding—the reverse of fluting; used on columns, pilasters, and furniture.

refraction The bending of a light, sound, or heat ray.

Regency A 19th century English style during the regency (1811–1820) of George IV.

Renaissance A period in Europe after the medieval and Gothic periods. Beginning in Italy in the fourteenth century, it was marked by a humanistic and classical period in which an unprecedented flourishing of the arts occurred.

replica An accurate reproduction.

repoussé Relief work done on metal, created by hammering the material on the reverse side.

reproduction A precise duplication of a historic style; a replica.

resilience The ability of a particular material to give or spring back when pressed.

rhythm Elements in a room that assist the eye in moving easily from one area to another.

riser The upright member between two stair treads.

rococo A phase of European art that had its roots in the late Italian Renaissance but developed in France during the reign of Louis XV in the first half of the eighteenth century. It was an extravagant style using symmetry, shells, rocks, and all manner of elaborate decoration.

Romanesque An architectural style popular in Europe from circa 800–1150; use of the semicircular arch, massive rusticated stone, and the horizontal line; revived during the late nineteenth century in Europe and America.

Rya rug A hand-hooked "shaggy" rug from Scandinavia.

salamander-back chair A ladderback chair in which each crossbar resembles two salamanders; a fitting piece for Country French. The salamander was the symbol of Francis I, king of France.

sash The framework (in a window or door) in which the glass is set. It may constitute a movable part.

Savonnerie Eighteenth-century French pile rug popular in Louis XIV period. Patterns often inspired by formal gardens.

scale Refers to the overall "size" of an object or its parts compared with other objects or parts.

sconce A lighting fixture secured to the wall.

Secession (ca. 1897) A group of progressive designers in Vienna, Austria, who "seceded" from using historic styles. Their motto was: "To each time its art; to each art its freedom."

shade A color that has been darkened by adding black; a low value.

shoji A basic element of a Japanese house, it is made of panes of rice paper and wooden mullions and used as an exterior window. Shoji panels are also employed as wall partitions and freestanding screens.

sick building syndrome An unhealthy environment with stale or polluted air.

simultaneous contrast When a hue, value, or chroma is perceived as different as a result of being viewed beside or on a different colored background.

soffit A lower section of a ceiling; area underneath this section.

spectral Pertaining to or made by the spectrum.

standard milled items Items of various kinds (e.g., doors, door frames, windows, window frames, and mantels) made in standard sizes in large quantities in the factory, thus making the cost much less than for custom-made items.

stepped gable A gable in which the sides ascend to the peak in steps; a style brought to America by the Dutch.

stile The vertical or upright supportive frame for a door.

stretcher The horizontal supportive crosspiece spanning the area between the legs of a chair or table.

stringcourse A narrow horizontal band placed on the exterior of the Georgian house between the first and the second floors.

stucco A type of plaster surface treatment used on exterior or interior walls.

swag A festoon of flowers, fruit, or drapery.

synthesis The step of bringing together all parts to form a whole or all information gathered in the programming process.

synthetic Something artificial simulating the genuine piece.

systems furniture Flexible type of component furniture that can be arranged and rearranged to accommodate various needs for workstations.

tambour The front of a piece of furniture made with strips of wood attached to fabric and adjusted on a track, allowing it to open and close.

task light Efficient and functional lighting especially designed for various types of work or tasks.

tatami mat A soft straw mat, approximately 3 ft by 6 ft by 1½ in., which is the basic element of the Japanese house and serves as a unit of measurement. It is the basis of organization and determines the size and proportion of all spaces. The dark lines of its binding form an overall grid pattern, according to which rooms are sized.

templates Small patterns of furniture (either to cut or trace) used as guides in planning rooms.

terrace Usually refers to a relatively level paved area adjoining a building.

thermoplastic Any plastic material that softens with heat and hardens when cooled. Examples include vinyls and acrylics.

tint A color that is lightened by adding white; a high value.

T lamp A tubular-shaped light bulb or lamp.

toile de Jouy Fabric made at Jouy, France, by Oberkampf in the late eighteenth and early nineteenth centuries; usually printed on cotton using only one color (red most popular) on a natural ground. Rural French and Chinese scenic designs are the most characteristic.

tokonoma A sacred recessed niche or alcove featured in the Japanese house.

tone A neutralized hue produced by adding gray or the color's complement.

tongue-and-groove joint The rib on one edge of a board is made to fit into a corresponding groove in the edge of another board to make a flush joint.

torchère A tall floor lamp with a design that casts light in an upward direction. Particularly popular for the Art Deco and Post-Modern styles.

tracery Decorative carved stone or wood openwork in the head of a Gothic window.

transept The lateral arms (across the nave) of cruciform churches.

tread The horizontal section of a stair.

trompe l'oeil French expression meaning "to fool the eye"; a term applied to wall decoration showing bookshelves full of books, cupboards with dishes of fruit, and so on, in remarkably realistic renderings.

tryglyph Greek for "thrice grooved." On a Doric frieze, the blocks that alternate with the metopes.

Tudor The name of the ruling house of England from 1485 to 1603.

Tudor arch A low or flattened elliptical arch.

tungsten-halogen lamp A highly efficient incandescent light source (also known as a quartz lamp) employing tubes, bulbs, or reflectors.

turning See *lathe*.

user The client or person who will use the designed space or environment.

user friendly Pertaining to computer software or hardware that is relatively easy to manipulate.

valance A short decorative fabric treatment at the top of a window that conceals drapery, curtains, and often lighting.

value The lightness or darkness of a color, ranging on a scale from white to black.

veneer Thin sheets of wood or other material (usually of a fine quality) used as a top surface over other more ordinary materials such as plywood.

veranda An open galley or portico (usually roofed) attached to the exterior of a building.

vernacular Reference to the distinguishing attributes or qualities of a certain culture.

Versailles The magnificent baroque palace built by Louis XIV in the late seventeenth century outside of Paris.

Victorian era (1837–1901) The period during the reign of Queen Victoria. A revival of many styles from the past. Coincides with the Industrial Revolution.

vigas The large exposed pole beams that support the roof in the Southwest Adobe structure.

villa (Italian) A large residential structure.

visual weight A visual (not necessarily actual) weight impression of a space and its components depending on various design elements including color, texture, light, and pattern.

volute The spiral-shaped decoration that tops the capital of the Ionic order.

wainscot Wood paneling that extends partway to the ceiling. Associated with the Medieval interior.

wall sconce An ornamental wall bracket to hold candles or electric bulbs.

wattle Interlacing twigs that function as infilling for timber-framed structures.

weft The horizontal cross-threads (or filler threads) of a textile. Also known as woof threads.

work triangle The work pattern in a kitchen connecting the three basic elements of sink, refrigerator, and stove.

wrought iron Ornamental iron that has been worked into a decorative shape or design.

zapata A carved decorative supportive bracket found on the Southwest Adobe house.

zones A term referring to the basic functional areas of a residential or nonresidential space, including social zones, work zones, and private zones.

BIBLIOGRAPHY

Abercrombie, Stanley. *A Philosophy of Interior Design.* New York: Harper & Row, 1990.

Albers, Josef. *Interaction of Color.* New Haven, Conn.: Yale University Press, 1975.

Alexander, Harold. *Design: Criteria for Decisions.* New York: Macmillan, 1976.

Alexander, Patsy. *Textile Fabrics and Their Selection.* Boston: Houghton Mifflin, 1976.

Allen, Edward, and Joseph Iano. *The Architect's Studio Companion.* New York: Wiley, 1989.

American National Standard for Buildings and Facilities— Providing Accessibility and Usability for Physically Handicapped People. A11.1–1986. Washington, D.C.: U.S. Department of Housing and Urban Development, 1986.

American National Standard Specifications for Making Buildings and Facilities Accessible to and Usable by Physically Handicapped People, ANSI A117.1–1980. New York: American National Standards Institute, 1980.

Anscombe, Isabelle. *Arts and Crafts Style.* New York: Rizzoli, 1991.

Aronson, Joseph. *The Encyclopedia of Furniture.* 3d ed. New York: Crown, 1965.

Ball, Victoria Kloss. *Architecture and Interior Design: Europe and America from the Colonial Era to Today.* 2 vols. New York: Wiley, 1980.

————. *The Art of Interior Design.* 2d ed. New York: Wiley, 1982.

Ballast, David Kent. *Practical Guide to Computer Applications for Architecture and Design.* Englewood Cliffs, N.J.: Prentice-Hall, 1986.

Baraban, Regina S., and Joseph F. Durocher. *Successful Restaurant Design.* New York: Van Nostrand Reinhold, 1988.

Barrows, Claire M. *New Decorating Book.* New York: Better Homes & Gardens, 1982.

Battersby, Martin, et al. (illus.) *History of Furniture.* New York: Morrow, 1976.

Bayley, Stephen (ed.). *Conran Directory of Design.* New York: Random House, Villard Books, 1985.

Bennett, Corwin. *Spaces for People.* Englewood Cliffs, N.J.: Prentice-Hall, 1977.

Bevlin, Marjorie Elliott. *Design Through Discovery.* New York: Holt, Rinehart and Winston, 1985.

Birren, Faber. *Color and Human Response.* New York: Van Nostrand Reinhold, 1978.

————. *Light, Color, and Environment.* New York: Van Nostrand Reinhold, 1969.

Blake, Jill. *Color and Pattern in the Home.* New York: Quick Fox, 1978.

Boger, Louise Ade. *Furniture, Past and Present.* Garden City, N.Y.: Doubleday, 1966.

Boyce, Charles. *Dictionary of Furniture.* New York: Roundtable Press, 1985.

Bradford, Barbara Taylor. *How to Solve Your Decorating Problems.* New York: Simon & Schuster, 1976.

Brett, James. *The Kitchen: 100 Solutions to Design Problems.* New York: Whitney Library of Design, 1977.

Brown, Erica. *Sixty Years of Interior Design.* New York: Viking Press, 1982.

Burde, Ernest. *Design Presentation Techniques.* New York: McGraw Hill, 1992.

Bush, Donald J. *The Streamlined Decade*. New York: George Braziller, 1975.

Bush-Brown, Albert. *Hospitable Design for Healthcare and Senior Communities*. New York: Van Nostrand Reinhold, 1992.

Carpenter, James M. *Visual Art: A Critical Introduction*. New York: Harcourt Brace Jovanovich, 1982.

Cheatham, Frank R., Jane Hart Cheatham, and Sheryl A. Haler. *Design Concepts and Applications*. Englewood Cliffs, N.J.: Prentice-Hall, 1983.

Clark, Robert Judson (ed.). *Arts and Crafts Movement in America*, 1876–1916. Princeton, N.J.: Princeton University Press, 1972.

Cobb, Hubbard H. *How to Paint Anything: The Complete Guide to Painting and Refinishing*. New York: Macmillan, 1972.

Conran, Terence. *The Bed and Bath Book*. New York: Crown, 1978.

———. *The House Book*. New York: Crown, 1976.

———. *New House Book*. New York: Random House, Villard Books, 1985.

Corbman, Bernard P. *Fiber to Fabric*. New York: McGraw-Hill, 1983.

Deasy, C. M., and Thomas E. Lasswell. *Designing Places for People*. New York: Whitney Library of Design, 1985.

Debaigts, Jacques. *Interiors for Old Houses*. New York: Van Nostrand Reinhold, 1973.

DeChiara, Joseph, Julius Panero, and Martin Zelnik. *Time-Saver Standards for Interior Design and Space Planning*. New York: McGraw-Hill, 1991.

De Sausmarez, Maurice. *Basic Design: The Dynamics of Visual Form*. New York: Van Nostrand Reinhold, 1983.

Design Criteria for Lighting Interior Living Spaces. New York: Illuminating Engineering Society of North America, 1980.

Diamonstein, Barbaralee. *Interior Design*. New York: Rizzoli International, 1982.

Eiland, Murray L. *Oriental Rugs: A Comprehensive Study*. Greenwich, Conn.: New York Graphic Society, 1973.

Emery, Marc. *Furniture by Architects*. New York: Harry N. Abrams, 1983.

Emmerling, Mary Ellisor. *American Country*. New York: Clarkson N. Potter, 1980.

The Encyclopedia of Wood. New York: Sterling, 1989.

Evans, Helen Marie, and Carla Davis Dumesnil. *An Invitation to Design*. New York: Macmillan, 1982.

Farren, Carol E. *Planning and Managing Interior Projects*. Kingston, Massachusetts: R. S. Means, 1988.

Faulkner, Ray and Sarah, and LuAnn Nissen. *Inside Today's Home*. 5th ed. New York: Holt, Rinehart & Winston, 1986.

Faulkner, Sarah. *Planning a Home*. New York: Holt, Rinehart & Winston, 1979.

Fehrman, Cherie, and Kenneth Fehrman. *Post-War Interior Design*, 1945–1960. New York: Van Nostrand Reinhold, 1986.

Ferebee, Ann. *A History of Design from the Victorian Era to the Present*. New York: Van Nostrand Reinhold, 1970.

Fetterman, Elsie, and Charles Klamkin. *Consumer Education in Practice*. New York: Wiley, 1976.

Fitzgerald, Oscar P. *Three Centuries of American Furniture*. Englewood Cliffs, N.J.: Prentice-Hall, 1982.

Flynn, John E., A. Segil, and G. Steffy. *Architectural Interior Systems*. 2d ed. New York: Van Nostrand Reinhold, 1988.

Foley, Mary Mix. *The American House*. New York: Harper & Row, 1980.

Friedmann, Arnold, John F. Pile, and Forrest Wilson. *Interior Design: An Introduction to Architectural Interiors*. 3d ed. New York: Elsevier, 1982.

Furuta, Tok. *Interior Landscaping*. Reston, Va.: Reston Pub. Co., 1983.

Gains, Patricia Ellisior. *Fabric Decoration Book*. New York: Morrow, 1975.

Garner, Philippe. *Contemporary Decorative Arts*. New York: Facts on File, 1980.

———. *Twentieth-Century Furniture*. New York: Van Nostrand Reinhold, 1980.

Gaynor, Elizabeth. *Scandinavia Living Design*. New York: Stewart, Tabori & Chang, 1987.

General Electric. *The Light Book*. Cleveland, Ohio: Nela Park, 1981.

Gerritsen, Frans. *Theory and Practice of Color*. New York: Van Nostrand Reinhold, 1975.

Gilliatt, Mary, and Douglas Baker. *Lighting Your Home: A Practical Guide*. New York: Pantheon, 1979.

Gowans, Alan. *Styles and Types of North American Architecture*. New York: Harper Collins, 1992.

Gosling, David, and Barry Maitland. *Design and Planning of Retail Systems*. New York: Whitney Library of Design, 1976.

Grosslight, Jane. *Light: Effective Use of Daylight and Electric Lighting in Residential and Commercial Projects*. Englewood Cliffs, N.J.: Prentice-Hall, 1984.

Gutman, Robert (ed.). *People and Buildings*. New York: Basic Books, 1972.

Halse, Albert O. *The Use of Color in Interiors*. 2d ed. New York: McGraw-Hill, 1978.

Hanks, David A. *Innovative Furniture in America from 1800 to the Present*. New York: Horizon, 1981.

Hardingham, Martin. *The Fabric Catalog*. New York: Simon & Schuster, Pocket Books, 1978.

Harness, S., and J. Groom. *Building without Barriers for the Disabled*. New York: Whitney Library of Design, 1976.

Harris, David A., et al. *Planning and Designing the Office Environment*. New York: Van Nostrand Reinhold, 1981.

Hartwigsen, Gail Lynn. *Design Concepts: A Basic Guidebook*. Boston: Allyn & Bacon, 1980.

Hawkseed Group. *The Passive Solar House Book*. New York: Rand McNally, 1980.

Helick, Martin R. *Varieties of Human Habitation*. Cambridge: MIT Press, 1970.

Hepburn, Andrew H. *Great Houses of American History*. New York: Bramhall House, 1972.

Hicks, David. *Style and Design*. Boston: Little, Brown, 1987.

Hitchcock, Henry-Russell, and Philip Johnson. *The International Style*. (1932, Reprint). New York: Norton, 1966.

Hope, Augustine, and Margaret Walch. *The Color Compendium*. New York: Van Nostrand Reinhold, 1990.

Horn, Richard. *Memphis: Objects, Furniture, and Patterns*. Philadelphia: Rushing Press, 1985.

Hurlburt, Allen. *The Design Concept*. Cincinnati: Watson-Guptill, 1981.

Hutchingson, Dale. *New Horizons for Human Factors*. New York: McGraw-Hill, 1981.

Itten, Johannes. *The Art of Color*. New York: Van Nostrand Reinhold, 1973.

_____ . *Design and Form: The Basic Course at the Bauhaus.* New York: Van Nostrand Reinhold, 1964.

Jackman, Dianne R., and Mary K. Dixon. *The Guide to Textiles for Interior Designers.* Winnipeg: Peguis, 1983.

Jacobson, Charles W. *Check Points on How to Buy Oriental Rugs.* Rutland, Vt.: Charles E. Tuttle, 1969.

Jaffe, Hans L. C. *De Stijl.* New York: Harry N. Abrams, 1967.

Jankowski, Wanda. *Designing with Light.* Glen Cove, New York: P. B. C. International, 1992.

Jencks, Charles, and William Chaitkin. *Architecture Today.* New York: Harry N. Abrams, 1982.

Jordan, R. Furneaux. *A Concise History of Western Architecture.* London: Thames & Hudson, 1969.

Joseph, Marjory L. *Essentials of Textiles.* 3d ed. New York: Holt, Rinehart & Winston, 1984.

Kahlenberg, Mary Hunt, and Anthony Berlant. *Navajo Blanket.* New York: Praeger, 1972.

Kaufman, Donald. *Color: Color Palettes for Painted Rooms.* New York: Clarkson Potter, 1992.

Kaufmann, John E. *IES Lighting Handbook Reference Volume.* New York: Illuminating Engineering Society of North America (IESNA), 1981.

Keiser, Marjorie Branin. *Housing: An Environment for Living.* New York: Macmillan, 1978.

Kicklighter, Clois E., and Joan C. Kicklighter. *Residential Interiors.* South Holland, Ill.: Goodheart-Wilcox, 1986.

Kilmer, Rosemary, and W. Otie Kilmer. *Designing Interiors.* New York: Harcourt Brace Jovanovich, 1992.

Kleeman, Walter B. *The Challenge of Interior Design.* New York: Van Nostrand Reinhold, 1981.

Klein, Dan. *Art Deco.* New York: Crown, 1974.

Knackstedt, Mary V. *The Interior Design Business Handbook: A Complete Guide to Profitability.* New York: Whitney Library of Design, 1992.

Kopp, Joel, and Kate Kopp. *American Hooked and Sewn Rugs.* New York: Dutton, 1975.

Kostof, Spiro. *History of Architecture.* New York: Oxford University Press, 1985.

Kron, Joan, and Suzanne Slesin. *High Tech: The Industrial Style and Source Book for the Home.* New York: Clarkson N. Potter, 1978.

Kuppers, Harold. *Color: Origins, Systems, Uses.* New York: Van Nostrand Reinhold, 1973.

Ladau, Robert F., Brent K. Smith, and Jennifer Place. *Color in Interior Design and Architecture.* New York: Van Nostrand Reinhold, 1989.

Larsen, Jack Lenor, and Jeanne Weeks. *Fabrics for Interiors.* New York: Van Nostrand Reinhold, 1975.

Libby, William Charles. *Color and the Structural Sense.* Englewood Cliffs, N.J.: Prentice-Hall, 1974.

Lightolier. *The Light Book.* Jersey City, N.J.: Lightolier, 1981.

Lucie-Smith, Edward. *Furniture: A Concise History.* London: Thames & Hudson, 1985.

Lyle, Dorothy Siegert. *Modern Textiles.* New York: John Wiley, 1983.

Maass, John. *The Victorian Home in America.* New York: Hawthorn, 1972.

Mackay, James. *Turn-of-the-Century Antiques: An Encyclopedia.* New York: Dutton, 1974.

Magnani, Franco (ed.). *Interiors for Today.* New York: Whitney Library of Design, 1975.

Mahnke, Frank H. and Rudolf H. Mahnke. *Color and Light in Man-made Environments.* New York: Van Nostrand Reinhold, 1987.

Maier, Manfred. *Basic Principles of Design.* New York: Van Nostrand Reinhold, 1977.

Malkin, Jain. *Hospital Interior Architecture: Creating Healing Environments.* New York: Van Nostrand Reinhold, 1992.

Mang, Karl. *History of Modern Furniture.* New York: Harry N. Abrams, 1979.

Massey, Anne. *Interior Design of the 20th Century.* New York: Thames and Hudson, 1990.

Mather, Christine, and Sharon Woods. *Santa Fe Style.* New York: Rizzoli International, 1986.

Mazzurco, Philip. *Bath Design.* New York: Whitney Library of Design, 1986.

McCorquodale, Charles. *A History of Interior Decoration.* New York: Vendome Press, 1983.

McFadden, David. *Scandinavian Modern Design.* New York: Harry N. Abrams, 1982.

Meadmore, Clement. *The Modern Chair.* New York: Van Nostrand Reinhold, 1975.

Meeks, Carol. *Housing.* Englewood Cliffs, N.J.: Prentice-Hall, 1980.

Minimum Guidelines and Requirements for Accessible Design. Washington D.C.: U.S. Architectural & Transportation Barriers Compliance Board, 1982.

Molesworth, H. D., and John Kenworthy-Browne. *Three Centuries of Furniture in Color.* New York: Viking Press, 1972.

Money Management Institute. *Your Home Furnishings Dollar.* Chicago: Household Finance Corp., 1973.

Moore, Fuller. *Concepts and Practice of Architectural Daylighting.* New York: Van Nostrand Reinhold, 1985.

Mount, Charles Morris. *Residential Interiors.* Glen Cove, New York: P. B. C. International, 1992.

Murphy, Dennis Grant. *The Business Management of Interior Design.* North Hollywood, CA: Stratford House Publishing Company, 1988.

National Council for Interior Design Qualification. *NCIDQ Examination Guide.* New York: National Council for Interior Design Qualification, 1989.

Naylor, Gillian. *The Bauhaus.* New York: Dutton, 1968.

Nicholson, Arnold. *American Houses in History.* New York: Viking Press, 1965.

Nielson, Karla J. *Window Treatments.* New York: Van Nostrand Reinhold, 1990.

Nielson, Karla J., and David Taylor. *Interiors: An Introduction.* Dubuque, IA: Wm. C. Brown, 1990.

Nuckolls, James L. *Interior Lighting for Environmental Designers.* New York: Wiley, 1976.

Ostwald, Wilhelm. *The Color Primer.* New York: Van Nostrand Reinhold, 1969.

Page, Marian. *Furniture Designed by Architects.* New York: Whitney Library of Design, 1980.

Panero, Julius, and Martin Zelnick. *Human Dimensions and Interior Space.* New York: Whitney Library of Design, 1979.

Papanek, Victor. *Design for Human Scale.* New York: Van Nostrand Reinhold, 1983.

Pevsner, Nikolaus. *Pioneers of Modern Design from William Morris to Walter Gropius.* 2d ed. New York: Museum of Modern Art, 1975.

Phillips, Derek. *Lighting in Architectural Design.* New York: Holt, Rinehart & Winston, 1968.

Pierson, William H., Jr. *American Buildings and Their Architects: The Colonial and Neoclassical Styles.* New York: Doubleday, 1970.

Pile, John. *Dictionary of 20th-Century Design.* New York: Facts on File, 1990.

———. *Interior Design.* Englewood Cliffs, N.J.: Prentice-Hall; New York: Harry N. Abrams, 1988.

———. *Interiors Third Book of Offices.* New York: Whitney Publications, 1976.

Piotrowski, Christine. *Interior Design Management: A Handbook for Owners and Managers.* New York: Van Nostrand Reinhold, 1992.

———. *Open Office Planning: A Handbook for Interior Designers and Architects.* New York: Whitney Library of Design, 1986.

———. *Open Office Space: The Office Book Design Series.* New York: Facts on File, 1984.

———. *Professional Practice for Interior Designers.* New York: Harper & Row, 1987.

Pomada, Elizabeth, and Michael Larsen. *Painted Ladies: San Francisco's Resplendent Victorians.* New York: Dutton, 1978.

Pool, Mary Jane, and Caroline Seebohm (eds.). *20th Century Decorating, Architecture and Gardens: 80 Years of Ideas and Pleasure from House and Garden.* New York: Holt, Rinehart & Winston, 1980.

Praz, Mario. *An Illustrated History of Furnishings.* New York: George Braziller, 1964.

Preiser, Wolfgang. *Post-Occupancy Evaluation.* New York: Van Nostrand Reinhold, 1988.

———. *Programming the Built Environment.* New York: Van Nostrand Reinhold, 1985.

Proshansky, Harold M., et al. (eds.). *Environmental Psychology: Man and His Physical Setting.* New York: Holt, Rinehart & Winston, 1970.

Radford, Penny. *Designer's Guide to Surfaces and Finishes.* New York: Watson-Guptill, 1984.

Radice, Barbara. *Memphis.* New York: Rizzoli International, 1984.

Reznikoff, S. C. *Interior Graphic and Design Standards.* New York: Whitney Library of Design, 1986.

———. *Specifications for Commercial Interiors.* New York: Whitney Library of Design, 1979.

Riggs, Rosemary. *Materials and Components of Interior Design.* 3d ed. Reston VA: Reston, 1993.

Robbins, C. C. *Daylighting Design and Analysis.* New York: Van Nostrand Reinhold, 1986.

Rooney, William F. *Practical Guide to Home Lighting.* New York: Van Nostrand Reinhold, 1980.

Rupp, William, and Arnold Friedmann. *Construction Materials for Interior Design.* New York: Whitney Library of Design/Watson-Guptill Publications, 1989.

Russell, Beverly. *Architecture and Design.* New York: Harry N. Abrams, 1989.

———. *The Interiors Book of Shops and Restaurants.* New York: Watson-Guptill, 1981.

Russell, Frank, Philippe Garner, and John Read. *A Century of Chair Design.* New York: Rizzoli International, 1980.

Scully, Vincent J., Jr. *Modern Architecture.* Rev. ed. New York: Braziller, 1974.

Sharp, Denis. *Showcase of Interior Design—Pacific Edition.* Grand Rapids, MI: Vitae, 1992.

———. *Twentieth Century Architecture.* New York: Facts on File, 1991.

Sharpe, Deborah T. *The Psychology of Color and Design.* Chicago: Nelson-Hall, 1975.

Siegel, Harry. *Business Guide for Interior Designers.* New York: Whitney Library of Design, 1976.

Siegel, Harry, and Alan Siegel. *A Guide to Business Principles and Practices for Interior Designers.* Rev. ed. New York: Whitney Library of Design, 1982.

Sinclair, Peg B. *Victorious Victorians: A Guide to the Major Architectural Styles.* New York: Holt, Rinehart & Winston, 1985.

Smith, C. Ray. *A History of Interior Design in 20th Century America.* New York: Harper & Row, 1987.

Smith, Fran Kellogg, and Fred J. Bertolone. *Bringing Interiors to Light.* New York: Whitney Library of Design, 1986.

Smith, S. Jane. *Elsie de Wolfe: A Life in the High Style.* New York: Atheneum, 1982.

Sommer, Robert. *Design Awareness.* Corte Madera, CA: Rinehart Press, 1972.

Sorcar, Prafulla C. *Architectural Lighting for Commercial Interiors.* New York: Wiley-Interscience, 1987.

Stimpson, Miriam. *Modern Furniture Classics.* New York: Whitney Library of Design, 1987.

Sulahria, Julie, and Ruby Diamond. *Inside Design: Creating Your Environment.* San Francisco: Canfield Press, 1977.

Tate, Allen. *The Making of Interiors: An Introduction.* New York: Harper & Row, 1987.

Tate, Allen, and C. Ray Smith. *Interior Design in the 20th Century.* New York: Harper & Row, 1986.

Tortora, Phyllis G. *Understanding Textiles.* New York: Macmillan, 1982.

Trachtenberg, Marvin, and Isabelle Hyman. *Architecture from Prehistory to Post-Modernism.* New York: Harry N. Abrams, 1986.

Veitch, Ronald, et al. *Professional Practice.* Winnipeg, Canada: Peguis, 1990.

Verity, Enid. *Color Observed.* New York: Van Nostrand Reinhold, 1982.

Wakita, Dr. Osamu A., and Richard M. Linde. *The Professional Practice of Architectural Working Drawings.* New York: Wiley, 1984.

Wanscher, Ole. *The Art of Furniture.* New York: Reinhold Pub. Corp., 1967.

Warren, Geoffrey. *Art Nouveau Style.* London: Octopus, 1972.

Watson, Sir Francis. *The History of Furniture.* London: Orbio, 1982.

Weale, Mary Jo, et al. *Environmental Interiors.* New York: Macmillan, 1982.

Whiton, Sherrill. *Interior Design and Decoration.* 4th ed. Philadelphia: J. P. Lippincott, 1974.

Wiffen, Marcus, and Frederick Koeper. *American Architecture, 1607–1976.* 2 vols. Cambridge, Mass.: MIT Press, 1981.

Wingate, Isabel B., Karen Gillespie, and Betty Mildram. *Know Your Merchandise for Retailers and Consumers.* 4th ed. New York: McGraw-Hill, 1975.

Wise, Herbert. *Kitchen Detail.* New York: Quick Fox, 1980.

Wrey, Lady Caroline. *Complete Book of Curtains and Draperies.* London: Ebury/Random Century, 1991.

Wright, David. *Natural Solar Architecture: The Passive Solar Primer.* 3d ed. New York: Van Nostrand Reinhold, 1984.

Wright, Frank Lloyd. *The Natural House.* New York: Bramhall House, 1954.

Yeager, Jan. *Textiles for Residential and Commercial Interiors.* New York: Harper & Row, 1988.

Zelanski, Paul, and Mary Pat Fisher. *Design: Principles and Problems.* New York: Holt, Rinehart & Winston, 1984.

Selected Periodicals

Abitare

Americana

American Craft

American Home

Antiques Magazine

Apartment Life

Architectural Digest

Better Homes & Gardens

Budget Decorating

Design and Environment

The Designer Magazine

Designers West

Domus

Elle

Home

House and Garden

House Beautiful

Interior Design

Interiors

Metropolis

Metropolitan Home

National Trust for Historic Preservation

1001 Decorating Ideas Home Library

Professional Builder

Sighting Dimensions

Southern Accents

Other Readings

Current *catalogs and brochures* are published and made available by major manufacturers of fabrics, wallpaper, wall paneling, hard floor coverings, carpets, and furniture.

How-to booklets on every phase of building, remodeling, and interior design are available to both the professional and nonprofessional and are advertised in current periodicals.

INDEX

furniture arrangement, 308–9
lighting, 78, 99
Ergonomics, 233, 302
Exotic revival style architecture, 379–80
Eyeball lighting fixtures, 71

Fabrics. *See also* Textiles
  for ceilings, 198
  combining, 134–38
  construction of, 126–27, 130
  decorative uses of, 131–34
  design problems solved with, 138–40
  for Early American style, 258
  formal and informal, 135–36
  for French style, 272, 274, 277
  for Georgian style, 261
  for modern rooms, 140
  for Neoclassic period, 264, 270
  for period rooms, 140–42
  for Spanish style, 256
  upholstery, 133, 250–51
  for Victorian style, 279
  for wall coverings, 188
  weaves of, 126–27
  window shades, 209–11
Factory-built (prefabricated) house, 410
Family rooms. *See also* Entertainment centers
  design factors, 100–101
  furniture arrangement, 313–14
  lighting, 79, 101
Felting, 130
Fibers
  for carpets, 163
  importance, 122, 124
  man-made, 125–26, 128–29
  natural, 124–25
Fireplaces
  construction of, 226–27
  drafting symbols, 95
  in entertainment areas, 104–5
  environmental limits, 226
  function and design, 224–26
  gas, 226
  in living areas, 99
  wood-burning stoves and heaters, 226
Fleeson, Plunket, 186
Flemish gables, 375
Flocked carpets, 164
Floor lighting, 74
Floor plans
  atrium style, 114
  basic shapes, 88, 109
  circular, 114–15
  closed or open plan, 109
  comparisons of poor and well-arranged,
    115–17
  drafting symbols, 95
  economic factors in, 88–89
  function of, 13
  for furniture arrangement, 303
  high-density units, 117
  importance, 94–95
  kitchens, 96–97
  L-shaped, 112–13
  multistoried, 112
  rectangle, 111
  scale, 95
  square, 111–12
  switches and outlets, 77
Floors/floor coverings. *See also* Carpets
    and rugs
  for disabled persons, 87
  for harmony, 22
  masonry, 150–51

nonresilient hard-surface flooring, 150–51,
    152–54, 156–57
  resilient hard surface flooring, 159
  soft, 159, 162
  use considerations, 150
  vinyl, 159
  wood, 151, 154–55, 158–59
Flowers, foliage, and plants as accessories,
    336–38
Fluorescent lamps, 65
Flush-mounted lighting, 74
Focal point, 20
Footcandles, 50, 61
Footlambert, 61
Form and shape, 11–12
Foundation for Interior Design Education
    Research, 426, 427
Frankl, Paul, 285, 399
Freestyle Movement, 404
Freideberg, Pedro, 289
French doors, 203, 204, 222
French rugs, 172–73
French style
  architecture, 370–75
  furniture, 272–77
Friedman, Stanley Jay, 70, 226
Fuller, Buckminster, 401
Furniture
  in dining room, 102
  in family room, 101
  function and design factors, 232–34
  for harmony, 21
  in living room, 100
  metal, 246
  modular, 310
  quality factors, 243–44
  rattan, cane, rush, and wicker, 247–48
  scale of, 14, 15–16
  slipcovers, 133–34
  of synthetic materials, 246–47
  systems, 243
  types of pieces, 234–42
  upholstered, 133, 248–51
  wood, 244–46
Furniture arrangement
  bedrooms, 314–15
  CAD for, 303
  clearance spaces, 306
  design factors, 300
  dining room, 313
  entrance hall, 308–9
  family room, 313–14
  guidelines for, 303–8
  living room, 309–13
  nonresidential projects, 315
  in programming phase, 300–303
  spatial aspects, 315–19
Furniture styles
  contemporary, 281–82
  Early American, 258–61
  French, 272–77
  Georgian, 261–64
  glossary of terms, 279, 281
  modern, 282–92, 399, 400, 402
  Neoclassic period, 264–72
  Oriental, 292–94
  selection criteria, 294–95
  Spanish, 254–58
  Victorian, 277–79

Gallé, Emile, 282
Gambrel roof style, 359
Gannet, W. C., 419
Garrison (jetty) style, 358

Gaudi, Antonio, 282, 393
Gehry, Frank, 289, 404, 405
General Grant style architecture, 378
Geodesic dome, 401
Geometric design, 7
Georgian style
  architecture, 360–65
  furniture, 261–64
German style architecture, 375–77
Gerritsen color system, 37
Gibbs, James, 361, 364
Gimson, Ernest, 282
Glass block, 219–20
Glass curtains (sheers), 132, 207
Godwin, Edward W., 282
Golden mean, 14
Gothic revival style architecture, 377
Gradation, 19
Graves, Michael, 94, 197, 289, 403, 404
Gray, Eileen, 285
Greek orders of architecture, 346–47
Greek proportions, 14
Greek Revival period style
  architecture, 367–70
  furniture, 270–72
Greene, Charles, 282, 391
Greene, Henry, 282, 391
Greening of interiors, 408
Grills, 216, 219
Gropius, Walter, 396
Grubbs, C. Smith, 21
Guimard, Hector, 282, 393
Gwathmey, Charles, 319

Halls, lighting, 80
Halogen lamps, 64–65
Hampton, Mark, 4, 421
Hancock, William, 270
Handcraft revival, 289
Handicapped persons. *See* Physically
    challenged persons
Harmony, 21–30
Hennigsen, Poul, 59
Henry, Carolyn, 123
Hepplewhite, George, 264
Hepplewhite furniture, 264–66
Hicks, David, 326
HID (high-intensity discharge) lamps, 65–66
High Tech style
  architecture, 404
  color, 28
Hints on Household Taste (Eastlake), 279,
    418
Historic preservation efforts, 382–85
Hitchcock, Henry-Russell, 396
Hoffmann, Josef, 282, 395
Home Fashions League, 56
Honey, Peggy, 90, 317, 342
Hooked rugs, 164, 175
Horizontal lines, 10
Horta, Victor, 392
Hue, 31–32, 37, 53, 136–37
Hunt, Richard Morris, 381, 382

Incandescent lighting, 63–64
Indirect lighting, 67–68
Institute of Business Designers, 432
Insulation, 89, 198
Intensity of color, 39
Interaction with Color (Albers), 37
Interior Design Educators Council, Inc., 432
Interior designers
  education and training, 426
  fee systems, 425–26

furniture arrangement, 315
systems furniture, 242
textile selection, 142–43

Octagonal style architecture, 379
Off-white, 51
Olbrich, Josef Maria, 282, 395
Opposition, 18–19
Organic architecture, 393–94
Oriental rugs, 169–72
Oriental style
architecture, 405–7
color, 27
furniture, 292–94
Ostwald, Friedrich Wilhelm, 33
Ostwald Color Wheel, 33–34
O'Toole, Tom, 227
Outdoor lighting, 80

Paints for wall coverings, 183–85
Palladian windows, 203, 205
Palladio, Andrea, 364
Panton, Vernor, 247, 285
Papillon, Jean, 185–86
Parquetry, 154
Pattern, 10
for emphasis, 21
in fabric combinations, 134–35
Paulin, Pierre, 239, 289
Pendants, 71
Perpendicular style, 393
Pesce, Gaetano, 289
Photographic design, 7
Phyfe, Duncan, 264, 266
Physically challenged persons
accessibility standards, 316
design factors, 87–88
furniture for, 233–34, 302
kitchen design, 96
Piano, Renzo, 404
Pigment colors, 32–33
Pile weave, 126, 127
Piretti, Giancarlo, 289
Plain weave, 126, 127
Plants as accessories, 336–38
Plaster ceilings, 197
Platner, Warren, 285
Plumbing fixtures, 107
Ponti, Gio, 289, 404
Pope, Thomas, 270
Pop furniture, 289
Portable lighting, 74–77
Portman, John, 143
Post-Modernism, 28, 403
Prairie style, 393
Prang color wheel, 33, 34
Predesigned home plan, 410
Prefabricated (factory-built) house, 410
Priscilla curtains, 209
Progression, 19
Proportion, 6, 13–14
Protein fibers, 124
Proxemics, 302
Psychological aspects of design
color, 28–29
lighting, 70
space planning, 86–88

Quartz-halogen lamps, 64–65
Queen Anne style
architecture, 378–79
furniture, 261, 262
Quervelle, Antoine Gabriel, 270

Radial balance, 16, 18
Radiation, 19
Rag rugs, 175
Rattan furniture, 247
Rauschenberg, Robert, 405
Realistic design, 7
Rectangle floor plan, 111
Rectangles, 11
Regency style, 266, 268–70
Related color schemes, 42, 44
Remodeling trend, 411–13
Renaissance and medieval styles, 353–56
Rennick, Michael, 104, 183, 302, 435
Repetition, 18
Reveillon, Baptiste, 186
Rhythm, 18–19
Richardson, Henry Hobson, 282, 380, 391–92
Riemerschmid, Richard, 282
Rietveld, Gerrit, 285, 395, 396
Robison, Jonna, 87, 428
Robsjohn-Gibbings, T. H., 285
Rococo style, 370–71
Rodgers, Richard, 404
Romanesque Revival architecture, 380
Roman shades, 209, 210
Rudolph, Paul, 401
Rugs. See Carpets and rugs
Ruhlmann, Jacques-Emile, 285, 399
Rush furniture, 247–48
Ruskin, John, 26
Rya rugs, 174–75

Saarinen, Eero, 254, 400–401
Saarinen, Eliel, 282, 285, 399
Saladino, John, 421
Saltbox style, 357–58
Santa Fe style
architecture, 351
color, 28
furniture, 256
Sapper, Richard, 76
Satin weave, 126, 127
Savonnerie rugs, 172
Scale
of accessories, 17
of furniture, 14, 15–16
importance, 15
in residential floor plans, 95
Scandinavian style architecture, 403
Scarpa, Afra, 289
Scarpa, Tobia, 289
Sconces, for lighting, 71
Screens, 216, 219
Sculpture, 329
Secession movement
architecture, 395
furniture, 282
Shades
fabric, 209–11
for light fixtures, 75–76
Shades of color, 38
Shape and form, 11–12
Sheerer, Tom, 133
Sheers, 132, 207
Shell framing, 410
Sheraton, Thomas, 264, 270
Sheraton furniture, 266, 267
Shibui color theory, 27, 46–47, 407
Shingle style architecture, 380
Shoji screens, 216, 219, 406
Showcase of Interior Design, 418
Shutters, 216
Silk, 124
Simmon, Montie, 242

Simplicity, in design, 6, 388
Site selection, 94
Skurka, Norma, 202
Skylights, 204
Slipcovers, 133–34
Smart House, 408
Sodium lamps, 65
Sofas, types of, 236, 239–40
Soffit lighting fixtures, 71
Solar house, 413
Solar orientation, 89, 94
Sottsass, Ettore, 251, 289, 405, 406
Southwest Adobe style
architecture, 351
furniture, 256
Space, defined, 12
Space planning. See Design; Floor plans
Spanish matrimonia rugs, 174
Spanish style
architecture, 347–53
furniture, 254–58
Spectre, Jay, 421
Split complement color schemes, 46
Square floor plan, 111–12
Squares, 11
Stained glass, 219–20
Stairways
drafting symbols, 95
function and design, 223–24
lighting, 80
Starck, Philippe, 289
Stein, Harry, 196
Stella, Frank, 405
Stern, Robert, 403
Stickley, Gustav, 282, 391, 418
Stick style architecture, 380
Stodola, Bruce, 3, 136, 235, 305, 337
Stone, Edward Durell, 403
Structural design, 6–7
Structural lighting fixtures, 76
Style. See also Design
developing, 4–5
in fabric coordination, 137
of fireplaces, 225–26
kitchen, 97
master bedroom, 105
personal, 4
Stylistic design, 7
Sullivan, Louis, 393
Suspended lighting fixtures, 71
Swedish style architecture, 376
Sydnor, Douglas, 310
Synthetic fibers, 125–26
Systems furniture, 243

Tables, types of, 237, 240, 241
Tandem floor plan, 117
Tapestry weave, 126
Task lighting, 68–69
Temperature, color and effect on, 51
Territoriality, 303
Tetrad color schemes, 46
Tew, Paul, 301, 424
Textile Products Identification Act, 125
Textiles. See also Fabrics
as art, 331
care and maintenance, 146–47
coloring of, 130
for commercial projects, 142–43
fibers, 122–26
finishing, 130–31
glossary of terms, 144–46
importance, 122
nonwoven, 127, 130